THE LETTERS AND
PROSE WRITINGS OF
WILLIAM COWPER
1787–1791

WILLIAM COWPER

From an engraving by Francesco Bartolozzi
after the portrait by Sir Thomas Lawrence (1793)

THE LETTERS
AND PROSE WRITINGS OF
William Cowper

VOLUME III
Letters 1787–1791

EDITED BY

JAMES KING

AND

CHARLES RYSKAMP

CLARENDON PRESS · OXFORD

1982

Oxford University Press, Walton Street, Oxford OX2 6DP
London Glasgow New York Toronto
Delhi Bombay Calcutta Madras Karachi
Kuala Lumpur Singapore Hong Kong Tokyo
Nairobi Dar es Salaam Cape Town
Melbourne Auckland
and associates in
Beirut Berlin Ibadan Mexico City Nicosia

Published in the United States by
Oxford University Press, New York

British Library Cataloguing in Publication Data
Cowper, William
The letters and prose writings of William Cowper,
Vol. 3: Letters 1787-1791
1. Cowper, William — Biography
2. Authors, English — 18th century — Biography
I. Title   II. King, James   III. Ryskamp, Charles
828'.608   PR3383.A4
ISBN 0-19-812608-5

Library of Congress Cataloguing in Publication Data
Cowper, William, 1731-1800.
The letters and prose writings of William Cowper.
Includes bibliographical references and indexes.
CONTENTS: v. 1. Adelphi and letters, 1750-1781. —
v. 2. Letters, 1782-1786. — v. 3. Letters, 1787-1791.
1. Cowper, William, 1731-1800 — Correspondence.
2. Poets, English — 18th century — Correspondence.
I. King, James.   II. Ryskamp, Charles.   III. Title.
PR3383.A3K5 1979   821'.6[B]   78-40495
AACR2

ISBN 0-19-812608-5

Set by Hope Services, Abingdon, Oxon
and Printed in Great Britain
at the University Press, Oxford
by Eric Buckley
Printer to the University

CONTENTS

ACKNOWLEDGEMENTS

The editors are deeply grateful to Miss Mary Barham Johnson who has so generously provided them with information on Cowper's Donne relations, especially John Johnson. Professor Harold F. Guite has translated Cowper's Greek and Latin into English. The editors would also like to thank the following who provided information and assistance for this volume: Professor J. M. Armistead, Mr Richard A. Arnold, Professor John D. Baird, Mr J. F. J. Collett-Wite, Mr S. J. Connolly, Mr E. H. Cornelius, Mr E. Davis, Mr P. Durrant, Professor Irvin Ehrenpreis, Mr M. W. Farr, Mr M. Frankel, Professor Donald Greene, Professor W. F. Hanley, Miss Olwen Hedley, Mr C. P. C. Johnson, Mr P. I. King, Mr Verlyn Klinkenborg, the late Dr W. S. Lewis, Mr I. F. Lyle, Mrs Edwine Montague Martz, Miss Gillian Morton, Mr K. C. Newton, Mr J. H. Prynne, Mr Michael Schroeder, Professor Robert Shackleton, Mr Peter Walne, Miss Joyce I. Whalley, Mr Clifford R. Wurfel.

LIST OF PLATES

SHORT TITLES AND ABBREVIATIONS

Standard encyclopedias, biographical dictionaries, peerages, baronetages, knightages, school and university lists, lists of clergy, town and city directories, and road guides have been used but will not be cited unless for a particular reason.

Bailey	*Poems of William Cowper*, ed. J. C. Bailey. London, 1905.
Burney Diary	*Diary and Letters of Madame d'Arblay (1778–1840)*, ed. Austin Dobson. 6 vols. London, 1904–5.
C	William Cowper.
GM	*The Gentleman's Magazine*, 1731–1880.
Hayley	William Hayley, *The Life, and Posthumous Writings, of William Cowper, Esqr.* 3 vols. Chichester, 1803–4.
Keynes	Geoffrey Keynes, 'The Library of Cowper', *Transactions of the Cambridge Bibliographical Society*, 1959–61.
Latin and Italian Poems	*Latin and Italian Poems of Milton Translated Into English Verse . . .* , ed. [William Hayley]. London, 1808.
Lives	Samuel Johnson, *Prefaces, Biographical and Critical, to the Works of the English Poets.* 10 vols. London, 1779–81.
The Madan Family	Falconer Madan, *The Madan Family*. Oxford, 1933.
Milford	William Cowper, *Poetical Works*, ed. H. S. Milford, 4th edition, revised. London, 1967.
OED	*The Oxford English Dictionary.*
OPR	*The Register of the Parish of Olney . . . 1665 to 1812.* Transcribed and indexed by Oliver Ratcliff. With an introduction by Thomas Wright, etc. Olney, [1907–10].
PRO	Public Record Office, London.
Russell	Norma Russell, *A Bibliography of William Cowper to 1837.* Oxford, 1963.

Ryskamp	Charles Ryskamp, *William Cowper of the Inner Temple, Esq.* Cambridge, 1959.
Southey	*The Works of William Cowper*, ed. Robert Southey. 15 vols. London, 1835-7.
VCH	*Victoria County History.*
Walpole	*The Yale Edition of Horace Walpole's Correspondence*, ed. W. S. Lewis. New Haven, 1937-.
Wright	*The Correspondence of William Cowper*, ed. Thomas Wright, 4 vols. London, 1904.
1782	*Poems by William Cowper, of the Inner Temple, Esq.* London, 1782.
1785	*The Task, A Poem, in Six Books. By William Cowper, of the Inner Temple, Esq. . . . . To Which Are Added, By the Same Author, An Epistle to Joseph Hill, Esq. Tirocinium or a Review of Schools, and the History of John Gilpin.* London, 1785.

CHRONOLOGY OF COWPER'S LIFE

15 November 1731 (OS)	William Cowper born in the rectory, Berkhamsted, Hertfordshire; son of the Revd John Cowper, and of Ann, daughter of Roger Donne of Ludham Hall, Norfolk.
13 November 1737 (OS)	Death of Ann Cowper.
c.1737	At school in Aldbury, Herts., under the Revd William Davis.
c.1737–9	At the Revd Dr William Pittman's boarding-school at Markyate Street, Herts.
c.1740–2	A boarder in the house of Mrs Disney.
April 1742	Enters Westminster School.
29 April 1748 (OS)	Admitted to the Middle Temple.
May 1749	Spends nine months at Berkhamsted.
1750–3	Is articled to Chapman, a London solicitor. He spends much time in the company of Theadora and Harriot, the daughters of his uncle, Ashley Cowper.
c.1753–4	Abandonment of hope of marrying Theadora Cowper.
November 1753	Experiences his first period of depression.
June 1754	Is called to the Bar.
9 July 1756	Death of his father.
1755–63	Association with the 'Geniuses' (Bonnell Thornton, Robert Lloyd, Charles Churchill, George Colman).
15 April 1757	Is admitted to the Inner Temple.
1763	Dispute erupts over the Clerkship of the Journals of the House of Lords; C is summoned to appear at the Bar of the House of Lords. Beginning of his second period of depression. Makes his third suicide attempt on the eve of his examination at the House of Lords. On the urging of his brother, he enters Dr

	Cotton's 'Collegium Insanorum' at St. Albans.
July 1764	Recovery and beginning of conversion to evangelicalism.
June 1765	Leaves St. Albans and settles in lodgings at Huntingdon.
*c.*September 1765	First acquaintance with the Unwin family.
11 November 1765	Becomes a boarder with the Unwin family.
2 July 1767	Death of the Revd Morley Unwin.
14 September 1767	Arrival of C and Mrs Unwin at Olney, where the Revd John Newton had offered to find a house for them.
15 February 1768	Move to Orchard Side, Olney.
20 March 1770	Death of C's brother, John.
1771	Begins *Olney Hymns* in collaboration with Newton.
1772	Engaged to Mrs Unwin.
January–February 1773	Engagement is broken. Third period of severe depression.
April 1773	Moves to Olney vicarage under the care of Newton.
October 1773	Makes another attempt to commit suicide.
23 May 1774	Returns to Orchard Side.
February 1779	*Olney Hymns* published.
December 1780	'The Progress of Error' and 'Truth' begun.
January–March 1781	'Table Talk' and 'Expostulation' written.
Spring 1781	'Charity' written.
July 1781	Meets Lady Austen.
August 1781	'Retirement' begun.
1 March 1782	*Poems by William Cowper, of the Inner Temple, Esq.* published.
October 1782	*John Gilpin* written.
*c.*October 1783	*The Task* begun.
May 1784	First acquaintance with the Throckmortons.

24 May–12 July 1784	Final breach with Lady Austen.
October 1784.	*The Task* completed.
November 1784	'Tirocinium' completed. The translation of the *Iliad* begun.
July 1785	*The Task* published.
October 1785	Resumes his correspondence with Lady Hesketh; receives financial assistance from her and 'Anonymous' (Theadora).
November 1786	Following Lady Hesketh's visit from June to November, C, at the invitation of the Throckmortons, moves to The Lodge, Weston Underwood.
January–June 1787	Fourth period of depression.
September 1788	Translation of the *Odyssey* begun.
January 1790	First acquaintance with his cousin, John Johnson.
July 1791	Translation of Homer published.
September 1791	Translation of Milton's Latin and Italian poems begun.
December 1791	Mrs Unwin's first paralytic stroke.
May 1792	Mrs Unwin's second paralytic stroke. First visit from William Hayley.
1 August–17 September 1792	C, Mrs Unwin, and John Johnson visit Hayley at Eartham, Sussex.
Autumn 1792	Renewed depression.
Autumn 1793	Further deterioration in Mrs Unwin's health. 'To Mary' written.
November 1793	Lady Hesketh arrives to take charge of C and his household.
January 1794	Beginning of his fifth severe depression, from which he never fully recovers.
April 1794	Granted a yearly pension of £300.
17 May 1794	Mrs Unwin's third paralytic stroke.
28 July 1795	C and Mrs Unwin removed by John Johnson to his home in East Dereham, Norfolk.
17 December 1796	Death of Mrs Unwin.
November 1797	Revision of Homer translation begun.
8 March 1799	Revision of Homer completed.

19 March 1799	'The Cast-away' begun.
31 January 1800	Treated for dropsy.
22 February 1800	Confined to his rooms.
25 April 1800	Death.
2 May 1800	Buried in the parish church of East Dereham.

INTRODUCTION

Cowper was occupied with further revisions to his translation of Homer until that work appeared in July 1791; after a short hiatus, he began work on his translation of Milton's Latin and Italian poems. Letters from this time are filled with apologies for delays in responding, and Cowper complains of the arduous life of a translator.

Cowper's friendship with the Throckmorton family deepened and intensified because of the proximity of Cowper and Mrs Unwin to their landlord's house at Weston. That congeniality also flourished because of the shared interests in art, literature, and current happenings which Cowper and the Throckmortons enjoyed.

In 1788, Mrs John King, who had known Cowper's brother and whose husband had been at Westminster with Cowper, wrote to him, and a devoted if somewhat formal correspondence commenced which terminated only in 1792, the year before Mrs King died. In January 1787, Samuel Rose, then a young man of twenty and a recent graduate of the University of Glasgow, called upon Cowper to pay his respects; their friendship was to be similar in intensity and style to that between Cowper and the late William Cawthorne Unwin.

Three years later, in January 1790, another young man, John Johnson of Norfolk, called upon Cowper at Weston, and this launched a relationship of tremendous consequences. Johnny was the son of Catharine Johnson, a niece of Cowper's mother. Although Cowper admired John Johnson for his charming and likeable personality, his sincere devotion to him, and his eagerness to do anything in his power to advance his work, he also found in his friendship with Johnny a re-establishment of a link with his Donne relations and with his long-dead but still mourned mother. He poignantly expressed these sentiments to his cousin Anne Bodham in his poem, 'On Receipt of My Mother's Picture,' and stated them strongly in a letter to her of 27 February 1790: 'There is in me, I believe, more of the Donne than of the Cowper, and though I love all of both names ... yet I feel the bond of nature draw me vehemently to your side.'

There were other significant events during these years. Cowper experienced a serious bout of depression from January to June 1787; Mrs Newton died in 1791; Mrs Unwin suffered her first paralytic stroke in December 1791; Cowper himself suffered from a troubling 'nervous fever' in the same year.

Lady Hesketh continued her visits and her letters, both of which were eagerly received by Cowper. And he had the additional pleasure and comfort of John Johnson's friendship and the rejuvenation of his relations with his Norfolk kinsmen. This volume of letters is testimony to friends, old and new, and friendship itself, and the history of Cowper's translation of Homer.

CORRESPONDENTS

JOHN BACON (1740–99), the sculptor. Although he was apprenticed to a porcelain manufacturer at the age of fourteen and quickly showed an aptitude for modelling figures, it was not until 1768 that Bacon entered the Royal Academy Schools where he achieved some attention in 1769 for a bust of 'Ossian' and a bas-relief entitled, 'Aeneas Escaping from Troy'. In 1770 he was elected an Associate of the Royal Academy and seven years later a full member. In that year Bacon made a bust of George III, who was thoroughly delighted with his work. Bacon remained a largely self-taught artist. He had strong connections with the Methodist Church and was a friend of Newton (he was also a member of the Eclectic Society), and it was through him that Bacon first approached Cowper to say how much he admired his verse. A shrewd and sometimes grasping man of business, Bacon once suggested that he could execute all the national monuments at a price below that fixed by Parliament.

WALTER BAGOT (1731–1806), of Pipe Hall, Staffs. He was the son of Sir Walter Wagstaffe Bagot, 5th baronet, and his wife Barbara (d. 1765), eldest daughter of William Legge, Earl of Dartmouth. The family of Bagot had held property at Blithfield and Bagot's Bromley, Staffs., since the Conquest. Bagot and Cowper were intimate friends at Westminster but drifted apart soon afterwards, and visited each other only twice in the years 1750–81. Bagot was very much like Cowper in his taste and in his simple, amiable, gentle manners, and had a similar relish for humour. He had been a handsome boy and a slovenly dresser; he published poety in his youth, and throughout his life; while he held the family livings (from 1759) of Blithfield and Leigh in Staffordshire, he spent hours of every day in reading — especially the classics. On 7 September 1773, he married Anne (d. 1786), daughter of William Swinnerton, of Butterton, Staffs. Bagot subsequently married Mary Ward. He visited Cowper in 1785 after the publication of *The Task*, and he used many of his family connections to obtain subscribers to Cowper's translation of Homer.

HARRIOT RIVAL DONNE, afterwards Mrs BALLS (1736–1808), the niece of Cowper's mother, and the sister of Anne Bodham, Catharine Johnson, and the Revd. Castres Donne. In 1759 she married Richard Balls (1736–84), a Catfield farmer. They had no children.

ANNE DONNE, afterwards Mrs BODHAM (1748–1846), the niece of Cowper's mother, also Ann Donne, and the sister of Harriot Balls and Catharine Johnson, John Johnson's mother. She married in 1781 Thomas Bodham (1741–96), of Gonville and Caius College, Cambridge (BA, 1764; MA, 1767; Fellow, 1767–79), who was curate of Brandon Parva, Norfolk. The Bodhams were childless, but they brought up their niece, Anne Vertue Donne (1781–1859), the daughter of Mrs Bodham's brother, the Revd Castres Donne (1744/5–1789). There are numerous references to Mrs Bodham and her husband in James Woodforde, *The Diary of a Country Parson*, ed. John Beresford (5 vols., Oxford, 1924–31). 'Rose' was Cowper's name for Mrs Bodham; she was known to other members of her family as 'Nancy' or 'Nanny'.

JOHN BUCHANAN (1772–1826), who lived in Weston a few doors from Cowper. Hayley in his *Life* provides an extensive description of Buchanan who served as curate of Weston Underwood and Ravenstone; he was subsequently vicar of South Grimston, Yorkshire: 'The ideas [for a poem on the four ages of man] had been suggested to [Cowper] in the year 1791, by a very amiable clerical neighbour, Mr. Buchanan, who in the humble curacy of Ravenstone (a little sequestered village within the distance of an easy walk from Weston) possesses, in a scene of rustic privacy, such extensive scholarship, such gentleness of manners, and such a contemplative dignity of mind, as would certainly raise him to a more suitable, and indeed to a conspicuous situation, if the professional success of a divine were the immediate consequence of exemplary merit. This gentleman who had occasionally enjoyed the gratification of visiting Cowper, suggested to him, with a becoming diffidence, the project of a new poem on the four distinct periods of life, infancy, youth, manhood, and old age. He imparted his ideas to the poet by a letter, in which he observed, with equal modesty and truth, that Cowper was particularly qualified to relish, and to do justice to the subject; a subject which he supposes not hitherto treated expressly, as its importance deserves, by any poet ancient or modern.'

WILLIAM BULL (1738–1814) was born at Irthlingborough, Northamptonshire, and baptized there on 17 December 1738. He was the son of John and Judith Bull but was reared by his grandfather, Francis Bull. In 1759 he was admitted to the Daventry Dissenting Academy and five years later he accepted the pastorship of Newport Independent Church. At about the same time as he settled at Newport, Bull first admitted students for instruction. He married Hannah Palmer (d. 1804), a daughter of Thomas Palmer of Bedford, on 7 June 1768. Bull's friendship with Newton began about this time, and it was through Newton that Bull was eventually introduced to Cowper. Bull's Academy for Dissenting Ministers, of which he was the first principal, was founded in 1782 and took in two students the following year. John Thornton provided a great part of the funds for the support of the Academy, and Bull's involvement with the Academy brough him into close contact with other members of the Clapham Sect:

Zachary Macaulay, Thomas Babington, and Mrs Wilberforce. Bull's only child to survive to maturity was Thomas Palmer Bull (1773–1859), who became co-pastor of Newport Independent Church in 1800.

William Bull placed the three volumes of Madame Guyon's *Spiritual Songs* in Cowper's hands about July 1782, not long after the publication of Cowper's first volume of poems. Cowper readily agreed, at his suggestion, to translate some of Madame Guyon's verse, and Bull eventually published the translations in a small volume printed at Newport Pagnell in 1801.

WALTER CHURCHEY (1747–1805) was born at Brecon, and was an attorney by profession. Having been deeply influenced by Thomas Coke and John Wesley, Churchey wrote to Cowper to ask his advice about publishing verse of a Methodist cast. Churchey eventually published *Poems and Imitations* in 1789, for which Wesley assisted him in obtaining subscribers. Among his other writings were *Lines on the Rev. J. Wesley* (1791), *An Elegy to the Memory of W. Cowper* (1800), and *An Apology by W. Churchey for his Public Appearance as a Poet* (1805). Churchey married Mary Brevan (d. 1822) and had six children.

ROBERT GLYNN, afterwards CLOBERY (1719–1800), physician, son of Robert Glynn of Brodes, Cornwall. After attending Eton, in 1737 he was elected a scholar of King's College, Cambridge (BA, 1741; MA, 1745; MD, 1752). Glynn practised medicine in Richmond for a short time, but he then returned to Cambridge permanently. In 1763, he became a Fellow of the College of Physicians at London, but he refused all further distinctions.

Glynn was extremely interested in literature, and is now chiefly remembered for his championing of the authenticity of Chatterton's Rowley poems. An early honour was the Seatonian prize in 1757.

DR JAMES COGSWELL (1746–92), surgeon, of New York City, had served as a surgeon in the American Army during the Revolutionary War, and the General Assembly had appointed him one of the committee of medical examiners for the state of Connecticut. He was the son of the Revd James Cogswell (1720–1807) who served as a clergyman in Canterbury, Connecticut, and who published at least three sermons (1757–76); his mother Alice (1725–72) was the daughter of Jabez Fitch of Canterbury. Dr Cogswell's younger brother, Mason Fitch Cogswell (1761–1830), was a prominent physician in Hartford, Connecticut, from 1789 until his death. James Cogswell died of yellow fever on 20 November 1792.

HENRY COWPER (1758–1840), the third son of General Spencer Cowper, and his wife, Charlotte Baber, was called to the Bar at the Middle Temple in 1775 and from 1785 to 1826 he was Deputy Clerk of the Parliaments and Clerk Assistant to the House of Lords. In 1783 he published a three-volume study, *Reports of Cases in the Court of King's Bench from Hilary term 14 George III to 18 George III*.

He married his cousin german Maria Judith, daughter of William Cowper of Hertingfordbury, but had no issue. By his will he left a sum of money for educating the poor children of Hertingfordbury parish. He died at Tewin Water on 28 November 1840.

MARIA FRANCES CECILIA MADAN, afterwards Mrs COWPER (1726–97), Cowper's cousin and Martin Madan's sister. An unusually accomplished woman, Mrs Cowper was sufficiently skilled in French to act in Racine's *Athalie*, and she was so successful in that endeavour that she tried to become an actress. On 5 August 1749, she married her first cousin, William Cowper (1721?–69).

Cowper's letter to Mrs Cowper of 23 January 1790 is the first surviving letter to her since 19 October 1781, a hiatus of almost nine years. From 1766 until 1781 they had been frequent correspondents. The bond of the early letters (see Volume I *passim*) is a community of intense religious feelings; the loosening of that bond may have been due to Cowper's antagonism to Martin's *Thelyphthora* (1781) or to the fact that religious ardour was the only strong tie which held them together. Like other members of her family, Mrs Cowper was a versifier, but *Original Poems, on Various Occasions, by a Lady* (1792) was her single publication in book form. Cowper revised the volume before it went to press, and only his name ('Revised by William Cowper, Esq. of the Inner Temple') appears on the title-page.

MAJOR-GENERAL SPENCER COWPER (1723 or 1724–1797), the first cousin of Cowper and Lady Hesketh. Educated at Westminster, and Worcester College, Oxford (matriculated December 1742), and admitted to the Inner Temple in 1741, he became a Major-General on 19 February 1779 and was gazetted Lieutenant-General in 1787. The General, who had commanded a brigade in the war in America, had earlier purchased Cowper's law books.

The General renewed his interest in the welfare and literary fortunes of his younger cousin after the publication of *The Task*, and he, together with Lady Hesketh, obtained the opinions of men of letters as to the merits of the translation of Homer and helped gather subscribers to the edition.

JOSIAH DORNFORD (*c*.1734–1810), who served as a member of the court of common council of the City of London, was the author of several pamphlets on the affairs of that court and on the reform of debtors' prisons. His son, Josiah (1764–97), also published various pamphlets and in 1795 was appointed inspector-general of the army accounts of the Leeward Islands. Dornford Sr. was in the Commission of the Peace at Kent when he died at Sydenham on 12 September 1810. In 1786, he published *Nine Letters to the Right Honorable the Lord Mayor and Aldermen of the City of London, On the State of Prisons and Prisoners within their Jurisdiction: Shewing a Necessity of a Reform of Them. Urging the Great Advantage of Solitary Confinement, and the Treating of Prisoners with Humanity* and *Seven Letters to the Lords and Commons of Great Britain, upon the Impolicy, Inhumanity, and Injustice of our Present Mode of Arresting the Bodies of Debtors*. One of these pamphlets, both of which were influenced by John Howard, was sent to Cowper by Dornford in 1786.

HARRIOT COWPER, afterwards LADY HESKETH (1733–

1807). Lady Hesketh, the daughter of Ashley Cowper, was Cowper's first cousin and the sister of Theodora Cowper, whom Cowper had wished to marry. She was the wife of Thomas Hesketh of Rufford Hall in Lancashire, who had been created a baronet in 1761 and had died in 1778, leaving Cowper a small legacy. The Heskeths had gone to Italy after Cowper had moved to Olney and they then lost touch with him. Lady Hesketh resumed correspondence with Cowper following the publication of *The Task* in 1785, and she henceforth devoted a great deal of her time to his welfare. A person of somewhat austere refinement, she sometimes put people off by her manner. Mrs Thrale in a diary entry of 10 January 1781 provides a full description of her: 'Dear Lady Hesketh! and how like a Naples Washball She is: so round, so sweet, so plump, so polished, so red, so white . . . with more Beauty than almost any body, as much Wit as many a body; and six Times the Quantity of polite Literature . . . I never can find out what that Woman does to keep the people from adoring her.' *Thraliana*, ed. K. Balderston (Oxford, 1942), i. 478.

JOHN HIGGINS (b. 1768) was a native of Weston and an admirer of Cowper's poetry. 'On learning that a neighbour of his was able to repeat any of his poems by heart, Cowper invited his youthful admirer to "a dish of tea"; which was the beginning of a friendship to which Mr. Higgins ever after reverted with affectionate delight and excusable pride.' (J. W. Burgon, *Lives of Twelve Good Men* (New York, 1888), ii. 348.) The earliest-known portrait of the poet is a profile drawing which Higgins made in 1791. In 1792 he inherited the estate of Turvey Abbey, several miles from Weston, from an uncle and left Weston. Although their regular contacts seem to have ceased at this time, Higgins's admiration for the poet was unflagging, and he cherished a collection of relics of the poet (he wore Cowper's shoe-buckles constantly).

JOSEPH HILL (1733–1811). Perhaps Cowper's closest friend during his Temple days, Joe Hill had been born near Chancery Lane, the son of Francis Hill (d. 1741), an attorney who was the nephew and secretary of Sir Joseph Jekyll, Master of the

Rolls, and Theodosia Sedgwick (d. 1784). He had been well known to Cowper's Uncle Ashley and his family, and soon after Cowper left Westminster he and young 'Sephus' became friends. Hill had been early bred to the law; he acted as a clerk in Chancery Lane (he served his articles of clerkship under Robert Chester of the Six Clerks' Office in Chancery Lane), later qualified as solicitor and attorney, and was appointed one of the Sixty, or Sworn Clerks in Chancery. He was made Secretary of Lunatics in 1778. He became a rich man owing to the justified esteem in which so many of his wealthy clients held him. During most of his life Cowper was financially dependent on Hill. Hill not only handled Cowper's small monetary matters — paying his London bills, apportioning his income for expenses in Huntingdon, Olney, etc. — but from his own pocket made it possible for Cowper to live as a gentleman, though a very poor one. Hill had married Sarah Mathews (1742-1824) in August 1771.

ROWLAND HILL (1744-1833), preacher. Hill was the sixth son of Sir Rowland Hill and was educated at Shrewsbury, Eton, and St. John's College, Cambridge (BA, 1769). Deeply influenced by the religious fervour of his brother, Sir Richard Hill (1732-1808), he was from an early age committed to theological views of a very evangelical cast. After being refused ordination by six bishops because of his unorthodox opinions, he was finally ordained on 6 June 1773. Hill became a renowned preacher, and in 1783 Surrey Chapel, London, was built for him. There were thirteen Sunday schools, with over 3,000 children enrolled, attached to Surrey Chapel. Hill was an enthusiastic supporter of vaccination, and he was an ardent defender of such institutions as the Religious Tract Society, the British and Foreign Bible Society, and the London Missionary Society.

Hill approached Cowper through Bull in 1789 to obtain assistance in revising his *Divine Hyms . . . for the Use of Children* (1790), which was intended primarily but not exclusively for the children in the Surrey Chapel Sunday schools. On 29 March 1790, Cowper wrote to Hill, whom he now knew to be the author of the book, telling him that he did not have to accept all his suggested revisions. In addition to revising Hill's book, Cowper contributed two hymns to the collection.

JAMES HURDIS (1763-1801), the poet, who was educated at the prebendal school at Chichester, St. Mary Hall, Oxford, and Magdalen College, Oxford (BA, 1785). He was appointed curate of Burwash, Sussex, in 1785; he remained there until he obtained the living of Bishopstone in 1791, which he held until his death. In November 1793, Hurdis was appointed Professor of Poetry at Oxford. He married Harriet Minet in 1799, and had two sons, one of whom was James Henry Hurdis (1800-1857), the amateur artist.

Hurdis's first collection of poetry, *The Village Curate* (1788), a deliberate imitation of Cowper's style, was well received and went through four editions. Joseph Johnson sent the manuscript of Hurdis's second work, a long poem entitled *Adriano; or the First of June*, to Cowper for an opinion in 1788; Cowper undertook a painstakingly detailed criticism of the poem which did not appear until 1790. At Johnson's instigation, Cowper also revised Hurdis's tragedy, *Sir Thomas More*. Having learnt of Cowper's involvement in his work, Hurdis wrote to him on 26 February 1791, inaugurating a correspondence which lasted several years. When Cowper's Homer was published, Hurdis sent him 'numerous packets' containing corrections and parallel passages from other translators.

CATHARINE JOHNSON (1767-1821), the daughter of John Johnson (1717-85), of Ludham, and Catharine Johnson, *née* Donne (1740-70), who had married in 1765. As Kate was only two when her mother died, she lived with her Donne grandparents, the Revd Roger Donne (1702-73) and his wife Harriot Judith Rival Donne (1706-76); when they died, she lived with Mrs. Balls and, later, with her father's half-sisters. After her father's death, she was chiefly with Mrs Bodham. When her brother, John Johnson, took a house in Dereham in 1791, she lived with him until her marriage in 1796 to Charles Hewitt, of Holt.

JOHN JOHNSON (1769-1833), the son of John Johnson

(1717–85), of Ludham, and Catharine Donne (1740–70), and the brother of Catharine Johnson. He was educated at Bungay Grammar School, Essex; Newpost Grammar School, Essex; and Gonville and Caius College, Cambridge (LLB, 1794; LLD, 1803). He was ordained as deacon at Norwich on 7 July 1793 and as priest the same year. He was appointed a curate of East Dereham, Norfolk, and vicar of Hempnall in 1793, and he became chaplain to the Bishop of Peterborough in the same year. He resigned the curacy at Dereham in 1795 and became curate of Yaxham and Welborne. On 1 January 1800, he was presented by Mrs Bodham to these two livings, which he held until his death on 29 September 1833. In 1807 he married Maria Dorothy Livius, daughter of George Livius, who was the head of the commissariat in India. Their children included William Cowper Johnson (1813–93), John Barham Johnson (1818–94), and Henry Robert Vaughan Johnson (1820–1900).

When John Johnson paid his first visit to Cowper in January 1790, the poet had not been in touch with any of his maternal relations for twenty-seven years. 'Johnny of Norfolk' took a kindly and devoted interest in his elderly cousin and in his writings; for his part, Cowper responded immediately to the vivacity and sincere kindness of 'the wild boy Johnson'. Cowper's friendship with Johnny led to renewed contacts with his Donne relatives.

JOSEPH JOHNSON (1738–1809), publisher and bookseller, was born at Everton, near Liverpool, and arrived in London in 1752. He established himself at St. Paul's Churchyard from 1772 onwards. A man of advanced, firmly held opinions, he published important works on surgery and medicine as well as some of the most innovative literary, social, and political books of his time. His authors included Joseph Priestley, Erasmus Darwin, Horne Tooke, Mary Woolstonecraft, Tom Paine, Henry Fuseli, and Maria Edgeworth. Johnson had been one of the booksellers concerned with the *Olney Hymns*. Newton, whom Cowper consulted at every stage of the publication of *Poems* in 1782, found his publisher for him. Johnson afterwards published *The Task* in 1785 and the translation of Homer in 1791.

MARGARET DEVEILLE, afterwards Mrs KING (1735–93). She was the daughter of the Revd Hans Deveille (d. 1741), Vicar of Saling, Essex (1732–41), and Felsted (1740–1). She married in 1752 the Revd John King (c.1727–6 October 1812), the son of John King (1696–1728), of Stamford, Lincs., a physician and classical scholar. The younger King entered Westminster in July 1738 and left in 1746, and was a fellow student with Cowper. King matriculated from Balliol College, Oxford, on 12 August 1746. He served as the patron and Rector of Pertenhall, Bedfordshire, from 1752 until 1800. King was also a Fellow of King's College, Cambridge.

HENRY MACKENZIE (1745–1831), the writer, was the son of Joshua Mackenzie, an eminent Edinburgh physician. Mackenzie attended Edinburgh University and was trained in the law, but with the publication of *The Man of Feeling* in 1771 his reputation was made and his career as a man-of-letters firmly established. He went on to write other novels (including *The Man of the World*, 1773, and *Julia de Roubigné*, 1777), plays (including *The Prince of Tunis*, 1773), and political writings. He edited *The Mirror* (1779–80) and *The Lounger* (1785–7), both of which were extremely successful periodicals. Mackenzie was involved wholeheartedly in the literary life of his time, partiularly that in Edinburgh; he was a friend of Hume, Home, Robertson, and Burns as well as Scott and Lockhart.

MARTIN MADAN (1725–90). Educated at Westminster (admitted 1736) and Christ Church, Oxford (BA, 1746), and the Inner Temple (admitted 1747), Madan was called to the Bar in 1748. He was a member of the Poetical Club from 1748 to 1750. He was deeply moved by hearing John Wesley preach in 1750 and in this year he obtained Wesley's licence to become an itinerant preacher and was eventually ordained deacon in the Church of England in 1757. Madan was much involved with the Wesleys, Lady Huntingdon, George Whitefield, and other distinguished Methodists. He was Chaplain at the Lock Hospital from 1762 to 1780 and in 1767 was involved in a simony scandal concerning the parish of Aldwinkle. A man of extraordinary faith and self-confidence, he had published several theological works (among others: *A Collection of Hymns, Extracted from Various Authors,* 1760; *A Scriptural Account of the Doctrine of Perfection,* 1763; and *A Scriptural Comment upon the Thirty-nine Articles of the Church of England,* 1771) before the appearance of the infamous *Thelyphthora* in 1781. On 17 December 1751, Martin had married Jane Hale (*c.*1723–91), daughter of Sir Bernard Hale (1677–1729), chief baron of the Irish Exchequer.

JOHN NEWTON (1725–1807) and MARY CATLETT, afterwards Mrs NEWTON (1729–90). Newton, a fervent, extremely dedicated, and sometimes over-zealous man, led a very strange and adventure-filled life before and after his conversion to evangelical Christianity in 1748. His auto-biography, *An Authentic Narrative* (1764), tells the story of his life as the master of a slave-ship and of his conversion. Newton had first gone to sea in 1736 and had made six journeys before 1742. After his marriage to Mary Catlett on 12 February 1750, he made three further voyages, but in 1754, owing to ill health, he relinquished the sea. After his retirement from the sea, Newton was surveyor of tides at Liverpool for five years, using his leisure time for the study of Greek, Hebrew, and theology. Newton applied for Holy Orders to the Archbishop of York in December 1758 but was refused. Afterwards he spent three months in charge of an independent congregation at Warwick in 1760, and was ultimately ordained deacon (29 April) and priest (17 June) in the Church of England in 1764. He accepted the curacy of Olney in 1764, where he remained until 1780, when he became rector of St. Mary Woolnoth in the City of London. In addition to his contributions to the *Olney Hymns* (published 1779), Newton was the author of some important theological works, including *Olney Sermons* (1767), *Omicron's Letters* (1774), and *Cardiphonia* (1781). Mrs Newton was a quiet, unassuming but firm person who suffered from ill health. The friendship between Cowper and Newton became very strained in 1785 when Newton learned that Cowper had asked William Unwin to act as his intermediary with Joseph Johnson in the publication of *The Task*; Newton had acted in a similar capacity with the *Poems* of 1782 and was offended when Cowper did not make use of his services a second time.

JOHN NICHOLS (1745–1826), editor, author, and publisher, was educated at Islington and apprenticed to William Bowyer the younger, whose partner he became in 1766. Nichols' involvement with the *Gentleman's Magazine* began in 1778 and his responsibilities in the management of that periodical increased until he became its editor in 1792, a post he held until his death. Cowper knew Nichols principally through the *Gentleman's Magazine*, but Nichols had written many works and was a scholar of genuine distinction. Among his projects were an edition of the works of William King (1776), *Biographical Anecdotes of Hogarth* (1781), *The History and Antiquities of Leicester* (8 vols., 1795–1815), and an edition of Swift's works (19 vols., 1801).

SAMUEL ROSE (1767–1804) was the son of William Rose who kept a highly regarded school at Chiswick. Rose graduated from the University of Glasgow in 1787, entered Lincoln's Inn, and was called to the Bar in 1796. While a student at Glasgow, Rose lodged with William Richardson, a man of strong literary interests; hence the commission from the professors when Rose called on Cowper in 1787. Cowper's enthusiastic response to the devotion of the younger man, led to the beginning of a cordial and lively friendship. Rose edited the minor works of Goldsmith, compiled two volumes of law reports, and contributed to the *Monthly Review*. His most famous client was William Blake, whom he defended at his trial for treason at Chichester. Although his health was always precarious and he had been quite ill a number of times, there is a legend that he caught a cold in Chichester while defending Blake from which he never recovered. Rose's wife, Sarah, was the eldest daughter of the distinguished physician, William Farr (d. 1809).

CLOTWORTHY ROWLEY (1731–1805). Rowley was the son of Sir William Rowley, KB, Admiral of the Fleet, of Tendring Hall, Stoke by Nayland, Suffolk. Of a robust and unruly nature, Rowley lived in accordance with the adventurous spirit of his extremely distinguished Admiralty family.

Rowley was admitted to Trinity Hall, Cambridge, and then to the Inner Temple in 1750. Rowley and Cowper were neighbours in the Temple. Rowley withdrew from there in 1768, at which time he was called to the Irish Bar, and later became MP for Downpatrick (1771-1801).

ROBERT SMITH (1752-1838), the third but eldest surviving son of Abel Smith (d. 1788), a partner in the family banking firm of Smith, Payne, and Company, of Nottingham and London. Robert, also partner in the family business, entered parliament in 1779 as the member for Nottingham as successor to his brother Abel. Smith opposed North's administration, voted for Shelburne's peace preliminaries, and eventually became a close personal and political friend of Pitt. On 11 July 1796 Smith was created Baron Carrington of Bulcot Lodge in the peerage of Ireland, and on 20 October 1797 he became Baron Carrington of Upton, Nottinghamshire. He served as President of the Board of Agriculture (1800-3) and Captain of Deal Castle (1802). On 6 July 1780 he had married Anne (d. 1827), daughter of Lewyns Boldero Barnard; on 19 January 1836 he married Charlotte (d. 1849), widow of the Revd Walter Trevelyan. Smith died on 18 September 1838 and was succeeded by his only son, Robert (1796-1868). Smith was generous with his money, and Cowper acted as his agent in distributing funds to the poor of Olney.

SAMUEL TEEDON (d. June 1798) seems to have come to Olney from Bedford in 1775. He lived in a cottage at the junction of Dagnell Street and High Street and was employed as the Olney schoolmaster. Teedon lived with Eusebius Killingworth and his mother Elizabeth. Eusebius, or 'Worthy' as Teedon called him, helped his cousin teach and also bound books for a livelihood. Although Cowper sometimes spoke of Teedon's religious fervour in a humorous way ('Mr. Teedon, who favors us now and then with his company in an Evening as usual, was not long since discoursing with that Eloquence which is so peculiar to himself on the many Providential interpositions that had taken place in his favor.' Cowper to Unwin, 7 February 1785), he began to pay more and more attention to Teedon's divinations of his spiritual fate, and the friendship was particularly intense from 1792 to 1794.

HENRY THORNTON (1760–1815), of Clapham, Surrey, was the third son of the wealthy merchant and devoted Evangelical, John Thornton (1720–90). After his apprenticeship to a merchant in 1778, Henry became a partner in his father's business, and in 1784 a partner in the bank of Downe, Thornton and Free of Bartholomew Lane, London. He was a substantial contributor to government loans in that capacity. From 24 September 1782 until his death, he served as the member of parliament for Southwark, and he generally supported the policies of Shelburne and Pitt. On 1 March 1796 he married Marianne, daughter of Joseph Sykes; he was the father of three sons and six daughters.

MARIA CATHERINE GIFFARD, afterwards Mrs JOHN THROCKMORTON, and later LADY THROCKMORTON (1762–1821), was the daughter of Thomas Giffard (d. 1775), by his first wife Barbara, daughter of the 8th Baron Petre, the son of the Baron in *The Rape of the Lock*. She married John Throckmorton (1753–1819) in 1782. The Giffards, like the Throckmortons and the Petres, were an old Catholic family, long established at Chillington Hall in Staffordshire. John Throckmorton succeeded in 1791 to the estate and baronetcy of his grandfather Sir Robert (1702–91) and went to live at Buckland House, Berks.

The cultivation, breeding, friendliness, and youthfulness of the Throckmortons captivated Cowper, and he was especially interested and involved in the activities of the family from 1786, when he moved to Weston and John Throckmorton became his landlord. John Throckmorton was a prominent recusant, being a member of the Catholic Committee; he was also a personal friend of Charles James Fox and a sympathizer with the Prince of Wales. Despite what must have been for Cowper objectionable sides to John's character so far as religious and political matters went, he nevertheless felt a real affection and devotion to the Throckmortons, and especially to Mrs Throckmorton, who was an eager copyist of his translation of Homer and who inspired three short poems and some charming letters. The Throckmortons as a family probably reminded Cowper of the cultivated and sophisticated society which he had once experienced in London and of which he had intermittent glimpses through the visits and letters of Lady Hesketh.

EDWARD THURLOW, FIRST BARON THURLOW (1731–1806), Lord Chancellor. Thurlow, eldest son of the Revd Thomas Thurlow (d. 1762), was born at Brecon Ash, Norfolk; educated at Seckars School, Scarning, Norfolk; King's School, Canterbury; and Gonville and Caius College, Cambridge, which he left without a degree. He then went to the office of Chapman, a solicitor of Ely Place, Holborn, where he was the workmate and companion of Cowper, who introduced him to his uncle Ashley and his family in Southampton Row. On 9 January 1752 Thurlow was admitted a member of the Inner Temple, and was called to the Bar on 22 November 1754. Thurlow was appointed solicitor-general in 1770, and attorney-general one year later. Thurlow's strong support of George III's North American policy led to his elevation to Lord Chancellor and to the title of Baron Thurlow in 1778. In April 1783 Thurlow was forced by the coalition of Fox and North to resign his post, but it was restored to him late in that year. He continued as Lord Chancellor until June 1792. A brilliant lawyer, skilful politician, and uncanny tactician, Thurlow was nevertheless often accused of vulgarity in his handling of legal cases and of duplicity in many of his administrative dealings.

OWNERS OF MANUSCRIPTS

There are 356 letters in this volume, 294 from holographs, 12 from manuscript copies, and 53 from printed sources. (The texts of two letters — 9 January 1788 and 31 October 1791 — are derived from both manuscript fragments and printed sources. The text of 10 February 1791 is a composite made from manuscripts and a manuscript copy.) Manuscripts or manuscript copies of Cowper's letters in this volume are, for the most part, in the collections of the Misses C. and A. Cowper Johnson (30), The Panshanger Collection, property of

Rosemary, Lady Ravensdale (28), The Pierpont Morgan Library (30), and Princeton University Library (126). In addition, the following own or owned holographs or manuscript copies of letters printed in this volume: The British Library (7), the Buffalo and Erie County Library (1), (formerly) Miss C. M. Bull (7), the Estate of Lord Charnwood (1), The Cowper and Newton Museum, Olney (15), The Harry L. Dalton Collection (1), (formerly) Mrs Augusta Donne (1), Fitzwilliam Museum, Cambridge (1), (formerly) Mrs Walter F. Harden (1), Harvard University Library (2), Haverford College Library (2), The Historical Society of Pennsylvania (3), The Henry E. Huntington Library and Art Gallery (1), Mrs Donald F. Hyde (1), Miss Mary Barham Johnson (9), Lehigh University Library (1), The City Library, Liverpool (1), H. C. Longuet-Higgins (3), (formerly) Hugh Longuet-Higgins (1), Maine Historical Society (1), McMaster University Library (1), The Carl H. Pforzheimer Library (6), The John Rylands Library (1), Charles Ryskamp (4), The Scottish Record Office (1), The Society of Antiquaries (1), The South African Library (1), Sir Robert Throckmorton (12), Trinity College, Cambridge (1), The Victoria and Albert Museum (1), The Earl Waldegrave (1), Yale University Library (4), including 1 in the Osborn Collection. (The text of Cowper's letter of 24 June 1788 is derived from two manuscript sources; the text of 31 October 1791 is derived from two manuscript sources as well as from print.)

LETTERS 1787–1791

JOSEPH HILL
Monday, 1 January, 1787

Cowper Johnson

My dear friend,

Your letter dated the 23d. of December did not reach me 'till this day the 1st. of January, having been a whole week on its travels no mortal knows whither, owing to a direction rather too Laconic. It reached me at last by the Cross Post[1] from Stratford. I thank you heartily for the Contents and for your friendly offer in the close of it, but hope to have no occasion to encroach any farther on your kindness, now. That Beast of a Frog,[2] what must we do with him? He is Welsh I suppose by his name, and I have no great opinion of the descendants of Cadwallader. I wish he would pay me my rent and go back to his mountains.

My friend, may all happiness attend you and yours, which is from my heart the sincere New-year's wish of your Affectionate

Wm Cowper.

Jan 1. 1787

Received of Joseph Hill Esqr. the Sum of Thirty pounds by Draft on Child and Co. by

£30.0.0

Wm Cowper
Weston Underwood
Near Olney
Bucks.

[1] The post, inaugurated by Ralph Allen in 1720, which carried letters on cross-country routes.

[2] Probably a reference to the Morgan who rented C's chambers at the Inner Temple. See n.1, C to Hill, 27 May 1777.

WALTER BAGOT   Wednesday, 3 January 1787

Weston Jan 3. 1787.

My dear friend,

You wish to hear from me at any calm Interval of Epic
frenzy. An Interval presents itself, but whether calm or not is
perhaps doubtful. Is it possible for a man to be calm who for
3 weeks past has been perpetually occupied in slaughter.
Letting out one man's bowels, smiting another through the
gullet, transfixing the liver of another, and lodging an arrow
in the buttock of a fourth? Read the 13th. book of the Iliad,
and you will find such amusing incidents as these the subject
of it, the sole subject.[1] In order to interest myself in it and to
catch the spirit of it, I had need discard all humanity. It is
woeful work, and were the best poet in the world to give us
at this day such a List of Killed and wounded, he would not
escape universal censure, to the praise of a more enlighten'd age
be it spoken. I have waded through much blood, and through
much more I must wade before I shall have finish'd. I determine in the mean time to account it all very sublime, and for
two reasons. First, because all the Learned think so, and 2dly,
because I am to translate it. But were I an indifferent by-
stander perhaps I should venture to wish that Homer had
applied his wonderful powers to a less disgusting subject. He
has in the Odyssey, and I long to get at it.

I have not the good fortune to meet with any of these fine
things that you say are printed in my praise. But I learn from
certain Advertisements in the Morning Herald, that I make a
conspicuous figure in the Entertainments of Free Masons' Hall.[2]

[1] Othryoneus' bowels are run through by Idomeneus' lance at line 458. Asius
attacks 'Idomeneus, who with his lance / Him reaching first, pierced him beneath
the chin / Into his throat, and urged the weapon through' (lines 479–81). Antilochus
then gashes the charioteer of Asius through the waist (lines 490–2). Next, a lance
glanced off Idomeneus' 'targe' and 'pierced the liver of Hypsenor, son / of Hippasus'
(lines 505–6). After much more slaughter, we read of the death of Harpalion:
'... swift flew the dart / To his right buttock, slipp'd beneath the bone, / His
bladder grazed, and started through before. / There ended his retreat; sudden he
sank / And like a worm lay on the ground, his life / Exhaling in his fellow-warrior's
arms / And with his sable blood soaking the plain' (lines 790–6).

[2] 'At the Free Mason's Tavern, this evening, December 19, will be presented an
Attic Entertainment, with variations and additions, in three parts. Consisting of

I learn also that my Volumes are out of print, and that a third Edition is soon to be published.[3] But if I am not gratified with the sight of Odes composed to my honour and glory, I have at least been tickled with some douceurs of a very flattering nature by the Post. A Lady[4] unknown addresses me by the appellation of the first of poets and the best of men — An unknown Gentleman[5] has read my inimitable poems and invites me to his seat in Hampshire. Another Incognito[6] gives me hopes of a Memorial in his garden, and a Welsh Attorney of Brecon[7] sends me his verses to revise, and obligingly asks

> Say, shall my little bark attendant sail,
> Pursue the triumph and partake the gale?[8]

If you find me a little vain hereafter, my friend, you must excuse it in consideration of these powerful incentives, especially the latter; for surely the poet who can charm an Attorney, especially a Welsh one, must be at least an Orpheus if not something greater.

Your Brother Chester[9] has been so kind as to give me a Morning call, and his visit though short was as sweet as the most obliging and friendly behaviour could make it. It makes me regret what I have seldom in my life regretted, that I keep no carriage nor even a horse. We are now 5 miles asunder, the ways are too dirty for a walk, and I am not quite so good at a walk of ten miles as I used to be, even when they are clean. But I know he will be so kind as not to hold me to a punctilio, and indeed he told me so at parting.

Mrs. Unwin is as much delighted as myself with our present situation, and often says that as far as situation is concerned she has not now a wish ungratified. But it is a sort of April weather life that we lead in this world. A little sunshine is

Readings and Imitations ... Part III. Poetical Extracts, from the Works of William Cowper, of the Inner-temple, Esq. by Mr. Phillips.' *The Morning Herald* for Tuesday, 19 Dec. 1786 (No. 1919).

[3] The third edition of *Poems* was published in 1787. 'The text follows the first edition of both volumes, with numerous minor corrections and revisions of spelling and punctuation and some verbal changes ...': *Russell*, pp. 56–7.

[4] Unidentified.   [5] Biddlecombe. See C to Lady Hesketh, 4 Dec. 1786.

[6] Unidentified.   [7] Walter Churchey.

[8] C is quoting lines 385–6 from Epistle IV from Pope's *Essay on Man*.

[9] Charles Chester. See n.2, C to Hill, 13 Feb. 1783.

generally the prelude to a storm. Hardly had we begun to enjoy
the change, when the death of her son cast a gloom upon
every thing. He was a most exemplary man; of your order;
learned, polite and amiable. The father of lovely children,
and the husband of a wife very much like dear Mrs. Bagot,
who adored him. Returning from a Western tour to his Living
in Essex he was seized with a putrid fever at Winchester and
died there.

Adieu my friend — remember me to your brother Richard[10]
when you see or write to him, and believe me with Mrs.
Unwin's best respects

> Your affectionate
> Wm Cowper.

LADY HESKETH Monday and Tuesday, 8–9 January 1787

Address: Lady Hesketh / New Norfolk Street / Grosvenor Square / London.
Postmarks: 10/IA *and* OULNEY
Panshanger Collection

The Lodge Jan. 8. 1787.

It costs me no great difficulty my Dear, to read your
letters; a strong inclination and a pretty deal of practise are
excellent qualifications. It happens now and then that a word
calls for closer attention than its neighbors and perhaps I am
forced to wipe my spectacles before I can perfectly master it,
but a hand-writing so good as yours is when you chuse to
write well, can never be inexplicable at the worst. At least I
have never found it so.

I have had a little nervous fever lately my Dear, that has
somewhat abridged my sleep, and though I find myself better
to-day than I have been since it seized me, yet I feel my head
lightish and not in the best order for writing. You will find
me therefore perhaps not only less alert in my manner than I
usually am when my spirits are good, but rather shorter. I
will however proceed to scribble 'till I find that it fatigues
me, and then will do as I know you would bid me do were
you here, shut up my desk and take a walk.

[10] Richard Howard. See n.2, C to Bagot, [24] Jan. 1786.

Trouble not thyself my sweet Coz to ask any questions concerning the Cardinal Epistle.[1] It is an affair of so little consequence that it would not be worth while to ask any body's permission to do it, especially as it is probable, the letter being genuine and its fair auth'ress living, that it would be deem'd improper.

The good General, who I find is still at Kingston, though through misapprehension of a passage in one of your late letters, I thought him settled in Town for the Winter, writes me word that his eye is much better, and seems to express himself as confident of a cure. News which gave me the greatest pleasure. He tells me that in the 8 first books which I have sent him he still finds alterations and amendments necessary, of which I myself am equally persuaded. And he asks my leave to lay them before an initimate friend of his of whom he gives a character that bespeaks him highly deserving of the Trust.[2] To this I have no objection. Desiring only to make the Translation as perfect as I can make it, if God grant me Life and health, I would spare no labour that might be necessary to secure that point. The General's letter is extremely kind and both for matter and manner like all the rest of his dealings with his Cousin the poet.

I had a Letter also yesterday from Mr. Smith, Member for Nottingham.[3] Though we never saw each other, he writes to me in the most friendly terms, and interests himself much in my Homer and in the success of my Subscription. Speaking on this latter subject, he says, that my poems are read by hundreds who know nothing of my Proposals, and makes no doubt that they would subscribe, if they did. I have myself always thought them imperfectly, or rather insufficiently announced, and shall send Johnson a line I believe by this post, to desire him to bind up an Advertizement of the Homer with the Edition of my poems that is just coming out. I blame myself that I did not think of this measure at the publication of the second Edition, having lost, I fear, some advantage by the neglect. Johnson should indeed have thought

---

[1] We do not know the document to which C refers.
[2] Unidentified.
[3] See List of Correspondents in this volume.

of it himself, but the Bookseller is almost as idle as his Author is inattentive.

I could pity the poor woman who has been weak enough [to clai]m[4] my song; such pilferings are sure to be detected. I w[rote] it, I know not how long, but I suppose 4 years ago. The rose in question was a rose given to Lady Austen by Mrs. Unwin, and the incident that suggested the subject occurred in the room in which you slept at the Vicarage, which Lady Austen made her Dining-room. Some time since, perhaps 2 years or more, Mr. Bull going to London I gave him a copy of it which he undertook to convey to *Nicholls* Printer of the Gentleman's Magazine. He show'd it to a Mrs. *Cardell*, who begg'd to copy it and promised to send it to the Printers by her servant. Three or 4 months after, and when I had concluded that it was lost, I saw it in the Gentleman's Magazine with my signature. W C. Poor simpleton! She will find now perhaps that the rose had a thorn and that she has prick'd her fingers with it.[5]

A basket my Dear that you announced some time since containing Crockery, is not yet arrived, and Rogers[6] assures us that it is not in the Warehouse in London. I mention it, lest any accident should have befallen it.

Mrs. Unwin begs me to mention her to you with affection. Our chairs are cushion'd and my study is much indebted to them for neatness and smartness of appearance.

Adieu! my beloved Cousin. I have done my possibles. That is to say, all that I can do without hurting my noddle. And I have a letter to write to the General beside. May God bless thee and preserve us both to another happy meeting!

Thine ever
Wm Cowper.

P.S.
Tuesday Jan 9
You have our best Love & thanks my Dear for the Basket and

[4] MS torn.

[5] C may be referring to the fact that Mrs Cardell would have been embarrassed by the notice which was printed with the poem ('The Rose') in the June 1785 issue of *GM* (474): 'We have a particular reason for telling this correspondent, that "the coxcomb in livery," DID NOT PAY the postage of his *last* favour. EDIT.'

[6] The waggoner.

Box which arrived last night and all the Contents safe. Sir Giles's thanks in particular for the Gingerbread.[7] With the Muslin came a puzzling. It measures just 2 yards & 3 quarters. Now as I always wear 3 corner'd neck-cloths which are cut across, a difficulty occurs how to make the whole into neck-cloths without waste. If there is any new fashion in the Cutting of them, you can inform us.

The Cups, Saucers &c are all very pretty & much admired. There being a whole dozen of Cups we suppose they are Tea or Coffee cups indiscriminately.

JOSEPH JOHNSON   Tuesday, 9 January 1787

Maggs Catalogue 266[1]

In a letter ... from Mr. Smith of Lombard Street he expresses himself thus: your poems are, I doubt not, read by hundreds who know nothing of your proposals.

I think this very probable, and as the best remedy that I can devize, propose it to you to bind up with the Edition that I understand you have now in preparation, an advertizement of my Homer ...[2] Present my compliments to Mr. Fuseli, an indisposition of the feverish kind has for these 2 or 3 days interrupted my progress in the Translation, but I hope soon to take it up again.

JOHN NEWTON   Saturday, 13 January 1787

South African Library

                                        Weston Underwood.
                                        Jan. 13. 1787.
My dear friend —
    It gave me pleasure, such as it was, to learn by a letter

---

[7] See C to Lady Hesketh, 24 Dec. 1786 and n.2.

---

[1] The present whereabouts of this MS, which is described as an 'A.L.S. 1 full page, small 4to. Weston Underwood, 9 Jany., 1787.', is unknown. Catalogue 266 (Easter 1911), item 313.

[2] An undated *Proposals* for C's translation of the *Iliad* and *Odyssey* did appear at the back of Volume II of the third edition.

from Mr. H. Thornton, that the Inscription for the tomb of poor Unwin has been approved of.[1] The Dead have nothing to do with human praises, but if they died in the Lord they have abundant praises to render to Him, which is far better. The Dead, whatever they leave behind them, have nothing to regret. Good Christians are the only creatures in the world that are truely good, and them they will see again and see them improved, therefore them they regret not. Regret is for the Living. What we get we soon lose, and what we lose we regret. The most obvious consolation in this case seems to be, that we who regret others, shall quickly become objects of regret ourselves, for Mankind are continually passing off in a rapid succession.

I have many kind friends who, like yourself, wish that instead of turning my endeavours to a Translation of Homer, I had proceeded in the way of Original poetry. But I can truely say that it was order'd otherwise; not by me, but by the Providence that governs all my thoughts and directs my intentions as he pleases. It may seem strange but it is true, that after having written a volume, in general, with great ease to myself, I found it impossible to write another page. The mind of man is not a fountain, but a cistern, and mine, God knows, a broken one. It is my Creed, that the Intellect depends as much both for the energy and the multitude of its exertions, upon the operations of God's agency upon it, as the Heart for the exercise of its Graces, upon the influences of the Holy Spirit. According to this persuasion I may very reasonably affirm that it was not God's pleasure that I should proceed in the same track, because he did not enable me to do it. A whole year I waited, and waited in circumstances of mind that made a state of non-employment peculiarly irksome. I long'd for the pen as the only remedy, but I could find no subject. Extreme distress of spirit at last drove me, as if I mistake not, I told you some time since, to lay Homer before me and to translate for amusement. Why it pleased God that I should be hunted into such a business, of such enormous length and labour, by miseries for which he did not see good to afford me any other remedy, I know not. But so it was.

[1] See, however, C to Newton, 25 April 1793.

And jejune as the consolation may be, and unsuited to the exigencies of a mind and heart that once were spiritual, yet a thousand times have I been glad of it, for a thousand times it has served at least to divert my attention in some degree from such terrible tempests as I believe have seldom been permitted to beat upon a human mind. Let my friends therefore who wish me some little measure of tranquillity in the performance of the most turbulent voyage that ever Christian mariner made, be contented that having Homer's mountains and forests to windward, I escape under their shelter from the force of many a gust that would almost overset me; especially when they consider that not by choice but by necessity I make *them* my refuge. As to fame and honour and glory that may be acquired by poetical feats of any sort, God knows that if I could lay me down in the grave with Hope at my side, or sit with Hope at my side in a dungeon all the residue of my days, I would cheerfully waive them all. For the little fame that I have already earned, has never saved me from one terrible night or from one despairing day since I first acquired it. *For* what I am reserved, or *to* what, is a mystery. I would fain hope not merely that I may amuse others, or only to be a Translator of Homer.

Sally Perry's[2] case has given us much concern ever since we heard it. I have no doubt that it is distemper, and heartily wish her cured. But distresses of mind that are occasion'd by distemper are the most difficult of all to deal with. They refuse all consolation, they will hear no reason. God only, by his own immediate impressions can remove them, as after an experience of 13 years' misery I can abundantly testify.

The Oysters after whose arrival you enquired reach'd us safe, and were excellent. The Cocoa nut was equally good in its way. Our thanks are due for both and we pay them heartily. Mrs. Unwin is pretty well, and I as well as I generally am at this season of the year, when an obstructed perspiration is apt to affect me feverishly. Accept our united love to yourself and Mrs. Newton, and believe me, as ever, Your affectionate

Wm Cowper.

[2] She may have been a daughter of Mr Perry of Lavendon Mills, a friend of Newton's.

LADY HESKETH   Sunday–Tuesday, 14–16 January 1787

Address: Lady Hesketh / New Norfolk Street / Grosvenor Square / London.
Postmarks: JANUARY/17/D *and* OULNEY
British Library

The Lodge Sunday Jan. 14. 1787

My dearest Cousin — I have been so much indisposed in the course of the last week with the fever that I told you had seized me, as not to be able to follow my last letter with another, sooner, which I should otherwise certainly have done, because I know that you will feel some anxiety about me. My nights during the whole week may be said to have been almost sleepless, for waking generally about One in the morning, I slept no more till toward the time when I commonly used to rise. The consequence has been that except the translation of about 30 lines at the conclusion of the 13th book, I have been forced to abandon Homer entirely. This was a sensible mortification to me, as you may suppose, and felt the more, because my spirits of course failing with my strength, I seemed to have peculiar need of my old amusement. It seemed hard therefore to be forced to resign it just when I wanted it most. But Homer's battles cannot be fought by a man who does not sleep well, and who has not some little degree of animation in the day time. Last night however, quite contrary to my expectation, the fever left me entirely, and I slept quietly, soundly, and long. If it please God that it returns not, I shall soon find myself in a condition to proceed. I would now take the Bark,[1] but my stomach will not bear it, either the gross bark or the Tincture. Hoffman,[2] and Daffy,[3] and now and then a very small quantity of Magnesia, are the only medicines that do not seem to poison me, and they in their turn have each of them done me service. I walk constantly, that is to say Mrs. Unwin and I together, for at these times I

[1] *The London Chronicle* for 1–3 July 1783 (liv): 'This Medicine, so universally celebrated for the cure of agues, intermittent and putrid fevers, nervous head-achs, &c. may be had in the highest perfection, either in tincture or in powder . . .'

[2] One of the many compounds devised by the German physician Friedrich Hoffman (1660–1742).

[3] The celebrated elixir, made from senna, jalap, aniseed, caraway seeds, juniper berries, treacle, and water, which was invented by the Revd Thomas Daffy (d. 1680). In *GM* lx, pt. 2 (Sept. 1790), C published a facetious letter in which he queries the origins of this medication. See *Russell*, p. 137.

keep her continually employ'd and never suffer her to be absent from me many minutes. She gives me all her time and all her attention and forgets that there is another object in the world.

I believe my Dear I sent you very slovenly thanks for the Contents of the Box and basket. If I did, it was owing partly to want of room at the top of my letter, and partly to a cause that always prevents my being very diffuse on that topic, which is that to a heart generous and kind as yours a great deal of acknowledgment is only another word for a great deal of trouble. I now however repeat my thanks for all in general, and for the green cloth I give my Uncle thanks in particular. Present my Love to him into the bargain, and tell him that I hope he will live to give me such another piece when this shall be worn out. The leaves for fruit and the baskets are beautiful, and we shall rejoice to see them filled with raspberries, strawberries and cherries for you. Thanks also for the neat smart Almanac. And now I am on the subject of Thanksgiving, I beg that when you shall next see or write to my name-sake of Epsom,[4] you will mention me to him with much gratitude and affection, for him alone of all my benefactors I seem to forget, though in fact I do not forget him but have the warmest sense of his kindness. I shall be happy if it please God to spare my life 'till an opportunity may offer, to take him by the hand at Weston.

Mrs. Carter thinks on the subject of dreams as every body else does, that is to say according to her own experience.[5]

---

[4] William Cowper (1750–98), Maria Cowper's son, who in 1786 had bestowed £10 per year on C. See C to Unwin, 10–11 July 1786.

[5] C seems to be referring to *Rambler* Number 44 (18 Aug. 1750) which was written by Elizabeth Carter (1717–1806), who also wrote *Rambler* Number 100. Mrs Carter does not specifically state that dreams are 'the ordinary operations of the Fancy', but she does describe how a frightening nightmare is succeeded by a pleasant dream: 'In this sad situation I spied on one hand of me a deep muddy river, whose heavy waves rolled on in slow sullen murmurs. Here I determined to plunge, and was just upon the brink, when I found myself suddenly drawn back. I turned about, and was surprised by the sight of the loveliest object I had ever beheld. The most engaging charms of youth and beauty appeared in all her form; effulgent glories sparkled in her eyes, and their awful splendours were softened by the gentlest looks of compassion and peace.' *The Rambler*, ed. W. J. Bate and Albrecht B. Strauss (New Haven, 1969), i. 238–9. Mrs Carter also describes how the beautiful creature, who calls herself 'Religion', eschews those who dwell on melancholy thoughts (i. 242): '"Return then with me from continual misery to

13

She has had no extraordinary ones, and therefore accounts them only the ordinary operations of the Fancy. Mine are of a texture that will not suffer me to ascribe them to so inadequate a cause, or to any cause but the operation of an exterior agency. I have a mind my Dear (and to you I will venture to boast of it) as free from superstition as any man living, neither do I give heed to dreams in general as predictive, though particular dreams I believe to be so. Some very sensible persons, and I suppose Mrs. Carter among them, will acknowledge that in old times God spoke by dreams, but affirm with much boldness that he has since ceased to do so. If you ask them, Why? They answer because he has now reveal'd his Will in the Scripture, and there is no longer any need that he should instruct or admonish us in dreams —. I grant that with respect to doctrines and precepts, he has left us in want of nothing; but has he thereby precluded himself in any of the operations of his Provid[ence?] Surely not. It is perfectly a different consideration; and the sam[e] need that there ever was of his interference in this way, there is still and ever must be, while man continues blind and fallible and a creature beset with dangers which he can neither foresee, nor obviate. His operations however of this kind are I allow very rare, and as to the generality of dreams, they are made of such stuff and are in themselves so insignificant, that though I believe them all to be the manufacture of others, not our own, I account it not a farthing matter who makes them. As to my own peculiar experience in the dreaming way I have only this to observe. I have not believed that I shall perish because in dreams I have been told it, but because I have had hardly any but terrible dreams for 13 years, I therefore have spent the greatest part of that time most unhappily. They have either tinged my mind with melancholy or filled it with terrour, and

moderate enjoyment, and grateful alacrity. Return from the contracted views of solitude to the proper duties of a relative and dependent being. Religion is not confined to cells and closets, nor restrained to sullen retirement. These are the gloomy doctrines of Superstition..."' From the context of C's letter, it would seem that Lady Hesketh, who was attempting to relieve C from the depression following a series of nightmares, cited Mrs Carter's essay or had discussed C's dreams with this renowned expert whom she sometimes entertained (see *Walpole*, ii. 236). In rebuttal, C is saying that Mrs Carter's ability to move from a nightmare to a pleasant dream is in accord with 'her own experience' but that his dreams are of 'a texture that will not suffer [him] to ascribe them to so inadequate a cause...'

the effect has been unavoidable. If we swallow arsenic we must be poison'd, and he who dreams as I have done, must be troubled. So much for dreams.

Tuesday.

I have always worn the three-corner'd kerchiefs, and Mrs. U. will easily find an use for the odd bit, therefore will not trouble you with the muslin again.

Thanks my Dear for the very handsome Turchas[6] dish which arrived safe last night. — My fever is not yet gone, but sometimes seems to leave me. It is altogether of the nervous kind and attended now and then with much dejection.

A young Gentleman called here yesterday who came 6 miles out of his way to see me. He was on a journey to London from Glasgow, having just left the University there. He came I suppose partly to satisfy his own curiosity, but chiefly as it seemed to bring me the thanks of some of the Scotch professors for my 2 volumes. His name is Rose, an Englishman and very genteel. Your spirits being good you will derive more pleasure from this incident than I can at present, therefore I send it.

Adieu Dearest, Dearest Cousin. Yours Wm C.

SAMUEL ROSE
Hayley, i. 240–1

Tuesday, 24 July 1787

Weston, July 24th 1787.

Dear Sir,

This is the first time I have written these six months, and nothing but the constraint of obligation could induce me to write now. I cannot be so wanting to myself as not to endeavour at least, to thank you both for the visits with which you have favoured me, and the Poems that you sent me; in my present state of mind I taste nothing; nevertheless I read; partly from habit, and partly because it is the only thing that I am capable of.

I have therefore read Burns's Poems,[1] and have read them

---

[6] Turquoise.

---

[1] Burns's poems (*Poems, Chiefly in the Scottish Dialect*) first appeared in print

twice. And though they be written in a language that is new to me, and many of them on subjects much inferior to the author's ability, I think them on the whole a very extra-ordinary production. He is, I believe, the only Poet these kingdoms have produced in the lower rank of life, since Shakespeare, I should rather say since Prior, who need not be indebted for any part of his praise, to a charitable consider-ation of his origin, and the disadvantages under which he has laboured. It will be pity if he should not hereafter divest himself of barbarism, and content himself with writing pure English, in which he appears perfectly qualified to excel. He who can command admiration, dishonours himself if he aims no higher than to raise a laugh.

I am, dear Sir, with my best wishes for your prosperity, and with Mrs. Unwin's respects,

Your obliged and affectionate humble servant,
W.C.

JOSEPH HILL   Saturday, 4 August 1787

Cowper Johnson

My dear friend —

I write no Letters; but when money comes it seems neces-sary that I should acknowledge the Receipt of it. I am obliged to you for the Draft of 30Ł which the last Post brought me, and the more, because it makes me, for a part of that Sum, your Debtor. A Rheumatic disorder in my back has lately made me almost a Prisoner to my chair, but I am better. You may not forget perhaps that I was once crippled by the same complaint when we were at Weymouth.[1] I give you joy of

in 1786 in an edition published at Kilmarnock. The second, enlarged edition appeared in Edinburgh on 17 Apr. 1787. C owned a copy of the Edinburgh edition (*Keynes*, 54), apparently the gift of Rose.

[1] *A Tour through the South of England . . . made during the Summer of 1791* (1793), pp. 39-40: 'The prospect [of Weymouth] consists of the town, situated in a low, but agreeable spot, commanding at the same time the sea, and a distant view of the Isle of Portland. Weymouth is a little, narrow, dirty place, ill-paved, and irregularly built. The new street, called the Esplanade, is well situated, and facing the sea, has a handsome appearance . . . . Was it not for its bathing place, and the

the appearance of summer coming at last, and wish that after long confinement in the shackles of business you may receive in the improvement and establishment of your health, all the benefit of a more favorable season than the present year has yet afforded.

Accept my thanks for repeated remittances of the finest fish and believe me with

my best respects to Mrs. Hill
affectionately Yours
Wm Cowper.

Weston Lodge
  Augt. 4. 1787.
  I have to acknowledge likewise the Receipt of a Note for 40£ that reached me in the Spring.

SAMUEL ROSE   Monday, 27 August 1787

Hayley, i. 242-4

Weston, Aug. 27, 1787.

Dear Sir

I have not yet taken up the pen again, except to write to you. The little taste that I have had of your company, and your kindness in finding me out, make me wish, that we were nearer neighbours, and that there were not so great a disparity in our years; that is to say, not that you were older, but that I were younger. Could we have met in early life, I flatter myself that we might have been more intimate, than now we are likely to be. But you shall not find me slow to cultivate such a measure of your regard, as your friends of your own age can spare me. When your route shall lie through this country, I shall hope that the same kindness which has prompted you twice to call on me, will prompt you again; and I shall be happy if on a future occasion, I may be able to give you a more cheerful reception, than can be expected from an invalid. My health and spirits are considerably improved, and I once more associate with my neighbours. My head

late visits of the King, few would resort to Weymouth for the pleasure it affords. It has, perhaps, the finest shore for bathing in the whole world.'

however has been the worst part of me, and still continues so; is subject to giddiness and pain, maladies very unfavourable to poetical employment; but a preparation of the Bark, which I take regularly, has so far been of service to me in those respects, as to encourage in me a hope, that by perseverance in the use of it, I may possibly find myself qualified to resume the Translation of Homer.

When I cannot walk, I read; and read perhaps more than is good for me. But I cannot be idle. The only mercy that I shew myself in this respect is, that I read nothing that requires much closeness of application. I lately finished the perusal of a book, which in former years I have more than once attacked, but never till now conquered; some other book always interfered, before I could finish it. The work I mean is Barclay's Argenis[1], and if ever you allow yourself to read for mere amusement, I can recommend it to you (provided you have not already perused it) as the most amusing romance that ever was written. It is the only one indeed of an old date that I ever had the patience to go through with. It is interesting in a high degree; richer in incident than can be imagined, full of surprizes, which the reader never forestalls, and yet free from all entanglement and confusion. The stile too appears to me to be such as would not dishonour Tacitus himself.

Poor Burns loses much of his deserved praise in this country, through our ignorance of his language. I despair of meeting with any Englishman who will take the pains that I have taken to understand him. His candle is bright but shut up in a dark lantern. I lent him to a very sensible neighbour of mine, but his uncouth dialect spoiled all and before he had half read him through, he was quite *ramfeezled*.[2]

W. C.

---

[1] *Argenis*, a satire in Latin on political faction and conspiracy, was published in 1621. The first English translation of the work by John Barclay (1582-1621) appeared in 1625 in London.
[2] This word occurs in line 13 of the second poem addressed to 'J. L******K, an Old Scotch Bard' in Burns's poems (see n.1, C to Rose, 24 July 1787); it means to be 'exhausted'.

LADY HESKETH   Thursday, 30 August 1787

Address: Lady Hesketh / New Norfolk Street / Grosvenor Square / London.
Postmarks: AU/31/87 *and* OULNEY
H. C. Longuet-Higgins

The Lodge
Augt. 30. 1787.

My dearest Cousin,

Though it costs me something to write, it would cost me more to be silent. My intercourse with my neighbors being renew'd, I can no longer seem to forget how many reasons there are why you especially should not be neglected; no neighbor indeed, but the kindest of my friends, and 'ere long I hope, an inmate.

My health and Spirits seem to be mending daily. To what end I know not, Neither will conjecture, but endeavor, as far as I can, to be content that they do so. I use exercise and take the Air in the Park and Wilderness. I read much, but, as yet, write not. Our friends at the Hall make themselves more and more amiable in our account, by treating us rather as old friends, than as friends newly acquired. There are few days in which we do not meet, and I am now almost as much at Home in their house, as in our own. Mr. T. having long since put me in possession of all his grounds, has now given me possession of his library. An acquisition of great value to me, who never have been able to live without books since I first knew my letters, and who have no books of my own. By his means I have been so well supplied, that I have not yet even look'd at the Lownger,[1] for which however I do not forget that I am obliged to you. *His* turn comes next, and I shall probably begin him to morrow. Mr. George Throck-n is at the Hall, and the whole party drink Tea with us this Evening. I thought I had known these Brothers long enough to have found out all their Talents and accomplishments; but I was mistaken. The day before yesterday after having walked with us, they *carried* us up to the Library (a more accurate Writer would have said *conducted* us) and there they show'd me the Contents of an immense Port-folio, the Work of their own hands. It was furnished with drawings of the Architectural

[1] See n.1, C to Mackenzie, 15 Sept. 1787.

19

kind, executed in a most masterly manner, and among others, contained outside and inside views of the Pantheon. I mean the Roman one.[2] They were all, I believe made at Rome. Some men may be justly enough estimated at the first Interview, but the Throcks must be seen often and known long before one can understand all their value.

They often enquire after you, and ask me whether you visit Weston this Autumn. I answer, yes; and I charge you, my Dearest Coz, to authenticate my information. Write to me, and tell us when we may expect you. We were disappointed that we had no Letter from you this Morning. — You will find me when you come, coated and Button'd according to your recommendation. Mr. Palmer[3] happening to go to Town, purchased the materials in person.

I write but little because writing is become new to me; but I shall come on by degrees. Mrs. U. begs to be affectionately mention'd to you. She is in tolerable health, which is the chief comfort here that I have to boast of.

A sudden twirl in my head says I have written enough. A hint which, at the end of my paper, I am forced to attend to. Yours, my Dearest Coz. as ever

Wm Cowper.

Mr. Wrighte[4] stopp'd here this Morning in his Phæthon, but we were out.

LADY HESKETH   Tuesday, 4 September 1787

Address: Lady Hesketh / New Norfolk Street / Grosvenor Square / London.
Postmark: SE/5/87
Panshanger Collection

The Lodge
Septbr. 4. 1787.

My dearest Coz,
Come when thou canst come, secure of being always

---

[2] C is making it clear that he is not referring to the Pantheon built on the south side of Oxford Street and designed by James Wyatt. The building opened in Jan. 1772 and was destroyed by fire in Jan. 1792.
[3] See n.1, C to Hill, 10 Aug. 1782.
[4] See n.2, C to Unwin, 3 Dec. 1778.

welcome. All that is here, is thine, together with the hearts of those who dwell here. I am only sorry that your journey hither is necessarily postponed beyond the time when I did hope to have seen you; sorry too, that my Uncle's infirmities are the occasion of it. But years *will* have their course and their effect; they are happiest, so far as this life is concerned, who, like Him, escape those effects the longest, and who do not grow old before their time. Trouble and anguish do that for some, which only longævity does for others. A few months since I was older than your Father is now, and though I have lately recover'd, as Falstaff says, some *smatch of my youth*,[1] I have but little confidence, in truth none, in so flattering a change, but *expect, when I least expect it*, to wither again. The Past is a pledge for the Future.

Touching your retinue, my Dear, you have nothing to consider but what will be most convenient to yourself. Here will be room for two men Servants, and I imagine you will find occasion for your Buttler as well as for your Coachman. Our Servant sleeps always at his own house, and yours may sleep together. Mrs. Eaton[2] will occupy the Chamber over my Study, and when the Bedstead arrives, the furniture for it which you know is now in our hands, shall be immediately made ready. As your arrival is likely to be in the Winter, at least upon the Verge of it, you will find your Coach an Indispensible. Mrs. T——n proposed to us when we drank Tea there last, to get a little cover'd Cart and a little horse and a little Boy to drive it, the days being now so short that before we can separate, it is dark. But you will probably like your own vehicle better. Some vehicle however you must have, for the passage from the Hall to the Lodge would be impracticable to you in an Evening.

One thing more I will premise, my dearest Coz, and by way of Encouragement. It is suggested to me by the mention that you make of the House at the end of the Village. That House, by the way, I hear is taken. No matter. There is no need of it. When you shall find yourself under this roof, you will find yourself under your own. From the time of your

[1] *2 Henry IV*, I. ii. 95-7: 'your lordship though not clean past your youth, hath yet some smack of age in you, some relish of the saltness of time.'
[2] Lady Hesketh's maid. See C to Lady Hesketh, 10 Apr. 1786.

rising 'till the hour of dinner, your hours will be absolutely at your disposal. We engage for ourselves that we will never intrude upon you, and that it shall be a Capital crime in any body to give you the least disturbance. There is no danger of it indeed, for we were never in our lives so quietly served as now. Sam our lacquey, and Molly[3] our Cook are never heard but when they answer a question. Sam's Wife, by the way, has long been engaged to officiate in the Scullery while you shall be with us, and she is the very counterpart of her husband for quietness and sobriety. — This being the case, I doubt not, that we shall fadge[4] notably together, my Dear, and that you will find yourself perfectly at your Ease.

Thanks for the Waistcoat which I shall rejoice to receive. To give bulk to the parcel, you may send us if you please, some Bohea. We drink no other Tea, either at the Hall, or here, and the Throcks always prefer ours, which is what you sent us, to their own. I think with reason.

Mr. Giffard is here, Mrs. Throck's Uncle.[5] He is lately arrived from Italy where he has resided several years, and is so much the Gentleman that it is impossible to be more so. Sensible, polite, obliging, slender in figure, and in manner most engaging. Every way worthy to be so nearly related to the Throckmortons.

I have read Savary's Travels into Ægypt.[6] Memoires du Baron de Tott.[7] Fenn's Original Letters.[8] The Letters of

---

[3] Molly Pears or Pierce. See n. 4, C to Lady Hesketh, 5 March 1789.

[4] 'To make things fit; hence to get on, succeed' (*OED*).

[5] John Giffard of Plâs-Ucha, Flintshire, married Elizabeth, daughter and heir of Robert Hyde, of Nerquis, and had two daughters. He was the younger brother of Maria's deceased father Thomas.

[6] Probably the English translation of *Lettres sur l'Égypte* (1785). The second edition of the English version was published in two volumes in 1787 with the title: *Letters on Egypt, Containing a Parallel Between the Manners of its Ancient and Modern Inhabitants, its Commerce, Agriculture, Government and Religion; With the Descent of Louis IX. at Damietta, Extracted from Joinville, and Arabian Authors: Translated from the French.* The only possibly earlier English translation that we have been able to locate is the Dublin edition, also of 1787.

[7] Although there were three English editions of this work out by 1787, C probably read the French version: *Mémoires du Baron de Tott sur les Turcs et les Tartares*, published in four parts in 1784 in Amsterdam.

[8] C is referring to the first two volumes of Sir John Fenn's (see C to John Johnson, 31 Mar. 1792) edition of the Paston Letters. This edition was published in 5 volumes from 1787 to 1823. The title-pages of volumes 1 and 2 read 'in two volumes'. The work is entitled: *Original Letters, Written During the Reigns of*

Frederic of Bohemia,[9] and am now reading Memoires d'Henri de Lorraine Duc de Guise.[10] I have also read Barclay's Argenis a Latin Romance, & the best Romance that was ever written. All these, together with Madan's Letters to Priestley[11] & several pamphlets within these 2 Months. So I am a great Reader

— Yours, my Dearest, ever — Wm. Cowper.

LADY HESKETH   Saturday, 8 September 1787
Southey, vi. 60–2

The Lodge, Sept. 8, 1787.
I continue to write, as you perceive, my dearest cousin, though, in compassion for my pate, you advised me for the present to abstain: — in reality I have no need, at least I believe not, of any such caution. Those jarrings that made my scull feel like a broken egg-shell, and those twirls that I spoke of, have been removed by an infusion of the bark, which I have of late constantly applied to. I was blooded indeed, but to no purpose; for the whole complaint was owing to relaxation. But the apothecary recommended phlebotomy,[1] in order to ascertain that matter; wisely suggesting that if I found no relief from bleeding, it would be a sufficient proof that weakness must necessarily be the cause. It is well when the head is chargeable with no weakness but what may be cured by an astringent.

Thanks to your choice, I wear the most elegant buttons in all this country: they have been much admired at the Hall.

Henry VI., Edward IV., and Richard III. by Various Persons of Rank or Consequence; Containing Many Curious Anecdotes, Relative to that . . . Period of Our History.
[9] Probably *A Collection of Original Royal Letters, Written by King Charles the First and Second, King James the Second, and the King and Queen of Bohemia . . . From the Year 1619 to 1665* (1787). Sir George Bromley compiled this work which includes letters by Friedrich I, King of Bohemia and Elector Palatine, 1596–1632.
[10] *Les Mémoires d'Henri de Lorraine, duc de Guise* (Paris, 1681).
[11] Martin Madan's *Letters to Joseph Priestley, LL.D. F.R.S. Occasioned by his Late Controversial Writings* was published by Dodsley in 1787.

[1] 'The action or practice of cutting open a vein so as to let blood flow, as a medical or therapeutical operation' (*OED*).

When my waistcoat is made I shall be quite accomplished. You have made us both happy by giving us a nearer prospect of your arrival. But Mrs. Unwin says you must not fix an early day for your departure, nor talk of staying only two or three weeks, because it will be a thorn that she shall lean upon all the time that you are here; and so say I. It is a comfort to be informed when a visitor will go whom we wish to be rid of, but the reverse of a comfort, my cousin, when you are in the question.

Your last letter to Mrs. U. never came to hand; and as to the bed, it is so long since you supposed it sent that I fear it is altogether lost. You never mentioned it in any of your letters, therefore we did not look for it; its non-arrival would otherwise have been noticed. It is possible, however, that either the upholsterer, or the book-keeper at the inn, or the waggoner, may be able to give us some tidings of it. Woe be to them, careless knaves! if they have lost it among them!

The Throcks, as you observe, are Foxites; but their moderation in party matters is such, that in all the interviews we have had this summer, the string of politics has never been touched. Upon recollection, I must except a single instance, in which Peter Pindar,[2] whose last piece Mr. Throckmorton lent me, furnished the occasion. But even then, though I took the opportunity of speaking my mind of that licentious lampooner of dignities very freely, we had no dispute. It was agreed on all hands to be great pity, considering the ill effect of such political ribaldry on the minds of the multitude, that the court has not stopped his mouth with a bribe; — nobody doubted that he would open it wide enough for the reception of a large one. How contemptible is wit so miserably misemployed!

[2] John Wolcot (1738–1819), under the name of Peter Pindar, wrote various satires against George III from 1785. The piece to which C refers is probably *Instructions to a Celebrated Laureat* (Aug. 1787) in which Pindar attacked Thomas Warton's 'Ode on His Majesty's Birth-day, June 4th, 1787'. 'The poet laureate is told that Spenser and even Dryden had better sovereigns to write about, and he is requested to put down only the truth ... the satirist portrays what George III actually did on his birthday: the monarch had visited Whitebread's brewery and had learned the art of brewing beer. The laureate is told that the way to write a birthday ode has been demonstrated; he is to stick to the truth and is not to praise kings for imaginary qualities.' Robert L. Vales, *Peter Pindar* (New York, 1973), pp. 45–6.

I admire as much as you the spirit of our young minister. The Emperor and Pitt seem to be the two greatest names of the present age.[3] They are both at present in circumstances that give them a noble opportunity to display their address, and we shall soon see how they will acquit themselves. If they can manage their respective difficulties without blood-shed, they will each deserve a statue. I entirely agree with you that the ardour of youth under the control of wisdom, are the two essentials to make a good minister. Were the old Duke of Newcastle[4] now at the helm, the French party in Holland[5] would carry all before them, and the French court would pull us by the nose. Sir Thomas, therefore, was right in his opinion, as indeed he generally was, — and in political matters, I believe, always.

Our neighbours rejoice that you are coming, and desire me to tell you so. Mrs. Throckmorton walked with us yesterday morning to gather mushrooms.

We send you two brace of partridges; — one brace from them, and one brace a present from Mr. John Higgins.[6]

With Mrs. U.'s affectionate respects,

Yours, my dear, ever,
Wm. Cowper.

[3] At this time, the Holy Roman Emperor, Joseph II (1741–90), was co-operating closely with Catherine of Russia. The matter to which C refers is probably Joseph's desire to gain Moldavia and Wallachia, which would have threatened the sovereignty of Prussia, England's ally.

[4] Thomas Pelham-Holles (1693–1768), created Duke of Newcastle-upon-Tyne in 1715. He served as First Lord of the Treasury from 1754 to 1756 and formed a coalition with Pitt from 1757 to 1762.

[5] 'Inside the United Provinces the aristocratic party, who were in the ascendant, valued the French alliance for its assistance in ejecting the stadholder from all influence in their affairs . . . The opposition at Westminster assailed Pitt for sitting back and watching France wax stronger and more malevolent, imperilling British trade routes and markets in Western Europe. This was the background of Fox's attack upon the commerical treaty with France in 1787. Soon, however, developments inside the United Provinces began to assist Pitt . . . By October 1787 Amsterdam had been taken [by the Prussians]. The prince of Orange was fully restored as stadholder. England hastened to show her approval in a practical form. In 1788 alliances were made between England and the United Provinces and between England and Prussia for mutual defence and the maintenance of the *status quo*.' J. Steven Watson, *The Reign of George III, 1760–1815* (Oxford, 1960), p. 294.

[6] See n.1, C to Newton, 16 Dec. 1786.

HENRY MACKENZIE   Saturday, 15 September 1787

Address: Henry Mackenzie Esqr. / Brown Square / Edinburgh
Postmarks: SE/20 *and* OULNEY
Olney

Weston Underwood
Septbr. 15. 1787.

Sir

I should not have delay'd so long to acknowledge your
obliging Letter and the welcome present that accompanied it
had I known my obligation sooner. An Indisposition of many
months' duration, that deprived me of all intercourse with my
friends at a distance was the cause that your Letter though
dated in May, did not reach me till yesterday. The volumes
indeed I have not yet received, but they are safe, and I shall
have them soon. I am no stranger however to the merits of
the Lounger, which were given me some time since by Lady
Hesketh, who much admires them. The Mirrours have long
had a place upon my shelf, and their younger Brothers, in all
respects worthy of that near relation, shall now occupy their
place beside them.[1] I highly honour the Authors of those
elegant and useful works, and account myself happy that any
production of mine has been worthy to procure me such distinguishing notice from you, Sir, in particular. An impertinent
curiosity perhaps, but a natural one, prompts me to wish
that you had favour'd me with a knowledge of your signature,
because I should read with additional pleasure the Essays that
bear the mark of a Writer who has so much obliged me.[2] If

---

[1] C already owned an edition of *The Mirror* (5th edn. in 3 vols., London,
1783; now at Olney), and he is thanking Mackenzie for an edition of *The Lounger*
(3 vols., Edinburgh, 1787). *Keynes*, 68. Lady Hesketh had sent C some volumes of
The Lounger prior to 30 Aug. 1787 when he thanks her for this journal and says
he hopes to start reading it the next day.

[2] When *The Mirror* (and later *The Lounger*) was reissued in book form, letters
were appended to the contributions of Club members (but not to those of correspondents) as a means of identification, though the names of the contributors
remained generally secret until the publication of the first volume of the ninth
edition of *The Mirror* in 1792, with a list of the authors. Mackenzie used the
three letter-signatures V, I, and Z indifferently: in *The Mirror* V is used 17 times,
I 16 times, and Z 16 times, while four of his pieces are without signature. See C
to Lady Hesketh, 27 Nov. 1787. *The Mirror* originally appeared in 110 issues
from 23 Jan. 1779 until 27 May 1780; *The Lounger* in 101 issues from 5 Feb.
1785 until 6 Jan. 1787.

you are not in possession of my poems already, and can inform me how they may be conveyed to you so as not to cost more than they are worth, I will immediately give orders to my Bookseller for that purpose.

You have many names in Scotland that I truly venerate, and among them are two of your Coadjutors, as I understand, Beattie and Blair,[3] to whom, if a Stranger make take that liberty, I will beg you to present my warmest respects, with a thousand thanks for the pleasure that I have received from their excellent writings. Nobody, I believe, has ever read Beattie, without a wish to know him.

I live in a delightful part of Buckinghamshire, Sir, and in a most agreeable neighbourhood. It is possible that you may sometimes travel Southward; I am at no great distance from the great North road, and have once already been so favour'd by a Gentleman from Scotland, whom I am now happy to number among my Correspondents.[4] If you could, without too much inconvenience, make Weston on your way either to London or back again, you will always find me happy to receive you. At all events, I beg you to believe me, Sir,

Your much obliged
and most Obedient humble Servant
Wm Cowper.

LADY HESKETH   Saturday, 15 September 1787

Address: Lady Hesketh / New Norfolk Street / Grosvenor Square / London.
Postmarks: SE/17/87 *and* OULNEY
British Library

The Lodge Sepbr. 15. 1787.

My dearest Cousin —

The partridges that you received on Monday, were from us. The others which you received, as we suppose, on Tuesday or Wednesday, were from the Throcks immediately. They did not communicate their sending any, to us, 'till after the parcel was gone. And alas! they are now gone themselves. Gone into

---

[3] For Beattie, see C to Unwin, *c*. Sept. 1782 and n.2; for Blair, see C to Unwin, 24 Nov. 1783 and n.1. See also C to Lady Hesketh, 27 Nov. 1787 and n.7.
[4] Samuel Rose.

Staffordshire on a Visit to Her brother,[1] and are not to be expected here again in less than a Month. They set off this Morning. Mrs. Throck regretted last night that they had no Game-keeper, because, for that reason, they cannot furnish us with Game in their absence. We have indeed lived there lately, and to such a degree, that Mrs. Unwin told Mrs. Throck, she had better take us to board at once. They have generally drank Tea with us twice a week, and all the other days we have either dined or drank Tea with *them*.

On Monday last I was invited to meet your friend Miss Jekyll there, and there we found her.[2] I had the pleasure of being in her company every day while she stay'd, one day excepted. Yesterday Morning she returned to Gayhurst. Mrs. Throck accompanied her. Mr. Cathcart[3] rode bodkin,[4] and they mounted at our door. In a few days she departs for Beckenham.[5] I ask'd her if she had any commands to you, for that I should write to you by this Post, and she replied, give my *hearty* love to her. Her good-nature, her humorous manner, and her good sense are charming, insomuch that even I who was never much addicted to speech-making, and who, at present, find myself particularly indisposed to it, could not help saying at parting — I am glad that I have seen you, and sorry that I have seen so little of you. We were sometimes many in company, on Thursday, we were 15, but we had not all together so much vivacity and cleverness as Miss Jekyll, whose talent at mirth-making has this rare property to recommend it, that nobody suffers by it.

We have this day been enquiring after the lost Bed-stead. We sent Sam to Olney with orders, if he found not John Rogers there to proceed to Sherrington in quest of him. But at Olney he was informed that on this day (Saturday) he always goes to Northampton. On Monday however we shall

---

[1] Thomas Giffard (d. Aug. 1823), 23rd of Chillington, married 23 June 1788, Hon Charlotte Courtenay, daughter of 2nd Viscount Courtenay, and sister of the 10th Earl of Devon.

[2] We have not been able to obtain further information concerning this lady, who was probably a niece of Mrs Wrighte (*née* Jekyll) of Gayhurst.

[3] Perhaps the Revd Archibald Hamilton Cathcart (1764–1841), 3rd son of Charles Schaw, 9th Baron Cathcart.

[4] 'A person wedged in between two others where there is proper room for two only' (*OED*).

[5] Probably Buckenham in Norfolk, a residence of the Petres.

be sure to find him at Olney, when the proper enquiries shall be made. The Waggoners, in the mean time, whom Samuel actually saw & conversed with about it, declare that they have no remembrance of any such thing having at any time been sent to their Inn in London. We are on the whole rather inclined, at present, to suspect, that the fault must lie with the Upholsterer.

A thousand thanks my Dear for my Waistcoat, which I wore the last time I dined at the Hall, to the great admiration of the Ladies. It is perfectly genteel and elegant.

I am making a gravel walk for Winter use, under a warm hedge in the Orchard. It shall be furnish'd with a low seat for your accommodation, and if you do but like it, I shall be satisfied. In wet weather, or rather after wet weather, when the street is dirty, it will suit you well, for lying on an easy declivity through its whole length, it must, of course, be immediately dry.

Mrs. Throck has just made a Pheasantry where some shrubs grew, which you may remember, on the South side of the Court. She has order'd the Smith to make a Key for me. You observe, my Dear, that I have everything at Weston that 3,000 a year would procure me. And for being at Weston I am indebted to you.

I have just been writing a longish letter, an Author's letter, and consequently rather a formal one, to Mr. Mackenzie at Edinburgh, in answer to his which you sent me. If I ever get it again I will show it you, but last night Mrs. Throck who drank Tea here alone, walk'd away with it, that she might show it to her husband, and I have heard no tidings of it since.

Mrs. Unwin bids me say that your injunctions on the articles of Coals and Beer shall be obeyed, and she also charges me with her most affectionate Compliments. We talk much and often about you, and you are very much wish'd for by our friends at the Hall; How much by me, I will not tell you till the 2d week in October.

Yours my Dear, W C.

P.S.

I am very sorry to hear that the General's health is no better. When you see him, my Cousin, tell him so, and present my love to him. Thanks for the Tea.

LADY HESKETH   Thursday, 20 September 1787

Southey, vi. 64–6

The Lodge, Sept. 20, 1787.

For the more effectual abatement of your furious ire, my dearest coz, on the subject of these same partridges, it is expedient you should be told that we sent you only a *part* of the last present of that sort which we received from the Hall. Know also that when we found ourselves disposed to stew or to pot, we have an abundant supply of pigeons for those purposes from our neighbour's dove-cote, Mrs. Throck having given us the use of it at discretion. I know not by what coach they sent the basket which you never received, but I suppose by the Northampton coach. That it *was* sent is certain, and when I answer a letter which I expect to receive from our fair neighbour soon, (for she has promised to write to us,) I will thank her on your behalf.[1]

Rogers the Great has himself at least been spoken with about the bedstead. He expressed much concern for the loss of it, but at the same time was pretty positive that no such *meûble* had ever been conveyed to his warehouse in St. John Street. He thinks it must have been carried to some other inn, but promises to make enquiry when he goes next to London.

Miss J** informed me that a conjugal connexion between herself and the Rev. Mr. **** having been proposed by *********,[2] she held it adviseable to mention the matter to me, that if I had any influence with that gentleman, I might employ it for the promotion of so desirable a purpose. I replied that she was the most fortunate of women in having directed her application in that instance to me, for that I had stronger interest with him than any body. I learned in the course of our conversation on the subject that she was principally enamoured of his *house*, for himself she had never seen. He does not visit at the Hall, and how it has happened that he does not I have never been able to learn, for of all the neighbouring clergy, he is in that respect almost

---

[1] C did not receive the expected letter. See C to Lady Hesketh, 5 Oct. 1787.

[2] Perhaps Miss Jekyll's intended was the Revd Robert Pomfret (see n.1, C to Newton, 31 July 1780). In his letter to Newton of *c*.15 Apr. 1785 C mentions a visit to Pomfret's home and the 'fine bed of Tulips' there.

a singular exception: it is an exception, however, that renders my interposition on the occasion the more expedient; and certain it is that for whatsoever name she should exchange her own, if the consequence might be her approximation to us, we should rejoice in it. He sent us yesterday a present of the finest perch that I have seen these seven years.

I read with much pleasure, my dear cousin, the account that you give of my uncle, his snug and calm way of living, the neatness of his little person, and the cheerfulness of his spirit. How happy is he at so advanced an age, to have those with him whose chief delight is to entertain him, and to be susceptible as he is of being amused. Longevity, that in general either deprives a man of his friends, or if not of the power of enjoying their conversation, deals with *him* more gently, and still indulges him in the possession of those privileges which alone make life desirable. May he long continue to possess them! I acquiesce entirely in the justness of your reasoning on this subject, and must need confess that were I your father, I should with great reluctance resign you to the demands of any cousin in the world. I shall be happy to see you, my dear, yet once again, but not till I can enjoy that happiness without the violation of any proprieties on your part, — not till he can spare you. Give my love to him, and tell him that I am not so much younger than he is, now, as I was when I saw him last. As years proceed, the difference between the elder and the younger is gradually reduced to nothing. But you will come; and in the mean time the rich and the poor rejoice in the expectation of you; to whom may be added a third sort, — ourselves for instance, who are of neither of those descriptions. Mrs. Unwin bids me present her love to you in the most affectionate terms, and says, Pray tell Lady Hesketh that all our featherbeds are used by turns.

I rejoice that Bully[3] is so merry, and long to see him. Remember me kindly to Jocky.[4] The *Marquis* is dead, and is

---

[3] Probably a bullfinch. C to Lady Hesketh, 4 Dec. 1787: 'Have no fears on account of poor Bully's security at Weston. I can place him, even in my study, where no cat can reach him.'

[4] C to Lady Hesketh, 10 Dec. 1787: 'Had I known or could I have suspected that poor Jockey was dead, my dog should have borne his name.'

succeeded by a *Beau*.[5] — I received a letter yesterday, enclosing a Bank-note, and copy it for your edification: —

Sir,

A friend of yours, hearing where you reside, begs your acceptance of a ten pound note.

I am, sir, &c.

Est ce par hazard le Monsieur Dalling dont vous m'avez jadis fait le récit?[6]

Yours, my beloved cousin,
Wm. Cowper.

WALTER BAGOT   Saturday, 22 September 1787

Address: The Revd. Walter Bagot.
Morgan Library

Weston Underwood
Septbr. 22. 1787.

My dear friend,

Not well, but better, I take an early opportunity to tell you that I am so. Perhaps I might have sent you a more satisfactory account of myself, had I postponed my letter yet a season; but Mrs. Unwin having engaged for me that I should write to you *myself* as soon as I should find myself able to do so, and my inclination prompting me to it likewise, Here I am! When I saw you, I could not speak to you. Now, I can write to you. An alteration at least so much for the better, as will serve to gratify the kindness of your feelings for me, and therefore you have a right to know it. It would be better with me than it is, were I capable of resuming my occupation in the plains of Troy. But at present I do not feel myself free for that service. In the last year I seem to have lived twenty years. While I was busied in that work I seemed secure of bringing it to a conclusion. At the present moment, Life appears so

[5] C to Lady Hesketh, 4 Dec. 1787: 'My dog Beau died of a dysentry, and I have now another of the same name.'
[6] 'Is it by any chance Mr. Dalling whose story you've already told me?' Dalling is a difficult person to identify; possibly he is Gen Sir John Dalling (d. 16 Jan. 1798), who was recalled in 1786 as governor and commander-in-chief at Madras with an annuity of £1,000 for life.

short, as not to afford me half scope enough for the under-taking. If my views in this respect should alter, I shall return to my work with pleasure, and in the mean time instead of producing any thing myself, must have recourse, for amuse-ment, to the works of others. So it fares with mankind in general. We have not judgment or strength of mind for an arduous enterprize 'till two thirds of our allotted time are spent, and then, if through any infirmity of mind or body we happen to be thrown back, the remainder is too short to allow the hope of recovering the ground that we have lost. To reach the goal, a man must have eyes to see it; but as for me, I have no prospect.

The day before yesterday I had a call from your Brother Chester,[1] accompanied by Mr. Legg.[2] A great part of the pleasure that your Brother's visit would have afforded me, I lost by being out when he arrived here, but fortunately return'd just when he was about to mount his horse again. He had been seeking me in Mr. Throckmorton's Garden and wilderness, and I met him as I was coming home from my walk exactly at the Garden door. When our neighbors return, Mrs. Throckmorton who is at present in your country, has promised to give me a cast[3] to Chicheley, and I shall be happy to embrace the opportunity of acknowledging under his own roof, the repeated favours that he has done me in this way, without any return on my part hitherto but of thanks only.[4]

Mrs. Unwin is tolerably well, and always speaks and thinks of you with affection and respect. We shall be glad to hear that you have entirely recover'd from all effects of your late Illness.

Yours, my friend, Wm Cowper.

[1] See n.2, C to Hill, 13 Feb. 1783.
[2] Probably Charles Chester's brother-in-law Heneage Legge (1747–1827). Chester had married Legge's sister, Catherine, in 1765.
[3] A 'lift' in a conveyance (OED).
[4] In his letter to Walter Bagot of 3 Jan. 1787 C expresses his regret for being unable to return Charles Chester's visits.

LADY HESKETH   Saturday, 29 September 1787

Address: Lady Hesketh / New Norfolk Street / Grosvenor Square / London.
Postmarks: OC/1/87 *and* OULNEY
Panshanger Collection

The Lodge Saturday Sepr. 29. 1787
My dear Coz, I thank you for your political Intelligence;
retired as we are, and seemingly excluded from the world,
we are not indifferent to what passes in it; on the contrary
the arrival of a Newspaper at the present juncture never fails
to furnish us with a theme for discussion, short indeed but
satisfactory, for we seldom differ in opinion. I agree with you
in admiring the alacrity and vigour so conspicuous in the
measures of our Minister, who proves himself the true son of
his Father, and the Inheritor of his resolute temper. The
Conduct of the French with regard to Holland reminds me
of the old story of the Scotsman, who having climbed into
his neighbour's Apple-tree, and being sharply questioned by
him, what he was doing? replied, Coming down again. Their
affected approbation of the King of Prussia's measures so
fatal to their own sly intentions (if it be true, and it is so
truly in their stile that I can hardly doubt it) is strikingly
ridiculous. If they prove but equally complaisant to the
Empress in her quarrel with the Turks,[1] the Farce will be
complete. But Farce as it will be on their part, the consequences are seriously to be desired, for then, I suppose,
there will be peace in Europe.

I have received such an impression of the Turks from the
Memoirs of Baron de Tott which I read lately, that I can
hardly help presaging the conquest of that Empire on this
occasion, by the Russians. The disciples of Mahomet are such
babies in modern Tactics, and so enervated by the use of
their favorite drug, so fatally secure in their predestinarian
dream, and so prone to a spirit of mutiny against their

---

[1] 'In 1786 Catherine the Great was fighting the Turks in the Caucusus and was
in occupation of the Crimea ... It seemed possible that Russia might draw Austria
and Prussia once more into her orbit and leave England alone in the face of
France. English sailors were forbidden to seek service with Russia while Pitt
waited apprehensively the outcome of the Turkish war.' J. Steven Watson, *The
Reign of George III* (Oxford, 1960), p. 295.

Leaders, that nothing less can be expected.[2] In fact, they had not been their own masters at this day, had but the Russians known the weakness of their enemies, half so well as they undoubtedly know it now. Add to this, that there is a popular prophecy current in both countrys that Turkey is one day to fall under the Russian sceptre. A prophecy, which from whatever authority it be derived, as it will naturally encourage the Russians and dispirit the Turks in exact proportion to the degree of credit that it has on both sides, has a direct tendency to effect its own accomplishment. In the mean time if I wish them conquer'd, it is only because I think it will be a blessing to them to be governed by any other hand than their own, for under heaven has there never been a throne so execrably tyrannical as theirs. — The heads of the innocent that have been cut off to gratify the humour or the caprice of their Tyrants, could they be all collected and discharged against the walls of their city, would not leave one stone on another.

I have given you a noble dish of Politics my Dear! more in quantity than I have written on any such subject this many a day. Now for a little Weston News, if I can find any. But first for Olney. Your Padre[3] of that place, bids fair, I believe, for the Living. He has made application to Lord Dartmouth, and having served the cure with diligence and fidelity, and being in all respects an unexceptionable Minister, will, I Suppose, succeed. I hope however that no pretensions of any other person a perfect stranger to the place, will be deemed of equal validity. De Coetlegan[4] must have lost himself very much at the Lock, if he can stoop so low as Olney. Our Padre of the Hall dined with us on Tuesday, and on the same day

[2] Passages such as these in *Memoirs of Baron de Tott, on the Turks and Tartars. Translated from the French, By an English Gentleman at Paris* (2 vols., 1785) are being referred to by C: 'Those amongst the Turks who give themselves up to an immoderate use of opium, are easily to be distinguished by a sort of ricketty complaint, which this poison produces in course of time' (i. 176); 'If the climate which the Turks inhabit relaxes their fibres, the despotism under which they groan transports them to violence. They are not unfrequently ferocious; — their system of predestination adds to their fierceness; and the same prejudice that in a cold climate would have rendered them courageous, in a hot one produces nothing but fanaticism and rashness . . .' (i. 7).

[3] Postlethwaite (see C to Newton, 20 Oct. 1787). Although C initiated a petition in favour of Postlethwaite, the living went to Mr Bean (see C to Lady Hesketh, 4 Dec. 1787), who remained as resident vicar until 1794.

[4] See C to Newton, 30 Nov. 1783 and n.2.

the Higginses opposite to our house, drank Tea with us. I am more and more pleased with Grigson; though dumb at home, for reasons that I am not perfectly aware of, he is extremely conversible here. The *proud Alcove*,[5] as a certain poet calls it, and which I hope you will often visit, is in a state of reparation; it will be fit to receive you by the time when you arrive. The Gravel for my new walk is now digging at Ra'nston, and I hope will be laid next week.

Oh that you were here this beautiful day! It is too fine by half to be spent in London. I have not yet heard from Mrs. Throck, consequently have not written to her. When I do, your thanks shall not be forgotten. I have a perpetual Din in my head, and though not deaf, hear nothing aright, neither my own voice nor that of others. I am under a Tub. From which Tub, accept my best Love joined with Mrs. Unwin's.

Yours, my Dearest Cousin, W.C.

I have inadvertently reversed the sheet, and written backwards, as you perceive.[6]

JOHN NEWTON   Tuesday, 2 October 1787

Princeton

Weston Underwood
Octr. 2. 1787.

My dear friend

After a long but necessary interruption of our Correspondence,[1] I return to it again; in one respect at least better qualified for it than before, I mean, by a belief of your identity, which for 13 years I did not believe. The acquisition of this light, if light it may be called which leaves me as much in the dark as ever on the most interesting subjects, releases me however from the disagreeable suspicion that I am addressing myself to you as the friend whom I loved and valued so highly in my better days, while in fact you are not that friend but a

[5] See Pope's *Epistle to Bathurst*, l. 307.
[6] C began his letter on the extreme left hand side of his paper; this was the space he normally devoted to the address.

[1] The previous extant letter to Newton is that of 13 Jan. 1787.

36

stranger. I can now write to you without seeming to act a part, and without having any need to charge myself with dissimulation. A charge, from which in that state of mind and under such an uncomfortable persuasion, I knew not how to exculpate myself, and which, as you will easily conceive, not seldom made my correspondence with you a burthen. Still indeed it wants and is likely to want that best ingredient which can alone make it truly pleasant either to myself or you, that spirituality which once enliven'd all our intercourse. You will tell me, no doubt, that the knowlege I have gained is an earnest of more, and more valuable information, and that the dispersion of the clouds in part promises in due time their complete dispersion. I should be happy to believe it, but the power to do so is at present far from me. Never was the mind of man benighted to the degree that mine has been; the storms that have assailed me would have overset the Faith of every man that ever had any, and the very remembrance of them, even after they have been long pass'd by, makes Hope impossible.

Mrs. Unwin whose poor bark is still held together, though shatter'd by being toss'd and agitated so long at the side of mine, does not forget yours and Mrs. Newton's kindness on this last occasion. Mrs. Newton's offer to come to her assistance, and your readiness to have render'd us the same service, could you have hoped for any salutary effect of your presence, neither Mrs. Unwin nor myself undervalue nor shall presently forget. But you judged right when you supposed that even your company would have been no relief to me; the company of my Father or my Brother, could they have returned from the dead to visit me, would have been none to me.

We are busied in preparing for the reception of Lady Hesketh whom we expect here shortly. We have beds to put up and furniture for beds to make, workmen and scow'ring and bustle. Mrs. Unwin's time has of course been lately occupied to a degree that made writing, to her, impracticable, and she excused herself the rather, knowing my intentions to take her office. It does not however suit me to write much at a time. This last tempest has left my nerves in a worse condition than it found them, my head especially, though better informed, is more infirm than ever. I will therefore only add our joint love to yourself and Mrs. Newton, and that I am, my dear friend,

> Your affectionate
> Wm Cowper.

LADY HESKETH   Friday, 5 October 1787

Southey, vi. 68–71

The Lodge, Oct. 5, 1787.

My dearest Cousin,

My uncle's commendation of my hand-writing was the more agreeable to me as I have seldom received any on that subject. I write generally in the helter-skelter way, concerning myself about nothing more than to be legible. I am sorry for his deafness, which I hope however, by this time, the doctor and the doctor's engine[1] have removed. It is well if he is cheerful under that malady, which oppresses the spirits of most men more than any other disorder that is not accompanied with pain. We have but few senses, and can spare none of them without much inconvenience. But I know that when my uncle's spirits are good, they are proof against all oppression.

Mrs. Throck has not written to me, and now will not. Mr. Gregson had a letter from one of them today, in which they send compliments to us, and tell us they will be at home on Tuesday. How should she find time to write to me, who has been visiting her brother,[2] one of the gayest young men in

[1] The 'doctor's engine' would have been a Leyden jar, a primitive type of battery which is described in *An Essay on the Theory and Practice of Medical Electricity* (first published 1780; edition cited here is 1781) by Tiberius Cavallo (1749–1809): '*Deafness*, except when it is occasioned by obliteration, or other improper configuration of the parts, is either intirely or partly cured by drawing the sparks from the ear with a glass-tube-director, or by drawing the fluid with a wooden point' (pp. 67–8).

[2] See n.8, C to Lady Hesketh, 26 Nov. 1786. 'Between 1756 and his early death in 1776 Thomas Giffard carried out important alterations to the park. He employed "Capability" Brown and James Paine . . . A string of three pools, about three-quarters of a mile south-west of the house, was formed into a roughly triangular expanse of water, with a dam at the lower end. The shores were planted with woodland . . . Thomas Giffard the younger, who came of age in 1785, employed Sir John Soane from 1786 onwards. Soane's first design was also for a completely new house, but this was modified to include Peter Giffard's buildings of 1724.' *VCH Staffordshire*, v. 29.

the world, who is building a great house, and has one of the finest pieces of water in England, with thirty boats on it? I am sorry to hear that his youth, and his riches together, bid fair to ruin him, — that he is a prey to his neighbours, plays deep, and consequently cannot be rich long. Excessive good-nature is a quality attended with so much danger to a young man, that, amiable as it is, one cannot help pitying the man that owns it.

Mrs. Chester[3] paid her first visit here last Saturday, a prelude, no doubt, to the visit that she intends to you. I was angry with her for her omission of a civility to which you are so highly entitled; but now that she discovers symptoms of repentance, feel myself inclined to pardon her. She is one of those women, indeed, to whom one pardons every thing the moment they appear, — not handsome, but showing a gentleness in her countenance, voice, and manner, that speaks irresistibly in her favour.

Your newspaper,[4] for which I thank you, my cousin, pleases me more than any that I have seen lately. The pertness of the Herald is my detestation, yet I always read it; and why? because it is a newspaper, and should therefore doubtless read it were it ten times more disgusting than it is. Fielding was the only man who ever attempted to be witty with success in a newspaper, and even he could not support it long. But he led the way in his Covent Garden Journal,[5] and a thousand blockheads have followed him. I am not pleased, however, with that furious attack upon the poor Abbé Mann.[6] The zealous Protestant who makes it, discovers

---

[3] See n.2, C to Hill, 13 Feb. 1783.

[4] *The Morning Herald*, which the Throckmortons subscribed to and which they passed on to C, was a London newspaper published from 1 Nov. 1780 to 31 Dec. 1869; this publication supported the Prince of Wales and his coterie. We have not been able to locate a copy of *The Morning Herald* to which C refers.

[5] *The Covent-Garden Journal* was issued bi-weekly from Jan. to Nov. 1752.

[6] Theodore Augustus Mann, called the Abbé Mann (1735–1809), historian, antiquarian, man of science, had studied law in London and then went to France in 1754, where he converted to Catholicism. The author of a great many reports, letters, and catalogues, he was made secretary and treasurer of the Brussels Academy in 1786 and was elected a Fellow of the Royal Society in 1788. The controversy in which Mann was involved at this time and to which C refers is Mann's interest in the conversion of Lord Viscount Montague to Catholicism. 'I find myself called upon to give the publick an account of the particulars and motives of the late Lord Viscount Montague's return to the faith of his ancestors

too much of that spirit which he charges upon the Papists. The poor Abbé's narrative was in a manner extorted from him; and when I read it, instead of finding it insidious and hostile to the interests of the Church of England, I was foolish enough to think it discreet, modest, temperate. The gentleman, therefore, has either more zeal, or a better nose at a plot, than I have.

The bedstead, my dear, suffered nothing by the long delay and the bad lodging that it met with: it could not have looked better than it does had it arrived at the time intended. It lost a screw indeed; but our neighbour the tailor happening to have an odd one exactly of the right size, supplied the deficiency. It will have its furniture to-morrow.

Poor Teedon, whom I dare say you remember, has never missed calling here once, and generally twice, a week since January last. The poor man has gratitude if he has not wit, and in the possession of that one good quality has a sufficient recommendation. I blame myself often for finding him tiresome, but cannot help it. My only comfort is that I should be more weary of thousands who have all the cleverness that has been denied to Teedon.

I have been reading Hanway's Travels,[7] and of course the history of Nadir Shah, alias Kouli Khan[8] — a hero! my dear, — and I am old enough to remember the time when he was accounted one. He built up pyramids of human heads, and had consequently many admirers. But he has found few, I imagine, in the world to which he is gone to give an account of his building. I have now just entered upon Baker's Chronicle,[9] having never seen it in my life till I found it in the Hall library.

... When all was finished, Lord Montague called me to his bed-side, and declared anew, in the presence of seven or eight persons besides myself ... "that he had renounced the Roman Catholic Faith, from the vilest of motives ... "' *GM*, lvii, pt. 2 (1787), 654–5.

[7] C either read Jonas Hanway's *An Historical Account of the British Trade over the Caspian Sea ... To which are added, the Revolutions of Persia during the present Century, with the particular History of the great Usurper Nadir Kouli* (4 vols., 1753), or he read the abridgement of that work in volumes 14 and 15 (1775) of *The World Displayed* (1762–90).

[8] Nadir Shah (1688–1747), Shah of Iran (1736–47).

[9] *A Chronicle of the Kings of England* by Sir Richard Baker (1568–1645) was first published in four parts in 1643.

It is a book at which you and I should have laughed immoderately, some years ago. It is equally wise and foolish, which makes the most ridiculous mixture in the world.

With Mrs. U.'s affectionate respects, my dearest cousin,

> I am ever yours,
> Wm. Cowper.

JOSEPH JOHNSON Thursday, 18 October 1787

Princeton (*copy*)

Weston Underwood, Oct. 18. 1787.

Sir,

Finding myself able to answer with my own hand your inquiries, directed to Mrs. Unwin, I take the first opportunity to do it. My time, since I began to recover my spirits, has been given to the means of establishing them. At present I find myself in that respect nearly as well as usual and am ready as soon as I shall receive the books of my translation, that are now in London, to proceed with the work. It has suffered a long interruption, and all interruptions of poetical labors are prejudicial not only on account of lost time, but because the mind by disuse becomes prosaic. But I will do my best to recover its poetical habit. I wrote last week to General Cowper, but have not yet received his answer. Whether the copy is in his hands or in Mr. Fuseli's, I know not, but shall be glad to have it sent as soon as possible.

I beg my respectful compliments to my kind coadjutor and am, sir, your most humble servant,

> Wm Cowper.

19 October 1787

SAMUEL ROSE   Friday, 19 October 1787

Address: Samuel Rose Esqr. No. 23 / Percy Street / Rathbone Place / London.
Postmarks: OC/20/87 *and* OULNEY
Princeton

> Weston Underwood
> Octbr. 19. 1787.

Dear Sir,

A summons from Johnson which I receiv'd yesterday, calls my attention once more to the business of Translation. Before I begin, I am willing to catch though but a short opportunity to acknowledge your last favour. The necessity of applying myself with all diligence to a long work that has been but too long interrupted, will make my opportunities of writing rare in future. Air and exercise are necessary to all men, but peculiarly so to the man whose mind labours; and to Him who has all his life been accustom'd to much of both, they are necessary in the extreme. My time, since we parted, has been devoted entirely to the recovery of health and strength for this service, and I am willing to hope, with good effect. Ten months have passed since I discontinued my poetical efforts; I do not expect to find the same readiness as before, 'till exercise of the neglected faculty, such as it is, shall have restored it to me.

You find yourself, I hope, by this time, as comfortably situated in your new abode, as in a new abode one can be. I enter perfectly into all your feelings on occasion of the change. A sensible mind cannot do violence even to a local attachment, without much pain. When my Father died I was young; too young to have reflected much. He was Rector of Berkhamstead, and there I was born. It had never occurred to me that a parson has no fee simple[1] in the House and glebe he occupies. There was neither Tree nor Gate nor stile in all that country to which I did not feel a relation, and the House itself I preferred to a palace. I was sent for from London to attend him in his last illness, & he died just before I arrived. Then, and not 'till then, I felt for the first time that

---

[1] 'An estate in land, etc. belonging to the owner and his heirs for ever, without limitation to any particular class of heirs' (*OED*).

I and my native place were disunited for ever. I sighed a long adieu to fields and woods from which I once thought I should never be parted, and was at no time so sensible of their beauties as just when I left them all behind me to return no more. Some little time since I had a very obliging [Letter] [2] from a Gentleman at Edinburgh who signs himself Henry Mackenzie, one of the Authors of the Lounger. It came to announce a present that he had order'd for me of those volumes. I answer'd it, but am afraid that in directing my answer I mistook his description, having entitled him Esquire, whereas I have been since informed that he is a Divine. [3] If you correspond with him, I beg you will make my Apology, and place my ignorance of a person so honorably known in the literary world to its true account, long illness, close retirement, and much employment in a work that has not permitted me to be well or indeed at all acquainted even with the best modern publications.

I am interrupted by company but not till I have only left myself room to subjoin Mrs. Unwin's Compliments and to assure you of the unfeigned esteem with which I am, Dear Sir, Your most Obedient & Affectionate Servant

Wm Cowper.

JOHN NEWTON   Saturday, 20 October 1787

Address: The Revd. John Newton
Princeton

Weston Underwood
Octbr. 20. 1787.

My dear friend,

My Indisposition could not be of a worse kind. Had I been afflicted with a fever or confined by a broken bone, neither of those cases would have made it impossible that we should meet. I am truely sorry that the impediment was insurmountable while it lasted, for such in fact it was. The sight of any

[2] MS torn.
[3] The information was not correct. Rose must have assured C that Esquire was the appropriate form of address when he also told him he was a friend of Mackenzie. See C to Mackenzie 10 Dec. 1787.

face except Mrs. Unwin's was to me an insupportable grievance; and when it has happen'd that by forcing himself into
my hiding-place, some friend has found me out, he has had
no great cause to exult in his Success, as Mr. Bull can tell you.
From this dreadful condition of mind, I emerged suddenly.
So suddenly, that Mrs. Unwin, having no notice of such a
change herself, could give none to any body; and when it
obtained, how long it might last, or how far it was to be
depended on, was a matter of the greatest uncertainty. It
affects me, on the recollection, with the more concern,
because I learn from your last, that I have not only lost an
interview with you myself, but have stood in the way of
visits that you would have gladly paid to others, and who
would have been happy to have seen you. You should have
forgotten (but you are not good at forgetting your friends)
that such a creature as myself existed.

It has happen'd indeed, and by means that it was not
possible for us to prevent, that our chambers have not had
beds in them till within this fortnight. Lady Hesketh undertook to furnish them for us, and by a strange blunder of the
people at the Inn or of the Waggoner, the materials that she
sent for the purpose, remained almost a twelvemonth in the
Warehouse. She order'd them hither without mentioning that
she had done it in any of her Letters to Mrs. Unwin, who
wonder'd indeed that they did not come, but could not
decently take any notice of their non-arrival.

I rejoice that Mrs. Cowper has been so comfortably supported. She must have severely felt the loss of her son.[1] She
has an affectionate heart toward her children, and could not
but be sensible of the bitterness of such a cup. But God's
presence sweetens every bitter. Desertion is the only evil that
a Christian cannot bear.

I have done a deed for which I find some people thank me
little. Perhaps I have only burn'd my fingers, and had better
not have meddled. Last Sunday se'nnight I drew up a short
petition to Lord D——h in behalf of Mr. Postlethwaite.[2] We
signed it, and all the principal inhabitants of Weston follow'd

---

[1] C is referring to the death of George Cowper (1754–87); see n.1, C to Mrs
Cowper, 20 Oct. 1766, and n.3, C to Mrs Cowper, 11 Mar. 1767.
[2] See n.9, C to Lady Hesketh, 24 Apr. 1786.

our example. What we had done was soon known in Olney, and an Evening or two ago, Mr. Raban called here, to inform me (for that seemed to be his errand) how little the measure that I had taken was relish'd by some of his neighbours. I vindicated my proceeding on the principles of Justice and mercy to a laborious and well-deserving Minister, to whom I had the satisfaction to find that none could alledge one serious objection, and that all, except one, who objected at all, are persons who in reality ought to have no vote upon such a question. The affair seems still to remain undecided. If his Lordship waits, which I a little suspect, 'till his Steward shall have taken the sense of those with whom he is likely to converse upon the subject, and means to be determined by his report, Mr. Postlethwaite's case is desperate.

I beg that you will remember me affectionately to Mr. Bacon. We rejoice in Mrs. Newton's amended health, and when we can hear that she is restored, shall rejoice still more. The next Summer may prove more propitious to us than the past; if it should, we shall be happy to receive you and yours. Mrs. Unwin unites with me in love to you all three. She is tolerably well, & her writing was prevented by nothing but her expectation that I should soon do it myself. Ever yours

Wm Cowper.

LADY HESKETH   Saturday, 27 October 1787

Address: Lady Hesketh / New Norfolk Street / Grovenor Square / London.
Southey, vi. 75–7.

The Lodge, Saturday,
Oct. 27, 1787.

My dearest Cousin,

Now that there is something like a time appointed, I feel myself a little more at my ease. Days and weeks slide imperceptibly away; November is just at hand, and the half of it, as you observe, will soon be over. Then, no impediment intervening, we shall meet once more, — a happiness of which I so lately despaired. My uncle, who so kindly spared you before, will I doubt not spare you again. He knows that a little frisk in country air will be serviceable to you, and even to my welfare, which is not a little concerned in the matter, I am persuaded he is not indifferent. For this and for many other reasons I ardently wish that he may enjoy and long enjoy the present measure of health, with which he is favoured. Our wants are included within the compass of two items. *I* want a watchstring, and we *both* are in want of certain things, called candle-ends, but of wax, not *tallow-fats*.[1] Those with which you furnished us at Olney are not quite expended indeed, but are drawing near to their dissolution. Should I after farther scrutiny discover any other deficiencies, you shall know them.

You need not, my dear, be under any apprehensions lest I should too soon engage again in the translation of Homer. My health and strength of spirits for this service are, I believe, exactly in *statu quo prius*. But Mrs. Unwin having enlarged upon this head, I will therefore say the less. Whether I shall live to finish it, or whether, if I should, I shall live to enjoy any fruit of my labours, are articles in my account of such extreme uncertainty, that I feel them often operate as no small discouragement. But uncertain as these things are, I yet consider the employment *essential* to my present well-being, and pursue it accordingly. But had Pope been subject to the same alarming speculations, had he waking and sleeping dreamt as I do, I am inclined to think he would not have been my predecessor in these labours; for I compliment myself with a persuasion that I have more heroic valour, of the passive kind at least, than he had, — perhaps than any man; it would be strange had I not, after so much exercise.

By some accident or other it comes to pass that I see the Throckmortons daily. Yesterday, soon after I had received your letter, I met them armed with bow and arrows, going to practise at the target in the garden. I consulted them on the subject of the best road from Newport hither, and the

[1] 'The alternative to wax was tallow, which was much cheaper, but the animal fat gave an unpleasant smell; owing to is low melting-point tallow was more prone to guttering and burned more quickly.' John Dummelow, *The Wax Chandlers of London* (1973), p. 10. Lady Hesketh evidently supplied the Weston household with the ends of her candles.

prevailing opinion was in favour of the road through Emberton. It is rough, indeed, but not so heavy as the road by Gayhurst. Mrs. Throck, anxious to put the matter past all doubt, cut a caper on the grass-plot, and said she would go ride to Olney immediately on purpose to examine the road. If her report contains any thing material, you shall hear it.

By *their* means I hear of Mrs. W**[2] daily. Their account of her yesterday was, that she begins to eat, and is somewhat more recollected. Dr. Kerr,[3] I believe, is *now* pretty confident of her recovery. But it has been a terrible malady.

I rejoice, my dear, that you have such a Cadwallader. Silent and sober is exactly the character of our household; we shall be as harmonious as any thing so noiseless can be.

I thank you for the Prologue.[4] There are, as you say, some good lines in it; and *so* good, that it is pity they have not a better ending. But the distinction between *Praise* and *Applause*, is too fine for an ordinary apprehension.

In a letter that I received yesterday from the General, he tells me that my MSS. are all safe: a piece of intelligence that refreshed me much. For missing some books that I did not remember to have sent, I began to be in no small *quandary*. I expect in a few days the old box brimful of heroics.

Farewell, my dearest coz.! the month that you speak of will be short indeed, unless you can contrive to lengthen it.

Ever yours,
Wm. Cowper.

LADY HESKETH   Saturday, 3 November 1787

Southey, vi. 78–81

The Lodge, Nov. 3, 1787.

Suffer not thyself, my dearest coz., to be seduced from thy purpose. There are those among thy friends and kindred who being covetous of thy company will endeavour to keep thee near them, and the better to effect their machinations,

[2] Mrs. Wrighte. See n.2, C to Unwin, 3 Dec. 1778.
[3] See n.6, C to Unwin, 3 Jan. 1784.
[4] We have not been able to identify this reference.

will possess thee, if they can, with many megrims concerning the roads and the season of the year. But heed them not. They only do what I should do myself were I in their predicament, who certainly should not fail, for my own sake, to represent your intended journey as an enterprise rather to be admired than approved — more bold than prudent. The turnpike, as you well know, will facilitate your progress every inch of the way till you come to Sherrington,[1] and from Sherrington hither you will find the way equally safe, though undoubtedly a little rough. Rough it was when you were here, such it is still, but not rougher than then, nor will it be so. The reason is this — that the soil being naturally a rock is very little, or rather not at all affected by the season, for as thou well knowest, no showers will melt a stone. The distance also from Sherrington toll-gate to our door is but four miles and a quarter. The only reason why I do not recommend the back road rather than this, is because it is apt to be heavy; in other respects it deserves the preferance, for it is just as safe as the other, and from the turning at Gayhurst, is shorter than that by a mile and a half. The Throcks travel them both continually, and so do all the chaises and coaches in the country, and I never heard of an accident to any of them in all the twenty years that I have lived in it. Mr. and Mrs. Throck, understanding that you are a little apprehensive on this subject, begged me yesterday evening to tell you that *they* will send their servant to meet you at Newport, who will direct your *cocher*[2] to all the best and most commodious quarters. As to the season of the year, I grant that it is November. It would be but folly to deny it. But what then? — Does not the sun shine in November? One would imagine that it did not, could not, or would not, were we to listen only to the suggestions of certain persons. But, my dear, the matter is far otherwise; nay it is even just the reverse; for he not only shines, but with such splendour too, that I write at this moment in a room heated by his beams, and with the curtain at my side let down on purpose to abate their fervour. Then let November have its just praise, and let not my cousin

---

[1] See n.1, C to Lady Hesketh, 6 Dec. 1785.
[2] Variant spelling of 'coacher' (*OED*).

fear to find the country pleasant even now. I have said it in verse, and I think it in prose, that as it is at all times preferable to the town,[3] so is it especially preferable in winter, provided I mean that you have gravel to walk upon, of which there is no scarcity at Weston.

Coming home from my walk yesterday I met Mr. Throck., on his return from Gayhurst. I was glad that I had so good an opportunity to inform myself concerning Mrs. W**. His account of her was in some respects favourable, but upon the whole not flattering. She eats, it is true, and knows those about her; but she almost keeps her bed, is torpid, and inattentive to all that passes, and can hardly be prevailed with to speak, unless constrained to it. Dr. Kerr professes himself perfectly master of her case, but I have more than once heard some wonder expressed that they have not called in other assistance. The present is an unfortunate period in that family: three or four days since, Mr. W * * had a terrible fall from his horse. He was fox-hunting; and in Yardley Chase,[4] the hounds chose to follow the deer. He rode violently to whip them off, when his horse plunged into a slough, pitched him over his head, and fell upon him. The softness of the ground saved him, but he was much hurt in both shoulders, and is now suffering by a fit of the gout, which the fall has brought upon him. Mr. Throck. and Mrs. Throck.'s brother, who is now at the Hall, happened to see him thrown, and very humanely assisted him to mount again, which without their help he could never have done. The rest of the company were too much fox-hunters to trouble themselves at all about him.

Many thanks, my dear cousin, both on Mrs. Unwin's part and mine for the gown you have purchased for her. She is even now proud of it, and will be prouder still when she shall put it on. I shall be glad of the paper; not that I am in immediate want, but it is good to be provided. I shall put the fourteenth Iliad into Mrs. Throck.'s hands in a day or two; I

---

[3] See, especially, *The Task*, iii. 675 ff.

[4] '[I]n the southern half of the parish [of Yardley Hastings, which lies on the border of Buckinghamshire on the road from Bedford to Northampton,] Yardley Chase consists of a deer park and a number of woods noted for their timber including oaks of great age . . . ' *VCH Northamptonshire*, iv. 296.

am at present only employed by blots and obliterations in making it more difficult for her to decipher.

Adieu, my dear. Our best love, and best wishes are always with you.

Yours affectionately,
Wm. Cowper.

I hear of three prints lately published.[5] Two of Crazy Kate, and one of the Lacemaker in 'Truth.' Mr. Wm. T——n[6] has said that he will send them to me.

I rejoice that we have peace, at least a respite from war. But you do well to suspect the French of a double meaning, or even of a treble one if that be possible. I believe they mean nothing so little, as to be honest.

LADY HESKETH   Saturday, 10 November 1787

Address: Lady Hesketh / New Norfolk Street / Grosvenor Square / London.
Postmarks: NO/12/87 *and* OULNEY
Yale

The Lodge Novbr. 10. 1787.

The Parliament my dearest Cousin, prorogued continually, is a meteor dancing before my eyes, promising me my wish only to disappoint me, and none but the King and his Minister can tell when you and I shall come together.[1] I hope however that the period, though so often postponed, is not far distant, and that once more I shall behold you and experience your power to make Winter gay and sprightly.

I have always forgotten (never say forgot) to tell you the reason why Mr. Bull did not fulfill his engagement to call on you in his return from the West. It was owing to an accident that happen'd to one of those legs of his. At Exmouth he chose to wallow in the sea and made use of a Bathing machine for that purpose. It has a Ladder, as you know, attach'd to its

---

[5] We do not have further information on these. See *Russell*, p. 307.
[6] Probably William Throckmorton (1762-1819), the brother of John and George. C ultimately thanks Hill in his letter of 24 May 1788 for providing him with two of these prints.

---

[1] The London season usually continued unabated while Parliament was sitting, and Lady Hesketh does not wish to leave the city until the season is over.

tail. On the lowermost step of that Ladder he stood, when it
broke under him. He fell of course, and with his knee on the
point of a large nail which pierced it almost to the depth of
two inches. The consequence was that when he reach'd
London, he could think of nothing but getting home as fast
as possible. The wound has been healed some time, but is
occasionally still painful, so that he is not without apprehensions that it may open again, which considering that he is
somewhat gross in his habit, is not impossible. But I have just
sent to invite him to dine with us on Monday.

I have a kitten my Dear, the drollest of all creatures that
ever wore a Cat-skin. Her gambols are not to be described,
and would be incredible if they could. She tumbles head over
heels several times together, she lays her cheek to the ground
and presents her rump at you with an air of most supreme
disdain, from this posture she rises to dance upon her hind
feet, an exercise that she performs with all the grace imaginable, and she closes these various exhibitions with a loud
smack of her lips, which for want of greater propriety of
expression, we call Spitting. But though all cats spit, no cat
ever produced such a sound as she does. In point of size she
is likely to be a kitten always, being extremely small of her
age, but time I suppose, that spoils every thing will make her
also a Cat. You will see her I hope before that melancholy
period shall arrive, for no wisdom that she may gain by
experience and reflection hereafter, will ever compensate the
loss of her present hilarity. She is dress'd in a tortoise-shell
suit, and I know that you will delight in her.

Mrs. Throck. carries us to-morrow in her chaise to Chicheley.
Mr. Chester has been often here, and Mrs. Chester as I told
you, once; and we are glad and obliged to our neighbor for
an opportunity to return their visits, at once so convenient
and inviting. The event however must be supposed to depend
in some degree on the elements, at least on the state of the
atmosphere which is at present turbulent beyond measure.
Yesterday it thunder'd. Last night it lighten'd, and at 3 this
morning I saw the sky as red as a city in flames could have
made it. I have a Leech in a bottle my Dear, that foretells all
these prodigies and convulsions of nature. No. Not as *you*
will naturally conjecture, by articulate utterance of oracular

notices, but by a variety of gesticulations which here I have not room to give an account of. Suffice it to say that no change of weather surprizes him, and that in point of the earliest and most accurate intelligence he is worth all the Barometers in the world. None of them all indeed even make the least pretence to foretell thunder, a species of sagacity of which he has frequently given the most unequivocal evidence. I gave but sixpence for him, which is a groat more than the market price, though he is in fact, or rather would be if Leeches were not found in every ditch, an invaluable acquisition.

Mrs. Throck. sola dined with us last Tuesday. She invited herself. The particular reason of her so doing was that her husband and brother dined at Horton.[2] The next day we Dined at the Hall.

Mrs. Wrighte's is still consider'd as a melancholy case, though we learn this evening that she has twice or thrice taken airings in the chaise, and must therefore I suppose be better. Pray my Dear add to what I have already desired you to bring with you, a roll or two of green wax candle to go upon a spindle, spindle, spindle.[3] I repeat it 3 times having more than once experienced how apt that circumstance is to escape the memory. I have no room for any other addition than that of our best Love, and to assure you how truely I am ever yours

Wm Cowper.

JOSEPH HILL   Friday, 16 November 1787

Address: Joseph Hill Esqre. / Chancery Office / London.
Postmarks: NO/20/87 *and* OULNEY
Cowper Johnson

My dear Friend,

I thank you for adverting to my occasions,[1] and that before I had made them known, you sent me so seasonable a supply.

---

[2] With the Gunnings. See n.2, C to Lady Hesketh, 4 Dec. 1787.
[3] 'Green' is a reference to the freshness, not the colour; wax tapers were coiled on a vertical shaft and cut off when needed.

---

[1] C's need of paper.

I thank you also for the Sollicitude that you express on the subject of my present studies. The work is undoubtedly long and laborious, but it has an end, and proceeding leisurely, with a due attention to the use of Air and exercise, it is possible that I may live to find it. Assure yourself of one thing, that though to a [By-stander it may seem an occupa] [2] tion surpassing the pow'rs of a Constitution never very Athletic, and, at present, not a little the worse for wear, I can invent for myself no employment that does not exhaust my spirits more. I will not pretend to account for this, I will only say that it is not the language of predilection for a favorite amusement, but that the fact is really so. I have ever found that those play thing avocations which one may execute almost without any attention, fatigue me and wear me away, while such as engage me much and attach me closely, are rather serviceable to me than otherwise.

I condole with you sincerely on the loss of a friend in the Duke of Rutland,[3] whom I know you valued highly. My Father used to say — The death of old men is necessary, but the death of a young man seems unnatural.

About ten days since I wrote to Archdeacon Heslop,[4] referring him to you. By your silence with regard to him, I conclude that he has not yet attended you. The delay however is no longer chargeable to me, with which reflection comforting myself as I may, and begging to be mention'd affectionately & respectfully to Mrs. Hill, I bid you heartily a good night

> and remain as ever
> Yours my dear friend
> Wm Cowper.

---

[2] These words are in someone else's hand.

[3] Charles Manners, 4th Duke of Rutland (1754–24 Oct. 1787), who had been educated at Eton (1762–70) and Trinity College, Cambridge (MA, 1774), had served as MP for Cambridge University (1774–9), and was Lord Lieutenant of Leicestershire from 9 July 1779 until his death.

[4] See n.1, C to Unwin, 31 Mar. 1770.

Weston near Olney
Bucks.
Your letters go the wrong way for want of this direction.
Novbr. 16. 1787
Received of Joseph Hill Esqr. the Sum of Forty pounds by
Draft on Child and Co.

£40.0.0   Wm Cowper.

LADY HESKETH   Saturday, 17 November 1787

Southey, vi. 83–5

Weston Lodge, Nov. 17, 1787.

My dearest Cousin,

We are therefore not to meet before Christmas. There is a
combination of King, Lords, and Commons against it, and we
must submit. I do it with an ill grace, but in a corner; and
nobody — not even yourself, shall know with how much
reluctance. In consideration of the necessity there is, that
should you come on this side Christmas you must return
immediately after the holidays, on account of those three
limbs of the legislature coming together again, I am so far
well content that your journey hither should be postponed
till your continuance here shall be less liable to interruption;
and I console myself in the mean time with frequent recollections of that passage in your letter, in which you speak of
frequent visits to Weston. This is a comfort on which I have
only one drawback; and it is the reflection that I make
without being able to help it, on the style and nature of my
constant experience, which has taught me that what I hope
for with most pleasure, is the very thing in which I am most
likely to meet with a disappointment; — but sufficient to the
past is the evil thereof;[1] let futurity speak for itself.

On Monday last — for headaches and other matters,
prevented our going sooner, Mrs. Throck. carried us to
Chicheley, viz. Mr. Chester's. It seemed as if all the world
was there to meet us, though in fact there was not above
half of it, their own family, which is very numerous, excepted.

[1] See Matthew 6:34: 'Sufficient unto the day is the evil thereof.'

54

17 November 1787

The Bishop of Norwich was there, that is to say, the little Doctor Lewis Bagot, and his lady.[2] She is handsome, and he in all respects what a Bishop should be. Besides these, Mrs. Praed was there, and her sister, Miss Backwell.[3] There might be many others, but if there were, I overlooked them. 'Foresaid little Bishop and I had much talk about many things, but most about Homer. I have not room to particularize, and will therefore sum up the whole with observing, that both with respect to our ideas of the original, of Pope's translation, and of the sort of translation that is wanted, we were perfectly at an agreement. As to the house, it is handsome, so is the pleasure-ground, and so are all the gardens, which are not less, I believe, than four in number. With respect to the family themselves, they are all amiable, and our visit was a very agreeable one.

We sent over to Olney this morning to enquire after the hamper; but the answer of Rogers was, that he and his book-keeper had searched the warehouse for parcels directed hither, but could find none. Either, therefore, something prevented your sending it at the time you mentioned, or it must have reached the inn too late, in which case we shall have it by the next waggon.

I write both to the General and to Mr. Hill by this post, the latter advises me to abstain from Homer, but I might as well advise him to abstain from parchment.

My dearest — farewell.
Thine ever,
Wm. C.

---

[2] For Lewis Bagot, see C to Unwin, 18 Dec. 1784 and nn.3–5. His wife was Mary (d. 17 Aug. 1799), daughter of the Hon Edward Hay.
[3] Elizabeth Tyringham Backwell (1749–1811), daughter of Barnaby Backwell and sole heiress of her brother Tyringham Backwell of Tyringham and St. Clement Danes, had succeeded her brother in 1777 and had married William Mackworth Praed in 1778. Jane Backwell (d. 1795) is the sister to whom C refers.

LADY HESKETH   Tuesday, 27 November 1787

Address: Lady Hesketh / New Norfolk Street / Grosvenor Square / London.
Postmarks: NO/28/87 *and* OULNEY
Panshanger Collection

The Lodge
Novr. 27. 1787.

It is the part of wisdom, my dearest Cousin, to sit down contented under the demands of Necessity, because they are such. I am sensible that you cannot, in my Uncle's present infirm state and of which it is not possible to expect any considerable amendment, indulge either us or yourself with a journey to Weston. Yourself, I say, both because I know it will give you pleasure to see Causidice mi[1] once more, especially in the comfortable abode where you have placed him, and because after so long an imprisonment in London, you who love the country and have a taste for it, would of course be glad to return to it. For my own part, to me it is ever new, and though I have now been an inhabitant of this village a twelvemonth, and have during the half of that time been at liberty to expatiate and to make discoveries, I am daily finding out fresh scenes, and walks which you would never be satisfied with enjoying. Some of them indeed are unapproachable by you either on foot or in your carriage. Had you twenty toes (whereas I suppose you have but ten) you could not reach them; and coach-wheels have never been seen there since the flood. Before it indeed, Bishop Burnet says, that the earth being perfectly free from all inequalities in its surface, they might be seen there every day.[2] But á l'heure qu'il est, we are never the better for that. But then, my Dear, we have other walks both upon Hill-tops and in vallies beneath, some of which by the help of your carriage, and many of them without its help, would be always at your command.

[1] Italian for 'my advocate'. Lady Hesketh added this note to the letter: 'the appellation which Sir Thos. used to give him in Jest when this Excellent Creature was of the Temple'.

[2] 'In the First Book we so far describ'd This new-found World, as to show it very different in form and fabrick from the present Earth; there was no Sea there, no Mountains, nor Rocks, nor broken Caves, 'twas all one continued and regular mass, smooth, simple and compleat as the first works of Nature use to be.' Thomas Burnet, *The Theory of the Earth* (first English edition: 1684), p. 174.

56

On Monday Morning last, Sam brought me word into the study that a man was in the kitchen who desired to speak with me. I order'd him in. A plain decent elderly figure made its appearance, and being desired to sit, spoke as follows. Sir, I am Clerk of the Parish of All Saints in Northampton.[3] Brother of Mr. Cox the Upholst'er. It is customary for the person in my office to annex to a Bill of Mortality which he publishes at Christmas, a Copy of Verses. You would do me a great favour, Sir, if you would furnish me with one. To this I replied — Mr. Cox, you have several men of Genius in your town, why have not you applied to some of them? There is a namesake of yours in particular, Cox the Statuary, who, every body knows, is a first-rate Maker of Verses. He is surely the man of all the world for your purpose. Alas Sir! I have heretofore borrowed help from him, but he is a Gentleman of so much reading that the people of our town cannot understand him. I confess to you, my Dear, I felt all the force of the Compliment implied in this speech, and was almost ready to answer, perhaps my good friend, they may find me unintelligible too for the same reason, but on asking him whether he had walked over to Weston on purpose to implore the assistance of my Muse, and on his replying in the affirmative, I felt my mortified vanity a little consoled, and pitying the poor man's distress which appeared to be considerable, promised to supply him. The waggon has accordingly gone this day to Northampton loaded in part with my effusions in the Mortuary stile. A fig for poets who write Epitaphs upon Individuals; I have written *one* that serves *200* persons.

If you have not yet open'd the parcel containing the Loungers[4] my Cousin, you must do it now; for I have immediate occasion to know whether they are stitched only or bound, and if bound in what manner. Few days since, I received a second very obliging Letter from Mr. McKenzie, in which he accepts avec beaucoup de politesse an offer that I made him of my two volumes. I would therefore give him a Rowland for his Oliver,[5] and order Johnson to transmit to

[3] John Cox (d. *c.*1791), who was succeeded in 1791–2 by Samuel Wright.
[4] See n.1, C to Mackenzie, 15 Sept. 1787.
[5] A proverbial expression meaning 'tit for tat'. Roland and Oliver, in the Charlemagne cycle of legends, were close friends.

his Bookseller Cadell,[6] just such a Set in respect of Binding as he has bestowed upon me. He tells me, in some sort confidentially, (for as decently as I could I had ask'd him who were the Authors of those papers) that Dr. Beattie wrote but two,[7] which are in the Mirrour and on the subject of dreams and which he afterward extended into an Essay. And that Dr. Blair had nothing to do with it; also that his own papers which are by far, he is sorry to say it, the most numerous, are marked V.I.Z. Accordingly, my Dear, I am happy to find that I am at last engaged in a Correspondence with Mr. Viz. a gentleman for whom I have always entertained the profoundest veneration. But the serious fact is, that the papers distinguished by those signatures, have ever pleased me most and struck me as the work of a sensible man who knows the world well and has more of Addison's delicate Humour than any body.

A Poor man begg'd food at the Hall lately. The Cook gave him some Vermicelli soup.[8] He ladled it about some time with the spoon and then returned it to her saying — I am a Poor man it is true, and I am very hungry, but yet I cannot eat broth with Maggots in it.

Once more, my Dear, a thousand thanks for your book full of good things, useful things, and beautiful things, and with Mrs. Unwin's affectionate remembrances — Ever Yours — Wm Cowper.

[6] Thomas Cadell (1742–1802), London bookseller, acted in association with the Scottish printer William Strahan until the latter's death in 1785 as the London co-publisher for William Creech (1745–1815), the most distinguished Edinburgh bookseller of the period, who had published both *The Mirror* and *The Lounger*.

[7] Nos. 73 (Tuesday, 18 Jan. 1780) and 74 (Saturday, 22 Jan. 1780); both papers were signed 'Insomnius'. 'Of Dreams' was printed as a portion of Chapter V in the general division 'Of Memory' in Volume I of *Dissertations Moral and Critical*: 'Extracts from this discourse were printed in a periodical paper called *The Mirrour*. The whole is here given, as, it was first composed.'

[8] 'A Wheaten paste, of Italian origin, now usually made of flour, cheese, yolks of eggs, sugar and saffron, prepared in the form of long, slender, hard threads, and used as an article of diet. . . . 1747 Mrs. Glasse *Cookery*, xix. 155 It will run up like little Worms, as Vermicella does' (*OED*).

LADY HESKETH   Tuesday, 4 December 1787

Address: Lady Hesketh / New Norfolk Street / Grosvenor Square / London.
Postmarks: DE/5/87 *and* OULNEY
H. C. Longuet-Higgins

The Lodge
Decr. 4. 1787.

I am glad my dearest Coz, that my last letter proved so very diverting. You may assure yourself of the literal truth of the whole narration, and that however droll, it was not in the least indebted to any embellishments of mine. Just at this moment I suspect that I shall not make my present dispatches quite so agreeable, having almost as many Aches in my mouth as teeth, the effect of a violent Cold, the second that I have had the address to catch within this fortnight.

We Dined yesterday at the Hall and mentioned your having seen Lady T——n[1] on Friday. Our friends laughed on the occasion, giving us to understand that we had unwittingly divulged a great secret, that Lady by no means intending that her present journey to town should have been known at Weston. Why she chose to be mysterious in that particular I cannot tell. We spent our 4 or 5 hours there, very agreeably, as we always do except when the company is too large for conversation. Mr. Postlethwaite was the only extrá ourselves excepted. By their desire I walked over to Olney on Saturday on purpose to invite him. The poor man is, as you know, bashful in the extreme, accordingly he said little and would in fact have said nothing, had I not twice or thrice constrained him to speak, on purpose that our friends might not run away with a notion that he could not. The Question whether he should be Vicar of Olney or not which hung so long in balance, is at last decided against him, and the living is given to a Mr. Behn. Of Mr. Behn I hear the highest character from a man of judgment who knows him well; but Mr. Postlethwaite I know well myself, which to me is a recommendation of *Him* in preference to any other man be he recommended by whom he may. I interested myself so much in his success that I drew up, a short representation in his favour to Lord D——h; Mrs. U. and I signed it, as did all the

¹ Sir Robert Throckmorton married Lucy, daughter of James Heywood in 1773; it was his third marriage.

principal Inhabitants of Weston. But Counter-petitions went from Olney and Letters in abundance to his prejudice, so that his Lordship at last and after long deliberation, with an intention (vain I fear, and soon to be proved such, of pleasing every body) has given them a Vicar of whom they are at present great admirers, having never seen him. Poor P. will however be provided for. John Thornton the Great is his patron, and there are hopes as I understand, that Lord Dartmouth will make application in his behalf to the Chancellor.

You say well, my Dear, that in Mr. T——n we have a peerless neighbour. We have so. I have now had an opportunity by His means of seeing nearly our whole neighborhood including all who live within about ten miles of our village. His great superiority to them all is always striking. In point of information upon all important subjects, in respect too of expression and address, and in short of every thing that enters into the idea of a Gentleman, I not only have not found his Equal here, but not often any where. Were I asked who in my judgment approaches the nearest to him in all his amiable qualities and qualifications, I should certainly answer — His Brother George — Who if he be not his exact counterpart, nor endued with precisely the same measure of the same accomplishments, is nevertheless deficient in none of them, and is of a character singularly agreeable in respect of a certain manly, I had almost said, heroic frankness with which his air strikes one almost immediately. He has too, a considerable share of drollery and quickness of thought and fancy, of a kind which none of the family seem to partake with him. As far as his opportunities have gone, he has ever been as friendly and obliging to us as we could wish him, and were he Lord of the Hall to-morrow, would, I dare say, conduct him self toward us in such manner as to leave us as little sensible as possible of the removal of its present Owners. But all this I say my Dear, merely for the sake of stating the matter as it is; not in order to obviate or to prove the inexpedience of any future plans of yours concerning the place of our residence. Providence and time shape every thing. I should rather say, Providence alone, for time has often no hand in the wonderful changes that we experience; they take place in a moment. It is not therefore worth while perhaps to consider much what we will or will not do in years to come, concerning which all that I can say with certainty at present, is that those years will be to me the most welcome in which I can see the most of You.

Mrs. Wrighte whom I forgot to mention in my last is much better; So much, that I am told there is no doubt of her recovery. You forgot to give me an account of my Loungers, in what manner they are attired. Have no fears on account of poor Bully's security at Weston. I can place him, even in my study, where no cat can reach him. My Love to Him & to Jockey, not forgetting the Finches. My dog Beau died of a dysentery, and I have now another of the same name. Miss Gunning² procured him and Mrs. Throck gave him to me. He is a very promising puppy. Ever yours

My dearest coz — W C.

WALTER BAGOT   Thursday, 6 December 1787

Address: The Revd. Walter Bagot
Morgan Library

Weston Underwood Decbr. 6. 1787
My dear friend,

A short time since by the help of Mrs. Throckmorton's Chaise, Mrs. Unwin and I reached Chichely. Now, said I to Mr. Chester, I shall write boldly to your Brother Walter, and will do it immediately. I have passed the gulph that parted us, and he will be glad to hear it. But let not the man who translates Homer be so presumptuous as to have a Will of his own, or to promise any thing. A fortnight has, I suppose, elapsed, since I pay'd this visit, and I am only now beginning to fulfill what I then undertook to accomplish without delay. The old Greecian must answer for it.

I spent my Morning there so agreeably, that I have ever since regretted more sensibly that there are five Miles of a dirty country interposed between us. For the encrease of my

---

² Sir Robert Gunning (1731–1816), a retired diplomat, lived at Horton, midway between Olney and Northampton. He had two daughters; the elder, Charlotte Margaret, was a maid of honour to the Queen.

pleasure, I had the good fortune to find your Brother the Bishop there. We had much talk about many things, but most, I believe, about Homer; and great satisfaction it gave me to find that on the most important points of that subject his Lordship and I were exactly of one mind. In the course of our conversation he produced from his pocketbook a translation of the first 10 or 12 lines of the Iliad, and in order to leave my judgment free, informed me kindly at the same time that they were not his own. I read them, and according to my best recollection of the Original, found them well executed. The Bishop indeed acknowledged that they were not faultless, neither did I find them so. Had they been such, I should have felt their perfection as a discouragement hardly to be surmounted; for at that passage I have laboured more abundantly than at any other, and hitherto with the least success. I am convinced that Homer planted it at the threshold of his work as a Scarecrow to all Translators. Now Walter, if thou knowest the Author[1] of this Version and it be not treason against thy brother's confidence in thy secrecy, declare him to me. Had I been so happy as to have seen the Bishop again before he left this country, I should certainly have asked him the question, having a curiosity upon the matter that is extremely troublesome.

The aukward situation in which you found yourself on receiving a Visit from an Authoress whose works, though presented to you long before, you had never read, made me laugh, and it was no sin against my friendship for you to do so.[2] It was a ridiculous distress and I can laugh at it even now. I hope she Catechized you well. How did you extricate yourself? Now laugh at me. The Clerk of the Parish of All Saints in the town of [North]ampton,[3] having occasion for a poet, has appoin[ted m]e to the Office. Some days since, he trudged on foot all those dirty miles that are between us, and enter'd my study before breakfast. Being seated and asked his business, he first told me who he was, then what he

---

[1] Lord Bagot. See n.3, C to Lady Hesketh, 30 Nov. 1785. C learned the name of the 'Author' from Walter Bagot by 5 Jan. 1788 (see p. 81).

[2] The authoress's name is not mentioned in any extant letter from Bagot to Cowper.

[3] MS torn.

wanted. I publish Sir, every year, a Bill of Mortality, and at the foot of it a Copy of Verses on the occasion; You will oblige me by furnishing me with such a copy. It must be printed before Christmas. I told him he lived in a large town in which no doubt are many poets, because there are many every where. But he had an Answer to all that I could urge, and I found myself obliged to comply. The Bellman comes next, and then I think, though even borne upon your Swans-quill, I can soar no higher. — I am, my dear friend, with Mrs. Unwin's Compliments — faithfully Yours —

Wm Cowper.

[ROBERT SMITH]   Friday, 7 December 1787

Morgan Library

Weston Underwood Decbr. 7. 1787.

My dear Sir,

It is long since I met with any thing that has given me so much pleasure as the account that I received this morning under your own hand, of your Return and Recovery. Many a time have I earnestly wished for Intelligence on the subject of your health, since I in some measure regained my own, for there is no man living now, in whose welfare I interest myself so much. The word *tolerable* that you make use of in describing the degree of reestablishment that you have found, is the only draw-back upon my satisfaction; perhaps you call that tolerable to which I should myself give a more qualified Epithet; but I will hope the best.

Your kind enquiries after me that you were so obliging as to make just before you went abroad, found me incapable of answering them myself, and even incapable of hoping that I ever should. I am however, as you say of yourself, *tolerably* restored; but I have now attained an age at which Nature not having such favorable materials to work upon, rather patches than mends, and seems by her best efforts to promise nothing more than a respite, and that a short one.

I have been rather anxious about that pacquet which you saw at Johnson's, and am therefore glad that you did see it.

He is a slovenly idle sensible fellow, and never sends me a syllable of information but when he cannot possibly avoid it. For aught I knew, or should have known for a long time to come, had it not fallen in your way to assure me of its arrival, it might have miscarried; in which case a labour would have been lengthen'd that seems already endless. Yet endless as it seems, I am neither weary of it, nor even wish to arrive soon at the conclusion. It is now become so habitual to me, to spend half my time with Homer, that it is impossible for me not to apprehend a tremendous Vacuum, when this work shall be accomplished. But thanks to the excellent and long-winded old Greecian, what with the difficulties with which he presents me, and the necessity that I find of sifting and searching and improving for ever my most successful attempts to represent him so as not grossly to wrong him, that dreaded consummation seems yet at a distance. The box that you saw contained the 12th and 13th books of the Iliad for Fuseli's revisal, and the 14th and 15th. are now ready to follow them.

Your note for 50£ with which you have favor'd us, is most seasonably arrived for many, and Mrs. Unwin and I have spent the day in enjoying the comforts that you have thus kindly enabled us to impart to others. The diseased, the naked, the hungry, are going to leap for joy, though ignorant of their Benefactor. No matter. He is known where by and by, but I hope not yet, he will be well rewarded. As to what concerns ourselves as your Almoners on these occasions, I know I can say nothing that will be more satisfactory to you, than that we are nice in the choice of our objects, considering ourselves, as in reason we ought, accountable to God for a discreet and judicious discharge of our office.

Mrs. Unwin joins with me, my dear Sir, in congratulating you warmly on your safe return to England, and in the Sincerest acknowledgments of all your kindness. I beg you to believe me, now and at all times, truly and Affectionately

Yours — Wm Cowper.

HENRY MACKENZIE   Monday, 10 December 1787

Address: Henry Mackenzie Esqre. / Brown Square / Edinborough.[1]
Postmarks: DE/12/[87], DE/15 *and* OULNEY
Princeton

Sir

   I esteem it a singular favor that unknown to you as I am
except in print, you have yet accounted me worthy of so
much of your confidence as is implied in the discovery you
make of the share, the large share that you had in Writing the
volumes that I so much admire.[2] Will you suspect me of
flattery, or will you give me credit for the truth of it? The
papers bearing the signature that you mention are those
which pleased me most, and how it came to pass I know not,
but of the three Letters, Z was my favorite in particular, so
that when it happen'd, as frequently was the case, that after
reading an Essay of yours I found an I or a V at the foot of it,
I was disappointed and puzzled. How can this be? said I to
myself. Have I so little discrimination of taste as to be thus
repeatedly mistaken? It is plain then that I am not so sagacious
in the affair of stile as I thought myself. In the mean time it
never occurred to me that a plurality of Letters might possibly be appropriate to the same person, though Addison's
Clio[3] and other instances of a similar kind might have served
me with a hint of it.

   I was once intimate with the Authors of a paper published
some years since in London, called the Connoisseur.[4] They
were Thornton[5] the Translator of Plautus, and Colman the

---

   [1] The letter is endorsed in Mackenzie's hand: 'Mr Cowper Author of the *Task*,
10 December 1787. The *Mirror* — Curious Anecdotes of the Author of the Connoisseur. His first Acquaintance with *Samuel Rose* whom he supposes to be a
relation of mine.'
   [2] See n.2, C to Mackenzie, 15 Sept. 1787.
   [3] Addison 'signed' his contributions to *The Spectator* with one or other of the
letters C.L.I. and O.
   [4] See *Russell*, pp. 2-3.
   [5] Bonnell Thornton (1724-68), though intended for medicine, turned to
literature while studying at Oxford, where he took his BA in 1747 and MB in
1754. He contributed both to *The Student*, the periodical associated with Smart,
and to *The Adventurer*. He enjoyed a reputation for wit and conviviality. His
translation of five comedies of Plautus, with the *Mercator* rendered by Richard
Warner and the *Captivi* by Colman, doubtless intended to complement Colman's
Terence, appeared in 1767, and was widely praised.

Translator of Terence. The former has been dead some time; with the latter I have lately renewed my correspondence, though it has been again broken off by illness. I had known them many months and had dined and supped with them an hundred times, before I even suspected that I was in company with authors. It may make you smile perhaps to be told that they so effectually cheated me upon this subject, that they even persuaded me to write for the Connoisseur, before they let me into the secret. They knew my hand-writing. I sent an Essay to the Printer. They read it, put it to the press, and on the day of its appearance sat together in a corner of the Coffee house[6] that I frequented, watching and enjoying the countenance with which I called for the paper. It was the countenance no doubt of a man trembling lest his first attempt should be rejected, and transported with joy to find himself actually in print. Your observation that Co-adjutors *may* write, but Principals *must*, brought to my mind this incident, and with it a maxim that I remember was frequently in Thornton's mouth — What *must* be done *will* be done.[7] Thursday was the day of publication; and being naturally of a dissipated turn, they would frequently suffer the week to elapse till Wednesday and sometimes the Evening of Wednesday was in fact arrived, before they had even thought on a subject. On such occasions he used to comfort himself with reflecting that the necessity of the emergence gave security for the performance, and though the first paragraph has been sometimes at the press before the second was written, he was never disappointed.

It is now about a year since I received a very obliging Call from a most amiable young Gentleman, and as I now understand, a friend of yours. His name is Rose. We have exchanged two or three letters and I intend to write to him to-morrow. If He be a fair sample of what your Universities in Scotland produce generally, we may well cry — fie upon ours! I forget whether I told you that I am translating Homer. This makes

[6] Dick's, or Richard's Coffee House, at 8 Fleet Street. See n.30, *Adelphi*.
[7] In both *The Mirror* and *The Lounger* the proportion of contributions by Mackenzie increases in the later months of publication. Clearly Mackenzie considered himself, despite the nominally joint editorship of both periodicals, as something more than simply *primus inter pares* — as indeed he was.

me a slack Correspondent, but I shall always be happy to hear from you, and will be as punctual in reply as the old Greecian will permit me to be.

I have order'd my two volumes to Cadell's with your address, and am, Sir,

Your most obliged
and obedient humble Servant Wm Cowper.
Weston Underwood
Decbr. 10. 1787.

LADY HESKETH   Monday, 10 December 1787

Address: Lady Hesketh / New Norfolk Street / Grosvenor Square / London.
Postmarks: DE/12/87 *and* OULNEY
H. C. Longuet-Higgins

The Lodge Decbr. 10. 1787.
My teeth are better my Cousin, all, save one, which nothing will cure but eradication; a remedy to which I am extremely unwilling to submit, because the corresponding tooth follows of course. But I thank you for your Recipe, which if that torment in the face should seize me, I will not fail to make trial of. I thank you likewise for the snip of Cloth commonly called a pattern. At present I have two coats and but one back. If at any time hereafter I should find myself possessed of fewer coats or more backs, it will then be of use to me, unless Mrs. Unwin, whose partiality to the puce seems invincible, should insist on my giving that colour the preference. — Had I known or could I have suspected that poor Jockey was dead, my dog should have borne his name. But it is now too late to Christen him again. Beau is his second name, and should I give him a third, he might possibly never answer to any at all. It is an old maxim of mine that he who multiplies connexions multiplies troubles. If this be true, it is consequently impolitic to keep a dog. Dogs as they are, they have yet good qualities that recommend them to our affections, and we cannot lose them without regret. Yet being myself a friend to the species, I cannot but wish *you* to keep one of them; because *that one* will be an individual added to the number of happy ones; a small number compared with the

thousands whom it would be mercy to poison or drown or knock on the head. While he lives he will entertain you, and when he dies, the loss is easily repaired.

Even as you suspect, my Dear, so it proved. The Ball was prepared for, the Ball was held, and the Ball passed, and we had nothing to do with it. Mrs. Throck knowing our trim did not give us the pain of an invitation, for a pain it would have been. And why? as Sternhold says — because, as Hopkins answers, we must have refused it.[1] But it fell out singularly enough that this Ball was held of all days in the year, on my Birth-day — and so I told them — but not 'till it was all over.

Neither Beattie nor Blair have any share at all in the Lounger. In the Mirrour, Beattie was the only one of the two who wrote, and he but two papers. I have read the third volume of the Loungers and a small part of the second, but none of the first. The first I lent to our neighbors at the Hall long since, and intend to recall it soon lest they should forget that they ever borrowed it. I like them well; and it happens luckily enough that Mackenzie's papers, with whom I am likely to correspond, are those which I liked the best. This I can tell him without flattery or the least violation of truth, and have accordingly told him so in a Letter that I send him by this very post.

Though I have thought proper never to take any notice of the arrival of my MSS together with the *other good things* in the box, yet certain it is that I received them. I have furbished up the Tenth Book 'till it is as bright as silver, and am now occupied in bestowing the same labour upon the eleventh. The 12th. and 13th. are in the hands of Fuseli, and the 14th. and 15th. are ready to succeed them. This notable job is the delight of my heart, and how sorry shall I be when it is ended! — The Smith and the Carpenter my Dear, are both in the room hanging a Bell, if I therefore make a thousand Blunders, let said intruders answer for them all. A reason that you are not aware of has occurred that would of itself have recommended the postponing of your Journey to Weston. The Small [pox] rages throughout the town, brought hither

---

[1] Thomas Sternhold (d. 1549) and John Hopkins (d. 1570) were joint versifiers of the Psalms, which were sung or read responsively.

from Newport first; now universally spread by innoculation. You indeed have nothing to fear from that distemper, nor, as I suppose, your servants. But our Hannah has never had them, and the probability that she will catch them now, and the consequent anxiety and trouble if she should, would have proved a drawback in some measure on the comfort you might have otherwise have found at Weston. Our Manservant has lost his eldest boy,[2] and has two children now in the crisis. Hannah doubtless draws the infection with every breath, and proper precautions have been taken to prepare her for the distemper.

I thank you my Dear for your history of the Gores.[3] What changes in that family! and how many thousand families have in the same time experienced changes as violent as theirs! The course of a rapid river is the justest of all Emblems to express the variableness of our scene below. Shakespeare says none ever bathed himself twice in the same stream,[4] and it is equally true that the world upon which we close our eyes at night is never the same with that on which we open them in a morning. I do not always say, give my Love to my Uncle, because he knows that I always love him. I do not always present Mrs. Unwin's love to you, partly for the same reason (deuce take the Smith and the Carpenter) and partly because I sometimes forget it. But to present my own I forget never, for I always have to finish my letter, which I know not how to do, my Dearest Coz! without telling you that I am ever yours.

W.C.

[2] Samuel Roberts's son. See C to Lady Hesketh, 1 Jan. 1788.

[3] The Gore family owned the manor of Marsworth, Buckinghamshire, just over the Hertfordshire border, from 1705 to 1786; the Gores were of 'Tring Park', the most splendid seat near Berkhamsted, where C was born. Charles Gore (d. 1810), as well as C, was named a beneficiary in the will of Sir Thomas Hesketh. See *Ryskamp*, p. 191.

[4] This does not occur in the work of Shakespeare; rather, C seems to be quoting Edward Young's *Night Thoughts*: 'Life glides away, Lorenzo, like a brook; / Forever changing, unperceived the change. / In the same brook none ever bathed him twice' (v. 401–3). Young's source, and possibly C's, must ultimately have been Plato. In *Cratylus* (402A), according to Socrates, 'Heraclitus is supposed to say that all things are in motion and nothing at rest; he compares them to the stream of a river, and says that you cannot go into the same water twice.' This translation is from the edition of Edith Hamilton and Huntington Cairns of *The Collected Dialogues of Plato* (Princeton, 1961).

SAMUEL ROSE Thursday, 13 December 1787

Address: Samuel Rose Esqre. No. 23 / Percy Street / Rathbone Place / London.
Postmarks: DE/17/87 *and* OULNEY
Olney

Weston Underwood
Decbr. 13. 1787.

My dear Sir,

    Unless my memory deceives me I forewarned you in my last that I should prove a very unpunctual correspondent. The work that lies before me engages unavoidably my whole attention. The length of it, the Spirit of it, and the exactness that is requisite to its due performance, are so many most interesting subjects of consideration to me, who find that my best attempts are only introductory to others, and that what to-day I suppose finished, to-morrow I must begin again. Thus it fares with a Translator of Homer. To exhibit the Majesty of such a Poet in a modern language is a task that no man can estimate the difficulty of 'till he attempts it. To paraphrase him loosely, to hang him with trappings that do not belong to him, all this is comparatively easy. But to represent him with only his own ornaments and still to preserve his dignity, is a labour that if I hope in any measure to atchieve it, I am sensible can only be atchieved by the most assiduous and unremitting attention. Our studies, however different in themselves, in respect of the means by which they are to be successfully carried on, bear some resemblance to each other. A perseverance that nothing can discourage, a minuteness of observation that suffers nothing to escape, and a determination not to be seduced from the strait line that lies before us by any images with which fancy may present us, are essentials that should be common to us both. There are perhaps few arduous undertakings that are not in fact more arduous than we at first supposed them. As we proceed difficulties increase upon us, but our hopes gather strength also, and we conquer obstacles which could we have foreseen them, we should never have had the boldness to encounter. May this be your experience, as I doubt not that it will. You possess by Nature all that is necessary to success in the profession that you have chosen, what remains is in

70

your own power. They say of poets that they must be born
such; so must Mathematicians, so must great Generals, and so
must Lawyers, and so indeed must men of all denominations
or it is not possible that they should excell. But with whatever
faculties we are born, and to whatever studies our Genius
may direct us, studies they must still be. I am persuaded that
Milton did not write his Paradise lost, nor Homer his Iliad,
nor Sir Isaac Newton his Principia, without immense labour.
Nature gave them a Bias to their respective pursuits, and that
strong propensity, I suppose, is what we mean by Genius.
The rest they gave themselves. Macte esto[1] therefore, and
have no fears for the issue.

I have had a second kind letter from your friend Mr.
Mackenzie which I have just answer'd. I must not I find
hope to see him here, at least I must not much expect it.
He has a family that does not permit him to fly Southward.
I have else a notion that we three could spend a few days
comfortably together, especially in a country like this
abounding in scenes with which I am sure you would both
be delighted. Having lived till lately at some distance from
the spot that I now inhabit, and having never been master
of any sort of vehicle whatever, it is but just now that I begin
myself to be acquainted with the beauties of our situation.
To you I may hope one time or other to show them, and
shall be happy to do it when an opportunity offers. In the
mean time, I am with Mrs. Unwin's best respects, Yours,
my Dear Sir,

most Affectionately
Wm Cowper.

LADY HESKETH   [Monday, 17 December 1787][1]

Southey, vi. 95–8

Saturday, my dearest cousin, was a day of receipts. In the
morning I received a box filled with an abundant variety of

---

[1] 'A blessing on you': Horace, *Satires*, I. ii. 31–2.

---

[1] Southey gives the date of the postmark of this letter as 'Dec. 19, 1787'.
In the opening paragraph C remarks that he received a letter 'yesterday — that is,

stationery ware, containing, in particular, a quantity of paper sufficient, well covered with good writing, to immortalize any man. I have nothing to do, therefore, but to cover it as aforesaid, and my name will never die. In the evening I received a smaller box, but still more welcome on account of its contents. It contained an almanack in red morocco, a pencil of a new invention, called an everlasting pencil,[2] and a noble purse, with a noble gift in it, called a Bank note for twenty-five pounds. I need use no arguments to assure you, my cousin, that by the help of ditto note, we shall be able to fadge very comfortably till Christmas is turned, without having the least occasion to draw upon you. By the post yesterday — that is, Sunday morning — I received also a letter from Anonymous, giving me advice of the kind present which I have just particularized; in which letter allusion is made to a certain piece by me composed, entitled, I believe, the Drop of Ink.[3] The only copy I ever gave of that piece, I gave to yourself. It is *possible*, therefore, that between you and *Anonymous* there may be some communication. If that should be the case, I will beg you just to signify to him, as opportunity may occur, the safe arrival of his most acceptable present, and my most grateful sense of it.

My toothache is in a great measure, that is to say, almost entirely removed; not by snipping my ears, as poor Lady Strange's ears were snipped,[4] nor by any other chirurgical

Sunday morning'. Therefore, this letter must have been written on Monday, 17 Dec. and posted on Wednesday, 19 Dec.

   [2] C's pencil was probably similar to the 'propelling pencil' described by Joyce Irene Whalley in *Writing Implements and Accessories* (1975), pp. 118–19: 'Graphite is a very fragile material and needs careful protection. It is also very soft and liable to leave traces on anyone or anything coming into contact with it. In order to overcome these problems manufacturers made a variety of decorative cases to protect the graphite. Some propelling pencils were very simple. A slim piece of lead was enclosed in a metal or ivory case.'

   [3] C included 'The Ink-glass Almost Dried in the Sun. An Ode to Apollo' in his letter to Unwin of 7 Sept. 1783; the poem was first published in *The Speaker* (1792).

   [4] Charlotte, *suo jure* Baroness Strange (1731–1805), married John, 3rd Duke of Atholl on 23 Oct. 1753. Although we have not located any reference to snipping ears for the relief of toothache, John Hunter in *Natural History of the Human Teeth, Part 2: A Practical Treatise on the Diseases of the Teeth* (2nd ed., 1786), p. 18 mentions the following approach: 'When there is no symptom except pain in the Tooth, we have many modes of treatment recommended, which can only be temporary in their effects. These act by derivation, or stimulus applied to

operation, except such as I could perform myself. The manner of it was as follows: we dined last Thursday at the Hall; I sat down to table, trembling lest the tooth, of which I told you in my last, should not only refuse its own office, but hinder all the rest. Accordingly, in less than five minutes, by a hideous dislocation of it, I found myself not only in great pain, but under an absolute prohibition not only to eat, but to speak another word. Great emergencies sometimes meet the most effectual remedies. I resolved, if it were possibe, then and there to draw it. This I effected so dexterously by a sudden twitch, and afterwards so dexterously conveyed it into my pocket, that no creature present, not even Mrs. Unwin, who sat facing me, was sensible either of my distress, or of the manner of my deliverance from it. I am poorer by one tooth than I was, but richer by the unimpeded use of all the rest.

When I lived in the Temple, I was rather intimate with a son of the late Admiral Rowley and a younger brother of the present Admiral.[5] Since I wrote to you last, I received a letter from him, in a very friendly and affectionate style. It accompanied half a dozen books, which I had lent him five and twenty years ago, and which he apologized for having kept so long, telling me that they had been sent to him at Dublin by mistake; for at Dublin, it seems, he now resides. Reading my poems, he felt, he said, his friendship for me revive, and wrote accordingly. I have now, therefore, a correspondent in Ireland, another in Scotland, and a third in Wales.[6] All this would be very diverting, had I a little more time to spare to them.

My dog, my dear is a spaniel. Till Miss Gunning begged him, he was the property of a farmer, and while he was their

some other part of the body. Thus to burn the ear by hot irons, has sometimes been a successful practice, and has relieved the Tooth-ach.' If burning ears was employed as a method of treatment, then snipping probably was too. In either case it can only have acted as a counter-irritant, and probably no lasting cure resulted, as the cause of the toothache would not have been treated.

[5] Clotworthy Rowley's father was Sir William Rowley, KB (1690–1768) who held various important positions in the Admiralty, including that of Rear-Admiral of Great Britain (1747), Lord of Admiralty (1751), the Admiral of the Fleet and Commander-in-Chief (1762); Clotworthy's brother, Sir Joshua (1730?–90), was created Rear-Admiral of the Blue in 1779 and Vice-Admiral of the White in 1787.

[6] Rowley, Mackenzie, and Churchey respectively.

property had been accustomed to lie in the chimney corner, among the embers, till the hair was singed from his back, and till nothing was left of his tail but the gristle. Allowing for these disadvantages, he is really handsome; and when nature shall have furnished him with a new coat, a gift which, in consideration of the ragged condition of his old one, it is hoped she will not long delay, he will then be unrivalled in personal endowments by any dog in this country. He and my cat are excessively fond of each other, and play a thousand gambols together that it is impossible not to admire.

Know thou, that from this time forth, the post comes daily to Weston. This improvement is effected by an annual subscription of ten shillings. The Throcks invited us to the measure, and we have acceded to it. Their servant will manage this concern for us at the Olney post office, and the subscription is to pay a man for stumping three times a week from Olney to Newport Pagnel, and back again.

Returning from my walk to-day, while I was passing by some small closes at the back of the town, I heard the voices of some persons extremely merry at the top of the hill. Advancing into the large field behind our house, I there met Mr. Throck, wife, and brother George. Combine in your imagination as large proportions as you can of earth and water intermingled so as to constitute what is commonly called mud, and you will have but an imperfect conception of the quantity that had attached itself to her petticoats: but she had half-boots, and laughed at her own figure. She told me that she had this morning transcribed sixteen pages of my Homer. I observed in reply, that to write so much, and to gather all that dirt, was no bad morning's work, considering the shortness of the days at this season.

Yours, my dear,
W. C.

LADY HESKETH   Monday, 24 December 1787

Southey, vi. 98–102

The Lodge, Dec. 24, 1787.

My dearest Cousin,

The Throcks do not leave Weston till after Easter. But this I hope will have no effect upon your movements, should an opportunity present itself to you of coming sooner. We dined there last Saturday. After dinner, while we all sat round the fire, I told them, as I related it to you, the adventure of my tooth. This drew from Mrs. Throck, (singular as it must appear,) a tale the very counterpart of mine. She, in like manner, had a tooth to draw, while I was drawing mine; and thus it came to pass (the world, I suppose, could not furnish such another instance) that we two, without the least intimation to each other of our respective distress, were employed in the same moment, sitting side by side, in drawing each a tooth: an operation which we performed with equal address, and without being perceived by any one.

This morning had very near been a tragical one to me, beyond all that have ever risen upon me. Mrs. Unwin rose as usual at seven o'clock; at eight she came to me, and showed me her bed-gown with a great piece burnt out of it. Having lighted her fire, which she always lights herself, she placed the candle upon the hearth. In a few moments it occurred to her that, if it continued there, it might possibly set fire to her clothes, therefore she put it out. But in fact, though she had not the least suspicion of it, her clothes were on fire at that very time. She found herself uncommonly annoyed by smoke, such as brought the water into her eyes; supposing that some of the billets might lie too forward, she disposed them differently; but finding the smoke increase, and grow more troublesome, (for by this time the room was filled with it,) she cast her eye downward, and perceived not only her bed-gown, but her petticoat on fire. She had the presence of mind to gather them in her hand, and plunge them immediately into the basin, by which means the general conflagration of her person, which must probably have ensued in a few moments, was effectually prevented. Thus was that which I have often heard from the pulpit, and have often had occasion myself to observe, most clearly illustrated, — that, secure as we may sometimes seem to ourselves, we are in reality never so safe as to have no need of a superintending Providence. Danger can never be at a distance from creatures who dwell in houses of clay.[1] Therefore take care of thyself, gentle Yahoo! and may a more vigilant than thou care for thee.

On the day when we dined as abovementioned at the Hall, Mrs. Throck had paid a morning visit at * * * *. When I enquired how she found Mrs. * * *,[2] her account of her was as follows: 'They say she is much better, but to judge by her looks and her manner, there is no ground to think so. She looks dreadfully, and talks in a rambling way without ceasing.' If this be a just description of her, and I do not at all doubt it, I am afraid, poor woman! that she is far from well, notwithstanding all that the physician of minds has done for her. In effect there is but One who merits that title; and were all the frantic who have been restored to their reason to make a reasonable use of it, they would acknowledge that God, and not man, had cured them.

I thank you, my dear, for your intentions to furnish me, had I not been otherwise accommodated with one, with an everlasting pencil. You may yet perhaps, on some distant day, have an opportunity to fulfil those intentions, for 'everlasting,' as it is called, it is not such in point of duration; but claims the title on this account only, that in the using, it perpetually works itself to a point, and never wants cutting. Otherwise it wastes and wears, as every thing made of earthly materials must.

When the Throcks happen to mention the chairs again, your directions shall be pursued. As to the balance due on the plate account,[3] it was, before the purchase of the silk handkerchiefs, &c., either six pounds or six guineas — we cannot recollect which. With the remainder, whatever it shall be found to be, Mrs. Unwin will be obliged to you if you will give it in commission to Mrs. Eaton, to buy for her some muslin for aprons, of the sort that you wore when you were at Olney, viz. with cross stripes. She thinks you called it an

[1] See Job 4:19.
[2] Mrs Wrighte of Gayhurst.
[3] See p. 88.

English muslin.[4] They must be ell and nail long.[5] But at the same time it does not appear probable to either of us, that there should be money remaining in your hands sufficient for this purpose.

I forgot to tell you that my dog is spotted liver-colour and white, or rather white and chestnut. He is at present my pupil as well as dog, and just before I sat down to write I gave him a lesson in the science of fetch and carry. He performs with an animation past all conception, except your own, whose poor head will never forget Tinker.[6] But I am now grown more reasonable, and never make such a dreadful din but when Beau and I are together. To teach him is necessary, in order that he may take the water, and *that* is necessary in order that he may be sweet in summer. Farewell, my dearest coz. I am, with Mrs. U.'s affections,

Ever thine, most truly,
Wm. Cowper.

LADY HESKETH   Tuesday, 1 January 1788

Address: Lady Hesketh / New Norfolk Street / Grosvenor Square / London.
Postmarks: JA/4/88 *and* OULNEY
Lord Charnwood Estate

The Lodge Jan. 1. 1788.

My dearest Coz — Mrs. Unwin was mistaken concerning the length of the Apron. The Ell without the Nail will be sufficient. She is obliged to you for your kindness in purchasing the Muslin for her, and especially for the interest you take in her very marvellous escape. The more marvellous, because her

---

[4] English muslin was the name given to extremely delicate woven cotton fabrics whereas French muslin was a sort of linen, made of cotton, which, although fine, was not close woven and thus not very smooth.
[5] Ell: 'A measure of length varying in different countries. The English ell = 45 in.' (*OED*).
Nail: 'A measure of length for cloth; 2¼ inches or the sixteenth part of a yard' (*OED*).
[6] Probably one of Lady Hesketh's deceased dogs.

petticoat was of Dimitty.[1] I have placed this at the head of my letter because at the end of it I am apt to find myself, after having allotted all my sheet to other matters, under some difficulty respecting room for the Needful.

Now for another story almost incredible; a story that would be quite such, if it was not certain that you will give *me* credit for any thing. I have read the poem for the sake of which you sent the paper and was much entertained by it. You think it perhaps, as very well you may, the only piece exactly of that kind that was ever produced. It is indeed Original, for I dare say Mr. Merry[2] never saw mine; but certainly it is not an Unique. For most true it is my Dear that 10 years since having a Letter to write to a friend of mine to whom I could write any thing, I filled a whole sheet with a composition both in measure and in manner precisely similar. I have in vain search'd for it. It is either burnt or lost. Could I have found it you would have had double postage to pay. For that one man in Italy and another in England who never saw each other, should stumble on a species of Verse in which no other man ever wrote (and I believe that to be the case) and upon a stile and manner too of which I suppose that neither of them had ever seen an example, appears to me so extraordinary a fact, that I must have sent you mine whatever it had cost you, and am really vex'd that I cannot authenticate the story by producing a voucher. The measure I recollect to have been perfectly the same, and as to the manner I am equally sure of that, and from this circumstance; That Mrs. U. and I never laughed more at any production of mine, perhaps not even at John Gilpin. But for all this my Dear, you must, as I said, give me credit; for the thing itself is gone to that Limbo of Vanity where alone says Milton,

---

[1] 'A stout cotton fabric, woven with raised stripes or fancy figures; usually employed undyed for beds and bedroom hangings, and sometimes for garments' (*OED*).

[2] Robert Merry (1755-98), the dilettante. Merry had returned from Italy to England in the spring of 1787, and he was engaged in a poetic correspondence with Hannah Cowley (1743-1809), who adopted the name of 'Anna Matilda' to Merry's 'Della Crusca'. The correspondence appeared in *The World* in 1787-8. C is probably referring to his 'Hop O' My Thumb' letter to Newton of 12 July 1781, and he is telling his cousin that 'Anna Matilda' and 'Della Crusca' are not unique as contemporary versifiers in the epistolary format.

things lost on earth are to be met with.[3] Said Limbo is, as you know in the Moon, whither I could not at present convey myself without a good deal of difficulty and inconvenience.

You desired that when Postlethwaite should be settled I would tell you where. I shall surprize you (so far as you concern yourself about him) first agreeably, and then otherwise. Mr. Thornton has given him a Living.[4] The income of it a 100£ per annum. The Church small and the congregation such of course. Circumstances very well adapted to his case, who could not many years survive the vociferation that he has been obliged to use at Olney. All this is well. But then the Living in question is in the Hundreds of Essex, where unless he drinks Brandy like small beer, which he will never do, he is sure to die of an Incurable Ague. The Natives of the country are seldom free from that distemper, and Foreigners, by necessity introduced among them, never. So farewell to poor P. — He is gone, he is fled — Gone to his death-bed — And we never shall see him again. So, I think Ophelia sings,[5] and so may we.

This morning, being the Morning of New year's day, I sent to the Hall a Copy of verses address'd to Mrs. Th——n, Entitled The Wish or the Poet's New year's gift.[6] We Dine there to-morrow when I suppose I shall hear News of them. Their kindness is so great, and they seize with such eagerness every opportunity of doing all they think will please us, that I held myself almost in duty bound to treat them with this stroke of my profession. By the way, Mrs. Throck——n has twice or thrice ask'd Mrs. Unwin if in any of your Letters to me, you have ever made mention of a Letter that you have had from her. I suppose therefore my Dear that either she wrote what you have never received, or you a Letter to Her which has miscarried.[7] Thou alone knowest.

[3] *Paradise Lost*, iii. 455-9, 495-6.

[4] Richard Postlethwaite, according to a list of clergy attending the visitation of the Archdeacon of Essex in 1793 (Essex Record Office D/AEM/ 2/3), was instituted Rector of Nevendon in Jan. 1788. He seems to have held this living until 1814. Postlethwaite succeeded the Revd John Powley (d. 21 July 1787).

[5] *Hamlet*, IV. v. 191-8.

[6] This poem was first published unsigned in *GM* lviii, pt. 2 (Dec. 1788), 1105.

[7] Lady Hesketh evidently answered this letter telling C that she had received a letter from Mrs Throckmorton which she had not and did not intend to answer (see C to Lady Hesketh, 9 Jan. 1788, pp. 84-5).

1 January 1788

The Small Pox has done, I believe, all that it has to do at Weston, and Hannah seems now secure. Jove has commanded sometimes Eurus and sometimes Zephyrus to puff forcibly at one end of the town so as to sweep the street even to the other, and the consequence is that we are all sweet again. None have died but our Samuel's eldest boy,[8] though old folks and even women with child have been inoculated. We talk of our freedom, and some of us are free enough, but not the poor. Dependent as they are upon Parish bounty they are sometimes obliged to submit to impositions which perhaps in France itself could hardly be parallell'd. Can man or woman be said to be free, who is commanded to take a distemper sometimes at least mortal, and in circumstances most likely to make it so? No circumstance whatever was permitted to exempt the Inhabitants of Weston. The old as well as the young, and the pregnant as well as they who had only themselves within them, have been all inoculated.[9] Were I ask'd Who is the most arbitrary Sov'reign on earth? I should answer — neither the King of France, nor the Grand Signor, but an Overseer of the Poor in England.[10]

I am as heretofore occupied continually with Homer. My present occupation is the revisal of all that I have done. Viz of the first 15 Books. I stand amazed at my own encreasing dexterity in the business, being verily persuaded that as far as I have gone I have improved the work to double its former value.

[8] The burial of Samuel Roberts's son is not recorded in *OPR*.

[9] 'Towards the end of the [eighteenth] century it became quite common to hold a general inoculation of the entire non-immune population of a village, when smallpox was raging uncontrolled. This was usually sponsored by the parish church and supported by its funds.' Genevieve Miller, *The Adoption of Inoculation for Smallpox in England and France* (Philadelphia, 1957), p. 155. A letter in *GM* lviii, pt. 1 (Apr. 1788), 283 from a clergyman in Bedfordshire mentions the fact that the poor in rural communities were frightened at the prospect of inoculation: 'I endeavoured to overcome the prejudice and fears of the people, and prevail on them to be inoculated. Accordingly, in the course of three days, a surgeon of the neighbourhood communicated the infection to 928 paupers, who were judged incapable of paying for themselves; and soon after to 287 more, mostly at their own charge.'

[10] According to the Act of Elizabeth of 1601, the 'poor were to be maintained and work was to be provided for the able-bodied. Overseers of the poor were to be nominated annually [in each parish, which was responsible for the maintenance of its own poor], and a poor-rate levied upon the inhabitants.' J. D. Marshall, *The Old Poor Law, 1795–1834* (1968), p. 10.

They have begun at Olney a Subscription for an Organ in the Church. Weary no doubt of the unceasing praises bestow'd upon a place well known by the name of Hogs-Norton,[11] they are determined to put in for a share of musical honour.

That you may begin the New year and End it in all health and happiness, and many more when the present shall have long become an old one, is the ardent wish of Mrs. Unwin, and of yours, my dearest Coz, most cordially

Wm Cowper.

WALTER BAGOT   Saturday, 5 January 1788

Address: The Revd. Walter Bagot.
Morgan Library

My dear friend —
I thank you for your information concerning the Author of the Translation of those lines. Had a man of less note and ability than Lord Bagot produced it, I should have been discouraged. As it is, I comfort myself with the thought that even He accounted it an atchievement worthy of his powers, and that even He found it difficult. Though I never had the honour to be known to his Lordship, I remember him well at Westminster, and the reputation in which he stood there. Since that time I have never seen him, except once, many years ago, in the House of Commons, when I heard him speak on the subject of a Drainage Bill, better than any member there.

My first 13 Books have been Criticized in London; have been by me accommodated to those Criticisms, returned to London in their improved state, and sent back to Weston with an Imprimantur. This would satisfy some poets, less anxious than myself about what they expose in public; but it has not satisfied me. I am now revising them again by the light of my own critical taper, and make more alterations than at the first. But are they improvements? you will ask — Is not the spirit of the work endanger'd by all this attention

[11] C is playfully recalling the proverbial expression, 'I think thou wast born at *Hoggs-Norton*, where piggs play upon the Organs.' See F. P. Wilson, *Oxford Dictionary of English Proverbs*, 3rd ed. (Oxford, 1970), p. 376.

to correctness? I think and hope that it is not. Being well aware of the possibility of such a catastrophe, I guard particularly against it. Where I find that a servile adherence to the Original would render the passage less animated than it should be, I still, as at the first, allow myself a liberty. On all other occasions I prune with an unsparing hand, determined that there shall not be found in the whole Translation an Idea that is not Homer's. My ambition is to produce the closest copy possible, and at the same time as harmonious as I know how to make it. This being my object, you will no longer think, if indeed you have thought it at all, that I am unnecessarily and overmuch industrious. The Original surpasses every thing, it is of an immense length, is composed in the best language ever used upon earth, and deserves, indeed demands, all the labour that any Translator, be he who he may, can possibly bestow on it. Of this I am sure, and your brother the good Bishop is of the same mind, that, at present, mere English readers know no more of Homer in reality than if he had never been translated. That consideration indeed it was which mainly induced me to the undertaking; and if after all, either through idleness or dotage upon what I have already done, I leave it chargeable with the same incorrectness as my predecessors, or indeed with any that I may be able to amend, I had better have amused myself otherwise. And you I know are of my opinion.

My friend! but very few days since I had almost lost Mrs. Unwin. She rises early and lights her own fire; had just performed for herself that service and placed the candle on the hearth, when it occurred to her that the flame of it might possibly catch her petticoat. She accordingly put it out. A very short time after, she perceived the room so full of smoke that it look'd like a thick mist, and brought the water into her eyes. Imagining that some of the billets might lie too forward, she busied herself in arranging them otherwise; but still the smoke continued and became more troublesome. When casting her eye downward she perceived her Bed-gown on fire, not flaming indeed (for then, being quite alone, she must have been burnt past remedy), but ready to break into a flame on the smallest encouragement. She had the presence of mind to gather it close at bottom and plunge it in the basin. The fire in fact had seized it before she extinguish'd the candle, and while she was thinking that such an accident might possibly happen, it had actually taken place. She came to me when it was all over and show'd me her gown with a hole in it much broader than my two palms, and her petticoat likewise burnt in two places. For the encrease of the wonder, they were both of Cotton.

I send you the Clerk's verses of which I told you.[1] They are very Clerk-like as you will perceive. But plain truths in plain words seemed to me to be the ne plus ultrá of Composition on such an occasion. I might have attempted something very fine, but then the persons principally concern'd, viz my Readers, would not have understood me. If it puts them in mind that they are mortal, its best end is answer'd.

My dear Walter, adieu!

Faithfully yours
Wm Cowper.

Weston Jan. 5. 1788.

Mrs. Unwin begs to be remember'd to you. She often gives me a jog and says, When do you write to your friend Mr. Bagot?

LADY HESKETH   Wednesday, 9 January 1788

Princeton *and Southey*, vi. 108–9[1]

The Lodge Decbr.[2] 9. 1788.
My dearest Coz, It has happen'd that this day I have had a double share of exercise, and am, in consequence, a little too weary and much too sleepy to be able to write you a very entertaining Epistle. In the Morning, the sky was of a true January cast, gloomy as black clouds could make it; the wind was cold in the extreme, and now and then it rained.

---

[1] With the letters from C to Bagot now in the Morgan Library are four Bills of Mortality which were sent by C to Bagot. They are those of 1787, 1788, 1789 (in part), and 1790. *Russell*, 244a, b, c, and d.

---

[1] Part of this letter is missing, and the last four paragraphs are supplied from *Southey*.

[2] Someone has altered C's incorrect dating of 'Decbr.' to 'Jany'.

In defiance of all these difficulties I took my walk; not so long a walk indeed as I gen'erally take, but long enough for the purposes that a walk is design'd to answer. At my return, as I was crossing the grove in front of the Hall, I saw all the family coming forth to do as I had done. I joined them and added their walk to my own. The effect is such as I have told you. But I will do my best.

We dined there yesterday. As soon as Tea-time arrived, I ascended to the Ladies in the Library. Mrs. Frog informed me that her Husband, at the end of the week, goes to London for a few days, leaving her at Weston. I replied — Then you must Dine with us in his absence. (For it has been some time a settled point, that when they are separated, she shall do so). She consented, but added, What is to become of George? He shall Dine with us too — But Mr. Frog who has never Dined with you yet, will be affronted — No. He shall not. For when he returns we will ask him too.

And thus it has come to pass, my Dear, that without any motion made toward it on our part, we find ourselves obliged to depart from our original resolve. I could not have answer'd otherwise than I did, without saying virtually — Pardon me Madam, we are always ready to partake of your good cheer, but as for our own, That we intend to keep to ourselves. We shall therefore now have occasion for the good things with which you have so plentifully furnished us, and now our Knives and forks of the newest construction will come into service. Not that we intend to perform any extraordinary feats in the feast-making way. Far from it. We shall measure ourselves and our own ability, not theirs, and shall consider what it becomes us to give and them to be content with at our table. After all, we mean not to establish a regular interchange of invitations, neither, I suppose, do they. Our present purpose is, to tell them that whenever it will be convenient to them to take a dinner at the Lodge, we shall always rejoice to see them; and having in that general way discharged the duty that Civility and reciprocal hospitality seem to demand from us, there to leave it.

I thought, my Dear, having a very sagacious nose in such matters, that your reason for not having answer'd Mrs. Frog was not perfectly and altogether sound. I determined therefore, unless she should repeat her question again (the question I mean, whether you had taken any notice in your Letters to me, of a Letter received from Her) to be, myself, silent upon the matter. Having always observed that an excuse which is not powerful enough to bear down all before it, does more harm than good; the peccadillo, whatever it be, which before was only suspected, is thenceforth ascertained and in effect acknowledged. It turned out as I expected. She said nothing, and I said nothing, and I dare say, nothing more will be said of it hereafter.

My verses, such as they were, had at least the effect that I wished. They pleased her, him, and theirs, as far as their fame has hitherto extended. Her brother Gifford in particular, who is excessively attached to his sister, and who arrived at the Hall last Sunday, though he has never given the smallest hint that he knows aught about them, has signified to me sufficiently by his manner, that he has both seen them and is obliged. These remarks of mine should rather have followed than have gone before them; but I am writing to you, and it is no matter; you will be sure to view them with a partial eye, and that may be highly necessary.

Many thanks, my dear, for your kind intentions in the oyster way. My stomach being in point of digestion better than it has been these fourteen years, I am now able to eat them raw. They are more agreeable to me raw than cooked, in whatever manner, and will now therefore be doubly welcome.

Depend upon it as a certainty, that I shall never be found a contributor to an organ at Olney: I never mention that vagary of theirs but with disapprobation. It is not much, indeed, that I say concerning any of their proceedings: they are generally so absurd, that it is impossible to give an opinion of them without offending all the parish.

My dearest coz! Heaven bless thee. I have more to say had I room, but nothing with which I can so well occupy the scanty remnant before me, as the often repeated assurance, and always true, that I am ever most affectionately thine,

Wm. Cowper.

LADY HESKETH   [Friday, 18 January] 1788

Address: Lady Hesketh / New Norfolk Street / Grosvenor Square / London.
Postmarks: JA/21/88 *and* OULNEY
Carl H. Pforzheimer Library

The Lodge Jan. 19. 1788.[1]

My dearest Coz — When I have Prose enough to fill my paper, which is always the case when I write to you, I cannot find in my heart to give a third part of it to Verse. Yet this I must do, or I must make my pacquets more costly than worshipful by doubling the Postage upon you which I should hold to be unreasonable. See then the true reason why I did not send you that same scribblement 'till you desired it. The thought which naturally presents itself to me on all such occasions is this. Is not your Cousin coming? Why are you impatient? Will it not be time enough to show her your fine things when she arrives?

Fine things indeed I have few. He who has Homer to Translate may well be contented to do little else. As when an Ass being harness'd with Ropes to a Sand-Cart, drags with hanging ears his heavy burthen, neither filling the long ecchoing streets with his harmonious Bray, nor throwing up his Heels behind frolicksome and airy, as Asses less engaged are wont to do — So I, satisfied to find myself indispensibly obliged to render into the best possible English Metre, eight and forty Greek Books of which the two finest Poems in the world consist, account it quite sufficient if I may at last atchieve that labour, and seldom allow myself those pretty little vagaries in which I should otherwise delight, and of which, if I should live long enough, I intend hereafter to enjoy my fill. This is the reason my Dear Cousin, if I may be permitted to call you so in the same breath with which I have utter'd this truly heroic comparison — this is the reason why I produce, at present, but few occasional poems, and the preceding reason is that which may account satisfactorily enough for my witholding the very few that I do produce. A thought sometimes strikes me before I rise; if it runs readily into verse and I can finish it before breakfast, it is

---

[1] 19 Jan. was a Saturday, although C states in his postscript that he is writing on a Friday.

well. Otherwise it dies and is forgotten; for all the subsequent hours are devoted to Homer.

Mr. Throckmorton told me that he would call on you if it were possible, but his Business (whatever it may have been, for I know not) lying among the Lawyers, and consequently very remote from you, seemed to make it doubtful whether he would have an opportunity or not. I therefore did not mention to you his intention; but it gave me great pleasure to find that he had executed it. If it were not more than almost a Bull,[2] I would say that we have lived with him ever since he has been gone. Twice we have Dined at his house, once we drank Tea there, and I have made Morning calls and have walked with them into the bargain. I forgot my Coz to tell you in my last, what since you have seen him it will be of very little use to mention, that his Brother Charles is lately married,[3] and that he and his Bride are gone with the youngest Brother Francis to Lisbon. Francis I have never seen, and understanding that he is an amiable young man and probably short-lived, am glad that I never have.[4]

The day before yesterday I saw for the first time Bunbury's new Print, the Propagation of a Lie.[5] Mr. Throck: sent it for the Amusement of the party. Bunbury sells Humour by the yard, and is, I suppose the first Vender of it who ever did so. He cannot therefore be said to have Humour without measure (pardon a Pun my Dear, from a man who has not made one before these 40 years) though he may certainly be said to be immeasurably droll. The Original thought is good, and the exemplification of it in those very expressive figures, admirable. A Poem on the same subject, displaying all that is display'd in those attitudes and in those features (for faces they can hardly be called) would be most excellent. The affinity of the two Arts, viz of Verse and Painting, has been often observed;

[2] 'A self-contradictory proposition' (*OED*).

[3] Charles Throckmorton, later 7th Baronet (1757–1840), married on 28 Dec. 1787 Mary Margaretta, daughter of Edmund Plowden.

[4] Journal of Sir John Throckmorton, Warwickshire Record Office, 16 Apr. 1788: 'at night I received the news of my Br. Francis's death at Lisbon'.

[5] Henry William Bunbury (1750–1811) was educated at Westminster School (1764–5) and St. Catharine's Hall, Cambridge (admitted 1768). Even while a student, Bunbury acquired a considerable reputation as a caricaturist, and his reputation was at its height at this time. 'The Propagation of a Lie', issued on 29 Dec. 1787, was published and engraved by William Dickinson (1746–1823).

possibly the happiest illustration of it would be found, if some Poet would ally himself to some such Draftsman as Bunbury, and undertake to write every thing that He should draw. Then let a Musician be admitted of the party. He should Compose said Poem adapting Notes to it exactly accommodated to the theme; so should the Sister Arts be proved to be indeed Sisters, and the World would die of Laughing.

It is now time, my Dear, that I should thank you, as I do most heartily, for a Barrel of excellent Oysters and for Brawn equally good. I shall not presently be reduced again to the necessity of sucking Eggs for supper.

Casting my eye over the Bill of Items that you lately sent relating to the expenditure of certain moneys arising from the sale of Plate, I observe that Muslin for me stands there with no charge opposed to it. This imports an obligation on my part to thank you my Cousin, on that account also. But I will do more than thank you. I will be grateful by God's help, and remember with affection both that and all your other kindnesses to my dying day.

Did Mr. Throck. tell you a diverting story of the arrival of a New Parson in this Village and of an Adventure that befell Me in consequence? If not, I will give it you in my next. At present I will add no more, because I cannot, than that I am with Mrs Unwin's best Love, most truely yours,

My dearest Cousin — Wm Cowper.

It has happen'd twice that I have written, as I do now, on a Friday and have dated my Letter accordingly, though you could not possibly receive it 'till Monday. This has occasion'd an appearance of unnecessary delay, though in reality there has been none. — My best respects to Mrs. Hill when you see her next.

JOHN NEWTON   Monday, 21 January 1788

Princeton

Weston Underwood. Jan 21. 1788

My dear friend —
Your last Letter informed us that you were likely to be

much occupied for some time in writing on a subject that must be interesting to a person of your feelings, the Slave trade.[1] I was unwilling to interrupt your progress in so good a work, and have therefore injoined myself a longer silence than I should otherwise have thought excuseable. Though to say the truth, did not our once intimate fellowship in the things of God, recur to my remembrance, and present me with something like a warrant for doing it, I should hardly prevail with myself to write at all. Letters such as mine to a person of a character such as yours, are like snow in harvest, and you well say that if I will send you a Letter that you can answer, I shall make your part of the business easier than it is. This I would gladly do, but though I abhor a Vacuum as much as Nature herself is said to do, yet a Vacuum I am bound to feel of all Such matter as may merit your perusal.

I expected that before this time I should have had the pleasure of seeing your friend Mr. Bean, but his stay in this country was so short that it was hardly possible he should find an opportunity to call. I have not only heard a high character of that Gentleman from yourself, whose opinion of Men as well as of other matters, weighs more with me than any body's, but from two or three different persons likewise not ill qualified to judge. From all that I have heard both from you and them, I have every reason to expect that I shall find him both an agreeable and useful neighbor; and if he can be content with me (for that seems doubtful, Poet as I am, and now alas! nothing more) it seems certain that I shall be highly satisfied with Him.

Here is much shifting and changing of Ministers; two are passing away and two are stepping into their places. Mr. Bull[2] I suppose, whom I know not, is almost upon the wing, and Mr. Postlethwait[3] with whom I have not been very much acquainted, is either going or gone. A Mr. Canniford[4] is come to occupy, for the present at least, the place of the former,

---

[1] Newton's *Thoughts upon the African Slave Trade* appeared at about this time, and C thanks Newton for a copy of the book in his letter to him of 19 Feb. 1788.

[2] Revd Thomas Bull, the lame curate of Weston Underwood.

[3] See n.9, C to Lady Hesketh, 24 Apr. 1786.

[4] Possibly the Revd Laurence Canniford who was preferred to the living of St. Helen's V. Abingdon in 1811. See *GM* lxxxi, pt. 2 (Aug. 1811), 187.

and if he can possess himself of the two Curacies of Ravenston and Weston, will I imagine take up his abode here. He lives now, with Mr. Socket,[5] who is lately become an Inhabitant of our village, and having, as I understand, no engagements elsewhere, will doubtless be happy to obtain a lasting one in this Country. What acceptance he finds among the people of Ravenston, I have not heard, but at Olney, where he has preached once, he was hailed as the Sun by the Greenlanders after half a year of Lamp-light. The Connoisseurs in preaching, or rather perhaps in Preachers, affirm that he resembles Mr. Whitefield[6] more than any man ever did *save and except Himself the said Mr. Whitefield.* Thus they speak of him at present, but the same persons had nearly the same opinion of Mr. Page[7] of wife-beating memory, for which reason I find myself rather slow to suppose them infallible.

Providence interposed to preserve me from the heaviest affliction that I can now suffer, or I had lately lost Mrs. Unwin, and in a way the most shocking imaginable. Having kindled her fire in the room where she dresses (an office that she always performs for herself) she placed the candle on the hearth, and kneeling addressed herself to her devotions. A thought struck her while thus occupied that the candle being short, might possibly catch her cloaths. She pinched it out with the tongs and set it on the table. In few minutes the chamber was so filled with smoke that her eyes water'd and it was hardly possible to see across it. Supposing that it proceeded from the chimney, she push'd the billets backward, and while she did so, casting her eye downward, perceived that her Bed gown was on fire. In fact, before she extinguished the candle, the mischief that she apprehended, was begun, and when she related the matter to me, she show'd me her Bed-gown with a hole burnt in it as large as this sheet, and her petticoat burnt also in two places. It is not possible perhaps that so tragical a death should overtake a person actually engaged in prayer, for her escape seems almost a Miracle. Her presence of mind, by which she was enabled, without calling for help or waiting

---

[5] Thomas Socket had worked as a stationer and bookseller at one time and he moved to London in 1792 to resume this profession.

[6] George Whitefield (1714–70).

[7] Benjamin Page. See C to Newton, *post* 15 Jan. 1785.

for it, to gather up her cloaths and plunge them burning as they were in water, seems as wonderful a part of the occurrence as any. The very report of fire, though distant, has render'd hundreds torpid and incapable of self-succour. How much more was such a disability to be expected, when the fire had not seized a neighbor's house or begun its devastations on our own, but was actually consuming the apparel that she wore and seemed in possession of her person?

It draws toward Supper-time, I therefore heartily wish you a good night, and with our best affections to yourself, Mrs. Newton and Miss Catlett, I remain, my dear friend,

truly and warmly Yours
Wm Cowper.

JOSEPH HILL   Sunday, 27 January 1788

Cowper Johnson

Weston Underwood Jan. 27. 1788
My dear friend,

In hope that my finances are able to bear it, and necessity enforcing the measure, I shall take the liberty to draw on you to-morrow for Forty pounds, the draft payable at sight to John Higgins Esqr.[1] or order.

Lady Hesketh in her last Letter mention'd your having lately had a fit of the Gout. I will not congratulate *you* on an acquisition not very desireable perhaps in any case to Him who makes it, but your friends, and among them myself in particular, I *will* congratulate, because it seems to promise us that we shall keep you long. Wishing you a short and slight visit from this rough intruder as often as he shall return, and at the same time all possible benefit from his attendance, I remain with my best respects to Mrs. Hill — Yours, my dear friend, affectionately

Wm Cowper.

P.S. Many thanks for a barrel of fine Oysters —

[1] See n.1, C to Newton, 16 Dec. 1786.

LADY HESKETH   Wednesday, 30 January 1788

Address: Lady Hesketh / New Norfolk Street / Grosvenor Square / London.
Postmarks: JA/31/88 *and* NEWPORT/PAGNEL
Carl H. Pforzheimer Library

My dearest Cousin. It is now a fortnight since I heard from you, that is to say, a week longer than you have accustom'd me to wait for a letter. I do not forget that you have recommended it to me on occasions somewhat similar to banish all anxiety, and to ascribe your silence only to the interruptions of company. Good advice, my Dear, but not easily taken by a man circumstanced as I am. I have learn'd in the school of adversity, a school from which I have no expectations that I shall ever be dismiss'd, to apprehend the worst, and have ever found it the only course in which I can indulge myself without the least danger of incurring a disappointment. This kind of experience continued through many years has given me such an habitual biass to the gloomy side of every thing, that I never have a moment's ease on any subject to which I am not indifferent. How then can I be easy when I am left afloat upon a sea of endless conjectures of which you furnish the occasion. Write, I beseech you, and do not forget that I am now a batter'd actor upon this turbulent stage, that what little vigour of mind I ever had, of the self-supporting kind I mean, has long since been broken, and that though I can bear nothing well, yet anything better than a state of ignorance concerning your welfare. I have spent hours in the night, leaning upon my elbow and wondering what your silence means. I entreat you once more to put an end to these speculations which cost me more animal spirits than I can spare; if you cannot, without great trouble to yourself, which in your situation may very possibly be the case, contrive opportunities of writing so frequently as usual, only say it and I am content. I will wait, if you desire it, as long for every letter, but then let them arrive, the period once fixt, exactly at the time, for my patience will not hold out an hour beyond it.

Mrs. Unwin desires me to thank you for the Muslin brought by the Throck——ns which is exactly what she wanted. There is nothing more that I can add at present, except that with her affectionate respects I am my Dearest Cousin

Sincerely Yours
Wm Cowper.

Jan. 30. 1788.

LADY HESKETH   Friday, 1 February 1788

Address: Lady Hesketh / New Norfolk Street / Grosvenor Square / London.
Postmarks: NEWPORT/PAGNEL *and* [illegible]
Panshanger Collection

The Lodge
Feb. 1. 1788

Pardon me, my dearest Coz, the mournful Ditty that I sent you last.[1] There are times when I see every thing through a medium that distresses me to an insupportable degree, and that letter was written in one of them. A fog that had for three days obliterated all the beauties of Weston, and a North East wind might possibly contribute not a little to the melancholy that indited it. But my mind is now easy; your letter has made it so, and I feel myself as blithe as a bird in comparison. I love you my Cousin, and cannot suspect, either with or without cause, the least evil in which you may be concern'd, without being greatly troubled. Oh trouble! the portion of all mortals, but mine in particular, would I had never known thee, or could bid thee farewell for ever, for I meet thee at every turn, my pillows are stuff'd with thee, my very roses smell of thee, and even my Cousin who would cure me of all trouble if she could, is sometimes innocently the cause of trouble to me. I now see the unreasonableness of my late trouble, and would, if I could trust myself so far, promise never again to trouble either myself or you in the same manner, unless warranted by some more substantial ground of apprehension.

What I said concerning Homer my Dear, was spoken or rather written merely under the influence of a certain Jocularity that I felt at the moment. I am in reality so far from thinking myself an Ass and my translation a Sandcart,

---

[1] C is referring to his letter to Lady Hesketh of 30 Jan. 1788.

93

that I rather seem, in my own account of the matter, one of those flaming steeds harness'd to the chariot of Apollo of which we read in the works of the antients. I have lately, I know not how, acquired a certain superiority to myself in this business, and in this last revisal have elevated the expression to a degree far surpassing its former boast. A few Evenings since, I had an opportunity to try how far I might venture to expect such success of my labours as can alone repay them, by reading the first book of my Iliad to a friend of ours. He dined with you once at Olney. His name is Greatheed.[2] A man of Letters and of Taste. He dined with us, and the Evening proving dark and dirty we persuaded him to take a bed: Pour passer le tems, I entertained him as I tell you. He heard me with great attention, and with evident symptoms of the highest satisfaction, which when I had finished the exhibition he put out of all doubt by expressions which I cannot repeat. Only this he said to Mrs. Unwin while I was in another room, that he had never enter'd into the spirit of Homer before nor had any thing like a due conception of his manner. This I have said knowing that it [will][3] please you, and will now say no more, except that [since yo]u set so little value on your sixpences, have [at the]m. I shall inclose what I wrote for the Clerk of All Saints Northampton, to convince you that I am not so squeamish on such occasions as to wait for ask[ing.]

The brawn has been admired by all that have partaken of it as the best they ever saw or tasted. Nor has Mrs. Unwin's gown, your present, been less admired, our neighbors with the long name having repeatedly paid that just tribute to its merits and Mr. T. in particular.

Adieu my Dear! Will you never speak of coming to Weston more?

Yours most affectionately
Wm C.

---

[2] See n.1, C to Newton, 4 June 1785.
[3] MS torn at the seal.

LADY HESKETH   Thursday, 7 February 1788

Southey, vi. 118–21

The Lodge, Feb. 7, 1788.

My dearest Cousin,

Thanks beforehand for the books which you give me to expect. They will all be welcome. Of the two editions of Shakespeare[1] I prefer that which is printed in the largest type, independent of all other considerations. Dox Quixote by any hand must needs be welcome, and by Smollett's[2] especially, because I have never seen it. He had a drollery of his own, which for aught I know, may suit an English taste as well as that of Cervantes, perhaps better, because to us somewhat more intelligible.

It is pretty well known, (the clerk took care it should be so,) both at Northampton and in this country, who wrote the Mortuary Verses. All that I know of their success is, that he sent a bundle of them to Maurice Smith at Olney, who sold them for threepence a piece, — a high price for a *Memento Mori*, a commodity not generally in great request. The other small poem, addressed to Mrs. Throck, has given, as I understand, great satisfaction at Bucklands. The old baronet and his lady, having heard that such a piece existed, (Mrs. Bromley

---

[1] The set of Shakespeare which went to C was a 1747 set of Sir Thomas Hanmer's edition of *Works, with a Glossary, carefully printed from the Oxford Edition* (*Keynes*, 64). This set was offered for sale in their Catalogue 30 (Feb. 1935) by Marks & Co., p. 169, but its present whereabouts is unknown. 'An interesting association item, having belonged to William Cowper ... containing some corrections or explanations of obsolete words, in his handwriting ... In addition to the corrections, each volume, with the exception of the last, has the signature "Wm. Cowper 1797" on title; his bookplate inside front covers, and crest in gilt on the backs of the binding. This set has an interesting pedigree: It was originally owned by Cowper's uncle, Ashley Cowper (autograph on title of Vol. I), then by his cousin [Lady] Harriet Hesketh, with her autograph inside each cover. From William Cowper, the Poet, the set appears to have passed to John Hardy, who notes the loss of the last volume in 1802, and finally to Thomas Hill Mortimer in 1833. The latter has written on verso of title to Vol. I: "Note, each volume contains some corrections or explanations of obsolete words, in Cowper's handwriting."' Kenneth Povey, who saw the set at Marks & Co., evidently felt that the manuscript notes were in Ashley Cowper's hand.

[2] C owned a four-volume set of the fifth edition of Smollett's translation of *Don Quixote* (London: W. Strahan, 1782). *Keynes*, 64. C's *Quixote* is now owned by the Misses Cowper Johnson.

Chester,[3] I suppose, must have been their informant,) wrote to desire a copy. A copy was sent, and they answered it with warm encomiums.

Mr. Bull, the lame curate, having been lately preferred to a living, another was of course wanted to supply his place. By the recommendation of Mr. Romaine,[4] a Mr. C * * *[5] came down. He lodges at Mr. Socket's in this village, and Mr. Socket lives in the small house to which you had once conceived a liking. Our lacquey is also clerk of the parish. C * * * a day or two after his arrival had a corpse to bury at Weston. Having occasion to consult with the clerk concerning this matter, he sought him in our kitchen. Samuel entered the study to inform us that there was a clergyman without: he was accordingly invited in, and in he came. We had but lately dined; the wine was on the table, and he drank three glasses while the corpse in question was getting ready for its last journey. The moment he entered the room, I felt myself incurably prejudiced against him: his features, his figure, his address, and all that he uttered, confirmed that prejudice, and I determined, having once seen him, to see him no more. Two days after he overtook me in the village. 'Your humble servant, Mr. Cowper! a fine morning, sir, for a walk. I had liked to have called on you yesterday morning to tell you that I had become your near neighbour. I live at Mr. Socket's.' I answered without looking at him, as drily as possible, — 'Are you come to stay any time in the country?' — He believed he was. — 'Which way,' I replied, 'are you going? to Olney?' — 'Yes.' — 'I am going to Mr. Throckmorton's garden, and I wish you a good day, sir.' — I was in fact going to Olney myself, but this rencontre gave me such a violent twist another way that I found it impossible to recover that direction, and accordingly there we parted. All this I related at the Hall the next time we dined there, describing also my appre-

---

[3] Elizabeth Lucy Chester (d. 9 Jan. 1799), the daughter of Richard Howe Chester of Haseley, married on 20 Apr. 1765 William Bromley (1738–80), who served as MP for Gloucestershire from 6 May 1776 until 12 Dec. 1780. At the time of his marriage, Bromley took the additional name of Chester, and thus C refers to his widow as Mrs Bromley Chester.

[4] The Revd William Romaine (1714–95), the Evangelical divine, who held the living of St. Anne's, Blackfriars, from 1766 until his death.

[5] Canniford. See n.4, C to Newton, 21 Jan. 1788.

hensions and distress lest, whether I would or not, I should be obliged to have intercourse with a man to me so perfectly disagreeable. A good deal of laugh and merriment ensued, and there for that time it ended. The following Sunday, in the evening, I received a note to this purport: 'Mr. C***'s compliments,' &c. Understanding that my friends at the Hall were to dine with me the next day, he took the liberty to invite himself to eat a bit of mutton with me, being sure that I should be happy to introduce him. Having read the note, I threw it to Mrs. Unwin. 'There,' said I, 'take that and read it; then tell me if it be not an effort of impudence the most extraordinary you ever heard of.' I expected some such push from the man; I knew he was equal to it. She read it, and we were both of a mind. I sat down to my desk, and with a good deal of emotion gave it just such an answer as it would have deserved had it been genuine. But having heard by accident in the morning that he spells his name with a C, and observing in the note that it was spelt with a K, a suspicion struck me that it was a fiction. I looked at it more attentively and perceived that it was directed by Mrs. Throck. The inside I found afterwards was written by her brother George. This served us with another laugh on the subject, and I have hardly seen, and never spoken to, Mr. C * * * since. So, my dear, *that's the little story I promised you.*

Mr. Bull called here this morning: from him I learn what follows concerning P * * *.[6] He waited on the Bishop of London, like a blundering ignoramus as he is, without his canonicals. The Bishop was highly displeased, as he had cause to be; and having pretty significantly given him to know it, addressed himself to his chaplain with tokens of equal displeasure, enjoining him never more to admit a clergyman to him in such attire. To pay this visit he made a journey from Clapham to town on horseback. His horse he left at an inn on the Lambeth side of Westminster Bridge. Thence he proceeded to the Bishop's, and from the Bishop's to Mr. Scott. Having finished this last visit he begged Mr. Scott's company to the inn where he had left his horse, which he said was at the foot of *London* Bridge. Thither they went,

---

[6] Postlethwaite. See n.4, C to Lady Hesketh, 1 Jan. 1788.

but neither the inn nor the horse were there. Then, says P * * *, it must be at Blackfriars' Bridge that I left it. Thither also they went, but to as little purpose. Luckily for him there was but one more bridge, and there they found it. To make the poor youth amends for all these misadventures, it so happened that the incumbent, his predecessor, died before the crops of last year were reaped. The whole profits of that year, by consequence, go into P.'s pocket, which was never so stuffed before.

Good night, my dearest coz. Mrs. Unwin's love attends you.

> Affectionately yours,
> Wm. Cowper.

MRS KING   Tuesday, 12 February 1788

Address: Mrs. King / Perton Hall near / Kimbolton / Huntingdonshire
Postmark: FE/13/88
Princeton

> Weston Lodge, near Olney, Bucks
> Feb. 12. 1788

Dear Madam,

A Letter from a lady who was once intimate with my Brother, could not fail of being most acceptable to me. I lost him just in the moment when those Truths which have recommended my volumes to your approbation, were become his daily sustenance, as they had long been mine. But the Will of God was done. I have sometimes thought that had his life been spared, being made brothers by a stricter tie than ever, in the bands of the same Faith, Hope and Love, we should have been happier in each other than it was in the power of mere natural affection to make us. But it was his Blessing to be taken from a world in which he had no longer any wish to continue, and it will be mine, if while I dwell in it, my time may not be altogether wasted. In order to effect that good end, I wrote what I am happy to find it has given you pleasure to read. But for that pleasure, Madam, you are indebted neither to me nor to my Muse, but (as you are well aware) to Him who alone can make divine Truths palatable in whatever vehicle convey'd. It is an establish'd philosophical axiom, that Nothing can communicate what it has not in itself; but in the effects of Christian Communion a very strong exception is found to this general rule, however self-evident it may seem. A man, himself destitute of all spiritual consolation, may by occasion, impart it to others. Thus I, it seems, who wrote those very poems to amuse a mind oppressed with melancholy, and who have myself derived from them no other benefit (for mere success in Authorship will do me no good) have nevertheless by so doing, comforted others, at the same time that they administer to me no consolation. But I will proceed no farther in this strain, lest my prose should damp a pleasure that my verse has happily excited. On the contrary I will endeavour to rejoice in your joy, and especially because I have been myself the instrument of conveying it.

Since the receipt of your obliging letter, I have naturally had recourse to my recollection to try if it would furnish me with the name that I find at the bottom of it. At the same time I am aware that there is nothing more probable than that my brother might be honour'd with your friendship without mentioning it to me, for except a very short period before his death, we lived necessarily at a considerable distance from each other. Ascribe it Madam not to an impertinent Curiosity, but to a desire of better acquaintance with you, if I take the liberty to ask (since Ladys' Names at least are changeable) whether yours was at that time the same as now.

Sincerely wishing you all happiness, and especially that which I am sure you covet most, the happiness which is from above, I remain — Dear Madam — early as it may seem to say it —

Affectionately Yours
Wm Cowper.

SAMUEL ROSE   Thursday, 14 February 1788

Address: Samuel Rose Esqr. / No. 23 Percy Street / Rathbone Place / London.
Postmarks: FE/[illegible]/88 *and* OULNEY
Morgan Library

Weston Lodge Feb. 14. 1788

My dear Sir,

Though it be long since I received your last, I have not yet forgotten the impressions it made upon me, nor how sensibly I felt myself obliged by your unreserved and friendly communications. I will not apologize for my silence in the Interim, because apprized as you are of my present occupation, the excuse that I might alledge will present itself to you of course, and to dilate upon it would be therefore waste of paper.

You are in possession of the best security imaginable for the due improvement of your time, which is a just sense of its value. Had I been, when at your age, as much affected by that important consideration as I am at present, I should not have devoted, as I did, all the earlier part of my life to amusement only. I am now in the predicament into which the thoughtlessness of youth betrays nine tenths of Mankind, who never discover that the health and good spirits which generally accompany it, are in reality blessings only according to the use we make of them, 'till advanced years begin to threaten them with the loss of both. How much wiser would thousands have been than now they ever will be, had a puney constitution or some occasional infirmity constrained them to devote those hours to study and reflection, which for want of some such check, they have given entirely to dissipation! I therefore account you happy, who young as you are, need not to be informed that you cannot always be so, and who already know that the materials upon which age can alone build its comfort, should be brought together at an earlier period. You have indeed, losing a father,[1] lost a friend, but you have not lost his instructions, his example was not buried with him, but happily for you (happily because you are

---

[1] William Rose (1719–86), educator and translator. He had been educated at Marischal College, Aberdeen, and he had conducted a school at Kew and, from 1758 until his death, he ran a highly respectable school at Chiswick. He published his translations from Sallust in 1757.

desirous to avail yourself of it) still lives in your remembrance and is cherish'd in your best affections.

Your last was dated from the house of a Gentleman who was, I believe, my schoolfellow, for the Mr. Capper[2] who lived at Watford[3] while I had any connexion with Hartsfordshire, must have been the father of the present, and according to his age and the state of his health when I saw him last, has probably been long dead. I was never acquainted with the family farther than by report which always spoke honourably of them, though in all my journeys to and from my Father's I must have passed the door. The circumstance however reminds me of the beautiful reflection of Glaucus in the 6th Iliad; beautiful as well for the affecting nature of the observation, as for the justness of the comparison and the incomparable simplicity of the expression. I feel that I shall not be satisfied without transcribing it, and yet perhaps *my* Greek may be difficult to decypher.

Ὅιη περ φυλλων γενεη, τοιηδε και ανδρων.
φυλλα τα μεν τ᾽ανεμος χαμαδις χεει, αλλα δε θ᾽ὑλη
τελεθωσα φυει, εαρος δ᾽επιγιγνεται ὥρῃ·
Ὥς ανδρων γενεη, ἡ μεν φυει, ἡδ᾽απολῆγει.[4]

Excuse this piece of pedantry in a man whose Homer is always before him. What would I give that he were living now, and within my reach! I of all men living have the best excuse for indulging such a wish unreasonable as it may seem, for I have no doubt that the fire of his eye and the smile upon his lips would put me now and then in possession of his full meaning more effectually than any Commentator. — I return

[2] C's schoolmate was the Revd Francis Capper (1735–1818), the second son of Francis Capper of Bushey near Watford in Hertfordshire. He was admitted to Westminster in 1742 and subsequently elected to Christ Church, Oxford (BA, 1757; MA, 1760) and admitted to Lincoln's Inn in 1746/7. He served as Rector of Monk Soham and East Soham in Suffolk from 1759. From the context of C's letter to Lady Hesketh of 12 Mar., it would seem that Rose's friend was Robert Capper, the heir of Richard Capper, Francis's older brother. Rose's friend was thus the nephew and not the son of Francis Capper.

[3] Watford is approximately 12 miles south-east of Berkhamsted.

[4] In his translation of vi. 175–8, C renders the lines: 'For, as the leaves, such is the race of man. / The wind shakes down the leaves, the budding grove / Soon teems with others, and in spring they grow. / So pass mankind.'

you many thanks for the Elegies which you sent me,[5] both which, I think deserving of much commendation. I should requite you but ill by sending you my mortuary verses, neither at present can I prevail myself to do it, having no frank and being conscious that they are not worth carriage without one. I have one copy left, and that Copy I will keep for you.

A thousand thanks, my dear Sir, for your kind offer of the books you mention. But I have already found myself obliged to decline similar offers, lest by connecting the study of writers *upon* Homer and *about* him with the study of *Homer himself*, I should not live long enough to reach the end of my undertaking. I am not vain enough to think that they could not assist me, but I am too old to have so much time to spare as they would cost me.

Mrs. Unwin who always speaks of you with much respect, joins in every wish for your happiness with, my Dear Sir,

Your affectionate & obliged
Wm Cowper.

LADY HESKETH   Saturday, 16 February 1788

Address: Lady Hesketh / New Norfolk Street / Grosvenor Square / London.
Postmarks: FE/18/88 *and* OULNEY
Panshanger Collection

The Lodge
Feb. 16. 1788

I have now three Letters of yours, my dearest Cousin, before me, all written in the space of a Week, and must be indeed insensible of kindness did I not feel yours upon this occasion. I cannot describe to you, neither could you comprehend it if I should, the manner in which my mind is sometimes impressed with melancholy on particular subjects. Your late silence was such a subject. I heard, saw and felt a thousand terrible things which had no real existence, and was haunted by them night and day 'till they at last extorted from me the doleful Epistle which I have since wish'd had been burn'd before I

---

[5] We cannot now identify these elegies; C is not referring to the criticism on Homer mentioned in his letter of 29 Mar. 1788.

sent it. But the cloud has pass'd, and as far as you are concern'd, my heart is once more at rest.

Before you gave me the hint, I had once or twice as I lay on my bed watching for the break of day, ruminated on the subject which in your last but one, you recommend to me. Slavery, or a release from slavery such as the poor Negroes have endured, or perhaps both those topics together, appeared to me a theme so important at the present juncture, and at the same time so susceptible of poetical management, that I more than once perceived myself ready to start in that career, could I have allowed myself to desert Homer for so long a time as it would have cost me to do them justice. While I was pondering these things, the public prints informed me that Miss Moore was on the point of publication, having actually finished what I had not yet begun.[1] The sight of her advertisement convinced me that my best course would be that to which I felt myself most inclined, to persevere without turning aside to attend to any other call however alluring, in the business that I have in hand. It occurred to me likewise that I have already borne my testimony in favour of our Black Brethren,[2] and that I was one of the earliest, if not the first of those who have in the present day, expressed their detestation of the diabolical traffic in question. On all these accounts I judged it best to be silent, and especially because I cannot doubt that some effectual measures will now be taken to alleviate the miseries of their condition, the whole nation being in possession of the case, and it being impossible also to alledge an argument in behalf of Man-merchandize that can deserve a hearing. I shall be glad to see Hannah Moore's poem; she is a favorite writer with me, and has more nerve and energy both in her thoughts and language than half

[1] Hannah More (1745-1833) published her long poem, *Slavery*, and her prose treatise, *Thoughts on the Importance of the Manners of the Great to General Society*, in 1788. In C's library there was a copy of *Slavery* (1788) bound with C's *Anti-Thelyphthora* (*Keynes*, 62). As his letter to Lady Hesketh of 12 Mar. makes clear, C was initially under the assumption that *Thoughts* had been written by Wilberforce; his letter to Lady Hesketh of 31 Mar. reveals that she had informed C that Hannah More was the author.

[2] C is referring to lines 137-243 from 'Charity', and to sentiments such as these (lines 137-40): 'But, ah! what wish can prosper, or what pray'r, / For merchants, rich in cargoes of despair, / Who drive a loathsome traffic, gage, and span, / And buy, the muscles and the bones of man?'

the He rhimers in the kingdom. The Thoughts on the manners of the great will likewise be most acceptable. I want to learn as much of the world as I can, but to acquire that learning at a distance, and a book with such a title promises fair to serve that purpose effectually. For poor Hannah's sake I thank you, as does Mrs. Unwin, heartily, for your kind intentions to send her Mrs. Trimmer's publication.[3] She is at present a very good girl, affectionate and studious to please, and will I verily believe turn that Lady's instructions to as good account as any of her little disciples.

I recommend it to you, my Dear, by all means to embrace the fair occasion, and to put yourself in the way of being squeezed and incommoded a few hours, for the sake of hearing and seeing what you will never have opportunity to see and hear hereafter, the trial of a man who has been greater and more feared than the Mogul himself, and of his Myrmidon Sir Elijah.[4] Whatever we are at home, we have certainly been Tyrants in the East; and if these men have, as they are charged, riotted in the miseries of the innocent, and dealt death to the guiltless with an unsparing hand, may they receive a retribution that shall make all future Governors and Judges of ours in those distant regions tremble. While I speak thus, I equally wish them acquitted. They were both my Schoolfellows and for Hastings I had a particular value. As to our friends at the Hall, whether on this subject or any other, I never find them violent. If they dispute, as they do sometimes, it is with each other, never with me. To me and to mine they are always equally obliging, kind and friendly. Poor Mrs. Throg is doing Lent pennance at this time, a

[3] Mrs Sarah Trimmer (1741-1810), a popular writer whose work had been commended by Samuel Johnson, published *The Oeconomy of Charity* in 1787, and this edition of the work was in C's library (*Keynes*, 65). The book for Hannah must have been *Fabulous Histories: Designed for the Instruction of Children, Respecting their Treatment of Animals* (1786).

[4] Warren Hastings (1732–1818) attended Westminster from 1743 to 1749, and Sir Elijah Impey (1732-1809) had a longer stay (1740–51) at the school. Hastings had been Governer-General of Bengal for 14 years when the House of Commons voted on 3 Apr. 1787 his impeachment on the grounds of corruption and cruelty in his administration of Indian affairs. Hastings's trial began on 13 Feb. 1788 and ended on 23 Apr. 1795 (the trial itself occupied 145 days) with his acquittal. Impey, who was Chief Justice of the Supreme Court of Bengal from 1774 to 1787, defended himself successfully at the bar of the House of Commons in 1788 of six charges, including the exercise of extended judicial powers contrary to his patent.

discipline which I assure you does not at all agree with her. A Diet differing so much from that which she allows herself in common, affects both her looks and her spirits. The Gentlemen, the Padre excepted, are less scrupulous than she, and consequently fare better. Mr. Throg goes to town to morrow, but designing to stay there only till Thursday next, he will hardly have time to call upon you.

I have lately had a Letter from a Lady unknown to me, tho' she tells me she was intimate with my brother. Her name is Margaret King, and she lives at Perton Hall near Kimbolton. I answer'd it 2 or 3 days ago, and shall probably hear from her again. The consequence will be that I shall have a new Correspondent; an acquisition that I can hardly afford to make.

The terrible Curate of whom I told you, is become to me less terrible, having left Weston and taken up his abode at Ravenstone. I have had the good hap to see him but once, and may now hope that I shall see him no more.

Farewell, my dearest Cousin, with Mrs. Unwin's affectionate respects, I conclude myself

Ever Yours
Wm Cowper.

All Advertisements that you may see in the name of Andrew Fridze[5] are my compositions.

The Letter that you mention of which Padre Postlethwaite was so much the subject, came safe to hand.

JOHN NEWTON   Tuesday, 19 February 1788

Princeton

Weston Feb. 19. 1788.

My dear friend —

I have much to thank you for. In the first place for your Sermon;[1] in which you have addressed your brethren with all

---

[5] *Russell* does not provide an account of C's use of this pseudonym, and we have not been able to locate the advertisements in question.

[1] *The Best Wisdom. A Sermon Preached in the Parish Church of St. Mary Woolnoth, on Wednesday, the 21st of November, 1787, the Day of the Annual Meeting of the Society for Promoting Religious Knowledge among the Poor* (1788).

the delicacy and fidelity that were due both to their character and your own. If they were not impressed by it, it must be because like the Rabbies of old, they are less impressible than others. Such I suppose they are, and will be, so long as Doctorship and Clerical honours of every degree shall have a tendency to make unenlighten'd simpletons imagine themselves the only interpreters of God. In the next place, for your thoughts on the Slave Trade; in which there is such evidence of conscientious candour and moderation as will make it, I doubt not, to all prudent persons the most satisfactory publication on the subject. It is a subject on which I can ruminate 'till I feel myself lost in mazes of speculation never to be unravell'd. Could I suppose that the cruel hardships under which millions of that unhappy race have lived and died, were only preparatory to a deliverance to be wrought for them hereafter, like that of Israel out of Ægypt, my reasonings would cease, and I should at once acquiesce in a dispensation, severe indeed for a time, but leading to invaluable and everlasting mercies. But there is no room, Scripture affords no warrant for any such expectations. A question then presents itself which I cannot help asking, though conscious that it ought to be suppressed. Is it to be esteem'd a sufficient vindication of divine justice, if these miserable creatures, tormented as they have been from generation to generation, shall at last receive some relief, some abatement of their woes, shall not be treated absolutely as brutes for the future? The thousands of them who have already passed into an eternal state, hopeless of any thing better than they found in this life, what is to become of Them? Is it essential to the perfection of a plan concerted by infinite wisdom, that such wretches should exist at all, who from the beginning of their Being through all its endless duration can experience nothing for which they should say, It is good for us that we were created? These reasonings and such as these engage me often and more intensely than I wish them to do, when the Case of the poor Negroes occurs to me. I know that the difficulty, if it cannot be solved may be sever'd, and that the answer to which it lies open is this or somewhat like it. God is Sovereign. All are his, and he may do what he will with his own. What passes upon this grain of sand which we call the earth, is trivial when consider'd with reference to those purposes that have the Universe for their object. And lastly — All these things will be accounted for and explained hereafter. An answer like this would have satisfied me once, when I was myself happy. For I have frequently thought that the Happy are easily reconciled to the woes of the Miserable. But in the School of affliction I have learn'd to cavil and to question, and finding myself in my own case reduced frequently to the necessity of accounting for my own lot by the means of an uncontroulable sov'reignty which gives no account of its matters, am apt to discover, what appear to me, tremendous effects of the same sov'reignty in the case of others. Then I feel — I will not tell you what — and yet I must. A wish that I had never been. A wonder that I am. And an ardent but hopeless desire not to be. Thus have I written to you my whole heart on a subject which I thought to have touched only and to have left it. But the pen once in my hand, I am no longer master of my own intentions. To make you some small amends, the best I can at present, after having thank'd you in the third place for a basket of most excellent fish (Hollybut and Lobsters) I will subjoin some stanzas in the mortuary stile composed at the request of the Clerk of All Saints parish Northampton. They were printed at the foot of his Bill of Mortality published at Christmas last. Some time in November the said Clerk was introduced to me one morning before breakfast. Being ask'd his business, he told me that he wanted verses, and should be much obliged to me if I would furnish them. I replied that in Northampton there must be many poets, because poets abound every where, and because the News-paper printed there was seldom destitute of a Copy. I then mention'd in particular his Nake-sake Mr. Cox the Statuary, who to my knowledge often wooes the Muse and not without some cause to boast of his success. To which he answer'd — What you say Sir is true. But Mr. Cox is a gentleman of much Reading, and the people of our town do not well understand him. He has written for me, but nine in ten of us were stone-blind to his meaning. Finding that he had an answer to all that I could urge, and particularly affected by the eulogium implied in his last, I suffer'd myself to be persuaded, and in due time wrote as follows.

19 February 1788

Pallida Mors æquo pulsat pede pauperum tabernas
Regumque turres.[2]

Pale Death with equal foot strikes wide the door
Of Royal Halls and Hovels of the Poor.

While thirteen Moons saw smoothly run
    The Nen's[3] barge-laden wave,
All these, Life's rambling journey done,
    Have found their home, the grave.
+

Was Man (frail always) made more frail
    Than in foregoing years?
Did Famine, or did Plague prevail
    That so much Death appears?
+

No: These were vig'rous as their sires;
    Nor Plague nor Famine came;
This annual tribute Death requires
    And never waives his claim.
+

Like crowded forest-trees we stand,
    And some are mark'd to fall;
The axe will smite at God's command,
    And soon shall smite us all.
+

Green as the Bay-tree ever green
    With its new foliage on,
The Gay, the Thoughtless I have seen,
    I pass'd — and they were gone.
+

Read ye that run the awful truth
    With which I charge my page,
A worm is in the bud of Youth,
    And at the root of Age.
+

[2] Horace, *Odes*, I. iv. 13–14.
[3] The river which runs through Northamptonshire, Cambridgeshire, and Lincolnshire.

No present health can health insure
   For yet an hour to come,
No Med'cine, tho' it often cure
   Can always baulk the tomb.
         +

And oh! that (humble as my lot
   And scorn'd as is my strain)
These truths, though known, too much forgot
   I may not teach in vain.
         +

So prays your Clerk with all his heart,
   And ere he quits the pen
Begs you for once to take his part,
   And answer All — Amen.

We are truly sorry to be informed as we were by Mr. Bull, that Mrs. N. is so much indisposed. Our affectionate remembrances and best wishes attend you both.

> Yours most sincerely, my dear friend,
> Wm Cowper.

CLOTWORTHY ROWLEY   Thursday, 21 February 1788

Southey, ii. 284–8

Weston Underwood, Feb. 21, 1788.

My dear Rowley,

I have not, since I saw you, seen the face of any man whom I knew while you and I were neighbours in the Temple. From the Temple I went to St. Albans, thence to Cambridge, thence to Huntingdon, thence to Olney, thence hither. At Huntingdon I formed a connexion with a most valuable family of the name of Unwin, from which family I have never since been divided. The father of it is dead; his only son is dead; the daughter is married and gone northward; Mrs. Unwin and I live together. We dwell in a neat and comfortable abode in one of the prettiest villages in the kingdom, where, if your Hibernian engagements would permit, I should be happy to receive you. We have one family here, and only one, with which we much associate. They are Throckmortons, descendants of Sir Nicholas of that name,[1] young persons, but sensible, accomplished, and friendly in the highest degree. What sort of scenery lies around us I have already told you in verse; there is no need, therefore, to do it in prose. I will only add to its printed eulogium, that it affords opportunity of walking at all seasons, abounding with beautiful grass-grounds, which encompass our village on all sides to a considerable distance. These grounds are skirted by woods of great extent, belonging principally to our neighbours above mentioned. I, who love walking, and who always hated riding, who am fond of some society, but never had spirits that would endure a great deal, could not, as you perceive, be better situated. Within a few miles of us, both to the east and west, there are other families with whom we mix occasionally; but keeping no carriage of any sort, I cannot reach them often. Lady Hesketh (widow of Sir Thomas, whose name, at least, you remember,) spends part of the year with us, during which time I have means of conveyance, which else are not at my command.

So much for my situation. Now, what am I doing? Translating Homer. Is not this, you will say, *actum agere*?[2] But if you think again, you will find that it is not. At least, for my own part, I can assure you that I have never seen him translated yet, except in the Dog-Latin, which you remember to have applied to for illumination when you were a school boy. We are strange creatures, my little friend; every thing that we do is in reality important, though half that we do seems to be push-pin. Not much less than thirty years since, Alston[3] and I read Homer through together. We compared Pope with his original all the way. The result was a discovery, that there is hardly the thing in the world of which Pope was so entirely destitute, as a taste for Homer. After the publication of my last volume, I found myself without employment. Employment is essential to me; I have neither health nor spirits

[1] Sir Nicholas Throckmorton (1515–71), the diplomat and statesman, was a younger brother of Sir Robert Throckmorton (d. 1570), who was a direct ancestor of the Throckmortons of Weston.
[2] 'Doing what's been done already.'
[3] William Alston. See n.5, C to Rowley, Aug. 1758. He had retired from the 1st Foot Guards in 1762 and succeeded his brother Thomas as 6th Baronet in 1774.

without it. After some time, the recollection of what had passed between Alston and myself in the course of this business struck me forcibly; I remembered how we had been disgusted; how often we had sought the simplicity and majesty of Homer in his English representative, and had found instead of them, puerile conceits, extravagant metaphors, and the tinsel of modern embellishment in every possible position. Neither did I forget how often we were on the point of burning Pope, as we burnt Bertram Montfitchet[4] in your chambers. I laid a Homer before me. I translated a few lines into blank verse; the day following a few more; and proceeding thus till I had finished the first book, was convinced that I could render an acceptable service to the literary world, should I be favoured with health to enable me to translate the whole. The Iliad I translated without interruption. That done, I published Proposals for a subscription, and can boast of a very good one. Soon after, I was taken ill, and was hindered near a twelvemonth. But I have now resumed the work, and have proceeded in it as far as to the end of the fifteenth Iliad, altering and amending my first copy with all the diligence I am master of. For this I will be answerable, that it shall be found a close translation: in that respect, as faithful as our language, not always a match for the Greek, will give me leave to make it. For its other qualifications, I must refer myself to the judgement of the public, when it shall appear. Thus I have fulfilled my promise, and have told you not only how I am at present occupied, but how I am likely to be for some time to come. The Odyssey I have not yet touched. I need not, I am confident, use any extraordinary arts of persuasion to secure to myself your influence, as far as it extends. If you mention that there is such a work on the anvil in this country, in yours perhaps you will meet somebody now and then not disinclined to favour it. I would order you a parcel of printed proposals, if I knew how to send it. But they are not indispensably

---

[4] According to Southey, 'Some liquid has fallen upon the letter, and completely obliterated all but the initial and last syllable of this word. But the *Monthly Review*, for April, 1761, notices "The Life and Opinions of Bertram Montficet, Esq. written by himself," as an humble imitation of Tristram Shandy.' We have been able to locate editions of 1761 and 1765 of this work.

necessary. The terms are, two large volumes, quarto, royal paper, three guineas; common, two.

I rejoice that you have a post, which, though less lucrative than the labours of it deserve, is yet highly honourable, and so far worthy of you. Adieu, my dear Rowley. May peace and prosperity be your portion.

Yours, very affectionately,
Wm. Cowper.

LADY HESKETH   Friday, 22 February 1788

Address: Lady Hesketh / New Norfolk Street / Grosvenor Square / London. / Single Sheet
Postmarks: FE/25/88 *and* OULNEY
Panshanger Collection

The Lodge Feb. 22. 1788

I thank you, my dearest Coz, for the Bank-note which I received this morning, and for your letter which accompanied it. I send my answer sooner by one Post than the usual time, that you may be apprized of its safe arrival as early as possible.

I do not wonder that your ears and feelings were hurt by Mr. Burke's severe invective.[1] But severe as it was, I am told that they who are to follow him threaten to bear still harder upon the culprit than he. So that whatever be the event of the trial, whether Hastings be condemned or acquitted, unpunished he cannot be; for perhaps there is not so much difference as one would at first imagine, between being

[1] Burke had been very instrumental in having Hastings impeached. P. J. Marshall, *The Impeachment of Warren Hastings* (Oxford, 1965), p. 78: 'Burke began the prosecution's case by expounding his views on Indian society and the importance of the impeachment in a speech of four days, embellished by sensational material not relevant to any of the articles.' Burke began his speech on the third day of the trial, Friday, 15 Feb., and he resumed it on the fourth day, 16 Feb. Fanny Burney, an ardent believer in Hastings's innocence, was, like Lady Hesketh, shaken by Burke's speech: 'Were talents such as these exercised in the service of truth, unbiassed by party and prejudice, how could we sufficiently applaud their exalted possessor? But though frequently he made me tremble by his strong and horrible representations, his own violence recovered me, by stigmatising his assertions with personal ill-will and designing illiberality. Yet at times, I confess, with all that I felt, wished and thought concerning Mr. Hastings, the whirlwind of his eloquence nearly drew me into its vortex.' *Burney Diary*, iii. 449.

pilloried and pelted with addled eggs, and placed at the Bar of such a court, a mark for all eyes and the theme of the most unmerciful reproaches. The main difference seems to be, that in the former case the Mob are the Agents and the Spectators, and in the latter, persons of consideration, quality and fashion. Otherwise, I do not know but that the tongue of a great Orator may be as formidable as the Hoot of an Irish Chairman, and a rhetorical flourish finely turned & pointed at least as painful in its effects as a handful of Boüe de Londres.[2] But you are to know, my Dear, or probably you know it already, that the prosecution of public delinquents has always and in all countries, been thus conducted. The stile of a criminal charge of this kind has been an affair settled among Orators from the days of Tully to the present, and like all other practises that have obtained for ages, this in particular seems to have been founded originally in reason and in the necessity of the case. He who accuses another to the state, must not appear himself unmoved by the view of the crimes with which he charges him, lest he should be suspected of fiction, or of precipitancy, or of a consciousness that after all he shall not be able to prove his allegations. On the contrary, in order to impress the minds of his hearers with a persuasion that he himself at least is convinced of the criminality of the prisoner, he must be vehement, energetic, rapid; must call him tyrant and traytor and every thing else that is odious, and all this to his face, because all this, bad as it is, is no more than he undertakes to prove in the sequel, and if he cannot prove it, he must himself appear in a light very little more desireable, and at the best to have trifled with the tribunal to which he has summon'd him. Thus Tully in the very first sentence of his first Oration against Cataline, calls him a Monster;[3] a manner of address in which he persisted, 'till said Monster unable to support the fury of his accuser's eloquence any longer, rose from his seat, elbow'd for himself a passage through the crowd, and at last burst from the Senate house in an agony, as if the Furies themselves had follow'd him. And now, my Dear, though I have thus

---

[2] 'London filth'.

[3] C is referring to the end of section 11 of the first *Invectivarum in L. Catilinam* in which Cicero calls Catiline a 'pestis'.

spoken, and have seemed to plead the cause of that species of eloquence which you and every creature who has your sentiments must necessarily dislike, perhaps I am not altogether convinced of its propriety. Perhaps at the bottom, I am much more of opinion, that if the charge unaccompanied by any inflammatory matter and simply detailed, being once deliver'd into the court and read aloud, the witnesses were immediately examined and sentence pronounced according to the evidence, not only the process would be shorten'd, much time and much expence saved, but Justice would have at least as fair play as now she has. Prejudice is of no use in weighing the question — Guilty or not guilty — and the principal aim, end, and effect of all such introductory harrangues is to create as much prejudice as possible. When you and I therefore shall have the whole and sole management of such a business entrusted to us, we will order it otherwise.

I have not quarrell'd with Hoffman,[4] on the contrary I admire him as much as ever. But I am become a better oeconomist in that particular than I was. Last year I took his anodyne 'till it had ceased to be one. I now only take it occasionally, and find the benefit of it. When I dine at the Hall, which we generally do twice a week, I talk five times more than at any other time. The consequence is a flurry of spirits which a spoonful of Hoffman presently composes. My health is, in the main, better than it has been these 30 years. I know not now what it is to have a disorder'd stomach. A fever of the nervous kind indeed, attends me Spring and Fall, for which I take a decoction of Bark that never fails to remove it, and which I am now taking. Except when that fever prevails, I sleep as well as any man.

I was glad to learn from the papers that our Cousin Henry shone as he did in reading the charge. This must have given much pleasure to the General. Yet alas! a thought comes across me that had he pursued his first career, he might have lived to press the Wool-sack himself, instead of addressing it in the humbler capacity of a reader.[5] — Mr. Throg returned

[4] See n.2, C to Lady Hesketh, 14–16 Jan. 1787.
[5] C is referring to the fact that Henry, who had attended the Middle Temple, was called to the Bar in 1775, but had not practised law as such.

from London yesterday. He arrived just at dinner time and found Uzz in his Hall ready to dine with him. — What shall I say? How shall I tell it you? Making a general sweep of loose papers out of my desk, I unwittingly threw into the fire along with them, your Birth-day copy of verses by our friend Frances.[6] I would with all my heart that thou wert here to box my ears for doing it.

Mrs. Unwin's love attends thee with that of thy ever affectionate

W C.

JOHN NEWTON   Saturday, 1 March 1788

Barham Johnson (*copy*)

Weston March 1. 1788.

My dear friend,

That my letters may not be exactly an echo to those, which I receive, I seldom read a letter immediately before I answer it, trusting to my memory to suggest to me such of its contents as may call for particular notice. Thus I dealt with your last, which lay in my desk, while I was writing to you. But my memory, or rather my recollection, failed me in that instance. I had not forgotten Mr. Bean's letter, nor my obligations to you for the communication of it,[1] but they did not happen to present themselves to me in the proper moment, nor till some hours after my own had been dispatched. I now return it with many thanks for so favourable a specimen of its author. That he is a good man and a wise man its testimony proves sufficiently, and I doubt not that when he shall speak for himself, he will be found an agreeable one. For it is possible to be very good, and in many respects very wise, yet at the same time not the most delightful companion.

Excuse the shortness of an occasional scratch which I send in much haste, and believe me, my dear friend, with our united

---

[6] Frances Hill. See List of Correspondents, Volume II.

---

[1] In his letter to Newton of 19 Feb., C did not thank him for the letter from Bean.

Love to yourself and Mrs. Newton, of whose health we hope to hear a more favourable account as the year rises, and with our love to Miss Catlett

Your truly affectionate
M Unwin
Wm. Cowper.

JOHN NEWTON   [Monday, 3 March 1788][1]

Princeton

My dear friend,

I had not, as you may imagine, read more than two or three lines of the enclosed, before I perceived that I had accidentally come to the possession of another man's property, who by the same misadventure has doubtless occupied mine.[2] I accordingly folded it again the moment after having open'd it, and now return it.

The Bells of Olney both last night and this Morning have announced the arrival of Mr. Bean. I understand that he is now come with his family. It will not be long therefore before we shall be acquainted. I rather wish than hope that he may find himself comfortably situated, but their admiration of Mr. Canniford, whatever the Bells may say, is no good omen. It is hardly to be expected that the same people should admire both. The parishioners of Ra'nstone[3] have been suitors to Mr. Finch[4] that he would appoint that Gentleman his Curate, to which suit of theirs Mr. Finch has graciously condescended, and he is gone to reside among them.

I have lately been engaged in a correspondence with a Lady whom I never saw. She lives at Pertenhall near Kimbolton and is the wife of a Dr. King who has the Living. She is, I understand, very happy in her husband, who for that reason I should suppose, is at least no enemy to the Gospel, for she

---

[1] The top of this letter has been dated 'Mar: 3. 1788.' and '[probable date Mar. 3. 1788.]' in an unknown hand and Newton's hand respectively.

[2] We do not know any further particulars of this mis-sent letter.

[3] See n.3, C to [Mrs. Newton], 5 Oct. 1780.

[4] The Hon Henry Finch was Rector of Ravenstone with Weston Underwood from 1786 to 1788.

is evidently herself a Christian and a very gracious one. I would that she had you for a correspondent rather than me. One letter from you would do her more good than a ream of mine. But so it is, and since I cannot depute my office to you, and am bound by all sorts of considerations to answer her this Evening, I must necessarily quit you that I may have time to do it.

Mr. Bull called here yesterday. His horse lately ran away with him, and threw him just at the entrance of Newport. He hurt his knees a little, received a bruise on the back of his head which however has not been attended[5]

LADY HESKETH   Monday, 3 March 1788

Address: Lady Hesketh / New Norfolk Street / Grosvenor Square / London. / Single Sheet
Postmarks: MR/5/88 *and* OULNEY
Panshanger Collection

The Lodge
Mar. 3. 1788 — Monday.

My dearest Coz — He who can sit up all night at a Gaming table,[1] knowing that he is to spend the next day in the accusation of another at the Bar of the first Court of Judicature in the world, is not a jot more innocent than he whom he accuses. If he has not committed the same offences it is only. because he never had the same opportunity, for profligate he must be to a degree that no Governor of Fort St. George[2] past, present, or to come can possibly surpass. This may look like an assertion built upon grounds too slight to bear it, but if I were not writing to my Cousin whom I would not entertain merely with logical deductions, I think I could make it appear probable at least, if not absolutely certain.

One day last Week, Mrs. Unwin and I having taken our

---

[5] The final page of this letter is missing.

[1] A reference to Charles James Fox.
[2] Fort St. George, an outpost completed in 1640, was the centre of British activity in Madras. Hastings served as second in council there from 1769 to 1772. In using the expression 'Governor of Fort St. George' C is referring figuratively to British rule in India.

morning walk, and returning homeward through the wilderness, met the three Throckmortons. A minute after we had met them, we heard the cry of hounds at no great distance, and mounting the broad stump of an Elm which had been felled, & by the aid of which we were enabled to look over the Wall, we saw them. They were at that time in our Orchard. Presently we heard a Terrier belonging to Mrs. Throg, which you may remember by the name of Fury, yelping with much vehemence, and saw her running through the thickets within few yards of us at her utmost speed as if in pursuit of something which we doubted not was the Fox. Before we could reach the other end of the wilderness, the hounds enter'd also; and when we arrived at the Gate which opens into the grove, there we found the whole dirty and weary cavalcade assembled. The Huntsman dismounting begg'd leave to follow his hounds on foot, for he was sure, he said, that they had killed him. A conclusion which I suppose he drew from their profound silence. He was accordingly admitted, and with a sagacity that would not have dishonour'd the best hound in the world, pursuing precisely the track which the Fox and the dogs had taken, though he had never had a glimpse of either after their first entrance through the rails, soon arrived where he found the slaughter'd prey, videlicet in the Pit of a certain place called Jessamy Hall,[3] into which both the Fox and the dogs had enter'd by a large aperture in the Brick-work at the bottom of it. Being himself by far too staunch to boggle at a little filth contracted in so honourable a cause, he soon produced dead Reynard, and rejoined us in the grove with all his dogs about him. Having an opportunity to see a ceremony which I was pretty sure would never fall in my way again, I determined to stay and to notice all that passed with the most minute attention. The Fox's tail, or brush as I ought to call it, was given to one of the Hall Foot-boys, who bearing it in his hat-band, ran with it to his mistress, and in the height of his transport offer'd it to her fair hand, neither so clean nor so sweet as it had been while the Fox possess'd it. Happily however for Mrs. Throg, not being quite so enraptured, she had the presence of mind to decline the offer. The boy

---

[3] Probably a lavatory.

therefore for aught I know, remains to this hour in possession both of the tail and the stink that belongs to it. The Huntsman having by the aid of a Pitchfork lodged Reynard on the arm of an Elm at the height of about 9 feet from the ground, there left him for a considerable time. The Gentlemen sat on their horses contemplating the Fox for which they had toiled so hard, and the hounds assembled at the foot of the tree with faces not at all less expressive of the most rational delight, contemplated the same object. The Huntsman remounted. He cut off a foot and threw it to the hounds. One of them swallow'd it whole like a Bolus. He then once more alighted, and drawing down the fox by his hinder legs, desired the people who were by this time rather numerous to open a lane for him to the right and left. He was instantly obey'd, when throwing the fox to the distance of some yards, and screaming like a fiend as he is — Tear him in pieces — at least six times repeatedly, he consign'd him over absolutely to the pack, who in a few minutes devour'd him completely. Thus, my Dear, as Virgil says, What none of the Gods could have ventured to promise me, time itself pursuing its accustom'd course has of its own accord presented me with.[4] — I have been In at the death of a Fox — and you now know as much of that matter as I, who am as well inform'd as any Sportsman in England.

A thousand thanks my Dear for your kind intention to furnish me not only with Books but with Shelves also to set them on. I am in reality equally in want of both, having no shelf in the world but an Encoignure[5] which holds a Lexicon and a Dictionary.

My Dog turns out a most beautiful creature but is at present apt to lift up his leg in the house, on which subject he and I had a terrible quarrel this morning. My Cat is the most affectionate of all her kind, and in my eyes a beauty also. — The Throgs with whom we walked this morning enquired after you as they often do, when I made your remembrances as you desired.

[4] *Aeneid*, ix. 6–7.   [5] Corner cupboard.

Adieu my dearest Coz, with Mrs. Unwin's very best and warmest respects, I remain ever Yours —

Wm Cowper.

I often think of my Uncle though I do not always mention him. Few days pass in which he is not in my thoughts — Give my Love to him.[6]

MRS KING   Monday, 3 March 1788

Address: Mrs. King / Pertenhall near / Kimbolton / Huntingdonshire
Postmark: MR/4/88
Princeton

Weston Underwood
March 3. 1788

I owe you many acknowledgments, Dear Madam, for that unreserved communication both of your history and of your sentiments with which you favour'd me in your last. It gives me great pleasure to learn that you are so happily circumstanced both in respect of situation and frame of mind. With your view of religious subjects, you could not indeed, speaking properly, be pronounced unhappy in any circumstances, but to have received from above not only that Faith which reconciles the heart to affliction, but many outward comforts also, and especially that greatest of all earthly comforts, a comfortable Home, is Happiness indeed. May you long enjoy it! As to Health or Sickness you have learn'd already their true value, and know well that the former is no blessing unless it be sanctified, and that the latter is one of the greatest we can receive, when we are enabled to make a proper use of it.

There is nothing in my story that can possibly be worth your knowledge, yet lest I should seem to treat you with a reserve which at your hands I have not experienced, such as it is, I will relate it. I was bred to the Law. A Profession to which I was never much inclined, and in which I engaged rather because I was desirous to gratify a most indulgent

---

[6] Lady Hesketh has written on this letter: 'I send this because it contains a Curious account of a Fox-Chace who wou'd believe that my Quiet humane Cousin shd. be in at the Death!'

Father, than because I had any hope of success in it myself. I spent 12 years in the Temple where I made no progress in that science to cultivate which I was sent thither. During this time my Father died; not long after him died my Mother in Law, and at the expiration of it a Melancholy seized me which obliged me to quit London, and consequently to renounce the Bar. I lived some time at St. Albans. After having suffer'd in that place long and extreme affliction, the storm was suddenly dispelled and the same Day-spring from on high which has arisen upon you, arose on me also. I spent 8 years in the Enjoyment of it, and have ever since the expiration of those 8 years been occasionally the prey of the same melancholy as at first. In the Depths of it I wrote the Task and the Volume which preceded it, and in the same Deeps am now Translating Homer. But to return to St. Albans. I abode there a year and half. Thence I went to Cambridge where I spent a short time with my brother, in whose neighborhood I determined, if possible, to pass the remainder of my days. He soon found a Lodging for me at Huntingdon. At that place I had not resided long, when I was led to an intimate connexion with a family of the name of Unwin. I soon quitted my Lodging and took up my abode with them. I had not lived long under their roof, when Mr. Unwin as he was riding one Sunday Morning to his Cure at Gravely, was thrown from his horse, of which fall he died. Mrs. Unwin having the same views of the Gospel as myself, and being desirous of attending a purer ministration of it than was to be found at Huntingdon, removed to Olney where Mr. Newton was at that time the preacher, and I with her. There we continued 'till Mr. Newton, whose family was the only one in the place with which we could have a connexion, and with whom we lived always on the most intimate terms, left it. After his departure, finding the situation no longer desireable, and our House threat'ning to fall upon our heads, we removed hither. Here we have a good house in a most beautiful village, and for the greatest part of the year a most agreeable neighborhood. Like you, Madam, I stay much at home, and have not travell'd 20 miles from this place and its Environs more than once these 20 years.

All this I have written not for the singularity of the matter (as you will perceive) but partly for the reason which I gave at the Outset, and partly that seeing we are become correspondents, we may know as much of each other as we can, and that, as soon as possible.

I beg Madam that you will present my best respects to Mr. King, whom together with yourself, should you at any time hereafter take wing for a longer flight than usual, we shall be happy to receive at Weston, and believe me Dear Madam His and Your

Obliged and Affectionate
Wm Cowper.

[SAMUEL ROSE]   Monday, [10 March 1788][1]

Princeton

My Dear Sir —

Your Letter finds me fagg'd after five hours spent with Homer, and in real need of fresh air and motion. For which reason I must be short.

We shall rejoice most sincerely in the sight of Mr. Clark.[2] We have no Letters for you nor any new Commissions, and are glad that you found your way though in the Dark, and through fields and woods to you so little known. As you say nothing of an earlier hour We suppose that Four will not be inconvenient.

Adieu! With the Ladys' best Compliments and with the least fear possible of your Uncle, to whom I beg my best respects — I remain Sincerely Yours

Wm Cowper.

Monday
Two o'clock

---

[1] C mentions Rose's recent visit in his letter to Lady Hesketh of Wednesday, 12 March 1788, and it would seem that this note was written to confirm a dinner engagement towards the latter part of Rose's sojourn in the area.

[2] Probably James Clarke (d. 1795) who, having served as one of the two bailiffs in 1775, was elected mayor of Northampton on 9 Aug. 1779.

LADY HESKETH   Wednesday, 12 March 1788

Address: Lady Hesketh / New Norfolk Street / Grosvenor Square / London.
Postmarks: MR/14/88 *and* OULNEY
Panshanger Collection

The Lodge
March 12. 1788

I judged it wisest and best, my dearest Coz, to answer your letter and to thank you, as I do most heartily, for the parcel which arrived yesterday, by one and the same opportunity. I should have done it last night, had we not dined at the Hall, whence we did not return 'till Nine o'clock. *Slavery* and the *Manners of the Great*[1] I have read. The former I admired as I do all that Miss More writes, as well for the Energy of the expression as for the tendency of the design. I have never yet seen any production of her pen that has not recommended itself by both those qualifications. There is likewise much good sense in her manner of treating every subject, and no mere poetic Cant, which is the thing that I abhor, in her manner of treating *any*. And this I say, not because you now know and visit her, but it has long been my avowed opinion of her works, which I have both spoken and written as often as I have had occasion to mention them. — Mr. Wilbeforce's little Book (if he is the Author of it) has also charmed me. It is so evidently the work of a liberal, sensible man, of a man of Letters and a Gentleman, that it must, I should imagine, engage the notice of those to whom it is addressed. In that case one may say to them, Either answer it, or be set down by it. But alas! They will do neither. They will approve, commend and forget it. Such has been the fate of all exhortations to Reform whether in Verse or in Prose and however closely pressed upon the conscience, in all ages. Here and there a happy Individual to whom God gives grace and wisdom to profit by the admonition, is the better for it ever after, but the *Aggregate Body*, as Gilbert Cooper[2] used to call the *multitude*, remain, though with a very good understanding of the matter, like Horse and Mule that have none. Hannah stood at my side last night with a face full of anxious expectation

---

[1] See n.1, C to Lady Hesketh, 16 Feb. 1788.
[2] John Gilbert Cooper (1723–69).

while I open'd the parcel. I had taken out half a dozen books before I produced those in which she was chiefly concerned. The delay encreased her anxiety so much, that when your kind present to Her at last appeared, and I read to her what you had written in the Cover, she received them with transport, and now begs me to return you her humblest and best thanks for the favor. Mrs. Unwin is reading one of them while I write, and is delighted with what she reads. — Shakespear and the Don and all came safe, and for all, my Coz, once more I thank you.

I have heretofore mentioned to you a Mr. Rose, who knowing nothing of me but my books and having a curiosity to know their author also, found me out soon after our settling at Weston. Mrs. Unwin and I had just sallied to our Morning walk last Saturday, when having reached the middle of the village, I heard myself greeted from behind. I turned and saw a smart young man whom I did not immediately recollect, but Mrs. Unwin's memory being better than mine, she recognized him in a moment, and I as soon as she had named him. He brought with him a Mr. Capper,[3] the nephew of a Schoolfellow of mine; his Uncle, a man of fortune, is in parliament, and lives at Watford in Hartfordshire. These striplings twain had walked from Watford, but on that day only from Newport-pagnel. They dined, supp'd and slept with us, and after breakfast on Sunday set off on foot for Northampton, where Mr. Rose has an Uncle the Leading man of the Corporation.[4] I was much pleased with their company, and admired them both as great rarities, very young, yet modest, sober, and sensible, and desirous of nothing so much as improvement and to escape contamination from the manners of their contemporaries.

We shall now soon lose our neighbours at the Hall. They depart the Week after Easter. They have behaved to us with such a friendly kindness, and have treated us always with

[3] See n.2, C to Samuel Rose, 14 Feb. 1788. Robert Capper's uncle was John Ord (1729–1814) who served as Member of Parliament for Wendover from 1784 to 1790. Ord's sister married Richard Capper, Robert's father, in 1759. John Ord's residence in Watford must have been of a temporary nature; he was active in the affairs of the Capper family, and C thus describes him as at Watford, but his residence was in Bingfield, Northumberland.

[4] See n.2, C to [Rose], [10 Mar. 1788].

such an intimate familiarity so far surpassing all that they have shown to any other of their neighbors, that we shall truly miss them and long for their return. Mr. Throg said to me last night with sparkling eyes and a face expressive of the highest pleasure — We compared you this morning with Pope. We read your 4th. Iliad and his, and I verily think we shall beat him. He has many superfluous lines and does not interest me. When I read your translation I am deeply affected. I see plainly your advantage, and am convinced that Pope spoil'd all by attempting the work in rhime. His brother George, who is my most active Amanuensis and who indeed first introduced the subject, seconded all he said. More would have passed, but Mrs. Throg having seated herself at the Harpsichord, and for my amusement merely, my attention was of course turn'd to her. George when she had ceased to play and Mr. Potts[5] to sing, concluded the Music of the Evening with a French song in the manner and with the countenance of an old Frenchman, and so admirably performed that it was impossible for any sides to stand it.

A few posts since I had a letter from our good Friend and Coz the General, in which he kindly offers to recruit my Cellar. An offer accepted joyfully by me, my Cellar standing much in need of it. The new Vicar of Olney is arrived, viz Mr. Bean, and we have exchanged visits. He is a plain, sensible, good man and pleases me much, a treasure for Olney if Olney can understand his value.

Adieu! my Dearest. With Mrs. Unwin's love

Ever truly thine, Wm Cowper.[6]

MRS HILL   Monday, 17 March 1788

Address: Mrs. Hill / Wargrave / Twyford / Berks
Postmarks: MR/19/88 *and* OULNEY
Cowper Johnson

My dear Madam,

A thousand thanks to you for your obliging and most

[5] Unidentified.
[6] Lady Hesketh has written on this letter: '*This* I send only on account of the Paragraph of H. More all he says in *her* praise I shou'd wish inserted.'

acceptable Present which I received this Evening. Had you known my occasions you could not possibly have timed it more exactly. The Throckmorton family who live in our near neighborhood and who sometimes take a Dinner with us, were by engagement made with them two or three days ago appointed to dine with us just at the time when your Turkey will be in perfection. A Turkey from Wargrove the residence of my friend, and a Turkey, as I conclude, of your breeding, stands a fair chance, in my account, to excell all other Turkeys, and the Ham its companion will be no less welcome.

I have to thank you likewise for an excellent piece of Cod with Oysters, which however singular it may seem, came also just in due season to furnish out a smart entertainment for the very same neighbours of ours, the Throckmortons.

I shall be happy to hear that my friend Joseph has recover'd entirely from his late indisposition, which I was informed was Gout, a distemper which however painful in itself, brings at least some comfort with it, both for the Patient and those who love him, the hope of length of days and an exemption from num'rous other evils. I wish him just so much of it as may serve for a confirmation of this hope, and not one twinge more.

Your husband, my Dear Madam, told me some time since, that a certain library of mine concerning which I have heard no other tidings these five and twenty years, is still in being.[1] Hue and Cry have been made after it in Old Palace yard,[2] but hitherto in vain. If he can inform a Bookless Student in what Region or in what Nook his long lost volumes may be found, he will render me an important service. I am likely to be furnish'd soon with shelves which my Cousin of Norfolk Street is about to send me, but furniture for those shelves I shall not presently procure unless by recov'ring my stray Authors. I am not young enough to think of making a new collection, and shall probably possess myself of few Books hereafter but such as I may put forth myself, which cost me

[1] The hopes which Hill raised concerning C's books were not to be fulfilled. See Norma H. Rusell, 'Addenda to "The Library of William Cowper"', *Transactions of the Cambridge Bibliographical Society*, vol. iii, No. 3 (1961), 226-7.
[2] Ashley Cowper's residence.

nothing but what I can better spare than money — Time and consideration.

I beg, my Dear Madam, that you will give my Love to my friend, and believe me with the warmest sense of his and your kindness

Your most obliged and Affectionate

Wm Cowper.

Weston Underwood
March 17. 1788.

JOHN NEWTON

Monday, 17 March 1788

Barham Johnson (*copy*)

Mar: 17. 1788.

My dear friend,

The evening is almost worn away, while I have been writing a Letter to which I was obliged to give immediate attention. An application from a Lady,[1] and backed by You, could not be less than irresistible. That Lady too, a daughter of Mr. Thornton's. Neither are these words of course. Since I returned to Homer, in good earnest, I turn out of my way for no consideration, that I can possibly put aside.

With modern Tunes, I am unacquainted, and have therefore accommodated my Verse[2] to an old one. Not so old, however, but that there will be Songsters found, old enough to remember it. The Song is an admirable one, for the purpose for which it was made, and, though political, nearly, if not quite as serious, as mine. On such a subject, as I had before me, it seems impossible not to be serious. I shall be happy if it meet with Your, and Lady Balgonie's approbation.

[1] Jane (1757–1818) daughter of John Thornton, and the wife (married 1784) of Alexander Leslie, styled Lord Balgonie, later 7th Earl of Leven (1749–1820). C transcribed Lady Balgonie's letter in his to Lady Hesketh of 21 Mar.

[2] The resulting poem was 'The Negro's Complaint' and its tune was taken from 'Admiral Hosier's Ghost' which was a well-known political ballad attacking Walpole's administration, written in 1739 or 1740 by Richard 'Leonidas' Glover (1712–85), whose posthumous epic, *The Athenaid*, C was to review in the *Analytical Review* in the spring of 1789. After *John Gilpin*, 'The Negro's Complaint' was the most frequently reprinted of C's poems, the earliest-known printing being in *Stuart's Star, and Evening Advertiser* for 2 Apr. 1789.

Of Mr. Bean, I could say much, but have only time, at present, to say that I esteem, and love him. On some future occasion, I shall speak of him, more at large.

We rejoice that Mrs. Newton is better, and wish nothing more than her complete recovery. Dr. Ford is to be pitied.[3] His Wife, I suppose, is going to heaven, a journey which she can better afford to take, than he to part with her.

I must now scribble the Copy, as fast as I can,[4] and bid you accordingly good night.

I am, my dear friend, with our united love to you all three,

most truly Yours,
Wm. Cowper.

WALTER BAGOT Wednesday, 19 March 1788

Address: The Revd. Walter Bagot.
Morgan Library

March 19. 1788

My dear friend —

The Spring is come, but not I suppose that Spring which our poets have celebrated. So I judge at least by the extreme severity of the Season, sunless skies and freezing blasts, surpassing all that we experienced in the depth of Winter. How do you dispose of yourself in this howling month of March? As for me, I walk daily be the weather what it may, take Bark, and write verses. By the aid of such means as these I combat the North East with some measure of success, and look forward with the hope of enjoying it, to the warmth of Summer.

Mr. Throckmorton brought with him from Chichely, some time since, the news of Lord Bagot's illness.[1] Though not personally known to his Lordship, it affected me with much concern, because I could pretty well guess the degree of trouble that it would cause to all his kindred, especially to

---

[3] *GM* (lviii, pt.1, 277) lists the death on 20 Mar. 1788 of 'Mrs. Margaret Ford, wife of Rev. Dr. Jn. F. of Bedford-row, Bloomsbury'.

[4] 'The Negro's Complaint' must have formed part of the original letter.

---

[1] See n.3, C to Lady Hesketh, 30 Nov. 1785.

two of them, whom I sometimes see, though not so often as I could wish. I rejoice however to learn that the alarm is over, and hope that his Lordship for the future if his way should happen to lie through furze or thorns will avail himself of the example of the εὐκνημίδες ᾿Αχαιοί[2] and arm his legs accordingly.

Have you seen a little volume lately published, entitled the Manners of the Great? It is said to have been written by Mr. Wilberforce; but whether actually written by Him or not, is undoubtedly the work of some man intimately acquainted with the subject, a Gentleman and a man of Letters. If it makes the impression on those to whom it is addressed that may be in some degree expected from his arguments and from his manner of pressing them, it will be well. But you and I have lived long enough in the world to know that the hope of a general reformation in any Class of men whatever, or of women either, may easily be too sanguine. The Author himself I hear is not very likely to be a witness of his own success, if any success should attend his pious labours, being though young, extremely infirm, and if I mistake not, inclined to a Consumption.

I have now given the last revisal to as much of my Translation as was ready for it, and do not know that I shall bestow another single stroke of my pen on that part of it, before I send it to the Press. My business at present is with the 16th. Book, in which I have made some progress, but have not yet actually sent forth Patroclus to the battle.[3] My first translation lies always before me; line by line I examine it as I proceed, and line by line reject it. I do not however hold myself altogether indebted to my Critics for the better judgment that I seem to exercise in this matter now than in the first instance. By long study of him, I am in fact become much more familiar with Homer than at any time heretofore, and have possessed myself of such a taste of his manner as is not to be acquired by mere cursory reading for amusement. But alas! 'tis after all a mortifying consideration that the majority of my judges hereafter, will be no judges of this.

---

[2] 'Well-greaved Acheans.' This expression is used in the *Iliad* (e.g. i. 17).
[3] Lines 332 ff. in C's translation.

Græcum est, non potest legi,[4] is a motto that would suit nine in ten of those who will give themselves airs about it, and pretend to like or to dislike. No matter. I know I shall please *you*, because I know *what* pleases you, and am sure that I have done it.

Adieu my good friend —
Ever affectionately Yours Wm Cowper.

Mrs. Unwin begs to be remember'd to you. She has lately been much troubled with a nervous disorder in her side of the spasmodic kind, but is I hope somewhat better.

LADY HESKETH

Friday, 21 March 1788

Address: Lady Hesketh / New Norfolk Street / Grosvenor Square / London. / Single Sheet
Postmarks: MR/24/88 *and* OULNEY
Panshanger Collection

The Lodge March 21. 1788

My dearest Coz —

I am, after all, become a contributor to the poetical effusions at this time produced on the subject of the Slave-trade. Since I wrote last the following reached me enclosed in a letter from Mr. Newton to whom it was address'd.

My dear Sir

We had some Gentlemen employed about the abolition of the Slave-trade with us the other day, they are very desirous of some good Ballads to be sung about the streets on that subject, which they mean to print and distribute, and think they might be of use to the cause. If you think Mr. Cowper could by your means be prevailed on to do this for them, they would be extremely obliged to him, and nobody could do it so well. — Yours in haste

J. Balgonie.

[4] Although this proverb is known in a wide variety of forms, John Strype (1643–1737), the ecclesiastical historian and biographer, in his biography (1705) of Sir John Cheke makes the following remark which follows C's statement precisely: 'This language was little known or understood hitherto in this realm. And if any saw a piece of Greek they used to say, Graecum est; not potest legi, i.e., "It is Greek, it cannot be read".' See *Oxford Dictionary of English Proverbs*, ed. F. P. Wilson, 3rd edn., (Oxford, 1970), p. 336.

130

Thus assailed, what could I do less than surrender all my resolutions to the contrary? Accordingly, I have sent up two pieces. One a serious Ballad to the Tune of Hosier's Ghost, called *the Negro's Complaint* — The other in a different strain and entitled — *Sweet meat has sower Sauce, or the Slave-trader in the dumps.*[1] This I tell you my Dear, that if they should happen to be sung within your hearing, you may pull your Bell and send for them, because they are your Cousin's. I have not however yet heard, nor has there been time for it, whether they have been approved or not. You know, I doubt not, that Lady Balgonie is Mr. Thornton's daughter. To the family of the Thorntons I have had particular obligations, and they are all Subscribers to my Homer. So that the application was on every account irresistible. I am, in fact, not sorry to have been constrained to abandon for a few hours the business of translation, that I might lend my shoulder, however insignificant, to this honourable attempt. I do not perfectly discern, at present, the probable utility of what I have done, for it seems an affair in which the good pleasure of King Mob is not likely to be much consulted; but at least it can do no harm, and I may perhaps hereafter have the comfort of flattering myself, that I help'd a little.

A House-breaker lately apprehended at Olney is to be executed at Aylesbury on Wednesday.[2] About a Week since, 3 of the principal inhabitants of Olney called on me just at Dinner-time, and put into my hand a letter addressed to one of them by the Prisoner. He begged hard that intercession might be made for him by Petition to the Judge, and their business with me was to entreat that I would draw it. I confess that I was rather averse to the employment for two reasons. First, because I knew the man to have been an offender for many years, and the fittest that could be to be

[1] For 'The Negro's Complaint', see n.2, C to Newton, 17 Mar. C probably wrote the words to 'Sweet Meat has Sour Sauce' in a ballad-like form without having any particular tune in mind; the poem first appeared in *Southey*, perhaps because the Committee for the Abolition of the Slave Trade found it too jocular for its purpose.

[2] Probably Jonathan Letts, Labourer, who, according to 'Clerks of Assize: South Eastern Circuit: Gaol Books' (PRO (ASSI 33) 7), was convicted at Buckinghamshire Lent Assize on 1 Mar. 1788 of burgling William Redbourn on 6 Feb. 1788. He was sentenced to be hanged but no date of execution is given.

made an example of, which was nowhere more wanted than at Olney. And secondly, because his case afforded not a single plea for mercy, or any thing which at all resembled one. On these grounds I remonstrated against the measure. But they still continuing to press it upon me, and I foreseeing that if the matter should hitch with me, the death of the prisoner would be charged on my refusal, I accordingly bent myself to this work also. I sent them a sheet full of what might be called a petition, that Evening; it seemed to say something but in fact said nothing, for nothing was there to be said. When, however, they came to offer it to their neighbors for attestation, nobody would sign it. [So] [3] this exercise of my ingenuity came to nothing. I hear that the poor wretch is very penitent and reconciled now to his fate, which makes the miscarriage an affair not at all to be regretted.

When I first began to think seriously of addressing myself to Homer again, (it is about 9 months since) Mrs. Unwin received a letter from Johnson enquiring after my health, in which he discover'd some anxiety to know if the work proceeded. In order to satisfy both him and Fuseli of the sincerity of my intentions to finish it, I immediately sent up the 12th and 13th books for Fuseli's revisal, which otherwise I should have sent to you as I had used to do, with a desire that you would transmit them to the General. From Johnson I have heard nothing since; so that had I not learn'd by a side wind that the parcel actually reached him, I must have concluded that it had miscarried. But a friend of mine saw it on his Counter, within few hours after its arrival. I am now in the 16th. Book, and my share of the business proceeding so much faster than that of Fuseli, am likely to be ready for the Press before he will have had leisure to criticise the remainder.

Looking back on what I have written I observe that the transitions in this letter are truely Pindaric. To finish it therefore in the same strain, I will just tell you that I have received this week a basket including a Turkey and Ham from the amiable Mrs. Hill. It comes just in time to make a Dinner for the Throcks, who next week take leave of Weston which I suppose they will see no more 'till Midsummer. — Mrs. Unwin

[3] MS torn.

reads Mrs. Trimmer to me after supper, with whose little books I am charmed.[4]

So now my Dear, good night to thee. Adieu. Not Peter,[5] but

William Pindar.

GENERAL COWPER   Thursday, 27 March 1788

Address: Lieutent. General Cowper / Kingston upon Thames / Surry.
Postmarks: MR/28/88 *and* OULNEY
Panshanger Collection

Weston. March 27. 1788

My dear Cousin[1]

A Letter is not pleasant which excites curiosity but does not gratify it. Such a letter was my last, the defects of which I therefore take the first opportunity to supply. When the condition of our Negroes in the Islands was first presented to me as a subject for Song, I felt myself not at all allured to the undertaking; it seemed to offer only images of horror which would by no means be accommodated to the Stile of that sort of Composition. But having a desire to comply, if possible, with the request made to me, after turning the matter in my mind as many ways as I could, I at last, as I told you, produced three, and that which appears to myself the best of those three, I here send you.

———

The Morning Dream.
To the tune of
Tweed-side.[2]

———

[4] See n.3, C to Lady Hesketh, 16 Feb. 1788.
[5] See n.2, C to Lady Hesketh, 8 Sept. 1787.

———

[1] C's word 'Cousin' has been obliterated and 'General' has been substituted in an unknown hand.
[2] The tune 'Tweedside' which C prescribes for his ballad is first known in connection with a song of the same name, the original words of which appear in Allan Ramsay's *Tea-Table Miscellany*, 9th edn. (1733), pp. 4–5. C's poem was first printed in *GM* lviii, pt. 2 (Nov. 1788), 1008–9.

27 March 1788

'Twas in the glad season of Spring,
   Asleep at the dawn of the day
I dream'd what I cannot but sing,
   So pleasant it seem'd as I lay.
I dream'd that on Ocean afloat
   Far West from fair Albion I sailed,
While the billows high-lifted the boat,
   And the fresh-blowing breeze never fail'd.

In the Steerage a woman I saw,
   Such at least was the form that she wore,
Whose beauty impress'd me with awe
   Ne'er taught me by woman before;
She sat, and a shield at her side,
   Shed light, like a sun, on the waves,
And smiling divinely, she cried,
   — I go to make Freemen of Slaves —
         ——

Then raising her voice to a strain
   The sweetest that ear ever heard,
She sung of the Slaves' broken chain
   Wherever her glory appear'd.
Some clouds which had over us hung
   Fled chased by her melody clear,
And, methought, while she Liberty sung
   It was Liberty only to hear.
         ——

Thus, swiftly dividing the flood,
   To a slave-cultur'd island we came,
Where a Dæmon, her enemy, stood,
   Oppression his terrible name.
In his hand, as the sign of his sway,
   A scourge hung with lashes he bore,
And stood looking out for his prey
   From Africa's sorrowful shore.
         ——

But soon as approaching the land
   That Goddess-like woman he view'd,
The scourge he let fall from his hand
   With blood of his subjects imbrued.

I saw him both sicken and die,
  And the moment the monster expired
Heard shouts which ascended the sky
  From thousands with rapture inspir'd.

———

Awaking, how could I but muse
  On what such a dream might betide?
But soon my ear caught the glad news
  Which serv'd my weak thought for a guide
That Britannia renown'd o'er the waves
  For the hatred she ever has shown
To the black-sceptred rulers of Slaves —
  Resolves to have none of her own.

———

Of the other two, One is serious, in a strain of thought perhaps rather too serious for a Ballad even of that cast — but the subject is serious, and I could not help it. The other, of which the Slave-Trader is himself the Subject, is somewhat ludicrous. If I could think them worth your seeing, I would, as opportunity should occur, send them also. If this amuses you at all, I shall be glad, and with my affectionate respects to Mrs. Cowper, I remain, my Dear Cousin,

Sincerely yours Wm Cowper.

SAMUEL ROSE   Saturday, 29 March 1788

Address: Samuel Rose Esqre. No. 23 / Percy Street / Rathbone Place / London.
Postmarks: MR/3[0]/[88] [1] *and* OULNEY
Princeton

Weston Underwood
March 29. 1788

My dear friend,
  I rejoice that you have so successfully performed so long a journey without the aid of hoofs or wheels, and that you met with nothing sinister by the way. Concluding that you would persevere as you had begun, I felt some anxiety for a

———

[1] The date stamp has been cropped.

letter from you that might assure me of your safe arrival once more in London. I do not know that a journey on foot exposes a man to more disasters than a carriage or a horse; perhaps it may be the safer way of travelling. But the novelty of the performance possessed me with some apprehensions on your account and Mr. Capper's which I am glad to be fairly rid of. I beg that you will mention me kindly to your fellow-pilgrim, in whom I discover more than meets the ear, at least the ear of a stranger.

It seems almost incredible to myself that my company should be at all desireable either to you or to any man. I know so little of the world as it goes at present, and labour generally under such a depression of spirits, especially at those times when I could wish to be most cheerful, that my own share in ev'ry conversation appears to me the most insipid thing imaginable. But you say you found it otherwise, and I will not for my own Sake doubt your sincerity. *De gustibus non est disputandum,*[2] and since such is yours, I shall leave you in quiet possession of it, wishing indeed both its continuance and encrease. I shall not find a properer place in which to say, accept of Mrs. Unwin's acknowledgments as well as mine of the kindness of your expressions on this subject, and be assured of an undissembling welcome at all times when it shall suit you to give us your company at Weston. As to Her, she is one of the sincerest of the Human race, and if she receives you with the appearance of pleasure, it is merely because she feels it. Her behaviour on such occasions is with her an affair of conscience, and she dares no more look a falsehood than utter one.

It is almost time to tell you that I have received the Books safe; they have not suffer'd the least detriment by the way, and I am much obliged to you for them.[3] If my Translation should be a little delay'd in consequence of this favour of yours, you must take the blame on yourself. It is impossible

---

[2] Proverbial: 'There's no arguing about taste.'
[3] C is referring to Samuel Clarke's *Ilias Graece et Latine* (2 vols., 1754). The inside cover of one of the volumes is inscribed: 'E libris Samuelis Rose. To William Cowper Esqr from his affectionate and much obliged Friend Saml Rose August 10th 1788.' Rose probably also gave C his copy of Clarke's *Odyssea Graece et Latine* (2 vols., 1740). *Keynes*, 57–8.

not to read the notes of a Commentator so learned, so judicious, and of so fine a taste as Dr. Clarke, having him at one's elbow. Though he has been but few hours under my roof I have already peep'd at him, and find that he will be *instar omnium*[4] to me. They are such notes exactly as I wanted. A Translator of Homer should ever have somebody at hand to say — That's a beauty — lest he should slumber where his Author does not, not only depreciating by such inadvertency the work of his Original, but depriving perhaps his own of an embellishment which wanted only to be noticed.

If you hear Ballads sung in the Streets on the subject of the hardships suffer'd by the poor Negroes in the islands, they are probably mine. I was lately applied to for assistance in that way by a society of Gentlemen enlisted in that laudable service. I have sent them 3. Two are serious, and one is not so. Of the former, one is called the *Negro's Complaint*, and one, the *Morning Dream*. The latter is entitled, *Sweet meat has sour sauce, or the Slave Trader in the dumps*. The subject, as a subject for Song, did not strike me much, but the application was from a quarter that might command me, and the occasion itself, whatever difficulties might attend it, offer'd pleas that were irresistible. It must be an honour to any man to have given a stroke to that chain, however feeble. I fear however that the attempt will fail. The tidings which have lately reached me from London concerning it, are not the most encouraging. While the matter slept or was but slightly adverted to, the English only had their share of shame in common with other nations, on account of it. But since it has been canvass'd and search'd to the bottom, since the public attention has been rivetted to the horrible theme, and we can no longer plead either that we did not know it, or did not think of it, woe be to us if we refuse the poor captives the redress to which they have so clear a right, and prove ourselves in the sight of God and man indifferent to all considerations but those of gain.

[4] 'Worth everything.' Source is probably Cicero, *Brutus*, 51.191: 'Plato mihi unus instar est omnium'. 'Plato is to me worth them all.'

Adieu, my dear friend, and believe me with Mrs. Unwin's affectionate respects

most truely Yours
Wm Cowper.

P.S.
Whatever confidence you may account me worthy of, of this you may rest assured; that though my opinion may not always be worth your having, your trust at least shall never be abused.

LADY HESKETH   Monday, 31 March 1788

Address: Lady Hesketh / New Norfolk Street / Grosvenor Square / London. / Single Sheet.
Postmarks: AP/1/88 *and* NEWPORT/PAGNEL
Panshanger Collection

The Lodge
March 31. 1788

My dearest Coz — I have received from the General six dozen of Oporto, four ditto of Sherry, and Madeira he says, shall follow soon. My thanks are due to *You* for thanking *him*, because it proves the interest that you take in my emoluments. — The Hen, I find, has hatch'd, and we have another Cousin.[1] The Throgs gave me this Intelligence, having found it in their paper, which as it happen'd I did not see. They leave Weston on Wednesday, and we dine with them to-morrow for the 3d. time within the week. I shall regret their going, but regret is vain. London has attractions irresistible by those who have youth and money. I shall amuse myself in their absence with raising Cucumbers in their garden which will be sent after them, and Melons on which they will regale themselves at their return. I have some thoughts, but have not absolutely resolved on it, that I shall charge Monsieur their Valet, with as much of my Homer as has been copied fair, to be consigned to you, and by you, when you have done with it, to the General. My doubts are

---

[1] 'On Monday last, the Lady of William Henry Cowper, Esq. of a son.' This birth announcement appeared in *The Morning Herald* for Thursday, 27 Mar. 1788 (No. 2318).

occasion'd only by the smallness of the quantity, four books or five at most being all that are in travelling order. But the General groans to see them, and you perhaps will not be sorry; I think therefore that I shall send them. — One day last week, on Thursday it might be, we met in the Grove, Mrs. Throg in company with two young Ladys and a Lady not so young as they. I soon learn'd that they were the Miss Knaps.[2] One of them, the eldest as I believe, addressing herself to me, gave me to understand that she had seen you lately, and spoke of you in terms that proved she knew you. The poor thing had walked from Gayhurst that Morning, and was at that moment setting out on her return by the same conveyance. When I saw her she was completely fagg'd, or as the Scots poet Burn calls it, ramfeezled. Therefore in what condition she reached Gayhurst, or whether she be still living, I neither know nor can conjecture. You are likely to be first informed, for if she still draws vital air, she goes to Town to-morrow. When you see her I beg that you will present her with my Compliments and assure her from me, that such journeys are not for a frame like hers. Her sister, who more prudently had committed herself to the back of an horse, fared better, and their friend Mrs. Roberts[3] who likewise performed on foot, seemed not to suffer much fatigue from doing so. Yet even she perhaps, for she is thin and delicate, might have migrated by means of a carriage or quadrupede with more advantage. Mrs. Throg has promised to write to me. I beg that as often as you shall see her you will give her a smart pinch and say — Have you written to my Cousin? — I build all my hope of her performance on this expedient, and for so doing these my letters not patent shall be your sufficient warrant. You are thus to give her the question 'till she shall answer — Yes. — I have written one more song and sent it. It is called the Morning Dream, and may be sung to the Tune of Tweed-side or any other Tune that will suit it, for I am not nice on that subject. I would have copied it for you, had I not almost filled my sheet

[2] Catharine, Mary, and Leonora Knapp of Little Linford Hall. They were the daughters of the Revd Primatt Knapp (d. 7 Dec. 1793) who was presented to the living of Shenley in 1755.
[3] Unidentified.

without it, but now, my Dear, you must stay till the sweet Sirens of London shall bring it to you. Or if that happy day should never arrive, I hereby acknowledge myself your Debtor to that amount. I shall now probably cease to sing of tortured Negroes, a theme which never pleased me, but which in the hope of doing them some little service, I was not unwilling to handle. What you tell me concerning the disposition of our great folks in this matter, is truely mortifying. It had been less dishonorable for England never to have stirred in it, than after having done so, to fall asleep again. Till now, we were chargeable perhaps only with Inattention, but hereafter, if the poor creatures be not effectually redressed, and all buying and selling of them prohibited for ever, we cannot be wrong'd by the most opprobrious appellations. Call us, who will, deliberately cruel and Tyrants upon principle, we are guilty and must acknowledge it.

If any thing could have raised Miss More to a higher rank in my opinion than she possessed before, it could only be your information that after all, she and not Mr. Wilberforce, is author of that volume. How comes it to pass, that she being a woman, writes so little like one? With a force, and energy, and a correctness hitherto arrogated by the men, and not very frequently displayed even by the men themselves? Adieu, my dearest Coz! Mrs. U. sends affectionate remembrances.

Ever thine — Wm Cowper.

P.S.

Your account of the Chancellor's behavior makes me wish you would touch the porcupine with more caution.

LADY HESKETH   Monday, 7 April 1788

Address: **Lady Hesketh | New Norfolk Street | Grosvenor Square | London. |
    Single Sheet**
Postmarks: **AP/9/88** *and* **OULNEY**
Panshanger Collection

The Lodge April 7. 1788

My dearest Coz —

I begin to scribble, but I do not say that I shall be able to fill the sheet. Interruptions have occurr'd and the Evening is far spent. But I will do my best.

We waited with the impatience that belongs to the Love we feel for the Donor, for the case announced in your last. But whether it did not reach the Inn in due season, which was probably the cause, or whether it were owing to any other less obvious reason, it came not. All that I can say therefore at present is, that when it comes, it will be most entirely welcome, and in the mean time I must be content to bestow my lumber where I can, which is in every nook and cranny that can be made to contain it. My very Dressing-table is filled with Homer, not to mention my drawer in the Secretary, and my Desk.

I sent you, my dear, by the Throcks the four first Books of the Iliad, which I hope have by this time reach'd you. This last Edition of it differs so much from that which you have seen, that I can venture to say you will at least find novelty in it. When you shall have seen enough of it, I will beg the favour of you by the safest means to convey it to the General. I have also this day written to Johnson, and have sent him a civil Hue and Cry after Fuseli, who has now been in possession of the 12th. and 13th books not less than nine months, and for aught that appears has done little or nothing to them. I have likewise suggested to him that having finish'd eleven books for the Press, and advanced in my translation as far as to the 17th, I cannot but suppose that it would be a good time to begin printing, and that I should be glad of his opinion upon that matter. What is the state of the Subscription I know not nor am at all able to conjecture, but I suppose it is such as may vindicate such a noble enterprize as that of going to Press immediately, from the imputation of rashness. You perhaps can inform me my Coz, whether the General and Henry have yet sent in their quotas. To me it appears doubtful, because in a letter which I received from Henry once on a time, he spoke of his list as not at that time deliver'd, saying that he had procured upwards of thirty Right Honourable names, and hoped at the meeting of Parliament to procure many more. The time indeed of which I speak has been long since past, but having never heard a syllable of the matter either from him, the General, or Johnson, I naturally suppose that the matter may rest where it did. All this I mention to you, as I do every thing else that interests me, because it does so, knowing that whatever falls under that description interests you likewise, and because I know that if I desire it, when you see Henry next you will ask him the question. — In the aforesaid Letter sent to Johnson by this Post, I have also desired him, as I did before, to send the 12th. and 13th. books to you, when Fuseli shall have revised them; which books I will also beg of you to send to the General at your own best leisure. Thou hast been, my dearest Coz, from the first, a principal mover of the wheels on which the business of my Subscription has rolled, to which kindness of yours you are indebted for the additional trouble with which this letter saddles you. — Having made the progress that I have mentioned, I begin to feel a wish that the Printer's share of the labour were begun. I know them to be tedious as Asses, and that having proceeded so far as I have, I shall have finished Iliad and Odyssey too long enough before they will come up with me, should they even set off to-morrow. There is therefore no reason why they should not, or at least as soon as possible.

Mr. Bean, the new vicar, drank Tea with us this Evening whom I like much. I like his wife also. I have seen her, but Mrs. Unwin has not. Dirty ways or high winds or rain or snow have hinder'd her walking to Olney ever since they have been settled there. As to Postlethwaite, of him I have heard nothing farther than that he never was so happy in his life, which is enough in all reason, and is probably all that I shall ever hear of *him*. I have the comfort to find on comparing notes with Mr. Bean, that the newly arrived parson so much my terrour once, was equally his.[1] It is plain therefore that I was not frighten'd for nothing. Adieu! If you see the Throcks, any or all, give my Love to them, and remember your Commission. — I am, with Mrs. Unwin's best remembrances — Ever thine — W C.

P.S. Rogers has this day had a particular charge to be careful of the Case, and to bring it by the next waggon, all which he has promised.

[1] Probably Canniford.

MRS KING   Friday, 11 April 1788

Address: Mrs. King / Perten Hall near / Kimbolton / Huntingdonshire
Postmark: Illegible
Princeton

Weston Underwood
April 11. 1788.

Dear Madam,

The Melancholy that I have mention'd and concerning which you are so kind as to enquire, is of a kind, so far as I know, peculiar to myself. It does not at all affect the operations of my mind on any subject to which I can attach it, whether serious or ludicrous, or whatsoever it may be. For which reason I am almost always employed either in Reading or writing when I am not engaged in Conversation. A vacant hour is my abhorrence, because when I am not occupied I suffer under the whole influence of my unhappy temperament. I thank you for your recommendation of a Medicine from which you have received benefit yourself, but there is hardly any thing that I have not proved, however beneficial it may have been found by others, in my own case, utterly useless. I have therefore long since bid adieu to all hope from human means, the means excepted of perpetual employment.

I will not say that we shall never meet, because it is not for a creature who knows not what shall be to-morrow, to assert any thing positively concerning the Future. Things more unlikely I have yet seen brought to pass, and things which if I had expressed my opinion of them at all, I should have said were impossible. But being respectively circumstanced as we are, there seems no present probability of it. You speak of insuperable hindrances, and I also have hindrances that would be equally difficult to surmount. One is, that I never Ride, that I am not able to perform a journey on foot, and that Chaises do not roll within the Sphere of that oeconomy which my circumstances oblige me to observe. If this were not of itself sufficient to excuse me when I decline so obliging an invitation as yours, I could mention yet other obstacles. But to what end? One impracticability makes as effectual a barrier as a thousand. It will be otherwise in other worlds. Either we shall not bear about us a body, or it will be more easily transportable than this. In the mean time, by the help of the Post, strangers to each other may cease to be such, as you and I have already begun to experience.

It is indeed Madam, as you say, a foolish world, and likely to continue such 'till the Great Teacher shall himself vouchsafe to make it wiser. I am persuaded that Time alone will never mend it. But there is doubtless a Day appointed when there shall be a more general manifestation of the Beauty of Holiness than mankind have ever yet beheld. When that period shall arrive, there will be an end of profane representations whether of Heaven or Hell on the Stage. The great realities will supersede them.

I have just discover'd that I have written to you on paper so transparent that it will hardly keep the contents a Secret. Excuse the mistake, and Believe me Dear Madam, with my respects to Mr. King,

Affectionately Yours
Wm Cowper.

LADY HESKETH Saturday, 12 April 1788

Address: Lady Hesketh / New Norfolk Street / Grosvenor Square / London. / Single Sheet
Postmarks: AP/13/88 *and* OULNEY
Carl H. Pforzheimer Library

The Lodge
April 12. 88

My dearest Coz — It is late in the Evening and I have only time to tell you that this day just after Dinner the expected Shelves or Chiffonieres[1] arrived. I have already furnished that which occupies a place in my study with about a dozen gay books of my own, and with Homers, Greek and English, that are not my own. People will now see that it is not called a Study for nothing, which never was the case 'till now. A thousand thanks to you my Dear for this neat Addition to

---

[1] 'A C18 French term for a piece of furniture for the storage of stuffs (*chiffons*) and small articles of clothing. It it usually, but not necessarily, a small, low chest-of-drawers (narrower than the normal commode).' John Fleming and Hugh Honour, *Dictionary of the Decorative Arts* (1977), p. 177.

our Meubles, which harmonizes exactly with the rest. These, like many other contrivances which administer to the comfort of life, have been invented since I saw the world, and, but for you, I should have died ignorant of their existence, but having now seen them, I see plainly too that I shall not be able to live without them hereafter.

I have Burnes' Poems by the gift of my lately acquired friend Mr. Rose who knows those who know the Author. It is true that he was a Ploughman when he composed them; but being a Ploughman in Scotland where the lowest of the people have yet some benefits of Education, makes the wonderment on that account the less. His poetical talent has however done that for *him*, which such a talent has done for few; it has mended his circumstances and of a ploughman has made him a Farmer. I think him an extraordinary Genius, and the facility with which he rhimes and versifies in a kind of measure not in itself very easy to execute, appears to me remarkable. But at the same time, both his measure and his language are so terribly barbarous, that though he has some humour and more good sense, he is not a pleasing poet to an English reader, nor do I think him worth your purchasing. Some time or other, surely, we shall see you at Weston, and then you will have an opportunity to taste for yourself, gratis. They came into my hands at a time when I was perfectly idle, and being so, had an opportunity to study his language, of which by the help of a Glossary at the Book's tail, I made myself master. But he whose hands are not as vacant as mine were at that moment, must have more resolution than I naturally possess, or he will never account it worth his while to study a Dialect so disgusting.

Half a dozen times since I have been writing I have turned my eyes from the paper to Squint at the Chiffonier.

Had I not supposed that, ere now, my songs would have greeted your ears, your eyes would probably have seen them. It is possible that my Suitors for that assitance may chuse not to avail themselves of it 'till next Winter. In which case I will contrive to send them to you in the Interim. To the General I have already sent twain, and in the only Letter that I have had from him since he received the first, he tells me that he was very much pleased with it.

12 April 1788

> Adieu, my Dear,
> I am ever thy most affectionate Coz.
> Wm Cowper.

N.B.
Your present suffer'd not the least damage in the journey.

GENERAL COWPER   Monday, 14 April 1788

Address: Lieutent. General Cowper / Kingston on Thames / Surry.
Postmark: AP/15/88
Princeton

> Weston Underwood
> April 14. 1788

My dear General —
Lest any mistake should have happen'd which you cannot otherwise be aware of, I thought it necessary to inform you that no Hamper has yet arrived. Sometimes our parcels have been carried to the wrong Inn. The Wind-mill in St. John Street is that from which ours sets out, and the best time to send is Tuesday night or Wednesday morning early, else the Waggon perhaps is loaded, and the parcel left to another Opportunity. I hope that your eye is so much better that you will be able to read what follows without distressing it, otherwise it will cost you much more than it is worth.

> The Negro's Complaint
> To the tune of
> Hosier's Ghost.
>
> ———
>
> Forced from Home and all its pleasures
>   Afric's coast I left forlorn,
> To encrease a stranger's treasures
>   O'er the raging billows borne;
> Men from England bought and sold me,
>   Pay'd my price in paltry gold,
> But though theirs they have enroll'd me
>   Minds are never to be sold.
>
> ———
>
> Still in thought as free as ever
>   What are England's rights, I ask,

146

14 April 1788

Me from my delights to sever,
    Me to torture, me to task?
Fleecy locks and black complexion
    Cannot forfeit Nature's claim;
Skins may differ, but Affection
    Dwells in White and Black the same.

———

Why did all-creating Nature
    Make the plant for which we toil?
Sighs must fan it, tears must water,
    Sweat of ours must dress the soil.
Think, ye Masters iron-hearted
    Lolling at your jovial boards,
Think, how many backs have smarted
    For the sweets your Cane affords.

———

Is there, as ye sometimes tell us,
    Is there One who reigns on high?
Has he bid you buy and sell us
    Speaking from his throne the sky?
Ask him if your knotted scourges,
    Fetters, blood-extorting screws
Are the means which Duty urges
    Agents of his Will to use?

———

Hark — He answers. Wild tornadoes
    Strewing yonder sea with wrecks,
Wasting Towns, Plantations, Meadows,
    Are the voice with which he speaks.
He foreseeing what vexations
    Afric's sons should undergo,
Fix'd their Tyrants' habitations
    Where his whirlwinds answer — No.

———

By our blood in Afric wasted
    'Ere our necks received the Chain,
By the mis'ries that we tasted
    Crossing in your barks the main,
By our suff'rings since ye brought us
    To the man-degrading mart,

147

All sustain'd with patience taught us
Only by a broken heart —

———

Deem our nation Brutes no longer
'Till some reason ye shall find
Worthier of regard and stronger
Than the Colour of our Kind.
Slaves of Gold! Whose sordid dealings
Tarnish all your boasted pow'rs
Prove that *You* have Human Feelings
'Ere ye proudly question *Ours*.

———

Lady Hesketh sent me this last week two neat little pieces of furniture which she calls Chiffonieres — What the word means I am not Frenchman enough to discover, but I have filled one of them with books, having only so many as will fill one of them. My own volumes make a conspicuous figure among them, and put me in mind of a Line of Pope's which not having seen these 30 years perhaps I may quote amiss.

— His Books, a slender store —
His own works neatly bound, and little more.[1]

When I left London my Library vanish'd. It was not sold with my furniture, but what became of it nobody seems to know. He that writes so much however and reads so little, may best shift without 'em. — I am, my dear Cousin — with my Love to Mrs. Cowper — Most affectionately yours — Wm Cowper.

JOHN NEWTON   Saturday, 19 April 1788

Address: The Revd. John Newton
Princeton

                                        Weston April 19
                                                    88
My dear friend—
    I thank you for your last, and for the Verses in particular

---

[1] We have been unable to trace these lines to Pope; C may be conflating passages from the *Dunciad* (see Book I, lines 127–42, Book IV, lines 319–20).

therein contained, in which there is not only rhime but reason; yet I fear that neither you nor I with all our reasoning and rhiming shall effect much good in this matter. So far as I can learn, and I have had intelligence from a quarter within the reach of such as is respectable, our Governors are not animated altogether with such heroic ardour as the occasion might inspire. They consult frequently indeed in the Cabinet about it, but the frequency of their consultations in a case so plain as this would be, did not what Shakespear calls Commodity[1] and what we call Political expedience cast a cloud over it, rather bespeaks a desire to save appearances than to interpose to purpose. Laws will, I suppose, be enacted for the more humane treatment of the Negroes, but who shall see to the execution of them? The Planters will not, and the Negroes cannot. In fact we know that Laws of this tendency have not been wanting enacted even amongst themselves, but there has been always a want of Prosecutors or righteous Judges; deficiencies which will not be very easily supplied. The News papers have lately told us that these merciful Masters have on this occasion been occupied in passing ordonnances by which the Lives and Limbs of their Slaves are to be secured from wanton cruelty hereafter.[2] But who does not immediately detect the artifice, or can give them a moment's credit for any thing more than a design, by this show of lenity, to avert the storm which they think hangs over them? On the whole I fear that there is reason to wish for the honour of England that the nuisance had never been troubled, lest we eventually make ourselves justly chargeable with the whole offence, by not removing it. The Enormity cannot be palliated; we can no longer plead either that we were not aware of it or that our attention was otherwise engaged, and shall be inexcuseable therefore ourselves if we leave part of it unredressed. Such arguments as Pharaoh might have used

---

[1] *King John*: II. i. 573–98.

[2] C's reference would seem to be to the forthcoming proposal (presented in Parliament on 21 May 1788) by Sir William Dolben (1726–1814) to 'limit, according to the tonnage of the vessel, the number of slaves she should carry: to secure for the slaves good and sufficient provisions: and to regulate other matters for their health and accommodation, until Parliament should decide on the general question, whether the Slave Trade should continue or not.' *Some Account of the Trade in Slaves from Africa* (1842), p. 81.

to justify his detention of the Israelites, substituting only Sugar for Bricks, may lie ready for our use also, but I think we can find no better.

The Vicarage at Olney begins once more to assume a comfortable aspect. Our new neighbours there are of a character exactly suited to our wish, conversible, peaceable, amiable. We drank Tea there yesterday; the first opportunity we have had of doing so; they, having waived all unnecessary ceremonials, drank Tea with us the day before. I had made several calls on them at Noon, and Mr. Bean several here in the Evening, but dirty ways, high winds, rain or snow had always interposed to prevent a meeting between the ladies. Mr. Bean has made a notable journey to Oxford in company with Thomas Bull. It is hardly fair to anticipate him in the account which he will doubtless give you of it himself, neither have I room to say much about it. I will only just mention that having but one horse between them, they availed themselves of him in every possible way. Mr. Bean having walk'd till he could walk no longer, mounted behind, but finding himself incommoded in the straddle that the horse's hips required, changed places with Mr. Bull; he thenceforth rode behind in the side-saddle fashion with both legs on a side, and thus they proceeded 'till they came near to Oxford.

We are tolerably well and shall rejoice to hear that as the year rises Mrs. N.'s health keeps pace with it. We expect Mr. and Mrs. Powley soon, but take it for granted, as they are gone first to Laytonstone,[3] that him, at least, you will see before we shall see him. Accept our best love to your whole Trio and believe me, my dear friend, affectionately

and truly yours — Wm Cowper.

---

[3] See n.1, C to Unwin, 26 Nov. 1781.

WALTER BAGOT   Thursday, 24 April 1788

Address: The Revd. Walter Bagot.
Morgan Library

My dear Walter. Shall I send you a song? I will. But I cannot begin to transcribe it 'till I have told you all the little News I have to communicate. — I have lately renew'd my correspondence with a Mr. Rowley,[1] once my familiar friend in the Temple. He is at present in an office of some dignity in Ireland. A Judge, I think he is called, of the Excise. I ask'd his interest in the business of my Subscription, and he has sent for 30 papers. — Item. I wrote lately to Johnson offering to go to Press directly if he was so inclined, but he answer'd that he never knew a work sent to the Printer before finish'd, but the Author repented of it, it being impossible to contrive the plan with any certainty. I am therefore, as the seamen say, thrown all aback for the present, but having reached almost the end of Book 17, am encouraged to hope for a gale, 'ere long, in my favour. Your Brother Chester was so kind as to call on us about 3 Mornings ago. Your Sister was coming with him, but they had hardly set out when they met Lord Stawell.[2] She return'd with her noble Visitor, and your brother came on. We are however soon to see them both here, when we shall settle a day to dine at Chicheley, your brother having kindly offer'd us his carriage. Now for the Song. But first for a short Preface. Having been lately applied to by Lady Balgonie with whose family I have some connexion (her name was Thornton) to write some songs on the subject of the Slave Trade I produced 3. Some Gentlemen, belonging, I suppose, to the society instituted in London for the abolition of said detestable traffic, had dined at Lord Balgonie's a day or two before, where they had come to a resolution that certain ditties to be sung in the streets and allies of London might have their use, and thus it came to pass that she applied to me.

[1] C's letter to Rowley was of 21 Feb. 1788.
[2] Henry (Bilson-Legge) Stawell (1757–1820), Baron Stawell of Somerton from 1780, was educated at Trinity College, Cambridge (MA, 1779), and served as Surveyor of Customs in the Port of London. He was the son of the Rt Hon Henry Bilson-Legge, *formerly* Legge (1708–64), the fourth son of the first Earl Dartmouth.

24 April 1788

The Morning Dream.

'Twas in the glad season of Spring,
    Asleep at the dawn of the day
I dream'd what I cannot but sing,
    So pleasant it seem'd as I lay.
I dream'd that on Ocean afloat
    Far West from fair Albion I sail'd
While the billows high-lifted the boat,
    And the fresh-blowing breeze never fail'd.

In the steerage a woman I saw,
    (Such at least was the form that she wore),
Whose beauty impress'd me with awe
    Ne'er taught me by woman before.
She sat, and a shield at her side
    Shed light like a sun on the waves,
And smiling divinely, she cried,
    I go to make Freemen of Slaves —

Then raising her voice to a strain
    The sweetest that ear ever heard,
She sung of the Slave's broken chain
    Wherever her glory appear'd.
Some clouds which had over us hung
    Fled chased by her melody clear,
And methought while she Liberty sung
    It was Liberty only to hear.

Thus swiftly dividing the flood
    To a slave-cultur'd island we came,
Where a dæmon, her enemy, stood,
    Oppression his terrible name.
In his hand, as the sign of his sway,
    A scourge hung with lashes he bore,
And stood looking out for his prey
    From Africa's sorrowful shore.

But soon as approaching the land
    That goddess-like Woman he view'd,
The scourge he let fall from his hand
    With blood of his subjects imbrued;
I saw him both sicken and die,
    And the moment the monster expired
Heard shouts which ascended the sky
    From thousands with rapture inspired.

Awaking, how could I but muse
    On what such a Dream might betide?
But soon my ear caught the glad news
    Which serv'd my weak thought for a guide —
That Britannia, renown'd o'er the waves
    For the hatred she ever has shown
To the black-sceptred rules of Slaves —
    Resolves to have none of *her own.*

Immediately on the receipt of your last I sent your brother Chester a Copy of my mortuary stanzas for which I was obliged to resort to my memory, having no copy at all left, and when he thank'd me for them he did it so heartily that I was *as* heartily glad I sent them. — Mrs. Unwin's best Compliments, who I thank God is in better health than when I wrote last, conclude me my dear Friend   Affectionately Yours

                                  Wm Cowper.

Weston
April 24. 88

Erratum. Instead of Mr. Wilberforce as author of *Manners of the Great*, read Hannah More.[3]
         I truly rejoice in Lord Bagot's recovery.

[3] C is correcting the information on this point that he gave to Bagot in his letter of 19 Mar. 1788.

LADY HESKETH   Thursday, 1 May 1788

Address: Lady Hesketh / New Norfolk Street / Grosvenor Square / London.
Postmarks: MA/2/88 *and* OULNEY
Yale

Weston Lodge
May 1. 1788

My dearest Cuzzy-wuzzy — Behold the Pill new-made and the Dose more brightly gilded![1] May the Patient be much the better for it and the Apothecary and Nurse well paid! Then You and I shall have no cause to complain.

I have lately sent you nothing but Scraps instead of Letters, but I shall soon grow more prolix, having more to communicate than the time will at this present writing, allow. Mrs. Frog told you indeed the truth. I have had a Letter from her, the brevity of which was the only cause of complaint with which it furnish'd me, though even of That I made no complaint in my answer to it, having too much Christian consideration of her various and multifarious engagements, to be so unreasonable. They have been now a Month in London, and if she and Mr. Frog are Men of their word, another Month brings them back again.

I told you that I admire Mrs. Maitland's Muse,[2] and I told you the Truth. She has no need to fear a Critical eye, an eye at least that is truly such. There are several very beautiful turns of expression and Versification in the Copy and the whole is good. Perhaps instead of *Gay* Hope (an Epithet that does not seem exactly to suit a Hope of the Religious kind) I should substitute some other term, and I know not that my fault-finding faculty discovers any other speck to lay its finger on.

To Copy my Verses inclosed and to scribble this morsel, is all that I am able to do before breakfast. Give my Love and Thanks to Mrs. Maitland when you write to her, and trust me my

---

[1] Probably 'On Mrs. Montagu's Feather-Hangings'. See n.1, C to Lady Hesketh, 12 May.

[2] 'She wrote many poems, chiefly religious, 1770–91 and earlier, many of which are preserved in Hog C. P. Bk. no. 3: two are on the death of the Countess of Huntingdon, and of her own son William.' *The Madan Family*, p. 125.

dearest Coz that with ardent wishes to see thee in the beautiful scenes with which I am here surrounded, I am ever Thine

Wm Cowper.

Mrs. Unwin's Love attends you.

LADY HESKETH   Tuesday, 6 May 1788

Address: Lady Hesketh / New Norfolk Street / Grosvenor Square / London. /
    Single Sheet
Postmarks: MA/7/88 *and* OULNEY
Princeton

The Lodge
May 6. 1788

My dearest Cousin — You ask'd me lately how I like Smollet's Don Q. I answer — Well. Perhaps better than anybody's. But having no skill in the Original, some diffidence becomes me. That is to say, I do not know whether I ought to prefer it or not. Yet there is so little deviation from other Versions of it which I have seen, that I do not much hesitate. It has made me laugh I know, immoderately, and in such a case, ça suffit.

A thousand thanks, my Dear, for the new Convenience in the way of Stowage which you are so kind as to intend me. There is nothing in which I am so deficient as Repositories for Letters, Papers, and Litter of all sorts, insomuch that as I told you before, the very Dressing-table and Beaufait are filled with my lumber. Your last Present has helped me somewhat, but not with respect to such things as require Lock and Key, which are numerous. A Box, therefore, so secured, will be to me an invaluable acquisition.[1] And since you leave it to my option, what shall be the size there of, I of course prefer a Folio. No matter how large. In my Study-Windows are seats broad enough to receive the largest. On the Back of the Book-seeming Box, some Artist expert in those matters may inscribe these words.

Collectanea Curiosa

The English of which is — A Collection of Curiosities. A title which I prefer to all others, because if I live, I shall take care that the Box shall merit it, and because it will operate as an

[1] The Solander. See C to Lady Hesketh, 5 July 1788 and n.5.

155

Incentive to open That which being Lock'd cannot be open'd. For in these cases, the greater the Baulk the more Wit is discover'd by the ingenious contriver of it. Viz myself.

The General, I understand by his last Letter, is in Town. In my last to Him, I told him news, which he being in Town may possibly have communicated to you before this can reach you. But the Letter in which I mention'd it, having been directed to Kingston, it is also possible that he may not. I will therefore relate it here, because it will give you pleasure and ought for that reason to be made known to you as soon as possible. My friend Rowley, who I told you has after twenty five years' silence, renew'd his correspondence with me, and who now lives in Ireland where he has many and considerable connexions, has sent to me for thirty Subscription papers, 6 for Royal Paper, and the rest for Common. They were transmitted to him about 3 weeks since by Johnson, and I expect soon to hear that they are disposed of. Such an addition to the List was very desireable, but by me lately not at all expected. Rowley is one of the most benevolent and friendly creatures in the world, and will, I dare say, do all in his power to serve me.

I have just recover'd from a violent Cold attended by a Cough which split my head while it lasted. I escaped these tortures all the Winter, but whose constitution or what skin can possibly be proof against our vernal breezes in England? Mine never were, nor will be. The Gayhurst Family set off yesterday for Bath, whence they are to go I know not whither, but they return not 'till July. Mr. and Mrs. Powley, Mrs. Unwin's daughter and Son in Law, are expected to arrive at the Lodge this Evening, where they will stay about a Fortnight.

When people are intimate, we say — They are as great as two Inkle-weavers[2] — On which expression I have to remark in the first place that the word *Great* is here used in a sense which the corresponding term has not, so far as I know, in any other language — and secondly, that Inkle weavers contract intimacies with each other sooner than other people, on account

---

[2] 'A weaver of inkle or linen tape; whence the phrase *as great* (or *thick*) *as inkle-weavers*, extremely intimate.' The *OED* cites Swift's *Polite Conversations*, i. 105: 'She and you were as great as two Inkle-weavers' as the first source for this expression.

of their juxtáposition in weaving of Inkle. Hence it is that Mr. Gregson and I emulate those happy weavers in the closeness of our connexion. We live near to each other, and while the Hall is empty are each other's only extraforaneous comfort.

I am, with Mrs. Unwin's best Love, most truely thine

Wm Cowper.

JOSEPH HILL   Thursday, 8 May 1788

Address: Joseph Hill Esqre / Chancery Office / London.
Postmarks: MA/9/88 *and* OULNEY
Cowper Johnson

Weston Underwood
May 8. 1788

My dear friend,

You judge well, as of all other things, so especially concerning poets and their occasions, and I am obliged to you for anticipating mine, by your draft for 30Ł which I received yesterday and not the day before as I ought to have done, your Letter being address'd to me in Northamptonshire, whereas my residence is in Bucks.

Walter Bagot wrote me word that he had seen you and that you look well, which I was heartily glad to hear. His Brother Chester called on me a few days since, who if we did not live 5 miles asunder would be more my comfort than under that predicament he can be. His carriage however is to waft us to Chicheley as soon as we can meet to settle a day for Dining with him. These trips are practicable at this season, but in the Winter the roads forbid them.

Alas! my Library — I must now give it up for a lost thing for ever.[1] The only consolation belonging to the circumstance is or seems to be, that no such loss did ever befall any other man, or can ever befall me again. As far as Books are concerned I am

——————— Totus teres atque rotundus[2]

and may set Fortune at defiance. Those Books which had

---

[1] See n.1, C to Mrs Hill, 17 Mar. 1788.
[2] 'I am complete in myself and perfectly round like a sphere': Horace, *Satires*, II. vii. 86.

been my Father's, had, most of them, his arms on the inside
Cover, but the rest, no mark, neither his name or mine. I
could mourn for them like Sancho for his Dapple,[3] but it
would avail me nothing.

You will oblige me much by sending me a Crazy Kate. A
Gentleman[4] last Winter promised me both Her and the Lace
maker, but he went to London, that place in which as in the
Grave — All things are forgotten — and I have never seen
either of them.

I begin to find some prospect of a conclusion, of the Iliad
at least, now opening upon me, having reached the 18th.
Book. Your Letter found me yesterday in the very fact of
dispersing the whole host of Troy, by the voice only of
Achilles. There is nothing extravagant in the idea, for you
have witnessed a similar effect attending even such a voice as
mine, at midnight, from a Garret window, on the dogs of a
whole parish whom I have put to flight in a moment.

I must beseech you if possible to send me a box of Elliot's
ointment, for with all its present faults, it is the only medicine
that renders me any effectual service. My last box was made
by this Irish bungler,[5] successor to Elliot, and has nevertheless
restored me to Eye sight a thousand times. If Kate be not on
the road before this reaches you, perhaps you can contrive to
send them together.

Present my very best respects to Mrs. Hill, and believe me,
my dear Friend —

most truly Yours — Wm Cowper

---

[3] *Don Quixote*, Part I, xxxiii.

[4] See C to Lady Hesketh, 3 Nov. 1787, and n.6.

[5] Mr O'Donnel, who had purchased the apothecary business of John Elliot, MD
(1747–87), testified at Elliot's trial for attempted murder in 1787. The treatment
which C found effectual was probably an ointment of quicksilver which used white
mercuric oxide. See John Elliot, *The Medical Pocket-Book* (4th edn., 1795), p. 69.

LADY HESKETH

Monday, 12 May 1788

Address: Lady Hesketh / New Norfolk Street / Grosvenor Square / London /
Single Sheet
Postmarks: MA/14/88 *and* OULNEY
Panshanger Collection

The Lodge
May 12. 1788

It is probable, my Dearest Coz, that I shall not be able to
write much, but as much as I can, I will. The time between
rising and Breakfast is all that I can at present find, and this
morning I lay later than usual.

I rejoice as much as you that you set me to work, and that
my labours have seemingly sped so well.[1] It may be a good
thing to have caught a *Lady* of Mrs. Montagu's eminence in
literary accomplishments and of her influence in the literary
world, by *the right ear*. My subscription perhaps may feel the
benefit of it. But I have learn'd not to be over-sanguine in
expectation, and recommend it to thee to guard against it.
The rather too, because thy natural temper is that way
inclined. What we much wish to believe in proportion, and
nobody I think has warmer wishes for my prosperity than
thou. In the Stile of this Lady's note to you, I can easily
perceive a smatch of her character. Neither men nor women
write with such neatness of expression, who have not given a
good deal of attention to language, and qualified themselves
by study. At the same time it gave me much more pleasure
to observe that my Coz, though not standing on a pinacle of
renown quite so elevated as that which lifts Mrs. Montagu to
the clouds, falls in no degree short of her in this particular;
so that should she make you a member of her Academy she
will do it honour. Suspect me not of flattering *you* for I

---

[1] Lady Hesketh, in hopes of gaining admission to the literary circle of Mrs
Montagu, *née* Elizabeth Robinson (1720–1800), the hostess and literary lady, asked
C to write a poem that would be helpful to her. C's poem, 'On Mrs. Montagu's
Feather-Hangings', is concerned with the 'feather-room' which Mrs Montagu had
been preparing at her house in Portman Square, now No. 22, since she had moved
there in Dec. 1781. The 'feather-hangings' appear not to have been completed
until 1791, when on 13 June 700 people gathered for the opening of the room:
'the walls are wholly covered with feathers, artfully sewed together, and forming
beautiful festoons of flowers and other fanciful decorations' (*St. James's Chronicle*,
11–14 June 1791, quoted in *Walpole*, xi. 290). C's poem first appeared in *GM*
lviii, pt. 1 (June 1788), 542.

abhor the thought. Neither *will* you suspect it, when you recollect that it is an invariable rule with me never to pay Compliments to those I love.

Two days en suite I have walked to Gayhurst, a longer journey than I have performed on foot these 17 years. The first day I went alone, designing merely to make the experiment, and chusing to be at liberty to return, at whatsoever point of my pilgrimage I should find myself fatigued. For I was not without suspicions that years and some other things not less injurious than years, viz melancholy and distress of mind, might by this time have unfitted me for such atchievements. But I found it otherwise. I reached the Church, which stands as you know in the garden, in 55 minutes, and return'd in ditto time to Weston. The next day, I took the same walk with Mr. Powley, having a desire to show him the prettiest place in the country. I not only performed these two excursions without injury to my health, but have by means of them gained indisputable proof that my ambulatory faculty is not yet impaired. A discovery which, considering that to my feet alone I am likely, as I have ever been, to be indebted always for my transportation from place to place, I find very delectable. My little dog was on the point of killing a most beautiful pheasant there, but fortunately the Gardener caught him in his arms time enough to prevent it. Beau, the handsomest creature in the world were it not for the extreme brevity of his tail, observing the pheasant's felicity in that respect whose tail was of a length unexampled, conceived envy at the sight and would have slain him. Foolish creature, could he by killing him have made that tail his own, who would not have laughed at a dog's rump adorned with a pheasant's tail! So little do we sometimes understand our own true advantage.

I forgot when I wrote last, and had almost forgotten now, to acquit your servants from all imputation of neglect in the affair of Letters. Though yours have twice been long delay'd, they have never been charged. A proof that the fault has been in the Olney post-office. Mrs. Marriot[2] indeed sent me an apology in the first instance, and told me that the letter had been overlook'd. Which how it should possibly happen is to

[2] See n.2, C to Lady Hesketh, 24 Apr. 1786.

me unintelligible, though it has often been produced to me as the reason of similar delay. — You will find in the last Gentleman's Magazine a Sonnet addressed to Henry Cowper, signed T. H.[3] I am the writer of it. No creature knows this but yourself. You will make what use of the intelligence you shall see good. But since I affronted Sephus[4] by praising him in print, I am become timorous and wary.

Ever thine
W C.

P.S.

Mrs. U. being woman is consequently curious, and impatient of course to see the List; you being woman too, will know how to pity her infirmity and to consult her case. — She sends you her best affections. — Johnson desires me not to Print 'till the whole is finished. — The affair is therefore settled.

LADY HESKETH

Monday, 19 May 1788

Address: Lady Hesketh / New Norfolk Street / Grosvenor Square / London. / Single Sheet
Postmarks: MA/20/88 *and* NEWPORT/PAGNEL
Olney

The Lodge
May 19. 1788

True, as you say, my Coz. Praise not sounded forth is lost, and the subject of it not at all advantaged. But the question is — Shall we publish our Eulogium on Mrs. Montagu in a Newspaper, or in the Gentleman's Magazine? Let us consider the matter. A Newspaper perhaps has more Readers than Mr. Urban. Yet Mr. Urban has many, and a majority of them are Literary men. No single Newspaper possibly is read by so many of the Literati as the publications of Mr. Urban; not to mention that he is perused by multitudes of Blockheads beside. Again — A Newspaper dies with the day, and its contents in general die with it. Not so the Gentleman's

---

[3] *GM* lviii, pt. 1 (Apr. 1788), 350.
[4] 'Sephus' has been crossed out and 'a good friend' written above the deletion in Lady Hesketh's hand.

Magazine. There are multitudes who perpetuate the long series of His labours; who Deliver them down to their posterity; one generation consigns them over to another, and they are consequently immortal. For these reasons therefore I deem a Compliment paid in a Magazine, twice as good as the same Compliment would be paid in a Newspaper. Especially considering that there is at least a Chance that some Daily paper may enrich itself with a Copy of said Compliment, stealing it from the Magazine. A practise not unfrequent. Thus far I have consider'd only Mrs. Montagu's interest in the affair, but I do not mean altogether to overlook my own concern in it. One good turn deserves another. Mr. Urban was not sparing either of his labours or his commendations in giving an account of the Task. On the contrary, he bestow'd on it a larger portion of both than any of his Brother Reviewers. I account myself therefore in some sort bound to give him now and then a proof that I am not insensible of the obligation, by sending him such scraps as the more weighty business of translating Homer, will permit me to produce. —

All these reasons maturely weigh'd a decision seems to result from them in favour of the Magazine. But after all I refer the whole to your arbitration. If in your next you should tell me that you are of my mind, I will transmit a Copy immediately to Mr. Nicols informing him at the same time that they are by the author of the Task. Shouldst thou differ from me thou wilt then do well to send them thyself to any newspaper which thou approvest most.[1]

It is generally a rule with me in writing to you to forget what is most important. Accordingly I forgot to tell you of Lord Cowper's Kindness. I was not aware of my obligations to Henry, neither did at all suspect that He had given his Lordship a Jog on the occasion. Of course when I answer'd his Letter I made him no acknowledgments on that behalf. I therefore entreat thee to be Proxy for me, and when you see him next to thank him heartily on my part for his friendly and seasonable intercession.

I also forgot to tell thee that in a Squabble that has fallen out between Maurice Smith and Mrs. Marriot of the Swan

---

[1] The poem appeared in *GM*. See n.1, C to Lady Hesketh, 12 May.

concerning the Post Office — viz. who should have the management of it, the new plan of a Daily Post has dropp'd to the ground, and we now have our Letters only 3 times in the Week as usual.

I beg that you will give my Love to Mrs. Frog, and tell her it is time she were gone to Bucklands. According to my reckoning which I know to be very exact, she has already stay'd her allotted time in London, where if she still continues frisking about, heedless how time goes, and is after all to take a frisk to Bucklands also, I shall be glad to know when we are likely to see her at the Hall again. It is true that Northerly winds have blown ever since she left us, but they have not prevented the most exuberant show of blossoms that ever was seen, nor the singing of Nightingales in every hedge. Ah my Cousin, thou hast lost all these luxuries too. But not by choice. Thine is an absence of necessity. The Wilderness is now in all its beauty. I would that thou wert here to enjoy it. Our guests leave us to-morrow. Fare thee well. Thanks for the two Lists of Subscribers, and for Mr. Vickery's most Admirable Puff.[2] Yours my Dearest ever —

Wm Cowper.

JOSEPH HILL   Saturday, 24 May 1788

Address: Joseph Hill Esqre. / Chancery Office / London.
Postmarks: MA/26/88 *and* OULNEY
Cowper Johnson

Weston Underwood
May 24. 1788

My dear Friend,

In the first place for an excellent Turbot with its concomitant Lobster, and in the second, for two excellent Prints, I return you my sincere acknowledgments. I cannot say that poor Kate resembles much the Original, who was neither so young nor so handsome as the pencil has represented her. But she is a figure well suited to the account given of her in the Task, and has a face exceedingly expressive of despairing melancholy. The Lacemaker is accidentally a good likeness

[2] Unidentified.

of a young woman once our neighbour, who was hardly less handsome than the Picture, twenty years ago. But the loss of one husband and the acquisition of another, have since that time impaired her much. Yet she might still be supposed to have sat to the Artist.

We dined yesterday with your friend and mine, the most companionable and domestic Mr. Chester. The Kingdom can hardly furnish a spectacle more pleasing to a man who has a Taste for true happiness, than himself, Mrs. Chester, and their multitudinous family. We talk'd much of you, and much was said that you would have blushed to hear, though without any real cause for doing so. Seven long miles are interposed between us, or perhaps I should oftener have an opportunity of declaiming on the same subject.

I am now in the nineteenth Book of the Iliad, and on the point of displaying such feats of Heroism performed by Achilles, as make all other atchievements trivial. I may well exclaim — Oh for a Muse of fire! — especially having not only a great host to cope with, but a great river also. Much however may be done when Homer leads the way. I should not have chosen to have been the original author of such a business, even though all the Nine had stood at my Elbow. Time has wonderfull effects. We admire that in an Antient for which we should send a modern Bard to Bedlam.

I saw at Mr. Chester's a great curiosity; an antique Bust of Paris in Parian Marble. You will conclude that it interested me exceedingly. I pleased myself with supposing that it once stood in Helen's Chamber. It was in fact brought from the Levant, and though not well mended (for it had suffer'd much by time) is an admirable performance.

Present my affectionate respects to Mrs. Hill,

and believe me truely Yours
Wm Cowper.

WILLIAM BULL   Sunday, 25 May 1788

My dear friend —
    Ask possibilities and they shall be performed, but ask not
Hymns from a man suffering by despair as I do. I could not
sing the Lord's song were it to save my life, banish'd as I am,
not to a strange land,[1] but to a remoteness from His presence
in comparison with which the distance from East to West is
no distance; is vicinity, and cohœsion. I dare not either in
Prose or Verse allow myself to express a frame of mind which
I am conscious does not belong to me; least of all can I
venture to use the language of absolute Resignation, lest only
counterfeiting, I should for that very reason be taken strictly
at my word, and lose all my remaining comfort. Can there
not be found among those Translations of Madame Guyon
somewhat that might serve the purpose? I should think there
might. Submission to the Will of Christ my Memory tells me
is a theme that pervades them all. If so, your request is performed already, and if any alteration in them should be
necessary I will with all my heart make it. I have no objection
to giving the Graces of the Foreigner an English dress, but
insuperable ones to all false pretences and affected exhibitions
of what I do not feel.
    Hoping that you will have the grace to be resigned most
perfectly to this disappointment which you should not have
suffer'd had it been in my power to prevent it, I remain,
with our best remembrances to Mr. Thornton,

                              Ever affectionately Yours
                                    Wm Cowper.
Weston
May 25. 1788

[1] Psalm 137:4.

165

WILLIAM BULL   [Monday, 26 May 1788][1]

Address: To / The Revd. Mr. Bull / Newport-pagnell.
Formerly Miss C. M. Bull

My Dear Mr. Bull —
   Distracted as I was yesterday with hurry and distress of
spirit I sent you a crazy note I believe, but you will pardon it.
   If you will be so kind as to deliver the enclosed to Mr.
Unwin[2] you will oblige

                           Yours most sincerely Wm Cowper.

LADY HESKETH   Tuesday, 27 May 1788

Address: Lady Hesketh / New Norfolk Street / Grosvenor Square / London /
   Single Sheet.
Postmarks: MA/28/88 *and* OULNEY
Panshanger Collection

                                        The Lodge
                                          May 27
                                           1788

My dearest Cuzwuzz
   The General in a Letter which came yesterday sent me
inclosed a Copy of my Sonnet, thus introducing it. — I send
you a Copy of Verses somebody has printed in the Gentleman's Magazine for April last.[1] Independent of my partiality
towards the subject, I think the Lines themselves are good. —
   Thus it appears that my poetical project has succeeded to
my wish, and I write to him by this Post on purpose to inform
him that the Somebody in question is Myself. I send him also
a Copy of the Montagu lines with a short History of that
matter. As Barebones[2] says, — They will Amuse him —

   [1] This letter followed C's letter to Bull of 25 May 1788 in the Bull book of
letters; therefore, it was probably written on 26 May 1788, C's 'crazy note' of
'yesterday' being the letter of 25 May 1788.
   [2] John Unwin of Croydon, Mrs Unwin's brother-in-law.

   [1] 'Sonnet, Addressed to Henry Cowper, Esq.' signed T.H. appeared on p. 350
of the Apr. issue (lviii, pt. i).
   [2] Perhaps a reference to Praise-God Barebones (c.1596–1679), the leather-
seller and Fifth Monarchy man, who was engaged in a number of religious and
political controversies.

I like your proposed method well. Begin therefore, and exhibit away to Right and Left as fast as possible. You will have 5 weeks complete for the exercise of your distributory function, for it is too late to get them inserted in the Magazine for May. The first Week in June I shall send them to my Trumpeter Mr. Urban, who will sound them forth to purpose.

I no longer wonder that Mrs. Montagu stands at the head of all that is called Learned, and that every Critic vails his Bonnet to her superior Judgment. I am now reading and have reached the middle of her Essay on the Writings and Genius of Shakespear, a Book of which, strange as it may seem, though I must have read it formerly, I had absolutely forgot the existence. The Learning, the Good sense, the sound Judgment and the Wit displayed in it, fully justify not only my Compliment but all Compliments that either have been already paid to her Talents, or shall be paid hereafter. Voltaire I doubt not rejoiced that his Antagonist wrote in English, and that his Countrymen could not possibly be Judges of the dispute. Could they have known how much she was in the right, and by how many thousand miles the Bard of Avon is superior to all their Dramatists, the French Critic would have lost half his fame among them.[3]

This Book I brought home with me on Friday from Mr. Chester's. He gave me a Morning call in the beginning of last week, and appointed with us that day for a jaunt to Chicheley. Mrs. and Miss Chester[4] accordingly render'd themselves at the Lodge between 12 and 1. and carried us to the place of our destination. We spent a most agreeable day, and in the Evening were sent home right honourably in his Chaise and four.

[3] '[Shakespeare] was approved by his own age, admired by the next, and is revered, and almost adored by the present. His merit is disputed by little wits, and his errors are the jests of little critics; but there has not been a great poet, or great critic, since his time, who has not spoken of him with the highest veneration, Mr. Voltaire excepted. His translations often, his criticisms still oftener, prove he did not perfectly understand the words of the author; and therefore it is certain he could not enter into his meaning. He comprehended enough to perceive he was unobservant of some established rules of composition; the felicity with which he performs what no rules can teach escapes him.' *An Essay on the Writings and Genius of Shakspeare, Compared with the Greek and French Dramatic Poets. With Some Remarks upon the Misrepresentations of Mons. de Voltaire* (1769), pp. 10–11. Mrs Montagu was attacking Voltaire's remarks on Shakespeare in *Letters Concerning the English Nation* (1733) and *Lettres philosophiques* (1734).
[4] Perhaps Barbara. See n.3, C to Mrs Throckmorton, 1 Apr. 1791.

They are a most amiable family and I am only sorry that we live seven miles asunder, and seven of the dirtiest miles, in winter, that can be found in all the country. At present, and while summer lasts, they are as good as any.

Those pieces of Burns which you mention'd with approbation in your letter before the last, are exactly the pieces which I should have recommended to your notice in particular. Could a Nightingale be so unhappy as to acquire the scream of a Jay, she would furnish an instance somewhat resembling the case of a good poet writing in a detestable language. A man may whistle well, but if his breath be offensive one would [not w]ish[5] to sit within the wind of him. Poor Burns [is eve]r in this predicament.

Once more our Post goes every day. A poor m[an for] the small sum of a Shilling per day undertakes to walk 90 miles per week. A London Porter would disdain such wages for such labour. Neither do I imagine that our Mercury will long prove equal to it. When he gives it up I will tell you.

I saw at Mr. Chester's a head of Paris. An Antique of Parian marble. His uncle who left him the Estate brought it, as I understood Mr. Chester, from the Levant. You may suppose that I viewed it with all the Enthusiasm that belongs to a Translator of Homer. It is in reality a great curiosity and highly valuable.

Our Friend Sephus has sent me two Prints. The Lacemaker and Crazy Kate. These also I have contemplated with pleasure, having, as you know, a particular interest in them. The former of them is not more beautiful than a Lacemaker once our neighbor at Olney, though the Artist has assembled as many charms in her countenance, as I ever saw in any countenance, *One* excepted. Kate is both younger and handsomer than the Original from which I drew, but she is in a good stile and as mad as need be.

How does this hot weather suit thee my Dear in London? As for me, with all my Colonades and Bowers I am quite oppress'd by it. With Mrs. Unwin's best Love

I am ever thine
Wm Cowper.

[5] MS torn at the seal. Readings conjectured.

LADY HESKETH

Tuesday, 3 June 1788

Address: Lady Hesketh / New Norfolk Street / Grosvenor Square / London. /
Single Sheet
Postmarks: JU/4/88 *and* OULNEY
Panshanger Collection

The Lodge June 3d. 88
cold as January.

My dearest Coz,

When you told me that you were going in quest of Florence wine[1] for my Uncle, I was not without apprehensions on his account, conjecturing from its known properties the nature of his disorder. But I never learn'd, 'till your last informed me of it, that there was any thing paralytic in his case. Slight, however, I am willing to hope it must be, if a change of weather be sufficient in so considerable a degree to relieve him, and in that hope I rejoice both for his sake and for the sake of all who love and interest themselves in him. For my own part, I am rather a sufferer by that which He has found beneficial. The excessive heat of those few days was indeed oppressive, but excepting the languor that it occasion'd both in my mind and body, it was so far from being prejudicial to me that I fared the better for it. It open'd 10,000 pores in this hide of mine, by which as many mischiefs, the effects of long obstruction, began to breathe themselves forth abundantly. Then came an East wind, baneful to me at all times, but following so closely such a sultry season uncommonly noxious. To speak in the seaman's phrase not entirely strange to you, I was *taken all a-back*; and the humours which would have escaped if old Eurus would have given them leave, finding every door shut, have fallen into my eyes, the lids of which they have swell'd considerably and the immaculate White of one of them suffused with crimson, not to mention a certain brown scurf which they have thrown out on the skin beneath them, less ornamental than it is inconvenient. But in a country like this poor miserable mortals must be content to suffer all that sudden and violent changes can inflict, and if they are quit for about half the plagues that

---

[1] Horace Walpole refers to this medicinal wine in his letter of 20 Nov. 1751 to Horace Mann (*Walpole*, xxi. 156).

Caliban calls down upon Prospero[2] they may say — we are well off, and may dance for joy if the Rheumatism or cramp will let them.

I have made a Copy of my Montagu verses for Mr. Urban which I shall send him by this post. The fame of them I perceive has already taken wing, for Mr. Newton speaks of such a report having reached him, in his last Letter to me. But this, I suppose, may be accounted for from his acquaintance with Mrs. Cowper. I believe I shall refer him to the Magazine for the gratification of his curiosity, for I have not time to transcribe for any body.

Did you ever see an Advertisement by one Towle[3] a Dancing master of Newport-pagnel. If not, I will contrive to send it you for your amusement. It is the most extravagently ludicrous affair of the kind I ever saw. The Author of it had the good hap to be crazed, or he had never produced any thing half so clever, for you will ever observe that they who are said to have lost their Wits have more than other people. It is therefore only a slander with which Envy prompts the malignity of persons in their senses to asperse wittier than themselves. But there are Countries in the world where the Mad have justice done them. Where they are revered as the Subjects of Inspiration and consulted as Oracles. Poor Towle would have made a figure there, and I perhaps a more illustrious one than I shall ever make in England.

Rogers the Great, the Waggoner I mean, is gone all to pieces. I do not mean that he is Burst (which, adverting to his size you might suppose to be my meaning) but that he is Broken. In other words, a Bankrupt. The consequence is an

---

[2] See *The Tempest*, I. ii. 320–40 and II. ii. 1–3.

[3] Christopher Towle, according to an advertisement from 1783, had schools in Oxford, Coventry, Northampton, Daventry, Holburn, Wellingborough, Wolston, and Hill, in addition to Newport Pagnell. 'Mr. Towle, undertakes Concerts, Balls, and Assemblies, and Assisteth at any undertaken by any other Person, either Public or Private, the purpose to have a Dance one night in Each Month, for the Grown Gentlemen and Ladies, and a Public Day for his Scholars at the Half-Years End, and a Public Ball at the Years End in every Town he Teaches in.' In outlining the special qualities of his teaching, Towle was concerned to emphasize the amazing results he could achieve in a relatively short time span: '. . . I will make a scholar or my scholars to understand the theare [*sic*] and practical parts of Dancing, &c. better in 12 months than all or any can or hath in 36 months, for any wager they will.'

universal uproar in this country, some poor people are ruined and some rich ones shaken, Maurice Smith among others is likely to be much a Loser. I have mention'd this catastrophe in terms that do not bespeak much pity for Rogers, and because, in truth, I do not feel much. Negligence and Drink have undone him, and just before he fell and even while he was falling he contrived by imposing on others and inveigling them to indorse his Bills, to pull them down with him. But the Waggon still goes, though under whose auspices I am not at present able to say — probably those of the Creditors.

With Mrs. Unwin's best Love, I am my Dearest Coz
Evermore thy affectionate
Wm Cowper.

P.S. You need be under no concern on the Letter carrier's account. He is at his own disposal, and if his legs prove unequal to the task he has imposed on them, he has only to return to his former occupation. Others who undertook it have done so before him.

JOHN NEWTON   Thursday, 5 June 1788

Princeton

Weston
June 5. 1788
My dear friend —
It is a comfort to me that you are so kind as to make allowances for me in consideration of my being so busy a man. The truth is, that could I write with both hands, and with both at the same time, Verse with one and Prose with the other, I should not even so be able to dispatch both my poetry and my arrears of correspondence faster than I have need. The only opportunities that I can find for conversing with distant friends are in the early hour (and that sometimes reduced to half a one) before breakfast. Neither am I exempt from hindrances which while they last are insurmountable, especially one, by which I have been occasionally a sufferer all my life. I mean an inflammation of the eyes, a malady under which I have lately labour'd, and from which I am at

this moment only in a small degree relieved. The last sudden change of the weather from heat almost insupportable to a Cold as severe as is commonly felt in mid-winter, would have disabled me entirely for all sorts of scribbling had I not favour'd the weak part a little and given my eyes a respite.

It is certain that we do not live far from Olney, but small as the distance is it has too often the effect of a separation between the Beans and us. He is a man with whom, when I can converse at all, I can converse on terms perfectly agreeable to myself. Who does not distress me with forms nor yet disgust me by the neglect of them, whose manners are easy and natural and his observations always sensible. I often therefore wish them nearer neighbours.

We have heard nothing of the Powleys since they left us a fortnight ago, and should be uneasy at their silence on such an occasion, did we not know that she cannot write, and that He on his first return to his parish after a long absence, may possibly find it difficult. Her we found much improved in her health and spirits, and him, as always, affectionate, and obliging. It was an agreeable visit, and as it was order'd for me, I happen'd to have better spirits than I have enjoyed at any time since.

I shall rejoice if your friend Mr. Phillips,[1] influenced by what you told him of my present engagements, shall waive his application to me for a poem on the Slave-trade. I account myself honour'd by his intention to sollicit me on the subject, and it would give me pain to refuse him, which inevitably I shall be constrained to do. The more I have consider'd it the more I have convinced myself that it is not a promising theme for verse. General censure on the iniquity of the practise will avail nothing, the world has been overwhelm'd with such remarks already, and to particularize all the horrors of it were an employment for the mind both of the poet and his readers of which they would necessarily soon grow weary. For my own part I cannot contemplate the subject very nearly without a degree of abhorrence that affects my spirits and sinks them below the pitch requisite for success in verse.

[1] James Phillips, the Quaker bookseller, stationer, and printer, who operated from 2 George Yard, Lombard Street, from 1775 to 1829. Ian Maxted, *The London Book Trades* (1977), p. 176.

Lady Hesketh recommended it to me some months since, and then I declined it for these reasons and for others which need not be mention'd here.

I return you many thanks for all your intelligence concerning the success of the Gospel in far countries, and shall rejoice in a sight of Mr. Van Lier's[2] letter, which being so voluminous I rather think you should bring with you when you can take your flight to Weston, than commit it any other conveyance.

Remember that it is now Summer and that the Summer flies fast, and that we shall be happy to see you and yours as speedily and for as long a time as you can afford.[3] We are sorry, truly so, that Mrs. Newton is so frequently and so much indisposed. Accept our best Love to you both and to your good niece Betsy, and believe me my Dear Friend,

affectionately Yours
Wm Cowper.

After what I have said on the subject of my writing engagements, I doubt not but you will excuse my transcribing the Verses to Mrs. Montagu, especially considering that my eyes are weary with what I have written this morning already. I feel somewhat like an impropriety in referring you to the next Gentleman's Magazine but at the present juncture I know not how to do better.

JOSEPH HILL   Sunday, 8 June 1788

Address: Joseph Hill Esqre / Chancery Office / London.
Postmark: NEWPORT/PAGNEL
Cowper Johnson

My dear friend —
Your Letter brought me the very first intelligence of the

---

[2] Helperus Ritzema van Lier (1764–93), a Dutch minister of the Reformed Church, settled in Cape Town in 1785 and died there. In 1790 C translated the letters in Latin from van Lier to Newton which appeared as *The Power of Grace Illustrated* in 1792.

[3] The Newtons stayed in Olney and Weston from 12 July until about the middle of Aug.

event it mentions.[1] My last Letter from Lady Hesketh gave me reason enough to expect it but the certainty of it was unknown to me 'till I learn'd it by your information. If a gradual decline, the consequence of great age, be a sufficient preparation of the mind to encounter such a loss, our minds were certainly prepared to meet it. Yet to you I need not say that no preparation can supersede the feelings of the heart on such occasions, while our friends yet live, inhabitants of the same world with ourselves, they seem still to live to *us*, we are sure that they sometimes think of us, and however improbable it may seem, it is never impossible that we may see each other once again. But the grave, like a great gulph, swallows all such expectations, and in the moment when a beloved friend sinks into it, a thousand tender recollections awaken a regret that will be felt in spite of all reasonings and let our warnings have been what they may. Thus it is that I take my last leave of poor Ashley, whose heart toward me was ever truly parental, and to whose memory I owe a tenderness and respect that can never leave me.

Every Letter of yours brings me some proof of your friendship, and lays me under some new obligation. Before I close this I must remember to thank you for the Ointment, which could not have arrived more seasonably; our late violent changes of weather from extreme heat to the opposite degree of cold, having inflamed my eyes exceedingly. By the same basket I received a very fine Turbot and Lobster, for which — Thanks also. I beg you to present my affectionate respects to Mrs. Hill, and to believe me

> My dear friend —
> Ever yours
> Wm Cowper.

Weston Underwood
June 8th. 1788

---

[1] Ashley Cowper died at Old Palace Yard, Westminster, on 6 June 1788, aged 87. C composed a poem lamenting his uncle's death at about this time, but he did not send it to Lady Hesketh or any other member of the family. 'Lines Composed for a Memorial of Ashley Cowper, Esq.' was first published in *Hayley*.

LADY HESKETH   Tuesday, 10 June 1788

Address: Lady Hesketh / New Norfolk Street / Grosvenor Square / London. /
    Single sheet
Postmarks: JU/11/88 *and* OULNEY
Panshanger Collection

The Lodge
June 10. 1788.

My dearest Coz —
  Your kind letter of precaution to Mr. Gregson sent him
hither as soon as Chapel service was ended in the Evening,
but he found me already apprized of the event that occasion'd
it by a line from Sephus received a few hours before. My dear
Uncle's death awaken'd in me many reflections, which for a
time sunk my spirits. A man like him would have been
mourned had he doubled the age he reached; at any age his
death would have been felt as a loss that no survivor could
repair. And though it was not probable that, for my own
part, I should ever see him more, yet the consciousness that
he still lived was a comfort to me. Let it comfort us now that
we have lost him only at a time when Nature could afford
him to us no longer, that as his life was blameless so his death
was without anguish, and that he is gone to heaven. I know
not that human life in its most prosperous state, can present
any thing to our wishes half so desireable as such a close of it.
  Not to mingle this subject with others that would ill sort
with it, I will add no more at present than a warm hope that
you and your Sister will be able effectually to avail yourselves
of all the consolatory matter with which it abounds. You
gave yourselves, while he lived, to a Father whose life was
doubtless prolong'd by your attentions, and whose tenderness
of disposition made him always deeply sensible of your
kindness. In this respect, as well as in many others, his Old
Age was the happiest that I have ever known, and I give you
both joy of having had so fair an opportunity, and of having
so well used it, to approve yourselves equal to the calls of
such a duty, in the sight of God and Man.
  Adieu! my Dearest Coz — I am with Mrs. Unwin's affectionate Compliments on the occasion. Ever thine —

Wm Cowper.

LADY HESKETH   Monday, 16 June 1788

Address: Lady Hesketh / New Norfolk Street / Grosvenor Square / London
Postmarks: JU/18/88 *and* NEWPORT/PAGNEL
Panshanger Collection

The Lodge Monday
June 16. 1788

My dearest Coz

Although I knew that you must be very much occupied on the present most affecting occasion, yet not hearing from you, I began to be uneasy on your account and to fear that your health might have suffer'd by the fatigue both of body and of Spirits that you must have undergone, 'till a Letter that reached me yesterday from the General, set my heart at rest so far as that cause of anxiety was in question. He speaks of my Uncle in the tenderest terms; such as show how truly sensible he was of the amiableness and excellence of his character, and how deeply he regrets his loss. We have indeed lost one who has not left his like in the present generation of our family, and whose equal in all respects no future generation of it will probably produce. My memory retains so perfect an impression of him that had I been painter instead of poet I could from those faithful traces have perpetuated his face and form with the most minute exactness. And this I the rather wonder at, because many with whom I was equally conversant five and twenty years ago have almost faded out of all recollection with me. But He made impressions not soon to be effaced, and was in figure, in temper and in manner, and in numerous other respects, such as I shall never behold again. I often think what a joyful interview there has been between him and some of his cotemporaries who went before him. The truth of the matter is, my Dear, that they are the happy ones, and that we shall never be such ourselves 'till we have joined their party. Could I hope for that felicity myself I should consider neither your parents nor my own as lost to me, but expect speedily to rejoin them. And in the mean time I should exult as often as I felt my clay totter, and look forward to its fall with rapture. For, almost to repeat what I said in my last, can there be any thing so worthy of our warmest wishes, as to enter on an eternal unchange-

176

able state in blessed fellowship and communion with those whose society we valued most and for the best reasons, while they continued with us? A few steps more through a vain foolish world and this happiness will be yours; but be not hasty my Dear to accomplish thy journey, for of all that live thou art one whom I can least spare, for thou also art one who shall not leave thy equal behind thee.

I am my Dearest Coz, with Mrs. Unwin's affectionate Compliments most truly thine

Wm Cowper.

WALTER BAGOT   Tuesday, 17 June 1788

Morgan Library

Weston June. 17. 1788

My dear Walter

You think me, no doubt, a tardy Correspondent, and such I am, but not willingly. Many hindrances have intervened, and the most difficult to surmount have been those which the East and North East winds have occasion'd, breathing Winter upon the roses of June, and inflaming my eyes ten times more sensible of the inconvenience than they. The vegetables of England seem like our Animals of a hardier and bolder nature than those of other countries. In France and Italy flowers blow because it is warm, but here, in spite of the Cold. The season however is somewhat mended at present, and my eyes with it, not to mention some other maladies with which I have been afflicted. Finding myself this Morning in perfect ease of body, I seize the welcome opportunity to do something at least toward the discharge of my arrears to you.

I am glad that you liked my song, and if I liked the others myself so well as that I sent you, I would transcribe for you them also. But I sent *that*, because I accounted it the best. Slavery, and especially Negro Slavery because the cruellest, is an odious and disgusting subject. Twice or thrice I have been assailed with entreaties to write a poem on that theme; but beside that it would be in some sort treason against Homer to abandon him for any other matter, I felt myself so much hurt in my spirits the moment I enter'd on the contemplation of it, that I have at least determined absolutely to have nothing more to do with it. There are some scenes of horror on which my imagination can dwell not without some complacence, but then they are such scenes as God not man produces. In earthquakes, high winds, tempestuous seas, there is the grand as well as the terrible. But when man is active to disturb there is such meanness in the design and such cruelty in the execution that I both hate and despise the whole operation, and feel it a degradation of poetry to employ her in the description of it. I hope also that the generality of my countrymen have more generosity in their nature than to want the fiddle of Verse to go before them in the performance of an act to which they are invited by the loudest calls of Humanity.

Since you heard from me last we have spent a day at Chicheley. I need not add a most agreeable one. Mrs. and Miss Chester came hither and coached us away at noon, and your brother sent us home in the Evening in his Chaise and four. The Waggoner of Sherrington having lately become bankrupt, the ingenuity of our neighbours immediately contrived by that circumstance to account for our jaunt to Chicheley. Mr. Chester, they said, had lost a thousand pounds by Rogers, and had sent for me being a Lawyer to consult with me on the likeliest means of recovery. It was with great pleasure I assured them that they were in this instance, as they are in all others in which they exercise conjecture, most entirely wrong. I am glad that I have seen so amiable a family, so happy in themselves and in each other. May they ever be so.

I congratulate you as you bid me on the recovery of your youngest child from innoculation, and was sincerely concern'd for your brother Richard's loss which I hope however will not prove irreparable. — Mrs. Unwin, a head-ach excepted is tolerably well, and begs to be remember'd to you. Breakfast calls, and then Homer.

Adieu — Ever Yours Wm Cowper.

PS My paper mourns and my seal.[1] It is for the death of a venerable Uncle — Ashley Cowper — at the age of 87.

[1] There is no seal on this letter, and no indication of mourning on the paper

MRS KING   Thursday, 19 June 1788

Address: Mrs. King / Pertenhall near / Kimbolton / Huntingdonshire
Postmarks: [J] U/20/88[1] *and* OULNEY
Princeton

Weston Underwood
June 19. 1788

My dear Madam,

You must think me a tardy correspondent, unless you have had charity enough for me to suppose that I have met with other hindrances than those of indolence and inattention. With these I cannot charge myself, for I am never idle by choice, and inattentive to you I certainly have not been, but on the contrary can safely affirm that every day I have thought on you. My silence has been occasion'd by a malady to which I have all my life been subject, an inflammation of the eyes. The last sudden change of weather from excessive heat to a wintry degree of cold, occasion'd it, and at the same time gave me a pinch of the rheumatic kind, from both which disorders I have but just recover'd. I do not suppose that our climate has been much alter'd since the days of our fore-fathers the Picts, but certainly the Human Constitution in this country has been alter'd much. Inured as we are from our cradles to every vicissitude in a climate more various than any other, and in possession of all that modern refinement has been able to contrive for our security, we are yet as subject to blights as the tenderest blossoms of Spring, and are so well admonished of every change in the atmosphere by our bodily feelings as hardly to have any need of a weather-glass to mark them. For this we are no doubt indebted to the multitude of our accommodations, for it was not possible to retain the hardiness that originally belong'd to our race under the delicate management to which for many ages we have now been accustom'd. I can hardly doubt that a Bull dog or a Game cock might be made just as susceptible of injuries from weather as myself, were he dietted and in all respects accommodated as I am. Or if the project did not succeed in the first

of the letter. The letter itself was probably enclosed in another sealed sheet, no longer extant.

---

[1] The date stamp is cropped.

instance (for we ourselves did not become what we are at once) in process of time however and in a course of many generations, it would certainly take effect. Let such a dog be fed in his infancy with pap, Naples biscuit,[2] and boiled Chicken, let him be wrapt in flannel at night, sleep on a good feather-bed, and ride out in a Coach for an Airing, and if his posterity do not become slight limb'd, puney and valetudinarian it will be a wonder. Thus our parents, and their parents, and the parents of both were managed; and thus ourselves; and the consequence is that instead of being weather-proof even without cloathing, furs and flannels are not warm enough to defend us. It is observable however that though we have by these means lost much of our pristine vigour, our days are not the fewer. We live as long as those whom on account of the sturdiness of their frame the poets supposed to have been the progeny of Oaks. Perhaps too they had little feeling, and for that reason also might be imagined to be so descended. For a very robust athletic habit seems inconsistent with much sensibility. But sensibility is the *sine quâ non* of real happiness. If therefore our lives have not been shorten'd and if our feelings have been render'd more exquisite as our habit of body has become more delicate, on the whole perhaps we have no cause to complain but are rather gainers by our degeneracy.

Do you consider what you do when you ask one poet his opinion of another? Yet I think I can give you an honest answer to your question and without the least wish to nibble. Thomson was admirable in description, but it always seemed to me that there was somewhat of affectation in his stile, and that his numbers are sometimes not well harmonized. I could wish too with Dr. Johnson that he had confined himself to this country,[3] for when he describes what he never saw, one

---

[2] Perhaps a form of arrowroot. *OED* gives several citations of this.

[3] Johnson did not make such a statement regarding Thomson. C may have been remembering inaccurately Johnson's review of Joseph Warton's *Essay on the Writings and Genius of Pope* in *The Literary Magazine*, i (1756), 36: 'Mentioning Thomson and other descriptive poets, he [Warton] remarks that writers fail in their copies for want of acquaintance with originals, and justly ridicules those who think they can form just ideas of valleys, mountains, and rivers in a garret of the Strand. For this reason I cannot regret with this author, that Pope laid aside his design of writing American pastorals; for as he must have painted scenes which he never saw, and manners he never knew, his performance, though it might have

is forced to read him with some allowance for possible misrepresentation. He was however a true poet and his lasting fame has proved it. Believe me, my Dear Madam, with my best respects to Mr. King —

> most truly Yours
> Wm Cowper.

P.S. I am extremely sorry that you have been so much indisposed, and hope that your next will bring me a more favorable account of your health. I know not why, but I rather suspect that you do not allow yourself sufficient air and exercise; the physicians call them Non-naturals. I suppose to deter their patients from the use of them.

SAMUEL ROSE
Monday, 23 June 1788

Address: Samuel Rose Esqre. No. 23 / Percy Street / Rathbone Place / London.
Postmark: JU/24/88
Princeton

> Weston Underwood
> June 23. 1788

Dear Sir —

When I tell you that an unanswer'd letter troubles my conscience in some degree like a crime, you will think me endued with a most heroic patience who have so long submitted to that trouble on account of yours not answer'd yet. But the truth is that I have been much engaged. Homer as you know affords me constant employment; beside which, I have rather what may be called, considering the privacy in which I have long lived, a numerous correspondence; to one of my friends in particular, a near and much loved relation, I write weekly, and sometimes twice in the week. Nor are these my only excuses. The sudden changes of the weather have much affected me, and especially with a disorder most unfavorable to the work of Letter-writing, an inflammation in my eyes. With all these apologies I approach you once more not altogether despairing of forgiveness.

been a pleasing amusement of fancy, would have exhibited no representation of nature or of life.'

It has pleased God to give us rain, without which this part of our County at least must soon have become a Desert. The meadows have been parched to a January Brown, and we have fodder'd our cattle for some time as in the winter. — The goodness and power of God are never, I believe, so universally acknowledged as at the end of a long drought. Man is naturally a selfsufficient animal, and in all concerns that seem to lie within the sphere of his own ability, thinks little or not at all of the need he always has of protection and furtherance from above. But he is sensible that the clouds will not assemble at his bidding, and that though clouds assemble, they will not fall in showers because he commands them. When therefore at last the blessing descends, you shall hear even in the streets the most irreligious and thoughtless with one voice exclaim — Thank God! Confessing themselves indebted to his favour, and willing, at least so far as words go, to give him the glory. I can hardly doubt therefore that the earth is sometimes parched, and the crops endanger'd, in order that the multitude may not want a memento to whom they owe them, nor absolutely forget the power on which all depend for all things.

Our solitary part of the year is over. Mrs. Unwin's daughter and Son-in-law have lately spent some time with us; we shall shortly receive from London, our old friends the Newtons. (He was once Minister of Olney.) And when they leave us, we expect that Lady Hesketh will succeed them, perhaps to spend the Summer here and possibly the Winter also. The Summer indeed is leaving us at a rapid rate, as do all the seasons, and though I have mark'd their flight so often, I know not which is the swiftest. Man is never so deluded as when he dreams of his own duration. The answer of the old Patriarch to Pharaoh may be adopted by every man at the end of the longest life — Few and evil have been the days of the years of my pilgrimage.[1] Whether we look back from 50 or from twice 50 the Past appears equally a dream, and we can only be said truly to have lived while we have been profitably employ'd. Alas then! Making the necessary deductions, how short is life! Were men in general to save themselves

---

[1] Genesis 48:9.

all the steps they take to no purpose, or a bad one, what numbers who are now active would become sedentary!

Thus I have sermonized through my paper. Living where you live you can bear with me the better. I always follow the leading of my unconstrained thoughts when I write to a friend, be they grave or otherwise. Homer reminds me of you every day. I am now in the 21st Iliad.

Adieu! Yours affectionately Wm Cowper.

LADY HESKETH   Monday, 23 June 1788

Address: Lady Hesketh / New Norfolk Street / Grosvenor Square / London.
Postmarks: JU/24/88 *and* NEWPORT/PAGNEL
Carl H. Pforzheimer Library

The Lodge June 23. 1788

My dearest Coz —

Mr. Newton and Mrs. and their niece, who, as you know, have long intended us a visit, will be here in about three weeks. I mention this as a necessary piece of information, and in the hope that at your own best time you also will find an opportunity to repair to Weston. They will not stay more than ten days, or at most a fortnight. This at least, I imagine, may be taken for granted, ministers who attend to their charge seldom allowing themselves a longer absence. I learn'd this day, you may guess that I had it from the quarter above-mention'd, the joyful news that you intend two trips hither. To this intelligence I owe the only glad moment that I have seen since I rose this morning. Ratify it yourself, and that one moment will multiply itself into many.

We expect the Frogs at home again by the end of the week. I yesterday received from them a large box containing a very handsome present of an Engraving to hang over the parlour Chimney. The subject is, Priam's interview with Achilles when he redeems the dead body of Hector. It is engraved after a picture of Hamilton, by Cunego.[1] I felt myself highly gratified on the receipt of it, and it will strike you I dare say

[1] The engraving, *Priam Redeems the Dead Body of Hector*, by Domenico Cunego (1726–1803) after Gavin Hamilton (1730–97) was issued in 1766. We do not know the present whereabouts of C's print. The engraving is reproduced as

as a well-judged and kind proof of their regard. They are on all occasions to the last degree friendly and obliging.

Being on the subject of presents I must mention a circumstance odd enough. Three baskets of fish have arrived within the last half year from some anonymous Donor. They are directed to me by the description of Mr. Cooper at Weston, and both the writing and Spelling are of the coarsest kind, in order, I suppose, to puzzle all conjecture. The first basket contained Lobsters, which while we were eating it struck me that they must have been designed for our neighbour Cooper the Taylor.[2] We made ourselves merry for a time with the thought that we had eaten lobsters never design'd for us, but on enquiry found that the taylor had no claim upon us for depredation. The second basket contained Maccarel remarkably large, and the third a very fine Turbot.

I send you Mrs. Montagu's copy[3] my Dear, but with a grudging mind, sorely unwilling to do it so much at your expence. The more, because in ten days' time the world will be in possession of them.

The late rains have revived us. 'Till they came, the fields were withering for want of water, but now they laugh again.

Mr. Pitt has charm'd me by the noble manner in which he has taken up the business of the Slave-trade. Mr. Newton who understands the Subject well, tells me that the limitation of the number of Slaves to the tonnage[4] will of itself go near to abolish the traffic, for that it will hardly be worth while, on those terms, to send any ships to Africa at all.

I hope, my Dear, thou wilt not make thy letters the less frequent because thou canst not frank them,[5] or by waiting to get them frank'd. Ten times the money or cash would not do me half so much good as always it does to hear from thee. I am, my Coz,

most affectionately Yours
Wm Cowper.

illustration 28 in Dora Wiebenson, 'Subjects from Homer's *Iliad* in Neoclassical Art', *Art Bulletin*, xlvi, No. 1 (Mar. 1964), 23–37.

[2] We cannot identify him further.

[3] C is referring to a copy of 'On Mrs. Montagu's Feather-Hangings' intended for the lady herself. See n.1, C to Lady Hesketh, 12 May 1788.

[4] See n.2, C to Newton, 19 Apr. 1788. For Pitt's support of Dolben's proposal, see John Ehrman, *The Younger Pitt* (1969), p. 394.

[5] Ashley Cowper had franked Lady Hesketh's letters to C.

A very good Quaker, named Phillips,[6] whom I never saw, but who wished me to write on the Slave Trade which I declined doing, sends me by Mr. Newton one of Wedgwood's original Cameos on that subject.[7] I understand that they are not purchaseable which makes it the more valuable. Wedgwood refused to sell them, affirming that it should never be said of him that he had sold a Negro.

JOHN NEWTON   Tuesday, 24 June 1788

Princeton *and* Charles Ryskamp[1]

Weston June 24.
1788

My dear friend —
    I rejoice that my letter found you at all points so well prepared to answer it according to our wishes. I have written to Lady Hesketh to apprize her of your intended journey hither, and she having as yet made no assignation with us herself, will easily adjust her measures to the occasion.
    I have not lately had an opportunity of seeing Mr. Bean. The late rains which have revived the hopes of the farmers, have intercepted our communication. I hear however that he meets with not a little trouble in his progress toward a reformation of Olney manners, and that the Sabbath which he wishes to have hallow'd by a stricter and more general observation of it, is through the brutality of the lowest order, a day of more turbulence and riot than any other. At the latter end of last week he found himself obliged to make

[6] See n.1, C to Newton, 5 June 1788.
[7] 'From July 1787 till the close of his life Wedgwood was more or less active in the cause of the Abolition of Slavery. He formed one of the Society's Committee, and attended it whenever he was in town.' Under Wedgwood's supervision, a design of a seal for the Society was modelled and presented on 16 Oct. 1787. The design shows a slave on his knees and carries the motto: 'Am I not a man and a brother?' 'Seals in all the various bodies, and cameos in jasper — the ground white, the relief black — were made in large quantities, and distributed gratuitously, as well as sold. . . . As a seal, a ring, a shirt-pin, or coat-buttons, gentlemen wore it; as also ladies, in every possible form, even mounted as pins for their hair.' Eliza Meteyard, *The Life of Josiah Wedgwood* (1866), pp. 565–6.

[1] The final paragraph and signature to this letter survive in a fragment in the possession of Charles Ryskamp.

another trip to the Justice, in company with 2 or 3 of the principal inhabitants. What passed I have not learn'd, but I understand their errand to have been, partly at least, to efface the evil impressions made on his Worship's mind by a rascal who had applied to him a day or two before for a warrant against the Constable; which however he did not obtain. I rather fear that the Constables are not altogether judicious in the exercise either of their justice or their mercy. Some who have seem'd proper objects of punishment they have released on a hopeless promise of better behaviour, and others whose offence has been personal against themselves, though in other respects less guilty, they have set in the Stocks. The Ladies however, and of course the Ladies of Silver End in particular, give them the most trouble, being always active on these occasions as well as clamorous, and both with impunity. For the sex are privileged in the free use of their tongues and of their nails, the parliament having never yet laid them under any penal restrictions. And they employ them accordingly. Johnson the Constable[2] lost much of his skin and still more of his coat in one of these Sunday battles, and had not Ashburner[3] hasted to his aid, had probably been completely stripp'd of both. With such a zeal are these Fair Ones animated, though unfortunately for all parties, rather erroneously.

What you tell me of the effect that the limitation of numbers to tonnage is likely to have on the Slave-trade gives me the greatest pleasure. Should it amount in the issue to an abolition of the traffic, I shall account it indeed an argument of great wisdom in our youthful minister. A silent and indirect way of doing it, is I suppose the only safe one. At the same time in how horrid a light does it place the trade itself when it comes to be proved by consequences, that the mere article of a little elbow room for the poor creatures in their passage to the islands could not be secured by an order of Parliament, without the utter annihilation of it! If so it prove, no man deserving to be called a man, can say that it ought to subsist a moment longer.

[2] Unidentified further.   [3] Unidentified further.

My Writing time is expended and breakfast is at hand. With our joint Love to the Trio and our best wishes for your good journey to Weston I remain my Dear Friend

> affectionately Yours
> Wm Cowper.

P.S. I beg that you will present my best respects to Mr. Phillips with many thanks for his obliging present which I shall highly value.

LADY HESKETH   Friday, 27 June 1788

Address: Lady Hesketh / New Norfolk Street / Grosvenor Square / London.
Postmarks: JU/30/88 *and* OULNEY
Princeton

> The Lodge
> June 27. 1788

For the sake of a longer visit, my dearest Coz, I can be well content to wait. The Country, this country at least, is pleasant at all times, and when Winter is come, or near at hand, we shall have the better chance for being snug. I know your passion for *Retirement indeed*, or for what we call here *Deedy*[1] Retirement, and the Frogs intending to return to Bath with their mother when her visit at the Hall is over, you will then find here exactly the retirement in question. I have made in the Orchard the best Winter walk in all the parish, shelter'd from the East and from the North East, and open to the Sun, except at his rising, all the day. Then we will have Homer and Don Quixote, and then we will have saunter and Chat, and one Laugh more before we die. Our Orchard is alive with creatures of all kinds, poultry of ev'ry denomination swarms in it, and pigs the drollest in the world. By that time indeed they will have ceased to be pigs and will probably be converted into pork or bacon, but we have also a most fruitful sow from whom we expect a continual and endless succession of pigs similar to these. At her first litter she produced Nine to the wonder of the whole village, and on that occasion all the Connoisseurs in such matters came to

---

[1] 'Actual, real' (*OED*). C is the only source given for this definition of the word.

visit her, with a man called John Watson[2] at the head of them who attends as man midwife at the production of all such births in the neighborhood. It is not common you must know, my Dear, for swine to produce so many at their first accouchement, and we were accordingly the envy of all around us.

I rejoice that we have a Cousin Charles[3] also, as well as a Cousin Henry, who has had the address to win the good-likings of the chancellor. May he fare the better for it! As to myself, I have long since ceased to have any expectations from that quarter. Yet if he were indeed mortified as you say (and no doubt you have particular reasons for thinking so) and repented to that degree of his hasty exertions in favour of the present Occupant, who can tell? He wants neither means nor management, but can easily at some future time redress the evil, if he chuses to do it. But in the mean time life steals away, and shortly neither he will be in circumstances to do me a kindness nor I to receive one at his hands. Let him make haste therefore or he will die a promise in my debt which he will never be able to perform. Your communications on this subject are as safe as you can wish them. We divulge nothing but what might appear in the Magazine, nor that neither without great consideration.

I have a stomach that is the plague of my life, and tomorrow morning, just when other people will be rising with a good appetite to their Breakfasts, I shall swallow Tartar Emetic,[4] alias one abomination in order to get rid of half a dozen. Till One o'clock this morning I was employed, sitting upright in bed, in the sort of exercise that such a stomach always makes necessary, and have for three or four days past been occupied in the same agreeable manner, after dinner. It is not possible tamely to submit to it any longer.

[2] Unidentified further.

[3] Charles Cowper (1765–1820), who had been called to the Bar in 1788 and who would serve as Commissioner of Bankrupts from *c.*1789 to 1801. See C to Mrs Cowper, 20 Oct. 1766.

[4] As he makes clear at the very opening of his letter to Lady Hesketh of 5 July, C was taking a form of fixed salt of tartar which is made from crude tartar as opposed to emetic tartar which is from cream of tartar. See John Quincy, *Pharmacopoeia Officinalis & Extemporanea or, A Complete English Dispensatory* ... (1726), pp. 345–7.

I must tell you a feat of my Dog Beau. Walking by the River-side I observed some Water-Lilies floating at a little distance from the Bank. They are a large white flower with an Orange colour'd Eye, and extremely beautiful. I [had a de]sire[5] to gather one, and having your long Cane in my hand, by the help of it endeavor'd to bring one of them within my reach. But the attempt proved vain and I walked forward. Beau had all the while observed me very attentively. Returning soon after toward the same place, I observed him plunge into the river while I was about 40 yards distant from him, and when I had nearly reached the spot, he swam to land with a Lily in his mouth, which he came and lay'd at my foot.

Mr. Rose, whom I have mentioned to you heretofore as a visitor of mine for the first time soon after you left us, writes me word that he has seen my Ballads against the Slavemongers, but not in Print. Where he met with them I know not. Mr. Bull begged hard for leave to Print them at Newport pagnel, and I refused, thinking that it would be wrong to anticipate the Nobility, Gentry and others at whose pressing instance I composed them, in *their* designs to print them. But perhaps I need not have been so squeamish, for the opportunity to publish them in London seems now not only ripe but rotten. I am well content. There is but one of the three with which I am myself satisfied, though I have heard them all well spoken of. But there are very few things of my own composing that I can endure to read when they have been written a month, though at first they seem to me to be all perfection.

Mrs. Unwin who has been much the happier since the time of your return hither has been in some sort settled, begs me to make her kindest remembrances — Yours my Dear most truly

Wm Cowper.

P.S. The Fish was not from Sephus.

---

[5] MS torn.

LADY HESKETH   Saturday, 5 July 1788

Address: Lady Hesketh / New Norfolk Street / Grosvenor Square / London.
Postmarks: JY/7/88 *and* OULNEY
Olney

The Lodge
July 5. 1788

Not *Emetic Tartar*, my Coz, but the *soluble Salt of Tartar*, has been of much sov'reign use to me. I have not ceased to take it since the time when Dr. Ash[1] prescribed it, and believe myself indebted to it in a great degree for the measure of health that I have enjoyed. But with all its virtues it has not superseded the necessity of now and then (once or twice in a year perhaps) a Dose of its namesake the Emetic. My stomach is much improved since the last operation, and yet is in all respects a troublesome, and in one, a very singular stomach. For you must know, my Dear, to carry on the *Johnsonianism* a little farther, that take what I will of the Emetic kind, I could not absolutely swear when the operation is over that I have *spuked*[2] at all. The only effect of it seems to be that it seems to be that it disturbs certain air-bubbles contained in the *organ* of *digestion*, which as they escape out of said organ through the gullet or throat, bring with them a part of what I wish to be rid of. But your true roaring vomit that pumps up the very dregs from the bottom, is an exploit to which I am by no means equal. Accordingly much is left where it was.

I have seen no more of Mrs. Piozzi's Letters than the Magazine and Review have afforded.[3] If I remember right, the Letters of Johnson pleased me chiefly on this account,

[1] Dr John Ash (1723–98) was born in Warwickshire and educated at Trinity College, Oxford (BA, 1743; MA, 1746; MB, 1750; MD, 1754). He founded the general hospital at Birmingham, where he remained until he moved to London in 1787. The recipient of many honours and distinctions, Ash established the Eumelian Club.

[2] C is using a variant spelling of spew.

[3] *Letters to and from the Late Samuel Johnson, LL.D.* had appeared on Saturday, 8 Mar. 1788. Some reviewers were hostile to Mrs Piozzi's publication on the grounds that it contained little of literary value. *The Gentleman's Magazine*, however, did not agree with this verdict: 'We cannot say that we think there is any thing unjustifiable, as some seem to imagine, in such a publication as this. Johnson himself would have answered those who think it unjustifiable, in some such way as this, perhaps: "No, sir; I cannot see any harm in the business. Do the

that though on all other occasions he wrote like nobody, in his Letters he expresses himself somewhat in the stile of other folks. For I hate Triplets in Prose, and can hardly think even *His* good sense a sufficient counterpoise for his affectation. I admire your New way to pay off old scores, and to save yourself from the Royal Durance alias the King's Bench, by printing my Letters.[4] You have my free permission to do it, but not 'till I am dead. No. Nor even then 'till you have given them a complete revisal, erasing all that the Critics in such matters would condemn. In which case my Dear thou wilt reduce thy Noble to ninepence, and must take thy seat in a gaol at last.

I shall be as happy in the arrival of my Solander[5] as he whose name it bears was to arrive once more in England after his circumnavigation. To be the proprietor of any thing that was once my Uncle's will make me rich. A mere trifle acquires value by having been the property of such a man; but his watch will be a Vade mecum with which I shall hold a thousand conversations when I am in the woods alone; nor will his Snuff-box fall a whit short of it as a most desireable companion. The Love I bore him, and the honour I have for his memory will make them both inestimable to me. The Box therefore charged with these treasures will both for its own sake and for the sake of its contents, be an addition not to my convenience only but likewise to my real comfort. Not forgetting the Dean's tooth-pick.[6] For the Dean also was justly one of the principal boasts of our family, and a man whom I loved and honour'd most devoutly. I have not words

Letters deduct from the man's good fame? Do they prove him to be in any respect less a man of virtue, or more a fool? No sir. Then where is the harm? He has written to women as wise men write when they write to women and he has written to children as wise men write when they write to children.''' (lviii, pt. 1, 233.) Arthur Murphy wrote the piece which appeared in *The Monthly Review* (lxxviii, 326) in which he avers: 'We see him in his undress, that is, the undress of his mind, which, unlike that of the body, was never slovenly.' There is an excellent discussion of this volume in James L. Clifford, *Hester Lynch Piozzi* (2nd edn., Oxford, 1952), pp. 314–30.

[4] The King's Bench was a debtors' prison in Southwark until 1842.

[5] A box made in the form of a book for holding papers, maps, and botanical specimens; this contrivance is named after the Swedish botanist, Daniel Charles Solander (see C to Hill, 8 Aug. 1779 and nn.3 and 4).

[6] C is referring to his cousin, Spencer Cowper (1713–74), who served as Dean of Durham from 1746 until his death. It was a tooth-pick case (see p. 220).

to tell you how much I feel myself obliged by the distinction made in my favour on this occasion, and I beg you will tell your sister so, giving her at the same time my sincerest thanks and acknowledgments. With respect to the conveyance of them hither, I think I shall be easier if they come by the Wellingbro' Coach, having more confidence in it than in the Waggon. The passage is quicker, the quantity of Lumber less, and the chances of damage are fewer in proportion. It is also an established law that the trusty Kitch meets always the Coach at its arrival, and brings hither our parcels immediately. Whereas we wait sometimes 2 or 3 days, and sometimes longer, for a parcel sent by the waggon. Thanks too for the Chocolate.

Beau's performance was exactly such as I represented it, without any embellishment. I may now add that the next time we walk'd to the same place together, he repeated it. With respect to his diet it is always of the most salutary kind; Lights he never eats, and liver, having observed that it makes him sick, we never give him now. Bread he eats in abundance, and it is the only thing for which he begs with much importunity. He is regularly comb'd, and his Ears which are remarkably handsome, are my own particular care. They gather burrs while he threads all the thickets in his way, from which I deliver them myself as soon as we get home. But having taught him to take the water and even to delight in it, I never give him a forced washing, lest he should contract an Hydrophobia and refuse the river. I have observed too that dogs often washed get Rheumatisms, because they do not dry themselves by exercise, but lie down in their damp coats which is hurtful to every thing but a Highlander.

The Frogs are to come home this day by Dinner.

I want much to see what Resolution the Chancellor moved against Mr. Rose.[7] At least he will give him a trimming, & a good one, I doubt not. Ever yours, my Dear!

Wm Cowper.

P.S. I forgot to tell you that my Watch is no Repeater, neither good for much in its kind. It was made at Cambridge for my

---

[7] We have not been able to locate such a resolution.

Brother and brought home the day after his death. A Metal one, for which I paid Six Guineas. — It has been one of my chief employments to wish for a better.

JOSEPH HILL   Sunday, 6 July 1788

Cowper Johnson

Weston. July 6. 1788.

My dear friend —
    Bitter constraint and sad occasion dear[1]
have compelled me to draw on you for the Sum of twenty pounds payable to John Higgins[2] Esqre. or Order. The draft bears date July 5th. — You will excuse my giving you this trouble in consideration that I am a poet, and can consequently draw for money much more easily than I can earn it.
    I heard of you a few days since from Walter Bagot who called here, and told me that you were gone, I think, into Rutlandshire, to settle the accounts of a large Estate[3] unliquidated many years. Intricacies that would turn my brains are play to you, but I give you joy of a long vacation at hand, when I suppose that even you will find it pleasant, if not to be idle, at least not to be hemm'd around by business.

Yours ever
Wm Cowper.

My best respects to Mrs. Hill.

LADY HESKETH   Friday, 11 July 1788

Address: Lady Hesketh / New Norfolk Street / Grosvenor Square / London
Postmarks: JY/12/88 *and* NEWPORT/PAGNEL
Charles Ryskamp

My dearest Coz
    Between Homer time and walking time I catch a few minutes to relieve you from all anxiety concerning the Solandrian volume and its contents precious to me, by informing you that neither the one nor the other sustained the

---

[1] *Lycidas*, line 6.
[2] See C to Lady Hesketh, 16 Dec. 1786.   [3] Unidentified.

11 July 1788

least damage by the road. Once more I beg you to give my affectionate thanks to your Sister for all her kind remembrances on this occasion not forgetting the books which I shall with the utmost pleasure expect by the waggon.

This short scribblement I shall send by special messenger to Newport, for the failure of Rogers the great having put an end to all Banking business at Olney, we have no longer the convenience of a daily post.

What is become of the General? It is so long since I heard from him that I wonder and am concerned. I wrote to him yesterday.

I must not forget to tell you that since I wrote last a cover frank'd by Mr. Arnott[1] brought me a Bank note for 25L *from Anonymous*. Those two words being all that it contained beside.

One Ounce of Castile soap scraped fine, beaten in a marble mortar, with as much honey as will bring it to a consistency for rolling into pills.

Liquorice powder is very proper to dust the patts with while forming it into pills, of which some should be shaken over the pills also to keep them from sticking together.

Have you seen the Gentleman's Magazine? There am I, and there am I abused likewise. Somebody has sent my mortuary verses,[2] who I know not. My censurer is neither a poet nor a good reasoner, therefore a fig for all such grumblings.

Mrs. Throg has a nervous fever, but is not very bad. We are loving neighbors & always together.

Mrs. Unwin's love and hearty good wishes that the pills may be as efficacious as ever.

The Newtons come to morrow. Could not come to day, his Grace of Bedford[3] having engaged all the chaises in the Town.

I have hung Grey[4] over the Chimney, and Solander lies on the Study-window-seat spread with a green Cloth to save him

[1] See n.1, C to Lady Hesketh, 7 Dec. 1785.
[2] 'The Verses Printed at the Bottom of the Yearly Bill of Mortality at Northampton' and 'On the Beautiful Feather-Hangings' appeared together with the attack on C ('The Question Answered: A Fragment') in *GM* lviii, pt. 1 (June 1788), 542-3.
[3] Francis Russell (1765-1802), 5th Duke of Bedford, who succeeded to the title in 1771.
[4] See n.1, C to Lady Hesketh, 23 June 1788.

194

from the Chafe and friction otherwise incident to his situation. He is perfectly [handso] me. Adieu my dearest Coz.

Thine, Jeremy Sago![5]

Saturday July 11.
1788.

LADY HESKETH   Monday, 28 July 1788

Hayley, i. 309–11

The Lodge, July 28, 1788.
It is in vain that you tell me you have no talent at description, while in fact you describe better than any body. You have given me a most complete idea of your mansion and its situation; and I doubt not that with your Letter in my hand, by way of map, could I be set down on the spot in a moment, I should find myself qualified to take my walks, and my pastime in whatever quarter of your paradise it should please me the most to visit. We also, as you know, have scenes at Weston worthy of description; but because you know them well, I will only say that one of them has within these few days been much improved; I mean the lime walk. By the help of the axe and the wood-bill,[1] which have of late been constantly employed in cutting out all straggling branches that intercepted the arch; Mr. Throckmorton has now defined it with such exactness, that no cathedral in the world can show one of more magnificence or beauty. I bless myself that I live so near it; for were it distant several miles, it would be well worth while to visit it, merely as an object of taste; not to mention the refreshment of such a gloom both to the eyes and spirits. And these are the things which our modern improvers of parks and pleasure grounds have displaced without mercy; because, forsooth, they are rectilinear. It is a wonder they do not quarrel with the sun-beams for the same reason.
Have you seen the account of five hundred celebrated

---

[5] Perhaps a signature used by C in his early rhyming correspondence (see p. 197).

[1] 'An implement used for cutting wood, pruning, etc.' (*OED*). This letter by C is the last source cited for this term.

Authors now living?[2] I am one of them; but stand charged
with the high crime and misdemeanor of totally neglecting
method. An accusation which, if the gentleman would take
the pains to read me, he would find sufficiently refuted.
I am conscious at least myself of having laboured much in
the arrangement of my matter, and of having given to the
several parts of every book of the Task, as well as to each
poem in the first volume, that sort of slight connection
which poetry demands; for in poetry (except professedly of
the didactic kind) a logical precision would be stiff, pedantic,
and ridiculous. But there is no pleasing some critics; the
comfort is, that I am contented whether they be pleased or
not. At the same time, to my honour be it spoken, the
chronicler of us five hundred prodigies bestows on me, for
ought I know, more commendations than on any other of
my confraternity. May he live to write the histories of as
many thousand poets, and find me the very best among
them! Amen!

I join with you, my dearest Coz. in wishing that I owned
the fee simple[3] of all the beautiful scenes around you; but
such emoluments were never designed for Poets. Am I not
happier than ever Poet was, in having thee for my Cousin;
and in the expectation of thy arrival here, whenever
Strawberry Hill[4] shall lose thee?

Ever thine,

W.C.

LADY HESKETH   Saturday, 9 August 1788

Hayley, i. 311–12

The Lodge, August 9, 1788.
The Newtons are still here, and continue with us I believe

[2] *Catalogue of Five Hundred Celebrated Authors of Great Britain, Now Living*
(1788). This anonymous work is attributed to a Mr Marshall by the British
Library. Among the comments on C's work is the following: 'His works are
poetical, and make two volumes in octavo. The style in which they are written is
nervous, manly and unaffected; but they are greatly deformed and obscured by
the total neglect of method.' (E3ᵛ and E4ʳ.)
[3] See n.1, C to Rose, 19 Oct. 1787.
[4] Lady Hesketh seems to have been at Twickenham from *circa post* 11 July

until the 15th of the month. Here is also my friend Mr. Rose, a valuable young man, who, attracted by the effluvia of my genius, found me out in my retirement last January twelve-month. I have not permitted him to be idle, but have made him transcribe for me the twelfth book of the Iliad. He brings me the compliments of several of the Literati, with whom he is acquainted in town; and tells me, that from Dr. Maclean,[1] whom he saw lately, he learns that my Book is in the hands of sixty different persons at the Hague, who are all enchanted with it; not forgetting the said Dr. Maclean himself, who tells him that he reads it every day, and is always the better for it. Oh rare we!

I have been employed this morning in composing a Latin motto for the King's clock.[2] The embellishments of which are by Mr. Bacon. That gentleman breakfasted with us on Wednesday, having come thirty-seven miles out of his way on purpose to see your Cousin. At his request I have done it, and have made two; he will chuse that which liketh him best. Mr. Bacon is a most excellent man, and a most agreeable companion: I would that he lived not so remote, or that he had more opportunity of travelling.

There is not, so far as I know, a syllable of the rhyming correspondence between me and my poor Brother left,[3] save and except the six lines of it quoted in yours. I *had* the whole

---

1788 until at least 13 Sept.; despite the fact that there are three extant holograph letters (21 Aug., 26 Aug., 13 Sept.) from C to Lady Hesketh addressed to her at Strawberry Hill, it would seem likely that she was staying somewhere in the neighbourhood and only had letters addressed to her at Strawberry Hill. This would explain the fact that Lady Hesketh and three others were given tickets to see Strawberry Hill on 14 Aug. (*Walpole*, xii. 231). The only reference to Walpole's visiting Lady Hesketh is in a letter to Mary Berry of 3 Apr. 1791 (*Walpole*, xi. 235, 236) and that seems to have been in London.

---

[1] The Revd Archibald Maclaine (1722–1804) was educated at Glàsgow, where he studied for the Presbyterian ministry. In 1746 he became assistant to his uncle, a pastor of the English church at The Hague, and was admitted as co-pastor a year later. He held this position until 1796, when he retired to Bath. He translated several theological tracts into English.

[2] 'Quæ lenta accedit, quam velox prætent hora! / Ut capias, patiens esto, sed esto vigil.' Hayley translated these lines thus: 'Slow comes the hour: its passing speed how great! Waiting to seize it — vigilantly wait.' The clock case, which was completed in 1789, is now at Buckingham Palace.

[3] This correspondence has not been found.

of it, but it perished in the wreck of a thousand other things when I left the Temple.

Breakfast calls. Adieu.

W.C.

SAMUEL ROSE   Monday, 18 August 1788

Hayley, i. 313-14.

Weston, August 18, 1788.

My dear friend,

I left you with a sensible regret, alleviated only by the consideration, that I shall see you again in October. I was under some concern also, lest, not being able to give you any certain directions myself, nor knowing where you might find a guide, you should wander and fatigue yourself, good walker as you are, before you should reach Northampton. Perhaps you heard me whistle just after our separation; it was to call back Beau, who was running after you with all speed to intreat you to return with me. For my part, I took my own time to return, and did not reach home till after one; and then so weary that I was glad of my great chair; to the comforts of which I added a crust, and a glass of rum and water, not without great occasion. Such a foot-traveller am I.

I am writing on Monday, but whether I shall finish my Letter this morning depends on Mrs. Unwin's coming sooner or later down to breakfast. Something tells me that you set off to-day for Birmingham; and though it be a sort of Iricism to say here, I beseech you take care of yourself, for the day threatens great heat, I cannot help it; the weather may be cold enough at the time when that good advice shall reach you, but be it hot or be it cold, to a man who travels as you travel, take care of yourself, can never be an unreasonable caution. I am sometimes distressed on this account, for though you are young, and well made for such exploits, those very circumstances are more likely than any thing to betray you into danger.

Consule quid valeant plantæ *quid ferre recusent.*[1]

[1] 'Take counsel as to what plants flourish and what they refuse to bear.' An adaptation from Virgil, *Georgics*, i. 51-3.

The Newtons left us on Friday. We frequently talked about you after your departure, and every thing that was spoken was to your advantage. I know they will be glad to see you in London, and perhaps when your summer and autumn rambles are over, you will afford them that pleasure. The Throckmortons are equally well disposed to you; and them also I recommend to you as a valuable connection; the rather, because you can only cultivate it at Weston.

I have not been idle since you went, having not only laboured as usual at the Iliad, but composed a *spick* and *span* new piece, called, 'The Dog and the Water-lilly;'[2] which you shall see when we meet again. I believe I related to you the incident which is the subject of it. I have also read most of Lavater's Aphorisms;[3] they appear to me some of them wise, many of them whimsical, a few of them false, and not a few of them extravagant. Nil illi medium[4] — If he finds in a man the feature or quality that he approves, he Deifies him; if the contrary, he is a Devil. His verdict is in neither case, I suppose, a just one.

LADY HESKETH   Thursday, 21 August 1788

Address: Lady Hesketh / Strawberry Hill / near / Twickenham / Surry
Postmarks: AU/22/88 *and* OULNEY
Princeton

The Lodge
August 21. 1788

My dearest Cozwoz

Our friends as you opine are gone, having made us (to ourselves at least) a very agreeable visit. We are now as quiet as Dormice in a hollow tree, but not always so, neither shall we be so today, no, nor yet to morrow. The Frogs dine with us to day, and to-morrow we with them. The Dowager and George arrived yesterday. They have also at their house An

---

[2] First published in the *Universal Magazine*, Apr. 1789.

[3] *Aphorisms on Man: Translated from the Original Manuscript of the Rev. John Caspar Lavater* (1788). The translator was Henry Fuseli. William Blake engraved the frontispiece. It was in C's library. (*Keynes*, 101).

[4] 'No middle way for him.' Perhaps an adaptation from Horace, *Satires*, I. ii. 28.

Aunt of Mrs. Frog's named Canning,[1] together with her husband. So we are likely to be a numerous party. But be not alarm'd my Dear lest such a feast should produce a Famine. There would I confess be danger of it were we to entertain such multitudes often, but we and our neighbours have, without a word said on the subject, fallen on the only method that could certainly prevent it. We receive 5 or 6 invitations, and sometimes more, for one that we give. A measure extremely salutary to the finances of a poet. And poet as I am, I could not eat with any comfort at their table, did I not occasionally set forth my board for them. Poor Mrs. Frog is far from well. In the morning she has tremblings and flutterings and other nervous affections as constantly as the Morning comes. Though as the day wears off so do her indispositions with it and she becomes herself again. I shall press her by and by to take the Medicine of your recommendation. George's company in the mean time bids fair to be of use to her. They love each other dearly, and he is ever droll and cheerful.

The behaviour of my little dog on the occasion which I related to you has given birth to the following, which I transcribe in the hope that it may entertain you at least as well as any thing that I could say in prose. It is spick and span, and unseen as yet by mortal eyes except Mrs. Unwin's.

The Dog and the Water-lily.
No Fable.

The Noon was shady, and soft airs
    Swept Ouse's silent tide,
When, 'scaped from literary cares,
    I wander'd on his side.

My Spaniel, prettiest of his race,
    And high in pedigree,
+Mrs Frog (Two+ Nymphs adorn'd with ev'ry grace
and Miss   That Spaniel found for me)
Gunning

[1] Francis Canning married Catherine Giffard; their son was Francis Canning (1772–1831).

21 August 1788

Now wanton'd lost in flags and reeds,
    Now starting into sight
Pursued the Swallow o'er the meads
    With scarce a slower flight.

It was the time when Ouse display'd
    His Lilies newly-blown;
Their beauties I intent survey'd,
    And One I wish'd my own.

With Cane extended-far I sought
    To steer it close to land,
But still the prize, though nearly caught,
    Escaped my eager hand.

Beau marked my unsuccessful pains
    With fixt consid'rate face,
And puzzling sat his puppy brains
    To comprehend the case.

But with a Chirrup shrill and strong
    Dispersing all his dream
I thence withdrew, and follow'd long
    The windings of the stream.

My ramble finish'd, I return'd.
    Beau trotting far before
The floating wreath again discern'd,
    And plunging left the shore.

I saw him with that lily cropp'd
    Impatient swim to meet
My quick approach, and soon he dropp'd
    The treasure at my feet.

Charm'd with the sight, the world, I cried,
    Shall hear of this thy deed,
My Dog shall mortify the pride
    Of Man's superior breed.

But, chief, myself I will enjoin
    Awake at Duty's call,
To show a Love as prompt as thine
    To Him who gives me all.

To me my Dear it seemeth that we shall never by any management make a deep impression on Mrs. Montagu. Persons who have been so long accustom'd to praise, become proof against it. — Mr. Walpole's opinion of me,[2] as I forebode, will not flatter much your predilections in favour of your Cousin. I know not why, but something tells me so.

My anonymous friend has again sent me fish. Three Cod with Oysters. I should like them better if he would announce himself. — I have made a new Frock — The Weston Uniform. We are all to meet so habited this day. — Mr. Newton has lately procured me several Subscriptions, and the General I suppose has told you that I am likely to get those of the Scots Universities.[3]

Farewell my Ever-beloved Coz

                  Thine most truly   Wm Cowper.

Touching the Mottos[4] in my next. They slipp'd through a hole in my memory.

LADY HESKETH   Tuesday, 26 August 1788

Address: Lady Hesketh / Strawberry Hill near / Twickenham / Surry / Single
Postmark: AU/27/88
Princeton

My dearest Coz! He who has thee for a friend will never want a warm one. — I send thee verbatim and literatim what I have sent to the Chancellor. His Letter is very kind and has given

[2] There is no opinion extant. Walpole owned the second edition (1786) of *1782*. See Allen Hazen, *A Catalogue of Horace Walpole's Library* (New Haven, 1969), ii. 471, Item 2827.

[3] The libraries of the University of Edinburgh, the Advocates, Edinburgh, the University of Glasgow, and King's College, Aberdeen, ordered fine copies. The University of St. Andrews subscribed to a common copy.

[4] Lady Hesketh probably had asked C for copies of the two mottos he mentioned in his letter of 9 Aug., but C forgot about them until he had finished this letter so intended to write about them in his next.

me much pleasure. — Give my Love to the generous Sir Archer[1] whom I honour highly for his bounty, and assure thyself that I love thee dearly and in every corner of my heart. — Adieu — Thine   W C.

My Lord,

Your Lordship will be very sure that though Lady Hesketh did not chuse to apprize me of her intentions to write to you, she has not thought it necessary to observe the same secresy with respect to your Lordship's answer. The sight of your Hand-writing (myself the subject) has awaken'd me feelings which with you I know will be my sufficient apology for following her example. They are such as would make it difficult for me to be silent, were there any propriety in being so. But I see none. Why should I seem indifferent where I ought to be warm and am so, and what honour would it do me to appear to have forgotten a friend who still affectionately remembers me?

Had my Cousin consulted me before she made Application to your Lordship in my favour, I should probably, at the same time that I had both loved and honour'd her for her zeal to serve me, have discouraged that proceeding. Not because I have no need of a friend, or because I have not the highest opinion of your constancy in that connexion, but because I am sensible how difficult it must be even for *you* to assist a man in his fortunes who *can* do nothing but write verses, and who *must* live in the country. But should no other good effect ever follow her application than merely what has already followed it, an avowal on your Lordship's part that you still remember me with affection, I shall be always glad that she acted as she did; she has procured me a gratification of which I shall feel the comfort while I have any sensibility left.

I know that your Lordship would never have expressed even remotely a wish to serve me, had you not in reality felt one, and will therefore never lay my scantiness of income to your account, but should I live and die circumscribed as I am, and have been ever, in my finances, will impute it always

---

[1] Sir Archer Croft, 3rd Baronet (d. 1790), was Lady Hesketh's brother-in-law. He had married Elizabeth Cowper. Sir Archer subscribed for one fine copy, and his wife ordered two fine copies.

to its proper cause, my own singularity of character, and not in the least to any deficiency of Good Will in your Lordship's dispositions toward me.

I will take this opportunity to thank you for having honour'd my Homer with your Subscription.[2] In that work I labour daily, and now draw near to a close of the Iliad, after having been, except an interruption of eight months occasion'd by Illness, three years employed in it. It seem'd to me, after all Pope's doings, that we still wanted an English Homer, and may I but be happy enough to supply the defect and to merit your Lordship's approbation, I shall envy no poet on the earth at present, nor many that have gone before me.

I have the honour to be my Lord your Lordship's most
> Obliged and affectionate
> Wm Cowper

Weston Underwood
Augt. 26. 1788

MRS KING   Thursday, 28 August 1788

Address: Mrs. King / Perten-Hall / Kimbolton / Huntingdonshire
Postmarks: AU/29/88 *and* OULNEY
Princeton

> Weston Underwood
> Augt. 28. 1788

My dear Madam —
Should you discard me from the Number of your Correspondents you would treat me as I seem to deserve, though I do not actually deserve it. I have lately been engaged with company at our house, who resided with us five weeks, and have had much of rheumatism into the bargain. Not in my fingers you will say — True — But you know as well as I that pain, be it where it may, indisposes us to writing.

You express some degree of wonder that I found you out to be sedentary, at least much a stayer within doors, without any sufficient Data for my direction. Now if I should guess your figure and stature with equal success, you will deem me

---

[2] 'The Lord High Chancellor' subscribed to two fine copies.

not only a poet but a conjuror. Yet in fact I have no pretensions of that sort. I have only formed a picture of you in my own Imagination, as we ever do of a person of whom we think much, though we have never seen that person. Your height I conceive to be about 5 feet 5 inches, which though it would make a short man is yet height enough for a woman. If you insist on an Inch or two more, I have no objection. You are not very fat, but somewhat inclined to be fat, and unless you allow yourself a little more air and exercise will incur some danger of exceeding in your dimensions before you die. Let me therefore once more recommend to you to walk a little more, at least in your garden, and to amuse yourself occasionally with pulling up here and there a weed; for it will be an inconvenience to you to be much fatter than you are at a time of life when your strength will be naturally on the decline. I have given you a fair complexion, a slight tinge of the rose in your cheeks, dark brown hair, and if the fashion would give you leave to show it, an open and well-formed forehead. To all this, I add a pair of eyes not quite black but nearly approaching to that hue, and very animated. I have not absolutely determined on the shape of your nose or the form of your mouth, but should you tell me that I have in other respects drawn a tolerable likeness, have no doubt but I can describe them too. I assure you that though I have a great desire to read him, I have never seen Lavater, nor have availed myself in the least of any of his rules on this occasion. Ah Madam! If with all that sensibility of yours which exposes you to so much sorrow, and necessarily must expose you to it in a world like this, I have had the good fortune to make you smile, I have then painted you, whether with a strong resemblance or with none at all, to very good purpose.

I had intended to have sent you a little poem[1] which I have lately finished but have no room to transcribe it. You shall have it by another opportunity. Breakfast is on the Table, and my time also fails as well as my paper. I rejoice that a Cousin of yours[2] found my volumes agreeable to him, for being your Cousin, I will be answerable for his good Taste and judgment.

[1] 'The Dog and the Water Lily'.
[2] Thomas Martyn (1735–1825), the distinguished botanist. He was educated at Emmanuel College, Cambridge, and became a Fellow of Sidney Sussex (MA,

When I wrote last I was in Mourning for a dear and much valued Uncle, Ashley Cowper. He died at the age of 86.

My best respects attend Mr. King, and I am

> Dear Madam,
> most truly Yours
> Wm Cowper.

CLOTWORTHY ROWLEY   Sunday, 31 August [1788][1]

Address: Clotworthy Rowley Esqr. / Dublin. / Single
Postmarks: SE/3/[illegible] *and* OULNEY
Princeton

> Weston Underwood near Olney
> Bucks.
> Last day of Augt.

My dear friend — I have been often in pain about you, and have anxiously mention'd you to Mrs. Unwin several times, fearing lest illness or some evil had befallen you. Your Letter inclosing a Bill of Exchange for sixteen Guineas[2] has rambled eleven days in quest of me, neither can I easily conjecture by what means it reach'd me at last, having set off with a wrong direction as the date of this will inform you. I cannot sufficiently express my sense of your kindness. Labouring as you do in my cause, you give me unequivocal proofs of a friendship superior to the influence of time, and to which I seem to make but a cold return, at least an inadequate one, when I only thank you for it. But what can I more? Poets are seldom

---

1758). He was an enthusiastic supporter of the Linnaean system and served as professor of botany at Cambridge from 1762 until his death. In 1774 he became rector of Ludgershall, Buckinghamshire, and in 1776 vicar of Little Marlow. He purchased the Charlotte Street Chapel, Pimlico, in 1784. In 1798 Martyn moved to Pertenhall.

---

[1] Although this letter has traditionally been assigned to 31 Aug. 1789, this is surely an error. (The year portion of the date stamp of the postmark is illegible.) In his letter, Rowley had obviously commented on the death of Ashley Cowper which took place on 6 June 1788. C also states in this letter that he is 'now finishing the 23d. book of the Iliad'. In his letter to Rose of 25 Sept. 1788, he writes that he finished the *Iliad* on 23 Sept. and started the *Odyssey* on the 24th. This would seem to place the letter in 1788, not 1789.

[2] Subscription money collected by Rowley for the Homer.

good for any thing except in rhime. It is however true that I both Love & Honour you for your fidelity & kindness.

I have from the beginning been aware that my Translation of Homer will have much prejudice to encounter, more perhaps than would have attended any other work that I could possibly have undertaken. I confess it a bold enterprize; not because Pope has succeeded in it, for he certainly has not; but because he is by thousands ignorantly supposed to have succeeded, and because it may perhaps be impossible to render justice to the Original in our language. All I can say is that I will do my best, and of one thing at least I will assure you, that according to all that I have seen or heard of other Translations of the same author, none of them have in any respect at all resembled mine. Whether mine shall be found to differ to a good purpose, probandum est.[3]

In answer to your question — When go I to the Press? I reply, When my Bookseller pleases. I am now finishing the 23d. Book of the Iliad, and being advanced so far could easily keep before the Printers, were they to begin to morrow. But Johnson recommends it to me by no means to Print till the whole is finish'd, alledging for his reason that the Printers cannot possibly plan the work 'till they shall have the Whole before them. And my most intelligent friends advise me to be determined by Johnson, who has universally the character of a sensible and an honest man.

I rejoice much in the account you give me of your domestic happiness. May it continue, and if possible encrease. You may safely present my Love to Miss Rowley. A present of that sort from a man old enough to be her father, can do her no harm, at least at this distance. Were we nearer to each other perhaps the approach might not be altogether so safe for me.

My Uncle, as you observe, died full of years, but not rich. The profits of the very lucrative office which he held so long were not his, but General Cowper's, whose interest in them determined on the death of Ashley. A gold Repeater[4] and a

[3] 'It remains to be seen.'

[4] This repeater is item 737 in the collection of the Cowper and Newton Museum, Olney; it was hallmarked in 1767 by Fra. Perigal. The tooth-pick case, once the property of Spencer Cowper, Dean of Durham, is mentioned in C's letters to Lady Hesketh of 5 July and to Mrs King of 25 Sept.

Tooth pick case are all that I have gained by the loss of a relation whom all who knew him most highly loved and valued, and whose Like I shall not presently see again.

M. Madan lives at Epsom, since the publication of his Thelyphthora little noticed I believe either by our family or his former friends. He and I have no correspondence. He neither has nor wants preferrment, his paternal Estate, as I have heard, bringing him in between 4 and 5000 per Annum. I pity the man, and time was when I felt much abhorrence of his book. But it is now a Dead thing, out of mind, and no longer a subject either of Liking or aversion.

I have scribbled in haste, being desirious that you may have the earliest possible advice of the safe though late arrival of yours. Nothing could have been more welcome to me than either your son William[5] or any of yours. Would I could see you all at the Lake-side!

I am happy that you are in health. May God keep you so. Except scratching now and then a Letter as fast as I can, I do nothing but Translate.

Ever yours my Dearest Friend
Wm Cowper.

JOHN NEWTON Tuesday, 2 September 1788

Princeton

Weston, Sep. 2. 1788

My dear friend — I rejoice that you and yours reach'd London safe, especially when I reflect that you perform'd the journey on a day so fatal, as I understand, to others travelling the same road. I found those comforts, in your visit, which have formerly sweeten'd all our interviews, in part restored. I knew you; knew you for the same shepherd who was sent to lead me out of the wilderness into the pasture where the Chief Shepherd feeds his flock, and felt my sentiments of affectionate friendship for you, the same as ever. But One thing was still wanting, and that thing the Crown of all. I shall find it in God's time, if it be not lost for ever. When I

[5] William Rowley (d. 1811) who served as MP for Kinsdale, Commander of the Customs, and Recorder of Kinsdale.

say this, I say it trembling, for at what time soever comfort shall come, it will not come without its attendant evil, and whatever good thing may occur in the interval, I have sad forebodings of the event, having learn'd by experience that I was born to be persecuted with peculiar fury, and assuredly believing that such as my lot has been, it will be to the end. This belief is connected in my mind with an observation I have often made, and is perhaps founded in great part upon it. That there is a certain stile of dispensations maintained by Providence in the dealings of God with every man, which, however the incidents of his life may vary, and though he may be thrown into many different situations, is never exchanged for another. The stile of dispensation peculiar to myself has hitherto been that of sudden, violent, unlook'd-for change. When I have thought myself falling into the abyss I have been caught up again; when I have thought myself on the threshold of a happy eternity, I have been thrust down to Hell. The rough and the smooth of such a lot taken together should perhaps have taught me never to despair, but through an unhappy propensity in my nature to forebode the worst, they have, on the contrary, operated as an admonition to me never to Hope. A firm persuasion that I can never durably enjoy a comfortable state of mind, but must be depressed in proportion as I have been elevated, withers my joys in the bud and in a manner intombs them before they are born. For I have no expectation but of sad vicissitude, and ever believe that the last shock of all will be fatal.

We have been careful to execute your commission of Compliments and Respects to the Throckmortons. They speak of you both in the handsomest terms, and I have little doubt that Mrs. Frog will visit Coleman's Buildings the first opportunity.[1]

Mr. Bean has still some trouble with his parishioners. The suppression of 5 public houses is the occasion. He called on me yesterday morning for advice, though discreet as he is himself, he has little need of such counsel as I can give him. Harold,[2] who is subtle as a dozen foxes, met him on Sunday exactly at his descent from the pulpit and proposed to him a

[1] The Newtons lived at No. 21, Coleman's Buildings.
[2] Unidentified.

general meeting of the parish in Vestry on the subject. Mr. Bean attack'd so suddenly, consented. But afterward repented that he had so done, assured as he was that he should be outvoted. There seem'd no remedy but to apprize them before hand that he would meet them indeed, but not with a view to have the question decided by a Majority. That he would take that opportunity to make his allegations against each of the houses in question, which if they could refute, well; if not, they could no longer reasonably oppose his measures. This was what he came to submit to my opinion. I could do no less than approve it, and he left me with a purpose to declare his mind to them immediately.

My Thanks attend Mrs. Newton for her Cambridge News.[3] The worthy Doctor might fairly be said to be in a sad scrape. — I beg that you will give my affectionate respects to Mr. Bacon, and assure him of my sincere desire that he should think himself perfectly at liberty respecting the Mottos, to chuse one or to reject both, as likes him best. I wish also to be remember'd with much affection to Mrs. Cowper and always rejoice to hear of her well-being.

Mrs. Unwin will speak for herself. She is going, she tells me, to write to Mrs. Newton. You will therefore present my best Love to Her and to Miss Catty and believe me, as I truly am, my Dear Friend,

Most affectionately Yours
Wm Cowper.

SAMUEL ROSE   Thursday, 11 September 1788

Address: Samuel Rose Esqr. / Dr. Hunter's[1] / York. / Single
Princeton

Weston Underwood
Septbr. 11: 1788

My dear friend
    It gave me much pleasure to learn that your pedestrian

---

[3] Unidentified.

[1] Alexander Hunter (1729-1809), who was educated at London, Paris, and Rouen, and who received his MD from Edinburgh in 1753. The founder of the York Lunatic Asylum, he practised at York from 1763.

ambition satisfied you have at length betaken yourself to a carriage. I seem to have the better chance to receive you here in good health in October. I have not, myself, performed any great matters on foot since your departure. I have indeed twice visited the Oak, and with an intention to push my enquiries a mile beyond it, where, it seems, I should have found another oak, much larger and more respectable than the former; but once I was hinder'd by rain, and once by the sultriness of the day. This latter oak has been known by the name of Judith many ages,[2] and is said to have been an oak at the time of the Conquest. If I have not an opportunity to reach it before your arrival here, we will attempt that exploit together, and even if I should have been able to visit it e'er you come, I shall yet be glad to do so, for the pleasure of extraordinary sights like all other pleasures, is doubled by the participation of a friend.

You wish a copy of my little dog's eulogium which I will therefore transcribe, but by so doing shall leave myself but scanty room for prose. Like a Tradesman, I must say the *needful*, and in as few words as possible, that my Muse may not be too much crowded, or perhaps in part excluded. — The Snuffers or rather Candle-snappers are come, and are perfect in their kind.[3] I admire an invention that has converted a disagreeable task into an amusement; such at least will be the effect for a time. — I shall be sorry if our neighbours at the Hall should have left it when we have the pleasure of seeing you, yet fear that they will, for in October they go

[2] Thomas Wright, *The Town of Cowper* (1886), pp. 120–1: 'the Yardley Oak, the tree to which the poem is addressed, the hollow tree, the tree said by Cowper to be 22 feet 6½ inches in girth, is the one now called "Cowper's Oak," situated three miles from Weston, just beyond Kilwick Wood, near Cowper's Oak farmhouse . . . the oak at Yardley Lodge, the perfectly sound tree, the tree that was formerly called Judith, the tree said by Cowper to be 28 feet 5 inches in girth, is the one now usually called Gog, and is situated a mile farther from Weston . . . near the old-fashioned farm-house of Chase Farm, which was formerly called the Ranger's Lodge . . . The name Judith, by which Gog was originally known, was possibly obtained from its having been planted by the Lady Judith, niece to the Conqueror, and wife of Earl Waltheof.'

[3] The 'necessary candle snuffers — often very delicate renderings of the scissor arrangement — once held proud places in the displays of many a cottage and farmhouse where they were brightly and regularly polished.' Gertrude Jekyll and Sydney R. Jones, *Old English Household Life* (1939), p. 88.

into Norfolk on a visit to Lord Petre's who has a seat there.[4]
I want you to see them soon again, that a little consuetudo[5]
may wear off restraint, and you may be able to improve the
advantage you have already gained in that quarter. It is but
lately, and since I wrote last, that Mr. Frog on hearing me
mention you, said, I like Mr. Rose. — I pitied you for the
fears which deprived you of your Uncle's[6] company, and the
more, having suffer'd so much by those fears myself. Fight
against that vicious fear, for such it is, as strenuously as you
can; it is the worst enemy that can attack a man destined to
the Forum. It ruin'd me, and will, I perceive, give you much
trouble, unless you take great pains to conquer yourself in
this particular. To associate as much as possible with the
most respectable company for good sense and good breeding,
is I believe the only, at least I am sure, is the best remedy.
The society of men of pleasure will not cure it, but rather
leaves us more exposed to its influence in company of better
persons. — Now for

The Dog and the Water-Lily.
No Fable.

The Noon was shady & soft airs
Swept Ouse's silent tide,
When 'scaped from literary cares
I wander'd on his side.
+
My Spaniel, prettiest of his race,
And high in pedigree,
(Two* Nymphs adorn'd with ev'ry grace
That Spaniel found for me)
+
Now wanton'd lost in flags & reeds,
Now starting into sight
Pursued the swallow o'er the meads
With scarce a slower flight.
+

[4] At Buckenham. For the Petres, see n.2, C to Unwin, 10–11 July 1786.
[5] 'Intimacy'.
[6] See n.2, C to [Rose], [10 Mar. 1788].

11 September 1788

It was the time when Ouse display'd
  His Lilies newly blown;
Their beauties I intent survey'd,
  And One I wish'd my own.
      +
With cane extended-far I sought
  To steer it close to land,
But still the prize, tho' nearly caught,
  Escaped my eager hand.
      +
Beau mark'd my unsuccessful pains
  With fixt consid'rate face,
And puzzling sat his puppy brains
  To comprehend the case.
      +
But with a chirrup clear & strong
  Dispersing all his dream
I thence withdrew, & follow'd long
  The windings of the stream.
      +
My ramble finish'd, I return'd.
  Beau trotting far before
The floating wreath again discern'd,
  And plunging left the shore.
      +
I saw him with that Lily cropp'd
  Impatient swim to meet
My quick approach, & soon he dropp'd
  The treasure at my feet.
      +
Charm'd with the sight, the world, I cried,
  Shall hear of this thy deed,
My dog shall mortify the pride
  Of man's superior breed;
      +
But, chief, myself I will enjoin
  Awake at Duty's call
To show a Love as prompt as thine
  To Him who gives me all.

———

11 September 1788

+Sir Robert Gunning's Daughters.

The little Gentleman above celebrated makes his affectionate Compliments to you, and hopes for your company again soon in his rambles round about Weston. Mrs. Unwin's Love attends you also with that of my Dear Sir

Yours truely
Wm Cowper.

LADY HESKETH   Saturday, 13 September 1788

Address: Lady Hesketh / Strawberry Hill / Twickenham / Surry. Single
Postmarks: SE/15/88 *and* OULNEY
Olney

The Lodge   Sepr. 13. 1788

My dearest Coz — Beau seems to have objections against my writing to you this morning that are not to be over-ruled. He will be in my lap, licking my face and nibbling the end of my pen. Perhaps he means to say, I beg you will give my Love to her, which I therefore send you accordingly.

There cannot be, this hindrance excepted, a situation more favorable to the business I have in hand, than mine at this moment. Here is no noise, *save* (as we poets always express it) that of the birds hopping on their perches and playing with their wires, while the sun glimmering through the Elm opposite the window, falls on my desk with all the softness of Moonshine. There is not a cloud in the sky nor a leaf that moves, so that over and above the enjoyment of the present calm, I feel a well-warranted expectation that such as the day is, it will be to the end. This is the month in which such weather is to be expected, and which is therefore welcome to me beyond all others, October excepted, which promises to bring you hither. At your coming, you will probably find us and us only, or to speak more properly, *uzz*. The Frogs, as I believe I told you, hop into Norfolk soon, on a visit to Lord Petre's, who beside his palace in Essex, has another in that county.[1] All the brothers are now at the Hall, *save* the

---

[1] Writtle, Essex and Buckenham, Norfolk.

214

Physician,[2] who is employed in prescribing med'cine to the Welsh at Cardiff. There lives he with Madame son Epouse, with an income of 300£ a year, all happiness and contentment. The mother is also here, and here is also our uncle Gifford, a man whom if you know, you must love, and if you do not, I wish you did.[3] But he goes this morning, and I expect every minute to see him pass my window. In volubility, variety, and earnestness of expression, he very much resembles your father, and in the sweetness of his temper too, so that though he be but a passenger, or rather a bird of passage, for his head quarters are in France and he only flits occasionally to England, he has much engaged my affections. I walk'd with him yesterday on a visit to an oak on the borders of Yardley Chase, an oak which I often visit, and which is one of the wonders that I show to all who come this way and have never seen it. I tell them all that it is a thousand years old, verily believing it to be so, though I do not know it. A mile beyond this oak stands another which has for time immemorial been known by the name of Judith, and is said to have been an oak when my namesake the Conqueror first came hither. And beside all this, there is a good coachway to them both, and I design that you shall see them too.

A day or two before the arrival of your last letter we were agreeably surprized by that of a Hamper stuff'd with various articles in the grocery way corresponding exactly with a Bill of parcels which accompany'd them. Though we had received no advise of the same, we were not at all at a loss for the sender, and hereby, my Dear, make you our very best acknowledgments for your kind present. Having had company this summer, and being also obliged now and then to feed the Frogs, our stock of Hams and Tongues is not at present, much. One of the former and two of the latter making up our whole store in that way.

I have, as yet, no News from the Chancellor. It is possible that none I may have 'till he can send me good. For to me it seems that after having expressed for me so much warmth of Friendship still subsisting, he has lay'd himself under pretty

[2] C's reference is to Charles Throckmorton, later 7th Baronet. We have not been able to find details of his medical training.
[3] See n.5, C to Lady Hesketh, 4 Sept. 1787.

strong obligations to do something for me, if any thing can be done. But though, in my time, my rest has been broken by many things, it never was yet by the desire of riches or the dread of poverty. At the same time I have no objection to all that he can do for me be it ever so much.

I am going this Morning with the Dowager Frog to Chicheley on a visit to the Chesters, which obliges me to shorten my scribble somewhat. Unless I finish my letter first, you will not get it by this poet. Therefore farewell my Dear! May God keep thee and give us a joyful meeting. So pray we both. Amen.

Ever thine   Wm C.

JOSEPH JOHNSON   Wednesday, 24 September 1788

Address: Mr. Johnson.
Carl H. Pforzheimer Library

Weston Underwood
Sepbr. 24. 1788

Dear Sir —

My thanks to you for the pleasure I have found in the perusal of Adriano come to you accompanied by some strictures on the work, of which you will make some use, or none, just as you shall see good. They will at least serve to convince you, that I have fulfill'd your request with a degree of attention that may prove the pleasure I had in doing it. I certainly have not objected to all that is objectionable, the passages which I censured are rather specimens of a greater number that call equally loud for alteration. Neither is the stile, which in many places creeps too much, the only circumstance that I could wish amended. The Writer has ability to remove all such blemishes with very little trouble to himself, if he will give but a short time to the business. The principal exception seems to lie against a particular passage in the story, on which passage nevertheless all that follows so immediately depends, that I have not been able to suggest any thing in the shape of a remedy. — Gilbert is supposed to have been cast away and buried by Frederic in the sands. Yet on the very Evening of the day that brings forth this shocking Catastrophe, the party, at first inconsolable for his loss, have so effectually overcome their grief, that Adriano amuses himself in his garden, and the young Ladies take a walk and a book; she in particular who had been destined to Gilbert, the shipwreck'd Lover, and who afterward marrys him, finding a commodious bench under a willow, actually falls fast asleep. — Oh what pity it will be if what is unnatural in this part of the story cannot be rectified! For surely the just reflections and the fine poety to which it gives birth, deserve to be immortal. I beseech you to recommend it to the Author to exert himself on an occasion in which his honour is so much concerned, and suffer him not idly to forego a degree of reputation which few men have the happiness to acquire. I am either much mistaken, and have read him through a false medium, or he has few, perhaps no equals in the present day. But, except on favourite occasions he does not put forth half his strength.

As I have not specified all his faults, so neither have I half his beauties; but what I have said will be Sufficient to express to you my opnion of his work, which is what you desired.

I am Dear Sir
Yours Wm Cowper.

SAMUEL ROSE   Thursday, 25 September 1788

Address: Samuel Rose Esq. / Post Office / Scarbro'[1]
Princeton

The Lodge
Sepr. 25. 1788

My dear friend —

The half hour next before breakfast I devote to you. The moment Mrs. Unwin arrives in the study, be what I have written much or little, I shall make my Bow and take leave, otherwise my Letter will not set off till Sunday which would be a loss of 3 days. — I was shock'd at what you tell me of my quondam friend's behavior.[2] Superior talents, it seems,

---

[1] This letter was originally addressed by C to 'Samuel Rose Esqe. / Dr. Hunter's / York / Single'. Someone has crossed out all but the first line of the address and substituted the address as given.   [2] Edward Thurlow.

give no security for propriety of conduct; on the contrary having a natural tendency to nourish pride, they often betray the possessor into such mistakes as men more moderately gifted, never commit. Ability therefore is not wisdom, and an ounce of grace is a better Guard against gross absurdity than the brightest talents in the world. If Markham[3] bore his rudeness patiently and without giving him any rebuff, he has learn'd in his Archepiscopal office a meekness for which prelates have not been always celebrated, and which he in particular had once no claim to. While he was Master of Westminster and before that period, he discover'd, on all trying occasions, a sturdiness and fortitude of temper, that on the occasion now in question, would have enabled him sufficiently to avenge his insulted dignity. Happy for you that you did not pay your visit 'till this tremendous man was departed! Where would you have hidden yourself from his frown, or what shield would you have presented against his arrows? Yet culpable as he is in some respects, I can assure you on second thoughts, that you would have had nothing to fear from him. For to modest men and diffident I have ever known him gentle and tractable as a lamb.

I rejoice that you are prepared for Transcriptwork. Here will be plenty for you. The day on which you shall receive this, I beg you will well remember to drink one glass at least to the success of the Iliad, which I finish'd the day before yesterday, and yesterday began the Odyssey. It will be some time before I shall perceive myself travelling in another road. The objects around me at present are [so much][4] the same; Olympus and a council of the Gods [meet m|e at my first entrance. To tell you the truth I am weary of Heroes and Deities, and with reverence be it spoken, shall be glad for variety-sake, to exchange their company for that of a Cyclops.

You speak of turning your *steps* Southward; by which expression you mean I suppose to signify that you intend to

---

[3] William Markham (1719–1807), archbishop of York from 1777 until his death. Markham had been a student with C at Westminster, which he entered in 1733. He was elected head into college in 1734, and went to Christ Church, Oxford, in 1738 (BA, 1742; MA, 1745; BCL, 1752; DCL, 1752). He was head-master of Westminster from 1753 until 1764.

[4] MS torn. The missing words are supplied from Thomas Wright, *Unpublished and Uncollected Letters of William Cowper* (1925), p. 47.

walk. Beware of over doing it; for though Mrs. Unwin is an excellent nurse, both she and I had rather that you should have no need of one. She has been lately much indisposed, having suffer'd excruciating pain from a Boil under her arm, which however has broken and she is now better. We shall both be happy to receive you. The Frogs will not be gone if you arrive at the time you mention. — I am sorry for it say you. Then there will be more terrours and tremblings for me. — But you need not fear them and that you know.

Mrs. Frog dines with us to day, sola. The rest are all going to Northampton races.[5] Young, handsome, and lively, she yet prefers serenity and silence.

Et sapit, et mecum facit, et dijudicat æque.[6]

I am, my Dear friend, with Mrs. Unwin's very best respects

Ever yours   Wm Cowper.

MRS KING   Thursday, 25 September 1788

Princeton (*copy*)[1]

                              Weston Underwood
                              Septr. 25. 1788.

My dearest Madam,

How surprised was I this moment to meet a servant at the gate who told me that he came from you! He could not have been more welcome unless he had announced yourself. I am charmed with your kindness and with all your elegant presents. So is Mrs. Unwin, who begs me in particular to thank you warmly for the housewife,[2] the very thing she had just begun to want. In the fire-screen you have sent me an ænigma which at present I have not the ingenuity to expound, but some muse will help me, or I shall meet with somebody able to instruct me. In all that I have seen beside, for *that* I have

[5] There were annual races in Northampton in Aug. or Sept., and advertisements or notices of them appear in the *Northampton Mercury*.

[6] 'She's a woman of taste, she's on my side, and she's a fair-minded critic': an adaptation of Horace, *Epistles*, II. i. 68.

[1] Note at head of letter states that it was 'copied by Maria D. Johnson Augt. 25th. 1841. The original of which I sent to Mr. Grimshaw — Aug. 26. 1841.'

[2] A housewife is a 'pocket-case for needles, pins, thread, scissors, etc.' (*OED*).

not yet seen, I admire both the taste and the execution. A tooth-pick-case I had, but one so large, that no modern waistcoat pocket could possibly contain it. It was some years since the Dean of Durham's,[3] for whose sake I valued it, though to me useless. Yours is come opportunely to supply the deficiency, and shall be my constant companion to its last thread. The cakes and the apples we will eat remembering who sent them, and when I say this I will add also, that when we have neither apples nor cakes to eat we will still remember you. — What the MSS poem can be that you suppose to have been written by me, I am not able to guess, and since you will not allow that I have guessed your person well, am become shy of exercising conjecture on any meaner subject. Perhaps they may be some mortuary verses which I wrote last year at the request of a certain Parish Clerk. If not, and you have never seen them, I will send you them hereafter.

You have been at Bedford.[4] Bedford is but 12 miles from Weston. When you are at home we are but 18 miles asunder. Is it possible that such a paltry interval can separate us always? I will never believe it. Our house is going to be filled by a cousin of mine, and her train who will I hope spend the winter with us. I cannot therefore repeat my invitation at present, but expect to be very troublesome on that theme next summer. I could almost scold you for not making Weston in your way home from Bedford. Though I am neither a relation nor quite 86 years of age, believe me I should as much rejoice to see you and Mr. King as if I were both.

Mrs. Unwin has this moment opened the screen which I admire, and shall find particularly useful.

I send you, my dear Madam, the poem I promised you, and shall be glad to send you any thing and every thing I write, as fast as it flows. Behold my two volumes! which though your old acquaintance, I thought might receive an additional recommendation in the shape of a present from myself.

What I have written I know not, for all has been scribbled in haste. I will not tempt your servant's honesty who seems

[3] See C to Lady Hesketh, 5 July and n.6.
[4] Mrs King had been visiting Mrs Battison of Brawbourn-Place, Kent, who died on 9 Nov. 1788; Mrs King must have gone through Bedford to and from Kent.

by his countence to have a great deal, being equally watchful to preserve uncorrupted the honesty of my own.

I am my dearest Madam with a thousand thanks for this stroke of friendship which I feel at my heart, and with Mrs. Unwin's very best respects

Most sincerely yours
Wm. Cowper.

P.S.

My two hares died little more than two years since.[5] One of them aged ten years, the other eleven years and eleven months.

Our compliments attend Mr. King.

MRS KING   Saturday, 11 October 1788

Address: Mrs. King / Pirten Hall near / Kimbolton / Huntingdonshire / Single
Postmarks: OC/13/88 *and* OULNEY
Princeton

Weston Underwood
October 11. 1788

My dear Madam,

You are perfectly secure from all danger of being over-whelm'd with presents from me. It is not much that a poet can possibly have it in his power to give; when he has presented his own works, he may be supposed to have exhausted all means of donation. They are his only superfluity. There was a time, but that time was before I commenced Writer for the Press, when I amused myself in a way somewhat similar to yours; allowing I mean for the difference between masculine and female operations. The scissors and the needle are your chief implements; mine were the chissel and the saw. In those days you might have been in some danger of too plentiful a return for your favours. Tables, such as they were, and Joint-stools, such as never were, might have travell'd to Pirtenhall in most inconvenient abundance. But I have long since discontinued this practise and many others which I

---

[5] 'Puss', one of the three hares who are the subject of C's *GM* essay of June 1784, died on 9 Mar. 1786 (see *Wright*, ii. 484) at 'eleven years and eleven months'. The hare who died at ten years cannot be either 'Tiney' or 'Bess', both of whom had died in or before 1784.

found it necessary to adopt, that I might escape the worst of all evils both in itself and in its consequences, an idle life. Many arts I have exercised with this view, for which Nature never design'd me, though among them were some in which I arrived at considerable proficiency by mere dint of the most heroic perseverance. There is not a Squire in all this country who can boast of having made better Squirrel houses, hutches for rabbits, or bird-cages than myself; and in the article of Cabbage-nets I had no Superior. I even had the hardiness to take in hand the pencil, and studied a whole year the art of drawing. Many figures were the fruit of my labours which had at least the merit of being unparallel'd by any production either of Art or Nature; but before the year was ended, I had occasion to wonder at the progress that may be made in despight of natural deficiency, but dint alone of practise; for I actually produced three Landscapes which a Lady thought worthy to be framed & glazed. I then judged it high time to exchange this occupation for another, lest by any subsequent productions of inferior merit, I should forfeit the honour I had so fortunately acquired. But Gardening was of all employments that in which I succeeded best, though even in this, I did not suddenly attain perfection. I began with Lettuces and Cauliflowers; from them I proceeded to cucumbers; next to Melons. I then purchased an Orange tree, to which in due time I added two or three Myrtles. These served me day and night with employment during a whole severe winter. To defend them from the frost in a situation that exposed them to its severity, cost me much ingenuity and much attendance. I contrived to give them a fire heat, and have waded night after night through the snow with the bellows under my arm, just before going to bed, to give the latest possible puff to the embers, lest the frost should seize them before Morning. Very minute beginnings have sometimes important consequences. From nursing 2 or 3 little ever-greens I became ambitious of a Greenhouse, and accordingly built one, which, Verse excepted, afforded me amusement for a longer time than any expedient of all the many to which I have fled for refuge from the misery of having nothing to do. When I left Olney for Weston I could no longer have a Greenhouse of my own, but in a neighbour's garden I find a better, of which the sole management is consign'd to me.

I had need take care when I begin a letter, that the subject with which I set off be of some importance, for before I can exhaust it, be it what it may, I have generally filled my paper. But self is a subject inexhaustible, which is the reason that though I have said little, and nothing, I am afraid, worth your hearing, I have only room to add that I am

My dear Madam,
Most truly Yours   Wm Cowper.

Mrs. Unwin bids me present her best Compliments and say how much she shall be obliged to you for the Receipt to make that most excellent Cake which came hither in its native pan. There is no production of yours that will not be always most welcome at Weston.

WALTER BAGOT   Tuesday, 14 October 1788

Address: The Revd. Walter Bagot.
Morgan Library

Weston Underwood
Octr. 14. 1788

My dear friend —

When I last saw your Brother Chester, to whom I lately pay'd a morning visit on board the chaise of the Dowager Throckmorton,[1] not being able readily to account for your long silence,[2] I ask'd him what had befallen you? He answer'd '— Oh — he is an idle rogue — it is a long time since I heard from him myself. But on recollection I believe I must acquit him of the charge of idleness, for he has been extremely busy gathering in his Tythes.' This being the case, I admit the excuse as available so long as that occupation engross'd you, but taking it for granted that your Barns have long since been fill'd, I once more express my wonder at your taciturnity, and that I may not mention it to no purpose, mention it to yourself. You will observe that I am in a predicament which

---

[1] See n.2, C to Unwin, 20 May 1784.
[2] C's previous letter to Bagot is of 17 June 1788; presumably Bagot did not answer that letter.

qualifies me to be thus clamorous, having written the last letter that has past between us. In what light my assiduity may appear to you I know not, but to me it seems highly meritorious, employ'd as I am day and night in a business less important indeed and less profitable, but equally laborious. It will give you pleasure to know (and therefore I tell it you) that I have finish'd the Iliad, and two books of the Odyssey. This last poem by the way, for the benefit of English readers, I want to entitle otherwise, for so long as Ulysses shall be the only name by which the Hero of it shall be known in this country, I cannot but suppose its present title unintelligible to all who are unacquainted with the Original. What think you therefore of the Ulyssiad? Myself, I know but one objection to the use of it. It may have the appearance of an affected departure from the practise of my predecessor, and all such appearances I would studiously avoid. Else, it would certainly answer the end of a Title much better than that which the poem bears at present, and I do not see why the Title should be so superstitiously preserved, when the name itself from which that Title is taken, is and ever has been varied. Give me your opinion.

I have lately made a new acquaintance with a young man whose name is Rose. His father was Dr. Rose of Chiswick where he kept an Academy. When I first saw him he had then lately left Glasgow where he had been finishing his education. He is sensible and a good scholar. This summer he spent three weeks with me, and determining to make him pay for his Lodging I employ'd him in transcribing for me. He copied, I believe, two books; but the circumstance from which I derived most advantage on the occasion was his own favourable opinion of them, which he express'd in such terms as gave me much encouragement. He compared all that he wrote with the Original. The passage in which Thersites plays his part[3] seem'd to please him much. I feel somewhat of an aukwardness when I write thus, and even though I write thus to you. But you will have the charity to judge that I venture on it rather for the sake of giving some pleasure to you, than to indulge a silly vanity of my

---

[3] *Iliad*, ii, lines 211–70 (lines 252–334 of C's translation).

own. At the worst, I am more excusable than Montesquieu,[4] who when he had ask'd a friend of mine if he had read his book, and had received an answer in the negative, replied, then you have not read the best book that ever was written.

Let me hear from you and believe me as I am

Yours my dear friend, most truly Wm Cowper.

Mrs. Unwin is pretty well and begs me not to forget her best respects.

JOSEPH HILL   Saturday, 25 October 1788

Address: Joseph Hill Esqre / Wargrave near Twyford / Berks
Postmark: OC/27/88
Cowper Johnson

Weston   October 25. 1788.
My dear friend
I am much obliged to you for taking the necessary measures to extort payment from the insolvent Welshman.[1] Frog I will not call him, because that is the name by which I call my valuable friends and neighbors the Throckmortons; for brevity sake, as you will suppose.

Nothing can be more picturesque than your description of Wargrove, nor, consequently more beautiful than the subject of it. And I would that I were at liberty for an excursion which I know I should find so perfectly agreeable and to which I have every inducement. But Homer, Homer, Homer, is my eternal answer to all invitations to a distance, and must be so long as I have that great stone to roll before me wherever I go. It will not I hope prove like that of Sisyphus. To Blithfield, to Bath, to Normandy have I been bidden, and

[4] In all his references to *L'Espirt des lois* (probably the book in question) Montesquieu is remarkably reticent and even, after he had run into trouble with the Church, moderately defensive. Other people described his work as the best book that ever was written and just conceivably he was quoting such an opinion in a semi-facetious way. C's friend, whom we cannot identify, must have visited Paris or the Bordeaux region between the end of 1748 and Montesquieu's death at the beginning of 1755.

[1] Mr Morgan. See n.1, C to Hill, 27 May 1777.

by friends whom I much love, but am forced to make the same reply to all.

The witness of my writing this agreeable Billet to Mr. Morgan, is my friend Mr. Rose of Rathbone place, a young Gentleman now engaged in the study of the Law under the auspices of a Special Pleader whose name I think is Praed.[2] He is at present with me, and because I know he will please you, I will with your permission recommend it to him to pay his respects to you next Winter in Great Queen Street.

My Love and Lady Hesketh's Love attend Mrs. Hill and your Sisters, of whose health I rejoice to hear and heartily wish them a continuance of the present delightful weather that they may have the most perfect enjoyment of the beauties of Wargrove.

Yours my dear friend most truly
Wm Cowper[3]

WALTER BAGOT   Thursday, 30 October 1788

Address: The Revd. Water Bagot.
Morgan Library

Weston October 30. 1788

My dear friend

The good fortune that you wish'd me I have actually enjoyed, having had an opportunity by means of Lady Hesketh's carriage to see your brother Howard at Chicheley. I had the pleasure of spending near an hour with him in the study, for the consequences of his unfortunate fall which he got in Norfolk, did not permit him to join the Ladies in the Salloon. It gave me much concern that not having seen him so many years, I should at last find him with a broken bone. He was, however, otherwise in good health, and as I told him, had suffer'd less in his looks by the lapse of time that has passed since we were all at School together, than any of us. Dr. Kerr of Northampton[1] has set the rib, and the only thing he complain'd of was the flannel bandage wrapt twice

---

[2] Unidentified.
[3] C's signature removed and substituted in another hand.

---

[1] See n.6, C to Unwin, 3 Jan. 1784.

about him, which he said occasion'd by the heat of it an itching where he could not scratch, and somewhat affected his respiration.

I was truly happy to be the instrument of bringing the Chesters and my Cousin to an acquaintance. She and your Sister would love each other more than people generally do in this neighborhood, could they come often together. Another year perhaps may afford more frequent opportunities than they are likely to find in the present, which is now far spent, and threatens us with foul weather soon and dirty roads which make Chicheley unapproachable by mortal wight who is subject to fear in a carriage. Menelaus tells Telemachus that had Ulysses return'd safe from Troy, it was in his intention to have built him a city and a house in Argos, that he and his people transferring themselves thither from Ithaca, might have become his neighbours.[2] Had I the thousands with which some people are favour'd, I would gladly build for the Chesters, not a city, which they would not want, but a house at least as good as that which Menelaus had design'd for Ulysses, in the precincts of Weston Underwood. Their non-residence here being the only defect in the situation. But I ought to account myself in my present circumstances and while Lady Hesketh continues here, if not so happy as in that case I should be, at least as happy as a world which I do not hold, as the saying is, in a string, is ever likely to make me. We are but one remove from brother and sister, and that distance has long since been absorb'd by a more than Cousinly affection.

I did not send you my verses in which I celebrated my little dog, because I knew that the Chesters being in possession of them, they would soon find their way to Blithfield. I rejoice that they pleased you. The Northampton Clerk has been with me again, and I have again promised him my assistance.[3] You may depend on my sending you a printed copy of this my second meditation upon Church-yard Subjects, as soon as I have received the impression. It is likely indeed to be an annual remittance, for said Clerk will, I dare say, resort to me for poetical aid till either he or I shall want an

[2] *Odyssey*, iv, lines 174–8 (lines 211–20 in C's translation).
[3] C's 1788 'Stanzas Subjoined to the Bills of Mortality . . . '

Epitaph for ourselves. I am not sorry to be employed by him, considering t[he] [4] task, in respect of the occasion of it, as even mor[e] important than Iliad and Odyssey together. To p[ut] others in mind of their latter end, is at least as proper an occupation for a man whose own latter end is nearer by almost sixty years than once it was, as to write about Gods and heroes. Let me once get well out of these two long stories, and if I ever meddle with such matters more, call me as Fluellin says, a fool and an ass and a prating coxcomb. [5]

It gives me much pleasure to hear that Lord Bagot is so well, and I sincerely wish that he may find the Naiads of Buxton [6] as propitious to him as those of Cheltenham. The Peerage can ill spare such Peers as he.

With Mrs. Unwin's best respects, I remain my dear friend, most truly Yours

Wm Cowper.

SAMUEL ROSE   Tuesday, 11 November 1788

Puttick and Simpson Catalogue[1]

Weston has not been without its tragedies since you left us. Mrs. Frog's piping Bull-finch has been eaten by a rat, and the villain left nothing but poor Bully's beak behind him. It will be a wonder if this event does not at some convenient time employ my versifying passion.[2] Did ever fair lady, from the Lesbia of Catullus to the present day lose her bird and find no poet to commemorate the loss? But, another tragedy, still more deplorable by me, though it did not happen, had almost happen'd, the very day I believe on which you left us.[3]

---

[4] Part of the letter is covered by the seal.   [5] *Henry V*, IV. i. 79–80.
[6] Buxton, 33 miles from Derby, had been a Roman bath and settlement; it was a popular spa in the 1780s.

---

[1] This letter is quoted in the Puttick and Simpson catalogue for 1 Aug. 1856. It was lot 205 of the first day's sale from Richard Capel Lambe's collection, and it is described as a four-page quarto. *Hayley* erroneously quotes this paragraph in his text (i. 319–20) of C to Rose, 25 Sept. 1788.
[2] 'On the Death of Mrs. Throckmorton's Bulfinch' was first published in the *GM* of Feb. 1789.
[3] According to the catalogue, the 'mishap occurred to *Beau*, his spaniel, and is circumstantially related.'

JOSEPH HILL   Thursday, 13 November 1788

Address: Joseph Hill Esqre / Chancery Office / London.
Postmarks: NO/14/88 *and* NEWPORT/PAGNEL
Cowper Johnson

Weston Underwood
Novr. 13. 1788

My dear friend,

That you may have the satisfaction to know that your
kind present suffer'd no unnecessary delay in its journey
hither, I give you the earliest information possible of its safe
arrival, together with many thanks for it. The Turkey has
been already an object of our joint admiration though in his
feathers, and will I doubt not excite still more when we
shall see him in querpo.[1] He does great credit to Mrs. Hill's
management, insomuch that I know not if she have not
brought upon herself some trouble of which perhaps she will
hear News 'ere long, but knowing that Lady Hesketh intends
shortly to write to her I forbear to mention it. It will serve
in the mean time to employ conjecture. I beg you will
present her with my very best respects, and with two thirds
of my thankful acknowledgements on the occasion, taking
the remainder to yourself. We were fortunate in receiving
your Letter so early. Mr. Throckmorton's servant happening
to go to Newport for his master's Letters brought mine too;
yours, otherwise, would not have reach'd me 'till the next
day, for we have not a daily Post.

We are kept, as they say, in hot water concerning the poor
King, but the last accounts having been the most favorable
encourage a hope that the important question of his Life or
Death, will soon be decided to our wish.[2] Should he die, the
best thing the Ministry, or rather the Parliament can do, will

---

[1] 'In the flesh.'
[2] Drs Ida Macalpine and Richard Hunter (*George III and the Mad-Business*,
1966) have speculated that the King's illness was a classic case of porphyria. John
Brooke, *King George III* (1972), agrees with them: 'It is a hereditary disease
which may take many forms. The porphyrins are pigments in the cells of the
human body, essential to its proper functioning, and the disease arises when the
body manufactures too many. Its symptoms include sensitivity of the skin to
sunlight or even to touch, colic, weakness of the limbs, difficulty in swallowing,
hoarseness, vomiting, and constipation. In acute stages it leads to irritability,
excitement, sleeplessness, delirium, and delusions, so that it may be mistaken for
mental illness' (p. 339). The attack which C describes in this and subsequent

be to Advertize for a Successor, for it does not presently occur Where we shall find a worthy one.[3]

I have been somewhat alarm'd lately for Mr. Chester, who I hear has a Carbuncle on his back; a very painful, and which is worse, a dangerous distemper, especially to a man like him, not qualified by great stength of constitution to contend with it. He spent the Summer at Harrow-gate, as the King at Cheltenham.[4] If such be the consequences of Water-drinking, let *Us* abstain from all such perilous bev'rage and drink Wine.

Lady Hesketh adds her best Compliments to mine both to yourself and Mrs. Hill. Believe me, my Dear Friend, most sincerely Yours

Wm Cowper

JOHN NEWTON   Saturday, 29 November 1788

Princeton

Weston. Novbr. 29. 1788

My dear Friend —
Not to fill my paper with apologies I will only say that you

letters began in June 1788 and was over by mid-Feb. 1789. Fanny Burney (6 Nov. 1788) provides a vivid picture of the tension between the King and the Queen: 'The King, in the middle of the night, had insisted upon seeing if his Queen was not removed from the house; and he had come into her room, with a candle in his hand, opened the bed-curtains, and satisfied himself she was there . . . This observance of his directions had much soothed him; but he stayed a full half-hour, and the depth of terror during that time no words can paint. The fear of such another entrance was now so strongly upon the nerves of the poor Queen, that she could hardly support herself.' (*Burney Diary*, iv. 135.)

[3] In Nov. 1788 there was real concern that the King would not survive. 'On 10 November he was two hours in a coma, the Lord of the Bedchamber in waiting attended at St James's to answer inquiries, and the Archbishop of Canterbury ordered prayers to be said for his recovery. Pitt went to Windsor and was told by the Prince of Wales that it was the unanimous opinion of the physicians "that His Majesty's understanding is at present so affected that there does not appear to them any interval in which any act that he could do could properly be considered as done with a consciousness and understanding of what it was about". "There was more ground to fear than to hope, and more reason to apprehend durable insanity than death." This was the situation about the middle of November. Once the danger of death had passed, it was the affliction of mind which gave most concern and dominated the picture of the King's illness. The Prince of Wales took charge at Windsor, and Pitt began to turn his thoughts towards carrying on the government by a regency.' Brooke, *King George III*, p. 327.

[4] The King stayed five weeks at Cheltenham in the summer of 1788. The waters at Cheltenham were supposed to be good for what at that time was thought

know my occupation, and how little time it leaves me for other employments, in which, had I leisure for them, I could take much pleasure. Letter-writing would be one of the most agreeable, and especially writing to you. It happens too that at this season of the year I lie in bed later than when the days are not so short; not for the sake of indulgence, but through necessity; for the servants lying later too, there is no room for me below till near 9 o'clock. Thus is my time, that part of it which I give to my correspondents, sadly abridged, so that I am at this moment in debt to them all, except one, who lives in Ireland. I have occasionally however heard of your well-being; you would otherwise notwithstanding all these hindrances have received at least a line or two, could I have sent no more. I know too that you have heard of mine; or if not of my *well*-being, at least of my being *as well* as when you saw me.

About three days since I was told that Mr. Wright, Lord Dartmouth's steward was at Olney, and yesterday I passed through Olney, ent'ring the town at one end and going out at the other, without once recollecting that such a person exists. This morning he is gone to London. My fault is therefore irreparable, unless you should at any time happen to see Mr. Wright and will be so good as to ask his pardon for me. He is one of the last men living to whom I would show disrespect, because he is truly respectable himself and the servant of a most valuable Master; the case too, seems the more flagrant, because I must have pass'd immediately before the window of the room in which he sat, whether he was at the Swan or at Mr. Gardener's[1] where he dined yesterday, and I pass'd at two o'clock. It gives me much pleasure however to understand by a message from Mr. Wright deliver'd here by Mr. Raban, that his Lordship enjoys better health than for years past. May he long enjoy it. — Poor Jenny Raban[2] is declining fast toward the grave and as fast aspiring to the skies. I expected to have heard yesterday of her death,

to be merely a bilious complaint, and the King found the waters 'most efficacious'. See *King George III*, pp. 322–3.

[1] Unidentified.
[2] Jenny, the daughter of Thomas and Elizabeth Raban, was christened 8 July 1768 (*OPR*, p. 353). C corrects this report on Jenny's health in his next letter to

but learn'd on enquiry that she was better. Dr. Kerr has seen her, and by virtue I suppose of his prescriptions, her fits with which she was frequently troubled, are become less frequent. But there is no reason, I believe, to look for her recovery. Her case is a Consumption into which I saw her sliding swiftly in the Spring. There is not much to be lamented, or that ought to be so, in the death of those who go to glory. She was a beautiful girl and perhaps may have left a heart-ach for a legacy to some poor Swain of Olney, though I never heard, beautiful as she was, that she had any Lovyers. Many an ugly bundle can find an husband in such a place as Olney, while Venus herself would shine there unnoticed. If you find many blots and my writing illegible, you must pardon them in consideration of the cause. Lady Hesketh and Mrs. Unwin are both talking as if they design'd to make themselves amends for the silence they are enjoin'd while I sit translating Homer. Mrs. Unwin is preparing the Breakfast, and not having seen each other since they parted to go to bed, they have consequently a deal to communicate.

I saw Mr. Bean lately and he is well. I called there yesterday but found him not. He also dined at Mr. Gardener's. It gave me concern to be told by the servant that Mrs. Bean is very much indisposed with the Rheumatism. — I have seen Mr. Greatheed[3] both at his own house and here, but his wife I have not seen, neither have I heard in what state of health and spirits she finds herself at present. Not long since she suffer'd a melancholy that seem'd rather alarming. Prosperity sits well on Mr. Greatheed, and I cannot find that this advantageous change in his condition has made any alteration either in his views or his behaviour.

When we return'd thanks for an excellent basket of Fish, Shrimps were not mention'd, because the Shrimps were not found 'till after the letter was sent, and then by mere accident. They were brought to light however soon enough to serve the purpose for which you were so kind as to send them.

The Winter is gliding merrily away while my Cousin is

Newton (9 Dec. 1788). According to *Wright*, after 'many years of mental derangement [Jenny] died in her brother George's house at Olney, about the end of February 1827.'

[3] See n.1, C to Newton, 4 June 1785.

with us. She annihilates the difference between Cold and Heat, gloomy skies and cloudless. Mrs. Unwin is well and joins me in the most affectionate remembrances of the Trio in Coleman's Buildings. I have written I know not what and with the dispatch of Leger de main, but with the utmost truth and consciousness of what I say, assure you, my Dear friend, that I am

Ever yours Wm Cowper

SAMUEL ROSE   Sunday, 30 November 1788

Address: Samuel Rose Esqre / Percy Street / Rathbone Place / London.
Postmarks: DE/3/88 *and* OULNEY
Princeton

Weston. Novbr. 30. 1788

My dear friend —

You are probably wond'ring at my silence, but I can give you a satisfactory account of it. Your Letter accompanying the books with which you have favor'd me and for which I return you a thousand thanks, though dated the 15th past, did not arrive here 'till yesterday. Johnson witheld it in hopes of being able to send me my MSS well Fuselied, but after all, his hopes proved frustrate. The Box reach'd me between 4 and 5 when I was on the way to the Hall where we dined; I had therefore no opportunity to open it 'till 10 at night, but I have this Morning dispatch'd the little parcel thither address'd to Mr. Frog. You are very good to think of me whether in an Oyster Cellar or elsewhere, and the Oysters themselves did great honour to your judgment in that commodity, but you had so loaded me with presents of one sort or other, that I could not for the life of me do less than exclaim — Ohe jam satis est![1] If Donors have their feelings, Donees must be permitted to have theirs also.

I shall have great pleasure in taking now and then a peep at my old friend Vincent Bourne,[2] the neatest of all men in his versification, though when I was under his ushership at Westminster, the most slovenly in his person. He was so

---

[1] Horace, *Satires*, I. v. 12: 'That's enough of that!'
[2] See n.4, C to Hill, 13 July 1777.

inattentive to his boys, and so indifferent whether they brought him good or bad exercises, or none at all, that he seem'd determined, as he was the best, so to be the last Latin poet of the Westminster line; a plot which I believe he executed very successfully, for I have not heard of any who has at all deserved to be compared with him.

We have hardly had either rain or snow since you left us; the roads are, accordingly, as dry as in the middle of Summer, and the opportunity of walking much more favorable. We have no season, in my mind, so pleasant as such a Winter, and I account it particularly fortunate that such it proves my Cousin being with us. She is in good health and cheerful, so are we all, and this I say, knowing you will be glad to hear it, for you have seen the time when this could not have been asserted of all your friends at Weston. If Mr. Praed can spare you, and you can allow yourself to be spared by Mr. Praed, we shall rejoice to see you here at Christmas, but I recollect that when I hinted such an excursion to you by word of mouth, you gave me no great encouragement to expect you. Minds alter, and yours may be of the number of those that do so, and if it should, you will be entirely welcome to us all.

It was with much pleasure I learn'd that you had been in Coleman's Buildings. We had the information yesterday in a letter from Mrs. Newton who speaks of your visit in terms of much complacency and satisfaction. Your introduction to Mr. Hill is the next thing to be consider'd. I believe I must give you a letter to him even though I should put you to the expence of double postage. If the measure succeed according to my wishes and hopes, you will hereafter find yourself reimbursed, and such a mode of introduction promises to be the easiest to your feelings which I know will need to be consulted on such an occasion.

We mourn daily for the King, and three times in the week, execrate the malignity and Viperism of the Morning Herald.[3] — Lady Hesketh says I must leave a little space for somewhat

---

[3] C was offended by the ready despair of that journal in discussing the King's illness and he was certainly not pleased by the very favourable treatment given the Prince of Wales. These passages from *The Morning Herald* of 10 Nov. 1788 (No. 2513) are typical of that newspaper's sentiments: 'It is with the deepest regret that we find ourselves under the painful necessity of informing the public, that according to the last dispatches from Windsor, received so late as half past

that she has to say to you. I will therefore only add Mrs. Unwin's affectionate Compliments and my own assurances that I am, my Dear Sir

most truly yours Wm Cowper.

The Frogs are gone this day, for 3 Weeks, into Norfolk; he returns you many thanks for the little book you sent him.[4]

Having had occasion to write this day to Mrs. Hill I have likewise given myself the pleasure of introducing you to Her. Shoes —[5]

JOSEPH HILL   Tuesday, 2 December 1788

Address: Joseph Hill Esqre / Great Queen Street / Lincolns Inn Fields.[1]
Princeton

My dear friend,

I told you lately that I had an ambition to introduce to your acquaintance my valuable friend Mr. Rose. He is now before you. You will find him a person of genteel manners and agreeable conversation. As to his other virtues and good qualities which are many, and such as are not often found in men of his years, I consign them over to your own discernment, perfectly sure that none of them will escape you. — I

eleven last night, there scarcely remained a ground for the continuance of those hopes which so long have been anxiously wished ... His Majesty's physicians have exhausted the last resources of their art ... The unremitting attention of the Prince of Wales towards his Majesty, gives such exemplary proof of duty and filial love, that creates to his Highness the most cordial attachments every hour. — Indeed he is the theme of national approbation and general affection.'

[4] Lady Hesketh has added the following note at this point: 'With one of the *delightfull* Pens with which Mr. Rose has so amply supplied Lady Hesketh, she desires to send him her best Compliments, with a thousand thanks for his polite and obliging attention to the various Commissions she took the liberty of troubling him with; she is a little hurt that acknowledgments so justly due, should have been so *long delay'd*, but for this — *Mr. Johnson only is to blame.* Lady H. takes this opportunity to thank Mr. Rose for the elegant praise he bestows on her fav'rite Mrs. Siddons; it has removed all her doubts, & perfectly satisfied all her partialitys, and tho' she had rather blame anybody than herself, fancies she must have been wrong in suspecting Mr. Rose did not think as justly on this subject, as he seems to do on all others. ——'

[5] Meaning unclear. Perhaps a note to remind C to ask Rose regarding the purchase of shoes. See C to Rose, 18 Dec.

[1] This letter of introduction was enclosed with C's letter to Rose of 30 Nov.

give you joy of each other and remain — my dear old Friend —

Most truly Yours
Wm Cowper.

Weston Underwood
Decr. 2. 1788

MRS KING   Saturday, 6 December 1788

Address: Mrs. King / Pirten Hall near / Kimbolton / Huntingdonshire / Single Sheet.
Postmark: DE/8/88
Princeton

Weston Underwood
Decbr. 6. 1788

My dear Madam,

It must, if you please, be a point agreed between us, that we will not make punctuality in writing the test of our regard for each other, lest we should incur the danger of pronouncing and suffering by an unjust sentence, and this mutually. I have told you, I believe, that the half hour before breakfast is my only Letter-writing opportunity. In summer, I rise rather early, and consequently at that season can find more time for scribbling than at present. If I enter my study now before nine, I find all at sixes and sev'ns, for servants will take, in part at least, the liberty claim'd by their masters. That you may not suppose us all sluggards alike, it is necessary however that I should add a word or two on this subject in justification of Mrs. Unwin, who because the days are too short for the important concerns of Knitting stockings and mending them, rises generally by Candle-light. A practise so much in the stile of all the Ladies of Antiquity who were good for any thing, that it is impossible not to applaud it.

Mrs. Battison being dead;[1] I began to fear that you would have no more calls to Bedford, but the marriage, so near at hand, of the young lady you mention with a gentleman of that place,[2] gives me hope again that you may occasionally approach us as heretofore, and that on some of those occasions

---

[1] See n.4, C to Mrs King, 25 Sept. 1788.
[2] Unidentified.

you will perhaps find your way to Weston. The deaths of some and the marriages of others make a new world of it ev'ry thirty years. Within that space of time the majority are displaced and a new generation has succeeded. Here and there one is permitted to stay a little longer, that there may not be wanting a few grave Dons like myself, to make the observation. This thought struck me very forcibly the other day, on reading a Paper called the County Chronicle[3] which came hither in the package of some books from London. It contain'd News from Hartfordshire, and inform'd me among other things that at Great Berkhamstead, the place of my birth, there is hardly a family left of all those with whom in my early days I was so familiar. The Houses no doubt remain, but the inhabitants are only to be found now by their Grave-stones, and it is certain that I might pass through a Town in which I was once a sort of principal figure, unknowing and unknown. They are happy who have not taken up their rest in a world fluctuating as the sea and passing away with the rapidity of a river. I wish from my heart that yourself and Mr. King may long continue, as you have already long continued, exceptions from the general truth of this remark. You doubtless married early, and the 36 years elapsed may have yet other years to succeed them. I do not forget that your relation Mrs. Battison lived to the age of 86. I am glad of her longævity because it seems to afford some assurance of yours, and I hope to know you better yet before you die.

Should you again Dream of an interview with me, I hope you will have the precaution to shut all doors and windows that no such Impertinents as those you mention may intrude a second time. It is hard that people who never meet awake, cannot come together even in Sleep without disturbance. We might I think be ourselves untroubled, at a time when we are so incapable of giving trouble to others, even had we the inclination.

I have never seen the Observer but am pleased with being handsomely spoken of by an old School fellow.[4] Cumberland

---

[3] *The County Chronicle, and Weekly Advertiser, for Essex, Herts, Kent, Surrey, Middlesex, &c.* which appeared from *c.*1787 until 1841.

[4] In No. XCV of *The Observer*, Cumberland cites *The Task* when he relates

and I boarded together in the same house at Westminster. He was at that time clever, and I suppose has given proof sufficient to the world that he is still clever, but of all that he has written it has never fallen in my way to read a syllable, except perhaps in a Magazine or Review, the sole sources, at present, of all my intelligence. Addison speaks of persons who grow dumb in the study of Eloquence,[5] and I have actually studied Homer 'till I am become a mere Ignoramus in every other province of Literature.

An almost Cessation of Egg-laying among the Hens has made it impossible for Mrs. Unwin to enterprize a Cake. She, however, returns you a thousand thanks for the receipt, and being now furnish'd with the necessary ingredients will begin directly. My Letter writing time is spent and I must now to Homer. With my best respects to Mr. King, I remain, Dear Madam —

Most Affectionately Yours   Wm Cowper.

When I wrote last, I told you, I believe, that Lady Hesketh was with us; she is with us now, making a cheerful winter for us at Weston. The acquisition of a new friend, and at a late day, the recovery of the friend of our youth, are two of the chief comforts of which this life is susceptible.

how he responded to the setting of the home in a distant country of a man called Attalus: 'It was a scene to seize the imagination with rapture; a poet's language would have run spontaneously into metre at the sight of it; "What a subject," said I within myself, "is here present for those ingenious bards, who have the happy talent of describing nature in her fairest forms! Oh! that I could plant the delightful author of *The Task* in this very spot! Perhaps, whilst his eye — *in a fine phrensy rolling* — glanced over this enchanting prospect, he might burst forth into the following, or something like the following, rhapsody —".' *The Observer: Being a Collection of Moral, Literary and Familiar Essays* (1785), iv. 16.

[5] C is referring to *Spectator* No. 231 of Saturday, 24 Nov. 1711 in which Addison remarks: 'But notwithstanding an Excess of Modesty obstructs the Tongue, and renders it unfit for its Offices, a due Proportion of it is thought so requisite to an Orator, that Rhetoricians have recommended it to their Disciples as a Particular in their Art. *Cicero* tells us, that he never liked an Orator, who did not appear in some little Confusion at the beginning of his Speech, and confesses that he himself never entered upon an Oration without trembling and concern.' *The Spectator*, ed. Donald F. Bond (Oxford, 1965), ii. 398.

JOSEPH JOHNSON   Saturday, 6 December 1788

Princeton (*copy*)

Weston Lodge, Dec. 6. 1788.
Dear sir,

I rejoice that Homer has once more set out on his travels to Ham.[1] I have no fear of Mr. Fuseli's remarks. He never finds fault in the wrong place. His delay has however sometimes affected me with concern, not because I am conscious of impatience, but because it has appeared to me too much like a symptom, that he found the revisal of my translation a burthen, which he could not conveniently bear. I set too high a value on his strictures and have been too much benefited by them not to regret this, if it be true. Yet at the same time it becomes me to say, that I should be sorry to owe even so great an advantage to his detriment and inconvenience.

The Analytical Review[2] comes close both in plan and execution to the idea I have always entertained of what a review ought to be. Perhaps before this work was thought on, certainly before I had heard that such a work was intended, I have expressed to my friends a wish, that such a performance were set on foot by persons liberal and well-informed and consequently well qualified to conduct it. That extreme bitterness of censure, which I have so often observed in the other reviews, and which nothing less than the immoral tendency of any work could at all justify, has frequently given me great disgust; and I doubt not, that it has operated as a restraint, if not on the press, at least on the pen of many a modest man as certainly and effectually as any prohibitory law could have done whatever.

I am, dear sir, with my best respects to Mr. Fuseli

your most obedient servant,
Wm. Cowper.

---

[1] General Cowper's residence.
[2] *Russell* (pp. 158–60) describes the reviews C undertook in this journal from 1789 to 1793.

JOHN NEWTON   Tuesday, 9 December 1788

Address: Revd. John Newton
Olney

My dear friend,

That I may return to you the Latin MSS[1] as soon as possible I take a short opportunity to scratch a few hasty lines, that it may not arrive alone. I have made here and there an alteration which appear'd to me for the better; but on the whole, I cannot but wonder at your adroitness in a business to which you have been probably at no time much accustom'd, and which for many years you have not at all practised. If when you shall have written the whole, you shall wish for a corrector of the rest, so far as my own skill in the matter goes, it is entirely at your service.

Our rural rumours in general deserve but little credit, and it seems now, that even a Father is not to be implicitly believed in what he relates of his own daughter. Mr. Raban called on purpose to tell us that Jenny was dying, but Dr. Kerr being consulted, instead of confirming has entirely falsified the report. He says that she is not only not in a dying state, but has never been in the least danger. I carried your Letter to Mrs. Raban myself, who informed me that the poor girl is better, though extremely weak through the operation of medicines prescribed to her by the Doctor. He pronounces it a case of worms.

Mrs. Unwin is much obliged to Mrs. Newton for her kind letter and will answer it soon. Lady Hes—h has had a cold and sore throat, but is recover'd. She is obliged to you for the part of your letter in which she is mention'd, and returns her Compliments. She loves all my friends and consequently cannot be indifferent to you. The Frogs are gone into Norfolk on a visit to Lord Petre's. They will probably return this day fortnight. Mr. Finch is now Preacher at Ravenstone.[2] Mr. Canniford[3] still preaches here. The latter is warmly attended, the former, of course, delivers himself to the walls. He has heard Mr. Canniford, having I suppose a curiosity to know

[1] See n.2, C to Newton, 5 June 1788.
[2] See n.4, C to Newton, [3 Mar. 1788].
[3] See n.4, C to Newton, 21 Jan. 1788.

by what charm he held his popularity; but whether he has
heard him to his own edification or not, is more than I can
say. Probably he wonders; for I have heard that he is a
sensible man. His successful competitor is wise in nothing
but his knowledge of the Gospel.

I am summon'd to Breakfast and am my dear friend with
our best Love to Mrs. Newton, Miss Catlett and yourself —

> most affectionately Yours
> Wm Cowper.

Weston. Decr. 9. 1788

I have not the assurance to call this an answer to your
letter, in which were many things deserving much notice;
but it is the best that in the present moment I am able to
send you.

JOSEPH HILL   *c.*Tuesday, 16 December 1788[1]

Address: Joseph Hill Esqre / Chancery Office / London
Postmarks: DE/16/88 *and* OULNEY
Cowper Johnson

My dear friend —

I write yet once again to give you notice of a draft payable
to John Higgins Esqre. or order for Thirty pounds, and dated
yesterday. My Bank, I should hope, is by this time somewhat
replenish'd, and in condition to answer the demand.

I have many acknowledgments to make you for your kind
reception of Mr. Rose. I consider him as my proxy at your
house, and all your favours to him as conferred on myself.
At Christmas I hope to have his company for a week. He is
a great walker in which respect he suits me well, for while
cold weather lasts I am a great walker too.

There seems to be a reasonable hope, judging by the opinion
of the faculty, that the King's malady may prove an affair of
no long continuance. He will be somewhat astonish'd, when
he shall be capable of learning it, to find at what a rate some
persons have driven during his derangement; And the longer
his disorder lasts, the more danger there will be of a relapse in

---

[1] The postmark, taken with the comments in the letter, suggests that it was
probably written on the morning of the sixteenth, before the post went out.

consequence of such discovery, for they seem to lose no opportunity of saying and doing every thing that would go near to turn the Head of any King, even of one whose head had never received a twirl before. No man wishes him well more warmly than myself, but I much fear that be the event of his Indisposition what it may, he has seen his happiest days, sensible as he must be if he live to be sensible of any thing

> How sharper than a Serpent's tooth it is
> To have an Heir like his.[2]

Lady Hesketh had last night a cold and was a little feverish; I have not heard of her this Morning, but hope soon to learn from herself that she is better. If she knew that I am writing she would say, remember me to them both, which thus doing and adding my own best respects to Mrs. Hill together with Compliments from the two Turkeys who are both in perfect health, I remain

my dear friend
Affectionately Yours
Wm Cowper.

MRS THROCKMORTON   Tuesday, 16 December 1788

Address: Mrs. Throckmorton / Buckenham place / near Brandon / Norfolk
Postmark: DE/17/88
Sir Robert Throckmorton

The Lodge
Decbr. 16 1788

My dear Madam —
    Not because I have eaten neither Ham nor Chicken, for I have actually eaten both, [   ][1] I forgot your direction, but because I fe[ared (I felt] very sure that I should hear from you) le[st our letters] should cross on the road, therefore it was [that I did] not write as you had good reason to expect I sh[ould.]
    The truth is however that though I sent no letter, I did

---

[2] See *King Lear*, I. iv. 297–8.

[1] The MS is badly torn and the words provided in square brackets are supplied from Hannay's transcription of Wright's copy of C's letter.

in fact begin one; but having risen that morning in very indifferent spirits, I found it so tinged with my own sable mood, that having filled one page, I burn'd it. You see then that I am not altogether so uncourteous a Knight, as on the first appearance of the affair I seem to have been; au contraire, I have great pleasure in writing to you, and had I not this everlasting labour of Translation on my hands, should have pelted you with letters ever since you have been absent.

On the day you went, setting forth to my walk, I met Charles with your milk-white palfrey at his side, who told me that you had found miserable roads and were obliged to ride two miles; but that at Astwood Bury[2] he had turn'd back, the pony being no longer wanted. I rejoiced, this being the case, that you had the discretion to take him with you, not [   ] the rest of your journey you would perform [   ]y alarm even to nerves susceptible as yours. [m]uch delighted with the late hours that you [Norf]olk. You do as you please, but I know [   ] you will please to do, so well, that I cannot but be a little apprehensive for the consequences. My chief comfort is that your present mode of living will be of no long duration, and that in another week you will come to settle once again in your tranquil abode at Weston.[3] You will find much less company there than you have been accustom'd to; the place will seem to you a perfect solitude in comparison with what it was; not that any of our neighbors are dead, or that the Natives will not come down upon you as usual, but because an army that had quarter'd itself within your walls, exists no longer. I cannot tell you exactly the numbers that have been destroy'd, but victory has daily d[   ] on the side of the Rat[ter whose success was] so brilliant, that 12, [   ] fallen victims to his [   ] he made among their [numb]ers. One in particular [   ] for his uncommon siz[e   ] as large as a Rabbit [   ] and the rats that occupy the [   ] in short worthy in

---

[2] c.5 miles south-east of Olney in Bedfordshire.
[3] According to John Throckmorton's diary (Coughton Court), they left Weston on 1 Dec. and arrived at Buckenham on 2 Dec. 1788 where they 'found the Lord, Lady and Miss Petre, Mr and Mrs Neare'. They 'left Buckenham and slept at Eton' on 22 Dec., returning to Weston the next day.

every respec[t   ] Rat-[   ] to his Majesty and to
y[ou.]

The puppy destined to be my Cousin's [has turned out] to
be a perfect beauty, handsomer even than his sire by a length
of tail which *he* must never hope for. He is beside the most
animated little fellow in the world, and though no bigger
than my thumb, when I open'd the stable door a day or two
since to visit him, sprang forward and bark'd at me.

Weston produces few incidents when you are absent. I
have told you, I believe, all the news. I rejoice that Mr. Frog
is well, that your nerves are, at least, not worse than they
were, and that George's gout rather threatens than executes.
We are well, and love you, and wish you at home again, and
the Compliments of all three attend you. For my own part
I am at all times and most perfectly Yours Wm C.

Here we have no snow, but bright suns and sharp frosts
for ever. Between *you and I*, did you ever feel it so intensely
cold as at this moment? Yet cold as it is, [I am so] occupied
with you, I have let the fire go out. My love to William. I
did not know that he was of the party.

SAMUEL ROSE   Thursday, 18 December 1788

Address: Samuel Rose Esqre / Percy Street / Rathbone Place / London.
Postmarks: [illegible] /88 *and* OULNEY
Charles Ryskamp

The Lodge Decbr. 18
1788

My dear friend —
I shall probably send you a scrap rather than a letter,
having slept this Morning later than usual, and consequently
shorten'd the Ante-breakfast opportunity, the only one I can
find for my correspondents.

Were there no other reason for your coming than merely
the pleasure it will afford to us, that reason alone would be
Sufficient; but after so many toils and with so many more in
prospect, it seems essential to your well-being that you should
allow yourself a respite, which perhaps you can take as
comfortably, I am sure you may as quietly, here as any where.

It gives me great pleasure to understand that you have paid your first visit in Queen Street with so much ease to yourself, and that my friend Hill perform'd so handsomely the part I expected from him. I shall rejoice still more if you find the connexion not only agreeable, but hereafter beneficial also. My friend Joseph is in point of good qualities all that I can say of him whether in verse or prose. But I owe you one caution which on account of its importance I should deal unfairly with you to withold; he is warm in temper, and consequently warm in disputation. Touch him, if you touch him at all, very gently on the subjects of Religion and Politics. You will presently feel how far you may venture to differ from him on either. He is, or was at least, extremely latitudinary on the former, and what is his precise mode of thinking on the latter I cannot inform you; but I believe him what we call a staunch Whig on the old plan, in short, just what I am myself.

Mrs. Hill, whom perhaps you have not yet seen, neither indeed have I, is by the report of those who know her well, a most amiable woman. Sensible, obliging, and gentle both in voice and manner. With her, I have no doubt you will find it easy to associate without the least danger of a clash; nor will you incur any danger of it with her husband, consulting only the dictates of your own discretion a little enlighten'd by this preliminary information.

You will be so kind as to let us know on what day we may look for you.[1] As for ourselves, we are all in good health at present. Lady Hesketh has had a cold which threat'ned to become something worse, but James's Powder expell'd the enemy in few hours, and she is now herself again. The Frogs, now in Norfolk, return next Tuesday. From her I learn that they are as well as usual, and will come home I suppose well prepared by the pleasures of Buckenham house [for][2] a merry Christmas at Weston.

My Shoes may come either before you, or with you, as may be most convenient. Accept our best remembrances

---

[1] The visit occurred before 19 Jan. In his letter of that date, C comments on the report Rose has sent him of his disagreeable trip back to London.
[2] This word has been covered by the seal.

together with those of my Coz, and believe me, my Dear Sir,

Sincerely Yours
Wm Cowper.

We have not yet tried the Blue.[3]

ROBERT SMITH　　　　　Saturday, 20 December 1788

Hayley (1809), 183–5

Weston-Underwood, Dec. 20, 1788.

My dear sir,

Mrs. Unwin is in tolerable health, and adds her warmest thanks to mine for your favor, and for your obliging enquiries. My own health is better than it has been many years. Long time I had a stomach that would digest nothing, and now nothing disagrees with it, an amendment for which I am, under God, indebted to the daily use of soluble tartar, which I have never omitted these two years. I am still, as you may suppose, occupied in my long labour. The Iliad has nearly received its last polish. And I have advanced in a rough copy, as far as to the ninth book of the Odyssey. My friends are, some of them, in haste to see the work printed, and my answer to them is — 'I do nothing else, and this I do day and night — it must in time be finished.'

My thoughts however are not engaged to Homer only. I cannot be so much a poet as not to feel greatly for the King, the Queen, and the country. My speculations on these subjects are indeed melancholy, for no such tragedy has befallen in my day. We are forbidden to trust in man, I will not therefore say, I trust in Mr. Pitt; — but in his counsels, under the blessing of providence, the remedy is, I believe, to be found, if a remedy there be. His integrity, firmness, and sagacity, are the only human means that seem adequate to the great emergence.

You say nothing of your own health, of which I should have been happy to have heard favorably. May you long enjoy the best. Neither Mrs. Unwin nor myself have a sincerer,

---

[3] C is perhaps referring to a gift from Rose of blue cheese.

or a warmer wish than for your felicity.

> I am,
> My dear Sir,
> Your most obliged and affectionate.
> W. C.

SAMUEL ROSE   Monday, 19 January 1789

Wright, iii. 340–2[1]

19 Jan. 1789.

My dear Sir,

We are all truly sorry that you were accompanied to London so disagreeably. Having the headache you had small need of fellow-travellers, and perhaps found yourself, though colder, yet more commodiously situated, than had you been obliged to exert yourself for the entertainment of others. If we had our pleasures while you were with us, as certainly we had, we have had our pains since. Poor Mrs. Unwin got a terrible fall on a gravel-walk covered with ice, the consequences of which have confined her to her chamber ever since. At first we feared a fracture, her pain being so extreme that she fainted under it, and continued in a fainting fit a considerable time; but it proves only a contusion. Her leg has been useless, however, a whole week, and whole weeks, I doubt not, must yet pass before it will recover its former ability. Evils never come alone. We lose my cousin to-morrow, unless the frost, which seems to have set in again this morning, should influence her to stay till the roads are again beaten. Yesterday they were full of water, consequently to-day they are full of ice, and though I shall think highly of her wisdom at any rate, yet my opinion of it will be advanced to a still sublimer height if she consent to a little delay. Mrs. Unwin's fall and my cousin's departure are a burthen, together, quite as heavy as I feel myself a match for, but I have been so many years accustomed either to feel trouble or to expect it, that habit

[1] Parts of paragraph 1 and 4 are quoted in the Puttick and Simpson catalogue of 1 Aug. 1856, lot 207 of the Richard Capel Lambe collection. Hayley and Southey erroneously placed parts of paragraphs 4 and 5 from C's letter of 19 Feb. 1789 under this date.

19 January 1789

has endued me with that sort of fortitude which I remember my old schoolmaster Dr. Nicol used to call the passive valour of an ass.[2] I have accordingly tolerable spirits in circumstances which twenty years ago would have left me none.

I thank you much for all the trouble you have taken on my account, for your call on Johnson, and for what you have done toward fitting out my parcel for its journey. It came not on Saturday, and I conclude that the candle-snappers not being included in time, occasioned the delay.

Johnson, no doubt, with the true sagacity of a bookseller smelt out your relationship to Mr. Griffiths,[3] and on that account, felt no small degree of alarm on discovering that you were made privy to the important secret. I am glad, however, that you had the address to compose his spirits. If he be at all an adept in the science professed by his friend Fuseli's friend Lavater, your aspect might serve in part to assure him that his fears were needless.

I do not at present feel myself so much amused by my new occupation as I hoped to be. The critic's task is not a pleasant one, unless he can find something to commend; and it has not yet been my fortune to stumble on an opportunity of much encomium. There are already three authors in my cupboard; ay, four, who will have small cause to bless their stars that it has been my lot to judge them.[4] On Saturday I read the first book of the *Athenaid*, and it is a sad thing, but a true, that I must read it again before I shall understand it. This bodes not much felicity to the memory of poor Glover, but I will hope that the gloom which hangs over his outset will clear away as I proceed. Apollo and all Parnassus know, or ought to know, that I enter on his work with the best dispositions in the world to be charmed with it.

[2] See n.6, *Adelphi*.

[3] Rose's father, William, was the brother-in-law of Ralph Griffiths, founder and publisher of *The Monthly Review* (see n.4, C to Unwin, 12 June 1782). Rose began reviewing for the *Monthly Review* in Aug. 1785 while a student at the University of Glasgow, and he continued to do so until his death. See Benjamin Christie Nangle, *The Monthly Review, Second Series, 1790–1815* (Oxford, 1955), pp. 58–9.

[4] It seems likely that Johnson did not publish C's most unfavourable reviews. Glover and Dwight are the two authors that C liked the best of the four he mentions in this letter. C's review of Richard Glover's *The Athenaid* (1787) appeared in the March (iii. 323–35) and Apr. (iii. 538–55) issues of the *Analytical Review*; his review of Timothy Dwight's *The Conquest of Canaan* (Hartford,

The ladies both beg to be affectionately remembered to you. My scribbling time and paper are both spent. — Adieu!

Truly yours,
Wm. Cowper.

We exult, and Lady Hesketh, in particular, in the persevering orthodoxy of your political sentiments. It is impossible that a man like you can do less than abhor daily more and more the conduct of a faction which makes itself duly more and more destestable. It is the natural antipathy of good to ill.

SAMUEL ROSE   Saturday, 24 January 1789

Puttick and Simpson Catalogue and *Hayley*, i. 323[1]

The Lodge, Jan. 24, 1789.

My dear sir,

We have heard from my Cousin in Norfolk-street; she reached home safely, and in good time. An observation suggests itself which, though I have but little time for observation making, I must allow myself time to mention. Accidents, as we call them, generally occur when there seems least reason to expect them. If a friend of ours travels far in indifferent roads, and at an unfavourable season, we are reasonably alarmed for the safety of one in whom we are so much interested. Yet how seldom do we hear a tragical account of such a journey! It is on the contrary at home, in our yard or garden, perhaps in our parlor that disaster finds us; in any place in short, where we seem perfectly out of the reach of danger. The lesson inculcated by such a procedure on the

---

Conn., 1785) appeared in the Apr. issue (iii. 531-44) of the same magazine. Both reviews were signed P.P. See *Russell*, pp. 158-9. C characterized Glover's poem 'the work of a man of considerable poetical merit, and of much classical information'; and he compared Dwight favourably to Pope: '. . . he is chiefly to be commended for the animation with which he writes, and which rather encreases, as he proceeds, than suffers any abatement.'

---

[1] In the Puttick and Simpson catalogue for 1 Aug. 1856 this letter occurs as lot 208 of the Richard Capel Lambe sale. It is described as '3 pages 4to'. Our text from the third sentence in the first paragraph to the end of the paragraph is taken from the sales catalogue; the rest of the letter is from *Hayley*.

part of Providence towards us, seems to be that of perpetual dependence.

Having preached this sermon, I must hasten to a close; you know that I am not idle, nor can I afford to be so; I would gladly spend more time with you, but by some means or other this day has hitherto proved a day of hindrance and confusion.

W. C.

MRS KING   Thursday, 29 January 1789

Princeton

My dear Madam —

This morning, I said to Mrs. Unwin, — I must write to Mrs. King — Her long silence alarms me — something has happen'd — These words of mine proved only a prelude to the arrival of your messenger with his most welcome charge, for which I return you my sincerest thanks. You have sent me the very things I wanted, and which I should have continued to want had not you sent them. As often as the wine has been set on the table, I have said to myself, this is all very well, but I have no bottle-stands; and myself as often replied — No matter — you can make shift without them. Thus I and myself have conferred together many a day, and you, as if you had been privy to the conference, have kindly supplied the deficiency and put an end to the debate for ever.

When your messenger arrived I was beginning to dress for dinner, being engaged to dine with my neighbour Mr. Throckmorton, from whose house I am just return'd, and snatch a few moments before supper to tell you how much I am obliged to you. You will not therefore find me very prolix at present, but it shall not be long before you shall hear farther from me. Your honest old neighbour sleeps under our roof, and will be gone in the morning before I shall have seen him.

I have more Items than one by which to remember the late frost; it has cost me the bitterest uneasiness. Mrs. Unwin got a fall on a gravel walk cover'd with ice, which has confined her to an upper chamber ever since. She neither broke nor dislocated any bone, but received such a contusion below the hip as crippled her completely. She now begins to recover, after having been helpless as a child for a whole fortnight, but so slowly at present, that her amendment is even now almost imperceptible.

Engaged however as I am with my own private anxieties, I yet find leisure to interest myself not a little in the distresses of the Royal Family, especially in those of the Queen. — The Lord Chancellor called the other morning on Lord Stafford; ent'ring the room he threw his Hat into a Sofa at the fire side, and clasping his hands, said — I have heard of distress and I have read of it, but I never saw distress equal to that of the Queen. — This I know from particular and certain authority.[1]

My dear Madam, I have not time to enlarge at present on this subject or to touch any other, once more therefore thanking you for your kindness of which I am truly sensible, and thanking too Mr. King for the favour he has done me in subscribing to my Homer,[2] and at the same time begging you to make my best compliments to him, I conclude myself, with Mrs. Unwin's acknowledgments of your most acceptable present to her — Your obliged and affectionate

Wm Cowper.

Weston Jan. 29. 1789

WALTER BAGOT   Thursday, 29 January 1789

Address: Revd. Walter Bagot
Morgan Library

Weston Jan. 29.
1789

My dear friend —

I shall be a better, at least a more frequent correspondent when I have done with Homer. I am not forgetful of any letters that I owe, and least of all forgetful of my debts in

[1] See n.2, C to Hill, 13 Nov. 1788. C had probably been made aware of the meeting between Thurlow and Granville Leveson-Gower, 1st Marquis of Stafford (1721–1803) through Joseph Hill.

[2] 'Mr. King, Fellow of Trinity College, Cambridge' subscribed for a common copy.

that way to you; on the contrary I live in a continual state of self-reproach for not writing more punctually, but the old Greecian whom I charge myself never to neglect lest I should never finish him, has at present a voice that seems to drown all other demands, and many to which I could listen with more pleasure than even his Os rotundum.[1] I am now in the eleventh book of the Odyssey, conversing with the Dead. Invoke the Muse in my behalf that I may roll the stone of Sisyphus with some success.[2] To do it as Homer has done it, is I suppose, in our verse and in our language, impossible, but I will hope not to labour altogether to as little purpose as Sisyphus himself did.

I see too little of Chicheley and of my friends there. We are at a cruel distance from each other. I feel that I love them and continually regret our long separations. My neighbour, however, Mrs. Throckmorton, intends to give me a cast thither to morrow. May it not prove a cast indeed! for the roads must now be as bad as a long frost succeeded by deluges of rain can make them. But where a Lady is not afraid to risque her bones, I ought not to fear for mine. Add too, that they cannot be hazarded in a better cause.

Poor Mrs. Unwin has been a sufferer by the frost and I, of course, with her. She fell on a gravel walk coated over with the smoothest ice and lying on a declivity. How came she there? you will ask. That has been a mystery both to herself and me ever since, for she is not very sure-footed at the best and less than any body given to perform exploits on the ice. So, however, it was, and the consequences she feels and will feel, I fear, a considerable time. She neither incurred fracture nor dislocation, but a terrible contusion just under the hip which for some time entirely deprived her of the use of one leg. She can now set it on the ground, but cannot move upon it unless supported by two, and then so very lamely that she is wheel'd in a chair from one room to another. This misfortune befell us above a fortnigh[t][3] since.

Though I meddle little with politics and can fi[nd] but little leisure to do so, the present state of things u[n]avoidably

---

[1] Horace, *The Art of Poetry*, 323: 'Well-rounded style.'
[2] *Odyssey*, xi, lines 593–600 (lines 726–33 in C's translation).
[3] The MS is torn.

engages a share of my attention. I depl[ore] the loss of a better King than we shall presently fin[d again,] and am much mistaken, if we do not soon feel [, in] every corner of this country, that the sceptre has pass'd into other hands. But as they say, Archimedes, when Syracuse was taken, was found busied in the solution of a problem,[4] so come what may, I shall be found Translating Homer.

Take my word for it in prose, if you cannot in verse, that your boys will do admirably well without Westminster.[5] It is a place, where — Effugere est triumphus[6] — and though the Bagots have all enjoyed that triumph hitherto, does it follow that they must for ever?

I rejoice in Lord Bagot's good state of health, and remain, with Mrs. Unwin's best respects — Sincerely Yours

Wm Cowper.

LADY HESKETH   Saturday, 31 January 1789

Address: Lady Hesketh / New Norfolk Street / Grosvenor Square / London.
Postmarks: FE/2/[cut off] *and* OULNEY
Olney

The Lodge Jan. 31. 1789

My dearest Cousin —

I have dined thrice at the Hall since we lost you, and this morning accompanied Mrs. Frog in her chaise to Chicheley. What vagary I shall perform next, is at present uncertain, but such violent doings must have proportionable consequences. Mrs. Unwin certainly recovers, but not fast enough to satisfy me. She now moves from chamber to chamber without help of wheels, but not without help of a staff on one side and a human prop on the other. In another week I hope she will be able to descend the stair-case, but it will probably be long e'er she will move unsupported. Yesterday an old man came hither on foot from Kimbolton; he brought a basket address'd

[4] Archimedes (*c.*287–212 BC), the most famous of the Greek mathematicians, was intent upon a problem when he was killed by a Roman soldier who was unaware of his eminence.

[5] All three of Bagot's sons attended Westminster, including Ralph (1791–1866), who was there from 1809 to 1813. See n.2; C to Bagot, 6 Sept. 1791.

[6] 'There is triumph in retreat': Horace, *Odes*, IV. iv. 52.

to me from my yet unseen friend Mrs. King; it contained two pair of Bottle-stands, her own manufacture, a Knitting-bag, and a piece of Plum-cake. The time seems approaching when that good Lady and we are to be better acquainted, and all these douceurs announce it.

I have lately had a Letter to write daily, and sometimes more than one; this is one reason why I have not sooner answer'd your last. You will not forget that you allow'd me a latitude in that respect, and I begin already to give you proof how much I am persuaded of the sincerity with which you did it. In truth I am the busiest man that ever lived sequester'd as I do, and am never idle. My days accordingly roll away with a most tremendous rapidity.

Mr. Chester, who if not a professed virtuoso is yet a person of some skill in articles of Virtù, produced for our amusement a small drawer furnish'd with seals and impressions of seals, Antiques. When he had display'd and we had admired all his treasures of this kind, I took the Ring from my finger which you gave me and offer'd it to his inspection, telling him by whom it was purchased, where, and at what price.[1] He examined it with much attention, and begg'd me to let him take an impression of it. He did so, and expressed still more admiration. I put it again on my finger, and in a quarter of an hour he begg'd to take another. Having taken another he return'd it to me, saying, that he had shown me an impression of a seal accounted the best in England (if I mistake not it was a Hercules, an antique in possession of the Duke of Northumberland) but that he thought mine a better, and much undersold at thirty Guineas. He took the impression with much address, and I never, myself, view'd it before to so great advantage.

It would be an easy matter to kill me by putting me into a chaise and commanding me to talk as I go. It is astonishing how exhausted I feel myself after rumbling and chattering incessantly for three hours.

Mrs. Frog of Bath is better and George continues at the Hall. Mr. and Mrs. Giffard are expected there next Tuesday.

---

[1] The ring cannot now be found.

Bully[2] is in perfect health and if I can secure him from such a fate, shall never be Cat's-meat. Take care of thyself for my sake that I may see thee yet again in due season. It is very kind in Mr. Rose to distinguish so honourably a poor poet like me, and it shall be my endeavour to merit by my future good behaviour as a bard the favour which he shows me now. Your kind expression on the same subject I will never forget, but I had a thousand times rather be as poor as all poets are, than you should ungown yourself to prevent it.

I sent my verses to the *World* at the wrong time. That Paper is certainly vearing and has been vearing for some weeks past. It was not likely therefore that the Printer of it should do any thing less than suppress a squib sent hissing at the Morning Herald,[3] the principal trumpet of the party he had just adopted. Farewell my dearest Coz — With Mrs. Unwin's affectionate respects I am ever thine

Wm C.

LADY HESKETH   Wednesday, 4 February 1789

Address: Lady Hesketh / New Norfolk Street / Grosvenor Square / London.
Postmarks: FE/6/89 *and* NEWPORT/PAGNEL
Olney

Weston Lodge
Feb. 4. 1789

My dear Cousin —

A Letter of mine is no sooner sealed and sent than I begin to be dissatisfied with and to hate it. I have accordingly hated the two Letters that I have sent to *you* since your departure, on many accounts, but principally because they have neither of them expressed any proportion of what I have felt. I have mourn'd for the loss of you and they have not said so. Deal with them as you desire me for another reason to deal with yours, burn them, for they deserve it.

The room over the study is still the place of our habitation, though Mrs. Unwin is certainly on the recovery. This day we

[2] Bully is probably Lady Hesketh's pet finch, which she left with C in Dec. 1787. See C to Lady Hesketh, 4 Dec. 1787.
[3] See n.4, C to Lady Hesketh, 5 Oct. 1787. The poem sent to *The World* has been lost, and the reference in this letter is all that is known about it.

have both been more sensible of an amendment in the part affected, than on any day since she received the hurt. Yet even now the chief subject of our boast is merely this — not that she walks, but that she limps with less labour. But we are, I hope, arrived at that stage of the affair when one day will do more toward her restoration than three days did at the beginning.

I thank you for all your politics and anecdotes of political persons, and you may depend on it that all the treason and treasonable matter with which you shall entrust me, shall be committed to the flames; I confide in you for the same prudent disposal of all my wicked and malicious communications. Perhaps a time is at hand when it may not be altogether so safe to give our free sentiments of public persons even in a private letter, as it has been these many years to express them with the utmost licentiousness in print. A vicious government is always a jealous and a vindictive one. But in the worst of times we may arch our eye-brows and shrug our shoulders; and that shall be our comfort when all other comforts fail.

This day's post brought me a Letter from the Bouton de Rose. Having told me that he call'd on you last Sunday Evening in his way from Chiswick and spent 3 most agreeable hours with you and your sister, he proceeds thus.

'Indeed, my Dear Sir, Lady Hesketh flatter'd and gratified me much by the polite and kind attentions with which she honour'd me. Since my Father's death I have not been exposed to the Temptation of much notice, therefore my feelings are not altogether blunted by the frequency of the occurrence, and I must feel sensibly obliged when Virtue, Understanding and Rank condescend to assure me of their regard. — I do myself an honour when I declare I love Lady Hesketh — but it is an honour I cannot forego, and I sincerely believe there are few persons to whom her Ladyship has been known who have not experienced a similarity of feelings with myself.'

I rejoice that my young friend has so just an estimation of what deserves his affections, and love him the better for it.

The Athenaid sleeps while I write this. I have made Tables of Contents for 12 Books of it, and have yet eight to analyse.

I must then give somewhat like a Critical account of the whole, as Critical at least as the brevity it will be necessary to observe, will allow. A Poem consisting of 20 Books could not perhaps hope for many Readers who would go fairly through it, and this has possibly miss'd a part of the praise it might have received had the story been comprized within more reasonable limits. I am the more persuaded that this is the case having found in it many passages to admire. It is condemn'd I dare say by those who have never read the half of it. At the same time I do not mean to say that it is on the whole a first-rate poem, but certainly it does not deserve to be cast aside as lumber, the treatment which I am told it has generally met with.

This Morning I had a visit from Mr. Greatheed. He has been lately in London and took the opportunity to get miniatures of himself and his wife. His wife's he show'd me. It seem'd to me admirably well done and I ask'd by whom. He said, by Englefeldt,[1] if I heard and remember the name aright. He then, fixing his eyes on me said, I wish I had yours. Mine I replied, is no-where extant. He *sigh'd* and said — That's a pity. I expect Englefeldt soon to call on me. Would you give me leave to bring him over to Weston that he may take your likeness? I should be happy to have it. I answer'd, I could not possibly refuse a request that did me so much honour. I shall not therefore at last die without leaving something behind me in my own likeness. If Fuseli should happen to come on the same errand I shall be multiplied with a witness. I felt myself however pleased with Mr. Greatheed's request, not because I am fool enough to think a Phiz like mine worthy to be perpetuated, but because it seem'd to bespeak him more warmly affected toward me, than I suspected.

Is it possible that the first Volume of Sir John Hawkins's Johnson[2] can have been put into any of your trunks or

[1] George Engleheart (1750–1829) was a renowned and fashionable miniature painter. He had been a pupil of Reynolds, many of whose works he had copied. Engleheart had a studio in Mayfair from 1775 to 1813, during which time he painted the likenesses of almost 5,000 persons. It is 'practically certain that the portrait [of C] was not painted' (*Russell*, p. 304).
[2] *The Works of Samuel Johnson, Together with his Life, and Notes on his Lives of the Poets by Sir John Hawkins* had appeared in eleven volumes in 1787;

boxes by mistake? for I can only find the second. I look'd
for it soon after you went, but forgot 'till now to mention it.

   With Mrs. Unwin's best Compliments I remain, my beloved
Coz

                                    most truly thine Wm C

LADY HESKETH   Sunday, 15 February 1789

Address: Lady Hesketh / New Norfolk Street / Grosvenor Square / London.
Postmarks: FE/16/88 *and* NEWPORT/PAGNEL
Princeton

                                    The Lodge February 15. 1789

My dearest Coz —

   Horace censures the Phæacian youth for having spent too
much of their time in taking care of their skins,[1] and I am in
danger, myself, of meriting to fall under the same censure.
My correspondents, at least, have cause to deplore the day
when you first recommended to me the flesh-brush,[2] in the
use of which I now spend most of the time which formerly
I could give to them. The practise is, I suppose, salutary, as
most things are that are troublesome, yet be it as salutary as
its most sanguine advocate can alledge, it is certainly either
not infallible or must be long pursued in order to be made
effectual, for yesterday the Lumbago seized me exactly in
the moment when I was currying the very part which the
Lumbago always seizes. But I am not discouraged, on the
contrary I scrub with redoubled ardour, and have this morning
received much benefit in said part by the operation.

   We are delighted with your accounts of the King, and
with the symptoms that now show themselves of his speedy
recovery. May a few more weeks confirm our hopes and place
him on his throne again to the everlasting mortification of
the dogs who now grin and go about the city, grudging that
they are not satisfied. When you sent us lately the anecdote

volume 1 of this edition contained the life of Johnson by Hawkins. C had mis-
placed the volume which contained Hawkins's biography.

───────────
   [1] *Epistles*, I. ii. 29–30.
   [2] 'A brush used for rubbing the surface of the body, in order to excite the
circulation' (*OED*).

of a Royal Duke,[3] who first Damn'd his precious self, and then told the Queen she was as mad as his Father, Mrs. Unwin observed upon it that if the Queen's tears could be congealed into gems she had no doubt but her sons would wear them for ornaments. Those tears, however, though they will never meet with such a transformation, yet if they prevail to obtain from a merciful God the restoration of her husband, will be invaluable in the estimation of all who have the grace to love a good sovereign and to tremble at the thought of seeing the worst men in the nation the most exalted. Heaven grant him health soon and a continuance of it 'till certain personages shall be either amended or dead, Amen!

The 10th. of this month was what we call here, A High-Buck-Holiday. On that day Mrs. Unwin descended for the first time since her fall, into the study. We have twice taken walks in the Orchard, limpingly indeed, with much labour and some pain, but much, I believe, to her benefit. For this reason I regret these perpetual storms which will not suffer a more frequent repetition of that remedy, but notwithstanding so much necessary confinement, she recovers strength and the use of her leg daily, and though thinner than before looks as well as ever. She bids me give you many thanks on her part for all your enquiries and kind mention of her.

Among the few events which occur at Weston, it seems one of the most worthy to be here recorded, that about a week since, I had an Evening visit from Mr. Canniford. His business was to solicit my subscription to a publication of antient inscriptions, but I had the barbarity to refuse it. He pleased me, when he went. I ought to add that the work is not his, nor by any friend of his, for which cause I found it the less difficult to be close-fisted.

My neighbour George is proceeding with the Transcript of my Homer, having taken it up where you left it. This Reviewing business I find too much an interruption of my main concern, and when I return the books to Johnson shall

---

[3] Lady Hesketh's anecdote concerns Frederick Augustus, Duke of York and Albany (1763–1827), and the incident probably took place at Kew on 6 Dec. 1788, after Pitt had visited the Queen to discuss the possibility of forming a regency. We are grateful to Miss Olwen Hedley for providing information on this matter.

desire him to send me either Authors less impatient, or no more till I have finish'd Homer. Mr. Frog goes to Town on Tuesday, on which day I dine at the Hall for the consolation of his wife in his absence. He returns on Thursday. Bully is in perfect health, and sings all day. I have planted all the Laurels you wish'd I should, viz. 2 dozen more. Adieu my beloved Cousin — Every truly Yours

Wm Cowper.

The Miniature of Mrs. Greatheed appear'd to me to be exceedingly well executed, with great freedom and elegance, and by what I have heard of her, must be as favorable a copy of her physiognomy as you can wish should be made of mine. Her husband will suffer no engraving to be made from it without my sov'reign permission. Of that you may rest assured.[4]

This subject reminds me of the Cameo of Sir Thomas[5] which you have so kindly destined to a place in my study. Can it not accompany the pamphlet you mention'd and which we long to see?[6] You cannot regret your late tranquil mornings and Evenings here, more than we regret that you do not still enjoy them. But — Le bon tems viendra.[7] I have owed Mr. Rose a Letter so long that the thought of it haunts me continually. I must pay him soon if it be only for peace of conscience.

Once more, my Coz — Farewell.

My Love to the Hillikins.[8]

JOSEPH JOHNSON   Tuesday, 17 February 1789

Address: Mr. Johnson.
Princeton

Weston Feb. 17.
1789

Dear Sir —

Lest you should think me tedious and I should become conscious of being so, I send you the little that I have been able to do in the few hours that I could steal from Homer.

[4] See C to Lady Hesketh, 4 Feb. 1789 and n.1.
[5] See C to Lady Hesketh, 5 Mar. 1789 for C's remarks on this cameo.
[6] See n.3, C to Lady Hesketh, 5 Mar. 1789.
[7] 'The good times will return.'   [8] The Hills.

You may possibly think that I have bestowed too much time on the Athenaid, and I am not sure that you are very desirous of Analysis. It occupies much room and, perhaps, is not always read. Send me a line to inform me of what you most wish, whether analytical revisals or Critical, and I will proceed with the two poems that I have not yet review'd, accordingly.[1]

You will perceive that my labours on the Athenaid end with the second volume; but you will find it necessary I suppose to distribute what I send into two separate Reviews, and shall receive from me an Analysis of the Third before you can possibly want it.

The Manuscript poem[2] I have not yet read, concluding that it could better afford to wait, than the others which you told me had been already too long delayed. For the future, if you please, you must send me Authors less impatient, for while I have Homer in hand it is but by occasion that I can give myself to this business.

Remember the hope you have given me that when the days shall be of a due length I shall have the pleasure to see you and Mr. Fuseli at Weston. I do not press it just now, Mrs Unwin having had a dreadful fall in the late frost, from the consequences of which she has not yet recover'd. But the approaching Spring will I hope restore her and bring us all together.

I beg my compliments to Mr. Fuseli and am

Dear Sir,
Your most obedient humble Servant
Wm Cowper

SAMUEL ROSE   Thursday, 19 February 1789

Address: Samuel Rose Esqre / Percy Street / Rathbone Place / London.
Postmarks: [torn] /89 *and* OULNEY
Victoria and Albert Museum

The Lodge Feb. 19
1789

My dear Sir —

If I were not the most industrious man alive, and if I were

[1] See n.4, C to Rose, 19 Jan. 1789.   [2] Unidentified.

not sure that you know me to be so, I should think a long apology necessary for so long a silence; but I will spare myself and you that trouble, assured that in consideration of my various employments you will excuse me.

It gave me much pleasure to hear of Mrs. Rose's complete recovery. May she long be continued to you. The loss of a good mother is irreparable; no friend can supply her place.

You mention your visit at Lady Hesketh's with much pleasure, and I can assure you (for I have it under her own hand) that you were not the only person much pleased on that occasion. Continue what you are, and I will insure you a welcome among all persons of her description.

I have taken, since you went, many of the walks which we have taken together, and none of them I believe, without thoughts of you. I have, though not a good memory in general, yet a good local memory, and can recollect by the help of a tree or a stile, what you said on that particular spot. For this reason I purpose, when the Summer is come, to walk with a book in my pocket. What I read at my fire-side I forget, but what I read under a hedge or at the side of a pond, that pond and that hedge will always bring to my remembrance; and this is a sort of Memoria technica[1] which I would recommend to you, did I not know that you have no occasion for it. But though I do not often find my fire-side assistant to my memory on other subjects, there is one on which it serves me faithfully at the present moment. We are indebted not only to your Uncle's[2] kindness for the coals by which we warm ourselves, but to his purse also. If that account be not already liquidated, you may settle it when you please with my Cousin, who will be responsible for the amount, and left me a commission to tell you so.

I am reading Sir John Hawkins, and still hold the same opinion of his book as when you were here. There are in it undoubtedly some awkwardnesses of phrase, and, which is worse, here and there some unequivocal indications of a vanity not easily pardonable in a man of his years; but on the whole I find it amusing, and to me at least, to whom every thing that has pass'd in the literary world within these five and

[1] 'Method of remembering.'
[2] See n.2, C to [Rose], [10 Mar. 1788].

twenty years, is news, sufficiently replete with information. Mr. Throckmorton told me about three days since, that it was lately recommended to him by a sensible man, as a book that would give him more insight into the history of modern literature and of modern men of letters, than most others. A commendation which I really think it merits. Fifty years hence perhaps the world will feel itself obliged to him.

I say nothing about Politics, persuaded that it becomes me more, situated as I am, to be a hearer on that subject than a speaker. But this I may and will say, that I rejoice in the fairer prospect that now seems to open on us, of the King's recovery.

Mrs. Unwin's restoration is slow, but I hope sure. She cannot walk at all without a support, nor long, with any; yet she walks better than she did a week ago. She must certainly have received some greater hurt than we were aware of, but what hurt we shall never know. It is sufficient that he knows who is able to heal the worst. With her best Compliments I remain, my dear friend, truly Yours Wm Cowper.

LADY HESKETH   Wednesday, 25 February 1789

Address: Lady Hesketh / New Norfolk Street / Grosvenor Square / London.
Postmarks: FE/27/89 *and* NEWPORT/PAGNEL
British Library

The Lodge Wednesday Feb 25
1789

My dearest Coz —

You dislike the crossing of Letters, and so do I, yet though I write at the hazard of that inconvenience, I feel that I must write this evening. My hands are at present less full than usual. Having lately sent Johnson as much Review-work as will serve to satisfy him for a time, I allow myself a little vacation from those labours, which, however, I must soon resume.

The King's recovery is with *us* a subject of daily conversation and of continual joy. It is so providentially timed, that no man who believes a providence at all, can say less of it than that *This is the finger of God*![1] Never was a hungry

[1] Exodus 8:19.

faction so mortally disappointed, nor the integrity of an upright administration more openly rewarded. It is a wonderful æra in the history of this country; and posterity will envy us the happiness of having lived at such a period. We who are loyal subjects and love our monarch, may now take up the old Jacobite ditty and say — *The King shall enjoy his own again.*[2] An application which, I fear, we should never have had an opportunity to make, had his recovery been delay'd but a little longer. The faction at home have driven too fast, and the Irish will feel that they have made a blunder. Now let us listen to the raptures that will be pretended on this occasion. Sheridan, I expect, will soar in rhetorical extasies; Burk will say his prayers are answer'd, and Fox will term it the happiest event that he has ever witness'd; and while they thus speak, they will gnash their teeth and curse inwardly. Oh they are a blessed Junto; may opposition to ministry be their business while they live!

You must not yet, my Dear, felicitate me on the double recovery of the King and Mrs Unwin too. I rather think it probable that the King will be able to rule us, before she will be able to walk. She boasts indeed that she is as active as old Farmer Archer,[3] but she would find few hardy enough to bet on her head were a trial to take place between them. My hopes are chiefly in the approach of a gentler season, for the progress of her amendment now, is almost imperceptible.

About a Fortnight since I received six bottles of Rum from Henry, who might, according to what the General told me, have sent seven had he pleased, no law forbidding it. I have written twice to the General and have had no answer. Is he ill? Or can you tell me what else it is that occasions his silence?

When you were here we told you a long story about my Brother's mare and the money due for her Keeping. Almost two years ago, when Mr. Heslop[4] wrote to me on that subject expressing a desire to have the account settled, I referred him to Mr. Hill as to my Agent in all money-matters, who I told

[2] This line occurs in the Jacobite song, 'The Constitution Restored, in 1711', which was set to the tune, 'Mortimer's Hole'. See James Hogg, *Jacobite Relics of Scotland* (Edinburgh, 1819), pp. 359-60.

[3] Unidentified.

[4] See C to Hill, 16 Nov. 1787, and n.1, C to Unwin, 31 Mar. 1770.

him would settle it with him and discharge the Balance. Nothing however ensued on this reference, and he never called on Mr. Hill for the purpose. The day before yesterday I received a Letter from him sent hither from Adstock[5] by a messenger who came on foot, requiring again a liquidation of the account, and threat'ning me with legal coercion if I delay'd to settle it any longer. This being rather a strange procedure and somewhat ungentlemanlike made me very angry, And the next day, that is yesterday, I wrote to him signifying as much, reminding him of my Letter of reference, and referring him to Mr. Hill again. What course he will deign to take now is in his own bosom, but he is an unreasonable man, if being at this moment in Town, he will rather chuse to trouble me with farther demands than to go to Great Queen Street to have them satisfied.

Mr. Newton writes me word that Martin Madan on his way to London where he intended to have spent a day or two with his sister whom he has not seen these 4 years, was seized with an Asthma and obliged to return to Epsom. His illness continued a fortnight and he was judged to be in great danger; he, however, recover'd, but by the report of his physician is not likely to last long.[6]

I dined yesterday at the Hall, where, notwithstanding the difference of our political sentiments, we were perfectly at peace with each other. Religion and Politics both excluded, we are sometimes threaten'd with a dearth of Topics, but in general make a tolerable shift without them. They are always kind and friendly.

Mrs. Unwin's best Compliments attend you. I am, my Dear, most truly Yours   Wm Cowper.

---

[5] A village in Buckinghamshire approximately 18 miles south-west of Weston.
[6] Martin Madan died in May 1790.

LADY HESKETH   Thursday, 5 March 1789

Southey, vi. 222-4 *and Henry Sotheran Catalogue*[1]

Weston Lodge, March 5th, 1789.

My Dearest Coz. —

Since I send you so much Verse[2] I shall send so the less Prose; desirous to forward the enclosed to you as early as possible I violate my engagements to Homer for once, and give this morning to the King, the Queen and you. On the word of a poet I can assure you that I have done my best, sensible that when verses are presented to a Royal personage they ought not to be slovenly put together, nor such as one might produce between sleeping and waking. I have bestowed praise which on these occasions is a thing of course, but have endeavoured to dress it so as to give it some air of novelty, and the best of the matter is, that though it be praise it is truth, and I could swear to it. Had the King and Queen been such as the world has been pestered with ever since such folks were heard of, they should have had no verse from me unless you had insisted, but being such as they are, it seemed necessary that I who am now a Poet by profession, should not leave an event in which their happiness and that of the Nation are so much concerned, uncelebrated.

Many thanks, my dear, for the parcel, which was truly welcome, especially on account of the cameo, in which, however, unless Sir Thomas altered much after I saw him last, I cannot trace much resemblance of him. In the nose, forehead, and eyes, some likeness; in cheek, chin, and mouth, none at all; which I wonder at the more because I have seen the strongest resemblances taken in that manner. But I am happy to have it, though but a remote copy of one whom

---

[1] The opening and closing paragraphs of this letter are incompletely quoted in the Henry Sotheran Catalogue, 648 (1904), lot 201, and the citations available there are used as copy-text. The remainder of the letter is from *Southey*.

[2] 'Annus Memorabilis 1789' is the poem to which C refers; and in his letter to Mrs King of 30 May, C is almost certainly referring to this poem and not 'On the Queen's Nocturnal Visit to London' when he says, 'Those stanzas on the Queen's Visit were presented some time since by Miss Goldsworthy to the Princess Augusta, who has probably given them to the Queen, but of their reception I have heard nothing.'

we both knew and loved. I have read the pamphlet,[3] and admire both the matter and manner of it; but how the deuce a country gentleman should be so accurately and intimately informed as the writer certainly is, has excited some wonder both in Mrs. Unwin and in me. Had he rather chosen to write in the character of a gentleman, resident in town, to his friend in the country, I should have found it a more natural procedure. His minute knowledge of the characters and views of both parties would then have been easily accounted for, whereas now it is rather mysterious. But this is no great matter, — *a faux pas*, if it be one, that does not at all affect the sequel. Permit me to add to all this, that Molly Pears[4] and Hannah,[5] together with their duty to your ladyship, send their love and thanks to Mrs. Eaton for her kind remembrance of them.

Mr. Bean called here last night, when I had the pleasure of conversing with him on the subject of the royal recovery. His heart is warm on that theme, and we had a hearty laugh at the Opposition and their blundering friends, the Irish. When the knowing ones are so completely taken in, it is no wonder if poor Teague[6] is entrapped also. I shall not forget to thank you, too, for your papers, which are really useful as an antidote to the baneful Herald.

Adieu my Dear — I can say no more just now, but that I am, with Mrs. Unwin's affectionate compliments, who is still a stick-propp'd walker —

> Ever yours,
> Wm. Cowper.

[3] The pamphlet to which C is referring is *A Letter from a Country Gentleman to a Member of Parliament on the Present State of Public Affairs*, which was published anonymously in 1789 by William Combe (1741-1823), the originator of 'Dr. Syntax'. Fanny Burney records in her diary for 16 Feb. 1789 her reaction to the pamphlet when it was presented to her by a friend: '"But I have got," cried he, "a pamphlet for you, well worth your perusal: 'tis a letter from a Member of Parliament to a country gentleman, and contains the characters of all the opposition; and here is your friend Mr. Burke, done to the life!" He insisted upon reading that passage himself: — 'tis skilfully written, but with extreme severity; though it allows to him original integrity, which is what I have never been induced to relinquish for him, and never can disbelieve.' (*Burney Diary*, iv. 257).

[4] Perhaps Mary Pierce who was christened on 23 Feb. 1769, the daughter of Thomas and Sarah Pierce (*OPR*, p. 353).

[5] See n.4, C to Newton, 3 May 1780.

[6] 'A nickname for an Irishman' (*OED*).

WILLIAM BULL   Friday, 6 March 1789

Formerly Miss C. M. Bull

Weston
Mar. 6. 1789

My dear friend

To travel so far and come back in no better health, hardly pays you for the trouble of the journey. A Southern trip would be more likely to benefit you than a Northern. He whose pores have been stopp'd during a whole English winter, need not go to Scotland to have them shut still faster. But Spring is at hand, and we hope that all your present complaints will give way to the influences of a warmer atmosphere.

Mrs. Unwin had a terrible fall which by its consequences confined her above stairs a whole month, and she is still so lame as to be able to walk only on smooth ground, and with a stick, and for not more than a quarter of an hour at a time.

As for me I am as well as usual. We shall rejoice to see you when it shall suit you to come over. Our affectionate Compliments to Mrs. Bull and your Son. I have not time to add more, but that I am Yours

W Cowper.

MRS KING   Thursday, 12 March 1789

Barham Johnson (*copy*)

March 12. 1789

My dear Madam,

I feel myself in no small degree unworthy of the kind solicitude which you express concerning me and my welfare, after a silence so much longer than I gave you reason to expect. I should indeed account myself inexcusable, had I not to alledge in my defence perpetual engagements of such a kind as would by no means be dispensed with. Had Homer alone been in question, Homer should have made room for you; but I have had other work in hand, at the same time, equally pressing, and more laborious. Let it suffice to say that I have not wilfully neglected you for a moment, and that you have never been out of my thoughts a day together. But I begin to perceive that if a man will be an author, he must live neither to himself nor to his friends, so much as to others whom he never saw nor shall see.

My promise to follow my last letter with another speedily, which promise I kept so ill, is not the only one which I am conscious of having made to you and but very indifferently performed. I promised you all the smaller pieces that I should produce, as fast as occasion called them forth, and leisure occurred to write them. Now the fact is, that I have produced several, since I made that fair profession, of which I have sent you hardly any. The reason is, that transcribed into the body of a letter, they would leave me no room for prose, and that other conveyance than by the Post, I cannot find, even after enquiry made among all my neighbours for a traveller to Kimbolton. Well, we shall see you, I hope, in the summer, and then I will shew you all. I will transcribe one for you every morning before breakfast, as long as they last, and when you come down you shall find it laid on your napkin. I sent one last week to London, which by some kind body or another, I know not whom, is to be presented to the Queen.[1] The subject, as you may guess, is the King's recovery. A theme that might make a bad poet a good one, and a good one excel himself. This too, you shall see when we meet, unless it should bounce upon you before, from some periodical Register of all such matters.

I shall commission my Cousin, who lately left us, to procure for me the Book you mention. Being and having long been so deep in the business of Translation, it was natural that I should have many thoughts on that subject. I have accordingly had as many as would of themselves perhaps make a volume, and shall be glad to compare them with those of any writer recommended by Mr. Martyn. When you write next to that Gentleman. I beg you, Madam, to present my compliments to him, with thanks both for the mention of Mr. Twining's Book,[2] and for the honour of his Name among

[1] See n.2, C to Lady Hesketh, 5 Mar. 1789.
[2] *Aristotle's Treatise on Poetry, Translated: with Notes on the Translation, and on the Original; and Two Dissertations, on Poetical and Musical, Imitation* was published in 1789 by Thomas Twining (1735–1804).

my Subscribers.[3]

Mrs. Unwin, though two months ago she fell, is still lame. The severity of the season, which has not suffered her to exercise herself in the open air, has, no doubt, retarded her recovery; but she recovers, though even more slowly than she walks. She joins me in best respects to yourself and Mr. King, and in hearty desires to see you both at Weston. Forgive the Past. I make no more promises, except to remain always, my dear Madam,

Your affectionate   Wm. Cowper.

LADY HESKETH Monday, 6 April 1789

Address: Lady Hesketh / New Norfolk Street / Grosvenor Square / London
Postmarks: AP/8/89 *and* NEWPORT/PAGNEL
Princeton[1]

The Lodge
April 6. 1789

My dearest Coz —

You received I suppose about a fortnight since, a Letter from me,[2] containing diverse matters of which you have hitherto said nothing. In that Letter I ask'd you what we should do with our verses on the King's recovery, for that they should be printed by some means or other seems expedient.[3] For my own part, I know not very well what course to take. I am not ambitious of figuring very often in the Magazine, for reasons which perhaps my vanity may suggest to me, and which your zeal for my success may possibly suggest to you. It seems rather a publication in which Candidates should wish to appear, than they who have

[3] See n.2, C to Mrs King, 28 Aug. 1788. 'The Rev. Mr. Martyn, Professor of Botany, Cambridge' subscribed for a fine copy.

---

[1] This letter is listed as item number 91 in the Sotheby Sales Catalogue for 18 Aug. 1941. It formed part of the 'Renowned Library of the late Henry Yates Thompson Esq.' Although the letter has been misdated 8 Apr. 1789 in this catalogue, the quotation given in the sales catalogue is taken from paragraph six of this letter.
[2] This letter is missing. The last extant letter to Lady Hesketh is of 5 Mar. 1789.
[3] The poem appeared in *The Morning Herald* c.1 Apr. (see C to Lady Hesketh, 14 Apr.).

acquired some little rank already. But the decision of this important point, as then, so still I refer absolutely to you. — I gave you also in that Letter some account of a melancholy one that I had received from the General, from whom I have heard nothing since. Send me what information you can about him, for he expressed himself in terms of such extreme dejection, that I often feel not a little anxiety on his account.

When you next see Mr. Rose, tell him that I love him though I do not write to him. It is to be hoped that none of my Correspondents will measure my regard for them by the frequency or rather *seldomcy* of my Epistles. It is very little that I can do, occupied as I am, toward satisfying their just demands upon me, and I am at this moment in debt to every creature to whom I ever write at all. Mr. Rose informed me in his last, that in conversation with the Archbishop of York[4] he had mention'd to him my Translation of Homer. It was News to his Grace, he had never heard of it before. Consequently he has not yet subscribed. But is there no way of getting at him? for his rank and literary repute are such, that would he give me his name, I had rather admit him to a place in my List for nothing, than go without it. He was Tutour to your late friend[5] and mine at Oxford.

Thanks for your preventive of any anxiety that I might entertain on the Archdeacon's account. Let him not come hither and I care not much what he does. After what has passed, I could not possibly be glad to see him.

We have had our Rejoicings also at Weston. Last Saturday fortnight Mr. Frog illuminated the front of his house in the handsomest manner, threw up many rockets, gave a large Bonfire and Beer to the people. I was there, and as my friends tell me, caught a violent cold on the occasion, though I was not sensible of it myself. Certain it is, however, that whether in consequence of that vagary or not, I have since been miserably tormented with a distemper called a Canker. It seized my tongue and affected me frequently both in the day and in the night with sensations which I could hardly bear and not at all describe. I now just begin to eat again as other people do, and shall dine at the Hall to-morrow.

[4] See n.3, C to Rose, 25 Sept. 1788.   [5] Sir Thomas.

My Dear, April is come and May cannot be very far off. In May you know, we are to see you here. Remember this. I know you will come if it be possible, because you assured me that nothing but impossibility should prevent you. Need I add that we shall both be happy to receive you? Certainly I need not, did not the custom established in all such cases require it. For it is true and doubtless you already know it, that we are never so comfortable as when you are with us. Mrs. Unwin heartily subscribes to this and sends you her best remembrances. She is still lame, but in a way of A-mend-ment, that is to say, mends very slowly.

Before you recommended to me the Hibernians for a subject, I had proceeded too far in my prior design, to drop it.[6] It is accordingly now finished, and being so, my poetical labours on this occasion are finish'd with it. The piece is not so long as I had hoped to make it, and would make no figure in a separate publication. It is, however, long enough for the theme on which it is written, and unless some interesting incident had presented itself, could not with propriety have been protracted. The Frogs go to London in Easter week, when I can transmit it to you by the hands of Mr. Menzie.[7]

Thanks for the Hymn.[8] Well-set and well performed it would certainly be very affecting. And thanks for his grace of Leinster's speech,[9] not so graceful and eloquent as some that I have read, but I hope not the less genuine on that account.

We rather suspect that the King has bound himself by a vow to offer up his Thanksgivings at St. Paul's.[10] In the mean

[6] Probably 'On the Queen's Visit to London' which first appeared in *The Times* of 15 June 1789.
[7] Unidentified.   [8] Unidentified.
[9] As the context of this letter makes clear, Lady Hesketh at about this time urged C to write a poem concerned with Irish affairs, and she probably sent C a book or pamphlet which contained a speech by the distinguished Irish peer and patriot, William Robert Fitzgerald (1749–1804), 2nd Duke of Leinster (1773–1804), who was advocating opposition to the Union, a position he was to renounce later. C's specific reference may be to the Duke's speech on 30 Mar. concerning the pensions bill. *The Times* of 6 Apr. gives the following account: 'The Duke of Leinster said, no man had a higher or a more loyal respect for his Majesty than he had, and he thought it necessary to rescue the characters of those gentlemen who had supported the bill in the other House, of the integrity of whose principles he was fully convinced.'
[10] King George 'insisted against the advice of his ministers on a thanksgiving service in St Paul's Cathedral on St George's Day, 23 April 1789. When the

time I cannot say that I am at all apprehensive of any evil consequences to his health from such a proceeding. Religious affections, provided they are such as the Scripture warrants, can hurt nobody, and as to the crowd and the Show they are nothing to heads that wear a crown. What would kill me, will be to him a medicine. O Wales and York and Sailor Will! What shall I say of you? Reform, ye Pow'rs! E'er George conclude his sway,
His graceless sons, or take them all away.[11]
This may serve you my Dear, for a Toast after Dinner.

Believe me as I truly am — Thine

Wm Cowper.

LADY HESKETH
Tuesday, 14 April 1789

Olney

Weston April 14. 1789
I threaten'd you with this, my Cousin, by the hands of Mr. Menzies, and it would have reached you sooner had he been the Bearer; but Mr. Bull gave me, yesterday, a Morning-call, and offer'd to be my Mercury on the occasion, promising, at the same time, to deliver any pacquet with which I should entrust him, into your own hands. He wanted, he said, an errand by way of introduction, and could not, on any other terms, find courage enough to call on you. To alleviate, therefore, his terrours, and to procure you a visit from a man whom I know you will be glad to see, I have substituted Him in the place of the first-intended.

Your Letter in which you postpone your visit to an uncertain period, though I felt the force of your reason, sunk my spirits for a time. Woodcocks, I said, should come in the Winter and go in the Spring, but the order of Nature

---

Archbishop of Canterbury remonstrated that perhaps the occasion might be too much for him, the King said: "My Lord, I have twice read over the evidence of the physicians on my case, and if I can stand that I can stand anything."' John Brooke, *King George III* (1972), p. 343.
[11] C is remonstrating against the King's sons: George, Prince of Wales (1762–1830), Frederick Augustus, Duke of York and Albany (see n.3, C to Lady Hesketh, 15 Feb. 1789), and William (1765–1837) Duke of Clarence and St. Andrews, who on 20 May 1789 had been appointed Admiral of the Fleet.

is reversed that I may be disappointed. But I depend on you with an absolute reliance, that you will return as soon as you can, and with this persuasion shall endeavour, in the mean time to compose my spirits.[1]

Place it entirely to the account of my forgetfullness that the receipt of your *favour* (such in a double sense) was not sooner acknowledged. It happen'd that the very Evening on which it arrived, Hannah was by invitation gone to the Hall to a Dance given on occasion of the King's recovery. Mrs. Unwin immediately sent it after her, and it was pinn'd before her then and there. She was not a little proud of being the only Lady in the company so distinguished, and is sorry that you have not been sooner thank'd for it. She is, truly, a good girl, and in no part of her behaviour blameable. Her chief occupation at present, in the day-time, is to make Black Lace for a cloak; which she does, by the account of the judicious in those matters, exceedingly well. In the Evening, she works at her needle. Ever since the first week or ten days of Mrs. Unwin's lameness, she has slept on the floor in a corner of her closet, that she might be at hand to assist her as often as she wanted help, and though sometimes called from her pallet twice or thrice in a night, has risen always with an affectionate readiness that no artifice can imitate.

You very reasonably supposed, my Dear, that I was not unacquainted with the figure I had made in the Morning Herald. Yet true it is, that the first notice I had of it, was from yourself. Whether the Frogs never sent me that paper, or whether I overlooked them (for I generally skim it hastily over) the information was entirely News to me. I am inclined with you to suppose that they sent them. I sent to the General Evening an account of their illumination, and to return the Compliment, they doubtless sent my Verses to the Herald.[2] I fully purposed to have fished it out yesterday

---

[1] Lady Hesketh's niece Elizabeth Charlotte, the eldest daughter of Lady Croft, married in 1778 James Woodcock (who changed his name to Croft in 1792). The Croft pedigrees describe him as 'of Berkhamsted' in recording the marriage, but *GM* (xlviii. 237) calls him 'of Jamaica'. Presumably he and his family were living there in 1789 and had come to England on a visit, which necessitated Lady Hesketh's change of plans.

[2] The Throckmortons illuminated their mansion, displayed fireworks, and gave beer to the people on 21 March. C sent a description of this event to *The*

when I dined there, but for want of a fair opportunity at first, afterward forgot it.

Mr. Frog goes to Town on Thursday and his wife follows him on the Monday after. She told me with a significant sort of a look, that she was going on purpose to be present at the Ball at Brooks's.[3] — I answer'd, it is indifferent to me on what account you go, if you do but take care of yourself while you are gone, and return in good health to Weston. Thus, and by such management as this, I contrive to avoid all party-disputation, a moderate course which I think myself the more at liberty to pursue, because my political principles are upon record, having long since been printed.

I have consider'd, and had indeed before I received your last, consider'd of the practicability of a new publication, and the result of my thoughts on that topic is, that with my present small stock of small pieces, the matter is not feasible. I have but few, and the greater part of those few, have already appeared in the Magazine. A circumstance which of itself would render a collection of them just at this time, improper. It is however an encreasing fund, and a month perhaps seldom passes in which I do not add something to it. In time, their number will make them more important, and in time possibly I may produce something *in itself* of more importance; then all may be pack'd off to the Press together, and in the Interim, whatsoever I may write, shall be kept secret among ourselves, that being new to the Public, it may appear, *when* it appears, with more advantage.

Two Copies accompany this — The Verses sent to the Queen, and the Queen's Visit —

The clock strikes 9. Good night, my Dear, and God Bless thee —

Yours ever Wm Cowper.

General Evening Post, and an excerpt from his letter was printed ('Extract of a Letter from Bucks', No. 8645, 21-4 Mar. 1789). The Throckmortons returned the courtesy by sending 'Annus Memorabilis' to *The Morning Herald*.

[3] 'Brooks's Club, St. James's Street: the Whig Club-house, No. 60 on the west side, but founded in Pall Mall in 1764, on the site of what was afterwards the British Institution' (the St. James's Street building was opened in October 1778). Henry Benjamin Wheatley, *London, Past and Present* (1930), i. 286.

JOSEPH HILL   Tuesday, 14 April 1789

Cowper Johnson

Weston Underwood
April 14. 1789

My dear friend —

My Cellar being nearly exhausted, I shall soon find it expedient to import a Hogshead of Wine from Lynn,[1] in which way of proceeding I supply myself much more advantageously than by Hampers from London. Other articles of expence also threaten me at this season, and make it necessary for me to beg that you will be so kind as to send me a Draft on your Banker for as much of my yearly revenue as you expect yet to receive.

Lady Hesketh has communicated to me what you told her on the subject of Mr. Archdeacon Heslop. He is a strange man, and one would think with all the fuss he has made about it, wants less his money, than an opportunity to be troublesome. I thank you however for the care you have taken of me in this particular by quieting my apprehensions on his account. So long as I have you at my back I fear him not, or if I fear him at all, it is only as a Visitor; even you cannot prevent his coming hither if he chuses it, and he has so managed for me that I feel it will be safest and best both for him and for me, that we should settle our accounts at a distance.

With my best respects to Mrs. Hill I remain, my Dear friend —

Sincerely yours
Wm Cowper.

SAMUEL ROSE   Monday, 20 April 1789

Address: Samuel Rose Esqre / Percy Street / Rathbone Place / London.
Postmarks: AP/22/89 *and* NEWPORT/PAGNEL
Princeton

The Lodge
April 20. 1789

My dear friend —

I *will* believe that you are not silent because I am so, but

[1] See n. 3, C to Hill, 26 May 1778.

because you are busy. This persuasion being necessary in some sort to that serenity of Spirit which I wish always to maintain, I encourage myself in it with the more resolution; for could I suspect that you are punctilious enough to insist on letter for letter, I should feel myself more than half inclined to scold you. That I am somewhat in fault myself, I will readily grant, or rather, upon recollection, I will not allow that I am in any fault at all; for since the woeful day when I commenced Reviewer, my opportunities of Letter-writing have been few indeed. I purpose however for the future to manage that matter with more discretion, and not to suffer an occupation by which I can gain neither money nor fame, to deprive me of the pleasure of corresponding with my friends, to me more valuable than either.

What you told me in your last concerning the Archbishop of York's coincidence with me in opinion concerning Mr. Ουτις,[1] flatter'd my vanity and consequently gave me pleasure. Had he felt himself equally flatter'd by my agreement in opinion with *him*, he would undoubtedly have enter'd himself immediately on the List of my subscribers. But He is an Archbishop and I am Ουτις, therefore the honour was all on my side. Would he give me his name, as I told my Cousin some time since, I could be content to admit him into my list gratis. Literatus as he is, and known to be so, the glory of numb'ring him among my friends would be a sufficient compensation. But observe. This is no hint to you, nor in the least designed as such. I forbid you on pain of my extreme displeasure to consider it in that view, or to move one step in

---

[1] Markham must have agreed with C's desicion not to translate the Greek 'Ουτις' which first occurs in the *Odyssey*, ix. (line 528 of C's translation). C's notes explain: 'Clarke, who has preserved this name in his marginal version, contends strenuously, and with great reason, that Outis ought not to be translated; and in a passage which he quotes from the *Acta eruditorum*, we see much fault found with Giphanius and other interpreters of Homer for having translated it. It is certain that in Homer the word is declined not as ουτις-τινος, which signifies no man, but as ουτις-τισος, making ουτιν in the accusative, consequently as a proper name. It is sufficient that the ambiguity was such as to deceive the friends of the Cyclops. Outis is said by some (perhaps absurdly) to have been a name given to Ulysses on account of his having larger ears than common.' (pp. 207–8).

'Outis, as a *name*, could only denote him who bore it; but as a *noun*, it signifies *no man*, which accounts sufficiently for the ludicrous mistake of his brethren.' (p. 210).

consequence of it. You have done your part already, and as I should be very sorry to attack an Archbishop myself in such a cause, even though it were to advance my own interest, so should I be very sorry to put any friend of mine on so painful a service. — I am now in the sixteenth Book of the Odyssey; and after having been so long engaged in it, begin with some impatience to look forward to the end of an undertaking almost too long and laborious for any creature to meddle with, the date of whose existence here is limitted to threescore years and ten!

I have heard of you from Lady Hesketh who always mentions you with pleasure, and would be glad to see you more frequently than she does. Our neighbours the Frogs went to London yesterday, and will be present I suppose at the approaching great celebrity. Their stay in town will be short. They have taken a house in St. James's Place. Perhaps if you should find yourself at the door, you might also find courage to lift the Knocker. I know that they would be glad to see you.

Mrs. Unwin begs me to thank you for the pencil and to tell you that the Carving Knives and Forks which would have been mentioned in my last had I not forgot are excellent. May we not hope that at least in the long vacation we may again enjoy your company? Mrs. Unwin still limps, walks with a stick, and soon grows weary, but is otherwise in as good health as usual. She sends you her affectionate Compliments. Beau, I have no doubt remembers you, and will prove it when he sees you next; His Compliments therefore added to hers shall conclude a scribblement very little worth sending, if it did not afford me an opportunity to assure you of the affection with which I think of you and subscribe myself sincerely Yours —

Wm Cowper.

MRS KING   Wednesday, 22 April 1789

Address: Mrs. King / Pirten Hall near / Kimbolton / Huntingdonshire.
Postmarks: AP/23/89 *and* NEWPORT/PAGNEL
Princeton

Weston April 22. 1789
My dear Madam —
   Having waited hitherto in expectation of the Messenger
whom in your last you mention'd a design to send, I have at
length sagaciously surmised that you delay to send him in
expectation of hearing first from me. I would that his errand
hither were better worth the journey. I shall have no very
voluminous pacquet to charge him with when he comes.
Such however as it is, it is ready, and has received an addition
in the Interim, of one copy which would not have made a
part of it, had your Mercury arrived here sooner. It is on the
subject of the Queen's Visit to London on the night of the
Illuminations. Mrs. Unwin, knowing the burthen that lies on
my back, too heavy for any but Atlantean shoulders, has
kindly performed the Copyist's part, and transcribed all that
I had to send you. Observe Madam — I do not write thus to
hasten your messenger hither, but merely to account for my
own silence. It is probable that the later he arrives, the more
he will receive when he comes, for I never fail to write when
I think I have found a favorable subject.
   We mourn that we must give up the hope of seeing you
and Mr. King at Weston. Had our correspondence commenced
sooner, we had certainly found the means of meeting, but it
seems that we were doom'd to know each other too late for
a meeting in this world. May a better world make us amends,
as it certainly will if I ever reach a better; our interviews here
are but imperfect pleasures at the best, and generally from
such as promise us most gratification we receive the most
disappointment; but disappointment is, I suppose, confined
to the planet on which we dwell, the only one in the Universe
probably that is inhabited by sinners.
   I did not know, or even suspect, that when I received your
last messenger, I received so eminent a disciple of Hippocrates;
A Physician of such absolute controul over disease and the
Human constitution, as to be able to put a pestilence into his

279

pocket, to confine it there and to let it loose at his pleasure. We are much indebted to him that he did not give us here a stroke of his ability.

I must not forget to mention that I have received, (probably not without your privity) Mr. Twining's valuable volume. For a long time I supposed it to have come from my Bookseller, who now and then sends me a new publication; but I find, on enquiry, that it came not from Him. I beg Madam, if you are aware that Mr. Twining himself sent it, or your friend Mr. Martin, that you will negotiate for me on the occasion, and contrive to convey to the obliging Donor my very warmest thanks; I am impatient 'till he receives them. I have not yet had time to do justice to a writer so sensible, elegant and entertaining, by a complete perusal of his work, but I have with pleasure sought out all those passages to which Mr. Martyn was so good as to refer me, and am delighted to observe the exact agreement in opinion on the subject of Translation in general, and on that of Mr. Pope's in particular, that subsists between Mr. Twining and myself. Ornament for ever! cries Pope — Simplicity for ever! cries Homer — No Two can be more opposite. — With Mrs. Unwin's best Compliments, I remain, my Dear Madam — your obliged and affectionate

Wm Cowper.

Our joint respects attend Mr. King —

MRS KING   Thursday, 30 April 1789

Address: Mrs. King / Pertenhall.
Princeton

Thursday April 30. 1789
My dear Madam,

I thought to have sent you by the return of your messenger, a Letter, at least something like one, but instead of sleeping here as I supposed he would, he purposes to pass the night at Lavendon a village 3 miles off. This design of his is but just made known to me, and it is now near 7 in the Evening. Therefore lest he should be obliged to feel out his way in an unknown country in the dark, I am forced to scribble a hasty word or two, instead of devoting, as I intended, the whole Evening to your service.

A thousand thanks for your basket and all the good things that it contained, particularly for my Brother's poems,[1] whose hand-writing struck me the moment I saw it. They gave me some feelings of a melancholy kind but not painful. I will return them to you by the next opportunity. I wish that mine which I send you may prove half as pleasant to you as your excellent cakes and apples have proved to us. You will then think yourself sufficiently recompensed for your obliging present. If a Crab-stock can transform a pippin into a Nonpareil,[2] what may not I effect in a translation of Homer? Alas! I fear nothing half so valuable.

I have learn'd at length that I am indebted for Twining's Aristotle to a relation of mine, General Cowper.

Pardon me that I quit you so soon, it is not willingly, but I have compassion on your poor messenger.

Adieu, my Dear Madam, and believe me with Mrs. Unwin's best Compliments

Affectionately yours
Wm Cowper.

WALTER BAGOT   Monday, 4 May 1789

Address: Revd. Walter Bagot.
Morgan Library

My dear friend —

I am obliged to you for your early and unreserved com- munication. There is so much of my old friend in the manner of it that I should have guessed it yours had I neither seen the hand nor the signature. You will not be said to have made a prudent choice, but may the event prove that you have made a fortunate one. If you are but happy, to Us at least it ought to be of small moment by whom you are made so. None of your friends will more sincerely rejoice than we, if you are able to tell us when we have the pleasure to see you next,

[1] These poems appear to be no longer extant. 'It is not improbable that Cowper was requested to consider the MS. as his own.' *Southey*, vii. 306.
[2] Philip Miller in *The Gardeners Dictionary* (1731) lists the 'Nonpariel' under 'Apples as are proper for a Desert'.

that the articles of birth and fortune excepted, you find yourself comfortably mated. I have not time for a long Epithalamium, I send you such a one as I could make while I shaved myself.

> Transcendit virtus, et opes, et avos, atavosque,
> Nobilis est uxor si modo fida viro.[1]

You can translate it to Mrs. Bagot to whom I beg my Compliments, and remain with Mrs. Unwin's affectionate and best wishes — most sincerely Yours

Wm Cowper.

Weston Underwood
May 4. 1789

MRS THROCKMORTON   Thursday, 14 May 1789

Address: Mrs. Throckmorton / St. Jamess Place / Westminster
Postmarks: MA/15/89 *and* OULNEY
Sir Robert Throckmorton

The Lodge May 14. 1789

My dear Madam,

I send you a Copy of Verses entitled and called a New Song,[1] and wanting nothing but a wooden Cut representing yourself, *Miss Stapleton* and me, to make it complete. I will beg the favour of you to pass it into the hands of that lady when you have done with it.

The little folks whom you left behind are, [all   ][2] in perfect health; they were so yesterday. We expect Miss Courtney to drink tea with us this Evening as she did on Monday, when she and I diverted ourselves with a game at Spillikins. Your tiny nephew[3] was here also, but fast asleep

---

[1] 'Virtue transcends wealth and grandfathers and great-great-grandfathers. A wife is of good lineage if she is faithfull to her husband.'

---

[1] This poem first appeared in *The Speaker* (1792) under the title 'Catharina'. Miss Catharine Stapleton (d. 22 Jan. 1839), the daughter of Thomas Stapleton, of Carleton, Yorkshire, was to marry George Throckmorton in 1792, who had by then assumed the name of Courtenay, to become Courtenay-Throckmorton.
[2] MS torn, reading conjectural.
[3] Thomas William, born 28 Mar. 1789, eldest child of Mrs Throckmorton's half-brother Thomas Giffard, 23rd of Chillington, who had married the Hon Charlotte Courtenay, daughter of the 2nd Viscount Courtenay. The Miss Courtenay who played spillikins was doubtless one of her twelve sisters, perhaps the youngest, Louisa Augusta, born 25 Dec. 1781.

the whole Evening, the most profitable way, I suppose, in which he can spend his time at present.

I pity you. You are going to Court, where the Heat and the crowd will half kill you. Make haste back again for your park and all your environs grow ev'ry day more and more delightful. With best love to Mr. Frog — I remain my dear Madam most truly Yours —

Wm C.

Mrs. Unwin's best Compliments.

SAMUEL ROSE   Wednesday, 20 May 1789

Hayley, i. 324-6

The Lodge, May 20, 1789.

My dear sir,

Finding myself between Twelve and One, at the end of the Seventeenth Book of the Odyssey, I give the interval between the present moment and the time of walking, to you. If I write Letters before I sit down to Homer, I feel my spirits too flat for Poetry, and too flat for Letter-writing if I address myself to Homer first; but the last I chuse as the least evil, because my friends will pardon my dullness, but the public will not.

I had been some days uneasy on your account when yours arrived. We should have rejoiced to have seen you, would your engagements have permitted: but in the autumn I hope, if not before, we shall have the pleasure to receive you. At what time we may expect Lady Hesketh at present I know not; but imagine that at any time after the month of June you will be sure to find her with us, which I mention, knowing that to meet you will add a relish to all the pleasures she can find at Weston.

When I wrote those Lines on the Queen's visit, I though I had performed well; but it belongs to me, as I have told you before, to dislike whatever I write when it has been written a month. The performance was, therefore, sinking in my esteem, when your approbation of it arriving in good time, buoyed it up again. It will now keep possession of the place it holds in my good opinion, because it has been favoured with yours; and a copy will certainly be at your service whenever you chuse to have one.

Nothing is more certain than that when I wrote the line,
God made the country, and man made the town.
I had not the least recollection of that very similar one, which you quote from Hawkins Brown.[1] It convinces me that critics (and none more than Warton, in his Notes on Milton's minor Poems)[2] have often charged authors with borrowing what they drew from their own fund. Brown was an entertaining companion when he had drank his bottle, but not before, this proved a snare to him, and he would sometimes drink too much; but I know not that he was chargeable with any other irregularities. He had those among his intimates, who would not have been such, had he been otherwise viciously inclined; the Duncombs,[3] in particular, father and son, who were of unblemished morals.

W. C.

JOHN NICHOLS   *c.*Friday, 29 May 1789[1]

Address: Mr. Nichols Printer / Red Lion Passage / Fleet Street / London. Post pd. 4d.
Postmarks: MA/29/89, NEWPORT/PAGNEL *and* POST/PAID
Princeton

To Mr. Urban
Sir
The underwritten Stanzas have for their subject a fact

[1] Rose had pointed out to C the similarity between line 749 from Book I of *The Task* ('And God made the country, and man made the town') and line 16 of 'The Fire-Side: A Pastoral Soliloquy' ('That the town is Man's world, but that this is of God') from *Poems Upon Various Subjects, Latin and English* (1768) by Isaac Hawkins Browne (1705–60).

[2] 'Among the English poets, those readers who trust to the late commentators will be led to believe, that our author imitated Spenser and Shakespeare only. But his style, expression, and more extensive combinations of diction, together with many of his thoughts, are also to be traced in other English poets, who were either his contemporaries or predecessors, and of whom many are now not commonly known. Of this it has been a part of my task to produce proofs.... Nor have his imitations from Spenser and Shakespeare been hitherto sufficiently noted.' Thomas Warton in his Preface (p. xx) to *Poems Upon Several Occasions ... By John Milton ... With Notes Critical and Explanatory* (1785).

[3] William and John Duncombe. See List of Correspondents, Volume I.

[1] The story on which this poem was based appears among the obituaries in

mention'd in your obituary for the Month of April last; should you think that the Lesson inculcated in verse may have its use, as the Author of these lines hoped it might, he will be obliged to you if you will give them a place in your Magazine when it can be done conveniently — And is Yours

W. C.

The Cock-fighter's Garland.[2]

Muse — Hide his Name of whom I sing,
Lest his surviving house thou bring
    For His sake, into scorn,
Nor speak the school from which he drew
The much or little that he knew,
    Nor Place where he was born.

That such a man once was, may seem
Worthy of record (if the theme
    Perchance may Credit win)
For proof to man, what man may prove,
If Grace depart, and dæmons move
    The source of guilt within.

This Man (for since the howling wild
Disclaims him, Man he must be stiled)
    Wanted no good below,
Gentle he was, if gentle birth
Could make him such, and he had worth,
    If wealth can worth bestow.

GM lix, pt. 1 (Apr. 1789), 374–5: '(*April*) 3. At Tottenham, John Ardesoif, esq., a young man of large fortune, and, in the splendour of his carriages and horses, rivaled by few country gentlemen. His table was that of hospitality, where, it may be said, he sacrificed too much to conviviality; but, if he had his foibles he had his merits also, that far outweighed them. — Mr. A. was very fond of cock-fighting, and had a favourite cock, upon which he had won many profitable matches. The last bet he laid upon this cock he lost; which so enraged him, that he had the bird tied to a spit and roasted alive before a large fire. The screams of the miserable animal were so affecting, that some gentlemen who were present attempted to interfere, which so enraged Mr. A. that he seized a poker, and with the most furious vehemence declared, that he would kill the first man who interposed; but, in the midst of his passionate asseverations, he fell down dead upon the spot.' The May 1789 issue of *GM* (465) published a retraction of the above account. The poem was not published until 1815 in *Posthumous Poetry*, edited by John Johnson.
    [2] The poem was transcribed by Mrs Unwin.

c.29 May 1789

In social talk and ready jest
He shone Superior at the feast,
   And qualities of mind
Illustrious in the eyes of those
Whose gay society he chose
   Possess'd of ev'ry kind.

Methinks I see him powder'd red,
With bushy locks his well-dress'd head
   Wing'd broad on either side,
The mossy rose-bud not so sweet;
His steeds superb, his carriage neat
   As lux'ry could provide.

Can such be cruel? — Such can be
Cruel as hell, and so was he;
   A tyrant entertain'd
With barb'rous sports, whose fell delight
Was to encourage mortal fight
   'Twixt birds to battle train'd.

One feather'd Champion he possess'd,
His darling far beyond the rest,
   Which never knew disgrace,
Nor e'er had fought, but he made flow
The Life-blood of his fiercest foe,
   The Cæsar of his race.

It chanced, at last, when, on a day
He push'd him to the desp'rate fray,
   His courage droop'd, he fled.
The master storm'd, the prize was lost,
And, instant, frantic at the cost,
   He doom'd his fav'rite dead.

He seized him fast, and from the Pit
Flew to his Kitchen, snatch'd the spit,
   And, bring me Cord, he cried —
The Cord was brought, and, at his word,
To that dire implement the bird,
   Alive and struggling, tied.

c.29 May 1789

The horrid sequel asks a veil,
And all the terrors of the tale
   That can be, shall be sunk —
Led by the suff'rer's screams aright
His shock'd Companions view the sight
   And him with fury drunk.

All, suppliant, beg a milder fate
For the Old Warrior at the Grate,
   He, deaf to pity's call,
Whirls round him rapid as a wheel
His Culinary club of steel,
   Death menacing on all.

But Vengeance hung not far remote,
For while he stretch'd his clam'rous throat
   And Heav'n and Earth defied,
Big with the Curse too closely pent
That Struggled vainly for a vent
   He totter'd, reel'd, and died.

Tis not for us, with rash surmize,
To point the judgments of the skies,
   But judgments plain as this,
That, sent for man's instruction, bring
A written label on their Wing,
   Tis hard to read amiss.

MRS KING   Saturday, 30 May 1789

Address: Mrs. King / Pertenhall
Princeton

Dearest Madam —
   Many thanks for your kind and valuable dispatches, none
of which, except your letter, I have yet had time to read, for
true it is and a sad truth too, that I was in bed when your
messenger arrived. He waits only for my answer, for which
reason I answer as speedily as I can.
   I am glad if my poetical pacquet pleased you. Those

287

stanzas on the Queen's Visit were presented some time since by Miss Goldsworthy[1] to the Princess Augusta,[2] who has probably given them to the Queen, but of their reception I have heard nothing. I gratified myself by complimenting two Sovereigns whom I love and honour, and that gratification will be my reward. It would indeed be unreasonable to expect that persons who keep a Laureate in constant pay, should have either praise or emolument to spare for ev'ry volunteer scribbler who may chuse to make them his subject.

Mrs. Unwin who is much obliged to you for your enquiries, is but little better since I wrote last. No person ever recover'd more imperceptibly, yet certain it is that she does recover. I am persuaded myself, that, though it was not suspected at the time, the thigh-bone was longitudinally fractured, and she is of my opinion. Much time is requisite to the restoration of a bone so injured, and nothing can be done to expedite the cure. My Mother-in-law[3] broke her leg-bone in the same manner and was long a cripple. The only comfort in the present case is, that had the bone been broken transversely, the consequences must probably have been mortal.

I will take the greatest care of the papers with which you have entrusted me and will return them by the next opportunity. It is very unfortunate that the people of Bedford should chuse to have the small-pox just at the season when it would be sure to prevent our meeting. God only knows Madam when we shall meet, or whether at all in this world, but certain it is that whether we meet or not, I am most truly Yours

Wm Cowper.

Mrs. Unwin presents her best respects, and I beg you will make mine to Mr. King.

Weston. May 30. 1789

---

[1] Martha Caroline Goldsworthy (*c*. 1740–1816), sub-governess to the younger sons and daughters of George III from 1774 to 1809.

[2] George III's second daughter, Augusta Sophia (1768–1840).

[3] C's stepmother, who had died in 1762.

SAMUEL ROSE   Friday, 5 June 1789

Address: Samuel Rose Esqre / Percy Street / Rathbone Place / London.
Postmarks: [JU] /8/89[1] *and* OULNEY
Princeton

The Lodge
June 5. 1789

My dear friend —

I am going to give you a deal of trouble, but London folks must be content to be troubled by country folks, for in London only can our strange necessities be supplied. You must buy for me, if you please, a Cuckow-Clock. And now I will tell you where they are sold, which, Londoner as you are, it is possible you may not know. They are sold, I am informed, at more houses than one in that narrow part of Holbourn which leads into broad St. Giles's. — It seems they are well-going clocks and cheap, which are the two best recommendations of any clock. They are made in Germany, and such numbers of them are annually imported, that they are even become a considerable article of commerce. A box I suppose will be wanted for the package of it, for which, as well as for said clock we will be your debtors and for all other incidental expences; it may come by Rogers's Waggon from the Windmill St. John Street.

We are here on the point of a general insurrection of Mops and Brooms, and the house for a week to come, at the least, will hardly be habitable even to ourselves. When these lustrations are finish'd we shall expect my Cousin, that is to say in about ten days' time, or perhaps a fortnight. That period arrived, we shall at any time and at all times be happy to receive you, and the longer you can stay the better.

I return you many thanks for Boswell's Tour.[2] I read it to Mrs. Unwin after supper and we find it entertaining. There is much trash in it, as there must be in every narrative that relates indiscriminately all that passed; but now and then the Doctor speaks like an Oracle, and That makes amends for all. Sir John[3] was a coxcomb, and Boswell is not less a coxcomb,

---

[1] The date stamp has been cropped.
[2] *The Journal of a Tour to the Hebrides, with Samuel Johnson* had been published in 1785.   [3] Sir John Hawkins.

though of another kind. I fancy Johnson made coxcombs of all his friends, and they in return made Him a coxcomb, for with reverence be it spoken, such he certainly was, and flatter'd as he was, was sure to be so.

I have sent up a new Edition to my Cousin of [the][4] Verses on the illumination-night, having at her request struck out two Stanzas which I think myself were no ornament to it, and given it a different conclusion.[5] We print it in the World, and it will probably make its appearance in a day or two. — Thanks for your invitation to London, but unless London can come to me, I fear we shall never meet. Persuade Fuseli if you can to send me all his Shakespear paintings[6] in a Box; I will gladly pay the carriage and honestly return them.

My Slippers are excellent — I was sure that you would love my friend Hill, when you should once be well acquainted with him, and equally sure that he would take kindly to you. Now for Homer —

I am with Mrs. Unwin's affectionate Compliments

Truly Yours   Wm Cowper.

LADY HESKETH

Saturday, 6 June 1789

Southey, vi. 240-3

The Lodge, June 6, 1789.

I know not, my dearest coz, that I have any thing to trouble thee about, save half a dozen tooth-brushes. Mrs. Unwin will be much obliged to thee also for a black summer cloak

---

[4] MS torn.

[5] For C's revisions, see n.1, C to Lady Hesketh, 13 June 1789. The poem was in fact published in *The Times* of 15 June because the editor of *The World* was too dilatory (see C to Lady Hesketh, 23 June).

[6] Fuseli executed nine paintings from Shakespeare for inclusion in Boydell's Gallery: 'Prospero, Miranda, Caliban, and Ariel — from the Tempest. Titania in raptures with Bottom, who wears the ass's head, attendant fairies, &c. Titania awaking, discovers Oberon at her side; Puck is removing the ass's head from Bottom — Midsummer Night's Dream. Henry the Vth with the Conspirators — King Henry V. Lear dismissing Cordelia from his Court — King Lear. Ghost of Hamlet's Father — Hamlet. Falstaff and Doll — King Henry IV. 2d part. Macbeth meeting the Witches on the Heath — Macbeth. Robin Goodfellow — Midsummer Night's Dream. — This gallery gave the public an opportunity of judging Fuseli's versatile powers.' John Knowles, *The Life and Writings of Henry Fuseli* (3 vols., 1831), i. 78.

untrimmed, because Hannah is making a trimming for it. Two of the brushes above-said must be for inside *scurryfunging*,[1] viz. they must be *hooked*. These wants satisfied, we have no other commissions with which to charge thee. The stiffer the brushes, the better.

My friend Walter Bagot, to whom I sent a copy of the Illumination verses, objected as thou didst to the concluding stanzas; but I could not alter them on the credit of his judgement only; — when thine and that of thy friends had confirmed it, I then thought it prudent to surrender my own, and am now glad that I did, for I think the copy much mended, and mended almost as much by the omission of the others.[2]

I have the satisfaction to find that the copy of which Miss Stapleton is the subject,[3] gratified much both her and her father. She wrote to Mrs. Frog lately, and told her, among other handsome things that she said on the occasion, that she showed them with not a little pride to all her acquaintance who could *read* and had *sense* to understand them. She expressed herself thus, because it happened that a young gentleman who could *not read*, being commissioned to read them at her father's table, he not only murdered them by his bad delivery, but feloniously attempted to maim them likewise by a puny criticism on one of the lines. It was, however, sufficiently vindicated by the company, and the young sprig of a critic, severely rallied by Mr. Stapleton, was made to blush for his misemployed sagacity. Mrs. Frog told me she never saw her friend so angry in her life.

I have composed since a small poem on a hideous subject, with which the Gentleman's Magazine for April furnished me; — it is nevertheless a true one, hideous as it is. Mr. Bull and Mr. Greatheed both have seen the man on whose death it is written, and know that he died as there related. It is entitled The Cockfighter's Garland.[4] Expecting to see thee soon, I shall not send it.

---

[1] 'To scrub, scour.' *OED* gives this letter as the source for this meaning of scurrifunge, which is 'a word of jocular formation, used in various senses with little or no discoverable connexion.'

[2] See C to Lady Hesketh, 13 June 1789, and n.1.

[3] See n.1, C to Mrs Throckmorton, 14 May 1789.

[4] See n.1, C to John Nichols, c.29 May 1789.

Running over what I have written, I feel that I should blush to send it to any but thyself. Another would charge me with being impelled by a vanity from which my conscience sets me clear, to speak so much of myself and my verses as I do. But I thus speak to none but thee, nor to thee do I thus speak from any such motives. I egotize in my letters to thee, not because I am of much importance to myself, but because to thee, both *Ego* and all that *Ego* does, is interesting. God doth know that when I labour most to excel as a poet, I do it under such mortifying impressions of the vanity of all human fame and glory, however acquired, that I wonder I can write at all.

Mr. Frog made his wife a short visit in his way from Bucklands to London, and on Thursday they dined with us, — the only dinner they have had here these seven months. He is gone again, and expects to be detained from home about a fortnight longer. In July they go to Tunbridge, and thence to Margate; after which they make another jaunt, I know not whither with certainty, but I think to Bucklands. Thus we are likely to be pretty much a trio, and to have none but ourselves to depend on for our entertainment. Well, we can fadge. On Monday I shall dine at Newport with Mr. Greatheed; he comes to give me a cast thither in his chaise and one. The artist who is to copy my phiz is expected in August. This falls out well, because you, I hope, will be here, who will settle what sort of a head he shall give me better than any body. I am now going to revise the last half of the eighteenth book of the Odyssey, and to-morrow shall begin the nineteenth. Mrs. Unwin makes her best compliments, and I am,

Ever thine,
Wm. Cowper.

P.S. Mrs. U. recollects that when you were here, and we had a dinner to get for the Frogs, you regretted that *sponge biscuits*, (so she thinks you called them,) were not to be had. Perhaps you would like to bring a small parcel of that commodity with you.

MARTIN MADAN   Monday, 8 June 1789

Address: The Revd. Martin Madan / Epsom / Surry
Postmark: JU/10/89
Haverford College

Weston Underwood
June 8. 1789

My dear Cousin —

I am much obliged to you for your late publication[1] which
I received a few days since from the hands of Mr. Bean my
neighbour, the Vicar of Olney, by whom Mr. Newton transmitted it to me. You have bestowed much pains on two
valuable Writers, and to very good purpose. It will not be
your fault if they are not more generally read than they have
been and better understood. As for me my time is so much
occupied with Homer, that I have not yet found leisure to
read more than the first Satyr of Juvenal and the chief part
of the second; such a sample as this however warrants sufficiently the judgment I have form'd of the whole, which is
that you have executed your undertaking well and that not
the Illiterati only but the Literati themselves also are much
obliged to you; for few even of *them* are so familiar with
Juvenal and Persius as to be superior to the aids which your
version and your Notes will afford them. Dr. Earl,[2] I remember, was a Master of both these authors, and could perhaps
have repeated the greatest part of Juvenal, but of all the
Scholars I have ever known He was the only one so well
acquainted with him. Juvenal, of all the Roman Writers,
was most his Favorite.

My labours, I hope, are drawing to a conclusion. I have
begun the 19th. Book of the Odyssey, and expect to finish
the Translation of that poem in about three months; I shall
then proceed to a revisal of the whole and to press with it as
soon as possible. Life wears away, and I have a curiosity to

---

[1] *A New and Literal Translation of Juvenal and Persius; with Copious Explan-*
atory Notes, by which these Difficult Satirists are Rendered Easy and Familiar
to the Reader (2 vols., 1789). *Keynes* (60) lists this set, now at the Lilly Library,
University of Indiana, as having been published in 1785.

[2] Jabez Earle (1676?–1768), the Presbyterian minister, was reputed to be able to
repeat easily a hundred lines at any given place from his favourite classical writers.

know the success of my long and arduous undertaking. In the Grave there is no remembrance of Homer.

I beg my affectionate Compliments to Mrs. and Miss Madan, and to Mr. Cowper[3] if he be with you, and remain

> My dear Cousin —
> Truly Yours
> Wm Cowper.

LADY HESKETH   Saturday, 13 June 1789

Address: Lady Hesketh / New Norfolk Street / Grosvenor Square / London
Postmark: JU/15/89
Princeton

> The Lodge
> June 13. 1789

I steal a few moments from the old Greecian my dear Cousin just to hint to you, in the way of admonition, that when this reaches your fair hands, the half of June will be over. You will know without my telling you, to what subject in particular this gentle insinuation applies.

Mrs. Unwin will be glad to have the Cloak with a Lining, but we hope for such a season in due time as shall supersede all occasion for wadding. At present we boast not much either of bright suns or genial airs; in this wonderful climate we have often sunless summers and clear-shining winters, but when once we meet we will not trouble ourselves about the weather.

It was with a little regret that I discarded the stanza ending with —   But when a nation's shouts arise
                That suffrage must be true.
The dismission however of the preceding stanza was necessarily attended with the dismission of that also, which had then no longer any propriety, wanting an introduction.[1] I shall be

---

[3] Probably Henry Cowper.

---

[1] 'On the Queen's Visit to London'. The MS sent to Walter Bagot by Mrs Unwin with her letter to him of 16 Apr. 1789 contains the two stanzas deleted between lines 44 and 45: 'She, Undiscover'd sat the While, / Yet, haply more Elate / Than When address'd in Solemn Stile / And in her Chair of State. / To periods clad in flowing guise / Some doubt, perhaps, is due, / But when a Nations shouts arise, / That suffrage must be true.' Both the MS in Mrs Unwin's hand and her

glad if the piece in its present form be consider'd as a Compliment in any measure worthy of those to whom it is paid. I have felt perhaps equal indignation with yourself at the behaviour of our three princes.[2] Were the nation of my mind, I know not to what throne they would stand related hereafter, certainly not to that of England, unless by manners very different from such as they have yet exhibited, they proved themselves more worthy of that honour.

I dined, as I told you I should, at Newport last Monday, and had an agreeable day. Mr. G——d came for me and carried me thither in a single-hors'd chaise almost as high as a Phaethon. At first I was rather alarm'd at such an extraordinary elevation, having never been accustom'd to ride in such triumphant sort; but having learn'd soon after I mounted, that Mrs. Greatheed frequently committed herself to it, I felt it a shame to fear that which held no terrours for a lady. I think them nevertheless dangerous. Should the horse fall, woe to the necks of the riders.

I forgot to tell thee that when thou wast here thou didst bid me refer the Rose-bud[3] to thee for the coal-money. It was accordingly at my instance that he sued thee for it.

Poor Mrs. Frog is still a widow, and I fear that her husband and she will receive no other recompense of their separation than a disappointment. The Chancellor is no friend to the measure which the Catholics are now pressing in parliament.[4]

I shall be glad if you can bring the Rose-bud with you. His

letter are at the Morgan Library. It is apparent from C's letter to Bagot of 16 June 1789 that Bagot had objected to the concluding stanzas which read as follows in Mrs Unwin's transcription: 'Such was the Royal visit paid / To Thousands in a Night, / Not formal, or with much parade, But with the more delight; / None knew her kind Intent to call, / Or hoped that she would come, / Yet, strange to tell, she saw them all / Though None she found at Home.' The poem was revised to conclude as follows: 'With more than astronomic eyes / She view'd the sparkling show; / One Georgian star adorns the skies, She myriads found below. / Yet let the glories of a night / Like that, once seen, suffice! / Heav'n grant us no such future sight, / Such previous woe the price!'

[2] See n.11, C to Lady Hesketh, 6 Apr. 1789.

[3] Samuel Rose. See C to Rose, 19 Feb. 1789.

[4] C means that Lord Thurlow is opposed to the proposed Catholic Relief Bill, delayed from 1788 because of the King's illness, which had been prepared mainly by Catholic laymen and which called for an end to the legal discriminations against Catholics. In fact, this bill did not receive royal assent until 10 June 1791. John Throckmorton was an active member of the committee which drafted the Bill and had to spend many months in London.

walking-scheme is a terrible one. Mrs. U. has twice taken a Morning-walk with me, but rather lamely. We are 2 hours performing a journey that used to cost us one.

Mrs. Hill's Turkey is become the father of 15 beautiful children, one of them white, and two or three of them Buff. If you see her pray tell her how much she has enriched us.

I am my dearest Coz. with Mrs. Unwin's best affections — Ever thine — Wm Cowper.

P.S

Many thanks for the Waistcoats. I have received a present of a silk one together with a silver snuff-box from a person who lays me under an unpleasant restraint, forbidding me absolutely to say from whom. Mrs. U. has a snuff-box also from the same quarter.[5]

WALTER BAGOT   Tuesday, 16 June 1789

Address: The Revd. Walter Bagot
Morgan Library

Weston — June 16. 1789

My dear friend —

You will naturally suppose that the letter in which you announced your marriage occasioned me some concern, though in my answer I had the wisdom to conceal it. The account you gave me of the object of your choice was such as left me at liberty to form conjectures not very comfortable to myself, if my friendship for you were indeed sincere. I have since, however, been sufficiently consoled. Your Brother Chester has informed me that you have married not only one of the most agreeable, but one of the most accomplish'd women in the kingdom. It is an old maxim, that it is better to exceed expectation than to disappoint it, and with this maxim in your view it was, no doubt, that you dwelt only on circumstances of disadvantage, and would not treat me with a recital of others which abundantly overweigh them. I now congratulate not you only but myself, and truly rejoice that my friend has chosen for his fellow-traveller through the remaining stages of his journey a companion who will do

[5] Perhaps from Mrs Throckmorton or possibly Mrs King.

honour to his discernment and make his way, so far as it can depend on a wife to do so, pleasant to the last.

The last news I heard from Chichely was not pleasant. Your Brother informed me in a note that he sat resting his legs on a stool, having bruised them by a fall in London. I am willing to hope, however, that by this time he is healed, having heard a bird sing that he is gone forth on a summer-ramble. To speak a Dublinism, I should have charming neighbours in that family were we not too far asunder. Some comfort we have in them, but little in comparison of what we should enjoy, were we neighbours in reality.

My verses on the Queen's visit to London either have been printed, or soon will be, in the World. The finishing to which you objected I have alter'd, and have substituted two new stanzas instead of it.[1] Two others also I have struck out, another Critic having objected to *them*. I think I am a very tractable sort of a poet. Most of my fraternity would as soon shorten the noses of their children because they were said to be too long, as thus dock their compositions in compliance with the opinion of others. I beg that when my life shall be written hereafter my Authorship's ductility of temper may not be forgotten.

I am, my dear friend, with poor lame Mrs. Unwin's best respects — Ever Yours —

Wm Cowper.

SAMUEL ROSE
Saturday, 20 June 1789

Address: Samuel Rose Esqre. / Percy Street / Rathbone Place / London.
Postmark: JU/22/89
Mrs Donald F. Hyde

The Lodge
June 20. 1789

Amico Mio —

I am truly sorry that it must be so long before we can have an opportunity to meet. My Cousin in her last letter but one, inspired me with other expectations, expressing a purpose, if the matter could be so contrived, of bringing you with her.

[1] See n.1, C to Lady Hesketh, 13 June 1789.

I was willing to believe that you had consulted together on the subject and found it feasible. A month was formerly a trifle in my account, but at my present age I give it all its importance, and grudge that so many months should pass in which I have not even a glimpse of those I love, and of whom, the course of nature consider'd, I must, e'er long, take leave for ever. — But I shall live till August.

Many thanks for the Cuckow which arrived perfectly safe and goes well, to the Amusement and Amazement of all who hear it. Hannah lies awake to hear it, and I am not sure that we have not others in the house who admire his music as much as she. The chief objection to it seems to be that should it happen to be out of order, we have no artist at hand to restore it. A common watch-maker would no doubt feel himself affronted by the offer of such a patient.

Nothing would please me more than to have you for a Tenant,[1] but the chambers of a man of my poor stint in temporals, cannot afford to stand empty long; yet can I hardly help wishing that they may continue so 'till you are ready to take them. Looking into Pump-court[2] in which there are Lime-trees, they are not unpleasant, and I can beside assure you on experience, that the sound of water continually pouring itself into pails and pitchers under the window, is a circumstance rather agreeable. In the country indeed, where we have purling brooks and such pretty things, a waterfall of the kind may be held rather cheap; but in the heart of London it has its value. They are also admirably well situated for business. It is certainly a truth that Attorneys are much decided in their choice of a Council by his situation, and, cœteris paribus,[3] will always prefer the man who is most easy to get at.

Having read both Hawkins and Boswell I now think myself almost as much a master of Johnson's character as if I had known him personally, and cannot but regret that our *Bards of other times*, found no such Biographers as these.

---

[1] See n.1, C to Hill, 27 May 1777.

[2] Pump Court, Middle Temple, 'was so called from the pump in the centre'. H. B. Wheatley, *London, Past and Present* (1930), iii. 131. This fountain, 'one of the sights of the city, rose . . . thirty feet' (*Ryskamp*, p. 69).

[3] 'All else being equal.'

They have both been ridiculed and the Wits have had their laugh, but such an history of Milton or of Shakespear as they have given of Johnson — Oh how desireable! I do not much wish you to take a tour to the Hebrides. The passage from island to island seems dangerous, and it does not appear from any thing that Boswel says, that there is aught to be seen that may not be much better imagined than visited; as to a curiosity to see uncivilized life, perhaps it somewhat resembles a curiosity to thrust one's nose into an ill smell. You in particular do not seem to me to be the sort of man for such a vagary. With your sensibilities you would meet with nothing that would make you amends for the coarseness of customs, manners, and accommodations that you would find there — With Mrs. Unwin's Love to you

Ever Yours. W. C.

JOSIAH DORNFORD   Sunday, 21 June 1789

Address: Josiah Dornford Esqre. / London
Postmarks: JU/22/89 *and* OULNEY
Princeton

Weston Underwood.
June 21. 1789

Dear Sir,

You have made me ample amends for any pleasure you might receive in reading the Translations you mention, by sending me that valuable little tract on the life and death of the excellent Mr. Fletcher.[1] I have not the happiness to have known or even to have seen him, but though of different sentiments with respect to some doctrines against which he disputed largely, have always entertained for him, as for a man of the most exemplary piety, the profoundest respect and veneration. If a man love God, which he cannot do without Faith in his son, his opinions are free, in my account, to settle themselves as they may. I shall not adopt them perhaps, but neither shall I value him the less because he differs from me.

It would not be easy, I fear, to make any considerable

---

[1] John Wesley's *A Short Account of the Life and Death of the Rev. John Fletcher* appeared in 1786.

addition to the small number of pieces which I have translated from Madame Guyon.[2] She was a woman of a most
heavenly mind and of very uncommon talents, but there is,
sometimes, in her most spiritual effusions a strain of familiarity, and sometimes of ænigmatical obscurity, which would
render most of her compositions useless at least, if not
disgusting, to the generality of readers. A life sequester'd as
hers, always begets peculiarities of sentiment, which they
who mix a little with the world, can by no means relish.

You are perfectly welcome, Sir, to a copy of those translations, though they have already been more dispersed than I
had any design they should be. It was a task which I performed
at a time when I had no other work in hand, merely for my
own amusement and to gratify a particular friend. They are
accordingly less finished than I should wish any thing of mine
to be that ventures into public. You will understand by this,
that I wish you neither to put them to the pres[s your] self,
nor to trust them in the hand of [   ][3] whose compliance with *that restriction* you cannot *perfectly* depend.

I am, Dear Sir,
Your obliged and most obedient Servant
Wm Cowper.

LADY HESKETH   Tuesday, 23 June 1789

Address: Lady Hesketh / New Norfolk Street / Grosvenor Square / London
Postmarks: JU/24/89 *and* OULNEY
Harvard

The Lodge
June 23. 1789

One more scrap of a Letter, my dearest Coz, and then I
hope it will be long before I shall have occasion to epistolize
thee again. I rejoice that the day is at last fixt for your
coming, and woe be to any whether Male or Female who

---

[2] C's translations of thirty-seven of the *Spiritual Songs* of Madame Guyon did
not appear until after his death, when Bull published them in a small volume
printed at Newport Pagnell in 1801. C apparently sent the translations he had
made in 1782-3 to Dornford, but refused a request by Dornford to translate
further poems by Madame Guyon.
[3] MS torn.

shall now interpose to hinder it! We have had much foul weather and the weather is still foul. This is tant mieux. It will be fair when you arrive, and the country the pleasanter for the deluge that has been pored down upon it. My laurels already give proof of the benefit they have received. A few days ago they were in appearance lifeless, but they are now almost cover'd with young leaves, save and except those under your parlour-window, which I am sorry to say are still but melancholy figures. Why they should have fared worse than the rest, I am at a loss to imagine, for they certainly have been more shelter'd and have a better aspect.

Mr. Frog has just pass'd by on his return to London. I dined with him yesterday. Mrs. Unwin being no longer able to walk in patterns or clogs was prevented by the dirt. The Catholic application to Parliament, I find, is not likely to speed at present.[1] The Bishop of London is not favorable to it; he leads all the other Bishops, and the Bishops all together lead Mr. Pitt. The Chancellor, on the other hand, is much their friend. But whether Chancellor alone will be able hereafter to preponderate against such a weight of Episcopacy, seems doubtful.

I learn from the Frogs that I am somewhat formidable to Mrs. B. Chester,[2] and that she trembles at the thought of encountering a man of my extraordinary consequence. I am glad of this. Nothing could so effectually relieve me from the fears that I should otherwise have of Her. Let her not detain you longer than the appointed Tuesday, and I will promise to frighten her as little as possible.

Thanks for the pains thou hast taken to promulgate my Illumination-verses, especially that thou didst take so sure a way to mortify the Printer of the *World*.[3] I dare say the rogue is now ready to hang himself. It would be a pleasant thing to see him the subject of an article in his own paper. —

---

[1] Bernard Ward in *The Dawn of the Catholic Revival in England, 1781–1803* (2 vols., 1909) provides information for June 1789 which confirms C's statement: 'Mr. Pitt intimated . . . that it was so very late in the sessions and that the Bishops considered it a business of so much importance that it must stand over till the next year. After some negotiations upon the subject, it was found impracticable to proceed; the delay was therefore acquiesced in.' (i. 159.)

[2] Mrs Bromley Chester. See n.3, C to Lady Hesketh, 7 Feb. 1788.

[3] See n.5, C to Rose, 5 June 1789.

The cause of this rash action we understand was the concern he felt at having neglected to print those incomparable stanzas by the Author of the Task, which appeared lately in the Times — Thus would complete justice be done to my violated importance, and an example held up in the eyes of all such vermin to deter them from taking such liberty with me in future.

Adieu — my Dear — The Bells are effectually muffled and you have no salute to fear from the steeple. Lady Spencer[4] is doubtless a respectable patroness and I can have no objection to her, should you persist in declining yourself the honour that I designed you.[5] But to tell you the truth I had rather have seen your name prefix'd to my labours than even hers or any body's.

We truly rejoice in the King's complete Restoration. A Restoration as worthy to be remember'd as any that has ever been commemorated in this country. The jaunt he proposes will probably be of great use to him and to the mortification of some enemies that he has in his own household, prove the means of lengthening his reign and our prosperity.

God give thee a good journey. So pray Mrs. Unwin and so, my dear Cousin —

Ever Yours Wm Cowper

MRS THROCKMORTON   Saturday, 18 July 1789

Address: Mrs. Throckmorton / Tunbridge-Wells.
Postmarks: JY/20/89 *and* NEWPORT/PAGNEL
Sir Robert Throckmorton

The Lodge — July 18. 1789

My dearest Madam,

You must not suppose that you have had all the rain at Tunbridge; we also have had our share; yet deluged as we have been, they have been still more drenched at Olney. There, no man could venture into the street who was not booted, and the inhabitants had a flood in their houses. Guess then the condition of your hay; yesterday and the day

---

[4] See n.5, C to Newton, 31 May 1783.
[5] See n.2, C to John Johnson, 23 May 1791.

before it was not visible, but this morning, as I walked down Hill-field,[1] I saw that it had emerged again. Some of the farmers, I understand, have resolved not to mow their meadow-grass at all, but to turn in their cattle as soon as the waters shall have subsided, that they may trample the crop into the soil and convert it into manure. But the scheme, I think, will hardly answer.

Your account of the attack that you sustained, on quitting your carriage, from the various artificers of the place, diverted me much; and I remember having sustained, myself, a similar one on the like occasion. I promised them all, my custom, dealing my gracious smiles about to the right and left, without giving preference to any. But the next morning I decamped; a measure which sufficiently explained my behaviour to them the Evening before, and as none of them had any reason to think himself particularly my favourite, they all bore my sudden departure with an equanimity that did them honour.

Many thanks, my dear Madam, for your extract from George's Letter. I retain but little Italian; yet that little was so forcibly muster'd by a consciousness that I was myself the subject, that I presently became Master of it. I have always said that George is a poet, and am never in his company but I discover proof of it; and the delicate address with which he has managed his Complimentary mention of me, convinces me of it still more than ever. Here are a thousand poets of us who have impudence enough to write for the public, but among the modest men who are by diffidence restrained from such an enterprize, there are those who would eclipse us all. I wish that George would make the experiment; I would bind on his Laurels with my own hand.

Your Gardener is gone after his wife, but having neglected to take his Lyre, alias fiddle with him, has not yet brought home Eurydice. Your Clock in the Hall has stopp'd, and strange to tell, it stopp'd at the sight of the Watchmaker, for he only looked at it, and it has been motionless ever since. Mr. Gregson is gone, and the Hall is a desolation. Pray don't think any place pleasant that you may find in your rambles,

---

[1] Hill-field was the field between the first spinney (Overbrook Spinnie) and Weston Park.

that we may see you again the sooner. Your Aviary is all in good health; I pass it every day and often enquire at the lattice; the Inhabitants of it send their duty and wish for your return. I took notice of the Inscription on your Seal, and had we an Artist here capable of furnishing me with such a one, you should read on mine — Sans encore une Lettre, je serai inconsolable[2] — I depend on your kindness that you will not suffer me to be so.

Lady Hesketh's and Mrs. Unwin's best Love attend you. You will assuredly find my Cousin here at your return. She is in our clutches and we shall not suddenly release her. May you derive in the mean time all possible benefit from the waters! These incessant rains, I know, dilute the mineral too much and make it less efficacious, but change of air is itself beneficial, and I hope you will find it so. I met Mr. Buchanan the other Evening in my walk and as I passed him called him Mr. Buchan. This is a sort of blunder that I was ever making when I lived in the world, and were I to return to it, should make it as often as ever — Adieu my dear Mrs. Frog — with my best Love to your husband — I remain affectionately

Yours.   Wm Cowper.

SAMUEL ROSE   Thursday, 23 July 1789

Address: Samuel Rose Esqre. / Percy Street / Rathbone Place / London.
Postmarks: [JY/2] 4/89[1] *and* OULNEY
Morgan Library

The Lodge July 23. 1789

You do well, my dear Sir, to improve your opportunity. To speak in the rural phrase, this is your sowing time, and the sheaves you look for can never be yours unless you make that use of it. The colour of our whole life is generally such as the three or four first years, in which we are our own masters, make it. Then it is that we may be said to shape our own destiny, and to treasure up for ourselves a series of future successes or disappointments. Had I employed my time as

---

[2] 'Without another letter, I shall be desolate.'

---

[1] The letter is torn and the date stamp has been covered by a patch over the tear.

wisely as you in a situation very similar to yours, I had never been a poet perhaps, but I might by this time have acquired a character of more importance in society, and a situation in which my friends would have been better pleased to see me. But three years mis-spent in an attorney's office were almost of course followed by several more equally mis-spent in the Temple, and the consequence has been, as the Italian Epitaph says — Sto qui[2] — The only use I can make of myself now, at least the best, is to serve in terrorem to others when occasion may happen to offer, that they may escape, so far as my admonitions can have any weight with them, my folly and my fate. When you feel yourself tempted to relax a little the strictness of your present discipline and to indulge in amusements incompatible with your future interests, think on your friend at Weston.

Having said this, I shall next with my whole heart invite you hither, and assure you that I look forward to approaching August with great pleasure because it promises me your company. After a little time (which we shall wish a longer) spent with us, you will return invigorated to your studies and pursue them with the more advantage. In the mean time, in point of season, you have lost little by being confined to London. Incessant rains and meadows under water have given to the summer the air of winter, and the country has been deprived of half its beauties. We begin to be seriously alarmed for the harvest. The hay has most of it already perished, and the corn having spired into a stalk of uncommon length, will consequently be productive of little. A very intelligent neighbour assured me two days ago, that the present wet weather continuing another fortnight will certainly cause a great dearth, if not a famine. The millers and Bakers even now find it difficult to procure wheat, and a lean crop succeeding will reduce us to a penury in the article of bread such as is seldom felt in England.

It is time to tell you that we are all well and often make you our subject. Lady Hesketh desires to be kindly remember'd to you, as does Mrs. Unwin. We comfort ourselves as well as we can under all these threatening appearances with cheerful

---

[2] 'I remain here.'

chat and the thought that we are once more together. This is the third meeting that my Cousin and we have had in this country, and a great instance of good fortune I account it in such a world as this, to have expected such a pleasure thrice without being once disappointed. Add to this wonder as soon as you can, by making yourself of the party — I am truly Yours

Wm Cowper

MRS KING   Saturday, 1 August 1789

Address: Mrs. King / Pirtenhall near / Kimbolton / Huntingdonshire
Postmark: AU/3/89
Princeton

Weston Augt. 1. 1789

My dear Madam —

The Post brings me no letters that do not grumble at my silence; had not you therefore taken me to task as roundly as others, I should have concluded you perhaps more indifferent to my Epistles than the rest of my Correspondents, of whom one says — I shall be glad when you have finished Homer, then possibly you will find me a little leisure for an old friend. Another says — I don't chuse to be neglected unless you equally neglect every one else — Thus I hear of it with both ears, and shall 'till I appear in the shape of two great Quarto volumes, the composition of which I confess engrosses me to a degree that gives my friends, to whom I feel myself obliged for their anxiety to hear from me, but too much reason to complain. Johnson told Mr. Martin the truth, but your inference from that truth is not altogether so just as most of your conclusions are. Instead of finding myself the more at leisure because my long labour draws to a close, I find myself the more occupied. As when a horse approaches the goal, he does not, unless he be jaded, slacken his pace, but quicken it, even so it fares with me. The end is in view; I seem almost to have reached the mark; and the nearness of it inspires me with fresh alacrity. But be it known to you that I have still two Books of the Odyssey before me, and when they are finished shall have almost the whole eight and forty to revise. Judge then, my dear Madam, if it is yet time for me to play, or to gratify myself with scribbling to those I love. No. It is still necessary that, waking, I should be all absorpt in Homer, and that, sleeping, I should dream of nothing else.

I am a great lover of good Paintings, but no Connoisseur, having never had an opportunity to become one. In the last forty years of my life I have hardly seen six pictures that were worth looking at; for I was never a frequenter of Auctions, having never had any spare money in my pocket, and the public exhibitions of them in London[1] had hardly taken place when I left it. My Cousin, who is with us, saw the Gentleman,[2] whose pieces you mention, on the top of a scaffold, copying a famous picture in the Vatican. She has seen of his performances and much admires them.

You have had a great loss,[3] and a loss that admits of no consolation except such as will naturally suggest itself to *you*. Such, I mean, as the Scripture furnishes. We must all leave or be left, and it is the circumstance of all others that makes long life the least desireable, that others go while we stay, 'till at last we find ourselves alone, like a tree on an Hill-top.

Accept, my dear Madam, mine and Mrs. Unwin's best Compliments to Yourself and Mr. King, and believe me, however unfrequent in telling you that I am so,

> Affectionately Yours
> Wm Cowper.

---

[1] In Chapter III, 'Forerunners: Exhibitions' (pp. 34–41), of *The History of the Royal Academy 1768–1968* (1968), Sidney C. Hutchison outlines the various attempts *c.*1760–8 to have public exhibitions of paintings in London. The first at the Royal Academy was in 1769 in Pall Mall.

[2] Probably Fuseli. 'He had from his boyhood admired Michael Angelo in engravings, and he adored him now in his full and undiminished majesty. It was a story which he loved to repeat, how he lay on his back day after day, and week succeeding week, with upturned and wondering eyes, musing on the splendid ceiling of the Sistine Chapel — on the unattainable grandeur of the Florentine.' Allan Cunningham, *The Lives of the Most Eminent British Painters, Sculptors, and Architects* (1830), ii. 280. Lady Hesketh was in Italy in 1770–1, the time at which the above incident would have taken place.

[3] This person is unidentified.

SAMUEL ROSE   Saturday, 8 August 1789

Address: Samuel Rose Esqre / Percy Street / Rathbone Place / London
Postmarks: AU/10/89 *and* OULNEY
Society of Antiquaries

> Weston Lodge
> Augt. 8. 1789

My dear friend —

Come when you will or when you can, you cannot come at a wrong time, but we shall expect you on the day mentioned.

To convince you that you execute my commissions in a manner that perfectly pleases me, I shall now charge you with a new one. You must bring me two or three pair of striped silk stockings. But how shall I give you an idea of the size? Your own size would exactly suit me were you exactly of my height; but my legs are a little longer than yours. This circumstance attended to, there is no danger of mistake, for we have, both, a plump calf and a shapely Small.[1]

If you have any Book that you think will make pleasant Evening reading, bring it with you. I now read Mrs. Piozzi's Travels to the Ladies after supper, and shall probably have finished them before we shall have the pleasure of seeing you. It is the fashion, I understand, to condemn them.[2] But we who make Books ourselves are more merciful to Bookmakers. I would that every fastidious judge of authors, were, himself, obliged to write; there goes more to the compilation of a volume than many Critics imagine. I have often wonder'd that the same poet who wrote the Dunciad, should have written these lines.

> The Mercy I to others show,
> That Mercy show to me.[3]

Alas for Pope, if the mercy he showed to others was the measure of the mercy he received! He was the less pardonable too, because experienced in all the difficulties of composition.

---

[1] 'The small, slender, or narrow part' of the leg (*OED*).
[2] *Observations and Reflections Made in the Course of a Journey through France, Italy, and Germany* had appeared on 4 June 1789. *The Morning Post* and *The European Magazine* were particularly hostile to Mrs Piozzi's way of writing. See James L. Clifford, *Hester Lynch Piozzi* (Oxford, 1952), pp. 342–8.
[3] 'The Universal Prayer', lines 39–40.

I scratch this between dinner and Tea; a time when I cannot write much without disordering my noddle and bringing a flush into my face. You will excuse me therefore, if through mere respect for the two important considerations of health and beauty, I conclude myself, with the Ladies' best wishes —

Ever Yours
Wm Cowper.

JOSEPH HILL   Wednesday, 12 August 1789

Address: Joseph Hill Esqre. / Wargrave near / Twyford / Berkshire
Postmarks: AU/14/89 *and* OULNEY
Cowper Johnson

Augt. 12 1789 — Received of Joseph Hill Esqre. by Draft on Child and Co. the Sum of Thirty pounds

Wm Cowper.

Weston Underwood
Augt 12. 1789

My dear friend —

Many thanks for the above, and I hold myself much indebted for it both to your kind vigilance in my favour and to the benevolence of my brethren at the bar. I rejoice that you and Mrs. Hill are so agreeably occupied in your retreat. August, I hope, will make us amends for the gloom of its many wintry predecessors. We are now gathering from our meadows not hay but muck, such stuff as deserves not the carriage, which yet it must have, that the after crop may have leave to grow. The Ouse has hardly deign'd to run in his channel since the summer began.

My Muse were a Vixen if she were not always ready to fly in obedience to your demands, but what can be done? I can write nothing in the few hours that remain to me of this day that will be fit for your purpose, and unless I could dispatch what I write by to-morrow's post, it would not reach you in time. I must add too that my friend the Vicar of the next parish engaged me the day before yesterday to furnish him by next Sunday with a Hymn to be sung on the occasion of his preaching to the children of the Sunday school.[1] Of which Hymn I have not yet produced a syllable. I am somewhat in the case of Lawyer Dowling in Tom Jones, and could I split myself into as many poets as there are Muses, could find employment for them all.[2]

You supposed I imagine that your Letter would have been with me sooner. It is now Wednesday Noon and I have this moment received it. The post as I said goes out again to-morrow morning, but after to-morrow, not till Sunday Evening. You will see therefore that unless I were more prompt-witted than I am, the opportunity is too short. For alas! In an afternoon I am good for nothing.

Lady Hesketh joins me in best Compliments to yourself and Mrs. Hill, not forgetting your sisters who have always my affectionate remembrances.

Adieu, my dear friend — I am
Ever yours — Wm Cowper.

JOHN NEWTON

Sunday, 16 August 1789

Princeton

Weston
Augt. 16. 1789

My dear friend —

Mrs. Newton and you are both kind and just in believing that I do not love you less when I am long silent. Perhaps a friend of mine who wishes me to have him always in my thoughts, is never so effectually possess'd of the accomplishment of that wish, as when I have been long his Debtor; for *then* I think of him not only every day, but day and night and all day long. But I confess at the same time that my thoughts of you will be more pleasant to myself, when I shall have exonerated my conscience by giving you the letter

---

[1] The request was made by the Revd James Bean. For a description of the complicated textual history of this hymn, see *Russell*, pp. 29–32.

[2] Lawyer Dowling 'lamented his great Hurry of Business, and wished he could divide himself into twenty Pieces, in order to be at once in twenty Places.' *The History of Tom Jones, A Foundling* (6 vols., 1749), iii. 205.

so long your due. — Therefore here it comes. Little worth your having, but payment, such as it is, that you have a right to expect, and that is essential to my own tranquillity.

That the Iliad and Odyssey should have proved the occasion of suspending my correspondence with you, is a proof how little we foresee the consequences of what we publish. Homer, I day say, hardly at all suspected, that at the fag end of time, two personages would appear, the one yclep'd Sir Newton and the other Sir Cowper, who loving each other heartily would nevertheless suffer the pains of an interrupted intercourse, his poems the cause. So, however, it has happen'd; and though it would not, I suppose, extort from the old Bard a single sigh if he knew it, yet to me it suggests the serious reflection abovementioned. An Author by profession had need narrowly to watch his pen, lest a line should escape it which by possibility may do mischief when He has been long dead and buried. What we have done when we have written a book, will never be known 'till the day of judgment, then the account will be liquidated, and all the good that it has occasion'd and all the Evil, will witness either for or against us.

I am now in the last book of the Odyssey, yet have still I suppose half a year's work before me. The accurate revisal of two such voluminous poems can hardly cost me less. I rejoice however that the goal is in prospect, for though it has cost me years to run this race, it is only now that I begin to have a glimpse of it. That I shall never receive any proportionable pecuniary recompense for my long labours is pretty certain; and as to any fame that I may possibly gain by it, *that* is a commodity that daily sinks in value, in measure as the consummation of all things approaches. In the day when the Lion shall dandle the Kid, and a little child shall lead him,[1] the world will have lost all relish for the fabulous Legends of antiquity, and Homer and his Translator may budge off the stage together.

The Ladies are coming down and Breakfast is at hand. Should I throw aside my letter unfinished, it is not probable that I shall be able to send it by this opportunity. Therefore

[1] See Isaiah 11:6.

311

that you may not wait longer for that for which you have waited too long already, I will only add that I always love and value you both as much as you can possibly wish, and that I am, with Mrs. Unwin's affectionate remembrances, my dear friend — Ever Yours —

Wm Cowper.

You know that Lady Hesketh is with us; you have had her Compliments before, and I send them now, because she would bid me, if she knew that I write to you. We have a snug summer. Our neighbours are out on a ramble, and we have all their pleasant places to ourselves. Not that their return in September will interrupt our pleasures, for they are always kind and agreeable, but it will give them a different cast.

Pray remember me to Mr. Bacon.

SAMUEL ROSE   Thursday, 24 September 1789

Hayley, i. 336–7 *and Puttick and Simpson Catalogue*[1]

Weston, Sept. 24, 1789.

My dear friend,

You left us exactly at the wrong time. Had you stay'd till now, you would have had the pleasure of hearing even my Cousin say — 'I am cold' — And the still greater pleasure of being warm yourself; for I have had a fire in the study ever since you went. It is the fault of our summers that they are hardly ever warm or cold enough. Were they warmer we should not want a fire, and were they colder we should have one.

I have twice seen and conversed with Mr. J——. He is witty, intelligent, and agreeable beyond the common measure of men who are so. But it is the constant effect of a spirit of party to make those hateful to each other, who are truly amiable in themselves.

Let me beg of you to settle for me, by a reference to your subscription-edition of Pope's Homer, the knotty

---

[1] The MS of this letter was listed for sale in the Puttick and Simpson catalogue for 1 Aug. 1856 (Richard Capel Lambe Sale, item 213, 4 pages 4to); the present whereabouts of the MS is unknown, and the printed versions of this letter are obviously very incomplete. The penultimate paragraph is supplied from the sales catalogue. *Wright* identifies Mr. J as Mr. Jekyll.

point that I mentioned to you, whether it be customary
for the patron of the work to be a subscriber.[2]

Beau sends his love; he was melancholy the whole day
after your departure.

W. C.

SAMUEL ROSE   Sunday, 4 October 1789

Address: Samuel Rose Esqre. / Percy Street / Rathbone Place / London
Postmarks: OC/7/89 *and* OULNEY
Yale

The Lodge
Octob. 4.
1789

My dear friend —

The Hamper is come and come safe, and the contents, I
can affirm on my own knowledge are excellent. Many thanks
for the Spirits, of which as it happen'd, I had particular need
in the moment of their arrival, having had an indifferent
stomach all the day. It chanced that another hamper and a
box came by the same conveyance, all which I unpack'd and
expounded in the hall, my Cousin sitting meantime on the
stairs, spectatress of the business. We diverted ourselves with
imagining the manner in which Homer would have described
the scene. Detailed in his circumstantial way, it would have
furnished materials for a paragraph of considerable length
in an Odyssey.

> The straw-stuff'd hamper with his ruthless steel
> He open'd, cutting sheer th' inserted cords
> Which bound the lid and lip secure. Forth came
> The rustling package first, bright straw of wheat
> Or oats or barley; next, a bottle green
> Throat-full, clear spirits the contents, distill'd

---

[2] There is no patron as such to Pope's translations of Homer. After thanking
many of the persons who have encouraged him in various ways, Pope in his
Preface to the *Iliad*, says: 'In short, I have found more Patrons than ever *Homer*
wanted.' *Poems of Alexander Pope*, Twickenham edition, ed. Maynard Mack
et alios (1967), vii. 25.

4 October 1789

Drop after drop odorous, by the art
Of the fair mother of his friend, the Rose.[1]

And so on —
I should rejoice to be the Hero of such a tale in the hands
of Homer.

It gives us all concern that you complain of Indisposition
both of mind and body. To say the truth, the only fear I feel
respecting your future success in the laborious profession
that you have chosen, arises from the consideration of the
natural delicacy of your frame. For delicate it is, notwithstanding the severe discipline with which you exercise it
occasionally. You will remember, I trust, that when the
state of your health or spirits is such as calls for rural walks
and fresh air, you have always a retreat at Weston.

I wish it had so happen'd that I had received the Botanic
Garden which your friend chose to water with wine, before
you had heard of a new Edition of it;[2] for the less expensive
your presents are, considering their frequency, the better I
like them. You certainly do not give like the Heathen,
expecting to receive as much again, for you know well that
I am not able to requite you.

I feel some impatience to see the Analytical which has
not reach'd me yet, especially since I find that I am not
an outside passenger, but shall loll with dignity in the body
of that vehicle.[3]

[1] First printed in *Hayley*.

[2] C owned a copy of *The Botanic Garden* (1791; 2 vols. in 1; 1st edn. of part
1, 2nd edn. of 1790 of part 2). These volumes (see *Keynes*, 55) are now in the
collection of Princeton University Library. C had reviewed part 2 (*The Loves of
the Plants* which had been published in 1789) in the *Analytical Review* for May
1789, and he would review part 1 (*The Œconomy of Vegetation* (1791)) in the
same journal's issue of Mar. 1793.

[3] That is, not a prospectus or advertisement of one of his works (which would
appear on the covers or as a supplement to, a journal), but — in this case — a
review written by him. C's review of *Ger. Nicolai Heerkens Groningani Aves
Frisicae. The Friesland Birds of G. N. Heerkens of Groningen* (Rotterdam, 1787)
appeared on pp. 47–51 of the *Analytical Review* (vol. 5) for Sept. 1789 under
the signature 'G.G.' Although Norma Russell feels that C is referring to his review
of *The Poems of Ferdosi*, which appeared in the October number of the *Analytical
Review*, C probably means the September issue which would be available during
October. The October issue would not be expected until November (cf. *Russell*,
p. 159, n.3).

We are all well, we all love you, down to the very dog, and shall rejoice to hear that you have exchanged languor for alacrity, and the debility that you mention, for indefatigable vigour.

The Hall is once more full. Poor George has the gout, which makes him an excellent Amanuensis for me, but I cannot rejoice *therein*. I wish rather that his feet were well, and the gout driven *therefrom*, then should I rejoice *therefore*. With the Ladies' best Compliments I am

> Sincerely Yours — Wm Cowper.

We shall perhaps trouble you for more Cheese in the course of the winter; so keep an exact account of our arrears sur cette article lá.

SAMUEL ROSE   Thursday, 5 November 1789

Address: Samuel Rose Esqre. / Percy Street / Rathbone place / London
Postmarks: NO/6/89 *and* OULNEY
Morgan Library

> The Lodge
> Nove. 5. 1789

My dear Sir —

Recollecting after you were gone that I could not send you my Tale[1] without more expence to you than it is worth, I have transmitted it, as we say here, *next ways* to Johnson, and hope that in the amusements of your Office you will find sufficient solace for so great a disappointment. The same oeconomical tenderness for you and the same modest opinion of my own works, are the only considerations that prevent my sending you *herein* enclosed, another new piece, a piece also finish'd since you went, a memento mori,[2] written for the benefit of the Northamptonians, but chiefly for the benefit of Mr. Cox my anniversary client and the Clerk of All Saints parish. All this I communicate to make you regret the more your short continuance at Weston, for you see that had

[1] Probably 'The Needless Alarm'.
[2] C is referring to the verses which he supplied in 1789 for the third time for the Bills of Mortality for the Parish of All Saints, Northampton.

you been more persuadeable on that subject, you would have had the earliest possible sight of both.

The day you went, a bottle of Spruce[3] was produced and the cork drawn in the study. A column of the contents immediately spouted to the cieling, nor did it cease to sally in this violent manner till more than two thirds of the liquor were expended. You will imagine that the remaining third[4] was excellent. But it did not prove so. As Mr. Pulteney,[5] while a patriot, speaking in the house of Commons on the subject of public measures, observed that the apparent energy of them was an ill symptom, that they bespoke the delirium of a fever in its last stage, and were not so much efforts as agonies, so it proved in the present instance. All the life, stength and spirit of the good creature were wasted in that last struggle

— placidâque ibi demúm morte quievit.[6]

The remaining bottles have been given to the servants, but the servants like it no better than ourselves.

Beau cannot forget Flora. Twice since you left us he has run away to Gayhurst alone, and this morning I have sent Samuel to bring him back again, judging that he will perhaps watch him more narrowly hereafter, when he finds that his escapes are attended with so much trouble to himself. I could by no means spare my dog, and yet it is not unlikely that I may lose him. He is very portable and would be an acquisition to any stranger.

Lady Hesketh forgot to thank you for the Croydon verses,[7] and therefore thanks you by me. She has taken a copy of them, and we all think them witty and elegant. It is earnestly recommended to you to follow punctually the good physical advice given you at Weston. We wish much to hear that your health is amended. Your brethren of the quill now at the Hall,

[3] Spruce beer, 'a femented beverage made with an extract from the leaves and branches of the spruce fir' (*OED*).

[4] C has marked the text here and inserted the following comment at the foot of the page: 'This would have done honour to an Irishman.'

[5] Daniel Pulteney (d. 1731) who served as MP for Tregony (Mar. 1721), Hedon (Nov. 1721), and Preston (1722–31).

[6] *Aeneid*, ix. 445: 'In the peace of death, he found rest.' The passage concerns the death of Nisus.

[7] We do not know the verses being referred to.

less industrious than yourself, mean to lengthen their holiday-time to the end of this week or the beginning of next. — Adieu, my Dear Sir, believe me with the Ladies' Compliments, who are just coming down to Breakfast, affectionately Yours

Wm Cowper

Mr. Throck—n has made me, since your departure, a handsome present. Villoisson's edition of the Iliad[8] elegantly bound by Edwards.[9] If I live long enough, by the contribution of my friends, I shall once more be possess'd of a Library.

SAMUEL ROSE   *pre* Sunday, 22 November 1789[1]

Address: Samuel Rose Esqre / Percy Street / Rathbone Place / London
Olney

My dear Sir —

I send you a line or two by the hands of a Bearer whom I am sorry so to employ, just to tell that your deliverance from your cough gives us the greatest pleasure, and to thank you for a barrel of remarkable fine Oysters, by which I was redeemed from the necessity of sucking eggs five nights successively, and to tell you that I will write to you soon when I will send you the Northampton Verses.

It is 10 at night and the cloth not yet laid. You have guess'd perhaps by this time that my Cousin is the Bearer alluded to above. She leaves us, to our great regret, to morrow.

Adieu — and Good night —
Yours with the Ladies' Compliments
Wm Cowper

[8] *Keynes* (58) lists *Villoison's Homer's Iliad* (Venice, 1788) as having belonged to C. An inscription in this volume reads, 'Presented by Mr. Throckmorton in 1789'.
[9] James Edwards (1757–1816), known as Edwards of Halifax. 'He opened his book-shop in Pall Mall in 1784, and early in 1785 was granted the patent for this binding process [designs on the under-surface of transparent vellum], which he and his brothers had been practising in Halifax for at least four years previously.' Ellic Howe, *A List of London Bookbinders, 1648–1815* (1950), p. 33.

[1] The MS is undated. The allusion to the Northampton verses and Lady Hesketh's departure would seem to place this letter between C's letters to Rose of 5 and 22 Nov. 1789.

SAMUEL ROSE   Sunday, 22 November 1789

Haverford College

The Lodge
Novr. 22. 1789

My dear Sir —

I mean to write to you, if a cough that interrupts me continually will permit. It is a sort of exercise which whether I will or not, I generally find myself obliged to take in the beginning of Winter, and which may perhaps be necessary to compensate the loss of my Evening-walks, no longer possible.

I thank you for your history of Dr. White and his borrowed plumes.[1] The man who could with any degree of complacence dress himself in a plumage so procured, was very likely to refuse payment for it when demanded. The same want of delicacy is observable on both occasions. He is I suppose the same Doctor whom I see mentioned in a Note of Hole's subjoined to a passage in his preface to his poem called Arthur. In that note he calls him Arabic Professor in the University of Oxford, and expresses something like a wish that he would favour the world with a new English version of the Arabian Nights Entertainments.[2] A work for which he is, probably, better qualified than for the composition of Sermons. Though his Arabic knowledge may perhaps prove at last as *unreal* a *mockery* as his Theological. The next time I dined at the Hall after the receipt of this intelligence, I promised myself that I should figure away with it and treat my host with a new story.

---

[1] Joseph White (1745–1814), the orientalist and theologian, at this time had been accused of having bought, but not having acknowledged, the services of the Revd Samuel Badcock (1747–88), the theologian and literary critic, in the composition of the Bampton lectures in 1784. After Badcock's death in 1788, his sister found a bond for £500 payable by White to Badcock. White at first refused to pay the bond, and when he finally agreed to do so, the story of Badcock's involvement with White was revealed in R. B. Gabriel's *Facts Relating to the Rev. Dr. White's Bampton Lectures* (1789).

[2] In his Preface to *Arthur; or, The Northern Enchantment* (1789), Richard Hole (1746–1803) refers to White's ownership of a manuscript of the *Arabian Nights Entertainment* and remarks (p. vii), 'Should it receive the advantage of being translated by that gentleman, it would no longer be considered as a book chiefly calculated for the entertainment of children.' C's review of *Arthur* appeared in the Dec. 1789 issue of the *Analytical Review*.

22 November 1789

But found already known what I for News
Had thought to have reported.

Indeed I never touched a subject yet which I found new to our neighbour, and on most, his information is accurate to a degree that surprizes one considering his retired situation.

We are now reduced from our square table to a small oval one, and from a party of sometimes four, and sometimes three, to our original duality. London is not only an abomination in my account, because it runs away with my friends, but because it steals them at a season when we should be especially glad of their company. But if we will live in the country we must be contented to bear the inconveniences of a situation which is not chargeable with many. Perhaps I have named the only one of any importance. For though the trees are now leafless, the days short and gloomy, and the walks dirty, there never was nor will be that metropolis on earth which I would prefer to the country even in this condition.

I promised you the Northampton verses, and should have transcribed them into this sheet, but my Cousin who has them, has undertaken to furnish you with a copy. I am glad that you were pleased with those which I sent to Johnson. I have two or three friends in the world, whom if I can please before publication, I give myself no trouble about the fate of the piece which has once had their approbation.

When my Cousin wrote to tell me of her safe arrival, she informed me that she had seen you, and you only. I rejoiced that you had given her so early a call, and should have rejoiced more had she seen you in the best health and spirits. We feel ourselves much interested in your welfare, and few days pass in which you do not furnish part of our conversation.

This accompanies a Turkey of which we beg your acceptance. Mrs. U. bids me say that you will perhaps find the fat of it somewhat yellow, but let not that discourage you when it appears on your table. It is owing to the particular manner of feeding it.

Mr. Rye[3] told me a few days since that he saw your uncle

[3] The Revd Joseph Jekyll Rye (1759–1819), with whom C corresponded in 1792.

319

Clarke[4] lately (at Lord Spencer's[5] if I am not mistaken) and that he was in perfect health and very cheerful.

Pardon a dull letter. My cold makes me uncommonly stupid. With Mrs. Unwin's best Compliments I am

Sincerely Yours — Wm Cowper.

JOHN NEWTON   Tuesday, 1 December [1789][1]

Address: The Revd. John Newton.
Princeton

My dear friend

On this fine first of December, under an unclouded sky and in a room full of sunshine, I address myself to the payment of a debt long in arrear but never forgotten by me, however I may have seemed to forget it. I will not waste time in apologies. I have but one, and that one will suggest itself unmention'd. I will only add that you are the first to whom I write of several to whom I have not written many months, who all have claims upon me and who I flatter myself are all grumbling at my silence. In your case perhaps I have been less anxious than in the case of some others, because if you have not heard from myself, you have heard from my better self, Mrs. Unwin. From her you have learn'd that I live, that I am as well as usual, and that I translate Homer. Three short Items, but in which is comprized the whole detail of my present history. Thus I fared when you were here, thus I have fared ever since you were here, and thus, if it please God, I shall continue to fare some time longer, for though the work is done it is not finished; a riddle which you who are a brother of the Press, will solve easily. I have also been the less anxious, because I have had frequent opportunities to hear of you, and have always heard that you are in good health and happy. Of Mrs. Newton too I have heard more favorable accounts of late, which have given us both the sincerest pleasure. Mrs. Unwin's case is at present my only subject of uneasiness that is not immediately

---

[4] See n.2, C to [Rose], [10 Mar. 1788].
[5] George, 2nd Earl Spencer (1758–1834).

[1] This letter is dated in Newton's hand 'Suppose 89/1 Dece.'

personal and properly my own. She has almost constant head-aches, almost a constant pain in her side which nobody understands, and her lameness, within the last half year, is very little amended. But her spirits are good, because supported by comforts which depend not on the state of the body, and I do not know that with all these pains her looks are at all alter'd since we had the happiness to see you here, unless perhaps they are alter'd a little for the better. I have thus given you as circumstantial an account of ourselves as I could; the most interesting matter, I verily believe, with which I could have filled my paper, unless I could have made spiritual mercies to myself the subject. In my next, perhaps, I shall find leisure to bestow a few lines on what is doing in France and in the Austrian Netherlands; though to say the truth I am much better qualified to write an essay on the siege of Troy, than to descant on any of these modern revolutions. I question if in either of the countries just mention'd, full of bustle and tumult as they are, there be a single character whom Homer were he living, would deign to make his hero. The populace are the heroes now, and the stuff of which gentlemen heroes are made, seems to be all expended.

I will endeavour that my next letter shall not follow this so tardily as this has followed the last, and with our joint affectionate remembrances to yourself and Mrs. Newton, remain as ever — Sincerely Yours

Wm Cowper

LADY HESKETH   Sunday, 13 December 1789

Address: Lady Hesketh
Princeton

The Lodge Decr. 13. 1789

My dearest Coz.

Unable to resist the temptation of a basket I take the opportunity that it affords, to send you a hasty and short scribblement though at an undue hour; for I write after Breakfast having overslept my usual time of rising. Homer will pardon me a trespass so seldom committed and by which he will be but little a loser.

In the first place I thank thee heartily, that with the patience and perseverance of an angler, in ponds *where fish are*, thou hast at length contrived to hook that great Gudgeon mention'd in thy last.[1] I do not think at the same time that thou wast guilty of any flattery in thy management of the matter, for to tell such a man that the absence of his name from my list of Subscribers would have been a dishonour to my book, considering especially what book it is, was telling him the truth. And now I will speak a proud word. He will be glad when he gets the book that he did subscribe to it. And this proud word I speak almost as much with a view to thy encouragement as to gratify my own vanity and self-complacence. Authors are not often good judges of themselves, but thou must know that I am an exception.

Again I thank thee for wine; for two dozen of excellent Madeira, not a bottle of which was broken by the way. Impatient to taste it, though it was hardly allowing it a fair trial, I open'd a bottle of it last night, and found it very superior to my last stock of that commodity which I doubt not had been kept too long.

Thanks also for the News-papers which I forgot like a beast to acknowledge in my last.

I sincerely rejoice with thee that thou hast succeeded in procuring a midshipmanship (there's a word for you!) for the poor young man in question;[2] may he live to command where he now serves!

We should sooner have had a daily post, could the people of Olney have settled the affair among themselves. Better now than never. — I must not forget to beg that you will make my best compliments to the lady, whoever she is, to whom I am indebted for a subscription so handsomely given.

Our poor neighbours have both been indisposed. Mrs. Frog with a terrible cold, from which she has just recover'd after a fortnight's illness, and Mr. Frog with his first fit of the gout which seized him about a week since by the foot, and which confines him still.

As to ourselves we are much in statû quo, except that Mrs. U. has a slight nervous fever accompanied with head-aches,

---

[1] Unidentified.   [2] Unidentified.

which she had not when you were here. She drinks limonade and finds it her best remedy.

Received from my master on account current with Lady Hesketh the sum of one Kiss on my forehead — witness my paw

Beau —+— his mark.

Mrs. U. sends her affectionate Compliments.

JOSEPH HILL   Monday, 14 December 1789

Cowper Johnson

Weston Underwood
Decr. 14. 1789

My dear friend

It is a shame that I should never write to you but for the Needful. The truth is, I write very few letters indeed that are not extorted from me by necessity. When I shall have fought all my Trojan battles, and have given Ulysses quiet possession of his own goods and chatels again, then I shall become a more reasonable correspondent.

I hope you have paid yourself out of Stock the amount of my last draft, my income not being adequte to such demands and to the supply of my necessities also. Those necessities oblige me to beg a farther supply at present, which I shall be happy to receive per first opportunity.

Our Grand Signor has produced — or rather his Sultanas — two families. The last, so late in the season, that we despaired of them. But they are now thriving Turks. Among the youngest are two perfectly white; if Mrs. Hill (to whom I beg my best Compliments) has any wish for such, Mrs. Unwin will send them in the Spring. They are now unequal to the journey.

I am, my dear friend,
Ever yours
Wm Cowper

Many thanks for a barrel of Oysters received some time since.

JOSEPH HILL   December 1789[1]

Cowper Johnson

My dear friend

Many thanks for your kind intentions and for the remittance above specified.

I think with you, though I have little leisure to think about them, that the French make rather a ludicrous figure in their new patriotic character. Their shoe-buckle subscriptions[2] and the childish enthusiasm with which they appear to be animated on that trivial occasion, are both truly laughable. By means of my neighbor Mr. Throckmorton, I have opportunity to see a French Newspaper which he receives regularly from Paris. It is that of Mlle. Caraillo,[3] if I spell her aright. It is not often that I have time to read it, but when I can, I generally find in it some provocation to mirth. On the whole, however, the present appears to me a wonderful period in the history of mankind. That nations so long contentedly slaves, should on a sudden become enamour'd of liberty and understand as suddenly their own natural right to it, feeling themselves at the same time inspired with resolution to assert it, seems difficult to account for from natural causes.

With respect to the issue of all this, I can only say, that if having discovered the value of liberty, they should next discover the value of peace, and lastly the value of the Word of God, they will be happier than they ever were since the rebellion of the first Pair, and as happy as it is possible they should be in the present life.

---

[1] Dated in pencil, perhaps by Hill: '18 Dec. 89'. A receipt has been cropped from the top of the page, and C's date was cut off with it. This dating is surely incorrect, since the Earl Cowper, whose death is mentioned in the postscript, did not die until 22 Dec. The letter probably belongs to the latter part of the month.

[2] 'During the month of September [1789] the State subsisted chiefly on patriotic gifts . . . The members of the Assembly gave up their silver shoe-buckles, and determined for the future they would only wear paste.' H. Morse Stephens, *A History of the French Revolution* (3 vols., 1886), i. 353. C read about these 'subscriptions' in the 26 Nov. 1789 issue of the French newspaper (see n.3 below) which Throckmorton received.

[3] *Journal d'Etat et du citoyen* . . . , edited by Louise-Félicité Guinement de Keralio-Robert, appeared from 13 Aug. to 27 Dec. 1789.

With my best Compliments to Mrs. Hill I am in much haste, most sincerely Yours

Wm Cowper.

I am truly sorry that I have lost so kind a Cousin & my intended patron.

SAMUEL ROSE   Sunday, 3 January 1790

Hayley, i. 340–1

The Lodge, Jan. 3, 1790.

My dear sir,

I have been long silent, but you have had the charity I hope, and believe, not to ascribe my silence to a wrong cause. The truth is, I have been too busy to write to any body, having been obliged to give my early mornings to the revisal and correction of a little volume of Hymns for Children, written by I know not whom.[1] This task I finished but yesterday, and while it was in hand, wrote only to my Cousin, and to her rarely. From her, however, I knew that you would hear of my well-being, which made me less anxious about my debts to you than I could have been otherwise.

I am almost the only person at Weston, known to you, who have enjoyed tolerable health this winter. In your next Letter give us some account of your own state of health, for I have had my anxieties about you. The winter has been mild; but our winters are in general such, that when a friend leaves us in the beginning of that season, I always feel in my heart a *perhaps* importing that we have possibly met for the last time, and that the Robins may whistle on the grave of one of us before the return of summer.

I am still thrumming Homer's lyre; that is to say, I am still employed in my last revisal; and to give you some idea of the intenseness of my toils, I will inform you that it cost me all the morning yesterday, and all the evening, to translate

[1] Rowland Hill. C revised his *Divine Hymns* in 1790 (see pp. xxv–xxvi). This work contained two new hymns by C: 'Hear, Lord, The Song of Praise and Pray'r' and 'Hymn For a Child That has Ungodly Parents'. Both hymns had been written in Aug. 1789, and the former was reprinted in the *Northampton Mercury* of 7 Aug. 1790 (see *Milford*, p. 683 and *Russell*, pp. 29–32).

a single simile to my mind. The transitions from one member of the subject to another, though easy and natural in the Greek, turn out often so intolerably awkward in an English version, that almost endless labour and no little address are requisite to give them grace and elegance. I forget if I told you that your German Clavis[2] has been of considerable use to me. I am indebted to it for a right understanding of the manner in which Achilles prepared pork, mutton, and goat's flesh for the entertainment of his friends, in the night when they came deputed by Agamemnon to negociate a reconciliation. A passage of which nobody in the world is perfectly master, myself only and Schaulfelbergerus excepted, nor ever was, except when Greek was a *live* language.

I do not know whether my Cousin has told you or not, how I brag in my Letters to her concerning my Translation; perhaps her modesty feels more for me than mine for myself, and she would blush to let even you know the degree of my self-conceit on that subject. I will tell you, however, expressing myself as decently as vanity will permit, that it has undergone such a change for the better in this last revisal, that I have much warmer hopes of success than formerly.

W. C.

MRS KING   Monday, 4 January 1790

Address: Mrs. King / Pirtenhall near / Kimbolton / Huntingdonshire
Postmarks: JA/5/90 *and* OULNEY
Princeton

Weston Underwood
Jan 4. 1790

My dear Madam,

Your long silence has occasion'd me to have a thousand anxious thoughts about you. So long it has been, that whether

---

[2] Johann Schaufelberger's *Nova Clavis Homerica*, 8 vols. (Turici, 1761–8). C is referring to his translation of 'κρεῖον μεγα' as 'an ample tray' in *Iliad*, ix, line 256 of his translation. 'It is not without authority that I have thus rendered κρεῖον μεγα. Homer's banquets are never stewed or boiled; it cannot therefore signify a kettle. It was probably a kitchen-table, dresser, or tray, on which the meat was prepared for the spit. Accordingly we find that this very meat was spitted afterward. — See Schaufelbergerus.' (i. 220).

I now write to a Mrs. King at present on earth, or already in heaven I know not. I have friends whose silence troubles me less though I have known them longer, because if I hear not from themselves, I yet learn from others that they are still living and likely to live. But if your letters cease to bring me news of your welfare, from whom can I gain the desireable intelligence? The birds of the air will not bring it, and third person there is none between us by whom it might be conveyed. Nothing is plain to me on this subject, but that either you are dead, or very much indisposed, or, which would affect me with perhaps as deep a concern, though of a different kind, very much offended. The latter of these suppositions I think the least probable, conscious as I am of an habitual desire to offend nobody, especially a lady, and especially a lady to whom I have many obligations. But all the three solutions abovementioned are very uncomfortable, and if you live and can send me one that will cause me less pain than either of them, I conjure you by the charity and benevolence which, I know, influence you on all occasions, to communicate it without delay.

It is possible, notwithstanding appearances to the contrary, that you are not become perfectly indifferent to me and to what concerns me. I will therefore add a word or two on a subject which once interested you, and which is for that reason worthy to be mentioned, though, truly, for no other. Meaning myself. I am well, and have been so (uneasiness on your account excepted) both in mind and body, ever since I wrote to you last. I have still the same employment. Homer in the morning and Homer in the evening, as constant as the day goes round. In the Spring I hope to send Iliad and Odyssey to the press. So much for me and my occupations. Poor Mrs. Unwin has hitherto had but an unpleasant winter; unpleasant as constant pain either in her head or side could make it. She joins me in affectionate Compliments to yourself and Mr. King, and in earnest wishes that you will soon favour me with a line that shall relieve me from all my perplexities. — I am, Dear Madam,

sincerely yours.
Wm Cowper.

WALTER BAGOT

*c.*January 1790[1]

Address: The Revd. Walter Bagot
Morgan Library

My dear friend

I know that you are too reasonable a man to expect any thing like punctuality of correspondence from a Translator of Homer, especially from one who is a Doer also of many other things at the same time; for I labour hard, not only to acquire a little fame for myself, but to win it also for others, men of whom I know nothing, not even their names, who send me their poetry, that by translating it out of prose into verse I may make it more like poetry than it was. Having heard all this, you will feel yourself not only inclined to pardon my long silence, but to pity me also for the cause of it. You may if you please believe likewise, for it is true, that I have a faculty of rememb'ring my friends even when I do not write to them, and of loving them not one jot the less though I leave them to starve for want of a letter from me. And now I think you have an apology both as to stile, matter, and manner, altogether unexceptionable.

Why is the winter like a Back biter? Because Solomon says that a Back biter separates between chief friends,[2] and so does the winter; to this dirty season it is owing that I see nothing of the valuable Chesters, whom indeed I see less at all times than serves at all to content me. I hear of them indeed occasionally from my neighbours at the Hall, but even of that comfort I have lately enjoyed less than usual, Mr. Throckmorton having been hinder'd by his first fit of gout from his usual visits to Chichley. The gout however has not prevented his making me a handsome present of a Folio edition of the Iliad published about a year since at Venice, by a literato who calls himself Villoison. It is possible that you have seen it, and that if you have it not yourself, it has at least found its way to Lord Bagot's library. If neither should be the case, when I write next (for sooner or later I shall

---

[1] The New Year reference and the mention of Earl Cowper's death place this letter in Jan. 1790.
[2] Proverbs 16:28.

certainly write to you again if I live) I will send you some
pretty stories out of his Prolegomena, which will make your
hair stand on end as mine has stood on end already, they so
terribly affect in point of authenticity the credit of the works
of the Immortal Homer.

Wishing you and Mrs. Bagot all the happiness that a new
year can possibly bring with it, I remain with Mrs. Unwin's
best respects, Yours, my dear friend, with all sincerity —

Wm Cowper.

My paper mourns for the death of Lord Cowper, my
valuable Cousin and much my Benefactor.

WALTER BAGOT   *c.*January 1790[1]

Address: Revd. Walter Bagot
Morgan Library

My dear friend —
I am a terrible creature for not writing sooner but the old
excuse must serve, at least I will not occupy paper with the
addition of others unless you should insist on it, in which case
I can assure you that I have them ready. Now to business —
From Villoison I learn that it was the avowed opinion and
persuasion of Callimachus[2] (whose hymns we both studied
at Westminster) that Homer was very imperfectly understood
even in *his* day; that his admirers, deceived by the perspicuity
of his stile, fancied themselves masters of his meaning, when,
in truth, they knew little about it.
Now we know that Callimachus, as I have hinted, was
himself a poet, and a good one; he was also esteemed a good
Critic; he almost, if not actually, adored Homer, and imitated
him as nearly as he could.
What shall we say to this? I will tell you what I say to it.
Callimachus meant, and he could mean nothing more by this
assertion, than that the poems of Homer were in fact an

[1] This undated letter seems to follow C's previous letter to Bagot (also undated
but definitely belonging to Jan. 1790): C expands his commentary, begun in the
previous letter, on Villoison. The MS is torn at the seal.
[2] Callimachus (*fl. c.*256 BC), the Hellenistic Greek poet and commentator.

Allegory, that under the obvious import of his stories, lay concealed a mystic sense, sometimes philosophical, sometimes religious, sometimes moral, and that the generality either wanted penetration or industry, or had not been properly qualified by their studies, to discover it. — This I can readily believe, for I am myself an Ignoramus in these points, and, except here and there, discern nothing more than the letter. But if Callimachus will tell me that even of *that* I am ignorant, I hope soon by two great volumes to convince him of the contrary.

I learn also from the same Villoison, that Pisistratus[3] who was a sort of Mæcenas in Athens where he gave great encouragement to literature and built and furnished a public library, regretting that there was no complete copy of Homer's works in the world, resolved to make one. For this purpose he advertized rewards in all the news-papers to those, who being possessed memoriter of any part or parcel of the poems of that bard, would resort to his house and repeat them to his secretaries that they might write them. Now it happen'd that more were desirous of the reward than qualified to deserve it. The consequence was that the non-qualified persons having, many of them, a pretty knack at versification, imposed on the generous Athenian most egregiously, giving hi[m][4] instead of Homer's verses which they had not to give, verse[s of the]ir own invention. He, good creature, s[uspecting] no s[uch frau]d, took them all for gospel, and en[tered] them [into his] volume accordingly. Hence, it seem[s we] have [Hom]er.

N[ow let] *Him* believe the story who can. That Homer's works were in this manner collected I *can* believe, but that a learned Athenian could be so imposed on, with sufficient means of detection at hand, I *cannot*. Would he not be on his guard? Would not a difference of stile and manner have occurred? Would not that difference have excited a suspicion? Would not that suspicion have led to enquiry, and would

[3] Pisistratus (*c.*605–527 BC), Greek statesman and tyrant of Athens, did much to enhance Athenian cultural prestige, and he was the first person to have an official text of Homer written down.

[4] MS torn at the seal; readings supplied from *Hayley* (1806), iii. 204 and by conjecture.

not that enquiry have issued in detection? For how easy was it in the multitude of Homer-conners to find two, ten, twenty possessed of the questionable passage, and by confronting them with the impudent impostor, to convict him? Abeas ergo in malam rem cum istis tuis hallucinationibus, Villoisone![5]

I have lately had the pleasure to see both your brother and sister Chester with two of your neices and a sister[6] of your own whose Christian name I know not, but perhaps you do. I have not had time to read the Sewardian controversy,[7] but feel myself most inclined to favour the Westonian side of it.

Lord Cowper left me a rent-charge[8] annuity of 40₤. I have not been called on for an Epitaph; the friend you mention, whom I conclude to be your brother also, would do me the greatest favour would he recover and permit me to see, the obliterated lines[9] you mention. — Adieu! with our best Compliments I remain

most sincerely Yours — Wm Cowper.

MRS KING   Monday, 18 January 1790

Address: Mrs. King
Princeton

Weston Underwood
Jan 18. 1790

My dear Madam,

The sincerest thanks attend you both from Mrs. Unwin and myself for your many good things, on some of which I have already regaled with an affectionate remembrance of

[5] 'Go and be damned along with your hallucinations, Villoison!'

[6] See n.4, C to Lady Hesketh, 1 May 1786.

[7] Perhaps a reference to a dispute between Anna Seward (1747–1809), known as the 'Swan of Litchfield', and her sometime friend, Penelope Sophia Weston (1752–1827), who married William Pennington in 1792. 'The correspondence with Anna Seward had ceased in 1791 or 1792, when the "Swan" felt it her duty to write Mrs. Pennington . . . "with an ingenuousness on my part which I thought necessary to her welfare, but which her spirit was too high to brook." The breach in their friendship was not healed till 1804.' *The Intimate Letters of Hester Piozzi and Penelope Pennington, 1788–1821*, ed. O. G. Knapp (1914), pp. 160–1.

[8] 'A rent forming a charge upon lands, etc., granted or reserved by deed to one who is not the owner, with a clause of distress in case of arrears' (*OED*).

[9] Not located.

the Giver. We have not yet open'd the Cocoa-nut, but it was particularly welcome. It is medicine to Mrs. Unwin, who finds it always more beneficial to her health than any thing properly called medicinal. We are truly sorry that you are so much a sufferer by the Rheumatism; I also occasionally suffer by the same disorder, and in years past was much tormented by it. I can therefore pity you.

The report that informed you of enquiries made by Mrs. Unwin after a house at Huntingdon was unfounded. We have no thought of quitting Weston, unless the same providence that led us hither, should lead us away. It is a situation perfectly agreeable to us both, and to me in particular who write much and walk much, and consequently love silence and retirement, one of the most eligible. If it has a fault, it is that it seems to threaten us with a certainty of never seeing you. But may we not hope that when a milder season shall have improved your health, we may yet, notwithstanding the distance, be favour'd with Mr. King's and your company? A better season will likewise improve the roads, and exactly in proportion as it does so, will in effect lessen the interval between us. I know not if Mr. Martyn be a mathematician, but most probably he is a good one, and He can tell you that this is a proposition mathematically true, though rather paradoxical in appearance.

I am obliged to that gentleman, and much obliged to him, for his favorable opinion of my translation. What parts of Homer are particularly intended by the Critics, as those in which I shall probably fall short, I know not; but let me fail where I may, I shall fail nowhere through want of endeavours to avoid it. The Under parts of the poems (those I mean which are merely narrative) I find the most difficult. These can only be supported by the diction, and on these, for that reason, I have bestowed the most abundant labour. Fine Similes and fine speeches take care of themselves, but the exact process of slaying a sheep and dressing it,[1] it is not so easy to dignify in our language and in our measure. But I shall have the comfort, as I said to reflect, that whatever may be hereafter laid to my charge, the sin of idleness will not. Justly, at least, it never will. In the mean time, my dear Madam, I whisper to

[1] *Iliad*, ix. 255-66 in C's translation.

you a secret. Not to fall short of the Original in every thing, is impossible.

I send you, I believe, all my pieces that you have never seen. Did I not send you Catharina?[2] If not you shall have it hereafter. Mrs. Unwin whose health is lately somewhat amended, unites with me in affectionate Compliments to yourself and Mr. King. I am, Dear Madam, ever, ever in haste

Sincerely yours — Wm Cowper.

MRS COWPER · Thursday, 21 January 1790[1]

Address: Mrs. Cowper / Devonshire Street / Bloomsbury / London.
Postmarks: JA/22/90 *and* OULNEY
Olney

Weston Underwood
Jan 21. 1789

My dear Cousin

I beg you will never want encouragement to write to me. I am neither so great nor so good for nothing as to have forgotten your many kindnesses to me in years past, but shall always rejoice to be informed of your well-being, and especially from yourself.

I thank you for your congratulations on the subject of my annuity. I was born to subsist at the expence of my friends; in that, and in that alone, God knows, resembling my Lord and Master. I shall ever, I hope, retain a grateful sense of the kindess of Lord Cowper to whom I was entirely a stranger; but his bounty is a proof that he did not account me one.

[I share] sincerely with you in the pleasure you receive from the continuation of Henry's emolument to your daughter and my good Cousin Maria. His Lordship could not have

---

[2] In his letter to Mrs King of 14 Aug. 1790, C promised to send 'Catharina' at the earliest opportunity but she did not receive it until his letter of 31 Dec. 1790.

[1] As the postmark and the mention of the death of Lord Cowper indicate, C misdated this letter when writing '1789'. The letter bears also the following note: 'NB The signature cut off this day by me to form part of a Collection of Autographs of Eminent persons by Miss Baker of Bayfordbury Herts. CC. June 17. 1819.' The words, presumably 'I share' (at the beginning of the third paragraph), were removed when the signature was cut away.

bestowed it on a more deserving woman, or who would make a better use of it.

My dear Cousin, I dwell in a snug corner of a beautiful country, in which are many walks, some in groves and some in fields and some by river's side, with which you would be delighted. If you would give indeed a pleasure to myself and Mrs. Unwin come and visit it. We are quiet folks and will give you your own way, be it what it will. And this I mention beforehand as an inducement which nobody need despise, even though it be offered to a person gentle as yourself and a promoter always of the convenience of others.

With my best love to all who belong to you, I remain my dear Cousin most affectionately Yours

LADY HESKETH   Saturday, 23 January 1790

Address: Lady Hesketh / New Norfolk Street / Grosvenor Square / London
Postmarks: JA/25/90 *and* OULNEY
Historical Society of Pennsylvania

The Lodge
Jan. 23. 1789[1]

A thousand thanks my dear for a basket full of excellent things on which I shall fare deliciously day and night.

> In lieu of deserts, unwholesome and dear,
> Pickled olives and Lodi[2] shall bring up the rear.

I had a letter yesterday from the wild boy Johnson, for whom I have conceived a great affection. It was just such a letter as I like, of the true helter-skelter kind, and though he writes a remarkable good hand, scribbled with such rapidity that it was barely legible. He gave in it a droll account of the adventures of Lord Howard's note, and of his own in pursuit of it, all which I presume were occasioned by me who forgot, as I suppose, when I told you that he was come to visit me, to tell you his name also. He feels very sensibly the kindness of your reception of him, is very much pleased with Mr. Rose

[1] As with his letter of 21 Jan. 1790 to Mrs Cowper, C wrote '1789' instead of '1790' when dating this letter.
[2] Cheese. Lodi, a town in the Piedmont 20 miles from Milan, produces more Parmesan cheese than Parma.

whom he had the good fortune to find with you, and adds that he is to meet him this day also — Saturday — at your dinner. He addressed his letter to Mrs. Unwin like an *inconsiderate* youth; on a presumption, as he says, that I should not be able to find time to read it; like an *inconsiderate* youth never recollecting that it would cost me as much time to hear it. The truth, I suppose was, that he thought he should have a better chance of an answer. In this he judged right, for Mrs. Unwin replied to him on the instant, which I could not have done, nor probably 'till he had returned to Cambridge.

The poem he brought me came as from Lord Howard with his Lordship's request that I would revise it.[3] It is in the form of a Pastoral, and is entitled the *Tale of the Lute or the beauties of Audley-End.* I read it attentively; Was much pleased with part of it, and part of it I equally disliked. I told him so, and in such terms as one naturally uses when there seems to be no occasion to qualify or to alleviate censure. I observed him afterward somewhat more thoughtful and silent, but occasionally as pleasant as usual, and in Kilwick wood[4] where we walked the next day, the truth came out; that he [was hi]mself the Author; that Lord H. not approving it altogether, and several friends of his own age to whom he had shown it, differing from his Lordship in opinion and being highly pleased with it, he had come at last to a resolution to be set down by my judgment, a measure to which Lord H by all means advised him. He accordingly brought it, and will bring it again in the summer, when we shall lay our heads together and try to mend it.

I have lately had a letter also from Mrs. King, to whom indeed I had written to enquire whether she were living or

[3] Johnson had pretended that the verses were written by Charles Howard, 11th Duke of Norfolk (1746–1815), who had succeeded to the title in 1786. In fact, Lord Howard had asked Johnson to celebrate Audley End, his seat near Saffron Walden. The poem, the manuscript of which is in the collection of Miss Mary Barham Johnson, is a pastoral eclogue reminiscent of Theocritus and Spenser, written in couplets grouped in four-line stanzas. The poem takes place at midday on the 'Road to Victory' at Audley End.

It is probable that Johnny had been given an introduction to Lord Howard by Sir John Fenn, who had traced a pedigree from Mrs Roger Donne, C's grandmother, through the female line to Mary Bolyn, sister of Henry VIII's queen, and to Mary Bolyn's grandfather, Thomas Howard, 1st Duke of Norfolk.

[4] A wood belonging to John Throckmorton.

dead. It was followed by a basket containing also good things but of a different kind from yours, chiefly Preserves and pastry. She tells me that the Critics expect from my Homer every thing in some parts, and that in others I shall fall short. These are the Cambridge Critics, and she has her intelligence from the Botanical Professor Martyn. That Gentleman in reply assures them that I shall fall short in nothing, but shall disappoint them all. — It shall be my endeavour to do so, and I am not without hope of succeeding.

Beau's Love and Mrs. Unwin's must finish, only let me not forget to thank you on my own part for your kindness shown to Johnson on my recommendation. For though he be my Cousin, to thee is he not at all related.

Ever yours, my Dear, Wm Cowper.

LADY HESKETH   Tuesday, 26 January 1790

Address: Lady Hesketh / New Norfolk Street / Grosvenor Square / London
Postmarks: JA/27/90 *and* OULNEY
Morgan Library

The Lodge
Jan 26. 1790

My blunder in thanking thee, my Dearest Coz, for a basket instead of a box,[1] seems to have had something prophetic in it; for in the Evening a basket sent from you and filled with excellent fishes, actually arrived. With some of them we have compensated our neighbors for pigs presented to us in times past, and on the remainder we have chiefly subsisted ever since, nor is our stock even now exhausted. Many thanks are due to thee for this supply, and we pay them with much sincerity.

Could I blunder as I did in the instance of my Norfolk Cousin always, always, I mean, with such ludicrous conse-quences, I should be tempted to do it daily. I have not laughed so much many a long day as at your and his droll account of the strange and unimaginable distresses that ensued on the mere omission of those two important syllables that compose the name of Johnson.

---

[1] See C to Lady Hesketh, 23 Jan.

JOHN JOHNSON
From a miniature in crayon and sepia wash
by William Blake

It gives me great pleasure that you are so much pleased with him because I was much pleased with him myself. There is a simplicity in his character that charms me, and the more because it is so great a rarity. Humour he certainly has, and of the most agreeable kind; his letter to you proves it and so does his poem, and that he has many other talents which, at present, his shyness too much suppresses, I doubt not. He has a countenance which with all the sweetness of temper that it expresses, expresses also a mind much given to reflection and an understanding that in due time will know how to show itself to advantage.

An indisposition from which Mrs. Frog was not sufficiently recover'd to see company, and especially a stranger, was the reason of our not being invited while he was with me. She is now however perfectly restored; I dined there the day after he went and dine there again to-morrow.

The young man begg'd that he might carry away with him 8 or 10 books of Homer, which he would transcribe for me, he said, at Cambridge. But I feared to trust them in that pestilent place, where some of his wild young Trigrymates[2] might have snatched them from him, and have done with them I know not what.

I wish you to read Adriano or the First of June, and tell me what you think of it. Johnson has sent it to me for my opinion and I must return it soon. It is rather a thin Octavo and will not occupy much of thy time.

Our friends at the Hall are all pretty well at present, but the Lord of the mansion has not perfectly recover'd his foot again. Mrs. Unwin still has her fever which chiefly attacks her in the night. Beau is well as are the two cats and the 3 birds whose cages I am going to clean, and all send their love to you. Yours, my dear, Wm C.

A Bank note will be most commodious and we have no fears about its safe arrival.

Johnson, I believe, is tolerably well incomed. I asked him if he depended on his success in the Church for a maintenance, and he answer'd — No.

---

[2] C is making a facetious reference to John Johnson's involvement with mathematics at Cambridge.

A rod is preparing for Miss Birch,[3] and when Enfield's Speaker[4] appears she will feel it.

> Tis hardly fair Miss Birch that you
> Should steal our hearts and poems too.

I am glad that the General dealt so kindly by your Protegé; he has dealt kindly too by me, having sent me a whole ream of paper.

Here end my Postscripts.

[3] Miss Birch probably claimed the authorship of a poem or poems by C, and he must have been anticipating that when a new edition of *The Speaker* appeared, her deceit would be exposed. This chastisement was, however, to be deferred until C's poems appeared in the 1792 edition.

Miss Birch may have been the Miss Selina Birch whom Sophia Streatfield brought to breakfast with Fanny Burney at Tunbridge Wells in 1779; Miss Birch being then 'a little girl but ten years old': 'Charmed as we all were with her, we all agreed that to have the care of her would be a distraction! "She seems the girl in the world," Miss Thrale wisely said, "to attain the highest reach of human perfection as a man's mistress! — as such she would be a second Cleopatra, and have the world at her command." Poor thing! I hope to heaven she will escape such sovereignty and such honours!' *Burney Diary*, i. 277, 280.

[4] The Revd William Enfield (1741–97), divine and author (LL D, Edinburgh, 1774), was tutor in belles-lettres and Rector of the Warrington Academy from 1770 until its dissolution in 1783. From 1785 until his death he was minister of the Octagon Chapel in Norwich. His works, most of them published by Joseph Johnson, include sermons and elocutionary works. *The Speaker*, which he first published in 1774 and which was many times revised and reprinted, achieved great popularity in England and in the United States as an anthology of pieces for reading and recitation. Poems by C ('The Faithful Friend', 'Pairing Time Anticipated', 'The Needless Alarm', 'The Moralizer Corrected', 'The Rose', 'The Poet's New Year's Gift to Mrs. Throckmorton', 'Ode to Apollo', 'Catharina', and 'On the Death of Mrs. Throckmorton's Bullfinch') were first included in the fifth edition (1792). It is likely that the negotiations were conducted through Joseph Johnson; there is no evidence that C knew Enfield personally or corresponded with him. The first four poems listed, all apparently previously unpublished, are fables or tales of a kind well adapted to recitation. Of the remaining five poems, three ('The Poet's New Year's Gift to Mrs. Throckmorton', 'Catharina', and 'On the Death of Mrs. Throckmorton's Bullfinch') are connected with the Throckmorton circle, and of the same five, at least three ('The Rose', 'The Poet's New Year's Gift to Mrs. Throckmorton', and 'On the Death of Mrs. Throckmorton's Bullfinch') seem to have been involved in some kind of 'piracy'. C's purpose in publishing several of these pieces was the dual one of publishing correct texts and of claiming the poems as his own.

CLOTWORTHY ROWLEY   Monday, 1 February 1790

Address: Clotworthy Rowley Esqre / Dublin
Postmarks: FE/[3?]/90[1] *and* OULNEY
Princeton

Weston Underwood
Feb. 1. 1790

My dear Rowley,

I shot a few lines after you to Holyhead[2] according to your desire, and considering the distance of the place from London I think it possible that you might find them there, though your letter did not reach me 'till the second day after your departure. But lest it should have happened otherwise, I take your letter first from an unasnwer'd heap, to tell you again what I told you there, that I am very sensible of your kindness, and considering our long separation, am sensible of it the more. Thou art the only one of all my Temple connections who has or seems to have adverted to me since I left them seven and twenty years ago. From many others I have received numerous acts of kindness, but none from them.

I told you also in that note that I would in due time take you roundly to task for being so long silent and for not giving me a day or two of your company while you were in England. The latter perhaps you could not, and if you could not I am so merciful that I will excuse you, much as I should have been gratified by a sight of you. But how you will make me amends for not visiting me once in a year and half by letter I am not able to conceive, unless by writing more frequently in future.

Alston's[3] connection with the Chancellor has been to him both honourable and useful and I am glad of it. I have applied, and application has been made for me to the same source of honour and profit, but in vain. I am indeed a man not easily served, being fit for nothing in the world but to write verses, which I do without intermission, and shall,

---

[1] The day on the date stamp is split at the overlap of the letter and therefore difficult to read.

[2] Rowley had probably told C that a letter addressed to him at Holyhead would reach him *en route* to Ireland. Holyhead, an island off the west coast of Anglesey, was the chief port for mail and passenger service to and from Dublin.

[3] See n.5, C to Rowley, Aug. 1758.

probably, while I can hold a pen. But it is late in the day, and every day the motives by which men are urged to distinguish themselves with me grow weaker. The Monumentum ære perennius[4] is of difficult acquisition and in fact of no worth to Him whose name it perpetuates. But write I must, because idleness is misery, and not to write my best would be absurd, because, though posthumous fame will do me no good, I could not well bear, while I live, to be called a blockhead.

This brings me naturally to answer your enquiries concerning Homer. Homer then, I hope, will go to press in the Spring; in April perhaps, or in May. I have finished the Odyssey pretty much to my mind, and fourteen books of the Iliad. When the Iliad has had the revisal which I am now giving it, I shall give the whole one more, in which I shall find but little to do, and then throw myself into the hands of the Public. On the sum of the matter I think it probable, nay certain, that the two volumes will come out next winter.

And now my friend adieu! Homer calls. I rejoice that your family are well and love them for your sake. Let me hear from you at some idle hour if you have any such, and believe me affectionately Yours —

Wm Cowper.

SAMUEL GREATHEED   *c.*1 February 1790[1]

Princeton

Shall be obliged to Mr. Greatheed if he will be so good as to give no copies 'till Enfield's Speaker — a new edition of it — is publish'd; he will then do with them as he pleases.

W C.

[4] 'Monument more enduring than bronze': Horace, *Odes*, I. iii. 30.

[1] This note probably accompanied the MS of one or more of the poems published in the fifth edition of *The Speaker* (1792). See n.4, C to Lady Hesketh, 26 Jan. 1790.

SAMUEL ROSE   Tuesday, 2 February 1790[1]

Hayley, i. 343–5

The Lodge, Feb. 2, 1790.

My dear friend,

Should Heyne's Homer[2] appear before mine, which I hope is not probable, and should he adopt in it the opinion of Bentley,[3] that the whole last Odyssey is spurious, I will dare to contradict both him and the Doctor. I am only in part of Bentley's mind (if indeed his mind were such) in this matter, and giant as he was in learning, and eagle-eyed in criticism, am persuaded, convinced, and sure (can I be more positive?) that except from the moment when the Ithacans begin to meditate an attack on the cottage of Laertes,[4] and thence to the end, that book is the work of Homer. From the moment aforesaid, I yield the point, or rather have never, since I had any skill in Homer, felt myself at all inclined to dispute it. But I believe perfectly, at the same time, that, Homer himself alone excepted, the Greek Poet never existed who could have written the speeches made by the shade of Agamemnon; in which there is more insight into the human heart discovered, than I ever saw in any other work, unless in Shakespeare's. I am equally disposed to fight for the whole passage that describes Laertes, and the interview between him and Ulysses.[5] Let Bentley grant these to Homer, and I will shake hands with him as to all the rest. The battle with which

---

[1] This letter was offered for sale as lot 274 ('A.L.S. from Cowper to S. Rose, 2 Feb. 1790.') in the F. Naylor Sale of Sotheby, Wilkinson & Hodge of 27–31 July, 1 Aug. 1855. According to the sale catalogue, the opening of the letter reads, 'Should Hughes' Homer appear . . . ', whereas Southey reads 'Heyne's', the more likely reading. The present whereabouts of the holograph is unknown.

[2] C is probably referring to Christian Gottlob Heyne (1729–1812), whose Greek edition of the *Iliad* did not appear until 1804.

[3] C seems to have misunderstood Bentley's stance on this issue; in his *Remarks Upon a Late Discourse of Free-thinking . . .* (1713), Bentley commented (p. 18): 'Take my word for it, poor *Homer*, in those Circumstances and early times had never such aspiring thoughts. He wrote a sequel of Songs and Rhapsodies, to be sung by himself for small earnings and good cheer, at Festivals and other days of Merriment; the *Ilias* he made for the men, and the *Odysseïs* for the other Sex. These loose songs were not collected together in the form of an Epic Poem, till *Pisistratus's* time about 500 years after.'

[4] xxiv. 484 ff. in C's translation.

[5] C is referring to the following three portions of his translation of the *Odyssey*: xi. 491–527, 535–58; i. 239–44; and xxiv. 272–427.

341

the book concludes is, I think, a paltry battle, and there is a huddle in the management of it altogether unworthy of my favourite, and the favourite of all ages.

If you should happen to fall into company with Dr. Warton again, you will not, I dare say, forget to make him my respectful compliments, and to assure him that I felt myself not a little flattered by the favourable mention he was pleased to make of me, and my labours.[6] The Poet who pleases a man like him, has nothing left to wish for. I am glad that you were pleased with my young cousin Johnson; he is a boy, and bashful, but has great merit in respect both of character and intellect. So far at least as in a week's knowledge of him I could possibly learn, he is very amiable, and very sensible, and inspired me with a warm wish to know him better.

W. C.

JOHN NEWTON   Friday, 5 February 1790

Address: Revd. John Newton
Princeton

The Lodge
Feb. 5. 1790

My dear friend

Your kind letter deserved a speedier answer, but you know my excuse, which were I to repeat always, my letters would resemble the fag-end of a news paper where we always find the price of stocks detailed with little or no variation.

When January returns you have your feelings concerning me, and such as prove the faithfulness of your friendship. I have mine also concerning myself but they are of a cast different from yours. Yours have a mixture of sympathy and tender solicitude which makes them perhaps not altogether unpleasant. Mine on the contrary are of an unmix'd nature and consist simply and merely of the most alarming apprehensions. Twice has that month returned upon me accompanied by such horrors as I have no reason to suppose ever made

---

[6] Joseph Warton (1722–1800), the critic, who, like C, did not admire the writings of Pope and his circle.

part of the experience of any other man.[1] I accordingly look forward to it and meet in with a dread not to be imagined. I number the nights as they pass, and in the morning bless myself that another night is gone and no harm has happened. This may argue perhaps some imbecillity of mind and no small degree of it, but it is natural I believe, and so natural as to be necessary and unavoidable. I know that God is not governed by secondary causes in any of his operations, and that, on the contrary, they are all so many agents in his hand which strike only when he bids them. I know consequently that one month is as dangerous to me as another, and that in the middle of summer, at noon-day, and in the clear sunshine, I am in reality, unless guarded by him, as much exposed as when fast asleep at midnight and in midwinter. But we are not always the wiser for our knowledge, and I can no more avail myself of mine than if it were in the head of another man and not in my own. I have heard of bodily aches and ails that have been particularly troublesome when the season returned in which the hurt that occasioned them was received. The mind I believe (with my own however I am sure it is so) is liable to similar periodical affection. But February is come; January, my terrour, is pass'd, and some shades of the gloom that attended his presence have pass'd [with][2] him. I look forward with a little cheerfulness to the buds and the leaves that will soon appear, and say to myself, 'till they turn yellow I will make myself easy. The year *will* go round and January *will* approach, I *shall* tremble again and I know it, but in the mean time I will be as confortable as I can. Thus in respect of peace of mind, such as it is that I enjoy, I subsist as the poor are vulgarly said to do, from hand to mouth, and of a Christian such as you once knew me, am by a strange transformation become an Epicurean philosopher, bearing this motto on my mind — Quid sit futurum cras, fuge quærere.[3]

I have run on in a strain that the beginning of your letter suggested to me with such impetuosity that I have not left

[1] See C to Newton, 16 Oct. 1785: 'I had a dream 12 years ago, before the recollection of which, all consolation vanishes ...'
[2] MS torn at the seal.
[3] Horace, *Odes*, I. ix. 13: 'ask not what the morn will bring'.

myself opportunity to write more by the present post, and being unwilling that you should wait longer for what will be nothing worth when you get it, will only express the great pleasure we feel on hearing as we did lately from Mr. Bull, that Mrs. Newton is so much better.

Mrs. Unwin has been very indifferent all the winter; harass'd by continual head-aches and want of sleep, the consequences of a nervous fever; but I hope she begins to recover.

With our best love to Mrs. Newton not forgetting Miss Catlett — I remain, my dear friend,

Truly Yours Wm Cowper

LADY HESKETH   Tuesday, 9 February 1790

Hayley, i. 345-6

The Lodge, Feb. 9, 1790.

I have sent you lately scraps instead of Letters, having had occasion to answer immediately on the receipt, which always happens while I am *deep in Homer*.

I knew when I recommended Johnson to you, that you would find some way to serve him, and so it has happened, for notwithstanding your own apprehensions to the contrary, you have already procured him a chaplainship.[1] This is pretty well, considering that it is an early day, and that you have but just begun to know that there is such a man under heaven. I had rather myself be patronized by a person of small interest, with a heart like yours, than by the Chancellor himself, if he did not care a farthing for me.

If I did not desire you to make my acknowledgments to Anonymous, as I believe I did not, it was because I am not aware that I am warranted to do so. But the omission is of less consequence, because whoever he is, though he has no objection to doing the kindest things, he seems to have an aversion to the thanks they merit.

You must know that two Odes composed by Horace, have lately been discovered at Rome;[2] I wanted them transcribed

---

[1] Johnny was appointed chaplain to Bishop Spencer Madan; no pay and no duty were required.

[2] The odes were spurious and they (*Ad Julium Florum* and *Ad librum suum*)

into the blank leaves of a little Horace of mine,[3] and Mrs. Throckmorton performed that service for me; in a blank leaf, therefore, of the same book, I wrote the following.

W. C.

———

To Mrs. THROCKMORTON,

On her beautiful Transcript of Horace's Ode, *Ad Librum suum.*

> *Maria, could Horace have guess'd*
>   *What honours awaited his Ode,*
> *To his own little volume address'd,*
>   *The honour which you have bestow'd;*
> *Who have traced it in characters here,*
>   *So elegant, even, and neat;*
> *He had laugh'd at the critical sneer,*
>   *Which he seems to have trembled to meet.*
>
> *And sneer, if you please, he had said,*
>   *Hereafter a Nymph shall arise,*
> *Who shall give me, when you are all dead,*
>   *The glory your malice denies;*
> *Shall dignity give to my lay,*
>   *Although but a mere bagatelle;*
> *And even a Poet shall say,*
>   *Nothing ever was written so well.*

were produced by Gaspar Pallavicini, Sub-Librarian of the Palatine Library, where he claimed to have found them. They were first published by Villoison in his edition of Longus in 1778. C's interest in these forgeries was awakened by a review in the *GM* of Jan. 1790 of an anonymous *Dissertation concerning Two Odes of Horace Which Have Been Discovered in the Palatine Library at Rome* (lx. 59).

[3] The 'little Horace' was J. Bond's edition of the *Poemata* (Orleans, 1767), now in the Rothschild Library. *Keynes* (59): 'Inscribed by Cowper on the verso of the fly-leaf: *Hunc librum Gulielmo dedit Johannes Cowper Frater ejus dilectissimus.* On the recto of the fly-leaf Cowper has written his poem, *To Mrs. Throckmorton On her beautiful transcript of Horace's Ode ad librum Suum. See the blank leaf at the end.* At the end are two odes transcribed by Mrs. Throckmorton.'

JOSEPH JOHNSON   Thursday, 11 February 1790

Hayley, ii. 274

Weston, Feb. 11, 1790.

Dear sir,

I am very sensibly obliged by the remarks of Mr. Fuseli, and beg that you will tell him so; they afford me opportunities of improvement which I shall not neglect. When he shall see the press-copy, he will be convinced of this, and will be convinced likewise, that smart as he sometimes is, he spares me often, when I have no mercy on myself. He will see in short almost a new Translation. * * * I assure you faithfully, that whatever my faults may be, to be easily or hastily satisfied with what I have written is not one of them.

LADY HESKETH   Friday, 26 February 1790

Address: Lady Hesketh / New Norfolk Street / Grosvenor Square / London
Postmark: FE/27/90
Princeton

Friday, I believe Feb 26. 1790
but am not sure.

You have set my heart at ease my Cousin, so far as you were yourself the subject of its anxieties. What other troubles it feels can be cured by God alone. But you are never silent a week longer than usual without giving an opportunity to my imagination ever fruitful in flowers of a sable hue, to teaze me with them day and night. London is indeed a pestilent place as you call it, and I would with all my heart that thou had'st less to do with it. Were you under the same roof with me, I should know you to be safe and should never distress you with melancholy letters.

Many thanks are due to you for adding Mrs. Howe[1] to the number of your acquaintance for my sake, and I shall be

---

[1] The 'Hon. Mrs. Howe' subscribed for a fine copy. Caroline Howe (*c.*1721–1814), daughter of Emanuel Scrope, 2nd Viscount Howe, married John Howe of Branslop, Bucks. in 1742. A noted intellectual, Mrs Howe was a friend of Mrs Montagu, and it is possibly through Lady Hesketh's involvement in Mrs Montagu's circle that she made the acquaintance of Mrs Howe and thus asked C to submit material to her.

glad if the measure answer to you, though I should never be much the better for it myself; to say the truth I have learn'd not to be very sanguine in expectations of advantage in this way. The rich and the great are so little apt to interest themselves in favour of such folks as I, that I believe I might scratch in the soil of this world a whole century, and never turn up a single jewel. I feel myself however well enough inclined to the measure that you propose, and will show her, with all my heart, a sample of my translation. But it shall not be, if you please, taken from the Odyssey. It is a poem of a gentler character than the Iliad, and as I purpose to carry her by a coup de main, shall employ Achilles, Agamemnon and the two armies of Greece and Troy in my service. I will accordingly send you in the box that I received from you last night, the two first books of the Iliad for that Lady's perusal. To those I have given a third revisal; for them therefore I will be answerable, and am not afraid to stake the credit of my work upon *them*, with her or with any living wight, especially who understands the Original. I do not mean that even they are finished, for I shall examine and cross-examine them yet again, and so you may tell her, but I know that they will not disgrace me, whereas it is so long since I have look'd at my Odyssey that I know nothing at all about it. They shall set sail from Olney on Monday morning in the Diligence, and will reach you, I hope, in the Evening. As soon as she has done with them I shall be glad to have them again, for the time draws near when I shall want to give them the last touch.

I am delighted with Mrs. Bodham's kindness in giving me the only picture of my own mother[2] that is to be found, I suppose, in all the world. I had rather possess it than the

[2] The portrait of Ann Cowper (1703–37) is now in the possession of Miss Mary Barham Johnson, of Norwich. It is a miniature (6¼ × 5 in.), oil on copper, by D. Heins. There seems to be some doubt as to the correct name of the painter. According to *Bryan's Dictionary of Painters and Engravers*, 4th edn., rev. Williamson, one D. Heins came from Germany to Norwich in about 1740, and about the same time fathered a son, John, who died in 1771. According to the *DNB*, John Theodore Heins (1732–71) was the son of John Theodore Heins, a German active in Norwich and Cambridge 1736–56. If the elder Heins began to work in Norwich in 1736, he would have been able to paint C's mother during the last year of her life. The *DNB* article may be slightly confused, however, inasmuch as it seems to credit this portrait to the younger Heins, which is impossible. The miniature is reproduced in *Ryskamp* (Plate I, facing p. 6).

richest jewel in the British crown, for I loved her with an affection that her death 52 years since has not in the least abated. I remember her too, young as I was when she died, well enough to know that it is a very exact resemblance of her, and as such, it is to me invaluable. Every body loved her, and with an amiable character so impress'd on all her features, every body was sure to do so. Should I mount when I die, I shall see her again, else, never.

I have a very affectionate and a very clever letter from Johnson who promises me the transcript of the books entrusted to him in a few days. I have a great love for that young man. He has some drops of the same stream in his veins that once animated the original of that dear picture.

Should the wretch be detected who has aspersed Lord Cowper in this second instance,[3] and should I learn his name, *Birth*, *parentage* and *education*, I may perhaps find an opportunity to pay him in *my* way. Should that happen, he shall not complain that he is overlook'd.

I am truly concerned for poor Rose and have little doubt that we shall lose him. Johnson the Bookseller told me lately that he was very so so, and intended writing to me in a few days. When he does, I will answer him soon, and say as you desire me.

The Oysters were not bad, but not so good as we have seen from your monger. The haddocks and lobsters are excellent.

As to Cambridge's[4] conclusion I shall only say that when you sent me a prose account of it, you express'd the thought yourself much better.

She has all she can wish, and she asks *for* no more. If you do not allow this to be a shabby line both on account of tautology and language, I shall say that you are partial, and admire That in Him which you would not endure in me. Adieu my Dearest Coz — with Mrs. U.'s best affections

Ever thine — Wm Cowper.

The Box contained also a letter from Mrs. Bodham which if I should have answer'd it before I screw up the box I will send you. Nothing can be kinder or better expressed.

---

[3] We do not know to what incident C is referring.
[4] Unidentified.

You will also receive per box two new pieces of mine, should Mrs. U. be well enough to copy them. They are both gone to Enfield's Speaker.[5]

MRS BODHAM   Saturday, 27 February 1790

Address: Mrs. Bodham / South Green / Mattishall / Norfolk
Postmarks: MR/1/90 *and* OULNEY
Barham Johnson

                        Weston Underwood near Olney, Bucks.
                                   Feb. 27. 1790

My dearest Rose,
   Whom I thought wither'd and fallen from the stalk but who I find are still alive, nothing could give me greater pleasure than to know it and to learn it from yourself. I loved you dearly when you were a child and love you not a jot the less for having ceased to be so. Every creature that bears any affinity to my own mother is dear to me, and you, the daughter of her brother, are but one remove distant from her; I love you therefore and love you much, both for her sake and for your own. The world could not have furnish'd you with a present so acceptable to me as the picture which you have so kindly sent me. I received it the night before last, and view'd it with a trepidation of nerves and spirits somewhat akin to what I should have felt had the dear Original presented herself to my embraces. I kissed it and hung it where it is the last object that I see at night, and, of course, the first on which I open my eyes in the morning. She died when I had completed my sixth year, yet I remember her well and am an ocular witness of the great fidelity of the Copy. I remember too a multitude of the maternal tendernesses which I received from her and which have endeared her memory to me beyond expression. There is in me, I believe, more of the Donne than of the Cowper, and though I love all of both names and have a thousand reasons to love those of my own name, yet I feel the bond of nature draw

---

[5] See n.4, C to Lady Hesketh, 26 Jan. 1790. The poems C mentions here must have been two of the following; 'Pairing Time Anticipated', 'The Needless Alarm', or 'The Moralizer Corrected', which were not published until 1792 in Enfield's *Speaker*.

me vehemently to your side. I was thought in the days of my childhood much to resemble my mother, and in my natural temper, of which at the age of 58 I must be supposed a competent judge, can trace both Her and my late uncle your father. Somewhat of his irritability, and a little, I would hope, both of his and of her — I know not what to call it without seeming to praise myself which is not my intention, but speaking to *you* I will e'en speak out and say — Good nature. Add to all this, that I deal much in poetry as did our venerable ancestor the Dean of St. Paul's, and I think I shall have proved myself a Donne at all points.[1] The truth is that whatever [I][2] am, I love you all.

I account it a happy event that brought [the] dear boy your nephew to my knowledge, and that, breaking through all the restraints which his natural bashfulness imposed on him, he determined to find me out. He is amiable to a degree that I have seldom seen, and I often long with impatience to see him again.

My dearest Cousin, what shall I say in answer to your affectionate invitation? I *must* say this. I cannot come now, nor soon, and I wish with all my heart I could. But I will tell you what may be done perhaps, and it will answer to us just as well. You and Mr. Bodham can come to Weston, can you not? The summer is at hand, there are roads and wheels to bring you, and you are neither of you translating Homer. I am crazed that I cannot ask you all together for want of House room, but for Mr. Bodham and yourself we have good room, and equally good for any third in the shape of a Donne, whether named Hewitt,[3] Bodham, Balls or Johnson or by whatever name distinguished. Mrs. Hewitt has particular claims upon me, she was my playfellow at Berkhamstead and has a share in my warmest affections. Pray tell her so. Neither do I at all forget my Cousin Harriot. She and I have been many a time merry at Catfield and have made the parsonage ring with laughter. Give my love to her. Assure yourself my

[1] It is possible, but not certain, that Thomas Dunne (d. 1592), the first Donne in C's ancestry we can be sure of, was related to the poet's father.

[2] MS torn.

[3] Elizabeth Donne (1724–96) was the daughter of the Revd Roger Donne (1702–73) and his first wife, Elizabeth Pacey (d. 1729). She married Thomas Hewitt of Mattishall in 1764.

dearest Cousin that I shall receive you as you were my sister, and Mrs. Unwin is for my sake prepared to do the same. When she has seen you she will love you for your own.

I am much obliged to Mr. B. for his kindness to my Homer, and with my love to you all and with Mrs. Unwin's kind respects, am

        my dear dear Rose — Ever yours   Wm Cowper.
P.S.

I mourn the death of your poor brother Castres[4] whom I should have seen had he lived, and should have seen with the greatest pleasure. He was an amiable boy and I was very fond of him.

P.S.

Your nephew tells me that his Sister in the qualities of the mind resembles you; that is enough to make her dear to me, and I beg you will assure her that she is so. Let it not be long before I hear from you.

Still another P.S. — I find on consulting Mrs. Unwin that I have under-rated our capabilities and that we have not only room for you and Mr. Bodham, but for two of your sex and even for your nephew into the bargain. We shall be happy to have it all so occupied.

JOHN JOHNSON   Sunday, 28 February 1790

Address: John Johnson Esqre / Caius' College / Cambridge.
Postmarks: FE/[illegible]/90 *and* OULNEY
Princeton

                      Weston near Olney Bucks
                             Feb 28
                              1790

My dear Cousin John —

I have much wished to hear from you, and though you are welcome to write to Mrs. Unwin as often as you please, I wish, myself, to be number'd among your correspondents.

[4] The Revd Castres Donne (1744/5–89) had married in 1780 Anne Vertue (1755–1839).

I shall find time to answer you, doubt it not; be as busy as we may we can always find time to do what is agreeable to us. By the way, had you a letter from Mrs. Unwin? I am witness that she address'd one to you before you went into Norfolk; but your Mathematico-poetical head forgot to acknowledge the receipt of it.

I was never more pleased in my life than to learn, and to learn it from herself, that my dearest Rose is still alive. Had she not engaged me to love her by the sweetness of her character when a child, she would have done it effectually now, by making me the most acceptable present in the world, my own dear mother's picture. I am perhaps the only person living who remembers her, but I remember her well, and can attest, on my own knowledge, the truth of the resemblance. Amiable and elegant as the countenance is, such exactly was her own. She was one of the tenderest parents, and so just a copy of her is therefore to me invaluable. I wrote yesterday to my Rose to tell her all this and to thank her for her kindness in sending it; neither do I forget your kindness who intimated to her that I should be happy to possess it. She invites me into Norfolk, but alas! she might as well invite the house in which I dwell, for, all other considerations and impediments apart, how is it possible that a translator of Homer should lumber to such a distance? But though I cannot comply with her kind invitation, I have made myself the best amends in my power by inviting her and all the family of Donnes to Weston. Perhaps we could not accommodate them all at once, but in succession we could, and can at any time find room for five, three of them being females and one a married one. You are a Mathematician; tell me then how five persons can be lodged in three beds, (two males and three females) and I shall have good hope that you will proceed a Senior optime.[1] It would make me happy to see our house so furnished. As to yourself, whom I know to be a Subscalarian or a man that sleeps under the stairs,[2] I should

---

[1] 'One of the highest merit.' Wrangler, Senior Optime, and Junior Optime are still the designation of a candidate who attains a first, second, and third class in Part II of the Mathematical Tripos at Cambridge.

[2] At Cambridge the rooms are usually grouped on staircases which are entered from the court.

have no objection at all, neither could you possibly have any yourself, to the garret as a place in which you might be disposed with great felicity of accommodation.

I thank you much for your services in the transcribing way, and would by no means have you despair of an opportunity to serve me in the same way yet again. Write to me soon and tell me when I shall see you. I have not said the half that I have to say, but breakfast is at hand which always terminates my Epistles. What have you done with your poem? The trimming that it procured you here, has not, I hope, put you out of conceit with it entirely. You are more than equal to all the alteration that it needs. Only remember that, in writing, perspicuity is always more than half the battle. The want of it is the ruin of more than half the poety that is published. A meaning that does not stare you in the face is as bad as no-meaning, because nobody will take the pains to poke for it. So now adieu for the present. Beware of killing yourself with problems, for if you do, you will never live to be another Sir Isaac.[3]

Mrs. Unwin's affectionate remembrances attend you. Lady Hesketh is most disposed to love you. Perhaps most who know you have some little tendency the same way.

Yours Wm Cowper.

LADY HESKETH   Monday, 8 March 1790

Address: Lady Hesketh / New Norfolk Street / Grosvenor Square / London
Postmarks: [MR]/11/90,[1] OULNEY *and* NEWPORT/PAGNEL
Princeton

The Lodge
March 8. 1790

My dearest Cousin,

I thank thee much and oft for negotiating so well this poetical concern with Mrs. Howe, and for sending me her opinion in her own hand. I should be unreasonable indeed

[3] Isaac Newton.

[1] The month portion of the date stamp was over the flap of the closure and is illegible.

353

not to be highly gratified by it, and I like it the better for being modestly expressed. It is, as you know, and it shall be some months longer, my daily business to polish and improve what is done, that when the whole shall appear, she may find her expectations answer'd. I am glad also that thou didst send her the 16th. Odyssey, though as I said before, I know not at all at present, whereof it is made, but I am sure that thou wouldst not have sent it, hadst thou not conceived a good opinion of it thyself, and thought that it would do me credit. It was very kind in thee to sacrifice to this Minerva on my account; being disposed to like what she has seen she will naturally say so in all her parties, which if it does me no other service, will at least redound to my honour. His Royal Highness of G.[2] is a prudent man, but I think he had done as well if being Royal himself he had dealt with me for Royal Paper. But it is no matter as you say, his name suffices, and I would send the volumes gratis to King, Queen and all, would they give me leave to place them among my Subscribers and promise to keep it secret by what means I won them to do so.

I am glad that my old friend the Knight of the wool-sack[3] was civiler to thee than usual; not that I have any hopes of good from that quarter, but I wish him and every body to show thee what thou well deservest, that is, all possible respect and kindness.

For my sentiments on the subject of the Test Act I cannot do better than refer thee to my poem entitled and call'd Expostulation.[4] I have there express'd myself not much in its favour, considering it in a Religious view, and in a Political one, I like it not a jot better. I am neither Tory nor High

[2] Prince William Henry, 1st Duke of Gloucester (1743–1805), had married Maria, dowager Countess of Waldegrave in 1766. The Duke and Duchess are both listed at the head of the subscription list for ordinary copies.

[3] Lord Chancellor Thurlow.

[4] C is referring to lines 376–89 from 'Expostulation', which begin: 'Hast thou by statute shov'd from its design / The Saviour's feast, his own blest bread and wine, / And made the symbols of atoning grace / An office-key, a pick-lock to a place, / That infidels may prove their title good / By an oath dipp'd in sacramental blood?' Although C's reference to the Test Acts, by which everyone holding public office was required to receive the sacrament publicly according to the Anglican Communion, in this letter is obscure, he may be commenting on the Oath of Allegiance which the Roman Catholics proposed to take as part of the Relief Bill (see n.4, C to Lady Hesketh, 13 June 1789).

Churchman, but an Old Whig as my father was before me, and an enemy consequently to all tyranical impositions.

I like the lines on the English and French Constitutions much.[5] They are clever, but it is a pity as thou observest that the author of them would chuse shivers for his word to rhime with. He might have broken his pot to *pieces* or to *shatters*, and in either case would have found it easy to accommodate his lines to the occasion.

Mrs. Unwin bids me return thee many thanks for thy enquiries so kindly made concerning her health. She is a little better than of late, but has been ill continually ever since last November. Head-aches, pains in the side, nights half sleepless, incessant noises in her ears, and every thing that could try patience and submission, she has had, and her submission and patience have answer'd in the trial, tho' mine on her account have often failed sadly.

I have written a new edition of the stanzas I presented to you on the occasion of your furnishing the house, less witty but more decent.[6] Mrs. Frog has a copy of them, and I will send one to thee by next opportunity.[7] The Frogs are all three in town on their way to Bucklands and Bath, and you will see the lady Frog should you be at home when she calls, which I know she intends.

I have a letter from Johnson, who tells me that he has sent his transcript to you, begging at the same time more copy. Let him have it by all means. He is an industrious youth and I love him dearly. I told him that you are disposed also to love him a little. A new poem is born on the receipt of my Mother's picture. Thou shalt have it.[8]

---

[5] Unidentified.

[6] C is referring to his verse letter of 14 Apr. 1788. It ('Benefactions') was revised ('a new edition') by C and resulted in the poem known as 'Gratitude'. In reworking his verse letter, C removed matter too personal, too intimate, and too ephemeral for the permanence of poetry.

[7] There is no surviving holograph of this poem; the poem was first printed in a pamphlet in 1798.

[8] There is no signature on this letter as C ran out of space.

SAMUEL ROSE   Thursday, 11 March 1790

Address: Samuel Rose Esqre / Percy Street / Rathbone Place / London
Postmarks: MR/12/90 *and* OULNEY
Harvard

The Lodge March 11 — 1790.

My dear Sir,

I was glad to hear from you, for a line from you gives me always much pleasure, but was not much gladden'd by the contents of your letter. The state of your health which I have learn'd more accurately perhaps from my Cousin, except in this last instance, than from yourself, has rather alarm'd me, and even she has collected her information on that subject more from your looks than from your own acknowledgments. To complain much and often of our indispositions does not always insure the pity of the hearer, perhaps sometimes forfeits it, but to dissemble them altogether, or at least to suppress the worst, is attended ultimately with an inconvenience greater still; the secret will out at last, and our friends unprepared to receive it, are doubly distressed about us. In saying this, I squint a little at Mrs. Unwin who will read it; it is with her, as with you, the only subject on which she practises any dissimulation at all; the consequence is that when she is much indisposed I never believe myself in possession of the whole truth, live in constant expectation of hearing something worse, and at the long run am rarely disappointed. It seems therefore, as on all other occasions so even on this, the better course on the whole to appear what we are, not to lay the fears of our friends asleep by cheerful looks which do not properly belong to us, or by letters written as if we were well, when in fact we are very much otherwise. On condition however that you act differently toward me for the future, I will pardon the past, and she may gather from my clemency shown to you, some hopes on the same condition of similar clemency to herself.

Mr. Farquhar's[1] opinion of your case, of whose judgment I think well because my Cousin does, affords me comfort,

---

[1] Sir Walter Farquhar (1738–1819), who was practising as an apothecary in London at this time. A Scotsman educated at Aberdeen and Edinburgh, he had served in the army before setting up his practice in London. He received the

and I shall rejoice sincerely to learn that the event confirms it. If on your return to town you find yourself restored, many days I hope will not elapse before you tell me of it. I shall not be easy on your account till more favourable news from yourself shall make me so.

About a fortnight since I had a letter from my Cousin in which she gave me cause to suspect that though not naturally much given to athletic feats she had beaten you, or at least threaten'd to beat you or had been guilty of some outrage or other on a certain evening when you found her, I conclude, not altogether so serene as she generally is. You know best in what manner she received you; if with less complacency than usual, break not your heart about it; I do not always escape a slap myself, and though such indications of esteem and friendship are less to be desired than many others, indications of that kind they certainly are when given by a lady. To a person indifferent to her or to whom she bears a dislike, she is all smiles on all occasions, but not such always to those whom she loves and values. Them, if she feels herself inclined to scratch, she scratches without ceremony, and this is the manner of all the ladies I ever knew and I question if you ever will meet with an exception. My Cousin however has more grace than most of them, for when she has indulged herself in a peak of this kind she is most heartily penitent, and such she appeared to be in the letter that gave me the account in question. With Mrs. Unwin's affectionate Compliments and best wishes for your complete recovery, I remain

most truly Yours   Wm Cowper.

P.S.
I do not rejoice that Oxford is disgraced as it is by such a generation as you describe, but I rejoice that being what they are, you have seen with your own eyes that they deserve not only what I have written about them, but even more. Had I nothing better to do I would give it them.

---

degree of MD from Aberdeen in 1796, was created a baronet the same year, and took a very high place in the medical profession.

MRS KING   Friday, 12 March 1790

Barham Johnson (*copy*)

March 12. 1790.

My dear Madam,

I live in such a nook, have so few opportunities of hearing news, and so little time to read it, that to me, to begin a letter, seems always a sort of forlorn hope. Can it be possible, I say to myself, that I should have any thing to communicate? These misgivings have an ill effect, so far as my punctuality is concerned, and are apt to deter me from the business of letter-writing as from an enterprise altogether impracticable.

I will not say that you are more pleased with my trifles than they deserve, lest I should seem to call your judgment in question; but I suspect that a little partiality to the brother of my brother enters into the opinion you form of them. No matter, however, by what you are influenced, it is for my interest that you should like them at any rate, because, such as they are, they are the only return I can make you for all your kindness. This consideration will have two effects, it will have a tendency to make me more industrious in the production of such pieces, and more attentive to the manner in which I write them. This reminds me of a piece in your possession, which I will entreat you to commit to the flames, because I am somewhat ashamed of it. To make you amends, I hereby promise to send you a new edition of it, when time shall serve, delivered from the passages that I dislike in the first, and in other respects amended. The piece that I mean, is one entitled — To Lady Hesketh on her furnishing for me our house at Weston[1] — or, as the Lawyers say, words to that amount.[2] I have likewise, since I sent you the last pacquet, been delivered of two or three other brats, and as the year proceeds, shall probably add to the number. All that come, shall be basketted in time, and conveyed to your door.

[1] See n.6, C to Lady Hesketh, 8 Mar. 1790.
[2] We have not been able to locate a direct reference to 'words to that amount' in any legal dictionary but assume from the context that C used it as the expression 'words to that effect' is used today. This is supported by the *OED* citation s.v. 'amount' when that word is used in a figurative sense: 'the full value, effect, a significance or import'.

I have lately received, from a female Cousin of mine in Norfolk, whom I have not seen these thirty years, a picture of my own mother. She died when I wanted two days of being six years old, yet I remember her perfectly, find the picture a strong likeness of her, and because her memory has been ever precious to me, have written a poem on the receipt of it. A poem which, one excepted,[3] I had more pleasure in writing than any that I ever wrote. That one was addressed to a lady whom I expect in a few minutes to come down to breakfast, and who has supplied to me the place of my own mother, my own invaluable mother, these six and twenty years. Some sons may be said to have had many fathers, but a plurality of mothers is not common.

Adieu my dear Madam, be assured that I always think of you with much esteem and affection, and am, with mine and Mrs. Unwin's best compliments to you and yours, most unfeignedly your friend and humble servant,

Wm. Cowper.

JOSEPH HILL   Saturday, 20 March 1790[1]

Cowper Johnson

My dear friend —

Forty pounds, as you observe, are a very material communication. As to communications of another kind, I can only say, that yours on whatever theme are always welcome, and that when they are made to me they are made to one who sincerely, as he ever did, loves and values you, and who is, with his best respects to Mrs. Hill

Affectionately yours
Wm Cowper.

[3] 'The Winter Nosegay'; first published in *1782*. See C to Mrs King, 14 Aug. 1790.

[1] The letter has been dated 'March 20, 1790.' in pencil, probably by Hill after removing the upper portion of the letter containing C's date and a receipt for the £40 mentioned in the opening paragraph.

MRS THROCKMORTON   Sunday, 21 March 1790

Address: Mrs. Throckmorton / Bath
Postmarks: MR/23/90 *and* OULNEY
Sir Robert Throckmorton

Lodge March 21. 1790
My dearest Madam, alias, my dear Mrs. Frog —

This comes to let you know that yours per post yesterday came safe to hand and found all well as we hope you are at this present.

I shall only observe on the subject of your absence that you have stretch'd it since you went and have made it a week longer. Weston is sadly *unke'd*[1] without you, and here are two of us who will be heartily glad to see you again. I believe you are happier at home than any where, which is a comfortable belief to your neighbours, because it affords assurance that since you are neither likely to ramble for pleasure nor to meet with many avocations of business, while Weston shall continue to be your home, it will not often want you.

The two first books of my Iliad have been submitted to the inspection and scrutiny of a great Critic of your sex,[2] at the instance of my Cousin as you may suppose. The lady is mistress of more tongues than a few (it is to be hoped she is single) and particularly she is mistress of the Greek. She returned with them expressions that if any thing would make a poet prouder than all poets naturally are, would have made me so. I tell you this because I know that you all interest yourself warmly in the success of said Iliad.

My periwig is arrived and is the very perfection of all periwigs, having only one fault which is that my head will only go into the first half of it, the other half or the upper part of it continuing still unoccupied. My artist in this way at Olney has however undertaken to make the whole of it tenantable and then I shall be 20 years younger than you have ever seen me.

I have produced another poem which awaits you at your return. It is in a stile very different from the last, not merry

[1] 'Lonely, dismal, forbiddingly dull'. The *OED* cites this letter as an authority for the use of the word.
[2] Mrs Howe. See n.1, C to Lady Hesketh, 26 Feb. 1790.

but sad, at least serious. The subject of it is my own Mother's picture, which I told you I had lately received out of Norfolk. She was the delight of my heart during the first six years of my [life, a]nd[3] then she died; but I have a perfect remembrance of her and of all her kindness.

I am glad, on more accounts than one that your Bill is not likely to come on this year. In the first place it will not call you to London, and in the next, I think it will be introduced with more probability of success when the present heat shall have somewhat abated. That our present Episcopacy should carry things with so high a hand, and that you should pay double price for living in your own country, are two grievances that I cannot bear.

Remember me affectionately to Mr. Frog and to your brother George whose absence I shall sincerely regret as well as you, for he is *jucundissimus omnium sodalium quot sunt, vel fuerunt, vel posthàc aliis erunt in annis*,[4] and when there are but two men of that description in a whole neighborhood it is not pleasant to be forced to dispense with one of them.

I am, my dear Mrs. Frog, with Mrs. Unwin's best remembrances ever Yours

Wm Cowper.

I heard of your birth day very early in the morning. The news came from the Steeple.

LADY HESKETH   Monday, 22 March 1790

Address: Lady Hesketh / New Norfolk Street / Grosvenor Square / London.
Postmarks: MR/23/90 *and* OULNEY
Panshanger Collection

The Lodge — March 22. 1790

I rejoice my dearest Coz that my MSS have roam'd the earth so successfully and have met with no disaster. The single book excepted that went to the bottom of the Thames and rose again, they have been fortunate without exception.[1]

---

[3] MS torn.
[4] 'The most pleasant of all the comrades who have ever been, or are, or will be.'

---

[1] See C to Hill, 10 Oct. 1786.

I am not superstitious, but have nevertheless as good a right to believe that adventure an omen and a favorable one, as Swift had to interpret, as he did, the loss of a fine fish which he had no sooner laid on the bank than it flounced into the water again. This, he tells us himself, he always consider'd as a type of his future disappointments, and why may not I, as well, consider the marvellous recovery of my lost book from the bottom of the Thames as typical of its future prosperity?[2] To say the truth, I have no fears now about the success of my translation, though in time past I have had many. I knew that there was a stile somewhere, could I but find it, in which Homer ought to be render'd and which alone would suit him. Long time I blunder'd about it e'er I could attain to any decided judgment on the matter. At first I was betrayed, by a desire of accommodating my language to the simplicity of his, into much of the quaintness that belong'd to our writers of the fifteenth century. In the course of many revisals I have deliver'd myself from this evil, I believe, entirely; but I have done it slowly, and as a man separates himself from his mistress when he is going to marry. I had so strong a predilection in favour of this stile at first that I was crazed to find that others were not as much enamoured with it as myself. At every passage of that sort which I obliterated, I groan'd bitterly, and said to myself I am spoiling my work to please those who have no taste for the simple Graces of antiquity. But in measure as I adopted a more modern phraseology, I became a convert to their opinion, and in the last revisal which I am now making am not sensible of having spared a single expression of the obsolete kind. I see my work so much improved by this alteration that I am filled with wonder at my own backwardness to assent to the necessity of it, and the more when I consider that Milton, with whose manner I account myself intimately acquainted, is never quaint, never twangs through the nose, but is every where grand and elegant without resorting to musty antiquity for

---

[2] C is referring to Swift's letter to Pope and Bolingbroke of 5 Apr. 1729: 'I remember when I was a little boy, I felt a great fish at the end of my line which I drew up almost on the ground, but it dropt in, and the disappointment vexeth me to this very day, and I believe it was the type of all my future disappointments.' *Correspondence of Jonathan Swift*, ed. Sir Harold Williams (5 vols., Oxford, 1963–5), iii. 329.

his beauties. On the contrary he took a long stride forward, left the language of his own day behind him, far behind him, and anticipated the expression of a century yet to come.

I have now, as I said, no longer any doubt of the event; but I will give thee a shilling if thou wilt tell me what I shall say in my preface. It is an affair of much delicacy and I have as many opinions about it as there are whims in a weather cock.

Send my MSS and thine when thou wilt. In a day or two I shall enter on the last Iliad. When I have finished it I shall give the Odyssey one more reading, and shall therefore shortly have occasion for the copy in thy possession, but you see that there is no need to hurry.

Thanks for all your labours and for all the new names which you have added. I leave the little remnant of paper for Mrs. Unwin's use, who means I believe to occupy it, and am

evermore thine most truly Wm Cowper.[3]

I want a new coat, but must first, it seems have a fashionable pattern. Wilt thou send me one when thou sendest or dost send the MSS.?

A pattern button is wanted also.

JOHN JOHNSON   Tuesday, 23 March 1790

Address: John Johnson Esqre / Caius College / Cambridge
Postmarks: MR/24/90 *and* OULNEY
Princeton

Weston Underwood
March 23. 1790

My dear Cousin,

Your cold has perhaps by this time left you, and if it has, I rejoice. But forget not the advice given you here, to furnish

---

[3] At this point, Mrs Unwin added a postscript: 'You cannot imagine how much your Ladyship would oblige your unworthy Servant if you would be so good as to let me know in what point I differ from you. All at present I can say is, that I will readily Sacrifice my own opinion, unless I can give you a Substantial reason for adhering to it. — I am with Egg for your Ladyships seeing Mr: Cowper's heart-touching Lines on his Mother's picture; Only give an address to a member, and they shall be sent you by the first opportunity. I bless the Lord my long ilness is now Come to a Crisis, therefore I hope to be well as usual in a short time. —'

yourself with a bed that may stand decently in your Keeping-room[1] (as I think you call it) for you will else incur consequences painful to yourself and to me, because I feel that I am interested in your well-being.

Your MSS have arrived safe in New Norfolk Street, and I am much obliged to you for your labours. Were you now at Weston I could furnish you with employment for some weeks, and shall perhaps be equally able to do it in the summer, for I have lost by best amanuensis in this place — Mr. George Throckmorton, who is gone to Bath.

You are a man to be envied who have never read the Odyssey, which is one of the most amusing story-books in the world. There is also much of the finest poetry in the world to be found in it, notwithstanding all that Longinus has insinuated to the contrary. His comparison of the Iliad and Odyssey to the Meridian and to the declining sun, is pretty, but, I am persuaded, not just. The prettiness of it seduced him; he was otherwise too judicious a reader of Homer to have made it.[2] I can find in the latter, no symptoms of impair'd ability, none of the effects of age. On the contrary it seems to me a certainty that Homer, had he written the Odyssey in his youth, could not have written it better, and if the Iliad in his old age, that he would have written it just as well. A Critic would tell me that instead of *written* I should have said *composed*. Very likely — but I am not writing to one of that snarling generation.

My Boy, I long to see thee again. It has happen'd some way or other that Mrs. Unwin and I have conceived a great affection for thee. That I should, is the less to be wonder'd

---

[1] 'The room usually occupied by a person or family as a sitting room' (*OED*).

[2] 'Hence is it, in my Opinion, that as *Homer* composed his *Iliad*, when his Mind was in its full Strength and Vigour, the whole Body of the Poem is Dramatical and full of Action; whereas the best Part of the *Odysseis* is taken up in Narrations, which seems to be the Genius of Old Age; so that one may compare him, in this last Work, to the setting Sun, who still appears with the same Magnificence, but has no longer the same Heat and Force. In a word, he has here quite lost his Tone; he has no more that Sublime which marches on in one equal Pace throughout the *Iliad*, and never stops or sinks; he has not in the *Odyseis*, so great a Variety of Turns and Passions heap'd one upon another; nor that Force and Volubility of Speech, so proper for Action, intermixed with such a Number of lively Images.' Leonard Welsted, *Epistles, Odes, &c. Written on Several Subjects. With a Translation of Longinus's Treatise on the Sublime* (1724), pp. 166-7.

My Boy, I long to see thee again. It has happen'd
some way or other that M.rs Unwin and I have con-
-ceived a great affection for thee. That I should, is
the less to be wonder'd at because thou art a shred
of my own mother; neither is the wonder great that
she should fall into the same predicament, for she
loves every thing that I love. You will observe
that your own personal right to be beloved
makes no part of the consideration. There is
nothing that I touch with so much tenderness as the
vanity of a young man, because I know how extremely
susceptible he is of impressions that might hurt him,
in that particular part of his composition. If you
should ever prove a coxcomb, from which character
you stand just now at a greater distance than any
young man I know, it shall never be said that I have
made you one. No — you will gain nothing by me

Cowper to John Johnson, 23 March 1790
The third page of the letter

at because thou art a shred of my own mother; neither is the wonder great that she should fall into the same predicament, for she loves every thing that I love. You will observe that your own personal right to be beloved makes no part of the consideration. There is nothing that I touch with so much tenderness as the vanity of a young man, because I know how extremely susceptible he is of impressions that might hurt him, in that particular part of his composition. If you should ever prove a coxcomb, from which character you stand just now at a greater distance than any young man I know, it shall never be said that I have made you one. No — you will gain nothing by me but the honour of being much valued by a poor poet who can do you no good while he lives and has nothing to leave you when he dies. If you can be contented to be dear to me on those conditions, so you shall be, but other terms more advantageous than these or more inviting, none have I to propose. Farewell. Puzzle not yourself about a subject when you write to either of us. Every thing is subject good enough from those we love. With Mrs. Unwin's best remembrances I am much Yours

Wm Cowper.

ROWLAND HILL   Monday, 29 March 1790

Southey, vi. 296–7

Weston Underwood, March 29, 1790.

My dear sir,

The moment when you ceased to be *incog.* I ought to have written you at least a few lines of apology for the liberties I had taken with your hymns, but being extremely busy at that time, and hoping that you would be so charitable as to pardon the omission, I desired Mr. Bull to be my proxy, charging him to make my excuses, and to assure you that I was perfectly satisfied with your making any alterations that you might see to be necessary in my text. If any thing fell from my pen that seemed to countenance the heresy of *universal redemption,* you did well to displace it, for it contradicted the Scripture, and belied me.

I am much obliged to you for the little volumes[1] which I received safe on Saturday; and because I suppose that your end will be best answered by dispersion, if I should have occasion for half a dozen more, will order them from your bookseller without scruple.

I am, my dear sir, with much respect, and with Mrs. Unwin's compliments,

Your affectionate humble servant,
Wm. Cowper.

Should you want me on any similar occasion hereafter, I am always at your disposal.

JOHN JOHNSON   Saturday, 17 April 1790

Address: John Johnson Esqre / Caius College / Cambridge
Postmarks: AP/19/90, OULNEY *and* NEWPORT/PAGNEL
Princeton

Weston April 17. 1790

My dear Cousin,

Your letter that now lies before me is almost three weeks old, and therefore of full age to receive an answer which it shall have without delay, if the interval between the present moment and that of breakfast should prove sufficient for the purpose. Yours to Mrs. Unwin was received yesterday for which she will thank you in due time. I have also seen and have now in my desk your letter to Lady Hesketh.[1] She sent it thinking that it would divert me, in which she was not mistaken. I shall tell her when I write to her next that you long to receive a line from her.

Give yourself no trouble on the subject of the politic device you saw good to recur to when you presented me with your Manuscript. It was an innocent deception, at least it could harm nobody save yourself; an effect which it did not fail to produce, and since the punishment follow'd it so closely, by me at least it may very well be forgiven. You ask, how I can tell that you are not addicted to practises of the

---

[1] Hill sent C six copies of *Divine Hymns.* See n.1, C to Rose, 3 Jan. 1790.

---

[1] This letter is not extant.

deceptive kind; and certainly if the little time that I have had to study you were alone to be consider'd, the question would not be unreasonable. But, in general, a man who reaches my years finds that

> Long experience does attain
> To something like prophetic strain.[2]

I am very much of Lavater's opinion, and persuaded that faces are as legible as books, only with these circumstances to recommend them to our perusal, that they are read in much less time, and are much less likely to deceive us. Yours gave me a favorable impression of you the moment I beheld it, and though I shall not tell you in particular what I saw in it, for reasons mentioned in my last, I will add that I have observed in you nothing since that has not confirm'd the opinion I then form'd in your favour. In fact, I cannot recollect that my skill in *phyznomy*[3] has ever deceived me, and I should add more on this subject had I room.

When you have shut up your Mathematical books, and have done with a study not likely to profit you any where out of Cambridge, you must give yourself to the study of Greek; not merely that you may be able to read Homer and the other Greek Classics with ease, but the Greek Testament and the Greek Fathers also. Thus qualified, and with the aid of your Fiddle into the bargain, together with some portion of the Grace of God (without which nothing can be done) to enable you to look well to your flock when you shall get one, you will be well set up for a parson. In which character, if I live to see you in it, I shall expect and hope that you will make a very different figure from most of your Fraternity.

We have had a terrible battle in our Orchard; one of our Turkey Hens has killed the other. Norfolk is famous for Turkeys;[4] do you think that you have ingenuity enough to

---

[2] *Il Penseroso*, lines 173–4.

[3] The *OED* does not cite this jocular variant spelling of physiognomy. ·

[4] 'The Norfolk housewives are characteristically famous for the feeding and dressing of poultry, and the county itself is no less so for the production of them. December 22nd and 23rd, 1793, one thousand seven hundred turkeys, weighing 9 tons, 2 cwt. 2 lbs. value 680£. were sent from Norwich to London in the various conveyances, and two days after half as many more.' [John Chambers], *A General History of the County of Norfolk*, 2 vols. (1829), ii. 1102.

procure us one of that breed at a proper season? For the present is not such. Yours, my dear boy, with Mrs. Unwin's best love —[5]

P.S. I have not heard from Norfolk.[6]

LADY HESKETH   Monday, 19 April 1790

Address: Lady Hesketh / New Norfolk Street / Grosvenor Square / London.
Postmarks: AP/20/90 *and* OULNEY
Panshanger Collection

The Lodge
April 19. 1790

My dearest Coz

I am much obliged to thee for thy negotiations in the Subscription way with my friend in the Church yard. My only comfort respecting the niggardly subscription of certain personages to my work, is, that it will presently be made known to the world as a matter of course; it does not often happen that an offended author can gratify himself with such safe vengeance, especially on the Great.

I have made known to the Frogs the satisfaction that the Executors feel on the subject of their brother's management at Florence,[1] and the information gave them, as it could not fail to do, great pleasure. If William should win the Dowager withal, which is not impossible, their pleasure would perhaps be still greater, for she is rich enough no doubt to recompense the toils of Courtship to a young lawyer of small fortune.

I thank thee also for my Cousin Johnson's letter which diverted me. I had one from him lately in which he expresses an ardent desire of a line from you and the delight he should feel on receiving it. I know not whether you will have the charity to satisfy his longings, but mention the matter thinking it possible that you may. A letter from a Lady to a youth immersed in the Mathematics must be singularly pleasant.

[5] The signature has been cut from the bottom of the letter.
[6] C means he has not heard again from Mrs Bodham since he wrote to her on 27 Feb. 1790.

___

[1] William Throckmorton eventually married on 19 Feb. 1788 Frances, a daughter of Thomas Giffard of Chillington.

I am finishing Homer backward, having begun at the last book and designing to persevere in that crab-like fashion till I arrive at the first. This may remind you perhaps of a certain poet's prisoner in the Bastile (thank heav'n! in the Bastile now no more)[2] counting the nails of his door, for variety's[3] sake, in all directions. I find so little to do in this last revisal that I shall soon reach the Odyssey, and soon, those books of it which are in thy possession, but the first two of the Iliad which are also in thy possession, much sooner. Thou may'st therefore send them by the first fair opportunity. I am in high spirits on this subject, and think that I h[ave a] t[4] last lick'd the clumsy cub into a shape that will secure to it the favorable notice of the public. Let not Fuseli retard me and I shall hope to get it out next winter.

Brother Gifford is at the Hall. He sent for the Frogs from Bath to Chillington, being, himself, in a state of moody melancholy to which he is subject. They brought him with them to Weston, where he has much recover'd his spirits, and in a week they return all together to Chillington that Mrs. Frog may attend the accouchement of her sister, which is expected to happen shortly.

I am glad that thou hast sent the General those verses on my mother's picture. They *will* amuse him — only I hope that he will not miss my Mother in law and think that she ought to have made a Third. On such an occasion it was not possible to mention her with any propriety. I rejoice at the General's recovery, may it prove a perfect one! Beau is in the best health and spirits. Mrs. U: better than in the winter but not well. What is become of Rose that he does not write? With Mrs. U.'s best love, I am ever

Thine Wm Cowper.

---

[2] C is referring to *The Task*, Book V, lines 379–445, specifically lines 425–31: 'To wear out time in numb'ring to and fro / The studs that thick emboss his iron door; / Then downward and then upward, then aslant / And then alternate; with a sickly hope / By dint of charge to give his tasteless task / Some relish; till the sum, exactly found / In all directions, he begins again—'.

[3] C has omitted the 's' after the apostrophe inadvertently because of the initial 's' in 'sake'.

[4] MS torn.

19 April 1790

News has arrived just as I finish'd my letter that Mrs. Gifford is deliver'd of a daughter[5] and is well for a Lady in such circumstances.

LADY HESKETH   Friday, 30 April 1790

Address: Lady Hesketh / New Norfolk Street / Grosvenor Square / London
Postmarks: MA/1/90 *and* NEWPORT/PAGNEL
Panshanger Collection

The Lodge
Weston — April 30. 1790

I did not write sooner, as thou hast no doubt supposed, because I waited for the arrival of the pacquet, which I can now inform thee, my dearest Coz, has reached my inky fingers safe. That is to say, all that it contained, for by some accident Book XX, viz: the fair copy of the twentieth Odyssey, which I suppose has been transcribed, came not. Thou wilt find it either in thy desk, or in thy Solander, that receptacle of all things lost. If it has happen'd that it was not copied, it is a matter of no consequence; Johnson will be here soon enough to do it for me.

I am glad that the Chancellor will now appear in my List a Subscriber for two copies Royal Paper. The greater will be both my honour and profit. He who subscribes for a single set, must be supposed to have done it on solicitation, but a subscription for two bespeaks him a volunteer; one who either is the author's friend or his humble admirer; both high honours where the Chancellor is in question. I feel myself also much indebted to Mrs. How for her unrequested application to him, and wish thee to tell her so on the first convenient occasion, and as for the note thou sent'st her, it was as all thy doings are, well-judged, and expressed my very mind on the matter.

To my old friend Dr. Madan thou could'st not have spoken better than thou didst. I have long'd to write this letter that the information it contains on the same subject might reach him from myself, while he is yet in town. Tell him I beseech

[5] Charlotte Giffard, who eventually married Samuel Campbell Simpson of Brockton.

370

you that I have not forgotten him, nor shall, so long as I can move and see the αυγας ηελιοιο.[1] Tell him also that to my heart and home he will be always welcome, nor he only, but all that are His. His judgment of my translation gave me the highest satisfaction, because I know him to be a rare old Greecian.

The General's approbation of my picture-verses gave me also much pleasure. I wrote them, not without tears, therefore I presume it may be that they are felt by others. Should he offer me my father's picture,[2] I shall gladly accept it. A melancholy pleasure is better than none, nay verily, better than most. He had a sad task imposed on him, but no man would acquit himself of such a one with more discretion or with more tenderness. The death of the unfortunate young man[3] reminded me of those lines in Lycidas

It was that fatal and perfidious bark
Built in the ecclipse and rigg'd with curses dark
That sunk so low that sacred head of thine![4]

— How beautiful!

I long to have a woman-wounder[5] caught and hang'd, hang'd in chains, hang'd with his heels uppermost, hang'd every way by which it is possible to hang a thing in human form. What a theme for music! Oh rare Astley![6]

I have not even now thank'd thee, monster as I am myself also, for thy labours in the transcribing way. But I now do it most heartily, and when I meet with a line which thou hast scored, will show it no favour.

Having misapprehended the matter and imagined that the Salmon would come with the papers, I invited Gregson to dine with us this day being a jour maigre.[7] Thus tantalizing the poor padré who must now keep fast indeed. Thanks for your design however to furnish us with such a banquet. With Mrs. U.'s best remembrances — Ever thine

W. C.

[1] 'Rays of the sun.' This expression occurs *passim* in both Homeric epics (e.g. *Odyssey*, xi. 498).

[2] There is an oil painting of John Cowper at the Cowper and Newton Museum, Olney; it is unsigned and measures 24 × 29¾ in. (item 641 in the collection).

[3] Unidentified.   [4] *Lycidas*, lines 100-2.   [5] Unidentified.

[6] Perhaps Philip Astley (1742-1814), the celebrated equestrian performer.

[7] 'A fast day.'

Thanks for the slip of News-paper are due likewise; I am obliged to Mr. Arno,[8] and if I knew him could render him a service, by telling him that he would write better, did he labour less. But he has done me much honour. So far he is to be esteem'd an excellent writer.

SAMUEL ROSE   Saturday, 1 May 1790

Address. Samuel Rose Esqre / Percy Street / Rathbone Place / London.
Postmarks: MA/3/90 *and* OULNEY
Princeton

The Lodge
May 1. 1790

My dear friend,

You could not have accounted for your silence in a manner more agreeable to me. I did not, I confess, willingly resign my pretensions to a letter, so long as I supposed your many hundred pages of precedents my only competitors, but finding that a future bride had interposed to prevent it, I am satisfied. The news gave me great pleasure, because the step you are about to take will, I trust, conduce much to the encrease of your own happiness. You may depend on our secresy till the affair shall be mature for publication.

I was very anxious on your account, 'till having an opportunity to ask news of you from Mr. Pitcairne,[1] I learn'd from him that your journey had done for you all that you expected from it, and that you found yourself perfectly recover'd. That young man is a great favorite with me, and I am glad to find that you are not altogether strangers to each other in London. My good opinion of him is not a hasty one, though my intercourse with him has been by no means frequent. I had lately sufficient proof, that his countenance and manner which speak much in his favour, are faithful indications of his real character, which is, I verily believe, that of a modest and virtuous man. You will wonder to what sort of circumstance I can possibly allude, and perhaps he would not,

---

[8] Unidentified.

[1] Probably Alexander Pitcairn (d. 1813) of Lincoln's Inn who married on 5 Apr. 1800. See *GM* lxx (1800), 589, and lxxxiv (1814), 100.

himself, be able to inform you, for persons of real worth are generally but little sensible of the striking propriety of their own conduct. When I see you, you shall know the matter, which at present I only mention that if it should happen to be convenient or desireable to you to cultivate an acquaintance with him, you may do it with the more assurance that he will not disappoint you.

We expect to receive the cheese to-day, and I shall be able to make my report of it before I close this letter which cannot go 'till to-morrow. It is now at Olney, and we should have been by this time intimate with both sorts had it not been for the Neglect of the waggoner to send it.

I am busied at present in transcribing my translation myself, and accommodating it as I proceed to my new ideas, which costs me no great trouble. By the end of the summer I shall hope that all will be in the press, at least ready to be so. Farewell my friend. A good journey and a prosperous one to Devonshire.

Mrs. Unwin adds her congratulations to mine on your approaching nuptials, and let not Beau's be omitted.

Ever yours
Wm Cowper.

Many thanks for another Subscriber.[2] You have perform'd nobly.

JOSEPH HILL

Sunday, 2 May 1790

Cowper Johnson

Weston Underwood
May 2. 1790

My dear friend —

My letters all begin with thanks, which is a proof that you are kind whether it prove my gratitude or not. *That* I should be glad to prove by longer and more frequent letters, did my situation afford me subjects or my occupation leisure.[1] At

---

[2] Unidentified.

---

[1] Hill evidently objected to the short note sent to him by C on 20 Mar.

present however I thank you for two parcels of excellent maccarel; the first at least was such teste me ipso,[2] and a few hours hence I shall be equally qualified, I doubt not, to attest the goodness of the latter.

I am still at the old sport; Homer all the morning and Homer all the Evening. Thus have I been held in constant employment, I know not exactly how many, but I believe these six years, an interval of eight months excepted. It is now become so familiar to me to take Homer from my shelf at a certain hour, that I shall no doubt continue to take him from my shelf at the same time, even after I have ceased to want him. That period is not far distant. I am now giving the last touches to a work, which had I foreseen the difficulty of it, I should never have meddled with, but which, having at length nearly finished it to my mind, I shall discontinue with regret.

My very best Compliments attend Mrs. Hill whom I love unsight unseen as they say, but yet truly.

Yours ever Wm Cowper.

LADY HESKETH   Sunday, 2 May [1790]

Address: Lady Hesketh / New Norfolk Street / Grosvenor Square / London.
Postmark: NEWPORT/PAGNEL
Harry L. Dalton Collection

May 2.
Sunday two o'clock
My dearest Coz
I send this in answer to yours just received, by express to Newport, to prevent if possible thy sending us any Salmon at the enormous price you mention. We shall not, in the mean time, die for want of fish, my friend Sephus having lately sent two baskets of Mackerel on the last of which we dine to-day, and Griggy dines with us on a turkey to-morrow. Therefore send no salmon, unless you wish us both to be choak'd, 'till it comes down to a price that one may swallow with safety.

[2] 'As I can affirm from personal experience.'

We were strictly charged not to mention the miscarriage[1] in a letter written by Mrs. Frog to Mrs. Unwin of considerable length, but secrets of that sort must be known I suppose to servants, for which reason all chance of their being kept is desperate.

Our hearts jump'd for joy at the Guardian's escape,[2] of which the Papers inform'd us, and we still sympathize with all parties concern'd.

I shall be happy also if thou hast been able to acquaint my dear friend Spencer,[3] either by means of his son, or by *personal intercourse* or otherwise with the joy that it will give me to see him here and his Reverend offspring with him. I shall not be altogether hopeless that he will call perhaps in his way downward.

Yours with the celerity of lightning
Wm Cowper.

MRS THROCKMORTON   Monday, 10 May 1790

Address: Mrs. Throckmorton / Bucklands / Farringdon / Berkshire
Postmark: MA/11/90
Sir Robert Throckmorton

The Lodge
May 10. 1790

My dear Mrs. Frog,

You have by this time I presume heard from the Doctor, whom I desired to present to you our best affections and to tell you that we are well. He sent an urchin (I do not mean a Hedge-hog, commonly call'd an urchin in old times, but a boy commonly so call'd at present)[1] expecting that he would

---

[1] Mrs Throckmorton evidently suffered a miscarriage at this time.

[2] C is referring to the incident on 23 Dec. 1789 when the ship *Guardian* struck an iceberg twelve days out from the Cape of Good Hope. The crew ultimately managed to get the badly damaged ship back to Table Bay on 21 Feb. C probably saw the extended account of this incident in *The General Evening Post* of 29 Apr.–1 May 1790 (No. 8323).

[3] Spencer Madan (1729–1813), bishop successively of Bristol and Peterborough, was the younger brother of Martin Madan; his eldest son, also Spencer (1758–1836), was ordained in 1782.

---

[1] *OED* gives hedgehog as the earliest meaning of urchin. Its first source is 1340, Hampole's *Psalter* ciii, 'An insectivorous quadruped of the genus *Erinaceus*,

find you at Bucklands, whither he supposed you gone on Thursday. He sent him charged, as I understand, with diverse articles, and among others I suppose with letters, or at least with a letter, which I mention that if the boy should be lost, together with his dispatches, past all possibility of recovery, you may yet know that the Doctor stands acquitted of not writing. That he is utterly lost (that is to say the boy, for the Doctor being the last antecedent as the Grammarians say, you might otherwise have supposed that *he* was intended) is the more probable, because he was never four miles from his home before, having only travell'd at the side of a plough-team, and when the Doctor gave him his direction to Bucklands, he ask'd, very naturally, if that pla-ace[2] was in England. So what is become of him heav'n knows!

I do not know that any adventures have presented themselves since your departure, worth mentioning, except that the Rabbit that infested your wilderness has been shot for devouring your carnations; and that I myself have been in some danger of being devoured in like manner by a great dog, viz Pearson's.[3] But I wrote him a letter on Friday (I mean a letter to Pearson, not to his Dog, which I mention to prevent mistakes, for the said last antecedent might occasion them in this place also) informing him that unless he tied up his great mastiff in the day time, I would send him a worse thing, commonly call'd and known by the name of an Attorney. When I go forth to ramble in the fields I do not sally like Don Quixot with a purpose of encount'ring monsters if any such can be found, but am a peaceable poor Gentleman and a poet who mean nobody any harm, the Fox-hunters and the two Universities of this land excepted.

I cannot learn from any creature whether the Turn-pike bill[4] is alive or dead, so ignorant am I and by such Ignoramuses

---

armed above with innumerable spines, and able to roll itself up into a ball with these bristling in every direction; an urchin'.

[2] C is imitating the local dialect.

[3] Unidentified further.

[4] C is referring to *A Bill for Amending, Widening, and Keeping in Repair the Road from Brombam Bridge, in the County of Bedford, to the Turnpike Road leading from Wellingborough to Olney, in the County of Bucks. and also the Road from the said Turnpike Road, at or near the South End of the Town of Olney aforesaid, to the Turnpike Road leading from Northampton to Newport Pagnell,*

surrounded. But if I know little else, this at least I know, that I love you and Mr. Frog, that I long for your return, and that I am, with Mrs. Unwin's best affections — Ever yours — W C.

LADY HESKETH   Tuesday, 11 May 1790

Address: Lady Hesketh / New Norfolk Street / Grosvenor Square / London
Postmark: MA/12/90
Olney

May 11. 1790

My dearest Coz
    We have of late exchanged dispatches with such frequency and nimbleness of finger, that it began to be necessary that we should allow ourselves time to breathe. It is well for us both that we spend much of our life with a pen in our hand, else I know not when we should have recover'd the effects of such severe exercise.
    Your news of Martin's death reach'd me in one of my melancholy moods and I reflected on it and felt it accordingly. What he was in reality God only knows. That he once seem'd to have grace is certain, and that no man had a mind more evangelically enlighten'd is equally so. The Giver of Grace and light, and He only, knows how to make allowance for the unavoidable effects of situation in life, constitution, errors in judgment, and those occurrences which give an unavoidable warp to the conduct. If by his providence he places one of his own people under the influence of any or all these possible causes of declension in spirituality of heart and mind, He will consider it, and to him, as you observe, the delinquent must be left; He has saved, I doubt not, thousands who in man's account have perish'd, and has left many to perish whom their survivors have been ready to canonize. Of Martin therefore in his present state I will hope the best, judging and condemning not Him, but his abominable and foolish book which for the sake of his connexions I wish that he had never written. The book

in the same County (30 Geo. III 1790, Northamptonshire Record Office Reference 931). Since the road ran right by his door at Weston, C was most interested in the provisions made for its maintenance.

indeed is pretty much forgotten, but it will never be forgotten that Polygamy has been defended and recommended in a Christian land and by a Minister of the Gospel, and that his name was Madan. When you shall have learn'd how he has disposed of the much that he left,[1] you will gratify my curiosity by informing me.

The Frogs made their transit from Chillington to Bucklands on Sunday last, and will come home again [the][2] last week of the month. From her I have had a letter which I answer'd yesterday. George is to join them here at their return, and then the village will seem peopled again.

Poor Beau has been much indisposed these two days and I have sent him this morning to Gayhurst to consult the Huntsman. What ails him or what is the cause of his ail I know not, but he is ever gulping as if swallowing somewhat that would hardly pass, or reaching, or coughing. Yet is not his vivacity in the least abated.

I have not heard lately from Johnson the Cantab: but wonder much more that I have had no answer from the Norfolk Rose, to whom I wrote immediately on the receipt of her letter, sending her a loving and pressing invitation to Weston. The only News of the place is that three great rogues have been apprehended at Olney and are gone to prison, one of whom will probably he hang'd.[3]

If thou has any such things as rags (pardon the expression) belonging to thee, Mrs. Unwin is ready to beg them on her knees for the use of two miserable women on the point of producing. We have not a rag left. When my odd book comes, they may come with it.

W C.

---

[1] According to his will (PRO Prob. 11/1192/252), which was proved on 12 May 1790, Madan left all his property to his wife, who was also sole executrix of the estate.

[2] MS torn.

[3] Unidentified. Buckinghamshire was on the Norfolk assize circuit, records of which have survived only sporadically; unfortunately, none survives for 1790.

JOSEPH HILL   Saturday, 22 May 1790

Cowper Johnson

Weston Underwood
May 22. 1790

My dear friend,

To have drawn for Forty pounds would have suited better the present state of my purse, which rather needs an immediate supply being altogether empty, but not being sure that you have cash of mine to that amount at present, I feared lest I should give myself an air to which I am not entitled. I shall however be much obliged to you if you will favour me with that Sum or with any other, for any will be welcome. In the mean time I remain yours

very affectionately Wm Cowper.

My best respects attend Mrs. Hill.

LADY HESKETH   Friday, 28 May 1790

Address: Lady Hesketh / New Norfolk Street / Grosvenor Square / London
Postmarks: MA/29/90 *and* OULNEY
Panshanger Collection

The Lodge
May 28. 1790

My dearest Coz —

I thank thee for the offer of thy best services on this occasion, but heaven guard my brows from the wreath you mention, whatever wreath beside may hereafter adorn them![1] It would be a leaden extinguisher clapp'd on all the fire of my genius, and I should never more produce a line worth reading. To speak seriously, it would make me miserable, and therefore I am sure that thou of all my friends woulds't least wish me to wear it.

Adieu! thine in a Homer-hurry
Wm Cowper.

[1] Henry James Pye (1745–1813) succeeded Thomas Warton (1728–90) as poet laureate in 1790. C in his letter to Churchey of 2 June 1790 mistakenly assumes the post had been offered to Robert Merry (see n.2, C to Lady Hesketh, 1 Jan. 1788).

Let me hear from thee again soon for it is long since I had thy last. — All best wishes from this place attend thee.

JOSEPH HILL   [Saturday, 29 May 1790][1]

Address: Joseph Hill Esqre / Chancery Office / London
Postmark: JU/1/90
Princeton

My dear friend
    I thank you heartily for your accustom'd readiness in furnishing me from your own bank, mine being as usual, exhausted. Should a day ever arrive when my treasury shall be more equal to my occasions, it will be well; in the mean time I will not seek to encrease it by soliciting the Laureatship, an office from which I believe it to be impossible to derive any honour, unless if it happens to be offer'd (as it never will be to me) the honour of refusing it.
    With my very affectionate remembrances to your sisters and my best Compliments to Mrs. Hill, I remain

                                    Ever yours   Wm Cowper.

WALTER CHURCHEY   Wednesday, 2 June 1790

Address: June four 1790 / London / Mr Churchey / Hay / Brecon / G Hardinge[1]
Postmarks: JU/4/90 *and* FREE P
Formerly Mrs. Walter F. Harden

                                    Weston Underwood
                                    June 2. 1790
Dear Sir
    I wish with all my heart that you wore the King's Laurel or that it were in my power to procure it for you, but did I

---

[1] The top portion of the letter has been torn away, and no date appears in C's hand on the MS. However, the MS is dated '29 May 1790' in an unknown hand, and the postmark and the reference to the laureateship would seem to confirm the accuracy of this dating.

---

[1] George Hardinge (1743–1816) of Pyrton, Wilts., was Member of Parliament for Old Sarum from 11 Mar. 1784 until 1802.

covet that honour for myself I should probably find the little interest that I can command far too insignificant to obtain it. I learn'd also some days since, but I cannot absolutely vouch for the truth of my information, that the appointment is already fixt, and that the place will be given to Mr. Merry[2] the Author of many Odes and other poems which have appeared in Newspapers and Magazines with the signature of Della Crusca.

You guess'd the true reason of my silence when you supposed it owing to want of leisure; I have indeed too little for any letters except those of absolute necessity. I gave orders to my Bookseller to enter your name on my List of Subscribers according to your request, and I understood that he sent you at the same time a few of my proposal papers as you likewise desired. If you never had them the neglect is chargeable on Him only.

I hope to send Iliad and Odyssey to the Press by the end of the Summer and remain with much respect

Yours   Wm Cowper.

LADY HESKETH Thursday, 3 June 1790

Hayley, i. 371–2

June 3, 1790.

You will wonder when I tell you, that I, even I, am considered by people, who live at a great distance, as having interest and influence sufficient to procure a place at Court, for those who may happen to want one. I have accordingly been applied to within these few days by a Welchman, with a wife and many children, to get him made Poet-Laureat as fast as possible. If thou wouldst wish to make the world merry twice a year, thou canst not do better than procure the office for him. I will promise thee that he shall afford thee a hearty laugh in return every birth-day, and every new-year. He is an honest man.

Adieu,

W. C.

<hr>

[2] See n.1, C to Lady Hesketh, 28 May 1790.

JOSEPH HILL   Friday, 4 June 1790

Cowper Johnson

Weston Underwood
June 4. 1790

My dear friend

Once more to trouble you in this business of Mr. Heslop.
I have at length had an interview with him and have finally
settled the account, the balance of which in his favour is
47. 10. 8. —

I entreat you therefore to send me a power of Attorney
that I may execute it to you immediately for the sale of 100
Consolidateds, and if it should not be inconvenient to you to
send him a Draft for the money in the meantime you will
much oblige me by doing it. I beg you to say Hush to any
arguments in favour of delay that your friendship for me may
dictate on the occasion, for my peace of mind and my health
are both concerned in the immediate payment. I have already
fretted myself more about it than either my mind or body is
able to bear.[1]

Mr. Heslop is at this time at the Bishop of Lincoln's Amen
Corner,[2] but is soon going to the sea side to join his family
there.

It vexes me not a little to give you so much trouble but the
necessity of the case must excuse me — I am, my dear friend

Yours ever
Wm Cowper

[1] For the financial difficulties with Luke Heslop, see n.1, C to Unwin, 31 Mar.
1770.
[2] Sir George Pretyman (1750–1827), who took the surname of Tomline in
1803, was Bishop of Lincoln from 1787 to 1820. Amen Corner was his London
residence as Dean of St. Paul's, a living he also held.

LADY HESKETH   Sunday, 6 June 1790

Address: Lady Hesketh / New Norfolk Street / Grosvenor Square / London
Postmarks: JU/7/90 *and* NEWPORT/PAGNEL
Princeton

The Lodge
June 6. 1790

Dearest Coz

I should sooner have acknowledged the receipt of thy charity box had I not been lately engaged more than usual, not in poetry alone, but in business also. I now tell you however that it came safe to our great joy and to the great joy especially of the two future mothers, whose children were in some danger not only of coming naked from the womb but of continuing naked afterwards. The money has been divided between them, and the linen, and by me they thank thee with unfeigned gratitude for thy bounty.

The business to which I allude above was my long un-liquidated account with the Revd. Luke Heslop. It has cost me many a fit of fretting and many a time has sunk my spirits; it has indeed been almost a continual vexation to me these 20 years. The delay has been occasion'd by himself, and were the account justly settled the Balance would be in my favour, for I have lost more by his negligence than I owe him for his services. Yet, notwithstanding these considerations which might, and ought perhaps to have consoled me, it is so detestable a thing to be considered as any man's debtor for so long a time, to be occasionally dunn'd for payment and always liable to it, that it has plaugued me past measure and was the cause of that depression of spirits which I mentioned in my last. I have however emerged sooner than I expected, for nervous fevers if they once seize me do not often leave me in a hurry. I pray God to keep me from them, for to me they are the most dreadful of all evils.

Heslop called here about a fortnight since, at which time I told him in pretty strong and severe terms my whole mind concerning the manner in which he had treated me. A day or two ago I wrote to my old friend Sephus, telling him how much the affair had hurt me, and entreating him to sell Stock immediately for satisfaction of my rev'rend creditor. My only fear now is that Joseph's friendship for me may determine him not to do it and to insist on a regular balance being struck between us. Should this be the case, the vexation will still continue, for Heslop is resolved never to go near him more, having been rather roughly handled by him when he saw him last.

Thus stands the matter, with which I did not mean to have occupied all my paper, but having told thee that I have been indisposed in my spirits, I thought it necessary to tell thee also the cause. A few days will, I hope, rid me for ever of the subject.

I am happy that Mrs. Howe is so well pleased with what she has seen of my Homer, and will take care that the whole shall not disgrace the sample.

I dined yesterday at the Hall where I spent my time merrily. Have no uneasiness about me, for I am I thank God at this present writing as well and in as good spirits as at any time these many years. Poor Mrs. Unwin, who was as much hurt as myself, is now well also, and sends you her best affections and her best thanks for your kind answer to her solicitations. I am

Ever thine   Wm Cowper.

Thanks for the papers and for the odd odd-yssey.[1]

JOHN JOHNSON   Monday, 7 June 1790

Address: J Johnson Esqr / Post Office / Norwich
Trinity College, Cambridge (*copy*)[1]

Weston Underwood   June 7, 1790

My dear John

You know my engagements and are consequently able to account for my silence. I will not therefore waste time and paper in mentioning them, but will only say that added to those with which you are acquainted I have had other hindrances, such as business and a disorder of my spirits to which I have been all my life subject. At present I am I thank

---

[1] Perhaps the fair copy of C's translation of Book XX of the *Odyssey*. See C to Lady Hesketh, 30 Apr. 1790.

---

[1] Add. MS Letters C. 1^{45}; this copy is in an unknown hand.

God! perfectly well both in mind [and body]. Of you I am always mindful whether I write or not and very desirous to see you. You will remember I hope that you are under engagements to us and as soon as your Norfolk friends can spare you will fulfil them. Give us all the time you can and all that they can spare to us.

You never pleased me more than when you told me you had abandoned your mathematical pursuits. It grieved me to think that you were wasting your time and doing perhaps irreparable injury to your constitution merely to gain a little Cambridge fame, not worth your having. I cannot be contented that your renown should thrive no where but on the banks of the Cam. Conceive a nobler ambition and never let your honours be circumscribed by the paltry dimensions of an University. It is well that you have already as you observe acquired sufficient information in that science to enable you to pass creditably such examinations as I suppose you must hereafter undergo. Keep what you have gotten and be content. More is needless.

You could not apply to a worse than I am to advise you concerning your studies. I was never a regular Student myself but lost the most valuable years of my life in an Attorney's office and in the Temple. I will not therefore give myself airs and affect to know what I know not. The affair is of great importance to you and you should be directed in it by a wiser than I. To speak however in very general terms on the subject, it seems to me that your chief concern is with History, Natural Philosophy, Logic and Divinity. As to Metaphysics I know little about them but the very little that I do know, has not taught me to admire them. Life is too short to afford time even for serious trifles. Pursue what you know to be attainable, make truth your object and your studies will make you a wise man. Let your Divinity, if I may advise, be the Divinity of the glorious Reformation. I mean in contra-distinction to Arminianism and all the *isms* that were ever broached in this world of error and ignorance. The Divinity of the Reformation is called Calvinism but injuriously; it has been that of the Church of Christ in all ages; it is the Divinity of St. Paul and of St. Paul's Master who met him in his way to Damascus.

I have written in great haste that I might finish if possible before breakfast. Mrs. Unwin is now come down and the tea things in a moment will begin to chatter. Adieu, let us see you soon; the sooner the better. Give my love to the silent Lady the Rose and to all my friends around you, and believe me with Mrs. U's warmest affections, yours most truly

Wm Cowper

SAMUEL ROSE   Tuesday, 8 June 1790

Address: Samuel Rose Esqre. / Percy Street / Rathbone Place / London
Postmarks: JU/9/90 *and* OULNEY
Princeton

The Lodge
June 8. 1790

My dear friend,

Among the many who love and esteem you there is none who rejoices more in your felicity than myself; far from blaming, I commend you much for connecting yourself, young as you are, with a well-chosen companion for life. Ent'ring on the state with uncontaminated morals you have the best possible prospect of happiness, and will be secure against a thousand and ten thousand temptations to which, at an early period of life in such a Babylon as you must necessarily inhabit, you would otherwise have been exposed. I see it too in the light that you do, as likely to be advantageous to you in your profession. Men of business have a better opinion of a candidate for employment who is married, because he has given bond to the world, as you observe, and to himself, for diligence, industry and attention. Neither is it a consideration of small importance that the Lady's father is in a situation that qualifies him to advance your interest. One such friend, who cannot fail you while he continues to love his own daughter, is worth many casual ones who are free to exchange you for another on any trivial inducement. This therefore must be added to the sum of your bride's portion, as a matter indefinite indeed in its value, but sure to be considerable. It is altogether therefore a subject of much congratulation, and mine, to which I add Mrs. Unwin's, is very sincere. Samson, at his marriage, proposed a Riddle to the Philistines.[1] I am no Samson neither are you a Philistine, yet expound to me the following if you can.

What are they which stand at a distance fro[m each][2] other and meet without ever moving?[3]

[Should yo]u be so fortunate as to guess it, you may propose it to the company when you celebrate your nuptials, and if you can win thirty changes of raiment by it as Samson did by his, let me tell you, they will be no contemptible acquisition to a young beginner.

You will not I hope forget your way to Weston in consequence of your marriage, where you and yours will be always welcome.

I am affectionately Yours

Wm Cowper.

MRS KING   Monday, 14 June 1790

Address: Mrs. King / Pirtenhall / Kimbolton / Huntingdonshire.
Postmark: JU/15/90
Olney

Weston June 14
1790

My dear Madam,

I have hardly a scrap of paper belonging to me that is not scribbled over with Blank verse, and taking out your letter from a bundle of others, this moment, I find it thus inscribed on the seal-side.

—— meantime his steeds
Snorted by Myrmidons detain'd, and loos'd
From their own master's chariot, foam'd to fly. —[1]

You will easily guess to what they belong, and I mention the

---

[1] Judges 14:14: 'Out of the eater came forth meat, and out of the strong came forth sweetness.'
[2] MS torn.
[3] C provides the answer ('The trees of a Colonnade') in his letter to Rose of 13 Sept. 1790.

---

[1] These are lines 611–13 in C's translation of Book XVI of the *Iliad*.

387

circumstance merely in proof of my perpetual engagement to Homer whether at home or abroad, for when I committed these lines to the back of your letter I was rambling at a considerable distance from home. I set one foot on a mole-hill, placed my hat with the crown upward on my knee, lay'd your letter upon it and with a pencil wrote the fragment that I have sent you. In the same posture I have written many and many a passage of a work which I hope soon to have done with. — But all this is foreign to what I intended when I first took pen in hand. My purpose then was to excuse my long silence as well as I could, by telling you that I am at present not only a laborer in verse but in prose also, having been requested by a friend to whom I could not refuse it, to translate for him a series of Latin Letters received from a Dutch minister of the Gospel at the Cape of Good Hope.[2] With this additional occupation you will be sensible that my hands are full, and it is a truth, that except to yourself, I would, just at this time, have written to nobody.

I felt a true concern for what you told me in your last concerning the ill-state of health and your much valued friend Mr. Martyn. You say, if I knew half his worth I should, with you, wish his longer continuance below. Now you must understand that ignorant as I am of Mr. Martyn except by your report of him, I do nevertheless sincerely wish it — and that, both for your sake and my own; nor less for the sake of the Public. For your sake because you love and esteem him highly; for the sake of the Public, because, should it please God to take him before he has completed his great Botanical work,[3] I suppose no other person will be able to finish it so well; and for my own sake, because I know he has a kind and favorable opinion beforehand of my Translation, and consequently, should it justify his prejudice when it appears, he will stand my friend against an army of Cambridge Critics. — It would have been a strange indeed if *Self* had not peep'd out on this subject. I beg you will present my best respects

[2] See n.2, C to Newton, 5 June 1788.
[3] In 1785, Martyn undertook an edition of Philip Miller's *Gardener's Dictionary*; his project was in fact an entirely new work based on the Linnaean system. The entire work was not completely finished until the 3rd ed. of 1807.

to him, and assure him that were it possible he could visit Weston, I should be most happy to receive him.

[Mrs Unwin would have been employed in translating my rhimes for you, would her health have permitted; but it is very seldom that she can write without being much a sufferer by it. She has almost a constant pain in her side, which forbids it. As soon as it leaves her, or much]⁴ abates, she will be glad to work for you.

I am like you and Mr. King an admirer of clouds, but only when there are blue intervals, and pretty wide ones too, between them. One cloud is too much for me, but a hundred are not too many. So with this riddle and with my best respects to Mr. King to which I add Mrs. Unwin's to you both — I remain, my Dear Madam — Truly yours — W. Cowper.

LADY HESKETH   Thursday, 17 June 1790

Hayley (1806), iii. 250–3

The Lodge, June 17, 1790.

My dear Coz,

Here am I, at eight in the morning, in full dress, going a visiting to Chicheley. We are a strong party, and fill two chaises; Mrs. F. the elder, and Mrs. G. in one; Mrs. F. the younger,¹ and myself in another. Were it not that I shall find Chesters at the end of my journey, I should be inconsolable. That expectation alone supports my spirits; and even with this prospect before me, when I saw this moment a poor old woman coming up the lane, opposite my window, I could not help sighing, and saying to myself — 'Poor, but happy old woman! Thou art exempted by thy situation in life from riding in chaises, and making thyself fine in a morning, happier therefore in my account than I, who am under the cruel necessity of doing both. Neither dost thou write verses, neither hast thou ever heard of the name of

---

⁴ These lines have been obliterated; our copy-text is *Southey*, vi. 314.

¹ Anna Maria Throckmorton, John's mother, and Maria, his wife, are 'Mrs. F.' the elder and younger respectively; 'Mrs. G' is probably Barbara Giffard (see n.2, C to Unwin, 10–11 July 1786), Maria's mother.

Homer, whom I am miserable to abandon for a whole morning!' This, and more of the same sort passed in my mind on seeing the old woman abovesaid.

The troublesome business with which I filled my last Letter, is (I hope) by this time concluded, and Mr. Archdeacon satisfied. I can, to be sure, but ill afford to pay fifty pounds for another man's negligence, but would be happy to pay an hundred rather than be treated as if I were insolvent; threatened with attornies and bums.[2] One would think, that, living where I live, I might be exempted from trouble. But alas! as the philosophers often affirm, there is no nook under Heaven in which trouble cannot enter; and perhaps had there never been one philosopher in the world this is a truth, that would not have been always altogether a secret.

I have made two inscriptions[3] lately at the request of Thomas Gifford, Esqr. who is sowing twenty acres with acorns on one side of his house, and twenty acres with ditto on the other. He erects two memorials of stone on the occasion, that when posterity shall be curious to know the age of the oaks, their curiosity may be gratified.

1.

INSCRIPTION.

Other stones the æra tell
When some feeble mortal fell.
I stand here to date the birth
Of these hardy sons of earth.

Anno 1790.

———

2.

INSCRIPTION.

Reader! Behold a monument
That asks no sigh or tear,
Though it perpetuate the event
Of a great burial here.

Anno 1791.

[2] A colloquial shortened version of bumbailiff, a contemptuous reference to a bailiff who is close at the debtor's back or who catches him in the rear. *OED* cites C's usage of the word in this letter.

[3] 'Inscription, for a Stone Erected at the Sowing of a Grove of Oaks at Chillington, the Seat of T. Gifford, Esq., 1790' and 'Another, for a Stone Erected on

17 June 1790

My works therefore will not all perish, or will not all perish soon, for he has ordered his lapidary to cut the characters very deep, and in stone extremely hard. It is not in vain then, that I have so long exercised the business of a poet. I shall at last reap the reward of my labours, and be immortal probably for many years.

Ever thine,
W. C.

WALTER BAGOT Tuesday, 22 June 1790

Address: The Revd. Walter Bagot / Blithfield / Litchfield / Staffordshire.
Postmark: OULNEY
Morgan Library

Weston
June 22. 1790

My dear friend,

I thought to have made you amends for putting you to the expence of double postage by not writing 'till you might receive me gratis,[1] but I have no patience to wait longer seeing that your last was written in April and it is now past Midsummer. So have at your purse, in defiance of all your oeconomy.

Villoison makes no mention of the serpent whose skin or bowels, or perhaps both, were honoured with the Iliad and Odyssey inscribed upon them, but I have conversed with a living eye-witness of an African serpent long enough to have afforded skin and guts for the purpose.[2] In Africa there are Ants also which frequently destroy these monsters. They are not much larger than ours but they travel in a column of immense length and eat through every thing that opposes them. Their bite is like a spark of fire. When these serpents have kill'd their prey, Lion, or Tiger or any other large

a Similar Occasion at the Same Place in the Following Year' were published respectively in 1803 and 1806 in *Hayley*. The Thomas Giffard who planted the oaks was Mrs Throckmorton's brother. Chillington Hall stands some six miles from Wolverhampton, in Staffordshire.

[1] Most of C's letters to Bagot were delivered by hand.
[2] John Newton may have supplied C with this information.

animal, before they swallow him, they take a considerable circuit round about the carcase to see if the ants are coming, because when they have gorged their prey they are unable to escape them. They are nevertheless sometimes surprized by them in their unwieldy state, and the ants make a passage through them. — Now if you thought your own story of Homer bound in snake-skin worthy of three notes of admiration, you cannot do less than add six to mine, confessing at the same time that if I put you to the expence of a letter, I do not make you pay your money for nothing. But this account I had from a person of most unimpeached veracity.

I rejoice with you in the good Bishop's removal to St. Asaph,[3] and especially because the Norfolk Parsons much more resemble the Ants abovementioned than he the serpent. He is neither of vast size, nor unwieldy, nor voracious, neither, I dare say, does he sleep after dinner according to the practise of the said serpent. But harmless as he is, I am mistaken if his mutinous clergy did not sometimes disturb his rest, and if he did not find their bite, though they could not actually eat through him, in a degree resembling fire. — Good men like him, and peaceable, should have good and peaceable folks to deal with, and I heartily wish him such in his new diocese. But if he will keep the clergy to their business, he shall have trouble let him go where he may; and this is boldly spoken considering that I speak it to one of that Reverend body. But ye are like Jeremiah's basket of figs,[4] some of you could not be better, and some of you are stark naught. Ask the Bishop himself if this be not true.

I draw fast to a close of my translating business, and expect to go to press in the Autumn.

I hope that Mrs. Bagot and all your family, who were well when you wrote, still continue so. Give my love to them all. Oeconomist like yourself I have scribbled with a pen which I have used 'till it has lost all point and is worn perfectly square, but it will yet serve to tell you that I am much and truly Yours Wm Cowper.

I was at Chichley a few days since and found all well — Adieu!

[3] C is referring to the removal of Bishop Lewis Bagot (see n.3, C to Unwin, 18 Dec. 1784) from Norwich to St. Asaph.   [4] Jeremiah 24:1-10.

LADY HESKETH   Monday, 28 June 1790

Address: Lady Hesketh / New Norfolk Street / Grosvenor Square / London
Postmarks: JU/29/90 *and* OULNEY
Princeton

The Lodge
June 28. 1790

My dearest Coz —

I write now merely to tell you that the Tea came safe and is excellent, for which you have my best thanks — and to entreat you to send forthwith either in a Bank note or Draft on your own Bank the money that you have in hand for me. It is the season of payment of Servants' wages, and we are liable also, or shall be shortly, to some demands of Rent, which will make the receipt of said money very convenient.

We proceed much at the usual rate, only Mrs. Unwin's constant pain in her side has at last produced a tumour on that part which distresses me more than it does her. Knowing neither the cause, nor in what it is likely to terminate, I cannot but be very uneasy about it. It has but lately appeared; as she describes it, is of half a hand's breadth in dimension, and projects to about a hand's thickness. If you should happen to see your skillful Apothecary[1] whose name I cannot now recover, but whom Mr. Rose consulted, I should be glad if you would ask his opinion. In the mean time I shall take the first opportunity to consult Mr. Gregson.

I expect to see shortly Mrs. Bodham here and her husband. If they come, which depends on the recovery of a relation of theirs at present very much indisposed, they will stay, I imagine, a parson's week, that is to say about a fortnight, and no longer. September in the mean time will be approaching and will arrive welcome, most welcome to us, because it promises to bring you with it. I dream'd last night that you are at Bath. Your next will inform [me][2] whether this is true or false. My dream was [owing] perhaps merely to your longer silence than usual, for which not knowing how to account while I am waking, I endeavoured to solve the difficulty in my sleep.

[1] Sir Walter Farquhar. See n.1, C to Rose, 11 Mar. 1790.
[2] MS torn.

393

Adieu! Let me hear from thee, and believe me, as I know thou dost, with Mrs. Unwin's affectionate Compliments.

> Ever thine
> Wm Cowper

The swelling is under the ribs at the side of the stomach, on the right.

MRS BODHAM   Tuesday, 29 June 1790

Address: Mrs. Bodham / Mattishall Green / Norfolk[1]
Postmark: JY/3/90
Princeton

> Weston Underwood
> June 29. 1790

My dearest Cousin,

It is true that I did sometimes complain to Mrs. Unwin of your long silence, but it is likewise true that I made many excuses for you in my own mind, and did not feel myself at all inclined to be angry nor even much to wonder. There is an aukwardness and a difficulty in writing to those whom distance and length of time have made in a manner new to us, that naturally give us a check when we would otherwise be glad to address them. But a time, I hope, is near at hand, when you and I shall be effectually deliver'd from all such constraints, and correspond as fluently as if our intercourse had suffer'd much less interruption.

You must not suppose, my Dear, that though I may be said to have lived many years with a pen in my hand, I am myself altogether at my ease on this tremendous occasion. Imagine rather, and you will come nearer to the truth, that when I placed this sheet before me I ask'd myself more than once, how shall I fill it? One subject indeed presents itself, the pleasant prospect that opens upon me of our coming once more together, but That once exhausted, with what shall I proceed? Thus I questioned myself; but finding

---

[1] This letter was missent first to Stoke, Norfolk, and then to Lynn, where a knowledgeable postman marked the address portion: 'Missent to Lynn' and added after Mattishall Green the direction 'Near Market Dereham / in Norfolk'.

neither end nor profit of such questions, I bravely resolved to dismiss them all at once, and to engage in the great enterprize of a letter to my quondam Rose at a venture. — There is great truth in a Rant of Nat: Lee's or of Dryden's, I know not which, who makes an enamour'd youth say to his mistress —

And Nonsense shall be Eloquence in Love.[2]

For certain it is that they who truly love one another are not very nice examiners of each other's stile or matter; if an epistle comes, it is always welcome, though it be perhaps neither so wise nor so witty as one might have wish'd to make it.

And now, my Cousin, let me tell thee how much I feel myself obliged to Mr. Bodham for the readiness he expresses to accept my invitation. Assure him that stranger as he is to me at present, and natural as the dread of strangers has ever been to me, I shall yet receive him with open arms, because he is your husband and loves you dearly. That consideration alone will endear him to me, and I dare say that I shall not find it his only recommendation to my best affections. May the health of his relation (his mother I suppose) be soon restored and long continued, and may nothing melancholy of what kind soever interefere to prevent our joyful meeting.[3] Between the present moment and September our house is clear for your reception, and you have nothing to [do but to give us a day or two] 's[4] notice of your coming. [In September we expect Lady Hesketh, and I only regret that our house is not large enough to hold all together,] for were it possible that you could meet, you would love each other dearly.

Mrs. Unwin bids me offer you her best love. She is never well, but always patient and always cheerful, and feels beforehand that she shall be loth to part with you.

[2] Jupiter, in the shape of Amphitryon (in Dryden's comedy of 1690 of the same name), addresses these words to Alcmena: 'And Nonsence shall be Eloquent, in Love' (I. ii. 111).
[3] Susanna Bodham (1717-97), Mr Bodham's aunt, was the widow of Thomas Bodham (d. 1785).
[4] The signature and some other portions of this letter have been cut off. The portions in square brackets have been supplied from *Hayley*; 'visit us' is a conjectured reading.

Give our best Love to Cousin John when you see him, and tell him that he is, like some other people, readier by half to receive letters than to answer them. His next I hope will tell us at what time he means to perform his promise to [visit us.

My love to all the dear Donnes of every name! — Write soon, no matter about what.

W. C.]

LADY HESKETH   Wednesday, 7 July 1790

Hayley, i. 378–9

July 7, 1790.

Instead of beginning with the saffron-vested morning to which Homer invites me, on a morning that has no saffron vest to boast, I shall begin with you.

It is irksome to us both to wait so long as we must for you, but we are willing to hope, that by a longer stay, you will make us amends for all this tedious procrastination.

Mrs. Unwin has made known her whole case to Mr. Gregson, whose opinion of it has been very consolatory to me. He says indeed it is a case perfectly out of the reach of all physical aid, but at the same time not at all dangerous. Constant pain is a sad grievance, whatever part is affected, and she is hardly ever free from an aching head, as well as an uneasy side, but patience is an anodyne of God's own preparation, and of that he gives her largely.

The French who like all lively folks, are extreme in every thing, are such in their zeal for Freedom, and if it were possible to make so noble a cause ridiculous, their manner of promoting it could not fail to do so. Princes and peers reduced to plain gentlemanship, and gentles reduced to a level with their own lacqueys, are excesses of which they will repent hereafter. Difference of rank and subordination, are, I believe of God's appointment, and consequently essential to the well being of society: but what we mean by fanaticism in reglion is exactly that which animates their politics, and unless time should sober the, they will, after all, be an unhappy people. Perhaps it deserves not much to be wondered at, that at their first escape from tyrannic shackles, they should act extravagantly, and treat their kings, as they have sometimes treated their idols. To these however they are reconciled in due time again, but their respect for monarchy is at an end. They want nothing now but a little English sobriety, and that they want extremely; I heartily wish them some wit in their anger, for it were great pity that so many millions should be miserable for want of it.

W. C.

JOHN JOHNSON   Thursday, 8 July 1790

Address: John Johnson Esqr. / Red-House, out Brazen Doors. / Norwich
Postmark: [illegible] /90[1]
Princeton

Weston July 8. 1790

My dear Johnny
    With a worse pen than yours, for I always use mine long after they have lost the very shape of a pen, I prepare to take vengeance on your illegibility by being more illegible myself. And first, to begin with the date of yours, so easy to read but so hard to understand — what in the name of common sense, is, or can be the meaning of, *Out Brazen doors*?[2] Explain these mysterious words I beseech you in your next, if explanation of them be possible, for I never saw the like in respect of perfect obscurity. Confiding however in this, that you were really awake and in your right mind when you dated your Letter, I shall direct mine accordingly.
    You do well to perfect yourself on the Violin. Only beware that an amusement so very bewitching as Music, especially when we produce it ourselves, do not steal from you *all* those hours that should be given to study. I can be well content

---

[1] The MS is torn, removing part of the date stamp.

[2] John Johnson to Mrs B. Parkyns, 20 Sept. 1826 (Princeton): 'In the days of my youth, that I might be near a music-master, I took lodgings just out of the walls of the City of Norwich at a place which went by the name of "*The Red House out Brazen Doors*;" and writing to Cowper soon after, I prefixed that date to my letter. In his reply to it, he asks — "What in the name of common sense is, or can be the meaning of, *Out Brazen Doors*?" .... On my inserting the word "*of*" between "*Out*" and "*Brazen*", his next Letter began thus — "To you, Dearest John, at your house, out o' doors."' (see C to John Johnson, 31 July 1790).

that it should serve you as a refreshment after severer exercises, but not that it should engross you wholly. Your own good sense will most probably dictate to you this precaution, and I might have spared you the trouble of it, but I have a degree of zeal for your proficiency in more important pursuits that would not suffer me to suppress it. Having delivered my conscience by giving you this sage admonition, I will convince you that I am a Censor not over and above severe, by acknowledging in the next place that I have known very good performers on the violin, very learned also; and my Cousin Dr. Spencer Madan is an instance.

I am delighted that you have engaged your sister to visit us, for I say to myself, if John be amiable, what must Catharine be? For we Males, be we angelic as we may, are always surpass'd by the Ladies. But know this, that I shall not be in love with either of you if you stay with us only a few days, for you talk of *a week or so*. Correct this Erratum I beseech you, and convince us by a much longer continuance here, that it was one. I lately answer'd a letter which I received about a fortnight since from your Aunt Bodham, in which answer I told her that 'till September we are free for the reception of all that can come from Norfolk, but that in September we expect Lady Hesketh. I would that our house would hold both Her and my Norfolk friends together, but it is too small and cannot be stretch'd. What then must be done? You must find some season in the interval. Mr. and Mrs. Bodham I trust will be able to do so, and as to you and your sister who are neither occupied in building nor planting, perhaps you may find one time as convenient as another. It will be a great pleasure both to me and to Mrs. Unwin to see you at any time, but the case standing as it does, it was necessary to apprize you of it. Give my best love to your sister, who I dare say is well entitled to it, and believe me my dear John, affectionately yours

Wm Cowper.

Mrs. Unwin has never been well since you saw her. You are not passionately fond of Letter-writing I perceive who have dropp'd a Lady; but you will be a loser by the bargain; for one letter of hers in point of real utility and sterling value is worth twenty of mine, and you will never have another from her 'till you have earn'd it.

P.S.

We will take care to find your sister a bed-fellow to whom she shall have no objection. Mrs. Unwin has a tender regard for her beforehand, and, recreant as thou art, sends her kind love even to thee. Remember Turkeys — they must be birds of last year.

WILLIAM BULL   *c.*Sunday, 11 July 1790[1]

Formerly Miss C. M. Bull

My dear friend —

Thanks for the papers which are come just in time to greet Mrs. King for whom the copies were made. I expect her here either on Monday or Tuesday. — I write with my Breakfast in my mouth, only just to tell you that we heartily wish you a good journey, and that I am with Mrs. Unwin's Love —

Sincerely yours
Wm Cowper.

Sund. Mor.

MRS KING   Friday, 16 July 1790

Address: Mrs. King / Pirten-hall / Kimbolton / Huntingdonshire
Postmarks: JY/17/90 *and* OULNEY
Princeton

Weston, July 16. 1790

My dear Madam,

Taking it for granted that this will find you at Pirtenhall, I follow you with an early line and a hasty one, to tell you how much we rejoice to have seen yourself and Mr. King, and how much regret you have left behind you. The wish

---

[1] Mrs King had departed before Friday, 16 July 1790 when C writes: 'we rejoice to have seen yourself and Mr. King'. The Kings probably arrived at Weston on 12 or 13 July, and this letter would then have been written on Sunday, 11 July 1790.

that we express'd when we were together, Mrs. Unwin and I have more than once express'd since your departure, and have always felt it, that it had pleased Providence to appoint our habitations nearer to each other. This is a life of wishes, and they only are happy who have arrived where wishes cannot enter. We shall live now in hope of a second meeting and a longer interview, which if it please God to continue to you and to Mr. King your present measure of health, you will be able I trust to contrive hereafter. You did not leave us without encouragement to expect it, and I know that you do not raise expectations but with a sincere design to fullfil them. Nothing shall be wanting on our part to accomplish, in due time, a journey to Pirtenhall. But I am a strange creature, who am less able than any man living to project any thing out of the common course with a reasonable prospect of performance. I have singularities of which I believe at present you know nothing, and which would fill you with wonder if you knew them. I will add however, in justice to myself, that they would not lower me in your good opinion, though perhaps they might tempt you to question the soundness of my upper story. Almost twenty years have I been thus unhappily circumstanced, and the remedy is in the hand of God only. That I make you this partial communication on the subject, conscious at the same time that you are well worthy to be entrusted with the whole, is merely because the recital would be too long for a letter, and painful both to me and to you. But all this may vanish in a moment, and if it please God, it shall; in the meantime, my dear Madam, remember me in your prayers and mention me at those times as one whom it has pleased God to afflict with singular visitations.

How I regret, for poor Mrs. Unwin's sake, your distance! She has no friend suitable as you to her disposition and character in all the neighborhood. Mr. King too is just the friend and companion with whom I could be happy, but such grow not in this country. Pray tell him that I remember him with much esteem and regard, and believe me, my dear Madam, with the sincerest affection — Yours entirely

Wm Cowper.

I have just left myself room to add Mrs. Unwin's true love.

JOHN JOHNSON   Saturday, 31 July 1790

Address: John Johnson Esqr. / Red-house out of Brazen Doors / Norwich
Postmark: AU/2/90
Princeton

Weston — July 31. 1790

> To you, Dearest John, at your house out o' doors
> I write from a room in the Inside of ours,
> And thus would proceed in metre and rhime
> Had I but opportunity, leisure, and time.

Yet this, though it be fine poetry, is not altogether true, for I could not proceed to answer in this jocular strain a letter containing so many sorrowful things as yours. I feel disappointed and grieved that I cannot see my Rose this summer, and am truly concern'd for the illness that threatens to deprive us also of the pleasure of your sister's company. But of her coming I do not absolutely despair; in the course of three weeks she may perhaps find herself so far restored as to be able to undertake the journey with you, and if she can, I shall rejoice truly. The journey itself and change of air may be of great service to her. My best love attends her.

Remember me affectionately to your Aunt Balls, and tell her I am very sensible of her kindness in taking upon herself so readily the trouble of furnishing us with Turkeys, and Mrs. Unwin begs to make her very best acknowledgments on the same subject.

You have by this time, I presume, answer'd Lady Hesketh's letter, if not, answer it without delay; and this injunction I give you, judging that it may not be entirely unnecessary, for though I have seen you but once, and then only for two or three days, I have found out that you are a scatter-brain and given to neglect your own interest. I made the discovery perhaps the sooner, because in this you very much resemble myself, who in the course of my life, have through mere carelessness and inattention lost many advantages. An insuperable shyness has also deprived me of many, and here again there is a resemblance between us. You will do well to guard against both, for of both I believe you have a considerable share as well as myself.

Mrs. Unwin was very much pleased with your letter to her,

401

yet I believe you must despair of an answer to it 'till she sees you. She will then answer it with all the kindness and affection which she has given you reason to expect from her. You will ascribe her silence to the true cause if you suppose it owing to head-ache and pain in her side, her two constant companions, which make writing inconvenient to her, and indeed hurtful.

We long to see you again, and are only concern'd at the short stay you propose to make with us. If time should seem to you as short at Weston as it seems to us, your visit here will be gone as a dream when one awaketh,[1] or as a watch in the night.[2] It is a life of dreams, but the pleasantest, one naturally wishes, longest.

I shall find employment for you, having made already some part of the fair copy of the Odyssey, a foul one. I am revising it for the last time, and spare nothing that I can mend. The Iliad is finish'd.

If you have Donne's poems, bring them with you, for I have not seen them many years and should like to look them over.[3] You may treat us too, if you please, with a little of your music, for I seldom hear any and delight much in it. You need not fear a rival, for we have but two fiddles in all the neighborhood, one a Gardener's, the other a Taylor's, terrible performers both. — My affectionate remembrances to all my friends whom you shall see, conclude me with Mrs. Unwin's Love to yourself — Yours, my dear John — Wm Cowper.

---

[1] Psalm 73:20.
[2] See Psalm 63:6.
[3] Mrs Balls sent a copy of Donne's poems to Weston with John Johnson (see C to Mrs Bodham, [9 Sept. 1790]) for C to read, but not keep.

JOSEPH HILL   [Sunday, 1 August] 1790[1]

Address: Joseph Hill Esqr / Great Queen Street / Lincolns Inn Fields / London
Postmarks: AU/2/90 *and* OULNEY
Cowper Johnson

My dear friend —

I feel considerably lighter in my spirit, as in fact I am in my purse, since it is in my power to satisfy the demands of Mr. Archdeacon, and devoutly wish with you that I may never have to deal with another like him. I shall this moment send him the joyful news that my money is at his service.

I feel myself in such perfect good humour that I cannot just now quarrel with any body, especially with you; but I can tell you that I am not delighted with your supposition that I might possibly be drawn to Wargrave by a desire of seeing your guests, though yourself have no such attractions for me. Were it possible that I could visit you at all, for your own sake should I come and for no other sake that can be mention'd. But you must understand that I have not slept from home these 19 years, and that I despair of being ever able to do it more. This is the effect of a cause with which I will not darken a letter that I have begun in good spirits. But if you are inclined to suspicions and surmises of duplicity, what do you think must mine be, who learn from yourself that you have been in the North and have return'd to the South, that is to say, that you have twice pass'd my door, without giving me so much as a call. Had I journey'd within little more than two miles of Wargrave and had served you so, it would have cost me much ingenuity to have exculpated myself from a charge at least of indifference, and I am curious to know which way even you will turn yourself to get rid of it.

My dear Sephus — If you and Mrs. Hill would come and spend part of your holidays with us, or the whole, either this year or the next, I would convince you in person with how much simplicity and sincerity I give you the invitation now, for I know nothing that would give me greater pleasure

---

[1] This letter bears a date stamp for 2 Aug. 1790. Since C usually wrote his letters the day before they were posted, it was probably written on 1 Aug. 1790. The letter is also dated in an unknown hand 'Augt. 1 90'.

than to see you; but whatever you do, never pass me more. With my best respects to Mrs. Hill

I am ever yours
Wm Cowper.

JOHN NEWTON   Wednesday, 11 August 1790

Princeton

Weston Augt. 11. 1790

My dear friend —

That I may not seem unreasonably tardy in answering your last kind letter, I steal a few minutes from my customary morning business (at present the translation of Mr. Van Lier's Narrative) to inform you that I received it safe from the hands of Judith Hughes[1] whom we met in the middle of Hill-field. Desirous of gaining the earliest intelligence possible concerning Mrs. Newton, we were going to call on Her, and she was on her way to us. It grieved us much that her news on that subject corresponded so little with our earnest wishes of Mrs. Newton's amendment, but if Dr. Benamer[2] still gives hope of her recovery, it is not, I trust, without substantial reason for doing so; much less can I suppose that he would do it contrary to his own persuasions, because a thousand reasons that must influence, in such a case, the conduct of a humane and sensible physician, concur to forbid it. If it shall please God to restore her, no tidings will give greater joy to us; in the mean time it is our comfort to know that in any event you will be sure of supports invaluable and that cannot fail you; though at the same time I know well that with your feelings, and especially on so affecting a subject, you will have need of the full exercise of all your faith and resignation. To a greater trial no man can be called than that of being a helpless eye-witness of the sufferings of one he loves, and loves tenderly. This I know by experience, but it is long since I had any experience of those communications from above

[1] 'Judith Hughes Widow' was buried on 20 Mar. 1810 (*OPR*, p. 476).

[2] Perhaps the Dr Benamor, a London MD, who was father of the Revd James Benamor, who had been admitted to Magdalene College, Cambridge, in 1786. He is otherwise unidentified.

which alone can enable us to acquit ourselves, on such an occasion, as we ought. But it is otherwise with you, and I rejoice that it is so.

With respect to my own initiation into the Secret of Animal Magnetism,[3] I have a thousand doubts. Twice, as you know, I have been overwhelmed with the blackest despair, and at those times every thing in which I have been at any period of my life concerned has afforded to the Enemy a handle against me. I tremble therefore almost at every step I take, lest on some future similar occasion, it should yield him opportunity and furnish him with means to torment me. Decide for me, if you can. And in the mean time present, if you please, my respectful Compliments and very best thanks to Mr. Holloway[4] for his most obliging offer. I am perhaps the only man living who would hesitate a moment whether on such easy terms he should, or should not accept it. But if he finds another like me, he will make a greater discovery than even that which he has already made of the principles of this wonderful art. For I take it for granted that He is the Gentleman whom you once mentioned to me as indebted only to his own penetration for the knowledge of it.

I shall proceed, you may depend on it, with all possible dispatch in your business. Had it fallen into my hands a few months later, I should have made quicker riddance, for before the Autumn shall be ended I hope to have done with Homer. But my first morning hour or two (now and then a letter which must be written, excepted) shall always be at your service till the whole is finished.

Commending you and Mrs. Newton with all the little power I have of that sort, to his fatherly and tender care in whom you have both believed, in which friendly office I am fervently joined by Mrs. Unwin, I remain, with our sincere love to you both and to Miss Catlett — My dear friend —

most affectionately Yours
Wm Cowper.

[3] Friedrich Anton Mesmer (1734-1815) was the principal proponent of this particular form of hypnotic therapy which claimed that a magnetic fluid or animal magnetism emanating from the operator to his patient could, while the patient was in a sleeping state, bring about cures from disease.

[4] John Holloway, younger brother of Thomas (1748-1827), the engraver, was a popular lecturer on animal magnetism.

MRS KING   Saturday, 14 August 1790

Address: Mrs. King / Pertenhall near / Kimbolton / Huntingdonshire
Postmark: AU/16/90
Princeton

Weston Underwood
Augt. 14. 1790

My dearest Madam —

My long silence may lead you to suppose the contrary, but you are never long out of my thoughts, silent as I am. I had no sooner received your commands than I began to obey them, and produced what you will find on the other side. To tell you the truth I had conceived a design to take your obliging present for a subject of verse, before your letter reached me; but what with Homer, and what with my other long job with which a friend of mine in London has furnished me, I am almost always at my wit's end for an opportunity to follow my own inclinations. Should my paper afford me room I may perhaps add another piece, such as it is, written since I wrote on the counterpane, and beg your acceptance of both not as what I wish them, for your sake, but as the best I have at present that can be contained in a letter. The verses to Mrs. Unwin you have already seen. They are those entitled the *Winter Nosegay* in my first volume.[1] She bids me present her best love to you, and is glad that the little book[2] she put into your hand has your approbation, she recommended it to you merely on account of the novelty of some of the arguments in it.

To Mrs. King
On her kind present to the Author
A patch-work counterpane
of her own making.[3]
———
The Bard, if e'er he feel at all,
Must sure be quicken'd by a call
Both on his heart and head
To pay with tuneful thanks the care
And kindness of a Lady fair
Who deigns to dress his bed.
———

[1] See C to Mrs King, 12 Mar. 1790.   [2] Unidentified.
[3] First published in *Hayley*.

406

14 August 1790

A Bed like this, in antient time,
On Ida's barren top sublime
   (As Homer's Epic shows)
Composed of sweetest vernal flow'rs,
Without the aid of sun or show'rs
   For Jove and Juno rose.

Less beautiful, however gay,
Is that which in the scorching day
   Receives the weary swain
Who, laying his long scythe aside,
Sleeps on some bank with daisies pied
   'Till roused to toil again.

What labours of the loom I see!
Looms numberless have groan'd for me!
   Should ev'ry maiden come
To scramble for the patch that bears
The impress of the robe she wears,
   The Bell would toll for some.

And Oh, what havoc would ensue!
This bright display of evr'y hue
   All in a moment fled!
As if a storm should strip the bow'rs
Of all their tendrils, leaves and flow'rs —
   Each pocketting a shred.

Thanks then to ev'ry gentle Fair
Who will not come to pick me bare
   As Bird of borrow'd feather,
And thanks to One above them all
The gentle Fair of Pertenhall
   Who put the whole together.

14 August 1790

On a mischievous Bull which the Owner of him sold at the
Author's instance.[4]

Go — Thou art all unfit to share
    The pleasures of this place
With such as its old tenants are,
    Creatures of gentler race.

The Squirrel here his hoard provides
    Aware of wint'ry storms,
And wood-peckers explore the sides
    Of rugged oaks for worms.

The Sheep here smooths the knotted Thorn
    With friction of her fleece,
And here I wander Eve and Morn,
    Like Her, a friend to peace.

Ah — I could pity thee exiled
    From this secure retreat —
I would not lose it to be stiled
    The happiest of the Great.

But thou canst taste no calm delight.
    Thy pleasure is to show
Thy magnanimity in fight,
    Thy prowess — therefore Go —

I care not whether East or North
    So I no more may find thee,
The angry Muse thus sings thee forth,
    And claps the gate behind thee.

My verses, my Dear Madam, have hardly left me room to
tell you how much, having once seen you, we long to see you
again. Another summer — and perhaps we shall meet once
more. Oh I love summer for a thousand reasons, but especially
because it now and then brings me and a friend together,
whom I should never see but for that blessed season. I wish

[4] First published in *Poems* (1808).

408

for summer to bring us together, and then, for winter to keep us so. With my very best respects to my dear old Schoolfellow I remain, my Dearest Madam

Ever yours —
Wm Cowper.

Catharina shall be copied and sent, by the first opportunity.[5]

JOSEPH HILL   Saturday, 4 September 1790

Cowper Johnson

Weston Underwood
Septbr. 4. 1790

My dear friend —

Felicitate me on an event in which I know you have interested yourself much and long. My Homer is finished, goes to London on Wednesday and in few days will be in the Press. It will not be long before I shall make my bargain with Johnson for the Copy, and then, once in my life I shall have money with which to purchase Stock instead of selling it. Shall even purchase more than I have sold out these many years. Necessities, that have no other cure oblige me at present to apply to you for the Sale of another Hundred, and that as soon as possible. You will oblige me much if you will issue your directions to your Agents in town accordingly. The Letter of Attorney that I executed lately in the Archdeacon's business will I presume empower them to obey you.

I had a Letter the other day from Lady Hesketh full of the beauties of Wargrove and of the hospitable and kind reception she found there. May you and Mrs. Hill have long life and long health to enjoy them! The week after next we expect to see my Cousin at Weston; she comes to spend the Autumn with us and I hope a good part of the Winter.

— If your sisters[1] are with you I beg you will present my affectionate remembrances to them, and tell them I have a

---

[5] The following MS fragment was included by Maggs Brothers with the holograph of this letter: 'Mrs. Unwin unites with me in best Compliments to yourself and Mr. King, and I am, my Dear Madam, very affectionately Yrs., Wm Cowper.'

---

[1] Frances and Theodosia. See List of Correspondents, Volume II.

409

sincere pleasure in thinking that my labour of five years will soon be spread before them.

> With my best Compliments to Mrs. Hill
> I remain my dear friend
> Truly Yours   Wm Cowper.

JOSEPH JOHNSON   Tuesday, 7 September 1790

Hayley, ii. 274

Sept. 7, 1790

It grieves me, that after all, I am obliged to go into public without the whole advantage of Mr. Fuseli's judicious strictures. My only consolation is, that I have not forfeited them by my own impatience. Five years are no small portion of a man's life, especially at the latter end of it, and in those five years, being a man of almost no engagements, I have done more in the way of hard work, than most could have done in twice the number. I beg you to present my compliments to Mr. Fuseli, with many and sincere thanks for the services, that his own more important occupations would allow him to render me.

JOHN BACON   Tuesday, 7 September 1790

Address: John Bacon Esqre / Portland Street. / London.
The Earl Waldegrave

Weston Underwood
Sepbr. 7. 1790.

Dear Sir

I have found no need to make a new Inscription, your own being in respect to the matter of it unimproveable. The alterations that I have made in the expression I have made merely on this principle, that the merit of all monumental writing consists in a strict adherence to classical neatness of phrase and connection, that the members of which the whole consists may slide handsomely into each other, and that there may not be one syllable redundant.

You will find my labours on the other side, for which I can say nothing but that I have done my best, which *best* is always most readily at your service.

I am with Mrs. Unwin's respects

Yours Dear Sir
very affectionately
Wm Cowper.

Sacred to the Memory of
John Howard[1]
Who
Devoted life and fortune to the service of his fellow-creatures.
Author of many merciful regulations
In the Gaols of his own native England
He compassed Europe
That he might communicate them
To other countries also.
Prompted forth a second time
By the desire and hope
Of alleviating that dreadful calamity the plague
He terminated his course of Benevolence
At this place,
Jan. 9. 1790. Aged 58.
He united in his character
Many virtues
Each worthy of a memorial
All springing from the Faith and animated by the Charity
Of a Christian.
He refused a Statue at home
But has here a Monument
That posterity may share with us the benefit of his example.

(over).[2]

---

[1] Howard was born on 2 Sept. 1726; he died on 20 Jan. 1790. C (and Bacon) had Howard's age and death wrong. Bacon designed a monument to him for Kherson in the Crimea where Howard died, but we have not found evidence that he executed any sculpture for this tomb, which has since become delapidated. A monumental statue to Howard by Bacon was installed at St. Paul's in 1795 but the inscription used was not C's. See *Russell*, p. 213.

[2] C wrote the text of this letter on the back of the epitaph.

WILLIAM BULL   Wednesday, 8 September 1790

Formerly Miss C. M. Bull

Weston
Sepbr. 8. 1790.

My dear friend —

We rejoice that though unhorsed and rather horseless you come safe home again, and shall be happy to hear that you are mounted again, because our having the pleasure to see you here depends on it.

Mrs. Unwin who is never well, is yet not worse than when you saw her last. As to myself, I am particularly frisky, having this very day sent all Homer to London.

Our joint best love attends yourself and family and I am most truly yours

Wm Cowper.

MRS BODHAM   [Thursday, 9 September 1790] [1]

Address: Mrs. Bodham / South Green / Mattishall / Norfolk
Postmarks: SE/10/90 *and* OULNEY
Princeton

My dear Cousin,

I am truly sorry to be forced after all to resign the hope of seeing you and Mr. Bodham at Weston this year; the next may possibly be more propitious and I heartily wish it may. Poor Catharine's unseasonable indisposition has also cost us a disappointment which we much regret, and were it not that Johnny has made shift to reach us, we should think ourselves completely unfortunate. But Him we have, and Him we will hold as long as we can, so expect not very soon to see him in Norfolk. He is so harmless, cheerful, gentle and good-temper'd, and I am so entirely at my ease with him, that I cannot surrender him without a *needs must* even to those who have a superior claim upon him. [He left us yesterday morning, and whither do you think he is gone, and on what errand?

---

[1] The top portion of the first page of this letter and the signature have been cut off; the date and those portions in square brackets are supplied from *Wright*, iii. 482–3.

412

Gone, as sure as you] are alive to London, and to convey my Homer to the Bookseller's. But he will return the day after to-morrow, and I mean to part with him no more 'till necessity shall force us asunder. Suspect me not, my Cousin, of being such a monster as to have imposed this task myself on your kind nephew, or even to have thought of doing it. It happened that one day, as we chatted by the fire-side, I expressed a wish that I could hear of some trusty body going to London, to whose care I might consign my voluminous labours, the work of five years. For I purpose never to visit that city again myself, and should have been uneasy to have left such a charge, of so much importance to me, altogether to the care of a stage-coachman. Johnny had no sooner heard my wish, than offering himself to the service, he fulfilled it; and his offer was made in such terms and accompanied with a countenance and manner expressive of so much alacrity, that unreasonable as I thought it at first to give him so much trouble, I soon found that I should mortify him by a refusal. He is gone therefore with a Box full of poetry, of which I think nobody will plunder him. He has only to tell what it is, and there is no commodity I think that a free-booter would covet less. — He has shown me the new edition of his poem on the Beauties of Audley End, which as he wrote it at the Red-House it is possible you may not have seen.[2] — I was forced to object to the copy that he showed me when he was here in the winter on account of the wildness of his notes, and he has now brought me another wilder by half than the first. But this is a good fault. An imagination too lively will be sober'd by time, but for a dull one there is no remedy. I shall make him write a third copy of it while he is here, and if it be possible to keep him from his vagaries I will do it.

If you see Mrs. Balls I beg that you will give my best love to her with many thanks for the sight of the Dean's poems with which she has favour'd me.

We expect Lady Hesketh soon after the twentieth of this month, and she will stay with us we hope chief part of the winter. I rejoice in this on all accounts, and particularly because Johnny has begun already to be a favorite with her, and hers is a connexion that may be of use to him.

[2] See n.3, C to Lady Hesketh, 23 Jan. 1790.

Mrs. Unwin as well as myself regrets much your not coming, and desires to be affectionately mentioned to you.

My Dearest Cousin — with my best respects to Mr. Bodham, I am most truly Yours

[Wm Cowper]

SAMUEL ROSE   Monday, 13 September 1790

Address: Samuel Rose Esqe / Percy Street / Rathbone Place / London.
Postmarks: SE/14/90 *and* OULNEY
Historical Society of Pennsylvania

The Lodge
Sepbr. 13. 1790

My dear Sir

Your letter was particularly welcome, not only because it came after a long silence, but because it brought me good news, news of your marriage and consequently I trust of your happiness. May that happiness be durable as your lives, and may you be the *Felices ter et amplius*[1] of whom Horace sings so sweetly! This is my sincere wish, and though expressed in prose, shall serve as your Epithalamium. You comfort me when you say that your marriage will not deprive me of the sight of you hereafter. If you do not wish that I should regret your union, you must make that assurance good as often as you have opportunity.

After perpetual versification during five years I find myself at last a vacant man and reduced to read for my amusement. My Homer is gone to the Press, and you will imagine that I feel a void in consequence. The proofs however will be coming soon, and I shall avail myself with all my force of this last opportunity to make my work as perfect as I wish it. I shall not therefore be long-time destitute of employment, but shall have sufficient to keep me occupied all winter and part of the ensuing Spring, for Johnson purposes to publish either in March, April or May. — My very Preface is finished. It did not cost me much trouble being neither long nor learned. An appearance of learning I could easily have given to it by the help of the Books with which you and another friend or two

[1] *Odes*, I. xiii. 17: 'Three times lucky and more'.

414

have supplied me, but I hate imposition and should be sorry to owe a grain of reputation to any such practise. I have spoken my mind, as freely as decency would permit, on the subject of Pope's version, allowing him at the same time all the merit to which I think him entitled.[2] I have given my reasons for translating in Blank verse,[3] and hold some discourse on the composition or mechanism of it, chiefly with a view to obviate the prejudices of some people against it. I expatiate a little on the manner in which I think Homer ought to be rendered and in which I have endeavoured to render him myself, and anticipate two or three cavils to which I foresee that I shall be liable from the ignorant and uncandid, in order, if possible, to prevent them.[4] These are the chief heads of my preface, and the whole consists of about 12 pages.

[2] 'I number myself among the warmest admirers of Mr. Pope as an original writer, and I allow him all the merit he can justly claim as the translator of this chief of poets. He has given us the *Tale of Troy divine* in smooth verse, generally in correct and elegant language, and in diction often highly poetical. But his deviations are so many, occasioned chiefly by the cause already mentioned, that, much as he has done, and valuable as his work is on some accounts, it was yet in the humble province of a translator that I thought it possible even for me to follow him with some advantage.

That he has sometimes altogether suppressed the sense of his author, and has not seldom intermingled his own ideas with it, is a remark which, on this occasion, nothing but necessity should have extorted from me. But we differ sometimes so widely in our matter, that unless this remark, invidious as it seems, be premised, I know not how to obviate a suspicion, on the one hand, of careless oversight, or of facetious embellishment on the other. On this head, therefore, the English reader is to be admonished, that the matter found in me, whether he like it or not, is found also in Homer, and that the matter not found in me, how much soever he may admire it, is found only in Mr. Pope. I have omitted nothing; I have invented nothing.' Preface, pp. vi–viii.

[3] 'Whether a translation of Homer may be best executed in blank verse or in rhime, is a question in the decision of which no man can find difficulty, who has ever duly considered what translation ought to be, or who is in any degree practically acquainted with those very different kinds of versification . . . No human ingenuity can be equal to the task of closing every couplet with sounds homotonous, expressing at the same time the full sense, and only the full sense of his original . . . Hence it has happened, that although the public have long been in possession of an English Homer by a poet whose writings have done immortal honour to his country, the demand of a new one, and especially in blank verse, has been repeatedly and loudly made by some of the best judges and ablest writers of the present day.' Preface, p. v.

[4] 'To those, therefore, who shall be inclined to tell me hereafter that my diction is often plain and unelevated, I reply beforehand that I know it — that it would be absurd were it otherwise, and that Homer himself stands in the same

It is possible that when I come to treat with Johnson about the copy I may want somebody to negotiate for me, and knowing none so intelligent as yourself in Books, or so well qualified to estimate their just value, shall beg leave to resort to and to rely on you as my negotiator. But I will not trouble you unless I should see occasion.

We are in your debt for two Cheeses. Let us know to what amount and Lady H—— shall pay you when you see her. We expect her here in about a fortnight. My Cousin Johnson was the bearer of my MSS to London. He went up on purpose and returns to-morrow. Mrs. Unwin's affectionate felicitations added to my own conclude me, my dear friend Sincerely yours

Wm Cowper.

Beau is well and heartily wishes *you* well.
P.S. The trees of a Colonnade will solve my riddle.[5]

CLOTWORTHY ROWLEY Thursday, 16 September 1790

Southey, vi. 330–1

Weston Underwood, Sept. 16, 1790.

My dear Rowley,

I have given you time to return to Dublin and to settle yourself there; and now perhaps you will find yourself at leisure to receive my thanks for the readiness with which you have resumed your enlisting labours, disagreeable in themselves, and which nothing but your friendship for him in whose service they are performed, could render supportable. You will not think it sufficient, I trust, when you shall have completed your list, to send the money only, but will transmit the names of the subscribers also. Pardon a hint which could not possibly be wanted, except by an Hibernian, or by one who has lived long in Ireland.

You are happy who, I presume, have not to deal with

predicament . . . By others I expect to be told that my numbers, though here and there tolerably smooth, are not always such, but have, now and then, an ugly hitch in their gait, ungraceful in itself, and inconvenient to the reader. To this charge also I plead guilty, but beg leave in alleviation of judgment to add, that my limping lines are not numerous, compared with those that limp not.' Preface, p. x.
[5] This is the answer to the riddle in C's letter to Rose of 8 June 1790.

booksellers and printers, the most dilatory of mankind, and who seem to exist only to torment and distract us miserable authors. My copy has been some weeks in Town, yet have I but this moment received the second proof-sheet. If you are possessed of any secret that will make a snail gallop — at least urge him to a trot, communicate it without delay, that I may accelerate with it the movements of these tedious vermin.

I find in my list the name of N. Westcomb, Esq.[1] This, I presume, is he whom we were formerly wont to call Cousin Westcomb. I much respect him, and feel the obligation he has conferred on me, very sensibly, and if you have any correspondence with him, which, considering your intimacy in old times, seems very probable, I shall be obliged to you if you will tell him so. I cannot help considering my subscription as a sort of test of their constancy who formerly professed a kindness for me. They in whom a spark of that kindness survives will hardly fail to discover it on such an occasion, and seeing the affair in this light, I feel myself a little grieved and hurt that some names which old friendship gave me a right to expect, are not to be found in my catalogue. The Lord Chancellor, however, has done handsomely, having twice honoured me with his name, once by solicitation, and in the second instance voluntarily. He is, like yourself, a man whose attachments are made of stuff that is proof against time and absence.

I revere your paternal character and am delighted with the anxiety you express about your children's welfare,[2] yet at the same time am a little apprehensive lest your solicitudes on that subject should so far exceed their proper limits as to make you at times unhappy. Remember, my friend, that He who gave them to you is able by his providence to preserve them also. The great success of the Rowleys at the last election[3] is a subject of congratulation, for which I

---

[1] Probably Nicholas Westcomb who matriculated at Trinity Hall, Cambridge, in 1750 and who may have been admitted to the Inner Temple in 1745. He subscribed for a fine copy.

[2] Rowley's children: William (see n.5, C to Rowley, 31 Aug. [1788]); Sir Josias (d. 1842), 1st and last Baronet Rowley; Samuel (b. 1774), Rear-Admiral of the White; the Revd John, Prebend of Christ Church, Dublin; and Mary.

[3] The Rowleys elected for the parliament in Ireland from 2 July 1790 until 11 July 1797 were five in number: Clotworthy Rowley for Downpatrick; his son William for Kinsdale; the Hon. Hercules Rowley for Antrim; the Right Hon.

ought to have left myself more room. I can now only say that I sincerely rejoice in it, and that I am most truly yours,

W. Cowper.

Will not your trip to Bath afford you an opportunity to take a peep at Weston? Some of your trips to England I hope will do it, for I should greatly rejoice to see you.

JOSEPH HILL   Friday, 17 September 1790

Cowper Johnson

Weston Sepbr. 17. 1790.

My dear friend —
Many thanks for your speedy answer to my importunate request. I enclose a receipt written on the Stamp which I presume you sent for that purpose.

I received last night a copy of my Subscribers' names from Johnson, in which I see how much I have been indebted to yours and to Mrs. Hill's solicitations. Accept my best thanks, so justly due to you both. It is an illustrious catalogue in respect of rank and title, but methinks I should have liked it as well had it been more numerous. The sum subscribed however will defray, or go near to defray the expence of printing, which is as much as in these unsubscribing days I had any reason to promise myself. I devoutly second your droll wish that the Booksellers may contend about me, the more the better, seven times seven if they please, and let them fight with the fury of Achilles!

> 'Till ev'ry rubric-post[1] be crimson'd o'er
> With blood of Booksellers in battle shed
> For me, and not a periwig untorn.

With my best love to your Sisters and my affectionate respects to Mrs. Hill I remain, my dear friend —

Most truly yours
Wm Cowper.

Hercules Langford Rowley (d. 1794) for Meath; and the Hon. Hercules Rowley, of Langford Lodge, for Langford.

---

[1] 'Inscribed with the titles of books' (*OED*).

JOSEPH HILL   Thursday, 30 September 1790

Address: Joseph Hill Esqr. / Wargrove near / Twyford / Berks
Postmarks: OC/1/90 *and* OULNEY
Cowper Johnson

Weston Underwood   Sepbr. 30. 1790.
Received of Joseph Hill Esqre. the Sum of Seventeen pounds twelve Shillings and Six-pence by Draft on Child and Co. by Me   Wm Cowper.

£17.12.6

My dear friend —
Many thanks for the remittance above specified, and for the Treatise on Planting[1] which my Cousin delivered to me this morning as a gift from you. An acceptable one as well because you are the Donor as for the sake of the subject; not that I plant much myself, for an obvious reason; but because I am every thing in theory that I have an opportunity to be and shall therefore find pleasure in studying it, and because I have a good neighbour in Mr. Throckmorton who delights much both in his Garden and Plantations, and will consequently be glad of the information he may collect from it.

My Cousin arrived yesterday Evening in perfect health and Spirits. Her best Compliments attend yourself and Mrs. Hill, and she bids me tell you beside how sorry she was that she could not possibly accept your kind invitation. I began to be out of patience that she stayed so long at Lady Fane's,[2] for twice she postponed her coming, but her arrival at last has made amends for all.

The world rings with the gaieties of your neighbourhood, to which ours is a perfect contrast. Here, we have no company but each other's, and all the little noise we hear is made by ourselves.

With my best respects to Mrs. Hill,
I remain my Dear Friend
most truly yours

Thursday   Wm Cowper.

[1] William Marshall's *Planting and Ornamental Gardening* (1785), which is 'inscribed "The gift of Joseph Hill Esqr. of Wargrove Berkshire." At the end of the book is a pencil sketch of the ground plan of a house with instructions in Cowper's hand': *Keynes*, 60.
[2] Probably the widow of Charles Fane, 2nd Viscount Fane (d. 1766), of

MRS BODHAM   Friday, 1 October 1790

Address: Mrs. Bodham / South Green / Mattishall / Norfolk
Postmarks: OC/2/90 *and* OULNEY
Princeton

Weston Underwood
Octbr. 1. 1790.

My dear Cousin —
    There will be some danger that I shall tell you what you
know already, for I am not sure that Johnny has not written
you an account beforehand of what my letter is likely to
inform you of. He is in bed at present and therefore I cannot
ask him. I told you in my last that he was gone to London
charged with the copy of my Homer for his namesake the
Bookseller. I expected his return in a day or two, but having
slept one night in town he slipp'd away into Essex and did
not return hither till he had been three weeks absent. His
reason for this sudden flight was a good one. Having embark'd
in the arduous enterprize of describing Audley End with all its
beauties in verse, he judged it necessary to revisit that place
that he might furnish himself with a distinct idea of it before
he began, or rather before he enter'd a third time on his great
labour. Labour enough he found at his arrival there, and
such as would have exhausted the patience and worn out
the temper of any other man living, having toiled from early
morning 'till Evening day and day continually in minuting
down a most circumstantial account of all the Contents of a
Pleasure-Ground six miles in circumference and of all the
prospects from it. Thus he proceeded, breakfasting late and
Dining almost at Supper-time, 'till he had filled two volumes
with materials for his future poem, and thus furnished he
came back to Weston. And what thinkest thou my Dear
Cousin has been the upshot of all this preparation? As soon
as I had seen the work and read a part of it, and expressed
my unfeigned amazement at the size of this Prose-description
of what he had seen, despairing that he would ever be able at
his early age to manage successfully in verse a subject so

Basildon, near Reading. Susanna (1706–92), the daughter of John Marriott and
the widow of Sir William Juxon, married Fane on 7 June 1749. 'Viscountess
Fane' subscribed for a common copy of the Homer.

unwieldy, I advised him by all means to postpone the versification of it, till time and experience shall have improved his powers and render'd him more equal to the work, and thus the matter rests.

When you see Mrs. Balls give my love to her and tell her that we have given all necessary cautions to our Waggoner concerning the Turkeys and have every reason to believe that he will bring them safely, being accustomed to the conveyance of such passengers and a man much in our interest. I forget whether I thank'd her in my last for a sight of Dr. Donne's poems, if not, you can do it for me now.[1]

Lady Hesketh arrived here the day before yesterday to take up her abode with us for some months. We are a *partie quarrée*[2] exactly suited to each other and consequently very comfortable together.

With your Nephew's best love[3] and Mrs. Unwin's affectionate Compliments I join my own to Mr. Bodham and remain my Dear Coz —

> Truly and much Yours
> Wm Cowper.

JOSEPH JOHNSON   Sunday, 3 October 1790

Hayley, ii. 275.

> Weston, Oct. 3, 1790.

Mr. Newton having again requested, that the preface, which he wrote for my first volume may be prefixed to it, I am desirous to gratify him in a particular, that so emphatically

---

[1] See C to John Johnson, 31 July 1790.   [2] 'A party of four.'

[3] John Johnson has added his own letter to this one; it reads in part: 'My dear Aunt — I will write to you in a few days — indeed I am quite ashamed that I have never written to you before — but I will be very good and write you a *long* letter — Our dear Cousin looks Charmingly well (thank God) & his spirits are quite alive — Every day we expect to hear from Johnson the Bookseller — I heartily pray that he may send Mr. Cowper some proof-sheets of his great work — as he is quite unemployed.

How is dear Cath? give my kindest Love to her. Only think of my having given up Audley End! My Cousin says it would be impossible for me to execute a poem of such length, and so full of circumstantial matter as Lord & Lady H[oward] require, at present — Congratulate me, my dear Aunt & Uncle, on the happy occasion that brought me to Weston. Among numberless other comforts that I

bespeaks his friendship for me; and should my books see another edition, shall be obliged to you if you will add it accordingly.[1]

MRS KING   Tuesday, 5 October 1790

Address: Mrs. King / Perten-Hall / Kimbolton / Huntingdonshire.
Postmarks: OC/6/90 *and* OULNEY
Princeton

Weston Underwood
Octbr. 5. 1790.

My dear Madam —
    I am truly concerned that you have so good an excuse for your silence. Were it proposed to my choice whether you should omit to write through illness or indifference to me, I should be selfish enough perhaps to find decision difficult for a few moments, but have such an opinion at the same time of my affection for you, as to be verily persuaded that I should at last make a right option, and wish you rather to forget me than to be afflicted. But there is One, wiser and more your friend than I can possibly be, who appoints all your sufferings, and who by a power altogether his own, is able to make them good for you.
    I wish heartily that my verses had been more worthy of the counterpane their subject. The gratitude I felt when you brought it and gave it to me might have inspired better, but a head full of Homer I find by sad experience is good for little else. Lady Hesketh, who is here, has seen your gift and pronounced it the most beautiful and best executed of the kind she ever saw.
    I have lately received from my Bookseller a copy of my Subscribers' names, and do not find among them the name of Mr. Professor Martyn. I mention it because you informed me

have obtained by coming hither I reckon it an happy circumstance that my Cousin's experience in poetical matters has pointed out to me the difficulties I was going to encounter by undertaking a subject too weighty for me.'
_____

[1] 'Now that Cowper's literary reputation was established, Johnson could waive his former objections [to Newton's Preface]; he reprinted the preface for the fifth edition of 1793, which he published for Cowper's benefit, and in this and in all subsequent editions of the *Poems* published by him it became an integral part of all copies.' *Russell*, p. 43.

some time since of his kind intentions to number himself among my encouragers on this occasion, and because I am unwilling to lose, for want of speaking in time, the honour that His name will do me. It is possible too that he may have subscribed, and that his non-appearance may be owing merely to Johnson's having forgot to enter him. Perhaps you will have an opportunity to ascertain the matter. The catalogue will be printed soon and published in the Analytical Review, as the last and most effectual way of advertizing my Translation, and the name of the Gentleman in question will be particularly serviceable to me in this first edition of it.[1]

My whole work is in the Bookseller's hands and ought by this time to be in the Press. The next Spring is the time appointed for the publication. It is a genial season, when people who are ever good-temper'd at all, are sure to be so, a circumstance well-worthy of an Author's attention, especially of mine, who am just going to give a thump on the outside of the Critics' hive that will probably alarm them all.

Mrs. Unwin I think is, on the whole, rather improved in her health since we had the pleasure of your short visit — I should say, the pleasure of your visit and the pain of its shortness. Our joint best Compliments attend yourself and Mr. King, and I am

My dearest Madam
most truly Yours
Wm Cowper.

JOHN NEWTON   Friday, 15 October 1790

Barham Johnson (*copy*)

October 15. 1790.

We were surprised and grieved at Mrs. Scott's sudden departure;[1] grieved, you may suppose, not for *her*, but for *him*, whose loss, except that in God he has an all-sufficient

[1] See n.2, C to Mrs King, 28 Aug. 1788 and n.3, C to Mrs King, 12 Mar. 1789. .

[1] *GM* lx, pt. 2 (Sept. 1790), 864 records Mrs Scott's death under 8 Sept. . 'In Chapel-street, after a short illness, Mrs. Scott, wife of the Rev. Mr. S. morning-preacher at the Lock Chapel.'

good, is irreparable. The day of separation, between those who have loved long and well, is an awful day, inasmuch as it calls the Christian's faith and submission to the severest trial. Yet I account those happy, who, if they are severely tried, shall yet be supported, and be carried safely through. What would become of me on a similar occasion! I have one comfort and only one; bereft of that, I should have nothing left to lean on: for my spiritual props have long since been struck from under me.

I have no objection at all to being known as the Translator of Van Lier's letters, when they shall be published; rather, I am ambitious of it as an honour. It will serve to prove that if I have spent much time to little purpose in the translation of Homer, some small portion of my time has, however, been well disposed of.

The honour of your preface prefixed to my Poems will be on my side; for surely to be known as the friend of a much favoured Minister of God's word, is a more illustrious distinction in reality than to have the friendship of any poet in the world to boast of.

We sympathise truly with you under all your tender concern for Mrs. Newton, and with her in all her sufferings from such various and discordant maladies. Alas! what a difference have 23 years made in us and in our condition — for just so long it is since Mrs. Unwin and I came into Buckinghamshire. Yesterday was the anniversary of that memorable æra. Farewell.

JOHN NEWTON   Tuesday, 26 October 1790

Princeton

                                   Weston October 26. 1790
My dear friend —

We should have been happy to have received from you a more favorable account of Mrs. Newton's health. Yours is indeed a post of observation, and of observation the most interesting. It is well that you are enabled to bear the stress and intenseness of it without prejudice to your own health or impediment to your ministry.

The last time I wrote to Johnson I made known to him your wishes to have your Preface printed and affixt as soon as an opportunity shall offer, expressing at the same time my own desires to have it done. Whether I shall have any answer to my proposal is a matter of much uncertainty, for he is always either too idle or too busy, I know not which, to write to me. Should you happen to pass his way, perhaps it would not be amiss to speak to him on the subject, for it is easier to carry a point by six words spoken than by writing as many sheets about it. I have asked him hither when my Cousin Johnson shall leave us, which will be in about a fortnight, and should he come, will enforce the measure myself.

A yellow shower of leaves is falling continually from all the trees in the country. A few moments only seem to have pass'd since they were buds, and in few moments more they will have disappeared. It is one advantage of a rural situation that it affords many hints of the rapidity with which life flies, that do not occur in towns and cities. It is impossible to a man conversant with such scenes as surround me, not to advert daily to the shortness of his existence here, admonished of it as he must be by ten thousand objects. There was a time when I could contemplate my present state and consider myself as a thing of a day with pleasure, when I number'd the seasons as they pass'd in swift rotation, as a school-boy numbers the days that interpose between the next vacation, when he shall see his parents and enjoy his home again. But to make so just an estimate of life like this is no longer in my power. The consideration of my short continuance here, which was once grateful to me, now fills me with regret. I would live and live always, and am become such another wretch as Mecænas was, who wish'd for long long life, he cared not at what expence of sufferings.[1] The only consolation left me on this subject is that the voice of the Almighty can in one moment cure me of this mental infirmity. That he can, I know by experience, and there are reasons for which I ought to believe that he will. But from hope to despair is a transition that I have made so often, that I can only consider the hope that may come, and that sometimes

---

[1] See Seneca (the Younger), *Epistles*, ci. 10–13.

I believe will, as a short prelude of joy to a miserable conclusion of sorrow that shall never end. Thus are my brightest prospects clouded, and thus to me is Hope itself become like a wither'd flower that has lost both its hue and its fragrance.

I ought not to have written in this dismal strain to you in your present trying situation, nor did I intend it. You have more need to be cheered than to be sadden'd, but a dearth of other themes constrained me to chuse myself for a subject, and of myself I can write no otherwise.

Adieu, my dear friend — we are well, and notwithstanding all that I have said, I am myself as cheerful as usual. Lady Hesketh is here, and in her company even I, except now and then for a moment, forget my sorrows.

With Mrs. U.'s best love to yourself and Mrs. N.

I remain sincerely Yours
Wm Cowper

JOSEPH JOHNSON   Saturday, 30 October 1790

Hayley, ii. 276

I beg that you will not suffer your reverence either for Homer, or his Translator to check your continual examinations. I never knew with certainty, till now, that the marginal strictures I found in the Task-proofs were yours. The justness of them, and the benefit I derived from them, are fresh in my memory, and I doubt not that their utility will be the same in the present instance.

Weston, Oct. 30, 1790.

MRS THROCKMORTON   Sunday, 31 October 1790

Address: Mrs. Throckmorton / Buckenham house / near Brandon / Norfolk
Postmarks: NO/1/90 *and* OULNEY
Sir Robert Throckmorton

Weston. Octr. 31. 1790

My dear Mrs. Frog —
I am not without expectations (too flattering perhaps) that I may receive a line from you to-day, but am obliged to write

before it can arrive, that I may catch the opportunity of sending this to the post.

I saw Tom[1] yesterday; have seen him indeed twice or thrice in the course of the week, but our other interviews were casual; yesterday I called on purpose to pay my respects to him. The little man is well, save and except (if it deserves to be mentioned) a slight cold that affects him only at the nose, and which he owes to the sudden change of our weather from sultry to very severe. *Tit*[2] I have not seen, but by the report of Mrs. Nunnerly[3] (if that be her name) and by the Doctor's report also, she is in perfect health. — You will be so good as not to make yourself uneasy in the smallest degree about Tom, suspecting that I represent the matter more favourably than truly, for I have told you all the worst.

Mrs. Nunnerly desired me to tell you that she has not heard from Mrs. Giffard, which is the reason *you* have not heard from *her*.

Homer, at length, goes on merrily. The difficulty of procuring paper that pleased him, was the cause of Johnson's tardiness which I mention'd in my last. Henceforth, he promises me six sheets every week, at which I rejoice for two reasons: First, because at that rate of proceeding we shall be ready for publication at the time appointed, and secondly, because in the interval I shall never want employment. The List of subscribers' names that I sent to the Hall a short time before you left it, was imperfect, the copyist having overlooked in his haste to obey my commands, no fewer than Forty and upward. I flatter myself therefore that with such additions as will not fail to be made before the subscription closes, the names will amount to full three hundred, which will pay the whole expence of printing. Seven hundred copies will be the number of the first impression.

A pretty subject this, to entertain a fair Lady withal! Rue the day that gave you a poet for a correspondent. Every man

---

[1] Thomas William Giffard (1789–1861), 24th of Chillington, the son of Mrs Throckmorton's half-brother, Thomas Giffard, 23rd of Chillington.

[2] Probably Charlotte Giffard. See n.5, C to Lady Hesketh, 19 Apr. 1790.

[3] Probably a servant in the Giffard household. This is C's mishearing or imitation of Tom's mispronunciation of 'Nanny Morley' (see C to Mrs Throckmorton, 19 Feb. 1791).

writes most of that which he has most at heart, and Authors, of course, about themselves and their labours.

Mrs. Unwin is as well as usual. My female and male Cousin are in perfect health, and all unite with me in affectionate remembrances to our dear friends in Norfolk. Adieu —

Ever yours
Toot.[4]

WILLIAM BULL   Monday, 1 November 1790

Formerly Miss C. M. Bull

My dear Mr. Bull

I thank you much for the communication of the inclosed,[1] which I read with a tender remembrance of the days that are past, and felt much sympathy with the writer of it. If you have not already answer'd it, present our kindest love to him when you do.

I must trouble you to beg Mr. Greatheed in Lady Hesketh's name, to return, if he has done with it, the Book[2] she lent him, sending it either to Olney or Weston as may be most convenient to him. Griggs the butcher[3] will take the charge of it.

Our best Compliments attend yourself, Mrs. Bull, and your son. Let us see you when the weather will permit. Yours ever

Wm Cowper.

Weston. Nove. 1. 1790

---

[4] Tom's name for C. See C to Mrs Throckmorton, 2 Feb. 1791.

---

[1] Bull must have informed C that John Thornton, who died on 7 Nov., was gravely ill, and he perhaps enclosed a note from Lady Balgonie (see C to Henry Thornton, 16 Nov.).

[2] Unidentified.

[3] Probably Joseph Griggs, butcher, who was christened on 22 Apr. 1762, aged 21 years (*OPR*, p. 338).

HENRY THORNTON   Tuesday, 16 November 1790

Scottish Record Office

Weston Underwood
Nove. 16. 1790

Dear Sir —

Lady Balgonie[1] having done me the honour to express a wish, in a letter of hers to Mr. Bull, that I would write something in remembrance of your late excellent father, I have endeavour'd to express my sense of that honour by doing it as soon and as well as a violent cold and my necessary attention to my Homer, now in the Press, would permit.

Should the Lines[2] be favour'd with your approbation, you will oblige me by forwarding them to her Ladyship, to whom I beg you to present my most respectful Compliments, and to believe me, Dear Sir, with much esteem

Yours —
Wm Cowper.

Mrs. Unwin sends best Compliments.

MRS BODHAM   Sunday, 21 November 1790

Address: Mrs. Bodham / South Green / Mattishall / Norfolk
Postmarks: NO/22/90 *and* OULNEY
Princeton

Weston Underwood
Nov. 21. 1790

My dear Coz —

I should more speedily have answer'd your last kind letter, but for the hindrance of a violent cold, which seized me in the beginning of the month and still holds me fast. It is with me a sort of anniversary disorder, which at the first approach of winter I have generally to undergo.

Our kindness to your nephew is no more than he must entitle himself to wherever he goes. His amiable disposition and manners will never fail to secure him a warm place in the affections of all who know him. The advice I gave respecting

---

[1] See n.1, C to Newton, 17 Mar. 1788.
[2] They were first published in 1803 in *Hayley*.

his poem on Audley end was dictated by my love of him and a sincere desire of his success. It is one thing to write what may please our friends, who, because they are such, are apt to be a little biass'd in our favour, and another to write what may please every body, because they who have no connexion with or even knowledge of the author, will be sure to find fault if they can. My advice however, salutary and necessary as it seemed to me, was such as I dare not have given to a poet of less diffidence than He. Poets are to a proverb irritable, and he is the only one I ever knew who seems to have no spark of that fire about him. — He has left us about a fortnight, and sorry we were to lose him, but had he been my son he must have gone, and I could not have regretted him more. If his Sister be still with you present my love to her, and tell her how much I wish to see them at Weston together.

The day before yesterday I received a letter from my dear old friend and Cousin Mrs. Balls. You mention in your last, expectations of seeing her in a few days. Should she be your guest when you receive this, remember me to her affectionately, give her my best thanks for her letter, and tell her that I will answer it as soon as the Turkeys arrive.

Mrs. Hewitt[1] probably remembers more of my Childhood than I can recollect either of hers or of my own. But this I know, that the days of that period were happy days compared with most that I have seen since. There are few perhaps in the world who have not cause to look back with regret on the days of Infancy. Yet, to say truth I suspect some deception in this. For Infancy itself has its cares, and though we cannot now conceive how trifles could affect us much, it is certain that they did. Trifles they appear now, but such they were not then.

My Love to Mrs. Hewitt — my best respects to Mr. Bodham, and believe my sweet Coz — though in haste,

most truly Yours — Wm Cowper.

Lady Hesketh is here, is obliged to you for your kind mention of her and sends her best Compliments to which Mrs. Unwin's are added most sincerely.

[1] See n.3, C to Mrs Bodham, 27 Feb. 1790.

MRS BALLS   Wednesday, 24 November 1790

Address: Mrs. Balls / Catfield / Norfolk
Postmark: NO/26/90
Princeton

Weston Underwood
Wednesday Novr. 24. 1790.

My dear Cousin —

I shall love the Turkeys the better for having procured me a letter from you my old friend and play-fellow in other days. We sent for them yesterday to the Waggoner's House in a village five miles off and they arrived safe at Weston in the Evening; safe, as I said, and in perfect health as they desire me to tell you, and to thank you for your kind enquiries. They have also had a good night, have rested well, and feel themselves much refreshed, and will shortly be made acquainted with all our premises, for it is early at present and they have not yet quitted their apartment. Mrs. Unwin, truly grateful for your kindness in sending them, bids me present you her very best thanks and acknowledgments. Mine accompany hers, and we both long for the Spring that we may thank you here in person.

Your Nephew whom I love as if he were my son, and who I believe is not unwilling to serve me in that capacity since I am likely never to have any other, has left us as you suppose and is now at Cambridge. Yesterday I had a letter from him in which he informs me that he has freed himself from all mathematical shackles, and after many frowns and many arguments from his Tutour has forsaken his unprofitable lectures and betaken himself to others in the Civil Law. The consequence of this will be that instead of injuring his health and wasting his time in a study that could never have been of use to him, he will be able to take an eternal leave of Cambridge in May and to pursue such studies at home as will be more suited to his future function. I am, myself, at the bottom of all this mischief; my evil counsels have perverted him. But I trust that neither I nor He nor his friends will have any reason to regret it hereafter. Dr. Cheatham[1] indeed is displeased, but that I presume is an affair of no great impor-

---

[1] Not further identified.

431

tance compared with the irretrievable loss of some of the best years that a man can give to study, a loss that he must have suffered had he continued to busy himself with Squares and Circles.

Do you consider, child, that when you call yourself an old woman you make it impossible for me to be young? Know you not that it is 40 years since we saw each other, that I was at that time at least two years older than you, and that consequently I continue to be so still? How then can you be old, when I who am so much your Elder, have still, as Falstaff says, a smatch of my youth, and am almost as active as ever?[2] Oh when shall we ride in a Whiskum-Snivel[3] again, and laugh as we have done heretofore? Should ever that day come, you must be the driver, for I have too great a value both for your neck and my own to aspire to that office myself. I never excelled in it, and have hardly been in a Whiskum since.

You have done wisely I dare say in selling your Estate at Catfield,[4] but I should have been glad would wisdom have permitted you to keep it. For of all places in the earth I love Catfield, and should then have had a chance of seeing it again.

Lady Hesketh will not allow that you are unknown to her though you call yourself so. Have you forgotten how she threatened one Evening to Kill you, and how you verily believed that she intended it and were frighten'd out of your wits? She however remembers it well, bids me present her best Compliments to you, and assure you that she has laid aside all such murtherous intentions.

Adieu my dear Cousin — Let me hear from you as often as you can, and believe me

with much affection — Yours
Wm Cowper.

[2] *2 Henry IV*, I. ii. 95–6: 'your lordship, though not clean past your youth, hath yet some smack of age in you.' C first misquotes this in his letter to Lady Hesketh of 4 Sept. 1787.

[3] 'Whisky' is a 'light two-wheeled, one-horse carriage' (*OED*), but, according to *Wright* (IV. 4), 'Whiskum-Snivel' was a 'name, coined by Lady Hesketh for a gig — the old fashioned gig, with bow springs.'

[4] Serious financial difficulty in 1790 prompted Mrs Balls to sell her property at Catfield, which is described in an advertisement: 'Manshion house, hall, kitchen, 2 parlors, 6 chambers, 3 garrets, Yards, Barns, Stables, Outhouse, Walled-in

JOHN JOHNSON   Friday, 26 November 1790

Address: John Johnson Esqe / Caius College / Cambridge
Postmarks: NO/27/90 *and* OULNEY
Princeton

> Friday Nov. 26. 1790.
> My Birth-day.

My dearest Johnny,

The Oysters and the snipes are safe arrived, and though these are dead and those are dumb, all have a voice that loudly demands our best acknowledgments. We often remember and mention you by one or other of your many names, and always regret that you have left us.

Your Oysters and snipes remind me of two fine pheasants which we lately received from Norfolk, and for which we are indebted to your Brother Heath.[1] I am not able to thank him not having his address, and though, since they came, I have written both to Mrs. Bodham and Mrs. Balls, forgot to desire either of them to do it for me. This makes me blush when I think of it, and lest I should still suffer by so painful a sensation, I must beg and even *insist* that you will take it on yourself to thank him on my part, and that you will do it as soon as possible; accepting at the same time the proportion of thanks so justly due to you as the first mover in this and in every emolument that I derive from Norfolk.

Your Aunt Balls wrote me a kind and cheerful letter, and I shall rejoice to number her among my correspondents. By the way, the Turkeys are arrived and, notwithstanding your defamatory dream, are no skeletons.

I am happy that you have escaped from the claws of Euclid into the bosom of Justinian. It is useful I suppose to *every* man to be well grounded in the principles of jurispru-
garden in front well staked with fruit-trees. 80 acres land. The Buildings are almost new.' Mrs Balls subsequently lived with Mrs Bodham.

---

[1] Johnny's father, John Johnson, a tanner by profession, was married three times. He married Mary Bacon and had a daughter Sarah (1749–75); the name of his second wife is unknown but she was the mother of Hannah Maria (1758–97) and Anne (1760–1807), who married in 1784 William Heath (1762–1825) of Hemblington, Norfolk. Catharine Donne, Johnny's mother, was John Johnson's third wife.

Both Johnny and his sister, Catharine, frequently stayed at Hemblington with 'Brother Heath', Johnny's brother-in-law.

dence, and I take it to be a branch of Science that bids much fairer to enlarge the mind and give an accuracy of reasoning than all the Mathematics in the world. Mind your studies and be a good boy and you will soon be wiser than I can hope to be.

I am glad that our Paste-board is not absolutely *Carte blanche*, and I am glad of it as much for your sake as my own. For I verily believe your zeal in my cause to be such that you would have been more mortified than myself had our project of pigeoning people at Merryl's[2] proved abortive. By no means forget to give my best Compliments to my old friend Dr. Glynn,[3] or to tell him how much I am obliged to him for serving me as a Decoy on the occasion.

Our Press goes on much at the old rate and I wrote yesterday to Rivington[4] the Printer to scold him. We now draw toward the latter end of the 5th. Iliad.

We had a visit on Monday from one of the first women in the world, in point of character I mean and accomplishments, the Dowager Lady Spencer.[5] I may receive perhaps some honours hereafter should my Translation speed according to my wishes and the pains that I have taken with it, but shall never receive any that I shall esteem so highly. She is indeed worthy to whom I should dedicate, and may but my Odyssey prove as worthy of her, I shall have nothing to fear from the Critics.

Farewell my Johnny — Let us see you when and as often as you can — Lady Hesketh sends her Love to you by every one of your titles, as does Mrs. Unwin. Mr. Rose in a Letter that I received from him lately enquires of me what is your address. Suppose you should send him a line to inform him.

> Yours my dear Johnny with much
> Affection — Wm Cowper.

[2] John (1731-1801) and Joseph Merrill (1735-1805) were booksellers and publishers in Cambridge, *c.*1773-95; they probably succeeded T. and J. Merrill at 3 Trinity Street. With C's permission, Johnson 'pasted me on a board and hung me in the shop' in order to attract subscribers for the edition of Homer. The plan was a great success. See C to Mrs King, 2 Mar. 1791.

[3] Robert Glynn, afterwards Clobery. See List of Correspondents for this volume.

[4] John Rivington (1720-92), the printer, was printing a portion of the edition of Homer for Joseph Johnson. C's letter to Rivington is missing. Deodatus Bye was the other printer engaged by Joseph Johnson to print the Homer.

[5] See n.5, C to Newton, 31 May 1783.

P.S. No Letter from Corke — We will call him no longer Kellet[6] but Kettle, and strike him out of the pedigree.
I am curious to know Quid in se tantum admisit.[7]

MRS KING   Monday, 29 November 1790

Address: Mrs. King / Pirten-hall near / Kimbolton / Huntingdonshire
Postmarks: NO/30/90 *and* OULNEY
Princeton

Weston Underwood
Novr. 29. 1790

My dear Madam,

It has not been owing to any neglect of mine that by my long silence I have reduced you to the necessity of concluding that your letter, inclosing that of Mr. Martyn, never reached me. The Post brought them safe and at the proper time, but an indisposition of the feverish kind attended by a violent cough seized me immediately after, and render'd me incapable of acknowledging both the kindness of your own letter and of Mr. Martyn's. All this was the effect of a Cold as you will suppose, and it proved the most obstinate that I ever had to deal with. So obstinate that I have but just conquer'd it, even by the aid of James's powder.

I value highly, as I ought and hope that I always shall, the favourable opinion of such men as Mr. Martyn. Though to say the truth, their commendations, instead of making me proud, have rather a tendency to humble me, conscious as I am that I am over-rated. There is an old piece of advice given by an antient Poet and Satyrist which it behoves every man who stands well in the opinion of others, to lay up in his bosom. — *Take care to be, what you are reported to be.* By due attention to this wise counsel, it is possible to turn the praises of our friends to good account, and to convert that which might prove an incentive to vanity, into a lesson of wisdom. — I will keep your good and respectable friend's letter very safely, and restore it to you the first opportunity.

[6] Johnny had written to Richard Kellett (1733–1828), an alderman of the city of Cork, to discover if he was related to the Kellet ancestor of Mrs Roger Donne, Senior. See C to Rowley, 1 Feb. 1791.

[7] 'What he committed in thought.'

I beg, my dear Madam, that you will present my best Compliments to Mr. Martyn when you shall either see him next, or write to him.

To that Gentleman's enquiries I am doubtless obliged for the recovery of no small proportion of my Subscription-list. For in consequence of his application to Johnson and very soon after it, I received from him no fewer than 45 names that had been omitted in the list he sent me, and that would probably never have been thought of more. No Author, I believe, has a more inattentive or indolent bookseller, but he has ev'ry body's good word for liberality and honesty; therefore I must be content.

The Press proceeds at present as well as I can reasonably wish. A month has passed since we began, and I revised this morning the first sheet of the sixth Iliad. — Mrs. Unwin begs to add a line from herself, so that I have only room to subjoin my best respects to Mr. King, and to say that I am truly, my dear Madam, yours

Wm Cowper.

SAMUEL ROSE Tuesday, 30 November 1790

Address: Samuel Rose Esqr. / Percy Street / Rathbone Place / London
Postmarks: DE/1/90 *and* OULNEY
British Library

Weston Underwood
Novr. 30. 1790

My dear friend,

I will confess that I thought your letter somewhat tardy, though, at the same time, I made every excuse for you, except, as it seems, the right. *That* indeed was out of the reach of all possible conjecture. I could not guess that your silence was occasion'd by your being occupied with either thieves or thief-takers.[1] Since however the cause was such, I rejoice that your labours were not in vain, and that the freebooters who had plunder'd your friend are safe in limbo. I admire too, as much as I rejoice in your success, the indefatigable spirit that prompted you to pursue with such

---

[1] We do not have further details of this incident.

unremitting perseverance an object not to be reached but at the expence of infinite trouble, and that must have led you into an acquaintance with scenes and characters the most horrible to a mind like yours. I see in this conduct the zeal and firmness of your friendship to whomsoever professed, and though I wanted not a proof of it myself, contemplate so unequivocal an indication of what you really are, and of what I always believed you to be, with much pleasure. May you rise from the condition of an humble prosecutor or witness to the bench of judgment, and instead of only bringing vilains to justice, may you live to inflict it upon them! You will not find even this a pleasant office, but the honour and the utility of it will be your sufficient compensation.

When your Letter arrived it found me indisposed with the worst and most obstinate Cold that I ever caught. This was one reason why it had not a speedier answer. Another is, that except Tuesday Morning, there is none in the week on which I am not engaged in the last revisal of my translation; the revisal I mean of my proof-sheets. To this business I give myself with an assiduity and attention truly admirable —, and set an example which, if other poets could be apprized of it, they would do well to follow. Miscarriages in Authorship I am persuaded are as often to be ascribed to want of pains-taking as to want of ability, and it shall for ever be an axiom with me, that, let a writer's ability be what it may, he has never done his best 'till he has done the same thing five times over. — I thank you for your ready compliance with my request to worry Johnson. I too have worried him, and not him only, but the Printer also. We now jog on, in consequence, merrily enough, and have begun the 6th. book of the Iliad. I am in good spirits respecting what is already printed, and see no reason to auger otherwise than well.

Lady Hesketh, Mrs. U. and myself, often mention you, and always in terms that, though you would blush to hear them, you need not be ashamed of; at the same time wishing much that you could change our Trio into a Quartetto. — Johnny of Norfolk left us about a fortnight since. He is now at Caius' College. But if you would wish that a line from you, which I know he will be happy to receive, should find him there, you must dispatch it soon, for he is hasting into Norfolk to settle with his guardians. The affectionate Compliments of all here attend you, and I am most truly Yours

Wm Cowper.

Nomen Univer. Glas.   cœteris non
     adscriptum   est.[2]

P.S.

Not being sure that you and Mrs. Rose, to whom we all beg our Compliments, have yet been able to settle yourselves in your new mansion, I direct to you as usual.

Your Books are all safe, but some of them I wish to keep till Homer is done with; especially Riccius.[3] — The rest attend your orders.

WALTER BAGOT   Wednesday, 1 December 1790

Address: The Revd. Walter Bagot.
Morgan Library

Weston Decr. 1. 1790

My dear friend —

It is plain that you understand Trap,[1] as we used to say at school, for you begin with accusing me of long silence, conscious yourself, at the same time, that you have been half a year in my debt, or thereabout. But I will answer your accusations with a boast. With a boast of having intended many a day to write to you again, notwithstanding your long insolvency. Your Brother and Sister of Chichely can both witness for me that, weeks since, I testified such an intention, and if I did not execute it, it was not for want of good will, but for want of leisure. When will you be able to glory of such designs, so liberal, and magnificent, you who have nothing to do by your own confession, but to grow fat and saucy? Add to all this that I have had a violent cold, such as I never have but at the first approach of winter, and such as

---

[2] 'The name of the University of Glasgow is listed, the rest are not.' Rose may have sent C a list of names, asking if any of them had subscribed to the Homer, to which this is C's reply.

[3] *Keynes* (63): Riccius, *Dissertationes Homericae* (Florence, 1740).

---

[1] 'To know one's own interest' (*OED*).

at that time I seldom escape. A fever accompanied it and an incessant cough.

> Ὡς δε κυων μεγαλως τε διηνεκεως τ᾽ ὑλακτει
> Ἱππων ωκυποδων η ανδρων δουπον ακουσας,
> Η διης εσιδων μεσονυκτιον ομμα σεληνης,
> Ὡς και εγων, αδινως ὑλακτων, δην εμογησα.[2]

Far be it from me to impose these lines upon you as an extemporaneous effusion, for, to tell you the truth, I made them on purpose for your edification before I rose this morning.

You measure the speed of Printers, of my Printer at least, rather by your own wishes than by any just standard. Mine, I believe, is as nimble a one as falls to the share of poets in general, though not nimble enough to satisfy either the Author or his friends. I told you that my work would go to the Press in Autumn, and so it did. But it had been six weeks in London e'er the Press began to work upon it. About a month since, we began to print, and at the rate of nine sheets in a fortnight have proceeded to about the middle of the sixth Iliad. No farther? you say. I answer, No. Nor even so far, without much scolding on my part both at the Bookseller and the Printer. But courage my friend! Fair and softly as we proceed we shall find our way through at last, and in confirmation of this hope, while I write this, another sheet arrives. I expect to publish in the Spring.

I love and thank you for the ardent desire you express to hear me bruited abroad, et per ora virûm volitantem.[3] For your encouragement I will tell you that I read, myself at least, with wonderful complacence what I have done, and if the world, when it shall appear, do not like it as well as I, we will both say and swear with Fluellin, that it is an Ass and a Fool, look you, and a prating coxcomb.[4]

I felt no ambition of the Laurel, else, though vainly perhaps, I had friends who would have made some stir on my behalf on that occasion. I confess that when I learn'd the

[2] 'As a dog howls long and loud when it hears the footsteps of men or of swift-footed horses, so I, when I looked upon the midnight eye of the heavenly moon, howled mightily and suffered long.'

[3] 'Flying alive on the lips of men'; C has adapted this from Ennius' elegaic epitaph on himself: '. . . volito uiuos per ora virum'.

[4] *Henry V,* IV. i. 79–80. C used this quotation in his letter to Bagot of 30 Oct. 1788.

new condition of the office, that Odes were no longer required and that the salary was encreased, I felt not the same dislike of it. But I could neither go to court, nor could I Kiss hands, were it for a much more valuable consideration. Therefore never expect to hear that Royal favours find out me.

Adieu my dear old friend! I will send you a mortuary Copy soon,[5] and in the mean time remain with Mrs. Unwin's best respects — Ever Yours

Wm Cowper

JOSEPH JOHNSON   Wednesday, 1 December 1790

Address: Mr. Johnson Bookseller / No. 72 / St Pauls Church Yard / London
Postmarks: DE/2/90 *and* OULNEY
Panshanger Collection

Weston Decr. 1. 1790

Dear Sir —

I suppose that my line and a half written on the margen of the sheet have escaped your notice, for it seems in vain that I solicit an answer to my question concerning the possibility of printing two or three Setts on Vellum.

Mrs. Frances Hill[1] of *Reading Berkshire* has not to this day received from you any proposal-papers though you promised to send them so long since. I shall be obliged to you if you will omit it no longer, for she finds the want of them a hindrance in her endeavours to procure Subscribers. Be pleased to send them, directed to her as above, to the house of Francis Annesley Esqe. Curzon Street — May Fair.[2]

I am Sir — Yours &c.
Wm Cowper.

---

[5] C sent his Northampton mortuary verses for 1790 to Bagot with his letter of 4 Jan. 1791.

---

[1] See List of Correspondents, Volume II.
[2] Francis Annesley (1734–1812) of Reading was MP for Reading from 1774 until 1806. He subscribed to the Homer.

JOHN NEWTON   Sunday, 5 December 1790

Princeton

Weston Decr. 5. 1790

My dear friend

Sometimes I am too sad, and sometimes too busy to write. Both these causes have concurred lately to keep me silent, but, more than by either of these, I have been hinder'd since I received your last, by a violent cold which oppressed me during almost the whole month of November. — Your letter affected us with both joy and sorrow. With sorrow and sympathy respecting poor Mrs. Newton, whose feeble and dying state suggests a wish for her release rather than for her continuance, and joy on your account, who are enabled to bear with so much resignation and cheerful acquiescence in the will of God, the prospect of a loss which even they who knew you best, apprehended might prove too much for you. As to Mrs. Newton's interest in the best things, none, intimately acquainted with her as we have been, could doubt it. She doubted it indeed herself, but, though it is not our duty to doubt any more than it is our privilege, I have always considered the self-condemning spirit to which such doubts are principally owing, as one of the most favorable symptoms of a nature spiritually renewed, and have many a time heard you make the same observation.

[Mr. Holloway]¹ has been shamefully betrayed, and I think he does wisely to anticipate the intended publication of his lean antagonist. The names of Mr. H[olloway's su]bscribers, you tell me, are not to be printed. I am glad of this, because it would give me pain to say — Nay — to any recommendation of²

---

¹ See n.4, C to Newton, 11 Aug. 1790.
² Parts of this final paragraph have been obliterated in ink, including the two references to Mr Holloway. This is all that remains of the letter.

JOSEPH HILL — Saturday, 11 December 1790

Cowper Johnson

Weston Decr. 11. 1790

My dear friend —

Presuming that by this time there are means of supply in my budget, I beg the remittance of £50 by a draft as usual.

I see you in the Papers appointed Clerk of the Peace[1] for your County. I know neither the quantum of emolument nor the business of your office, but you do, and since you deemed it worth your having, I heartily give you joy of it.

You have heard I presume that I am in the Press. The intelligence is true. It groans every day with my labours, and will continue groaning for some months to come. I expect to be born in April. This moment I receive a sheet, part of the last half of the eighth Iliad, and am, if possible, now more occupied than ever, retouching for the last time before it meets the public eye, my long translation. I flatter myself that I have not bestowed such unremitting study on it in vain, but that in the end these two great volumes will do me credit, and then I know you will rejoice with me.

Lady Hesketh is in the best health and spirits and presents her best Compliments to Yourself and to Mrs. Hill, in which she is most sincerely joined

by Yours ever
Wm Cowper.

JOSEPH JOHNSON — Friday, 17 December 1790

Address: Mr. Johnson Bookseller / No. 72 / St. Pauls Church Yard / London.
Postmarks: DE/18/90 *and* NEWPORT/PAGNEL
Maine Historical Society

Weston Decr. 17. 1790

Dear Sir —

It will save the Printer trouble if you will give him the following lines to be substituted in the place of the present concluding lines of the tenth book.

[1] According to *The Clerks of the Counties, 1360–1960* (1961), Joseph Hill served as Clerk of the Peace for Berkshire from 1790 until his death in 1811.

After this line —
Of Tydeus' son, with winnow'd wheat supplied.
He will proceed thus.

Ulysses in his bark the gory spoils
Of Dolon placed, designing them a gift
To Pallas. Then, descending to the sea
Neck, thighs and legs from sweat profuse they cleansed,
And, so refresh'd and purified, their last
Ablution in bright tepid baths performed.
Each thus completely laved and with smooth oil
Anointed, at the well-spread board they sat,
And quaff'd, in honour of Minerva, wine
Delicious, from the brimming beaker drawn.[1]

It is not without concern that by such numerous and sometimes long alterations I occasion so much trouble to the Printer, but in a work like this they are unavoidable; of which, experience has long since persuaded me. For could the utmost previous care and attention have secured the point, there would have been no occasion for a single alteration at the present moment. I have revised the MSS several times, and never without making many improvements, or without saying to myself — Now it is as it should be. Yet in this last revisal I still find occasion to alter. The truth is, that I could, more easily perhaps, satisfy the majority of readers, than I can satisfy myself.

I am, Dear Sir —
Yours Wm Cowper.

JOHN JOHNSON   Saturday, 18 December 1790

Address: John Johnson Esqr. / South-Green / Mattishall / Norfolk
Postmarks: DE/20/[90], DE/22/90 *and* OULNEY
Barham Johnson

Weston Decr. 18. 1790.

My dearest Johnny —
I address you with a new pen, a great rarity with me, and for which I am indebted to my Lady Cousin. And this I do,

---

[1] *Iliad*, x. 674–83 in C's translation.

the very day after the receipt of your letter, having an ardent desire to tell you in legible characters, how much I, and how much we all love and are obliged to you. The Oysters, like those you sent first, surpass all encomium, and the Cottenham cheeses[1] were especially welcome, being always cheeses that deserve to be number'd among the best in the world, and cheeses beside, such which we have not tasted many years. We thank you with no common thanks, but with such as your kindness merits.

But what thanks can I render you proportioned to your zeal exerted in favour of my Subscription? Be assured that I shall never forget it, speed as it may, and in order to immortalize it will record it immediately in verse, which must be of the extempore kind, because I have no time for any thing better.

> There was no Market-town in all
>   The land of the Icene[2]
> Where Johnny did not loudly call
>   For every body's Guinea.

> But gold was scarce; and we regret
>   That folks were grown so wise
> That few thought Homer half so sweet
>   As sausage and mince-pies.

I fear my Johnny that this will prove the case, but whether it should or not, my obligation to thee is equal. In the mean time I perceive myself so flattered by the instances of illustrious success mentioned in your letter, that I feel all the amiable modesty for which I was once so famous, sensibly giving way to a spirit of vain-glory.[3] The King's College subscription makes me proud, the effect that my verses have had on your

---

[1] This cream cheese, manufactured at Cottenham, *c.* 7 miles from Cambridge, was said to owe its superiority to the rich grasses growing on the fens in that region. See Arnold James Cooley, *A Cyclopædia of Practical Receipts* (1845), p. 247.

[2] C is humorously forecasting poor results for Johnny's efforts to raise subscriptions in his home area at Christmas time. The Iceni, Boadicea's tribe, lived in Norfolk; hence the allusion in the verses. First published in *Bailey*.

[3] Fifteen libraries at Cambridge subscribed for the Homer, including King's College.

444

two young friends, the Mathematicians,[4] makes me proud, and I am, if possible, prouder still of the contents of the Letter that you inclosed. You must give my most respectful Compliments to Mr. Reeve[5] the writer of it, and you must tell him how much I feel myself obliged to him for his own subscription so handsomely given, and for the readiness with which he gives me also his interest with others. I know not what Mr. Cowper that Gentleman can have met at Saffron Walden, and whom he supposes me. A Cousin of mine he must have been, but which of my Cousins I cannot even conjecture.[6] For my own part I was never there, nor ever had the happiness to be in his company.

You complained of being stupid, and sent me one of the cleverest letters. I have not complained of being stupid, and have sent you one of the dullest. But it is no matter; I never aim at any thing above the pitch of every-day scribble when I write to those I love.

Homer proceeds — my boy — we shall get through in time, and I hope by the time appointed. We are now in the tenth Iliad. I expect the Ladies every minute to breakfast, and will be responsible to you for a letter in due time from each. You have their best love. Mine attends the whole army of Donnes at Mattishall Green assembled. How happy should I find myself were I but one of the party! My capering days are over, but do you caper for me, that you may give them some idea of the happiness I should feel were I in the midst of them. — I am my dearest Johnny, Yours Wm C.

You will remember, I hope, your promised call here in January, or at whatever time you leave Norfolk.

Mrs. Hewitt, Mrs. Balls, Mrs. Bodham, and Kate! May God bless you all together, and yours with you — Amen!

I admire your advertizing boards; that which you sent hither is gone to Newport pagnel to catch as many gudgeons there as will bite, and then it will go to catch others at Wooburn.

[4] Not identified.

[5] 'The Rev. Mr. Thomas Reeve, Master of the Grammar School at Bungay' is entered for a common copy. Reeve (1745–1824) was Rector of Brockley at this time, and was sometime headmaster of the school at Bungay, which Johnny had attended.

[6] Unidentified.

I shall insist on defraying the cost.
Remember to thank Mr. H.[7] for pheasant and The Gods go
a-hunting.

WALTER CHURCHEY   Friday, 24 December 1790

Address: Mr. Walter Churchey Attorney at law / Hay / Brecon / Post pd. 9d.
Postmarks: DE/25/90, POST/PAID *and* OULNEY
Princeton

Dear Sir —
You know my occupation, and will be more charitable, I
trust, than to impute to negligence my tardiness in replying
to your obliging letters.

I have much to thank you for. Imprimis for your remarks
on the Specimen; which, I dare say, were favorable enough
to me. I know not if they have been published according to
your desire, but I apprehend that Johnson, who is my *fac
totum* in every thing that relates to Homer, may have judged
it to be rather too late in the day to print a commentary on
that passage now, which was itself printed five years ago, and
which the Critics have already mumbled.

I thank you also for the respectable names which you have
procured me, and have added them to my catalogue.

To say that I was grieved at the treatment you have received
from the Reviewers,[1] is saying little, for I felt myself not
more grieved than angry. To censure a book in that general
manner is neither just to the author of it, nor satisfactory
to their own readers. Extracts should always be given, first,
as a proof that they have read what they condemn, and
secondly, that the Public may judge for themselves.

[7] William Heath. See n.1, C to John Johnson, 26 Nov. 1790.

---

[1] The notice in the Monthly Catalogue portion of the *Monthly Review* for
Nov. 1790 (New Series, vol. 3, 339) of his *Poems, and Imitations of the British
Poets; with Odes, Miscellanies, and Notes* (1789) must have incensed Churchey:
'If the value of poetry were estimated, like a Dutch beauty, by its weight, this
immense volume would be worth some thing considerable; for really it is *very*
heavy. Such uniform solidity runs through the numerous pages, that the author
must excuse us from assenting to his request, "that the critics will neither condemn,
nor commend, by the *lump*, but deal out *specimena*," as he terms them: indeed,
by thus refusing, we are doing Mr. Churchey a kindness, for though we might
easily select passages to censure, we should be puzzled to find much to praise.'

446

I sent your publisher's address to Johnson and directed *him* to send me your volume, but though he is a sensible man and an honest one, I have not a few reasons to suspect that he is rather indolent, and to that cause ascribe it that I have never yet had the pleasure you intended me. Should it be convenient to you to order your own Bookseller to send it by the Olney waggon, I shall be sure of it. The waggon will be found at the Windmill — St. John Street, Smithfield.

I never feel myself poor but when I see or hear of a valuable man whose exigencies exceed my ability to relieve them. How heartily and gladly I would administer to the complete removal of yours, were it in my power, God knows.

I am, Dear Sir,
with much respect
Your obliged humble Servant
Wm Cowper.

Weston Underwood
Decr. 24. 1790.
You may tell your friends that my work is in the Press and will be published in the Spring.

ROBERT GLYNN   Saturday, 25 December 1790

Wright, iv. 14–16[1]

Weston Underwood near Olney, Bucks
25 Dece. 1790.

My dear Doctor,
Not to send you a line to thank you for the kindness you have shown me in subscribing to my work yourself, and procuring me other names that will reflect so much honour on the publication, would be an omission that I could never forgive myself. I do most heartily thank you for all that you have spoken of me, and all that you have done for me, having learned it minutely from my young cousin of Caius. This kindness of an old friend both of my brother's and mine has touched me too nearly not to be noticed, or ever to be forgotten. .

---

[1] In 1904 or thereabouts, the holograph of this letter was in the possession of Edward Henry Perowne (1826–1906), Master of Corpus Christi College, Cambridge, from 1879 until his death. We do not know its present whereabouts.

My translation is in the Press, as you have doubtless been informed, and we have arrived in an impression at the middle of the eleventh book of the *Iliad*, yet I want a better spur than I am master of to prick the printer forward. Such folks are the slowest of all that are slow, and the rogue takes the advantage of my living almost sixty miles off in the country; but we shall publish, I trust, in the spring, at least by the opening of the first roses.

I have found this work, laborious as it has been, during the five years a perpetual source of amusement to me, and of amusement so delightful that I despair of ever stumbling on the like again. My only want has been some fine old Grecian in my neighbourhood whom I might have occasionally consulted, and who would have enjoyed my author with me. Oh that you had been at hand yourself to have acted in that capacity.

Remember me kindly to the good Master of Benet,[2] thanking him heartily for his name on this occasion. — And believe me, my dear doctor, truly and affectionately yours,

Wm. Cowper.

You have obliged me much by your kind notice of my cousin Johnson, and I am happy to add that you will find him not unworthy of your encouragement. He spent a part of the summer and all the autumn with me, and I can affirm from a thorough knowledge of him, that there is nothing amiable either in temper or manners that I have not found in him.

[2] William Colman (1728-94), who was educated at Corpus Christi College, Cambridge, was elected Master on 25 June 1778; he subsequently served two terms (1779-80, 1793-4) as Vice Chancellor of the University. He is entered as 'Dr. Coleman, Master of Bene't College, Cambridge' in the subscription list.

MRS KING

Friday, 31 December 1790

Princeton

Weston-underwood
Decr. 31st. 1790.

My dear Madam —

Returning from my walk at half past three, I found your welcome messenger in the kitchen, and ent'ring the study found also the beautiful present[1] with which you had charged him. We have all admired it (for Lady Hesketh is here to assist us in doing so) and for my own particular I return you my sincerest thanks, a very inadequate compensation. Mrs. Unwin, not satisifed to send you thanks only, begs your acceptance likewise of a Turkey, which, though the figure of it might not much embellish a counter-pane, may possibly serve hereafter to swell the dimensions of a Feather-bed.

I have lately been visited with an indisposition much more formidable than that which I mentioned to you in my last, a nervous fever. A disorder to which I am subject, and which I dread above all others, because it comes attended by a melancholy perfectly insupportable. This is the first day of my complete recovery, the first in which I have perceived no symptoms of my terrible malady, and the only drawback on this comfort that I feel is the intelligence contained in yours that neither Mr. King nor yourself are well. I dread always, both for my own health and for that of my friends, the unhappy influences of a year worn out; but, my dear Madam, this is the last day of it, and I resolve to hope that the new year shall obliterate all the disagreeables of the old one. I can wish nothing more warmly than that it may prove a propitious year to you.

My poetical operations, I mean of the occasional kind, have lately been pretty much at a stand. I told you, I believe, in my last, that Homer in the present stage of the process, occupied me more intensely than ever. He still continues to do so, and threatens, 'till he shall be completely finished, to make all other composition impracticable. I have however written the mortuary verses as usual, but the wicked Clerk for whom I write them, has not yet sent me the impression.

[1] Unidentified.

449

31 December 1790

I transmit to you the long-promised Catharina, and were it possible that I could transcribe the others, would send them also. There is a way however by which I can procure a Frank, and you shall not want them long.

With Mrs. Unwin's best Compliments to yourself and Mr. King, together with our joint wishes for his and your complete recovery, I remain Dearest Madam — Ever yours
Wm Cowper.[2]

WALTER BAGOT

Tuesday, 4 January 1791

Address: The Revd. Walter Bagot
Morgan Library

Weston. Jan. 4. 1791

My dear friend —
You would long since have received an answer to your last, had not the wicked Clerk of Northampton[1] delayed to send me the printed copy[2] of my annual dirge which I waited to enclose. Here it is at last, and much good may it do the readers!

I have regretted that I could not write sooner, especially because it well became me to reply as soon as possible to your kind enquiries after my health, which has been both better and worse since I wrote last. The Cough that made me write Greek,[3] was cured, or nearly so, when I received your letter, but I have lately been afflicted with a nervous fever, a malady formidable to me above all others, on account of the terrour and dejection of spirits that, in my case, always accompany it. I ever look forward, for this reason, to the month now current, with the most miserable apprehensions, for in this month the distemper has twice seized me. I wish to

[2] Lady Hesketh has added a note to the foot of the letter: 'Lady Hesketh, tho.' unknown desires to present, her Compliments and best Wishes to the good and amiable Friend of her dear Cousin. — '

[1] John Cox died before 2 Mar. 1791. In his letter to Mrs King of that date, C explains that the 'clerk sent me only half the number of printed copies for which I stipulated with him at first, and they were all expended immediately. The poor man himself is dead now.'
[2] Now at the Morgan Library.
[3] See C to Bagot, 1 Dec. 1790.

be thankful however to the sov'reign dispenser both of health and sickness, that though I have felt cause enough to tremble, he gives me, now, encouragement to hope that I may dismiss my fears and expect, for this January at least, to escape it.

I think any man extremely rash who ventures to write, especially Verse, in any language save his own, neither would it have been possible that I should myself have played the fool so egregiously, except in a letter to you who have known me play the fool so often. I was conscious nevertheless of the perilous nature of the enterprize, and watched my quantities accordingly with a most jealous attention, taking care that the syllable in question, about which I had my own doubts, should not trespass, in my use of it, against the authority of my good old Greecian. You will find him in the following line using it long —

Εξαπινης δ᾽Οδυσηα ιδον κυνες ὑλακομωροι.[4]

I presume therefore, that it is one of those good-natured syllables that is contented to be either long or short at the poet's pleasure. It is the 29th. line of Odyssey 14. — The mention of Quantity reminds me of a remark that I have seen somewhere, possibly in Johnson, to this purport. That the syllables in our language being neither long nor short, our verse accordingly is less beautiful than the verse of Greeks or Romans, because requiring less artifice in its construction.[5] But I deny the fact, and am ready to depose on oath that I find every syllable as distinguishably and clearly either long or short in our language as in any other. I know also, that without an Attention to the quantity of our syllables, good

[4] *Odyssey*, xiv.29 (lines 35-6 in C's translation): 'Soon as those clamorous watch-dogs the approach / Saw of Ulysses...' Bagot had apparently observed that the υ in 'ὑλακτει' and 'ὑλακτων' (p. 439), scanned long by C, was always short in Homer, which is the case. C replies by citing an example not of 'ὑλακτέω' but of its cognate 'ὑλακόμωρος', where Homer in fact does scan the υ long.

[5] C may be referring to *The Rambler*, 94 (9 Feb. 1751): 'The measure of time in pronouncing may be varied so as very strongly to represent, not only the modes of external motion, but the quick or slow succession of ideas, and consequently the passions of the mind. This at least was the power of the spondaick and dacty-lick harmony, but our language can reach no eminent diversities of sound.' See also *Rambler*, 86 (12 Jan. 1751): 'The ancients, who had a language more capable of variety than ours, had two kinds of verse, the Iambick, consisting of short and long syllables alternately, from which our heroick measure is derived, and the Trochaick, consisting in a like alternation of long and short.'

verse cannot possibly be written, and that ignorance of this matter is one reason why we see so much that is good for nothing. The movement of a verse is always either shuffling or graceful according to our management in this particular, and Milton gives almost as many proofs of it in his Paradise Lost as there are lines in the poem. — Away therefore with all such unfounded observations, I would not give a farthing for many bushels of them — nor you perhaps for this letter — yet, upon recollection, for as much as I know you to be a dear lover of literary gossip, I think it possible that you may esteem it highly.

Give my love to Mrs. B and if you please to all your family — Mrs. U. begs to be respectfully remember'd to you. Believe me, my dear friend, most truly yours

Wm Cowper.

PS. About a fortnight since I had the happiness of a morning call from your brother Howard.

JOHN NEWTON   Thursday, 20 January 1791

Princeton

Weston Jan. 20. 1791

My dear friend —

Had you been a man of this world, I should have held myself bound by the law of ceremonies to have sent you long since my tribute of condolence. I have sincerely mourned with you, and though you have lost a wife,[1] and I only a friend, yet do I understand too well the value of such a friend as Mrs. Newton, not to have sympathized with you very nearly. But you are not a man of this world, neither can you who have both the Scripture and the Giver of Scripture to console you, have any need of aid from others, or expect it from such spiritual imbecillity as mine. I consider'd likewise that receiving a letter from Mrs. Unwin, you in fact received one from myself, with this difference only, that hers could not fail to be better adapted to the occasion and to your own frame of mind than any that I could send you.

---

[1] Mrs Newton died on 15 Dec. 1790.

20 January 1791

You are now, long as it is since I wrote, the first of my correspondents to whom I write, though I am actually in arrear to all. The reason of my insolvency would probably obtrude itself upon you, even if I did not mention it, but, in justice to myself, it is necessary for me to say, that in the present stage of my long work, my two great volumes being now in the Press, I find Letter-writing a difficulty and indeed almost impracticable. As fast as proof-sheets arrive, which is almost by every post, I am called to consider, for the last time, every line before me with the most exact attention, that the whole may be prepared to meet the eye of public and critical scrutiny, which I have reason enough to expect will examine me with all the zeal that an ambition to find fault inspires. This state of the matter renders the closest application necessary, and equally necessary it will continue to be[2]

JOHN JOHNSON   Friday, 21 January 1791

Address: John Johnson Esqre. / Caius College / Cambridge
Postmarks: JA/22/91 *and* OULNEY
Princeton

Weston-underwood
Jan. 21. 1791.

My dearest Johnny,
I know that you have already been well catechized by Lady Hesketh on the subject of your return hither before the winter shall be over, and shall therefore only say that, if you *can* come, we shall be happy to receive you. Remember also that nothing can excuse the non-performance of a promise, but absolute necessity. In the mean time my faith in your veracity is such, that I am persuaded you will suffer nothing less than necessity to prevent it. Were you not extremely pleasant to us and just the sort of youth that suits us (though not at all a Croydon)[1] we should neither of us have said half so much, or perhaps a word, on the subject.

[2] The rest of the MS is missing.

---

[1] 'Sir John Croydon' was Lady Hesketh's nickname for John Johnson; Lady Hesketh may have coined it from misreading the name 'Corydon' in 'Audley End'.

453

21 January 1791

I want to know exactly the manner of your interview with your guardian[2] and how it ended. What heats, what altercation and bickerings occurred, how angry others were, and how miserable you were yourself, sitting motionless and saying nothing. All this will interest and consequently amuse. It will interest, because the concern is yours, and amuse because it is now all over.

Forsan et hæc olim meminisse juvabit.[3]

Homer proceeds at the old rate, sometimes a sheet, sometimes two, and sometimes none. The work would be printed much sooner were you but here to sit cross-legg'd for me. For though we have three pair of legs amongst us, I have had cause to observe that yours only are worth crossing. You are sensible of this I presume yourself, and therefore not contented to cross them while seated, you throw them athwart each other when you walk. Yours, my dear Johnny, are vagaries that I shall never see practised by any other, and whether you slap your ancle, or reel as if you were fuddled, or dance in the path before me, all is characteristic of yourself, and therefore to me delightful. I have hinted to you indeed, sometimes, that you should be cautious of indulging antic habits and singularities of all sorts, and young men in general have need enough of such admonition; but yours are a sort of Fairy habits, such as might belong to Puck or Robin Good fellow, and therefore good as the advice is, I should be half sorry should you take it. This allowance at least I give you — Continue to take your walks, if walks they may be called, exactly in their present fashion, 'till you have taken Orders. Then indeed, forasmuch as a skipping, curvetting, bounding Divine might be a spectacle not altogether seemly, I shall consent to your adoption of a more grave demeanour.

[2] William Clopton Johnson, the husband of Johnny's sister, Hannah Maria. The Ludham estate and the guardianship of Johnny and Catharine had been left to Hannah's husband. Johnny's inheritance was not payable to him until he was thirty, and, in the intervening period, he was allowed £100 a year maintenance while at Cambridge. At the time of this letter, Johnny was probably trying to convince his guardian to continue his maintenance grant for a further year, despite the fact he was no longer in residence at Cambridge (although his name was still entered on the books).

[3] Virgil, *Aeneid*, i. 203: 'The suffereing will yield us yet a pleasant tale to tell.'

You will have the Grace I presume to answer Lady Hesketh's letter some time or other. How goes the Subscription on at Cambridge and in the Market-towns of Norfolk and Suffolk? Or do you judge it yet too soon to glory, and that you had better wait till other names are added in the two sister counties, to the *None* already enter'd? In this use your own discretion. My List will appear in the next Analytical Review — not numerous, but splendid, as you know, in the extreme. Respectable names have been added since you saw it. Tell me if you can, if Dr. Glynn had a Letter from me, and how he does, and give my love to him.

The Ladies are mindful of you, as is always my dear Johnny — Yours affectionately

Wm Cowper.

SAMUEL ROSE   Sunday, 23 January 1791

Address: Samuel Rose Esqre / Chancery Lane / London
Princeton

The Lodge
Jan. 23. 1791

My dear friend,

I should have acknowledged much sooner the receipt of your letter, not by the hand of my Secretary Cousin, Lady Hesketh, but under my own, had it not been for the old story, which engages my time, at present, more than ever. Lady Hesketh's I presume you have received, though not less occupied perhaps than myself, you have not yet been able to answer it. She informed you, as I remember, of the ground on which Johnson's stricture stands. It was originally the stricture of Fuseli,[1] but is now, I trust, pretty well superseded by the alterations that I have made in conformity to it. Nothing, I believe, resembles so much the tenderness of a parent as that of an author, different indeed in kind, but similar in degree. I could never otherwise have been so much hurt by a censure, which I was conscious that I had obviated long ago.

[1] See n.1, C to Joseph Johnson, 25 Jan. 1786, and n.1, C to Lady Hesketh, 9 Feb. 1786.

I have received a letter which has given me much pleasure, and is likely to cost you some trouble. This is a paradox which your friendship for me will not suffer you to understand 'till I have explained it. You must know then that I have received a very polite and flattering letter from Mr. Mackenzie. In which he informs me that — as it was then holiday-time when he received mine, he could not immediately meet with the Gentlemen to whom it was necessary to apply to attain the ends of it; but that he is now glad to acquaint me that his endeavors have been successful, and that he has it in Commission from the Principal of the College and the Curators of the Advocates Library to desire that I will set down '*The University of Edinburgh and the Advocates Library of Edinburgh*' as subscribers to my work, each for a Royal paper copy.[2]

Hence will arise, in part, your trouble. For I shall beg the favour of you, in order that there may be no omissions or mistakes, otherwise too likely to happen, to take this affair into your own hands, and to see the entrance of these subscriptions made according to the true stile and title of the Subscribers; telling Mr. Johnson at the same time, that if it be not now too late, I shall be happy to have them printed in the List to be annext to the Analytical. —

But this is not all. Other trouble still hangs over you. During my correspondence some time since with Mr. Mackenzie I promised him that my two Volumes as a present to him should be sent to Mr. Cadell's[3] to be forwarded thence to Scotland. This promise so far as depended on myself, I performed, having given directions accordingly. But an omission has happened somewhere, as Mr. Mackenzie says (and I guess where) he has never received them. This favour therefore I also beg of you, that you will see to the due performance of this business yourself, and that the poems in the *best edition of them and neatly bound* be sent to

[2] The libraries of 'the University of Edinburgh' and 'the Advocates, Edinburgh' are both listed for fine copies of the Homer. Only two more libraries of the thirty-two to subscribe ordered Royal Paper copies.

[3] See n.6, C to Lady Hesketh, 27 Nov. 1787. In his letter to Mackenzie of 10 Dec. 1787, C states that he has ordered his two volumes to be sent to Cadell's with Mackenzie's address.

Cadell's immediately. If you will be my scribe and Representative on the occasion, and mark them in the blank leaf as a gift from the Author, you will oblige me still more.

The Ladies send their best Compliments. — Mrs. Unwin is filling her Tea-pot and breakfast will be here in a minute. Well for you — for I must now, after having loaded you with commissions, of necessity release you, saying nothing more, except that I am most truly

Yours
Wm Cowper.

Mr. Mackenzie — so he writes his name — sends his particular Compliments to you.

HENRY MACKENZIE   Thursday, 27 January 1791

Princeton

Dear Sir —

I cannot too soon express the sense I have of the kindness with which you have managed for me, so successfully, a business that I had much at heart, and should have done it sooner but that I waited for the opportunity of a Frank.

I no sooner had received your obliging answer than I made Mr. Rose acquainted with the contents of it, who had left us few days before, desiring him to get the names of the University of Edinburgh and the Curators of the Advocates Library there, inserted, if possible, in a list of my Subscribers which will be publish'd with the next Analytical Review. But should it be now too late to do so, for we are at the end of the month, at any rate I shall have the pleasure of seeing them in the list prefixt to my volumes, and none shall I see there that will do me more honour or afford me a more sensible gratification.

I blushed when I learned that you had not yet received my volumes, but not through consciousness of any neglect of my own, for I actually sent the necessary instructions to my Bookseller at the time I mentioned. But though he is an honest man and a sensible one, he gives me frequent occasion to regret that he has not either a better memory or more attention. With this commission also I have now charged Mr. Rose, who I doubt not will execute it with the dispatch I have desired. The books are by this time, I imagine, sent to Cadell's, and will soon have the honour to stand on your shelf at Edinburgh.

I beg, Sir, that should you see it proper to do so, you will make my acknowledgments to the Gentlemen who have so readily and so obligingly favoured me with their distinguishing patronage, and believe me at all times with much respect and esteem

Sincerely yours
Wm Cowper.

Weston-Underwood
Jan. 27. 1791.

CLOTWORTHY ROWLEY   Tuesday, 1 February 1791

Address: Clotworthy Rowley Esqr. / Dublin
Postmarks: FE/2/91, OULNEY *and* [illegible]
Princeton

Weston-Underwood
Feb. 1. 1791

You must know, my dear Rowley, that a man having two great volumes in the Press, is no more master of his time than the greatest man in the Kingdom, and, therefore, that though I have somewhat delay'd my answer, I am clear of the charge to which you plead guilty, the charge of procrastination.

Your expectations that my Homer (or *our* Homer as you kindly call it) will appear in the middle of this month, it is to be hoped are not very sanguine, because in proportion as they are such, you will infallibly be disappointed. Not that I have lately had cause to complain of the Printer. He proceeds, leisurely indeed, but regularly, and, which is still better, very correctly. But it is a bulky business and will not be accomplish'd, I presume, 'till the Spring is nearly over. We are now in the 18th. Iliad. Burke's pamphlet[1] stood in

---

[1] C is referring to Burke's *Reflections on the Revolution in France, and on the Proceedings in Certain Societies in London Relative to That Event* which was first published on 1 Nov. 1790. Six editions appeared in 1790, and five more in 1791. Joseph Johnson published Mary Wollstonecraft's *A Vindication of the Rights of*

my way when I wrote last, for every press, and consequently mine, groan'd with answers to it, so that the old Greecian and his not very young Translator were sorely neglected.

You have not I hope lost your catalogue of Subscribers' names, and you will not I hope forget to send them time enough to be inserted in the volume.[2] It will be worth your while to attend to this matter, for as sure as you live if I get them not, I will chronicle them in the last edition of the list by the stile and title of *sixteen Irish, names and sex unknown.* — Unless you wish us therefore a laugh at the expence of your present countrymen, I recommend it to you by all means to send them in your next letter, and not to suffer that next letter to be very long in arrear. To tell you a sober truth, I should have been glad to have received them sooner, had it consisted with your procrastinating moods to have sent them, for the first edition of my [List][3] is published this very day, annext to the Analytical Review, and their appearance in it would have gratified me and would have done me honour; would have help'd likewise to decoy others, which is the view with which this present list is published.

I rejoice that you look so young. I too, I believe, am older than I seem, or the Ladies flatter me; and why they should I know not, for I have long since ceased to be worthy of so much favour and goodness at their [delicate hands. I would with all my heart][4] that you were not still accompanied by the Rheumatism, after so many years' cohabitation; but it is better than the gout, and we must have something. *Felicissimus ille Qui minimis urgetur.*[5]

Men, in a Letter to the Right Honourable Edmund Burke; Occasioned by His Reflections on the Revolution in France (1790); Capel Lofft the Elder's *Remarks on the Letter of the Right Honourable Edmund Burke, Concerning the Revolution in France* . . . (1790), and the second edition of this work in 1791; Lofft's *Remarks on the Letter of Mr. Burke, to a Member of the National Assembly* (1791); Part I of Paine's *Rights of Man* (1791); Thomas Christie's *Letters on the Revolution of France . . . Occasioned by the Publications of the Right Honourable Edmund Burke . . .* (1791).

    [2] The 16 names were received by C from Rowley on 26 Feb. See C to John Johnson, 27 Feb. 1791.

    [3] The word was removed with the seal.

    [4] This portion of the letter was removed with the closing salutation and signature. The missing portions are from *Southey*, vi. 352.

    [5] C has misquoted Horace's lines: ' . . . optimus est, / Qui minimum urgetur' (*Satires*, I. iii. 68–9). Christopher Smart translated these lines: 'He is the best

I can assure you, my dear old friend, that a journey from Bath hither is not like a journey to the world's end,[6] and the next time you visit the Nymph of that Spring, I shall hope that you will make the experiment. There is no creature whom I should receive with more true pleasure, for I am [most affectionately yours,

Wm Cowper.]

Is it possible that you should know any thing of a Mr. Kellet a banker at Corke,[7] and, as I understand, in some sort a relation of mine?

MRS THROCKMORTON   Wednesday, 2 February 1791

Address: Mrs. Throckmorton / No. 11 / New Burlington Street / London.
Postmarks: FE/3/91 *and* OULNEY
Sir Robert Throckmorton

The Lodge
Feb. 2. 1791

My dear Mrs. Frog —
Tom and Tit[1] are in perfect health. Either Lady Hesketh or I have seen them daily since you went. He gave my Cousin yesterday a sprig of Box, desiring her, in *his* way, to give it to Toot as a present from himself, on which occasion, Toot seized with a fit of poetic enthusiasm, said or seemed to say —

Dear Tom! my muse this moment sounds your praise,
And turns, at once, your sprig of Box to Bays.

No other news has occurred at Weston, none at least that has reached me, except that the long unseen Joe Rye[2] called yesterday. I made my Cousin a present of his company for near 2 hours, when he and I set forth to walk together, he in his great coat and boots, and I great-coated and in my boots also. We had a very agreeable tour to Dingle-derry and over

man who is incumbered with the least vice' (*The Works of Horace*, 2 vols. (1756), ii. 33).
  [6] It was *c.*130 miles by road from Weston to Bath.
  [7] See n.6, C to John Johnson, 26 Nov. 1790.

  [1] See notes 1 and 2, C to Mrs Throckmorton, 31 Oct. 1790.
  [2] See n.3, C to Rose, 22 Nov. 1789, and List of Correspondents, Volume IV.

the hill into Hoe-brook valley.[3] Agreeable, I mean, as it could be while the wind blew a hurricane, and the hail pelted us without mercy. But Joe is fond of a high wind, so at least he assured me, and if he does but like hailstones as well, he must have supposed himself in paradise.

We have had nothing but high winds ever since you left us. It must have been on occasion of some such stormy season as the present that the following beautiful lines were produced. Did you ever see them, and whose are they?

> Such was the agitation of the Deep,
> ·That ev'n a *Fish* did *wish* a sleeping potion,
> And yawning said — One drop to make me sleep
> Were now, methinks, worth all this troubled ocean.
>
> ———————
>
> The sprats were bulged against the rocks and split,
> The *whales*, with broken *tails*, were cast away,
> And ev'ry Lobster's shell did lose a bit,
> And crabs, in vain, with all their claws, griped hard
> ·   the bottom clay.[4]

It is impossible that I should follow this singular description of a storm at sea, the sublimity of which I must needs envy the poet who wrote it, with any thing equally worthy of your notice; I shall therefore conclude with my best love to Mr. Frog, and with the Ladies' joint best Compliments, and am

most truly yours
Wm Cowper alias W. Toot.

[3] 'Dingle-derry' is probably the field next to Kilwick wood which C describes in 'The Needless Alarm'; 'Ho-brook' is 'a diminutive stream that crosses the road about half way from Olney to Weston . . . Bounded on one side by the Ho-brook is a long narrow plantation called, locally, the First Spinnie, but better known to readers of Cowper as the Shrubbery': Thomas Wright, *The Town of Cowper* (1886), pp. 186–7.

[4] Unidentified. Perhaps C is the sublime author and is teasing Mrs Throckmorton (see his letter to her of 19 Feb. 1791); if this is so, he may be parodying lines from Thomas Heyrick's *The Submarine Voyage* (1691).

SAMUEL ROSE   Saturday, 5 February 1791

Address: Samuel Rose Esqr / Chancery Lane / London
Postmarks: FE/7/91 *and* OULNEY
Princeton

The Lodge Sat. Feb. 5. 1791

My dear friend —

My letters to you are all either petitionary or in the stile of thanks and acknowledgment, and such nearly in an alternate order. In my last I loaded you with commissions, for the due discharge of which I am now to say, and to say truly, how much I feel myself obliged to you. Neither can I stop there, but must thank you likewise for new honours from Scotland, which have left me nothing to wish from that Country, for my list is now, I believe, graced with the subscription of all its Learned bodies. I regret only that some of them arrived too late to do honour to my present publication of names, but there are those among them, and from Scotland too, that may give a useful hint perhaps to our own Universities. All these with many others, I owe to you, and should we balance the account of obligation (for you lately spoke highly of yours to me) it would be found, I believe, that I am much your debtor. Your very handsome present of Pope's Homer has arrived safe notwithstanding an accident that befell him by the way.[1] The Hall servant brought the parcel from Olney resting it on the pommel of his saddle, and his horse fell with him. Pope was, in consequence, roll'd in the dirt, but being well coated got no damage. If augurs and soothsayers were not out of fashion I should have consulted one or two of that order in hope of learning from them that this fall was ominous. — I have found place for him on the chiffonier in the parlour where he makes a splendid appearance, and where he shall not long want a neighbor; one, who if less popular than himself, shall at least look as big as he.

Johnson was not mistaken in the judgment he formed of

---

[1] *The Iliad of Homer*, 6 vols. in 3 (1715-20). The inside cover of the first volume is inscribed: 'To William Cowper of Weston Lodge Esqr. from his Affectionate Friend Samuel Rose'. Apparently the *Odyssey* in Pope's translation had already been given to C; in his copy of that translation (5 vols., 1725-6) 'on the fly-leaves are presentation inscriptions from John Unwin in Cowper's hand. Some underlinings and notes by him.' *Keynes*, 58-9.

the Odyssey, and I was. I had supposed it [more] [2] finished, than when I had received the copy again I found it. I could not have believed [he was s]o justly chargeable with the fault [of] a too frequent, and, sometimes, a too violent inversion and contortion of Syntax; nor can I otherwise account for its being so, and for my own blindness to that blemish, than by supposing myself, after such long and close study of the original, infected to the very bone with the Greecian manner of misarrangement. In other respects I verily think that I have executed this work well, and that in this respect also it may merit at least my own good opinion, I am now busy in delivering it from all possibility of such objection; in which last labour I have proceeded as far as to the 7th. Book.

How has it happen'd that since Pope did certainly dedicate both Iliad and Odyssey, no dedication is found in this first Edition of them? [3]

You know, I presume, having seen William, that the Throckmortons are in town. They are to be found at No. 11 New Burlington Street. Our Ladies, seeing that you are now a husband, take courage and send their love to you. Our best Compliments attend Mrs. Rose also.

I am, truly Yours — Wm Cowper.

MRS BODHAM   Thursday, 10 February 1791

Address: [Mrs. Bodh]am / [South] Green / [Ma]ttishall / Norfolk
Princeton *and* Panshanger Collection (*copy*)[1]

Weston-Underwood
Feb. 10. 1791

My dearest Cousin —

A hasty line, and a very hasty one, must plead my excuse for not writing sooner, and must say little more. I have waited weeks for an opportunity to give you an answer to

---

[2] MS torn at the seal. The words in brackets have been supplied in an unknown hand.

[3] Pope did not dedicate either translation.

---

[1] This letter is derived from two manuscript fragments at Princeton and a copy of the entire letter in the Panshanger Collection. The first fragment comprises the

your last kind letter, more worthy of it than this is likely to prove, but have found none, my long work in the present state of it occupying me continually. In a few weeks the whole, I hope, will be printed; *my* labours, at least, will be at an end; and I will gladly then make you the best amends in my power, for having seemed to neglect you now. But you will come, I hope, and receive those amends in person. The Spring comes on; Lady Hesketh left us the day before yesterday, and the loss of one Cousin whom I dearly love cannot be better supplied than by another.

Remember me most affectionately to my dear Johnny if he is now at Mattishal, and tell him that he owes me a letter and has been long in my debt, though mine perhaps which was addressed to him at College may have never reach'd him. Tell him also that my list of Subscribers is published in the Analytical Review of this month and in the Gentleman's Magazine, and that it will not be long, not longer I suppose than April, before the final list must be printed that is to appear in the volume. I mention this, lest his zeal to accumulate names and guineas should occasion him to delay too long the delivery of his collection at the booksellers'. Tell him too, in the last place, that we love him dearly and wish above all things to see him again at Weston, and that Lady Hesketh, though not here to speak for herself, keeps pace with us in a sincere affection and strong partiality toward him.

As to yourself, my dear Cousin, I can with truth say, that you, as well as he, are in my thoughts daily, and that nothing will give us greater pleasure than to see you as well as to think of you.

Mrs. Unwin joins me in very best Compliments and respects to all at Mattishall, and now I must say, farewell for the present, my dearest Rose, and with my love to you and yours conclude myself, though on the wings of all an author's hurry,

Sincerely Yours
Wm Cowper.

text of the letter from its opening until 'Weston, and' in the fourth sentence in the second paragraph; the second manuscript fragment runs from where the first fragment ends to the end of the second paragraph; the remainder of the letter is derived from the copy.

LADY HESKETH   Sunday, 13 February 1791

Address: Lady Hesketh / New Norfolk Street / Grosvenor Square / London
Postmarks: FE/14/91 *and* OULNEY
Panshanger Collection

Feb 13. 1791

My dearest Coz —

    I can now send you a full and true account of this business — Having learn'd from the Bull at Olney that your Inn at Wooburn was the George, we sent Samuel thither yesterday. I furnish'd him with a set of written Queries that produced the following answer, with which he return'd about Noon.

    Mr. Martin, master of the George told him that his two guests, James and Edward drank only sixpen' worth of either brandy or rum and water between them, and in 5 minutes after you had left the house, James follow'd. When he mounted the horse Martin told him that if he would be contented to trot him only, he would carry him 12 miles in the hour, but that his wind was not good, and if he gallop'd him, especially at first setting off, he would lose his wind presently and become unserviceable. — James furnished with these instructions immediately set off on a full gallop, and the consequence was such as had been foretold him. Long before he reached Dunstable the poor animal had no breath, and James, not wise enough to consider that without breath it was impossible that he should go fast, was spurring and flogging him till at last he fell under him, when a boy belonging to the George and who was returning from Dunstable with a horse which he had been sent thither to bring back to Wooburn, found him thus occupied, namely, belabouring the horse which seemed more likely to die than to live. The boy proposed a change of horses, to which James of course consented, and rode on to Dunstable; the boy, instead of proceeding to Wooburn, following him thither slowly on the disabled horse, that he might take both back with him to his master's. The boy says moreover, that arriving at Dunstable some time after James was gone forward to the next stage, he learn'd there that your carriage had proceeded from that place half an hour before James reached it. But whether he went away on horse back or Coach-back he knew not, not having had the curiosity to ask any farther questions about him. — Thus James's faults appear to have been two. First that he made the horse useless by sinning against the admonition given him by his owner, who knew what the poor beast could do, and what he could not; and 2dly — that when he had thus disabled him, he show'd him no mercy. — It remains for himself to explain his last desertion of you, since only he can do it.

I have now only time to add that we regret you always, and wish heartily that you could have stayed to hear our music, far more antient than that you mention — the music of our nightingales &c which will soon begin.

Johnson's week is expired, and the sheet now before me only begins the 23d. book.—Hang him for hurrying me.—I have even an affectionate letter from Walter Churchey, who promises, should he be called into England, to give me a sight of him at Weston. He hopes also to procure me more subscribers. Adieu my dearest Cousin, once more I say, beware of candle flame and hot pokers, and with Mrs. Unwin's best affections

remain ever Thine
Wm Cowper

N.B. The horse is recover'd and is as well as usual.

P.S. — I cannot help adding a circumstance that will divert you. Martin having learn'd from Sam whose servant he was, told him that he had never seen Mr. Cowper, but he had heard him frequently spoken of by the companies that had called at his house, and therefore, when Sam, would have paid for his breakfast, would take nothing from him.

Who says that fame is only empty breath? On the contrary it is good ale and cold beef into the bargain.

MRS THROCKMORTON   Saturday, 19 February 1791

Address: Mrs. Throckmorton — No. 11 / New Burlington Street / London
Sir Robert Throckmorton

The Lodge
Feb. 19. 1791

My dear Mrs. Frog —

I will be very good to you and will send you another letter, though you delay so long to answer my last and to tell me who was the author of the fine verses I sent you lately, and how much you admire them.

I was in hope that by this time you would have won your other ten guineas at Commerce,[1] and have flown upon the wings of that good fortune back to Weston. Methinks you are a long time about it. But if you have not won so much, I hope at least that you have taken care not to lose it. As for me, I grow rich, and have at this moment three guineas before me which my poetry, such is its power of attraction, has drawn into my desk from the distance of three miles and a half. I question if Orpheus ever performed such a feat in his life. It is Mr. Wrighte's subscription money to my Homer,[2] which he sent me the other day by the hands of Joe Rye, by whom he told me also that he should have paid it much sooner had he not feared to offend my delicacy. Now I wish him to know that my delicacy is never offended by the receipt of money. On the contrary, I esteem the want of money, commonly called poverty, the most indelicate thing in the world, and so did the antient Romans, who therefore always annex to the word *paupertas* an epithet expressing their contempt and abhorrence of it — such for instance as *squalida*, or *sordida*, or some such reproachful appellation.

But it was not with an intention to say this, or any part of this, that I have taken the pen at present. I meant only to relate to you a pretty little story of Tom, for I know it will do your heart good to hear it. — You know perhaps, if you have not forgot it in the hurry of other matters, that you lately sent a gown to be made at Weston. Nanny Morley[3] carried it into the nursery, and being seated there, said — Tom, or Master Giffard rather, this is your Aunt's gown. Which he no sooner heard, than walking up to it and taking a fold of it in his hand, he kiss'd it.

I made the Doctor[4] swear that he would not t[ell][5] this

---

[1] 'Commerce is a very old-fashioned English card-game, and is, perhaps, one of the most primitive of the Poker family. There are a number of varieties; all are played with the full pack of fifty-two cards, and all are very simple.' *Hoyle's Games Modernized*, rev. Lawrence H. Dawson (1950), p. 231.

[2] 'Geo. Wrighte, Esq; Gayhurst' subscribed for a fine copy.

[3] Nanny Morley was Thomas Giffard's nanny or nursemaid.

[4] Charles Throckmorton.

[5] The MS is torn at the seal.

anecdote, because I resolved to have the [pleasure] of telling it to you myself.

Give my best love to Mr. Frog — and my Compliments to Messrs. Cruise[6] and Pitcairne[7] when you see them, and believe me sincerely yours

Wm Cowper.

Tom and Tit are both in perfect health. Mrs. U. sends her very best respects. — Remember me to William.

JOHN BACON   Friday, 25 February 1791

Address : John Bacon Esqe. / Newman Street / Oxford Street / London
Postmarks : FE/26/91 *and* OULNEY
Princeton

Weston Underwood
Feb. 25. 1791

Dear Sir —

I take the first opportunity that my long work now in the press affords me, to make you my sincere acknowledgments in return for the very elegant and instructive specimen of your art conveyed to me by the hands of Mr. Bean.[1] — How happy are you! who if it had so pleased God, instead of exemplifying to the eye the virtue of a believing application to the Saviour, might have been a maker of images in honour of Diana of Ephesus! But he has furnished you with better subjects, and will pay you with a better reward than the praises of all the Heathen. — Should it happen at any time that you can possibly let us peep at you once again at Weston, you will find us always happy to receive you.

I am, Dear Sir, with Mrs. Unwin's respectful Compliments your much obliged friend and Servant

Wm Cowper.

[6] William Cruise (d. 1824), a legal writer of some stature. Although he was admitted as a member of Lincoln's Inn on 5 Nov. 1773, he was a Roman Catholic and was not able to be called to the Bar until the autumn of 1791; his major interest before and after being called to the Bar was conveyancing.

[7] See n.1, C to Rose, 1 May 1790.

[1] The MS is endorsed: 'Letter from Mr. Cowper to J. Bacon Esqe. R.A., on receiving from [him] a Cameo in paste from a seal modelled by him for Mrs. Onslow representing the woman touching the hem of our Saviour's garment.'

WALTER BAGOT   Saturday, 26 February 1791

Address: The Revd. Walter Bagot
Morgan Library

Weston Underwood
Feb: 26. 1791

My dear friend —

It is a maxim of much weight
Worth conning o'er and o'er,
He who has Homer to translate
Had need do nothing more.[1]

But notwithstanding the truth and importance of this
apothegm to which I lay claim as the original author of it, it
is not equally true that my application to Homer, close as it
is, has been the sole cause of my delay to answer you. No. In
observing so long a silence I have been influenced much more
by a vindictive purpose, a purpose to punish you for your
suspicion that I could possibly feel myself hurt or offended
by any critical suggestion of yours that seemed to reflect on
the purity of my nonsense verses. Understand, if you please
for the future, that whether I disport myself in Greek or
Latin, or in whatsoever other language, you are hereby,
henceforth and for ever entitled and warranted to take any
liberties with it to which you shall feel yourself inclined,
not excepting even the lines themselves which stand at the
head of this letter.

You delight me when you call *Blank* verse the English
heroic; for I have always thought and often said, that we have
no other verse worthy to be so entitled. When you read my
preface you will be made acquainted with my sentiments on
this subject pretty much at large, for which reason I will curb
my zeal and say the less about it at present. That Johnson,
who wrote harmoniously in rhime, should have had so
defective an ear as never to have discover'd any music at all in
Blank verse till he heard a particular friend of his reading it,
is a wonder never sufficiently to be wonder'd at. Yet this is
true on his own acknowledgment, and amounts to a plain
confession (of which perhaps he was not aware when he
made it), that he did not know how to read Blank verse

[1] These lines were first published in *Hayley*.

469

himself.[2] In short, he either suffer'd prejudice to lead him in a string whithersoever it would, or his taste in poetry was worth little. I don't believe he ever read any thing of that kind with enthusiasm in his life. And as good poetry cannot be composed without a considerable share of that quality in the mind of the author, so neither can it be read or tasted as it ought to be without it.

I have said all this in the morning fasting, but am soon going to my tea and toast, when, therefore, I shall have told you that we are now, in the course of our printing, in the second book of the Odyssey, I shall only have time to add, that I am, my dear friend, most

truly Yours Wm Cowper.

Mrs. Unwin joins me in best Compliments.

I think your Latin quotations[3] very applicable to the present state of France. But France is in a situation new and untried before. When she is a little more accustom'd to it and has had time to digest coolly and arrange the chaos of business before her, she will acquit herself better. At least, I think, she will never be enslaved again.

JOHN JOHNSON   Sunday, 27 February 1791

Address: John Johnson Esqe / Caius College / Cambridge
Postmarks: MR/1/91 *and* OULNEY
Princeton

Cowper's Homer.

All Booksellers and others of the Counties of Norfolk and Suffolk, at whose houses subscriptions to this work have

[2] Boswell relates the incident to which C refers: '"Mr. Langton, when a very young man, read Dodsley's 'Cleone, a Tragedy,' to him, not aware of his extreme impatience to be read to. As it went on he turned his face to the back of his chair, and put himself into various attitudes, which marked his uneasiness. At the end of an act, however, he said, 'Come, let's have some more, let's go into the slaughter-house again, Lanky. But I am afraid there is more blood than brains.' Yet he afterwards said, 'When I heard you read it, I thought higher of its power of language: when I read it myself, I was more sensible of its pathetick effect . . .'"' James Boswell, *Life of Johnson*, ed. George Birkbeck Hill (6 vols., Oxford, 1934–50), iv. 20.

Since Boswell's *Life* did not appear until May 1791, C's source must be a newspaper account or gossip passed on by a friend.

[3] Bagot's letter to C does not appear to have survived, and we have no record of the Latin quotations.

been entered, are hereby requested to accept the thanks of the Translator for their services rendered him on this occasion, and to deliver in their respective Lists and first payments to Mr. Stevenson Stationer of Norwich[1] in such time as that he may have opportunity to transmit the whole to the Publisher in London before the first of April next, the day already fixt by advertisement for closing the Subscription.

Weston-underwood Feb. 27. 1791

And now my dearest Johnny I must tell thee in few words how much I love and am obliged to thee for all thy affectionate services. My Cambridge honours are all to be ascribed to you and to you only. Yet you are but a little man neither, and a little man into the bargain who have kick'd the Mathematics, their idol, out of your study. So important are the endings which Providence frequently connects with small beginnings. — Had you been here, I could have furnished you with much employment, for I have so dealt with your fair MSS in the course of my polishing and improving, that I have almost blotted out the whole. Such however as it is, I must now send it to the Printer and he must be content with it, for there is not time to make a fresh copy. — We are now printing the second book of the Odyssey.

Should the Oxonians bestow none of their notice on me on this occasion, it will happen singularly enough that as Pope received all his university-honours in the subscription way from Oxford, and none at all from Cambridge, so I shall have received all mine from Cambridge and none from Oxford.[2] This is the more likely to be the case, because I understand that on whatsoever occasion either of those learned bodies thinks fit to move, the other always makes it a point to sit still. Thus proving its superiority.

[1] William Stevenson (1741–1821), of the firm of Stevenson, Matchett, & Stevenson, was a printer and publisher in the marketplace at Norwich; he had been publisher of the *Norfolk Chronicle* for more than thirty-five years at the time of his death, and was a fellow of the Society of Antiquaries.

[2] Fifteen separate Oxford libraries (10 for the *Iliad*; 13 for the *Odyssey*) subscribed to Pope's translation; in addition, 8 persons listed with addresses at Oxford subscribed to the translations; 4 college libraries at Cambridge subscribed to his *Odyssey* translation. C's list, on the other hand, contains 28 names associated with Cambridge colleges; 3 members of Oxford colleges; he also had 15 subscriptions from Cambridge college libraries, and none from Oxford college libraries.

I shall send up your letter to Lady Hesketh in a day or two, knowing that the intelligence contain'd in it will afford her the greatest pleasure. Know likewise for your own gratification that all the Scotch universities have subscribed, none excepted, and that I am now going to transmit to Johnson the names of 16 Irish subscribers, which I received from my friend Rowley yesterday. Several additions have also been made since the List was publish'd.

I esteem myself much obliged to Lord Howard[3] for his own name and for the names that have accompanied it, and should you write to his Lordship I beg you to tell him so.

I am happy that you left your sister and all my Norfolk friends in good health, and that you are in such good spirits yourself. We also are as well as usual, that is to say as well as reasonable folks expect to be on the crazy side of this frail existence. I rejoice that we shall so soon have you again at our fire-side, and remain with Mrs. Unwin's best love your affectionate

Wm C.

Should you see any alteration necessary in the above notice, make it.

MRS KING   Wednesday, 2 March 1791

Address: Mrs. King / Pirten-hall near / Kimbolton / Huntingdonshire
Postmarks: MR/3/91 *and* OULNEY
Princeton

Weston-underwood
March 2. 1791

My dearest Madam,

I am sick and ashamed of myself that I forgot my promise, but it is actually true that I did forget it. You, however, I did not forget, nor did I forget to wonder and to be alarmed at your silence, being, myself, perfectly unconscious of my arrears. All this, together with various other trespasses of mine must be set down to the account of Homer, and,

[3] Perhaps Lord Howard de Walden (1718–97), who subscribed for a fine copy. Charles Howard, 11th Duke of Norfolk, is not listed as a subscriber (see n.3, C to Lady Hesketh, 23 Jan. 1790).

wherever he is, he is bound to make his apology to all my correspondents, but to you in particular. True it is, that if Mrs. Unwin did not call me from that pursuit, I should forget in the ardour with which I persevere in it, both to eat and drink and to retire to rest. This zeal has encreased in me regularly as I have proceeded, and in an exact ratio as a mathematician would say, to the progress I have made toward the point at which I have been aiming. You will believe this when I tell you that, not contented with my previous labours, I have actually revised the whole work and have made a thousand alterations in it, since it has been in the press. I have now, however, tolerably well satisfied myself at least, and trust that the printer and I shall trundle along merrily to the conclusion. I expect to correct the proof-sheets of the third book of the Odyssey to day.

Thus it is, as I believe I have said to you before, that you are doom'd to hear of nothing but Homer from me. There is less of gallantry than of nature in this proceeding, when I write to you I think of nothing but the subject that is uppermost, and that uppermost is always Homer. Then I consider that though as a Lady you have a right to expect other treatment at my hands, you are a Lady who has a husband, and that husband an old school-fellow of mine, and who, I know, interests himself in my success.

I am likely after all to gather a better harvest of Subscribers at Cambridge than I expected. A little Cousin of mine, an undergraduate of Caius' College, suggested to me when he was here in the summer that it might not be amiss to advertize the work at Merryl's the bookseller.[1] I acquiesced in the measure, and at his return he pasted me on a board and hung me in the shop, as it has proved in the event, much to my emolument. For many, as I understand, have subscribed in consequence, and among the rest several of the public libraries.

I am glad that you have seen the last Northampton dirge, for the rogue of a Clerk sent me only half the number of printed copies for which I stipulated with him at first, and they were all expended immediately. The poor man himself

---

[1] See n.2, C to John Johnson, 26 Nov. 1790.

is dead now, and whether his successor will continue me in my office, or seek another Laureate, has not yet transpired.[2]

I began with being ashamed and I must end with being so. I am ashamed that when I wrote by your messenger I omitted to restore to you Mr. Martyn's letter. But it is safe, and shall be yours again. — I am truly sorry that you have suffer'd so much this winter by your old complaint the rheumatism. We shall both I hope be better in a better season, now not very distant; for I have never, myself, been free from my fever since the middle of January, neither do I expect to be released till Summer shall set me free.

I am, my dear Madam, with Mrs. Unwin's best Compliments to yourself and Mr. King, affectionately yours

Wm Cowper.

Lady Hesketh has left us about a month.

JOSEPH HILL   Sunday, 6 March 1791

Cowper Johnson

Weston-underwood
Mar. 6. 1791

My dear friend —

The old theme recurs, I want money, fifty pounds of good and lawful money of Great Britain.

After all this plowing and sowing on the plains of Troy, once fruitful, such at least to my translating predecessor, some harvest, I hope, will arise for me also, which will enable me to restore what I have spent of yours, and to replace some of my own annihilated hundreds.

My long work has received its last, last touches, and I am now giving my preface its final adjustment. We are at the 4th. Odyssey in the course of our printing, and I expect that I and the swallows shall appear together. They have slept all the winter, but I on the contrary have been extremely busy, yet if I can but — virûm volitare per ora[1] — as swiftly and as

---

[2] The new clerk for All Saints, Northampton, was Samuel Wright who reprinted verses from an old bill for the Mortuary Bill of 1791 and approached C for new verses for the Bills of 1792 and 1793.

---

[1] Virgil, *Georgics*, iii. 9: 'To fly on the lips of men'.

widely as they through the air, I shall account myself well requited.

With my best Compliments to Mrs. Hill, I remain
my Dear friend — most truly Yours
Wm Cowper

JAMES HURDIS   Sunday, 6 March 1791

Hayley, ii. 6–8

Weston, March 6, 1791.

Sir,

I have always entertained, and have occasionally avowed, a great degree of respect for the abilities of the unknown Author of the Village Curate, unknown at that time, but now well-known, and not to me only, but to many. For before I was favored with your obliging Letter, I knew your name, your place of abode, your profession, and that you had four Sisters;[1] all which I learned neither from our Bookseller, nor from any of his connexions: you will perceive, therefore, that you are no longer an Author incognito. The writer, indeed, of many passages, that have fallen from your pen, could not long continue so. Let genius, true genius, conceal itself where it may, we may say of it, as the young man in Terence of his beautiful Mistress — *'diu latere non potest.'*[2]

I am obliged to you for your kind offers of service, and will not say that I shall not be troublesome to your hereafter; but at present I have no need to be so. I have within these two days given the very last stroke of my pen to my long Translation, and what will be my next career I know not. At any rate we shall not, I hope, hereafter be known to each other as Poets only: for your Writings have made me ambitious of a nearer approach to you. Your door, however, will never be opened to me. My fate and fortune have combined with my natural disposition, to draw a circle round me

---

[1] Hurdis lived at Burwash in Sussex from 1785 until 1792; his sisters were Mary (1762–1824), Jane (1765–1809), Elizabeth (1767–1831), Catharine (1768–92), and Sarah Naomi (1769–1847).

[2] C has misquoted part of line 295 of *Eunuchus*: 'diu celari non potest'. 'She cannot be hidden for long.'

which I cannot pass; nor have I been more than thirteen miles from home these twenty years, and so far very seldom. But you are a younger man, and therefore, may not be quite so immoveable: in which case should you chuse at any time to move Weston-ward, you will always find me happy to receive you; and in the mean time I remain with much respect,

Your most obedient servant, critic, and friend,

W. C.

P. S. I wish to know what you mean to do with Sir Thomas.[3] For though I expressed doubts about his theatrical possibilities, I think him a very respectable person, and with some improvement well worthy of being introduced to the public.

JOSEPH HILL   Thursday, 10 March 1791[1]

Cowper Johnson

My dear friend

Having my hands full of Homer at present whom I am employed every day in correcting for the press, I must content myself with thanking you for your speedy supply. Give my affectionate remembrances to your sisters and tell them I am impatient to entertain them with my old story new-dress'd. I have two French prints[2] hanging in my study both on Iliad subjects, and I have an English one[3] in the Parlour on a subject from the same poem. In one of the former Agamemnon addresses Achilles exactly in the attitude of a Dancing master turning Miss in a minuet; in the latter the figures are plain and the attitudes plain also. This is in some considerable measure, I believe, the difference between my translation and Pope's, and will serve as an exemplification of what I am going to lay before you and the public — Adieu,

[3] Hurdis's play, *Sir Thomas More: A Tragedy*, was published by Joseph Johnson in 1792.

[1] There is a note by N. C. Hannay on this MS: 'This letter is undated by Cowper in its present state; but a strip has been torn off the top (the remaining portion is only 5 7/8" from top to bottom). Apparently a Receipt has been removed & with it Cowper's date. The date has been inserted in the upper r.h. cor. of f.1 in pencil.'
[2] We have no details on the French prints.
[3] See n.1, C to Lady Hesketh, 23 June 1788.

my dear friend, with my best respects to Mrs. Hill, I remain
yours with much affection and in great haste   Wm Cowper

LADY HESKETH   Saturday, 12 March 1791

Address: Lady Hesketh / New Norfolk Street / Grosvenor Square / London.
Postmarks: MR/14/91 *and* OULNEY
British Library

The Lodge Mar. 12. 1791

You are very kind, my dearest Coz, to accede so readily to
our purposed alterations. They are begun, and it will not cost
much time to finish them. The chamber allotted to your
maiden will be a snug and commodious one enough, and as to
the Pantry there will be no need either to mount or descend
to it, from which account of the matter you will conclude
that it is on ground. So in fact it is, but in a nook so perfectly
retired, that well as I may be supposed acquainted with the
house, I knew not that such a place existed. To give you an
idea therefore of its situation would be difficult, perhaps
impossible. Suffice it to say that it served our predecessors
in the house in that very capacity, that it has exactly the
aspect of the present pantry, consequently will be cool and
airy, and that it adjoins the Kitchen.

We were sure that Johnny's letter would give you pleasure
and therefore sent it. The little man has performed wonders.
Professors and Doctors and whole Colleges you see have troop'd
to his whistle; should Norfolk and Suffolk have been equally
ready to follow him our Subscription-list already splendid,
will be as numerous as it is respectable, and his success will
remind me (it does indeed already) of Fielding's droll simile

> So a cock-sparrow in some farmer's yard
> Hops at the head of a huge flock of Turkies.[1]

Thou may'st remember perhaps that, long since (not less
I suppose than a year and half) I sent some ridiculous Queries

---

[1] *Tom Thumb*, *A Tragedy* (1730), I, i. 7–12: 'The mightly Thomas Thumb
victorious comes; / Millions of Giants crowd his Chariot Wheels, / Who bite their
Chains, and frown and foam like Mad-Dogs. / He rides, regardless of their ugly
Looks. / So some Cock-Sparrow in a Farmer's Yard, / Hops at the Head of an
huge Flock of Turkeys.'

to the Gentleman's Magazine, in hope that either the answers to them, or some grave gentleman's censure of them would afford me an opportunity to kick up a controversy about them, for the amusement·of myself and my friends at the Hall. Long time they remained unprinted, but at last they appeared and were answer'd not only in the Magazine, but soon after in several news-papers also.[2] But nothing occurr'd that furnish'd me with the occasion of wrangling that I had sought. At length however, in the last magazine, a musty and insipid Antiquarian has thought proper to animadvert on the frivolous nature of my Queries with an air of great gravity and self-importance. I have accordingly enter'd the lists; that is to say, I have this very morning written and sent to the Post a letter to Mr. Urban, complaining of the undue severity of old square toe's stricture, and proving him to be altogether as ignorant and a more frivolous writer than myself. Now, therefore at last I hope that my end will be answer'd, and that there will be some sport between us. On my part at least nothing shall be wanting, for it will be delightful to me to plague him, and the occasion presents itself just at a time when I have leisure to improve it.

Surely we shall get Horace Walpole's name at last,[3] for I wrote, myself, to Johnson about it but a few days ago, and just before thou told'st me that thou hadst done it.

---

[2] In the Sept. 1790 edition of *GM* (lx, pt. ii. 301), C published a letter signed *Indagator* containing a series of mock queries as to the origin of 'Daffy's Elixir' and the expression 'an't please the pigs?', among other things. In this letter, C is complaining about the sixth answer to his letter in the *GM* (lxi, pt. i, 103–4) which appeared in the February 1791 issue as part of a pedantic letter from 'E' dated 'Feb. 17.' The paragraph which offended C reads: 'The stories about cant-words are beneath the dignity and reputation of the Gentleman's Magazine; foolish phrases about "pleasing pigs," and the like, have been descanted on, which I profess I never heard before; and that the people who deal most in such nonsense are the most uneducated and vulgar of mankind. I am obliged to your Magazine for much both of entertainment and information continually, and wish to guard it against descending to any thing mean and low.' C's letter to Mr Urban was not published (see *Russell*, pp. 137–8).

[3] 'The Hon. Horace Walpole' eventually did subscribe for an ordinary copy. Allen T. Hazen concludes that it was Walpole's cousin, the Hon. Horatio Walpole (1752–1822), later 2nd Earl of Orford of the 2nd creation, who was the subscriber. See Allen Hazen, *A Catalogue of Horace Walpole's Library* (New Haven, 1969), ii. 471–2.

12 March 1791

I leave the ends of my paper by Mrs. U's desire for her use,[4] and remain, my Dearest Coz. ever affectionately

Thine Wm Cowper.

CLOTWORTHY ROWLEY   Monday, 14 March 1791

Southey, vii. 7–9

Weston Underwood,
March 14, 1791.

My dear Rowley,

Monday morning is a time that I now devote to my correspondents in particular, and therefore I devote the present morning to you. Monday is a *dies non Homericus*, a day on which, having dispatched all the proof sheets of the preceding week, and as yet received no others, I am free from all engagement to Homer.

I have sent my bookseller the names which you transmitted to me (for which I now thank you, with a lively sense of the kindness you have shown, and of the honour they will do me). I have sent them copied with the greatest care. There is no danger, I hope, that they will not be accurately printed, for I shall revise the proofs of the subscription list myself. I have also given him the minutest instructions, and the clearest possible, concerning the conveyance of the books to your country as soon as they shall be ready for exportation, copying them from your letter. Thus nothing has been or shall be wanting on my part to promote the proper management, and effect a decent conclusion of this business.

---

[4] The following was added to the letter in Mrs Unwin's hand: 'I can assure your Ladyship that no one reveres the Clergy more than I do, when they give proofs of their own sense of the importance, the tremendous importance of their sacred office. I was grieved, indeed I was sincerely so, to find that the Author of all our happiness here and hereafter-purchased by His own blood, and transmitted to us through His alone intersession, should not so much as once be mentioned in the otherwise, charming Sermon at St. Pauls. May all the Bishops be stirred up to a faithful discharge of their duty here, and shine like stars in the heavenly kingdom. I am afraid I shall not have an opportunity 'till I have the honour & pleasure of waiting upon your Ladyship here, of seeing the new publication. However it will have my warmest wishes for its success. Your Ladyships recommendation must always have its due weight with me. — '

479

And now I will say, Oh my poor worried and tormented friend! why wast thou not, like me, a writer of verses, or almost any thing rather than a member of parliament? Had you been only a poor poet, the critics indeed might probably have given you some trouble; for that inconvenience no poet may hope to escape entirely, but the trouble that they can give, how trivial is it compared with that of a contested election![1] I heartily wish you well out of all this troublesome business, and hope that you will be able to tell me in your next that you are, and that all is settled to your mind.

I inquired of you in my last, if you knew aught, or had ever by accident heard of such a person as a Mr. Kellet of Cork, a banker.[2] Application was made to him long since for a subscription to my Homer, and for his interest on that behalf, but he has returned no answer. He is a sort of relation of mine by marriage, having chosen his wife out of my own mother's family, and his silence on this occasion makes me curious to know whether, as Homer says, he still opens his eyes on the bright lamp of day, or have already journeyed down into the house of Hades.[3] If you can possibly, without giving yourself the least trouble, — for of that you have already as much as may content any reasonable man, — procure me any intelligence respecting this dumb body, you will oblige me by doing so.

My subscribers' names, all that had entered at that time, were published in the Gentleman's Magazine and in the Analytical Review of the last month. Should either of them

---

[1] C may be referring to an incident recorded in Vol. XIV of *The Journals of the House of Commons in the Kingdom of Ireland From the Second Day of July, 1790, Inclusive, to the Fifth Day of May, 1791, Inclusive* . . . (Dublin, 1797), p. 78: 'The Right Honourable Mr. *Speaker* informed the House that he had received a Letter from the Honourable *Hercules Rowley*, at *Bath*, stating that having been chosen a Knight of the Shire for the County of *Antrim*, and also a Burgess for the Borough of *Longford*, in the county of *Longford*, he desired to make his Election to serve for the County of Antrim.

'*Ordered*, that Mr. *Speaker* do issue his Warrant to the Clerk of the Crown to make out a new Writ for electing a Burgess to serve in this present Parliament for the Borough of *Longford*, in the Room of the said Honourable *Hercules Rowley*.' There is no evidence that Clotworthy Rowley was himself personally involved in a contested election.

[2] See n.6, C to John Johnson, 26 Nov. 1790.

[3] *Iliad*, xxii. 52 (lines 57–8 in C's translation): 'But should they both, / Already slain, have journey'd to the shades . . .'

fall in your way, you will see that I shall introduce you and your friends into no unworthy company; several splendid names have also been added since.

I am, my dear Rowley, most truly yours,

Wm. Cowper.

MRS THROCKMORTON   Tuesday, 15 March 1791

Address: Mrs. Throckmorton
Sir Robert Throckmorton

The Lodge Mar. 15. 1791

My dear Mrs. Frog,

I send you my dispatches by a messenger who never was in town before, viz, by a pig. We hope however that by the help of a trusty guide he will arrive safe at the end of his journey.

I rejoice, though not in the cause of your return, the Cold that you say has attended you in London, yet in the consequence of it, that it sends you down to us again so soon. Soon I call it, because you return sooner than Mr. Frog, and sooner I suppose therefore than you intended. I shall know perhaps when we meet how much longer we must want your husband, and yet that may be a subject, one of the few subjects, on which he is not yet, himself, perfectly enlighten'd. Give my love to him and tell him that my charity for his religion will be all exhausted, if it prove the occasion of keeping him in town all the summer. I have none even now for those who have thrown impediments in your way, though of your own persuasion. The Doctor[1] dines with us to-day, and I shall endeavour to learn from him what can possibly be their motives, for they are far out of the reach of all my most ingenious conjecture. I hope, however, that maugre all such opposition you will soon hold your lands on the same terms as others, and be as rich as providence design'd you should be.

If you have not seen my Cousin of Norfolk Street very lately, I shall now tell you a piece of news, for which, if the thing pleases you as much as it has pleased me, you will thank me. The Queries that I sent to Mr. Urban are at last

[1] Probably Charles Throckmorton.

481

censured,[2] censured severely, and censured by the man of all the world whom I should have most wished to censure them, a grave, fusty, worm-eaten Antiquarian. I have already sent up a reply in which I have given him a good dressing, and should it but make him as angry as I think it cannot fail to do, we shall have rare sport all the summer. I had actually given up all hope of such good fortune, and the arrival of it now, at so late a day, is therefore doubly agreeable.

Little Mr. Buchanan will be of our party to day, who the last time he was here, desired that when I wrote next I would make his particular Compliments. — Mrs. Unwin's accompany them, which is all at present from your Lofing Frind and Nighbor[3]

Wm Cowper

I ought to have told you in my last that Tom has now found a shoemaker who fits him well, but I forgot it. He and Tit are in perfect health, and Tom talks of your coming home as well as he can, and with much pleasure.

WALTER BAGOT   Friday, 18 March 1791

Address: The Revd. Walter Bagot
Morgan Library

Weston-underwood
March 18. 1791

My dear friend —

I give you joy that you are about to receive some more of my elegant prose, and I feel myself in danger of attempting to make it even more elegant than usual, and thereby of spoiling it, under the influence of your commendations. But my old helter-skelter manner has already succeeded so well, that I will not, even for the sake of entitling myself to a still greater portion of your praise, abandon it.

I did not call in question Johnson's true spirit of Poetry because he was not qualified to relish Blank Verse[1] (though,

---

[2] See n.2, C to Lady Hesketh, 12 Mar. 1791.
[3] C is playfully imitating the local dialect.

---

[1] See n.2, C to Walter Bagot, 26 Feb. 1791.

to tell you the truth, I think That but an ugly symptom) but if I did not express it, I meant however to infer it from the perverse judgment that he has formed of our poets in general; depreciating some of the best, and making honourable mention of others, in my opinion, not undeservedly neglected. I will lay you sixpence that had he lived in the days of Milton, and by any accident had met with his Paradise Lost, he would neither have directed the attention of others to it, nor have much admired it himself. Good sense, in short, and strength of intellect, seem to me, rather than a fine taste, to have been his distinguishing characteristics. But should you still think otherwise you have my free permission, for so long as you have yourself a Taste for the beauties of Cowper, I care not a fig whether Johnson had a taste or not.

I wonder where you find all your quotations[2] pat as they are to the present condition of France. Do you make them yourself, or do you actually find them? I am apt to suspect sometimes that you impose them only on a poor man who has but twenty books in the world,[3] and two of them are your brother Chester's.[4] They are, however, much to the purpose, be the author of them who he may.

I was very sorry to learn lately that my friend at Chicheley has been some time indisposed, either with gout or rheumatism (for it seems to be uncertain, which) and attended by Dr. Kerr.[5] I am at a loss to conceive how so temperate a man should acquire the gout, and am resolved therefore to conclude that it must be the rheumatism, which, bad as it is, is in my judgment the best of the two, and will afford me, beside, some opportunity to sympathize with him, for I am not perfectly exempt from it myself. Distant as you are in situation, you are yet, perhaps nearer to him in point of intelligence than I, and if you can send me any particular news of him, pray do it in your next.

I love and thank you for your benediction. If God forgive me my sins, surely I shall love him much, for I have much to

[2] Bagot had perhaps sent C some more Latin epigrams.

[3] 'These protestations of booklessness must . . . have been largely rhetorical unless he embarked on a course of intensive book buying between 1792 and 1797. When Cowper died he was possessed of several hundred volumes . . . ': *Keynes*, 47.

[4] See n.4, C to Bagot, 20 May 1786.

[5] See n.6, C to Unwin, 3 Jan. 1784.

be forgiven. But the Quantum need not discourage me, since there is one, whose atonement can suffice for all.

Του δε κατ' αιμα ρεεν, και σοι, και ε μοι, και αδελφοις
Ἡμετεροις, αυτου σωξομενοις θανατω.[6]

Accept our joint remembrances and believe me affectionately Yours

Wm Cowper.

JOHN JOHNSON   Saturday, 19 March 1791

Address: John Johnson Esqe. / Caius' College / Cambridge
Postmarks: MR/21/91 *and* OULNEY
Princeton

Weston-underwood
Saty. March 19. 1791

My dearest Johnny —

Mrs. Unwin's letter has anticipated mine in almost every point to which yours required an answer, yet I must nevertheless write, because she, writing in haste and with Mr. Bean all the time in the room, forgot to mention the only subject on which you desire immediate information. You ask if it will not, or may not possibly be improper to solicit Lady H——'s subscription to the poems of the Norwich maiden.[1] To which I reply that it will be by no means improper, on the contrary I am persuaded that she will give her name with a very good will, for she is much an admirer of poesy that is worthy to be admired, and such, I think, judging by the specimen, the poesy of this maiden is likely to prove. Not

---

[6] 'His blood ran down for you, for me, and for our brothers, and we are all being saved by his death.'

---

[1] The 'Norwich Maiden' was Elizabeth Bentley (1767–1839); the work in question was *Genuine Poetical Compositions on Various Subjects* (Norwich, 1791). *Keynes*, 53.

John Johnson was probably particularly interested in this subscription list because the publisher was William Stevenson (see n.1, C to John Johnson, 27 Feb. 1791), who had taken in subscriptions to the Homer. ' . . . [I]t was through his patronage that Mrs. Elizabeth Bentley, an extraordinary self-educated poetess in the City of Norwich, was first known to the public' (*GM* xci, pt. i (1821), 473). Lady Hesketh's subscription must have arrived too late to be listed (see C to Lady Hesketh, *pre* 22 Apr. 1791).

that I am, myself, inclined to expect in general great matters in the poetical way from persons whose ill-fortune it has been to want the common advantages of education; neither do I account it, in general, a kindness to such, to encourage them in the indulgence of a propensity more likely to do them harm in the end than to advance their interests. Many such phoenomena have arisen within my remembrance, at which all the world has wonder'd for a season, and has then forgot them. The fact is, that though strong natural genius is always accompanied with strong natural tendency to its object, yet it often happens that the tendency is found where the Genius is wanting. In the present instance however, (the poems of a certain Mrs. Leapor excepted,[2] who published some 40 years ago) I discern, I think, more marks of a true poetical talent than I remember to have observed in the verses of any, whether male or female, so disadvantageously circumstanced. I wish her therefore good speed, and subscribe to her with all my heart.

The reason, I presume, why Johnson appointed so early a day for the termination of my subscription, must have been this — that a sufficient quantity of cash being already collected to defray the expences of the press, he deem'd it more for my purpose to cry — Halt! than to proceed any farther, designing to sell the unsubscribed part of the edition at an advanced price. If this at least were not his reason, I know it not, for it is pretty certain that we shall not publish sooner than the end of May, since we are now only in the 6th book of the Odyssey.

You· will rejoice when I tell you that I have some hope, after all, of a harvest from Oxford also. Mr. Throck——n has writ to a person of considerable influence there, which he has desired him to exert in my favour, and *his* request, I should imagine, will hardly prove a vain one.[3]

---

[2] Mary Leapor (1722–46), a cooking maid, composed verse from an early age, chiefly in imitation of Pope. Her *Poems on Several Occasions* (Vol. I, 1748; Vol. II, 1751) were edited by Isaac Hawkins Browne the Elder. A selection of her poems appeared in Mrs Barber's *Poems by Eminent Ladies* (1755).

[3] He had written to the Revd John Rawbone (1743–1825), vice-principal of St. Mary's Hall, Oxford (see C to Rose, 29 Apr. 1791); he ultimately subscribed for an ordinary copy.

Adieu, my dear Johnny, I long to see thee, and remain in the mean time with Mrs. U.'s best love — Your affectionate

Wm Cowper.

I have broken my seal to write a Postscript.

Mrs. Chester pay'd us a morning visit yesterday with two of her daughters, when she subscribed for herself and the eldest. Enter us all therefore in this order.

Mrs. Chester — Chicheley — Bucks
Miss Chester of do.
W. C. Weston-U — Bucks.[4]

Mr. Throck——n is in town and not expected here for some time, I cannot therefore get him for a subscriber, and here is nobody else who would give a farthing either to Poet or poetess. — I shall therefore be indebted to you in the sum of 15s and 6d.

UNIDENTIFIED RECIPIENT

Wednesday, 23 March 1791

Wednesday March 23. 1791

I dream'd that I walk'd up-hill in rather a deep snow, and that coming at the top of the hill to a long brick-wall which turn'd me to the right, while I pass'd under it I thought on you, and said — Shall I ever neglect Her? — Let me die first! Then lifting my eyes to heaven and having much of the presence of God with me, I exclaim'd — Think what I expected, and think how dreadfully disappointed I have been — Let it plead with thee for Pity, pardon, and peace — Oh my Father!

This I utter'd with such divine agitation as almost took my breath away.

---

[4] On the subscription list to *Genuine Poetical Compositions* . . . , C is entered as 'Cowper William Esq.'; the Chesters are under subscribers from 'Cambridge, &c.' as 'Chester Mrs. Chicheley' and '—— Miss, ditto'. The subscription price must have been 5s. 2d.

24 March 1791

SAMUEL ROSE   Thursday, 24 March 1791

Wright, iv. 48–9[1]

Weston, March 24, 1791.

My dear Friend,

You apologise for your silence in a manner which affords me so much pleasure, that I cannot but be satisfied. Let business be the cause, and I am contented. This is a cause to which I would even be accessary myself, and would increase yours by an means, expect by a lawsuit of my own, at the expense of all your opportunities of writing oftener than thrice in a twelvemonth.

I am glad that the prosecution of which you have had the conduct, troublesome as it must have been, has not been unsuccessful, and admire much that in the heart of a man who chose to subsist by plunder, that noble flame, the love of his country, should burn so bright, that he is offended at being sent abroad, after meriting to die at home. You must have been very merciful to him, or I see not how he could have escaped it.

Your application to Dr. Dunbar[2] reminds me of two lines to be found somewhere in Dr. Young: —

And now a poet's gratitude you see,
Grant him two favours, and he'll ask for three.[3]

In this particular, therefore, I perceive that a poet, and a poet's friend, bear a striking resemblance to each other. The Doctor will bless himself that the number of Scotch universities is not larger, assured that if they equalled those in England, in number of colleges, you would give him no rest till he had engaged them all. It is true, as Lady Hesketh told you, that I shall not fear in the matter of subscription a comparison even with Pope himself; considering (I mean) that we live in days of terrible taxation, and when verse, not being a necessary of life, is accounted dear, be it what it may,

---

[1] This letter was listed in the Puttick and Simpson catalogue for 1 Aug. 1856 as lot 218 of the Richard Capel Lambe collection.

[2] James Dunbar (d. 1798), the philosopher, was educated at King's College, Aberdeen, of which he was elected a regent in 1766; in that capacity he taught there for thirty years.

[3] *Love of Fame, The Universal Passion*, Satire III. 3–4.

even at the lowest price. I am no very good arithmetician, yet I calculated the other day in my morning walk, that my two volumes, at the price of three guineas,[4] will cost the purchaser less than the seventh part of a farthing per line. Yet there are lines among them that have cost me the labour of hours, and none that have not cost me some labour.

W. C.

LADY HESKETH   Friday, 25 March 1791

Friday Night   Mar. 25. 1791
My dearest Coz — The Subscription is so near a close, that it is too late to give Meryl[1] fresh instructions to any purpose. Beside which, there must I think, be a mistake in this matter; that he has received the Subscription-money of some is certain, and it is difficult to conceive, that being the case, for what reason he should refuse the money of others. Every Post that comes I expect will bring me the whole Cambridge account made up by Johnny, and a copy of it shall be immediately transmitted to you.

Johnson writes me word that he has repeatedly called on Horace Walpole,[2] and has never found him at home; he has also written on him and received no answer. I charge thee therefore on thy allegiance that thou move not a finger more in this business. My back is up, and I cannot bear the thought of wooing him any farther, nor would do it, though he were as pig a Gentleman, look you, as Lucifer himself.[3] I have Welsh blood in me, if the pedigree of the Donnes say true,[4] and every drop of it says — Let him alone.

---

[4] Three guineas was the price for a 'fine' or Royal Paper copy. Common paper copies sold for 2 guineas, unbound, and most of the subscriptions were for this version.

---

[1] See n.2, C to John Johnson, 26 Nov. 1790.
[2] See n.3, C to Lady Hesketh, 12 Mar. 1791.
[3] C probably has in mind *Henry V*, IV. vii. 146: 'As good a gentleman as the devil is, as Lucifer and Belzebub himself.'
[4] See n.1, C to Mrs Bodham, 27 Feb. 1790. 'According to Walton, [Donne] was "masculinely and lineally descended from a very antient Family in *Wales*".

I should have dined at the Hall to day, having engaged myself to do so, but an untoward occurrence that happen'd last night, or rather this morning prevented me. It was a thundering rap at the door just after the clock struck three. First I thought the house was on fire, then I thought the Hall was on fire, then I thought it was a Housebreaker's trick, then I thought it was an Express. In any case, I thought that if it should be repeated, it would awaken and terrify Mrs. Unwin and kill her with spasms. The consequence of all these thoughts was the worst nervous fever I ever had in my life, altough it was the shortest. Mrs. Unwin awoke in about half an hour, and having learn'd from me what had happened, would rise to give me some Hoffman.[5] I took it, and was never so benefitted by it before. It took off my fever, gave me quiet sleep, and enabled me to rise in tolerable spirits, yet not so well as to be fit for any place but home. The rap was given but once though a multifarious one. Had I heard a second, I should have risen myself at all adventures. It was the only minute since you went, in which I have been glad that you were not here. Soon after I came down, I learn'd that a drunken party had passed through the village at that time, and they were no doubt the authors of this witty, but troublesome invention.

Our thanks are due to you for the book[6] you sent us by Mrs. Frog. Mrs. Unwin has read to me several parts of it which I have much admired. The observations are shrewd and pointed, and there is much wit in the Similes and illustrations. Yet a remark struck me which I could not help making vivâ voce on the occasion. If the book has any real value, and does in truth deserve the notice taken of it by those to whom it is addressed, its claim is founded neither on the expression, nor on the stile, nor on the wit of it, but altogether on the Truth that it contains. Now the same Truths are deliver'd, to my knowledge, perpetually from the pulpit, by Ministers whom the admirers of this writer would disdain to hear. Yet the Truth is not the less important for

His earliest portrait, made in 1591, displays a coat of arms which he also used on one of his seals . . . These arms, azure a wolf salient, with a crest of snakes bound in a sheaf, are those of the ancient family of Dwn of Kidwelly in Carmarthenshire . . .': R. C. Bald, *John Donne, A Life* (Oxford, 1970), p. 20.

[5] See n.2, C to Lady Hesketh, 14–16 Jan. 1787.   [6] Unidentified.

not being accompanied and recommended by brilliant thoughts and expressions, neither is God, from whom comes all truth, any more a respecter of wit than he is of persons. It will appear soon, whether they applaud the book for the sake of its unanswerable arguments, or only tolerate the argument for the sake of the splendid manner in which it is enforced. — I wish as heartily that it may do them good, as if I were myself the author of it — but alas! my wishes and hopes are much at variance — It will be the talk of a day, as another publication of the same kind has been, and then the noise of Vanity-Fair will drown the voice of the Preacher.

I am glad to learn that the Chancellor does not forget me, though more for his sake than my own, for I see not how he can ever serve a man like me. Adieu, my Dearest Coz — Mrs. U will speak for herself.

MRS THROCKMORTON   Friday, [25 March 1791] [1]

Olney (*copy*)

My dear Mrs Frog

I have waited to the present hour that I might be able to ascertain what measure of strength and spirits I should be able to bring with, if I should dine with you to day and find Myself a miserable, fit only to go to sleep — for which reason if you please I will postpone it till I can be more agreeable —

The cause of all this is a disturbance that occurred last night or rather this morning. A party of Drunkards returning to Olney thro' Weston I know not whence, at three o'clock amused themselves with thundering at our door. I had just then awaked and concluding that either our own house or yours, was in flames, was immediately siezed with a Fever, which has quite exhausted me. The fever is gone, but not the effects of it, which will make it better for me to dine with you to morrow.

Adieu
Yours ever Wm Cowper

Friday one o'clock.

[1] This copy was made for Hayley; the letter can be dated from the reference to a 'drunken party' in the letter to Lady Hesketh of 25 Mar. 1791.

JOHN NEWTON   Tuesday, 29 March 1791

Princeton

Weston. Mar. 29. 1791

My dear friend —

It affords me sincere pleasure that you enjoy serentity of mind after your great loss. It is well in all circumstances, even in the most afflictive, with those who have God for their comforter. You do me justice in giving entire credit to my expressions of friendship for you; no day passes in which I do not look back to the days that are fled, and consequently none in which I do not feel myself affectionately reminded of you and of Her whom you have lost for a season. I cannot even see Olney spire from any of the fields in the neighbourhood, much less can I enter the town, and still less the vicarage, without experiencing the force of those mementos, and recollecting a multitude of passages to which you and yours were parties.

The Past would appear in a dream, were the remembrance of it less affecting. It was, in the most important respects, so unlike my present moment, that I am sometimes almost tempted to suppose it a dream. But the difference between dreams and realities long since elapsed, seems to consist chiefly in this, that a dream however painful or pleasant at the time, and perhaps for a few ensuing hours, passes like an arrow through the air, leaving no trace of its flight behind it; but our actual experiences make a lasting impression; we review those which interested us much when they occurred, with hardly less interest than in the first instance, and whether few years or many have intervened, our sensibility makes them still present; such a mere nullity is time to a creature to whom God gives a feeling heart and the faculty of recollection.

That you have not the first sight, and sometimes perhaps have a late one, of what I write, is owing merely to your distant situation. Some things I have written not worth your perusal, and a few, a very few, of such length, that engaged as I have been to Homer, it has not been possible that I should find opportunity to transcribe them. At the same time Mrs. Unwin's constant pain in her side has almost forbidden her the use of the pen; she cannot use it long without encreasing that pain, for which reason I am more unwilling than herself that she should ever meddle with it. But whether what I write be a trifle, or whether it be serious, you would certainly, were you present, see them all. Others get a sight of them by being so, who would never otherwise see them, and I should hardly withold them from you whose claim upon me is of so much older a date than theirs. It is not indeed with readiness and good will that I give them to any body, for, if I live, I shall probably print them, and my friends who are previously well acquainted with them, will have the less reason to value the book in which they shall appear. A trifle can have nothing to recommend it but its novelty. I have spoken of giving copies, but in fact I have given none; they who have them, made them; for till my whole work shall have fairly pass'd the press, it will not leave me a moment more than is necessarily due to my correspondents. Their number has of late encreased upon me, by the addition of many of my maternal relations, who having found me out about a year since, have behaved to me in the most affectionate manner, and have been singularly serviceable to me in the article of my Subscription. Several of them are coming from Norfolk to visit me in the course of the Summer.

I enclose a copy of my last mortuary verses. The Clerk for whom they were written is since dead, and whether his successor the late Sexton, will chuse to be his own dirge-maker, or will employ me, is a piece of important news that has not yet reached me.

Our best remembrances attend yourself and Miss Catlett, and we rejoice in the kind providence that has given you, in her, so amiable and comfortable a companion.

Adieu — my dear friend — I am sincerely yours. Wm C

MRS THROCKMORTON   Friday, 1 April 1791

Address: Mrs. Throckmorton — No. 11 / New Burlington Street / London
Postmark: AP/2/91
Sir Robert Throckmorton

The Lodge
April 1. 1791

My dear Mrs. Frog —

A word or two before breakfast, which is all that I shall have time to send you.

You have not, I hope, forgot to tell Mr. Frog how much I am obliged to him for his kind, though unsuccessful attempt in my favour at Oxford. It seems not a little extraordinary that persons so nobly patronized themselves on the score of Literature, should resolve to give no encouragement to it in return. Should I find a fair opportunity to thank them hereafter, I will not neglect it.

> Could Homer come himself, distress'd and poor,
> And tune his harp at Rhedicyna's door,
> The rich old vixen would exclaim, I fear,
> Be gone — no Tramper gets a farthing here.[1]

I have read your husband's pamphlet[2] through and through. You may think perhaps, and so may he, that a question so remote from all concern of mine, could not interest me; But if you think so, you are both mistaken. He can write nothing that will not interest me, in the first place, for the writer's sake, and in the next place because he writes better and

---

[1] This 'Epigram On the Refusal of the University of Oxford to Subscribe to His Translation of Homer' was first published in *Hayley*. Henry Cotton, *The Tyrographical Gazeteer* (Oxford, 1825), p. 116: 'In Welsh books this city [Oxford] is called *Rhed-y-chen* (i.e., ford of the Oxen) from which has been coined the word *Rhedycina*.'

[2] *A Second Letter Addressed to the Catholic Clergy of England on the Appointment of Bishops, in which the Objections to the First Letter Are Answered*. Throckmorton's first pamphlet (C owned both: *Keynes*, 65), which appeared in 1790, had attempted to convince Roman Catholics that they had the right to choose their own bishops without recourse to Rome; his aim was also to encourage fellow Catholics to accept the provisions of the Catholic Relief Act (finally passed on 7 June 1791) by which after publicly declaring their faith and signing a formal oath of allegiance to the King, they were allowed the full legal rights formerly denied them. Throckmorton's *Letter* of 1790 was answered by Bishop John Milner (1752–1826) in *The Clergyman's Answer to the Layman's Letter on the Appointment of Bishops*, and he wrote his *Second Letter . . .* in response to Miller.

reasons better than any body, with more candour and with more sufficiency, and consequently with more satisfaction to all his readers, save only his opponents. They, I think, by this time wish that they had let him alone.

Tom is delighted past measure with his wooden nag, and gallops at a rate that would kill any horse that had a life to lose. Mrs. Nunnerly bids me tell you that both He and his sister have got rid of their colds, and are in perfect health. He has travell'd so much in his nursery that I have not had the good fortune to meet him since you went, but I sent Samuel yesterday in the evening to enquire after him, who found him riding and as happy as even you can wish him.

Miss Bab Chester[3] came hither yesterday on her pony to introduce to me Lord Bagot's eldest son[4] accompanied by his Tutour.[5] I like them both. The young man has a handsome countenance, sensible and expressive, and his Tutour, whose name if I remember it is Harlock, seems gentle and amiable and well qualified for his office. *It* happened that I was not in one of my shy moods, so we were all chatty and agreeable.

We have met with some rubs lately in the affair of the By-post,[6] and I began to fear that I should have occasion to give Mr. Frog some trouble about it, lest that convenience should be lost to us. All the danger that seem'd to threaten us was occasion'd by the Post-mistress at Olney, but at present we go on in our old train.

With our joint best Compliments to you both I remain

> my dear Mrs. F — Sincerely yours   Wm C.

[3] Barbara Chester, eldest daughter of Charles Chester of Chicheley Hall. In May 1806 she married John Drummond, a banker; at that time she was a Maid of Honour to the Queen.

[4] William, later 2nd Baron Bagot (1773-1856).

[5] James Thomas Hurlock (1766-1847), who entered St. John's College, Cambridge, in 1784 (BA, 1789; MA, 1792; DD, 1809). He was ordained deacon at Norwich in Sept. 1789 and became curate of Little Wratting, Suffolk, the same year. He subsequently became Prebend of Salisbury Cathedral (1821–47) and Rector of Langham, Essex (1829–47).

[6] A reference to the person who carried the mail from Weston to Olney; the difficulty mentioned here was resolved by 17 May (see C's letter of that date to Mrs Throckmorton).

JOHN JOHNSON   Wednesday, 6 April 1791

Hayley, i. 402–3

Weston, April 6, 1791.

My dear Johnny,

A thousand thanks for your splendid assemblage of Cambridge luminaries.[1] If you are not contented with your collection, it can only be because you are unreasonable; for I, who may be supposed more covetous on this occasion than any body, am highly satisfied, and even delighted with it. If indeed you should find it practicable to add still to the number, I have not the least objection; but this charge I give you,

Αλλο δε τοι ερεω, συ δ᾽ενι φρεσι Βαλλεο σησι.[2]

Stay not an hour beyond the time you have mentioned, even though you should be able to add a thousand names by doing so; for I cannot afford to purchase them at that cost. I long to see you, and so do we both, and will not suffer you to postpone your visit for any such consideration. No, my dear boy, in the affair of subscriptions, we are already illustrious enough; shall be so at least when you shall have inlisted a College or two more, which, perhaps, you may be able to do in the course of the ensuing week. I feel myself much obliged to your University, and much disposed to admire the liberality of spirit they have shewn on this occasion. Certainly I had not deserved much favour of their hands, all things considered; but the cause of literature seems to have some weight with them, and to have superseded the resentment they might be supposed to entertain on the score of certain censures that you wot of. It is not so at Oxford.

W. C.

---

[1] According to C's letter to Lady Hesketh of *pre* 22 Apr. 1791, John Johnson had obtained subscriptions worth a 100 guineas. On the subscription list, 28 names are associated with Cambridge, and of these 5 asked for fine copies; there were also subscriptions from 15 Cambridge college libraries. There must have been some subscribers enlisted by John Johnson who did not place Cambridge after their name, since the total subscription money for the known Cambridge copies amounts to 91 guineas.

[2] 'I'll tell you another thing, and see you lay it to heart.' A formulaic line that recurs with variations in Homer (see *Iliad*, i. 297).

JOSEPH HILL   Wednesday, 6 April 1791

Cowper Johnson

Weston-Underwood
April 6. 1791.

My dear friend —

Many thanks for your early information.[1] I send you as
speedily a short line in return, merely to assure you that I
did not boast of more philosophical fortitude than I really
possess, but am as easy and as well contented with my lean
purse as ever. I have heard vulgar people say — No butter will
stick upon my bread — An adage which, when I review the
Past, vulgar as it is, I feel myself ready to adopt; but I will
not at present adopt it, in Hopes that Homer may yet butter
a crust or two for me before I die.

With my Love to Mrs. Hill and your Sisters I remain —
Ever yours — Wm Cowper.

My intelligence was not from Lady H—— but from General
Cowper.

SAMUEL ROSE   Thursday, 7 April 1791

Address: Samuel Rose Esqr. / Chancery Lane / London
Postmark: AP/9/91
Carl H. Pforzheimer Library

The Lodge Thursd. Eve
April 7. 1791

My dear friend —

Admit a Client by whom you will get nothing but trouble.
It is the lot of all you Londoners who have friends in the
country, and was once my own. I have two wants and only
you can supply them.

In the first place I want shoes; which indeed I told you
when I had last the pleasure to see you here, and you noted
it in your tables. Be so kind as to order your artist in the
leather way to make me three pair of the common sort, and
two pair of walking shoes, substantially put together and that

---

[1] This is a reference to the 'unclaim'd Dividend', which did not exist, mentioned
in C's letter to Lady Hesketh of *pre* 22 Apr.

may serve me two years, for so long I used those which I have lately discarded. He must allow himself no delay, but must work double tides, lest I go barefoot or be obliged to have recourse to the Farrier, a more eligible assistant in such a case than any of the Coblers hereabout.

Secondly, I want Cheese — a Cheshire cheese — a large one. Mrs. Unwin says, a cheese of about 60 or 70 lb weight. The last you procured for us was excellent and did great honour both to the Taster and the country that produced it. At present, we have not about two ounces of it left, which I mention that you may judge of the greatness of the emergency and how much need there is of expedition in this case also. Lady Hesketh has given bond to pay for it, and I will take care that in my next letter she shall hear of it with both ears.

I hope that Mr. Frogat[1] continues true to you. Of this I am sure, that you will not lose *him* as I lost a legion of Attorneys myself — by never doing the business they brought me.

My Cousin Johnson has done great things for me at Cambridge. He is such another friend as you, active and warm in my interest to a degree that suits me exactly; me, who never could do myself any good, and had therefore always great need of such as would do it for me. I expect him here tomorrow se'nnight.

My Printer wants no good quality save that of expedition. I scold him but he will not budge. Should you happen to go near Johnson's house you will oblige me by giving him a gentle hint. Only ask him, when he thinks the Town will adjourn to the Country, and when we are likely to publish; for I get but 5 sheets a week, and we are now only in the eleventh Odyssey.

With our joint best Compliments to yourself and Mrs. Rose

I remain sincerely Yours — Wm Cowper.

I sent your books according to notice and hope they arrived safe.[2]

---

[1] 'A New, Complete, and Accurate List of all the Certificated Attorneys, Residing in London . . .' in John Hughes, *The New Law List* (1799), p. 22, gives a William Froggatt whose office was at 26 Castle Street in Leicester Square; he was a specialist in common-pleas.

[2] C must have returned some of the Homer books lent to him by Rose.

MRS BODHAM   Friday, 8 April 1791

Address: Mrs. Bodham / South Green / Mattishall / Norfolk
Postmarks: AP/9/91 *and* OULNEY
Princeton

Weston-Underwood
Friday April 8. 1791

My dearest Coz —

If you knew how pleasant I find all your letters you would write more frequently, for I know you have a world of good-nature and love to do kind things. My affection for my own mother's kindred is the same as if my intercourse with them had been constant even from my cradle, and, by consequence, I account this late revival of it, late indeed as it is, one of the most fortunate occurrences that in the evening of my days could possibly have befallen me.

I lament your poor Aunt Bodham's[1] great and distressing infirmities on all accounts, and among others on a selfish one, because I cannot but fear lest they should prove a hindrance yet again to your promised journey hither. There is One however who orders all things, and all things for the best to those who trust him; you, I dare say, are of that happy number, and should That happen which you expect and fear, will remember that whether he gives or takes away, he is equally gracious, and in both cases designs nothing but the welfare of his children.

Your nephew has perform'd wonders in the way of gathering subscriptions at Cambridge. There is no end of Doctors and Professors and Heads of Houses in the List that he has sent me, and the best of all is that he will be here himself on this day se'nnight. To him I am indebted for all these honours, and cannot enough wonder (the effect seems so dispro-portion'd to the cause) that such a whipper-snapper as he should have atchieved such great exploits. Had he been of Oxford, though his best wishes would have been equally mine his success would not have been the same; for Oxford has been applied to and powerfully too, but has return'd for answer — That it is a Rule with *Them*, never to subscribe to

---

[1] See n.3, C to Mrs Bodham, 29 June 1790.

any thing — Could you have believed it my Dear? Ask Mr. Bodham if he could have believed it possible, that a University, an Institution owing its very existence to the liberal encour- agement given to literature, should itself resolve to give literature no encouragement? For that is the plain and unavoidable construction of their answer. — So let it be — I shall make shift without them, and may live perhaps to pay them a Compliment such as they deserve.[2]

I am sorry for poor Catharine's illness. She must permit me to be her physician and to prescribe Weston to her. If large fashionable parties are hurtful to her, and I believe they do nobody good, here she will find exactly the remedy that her case requires, Early hours, stillness and peace. Her I expect to see and your Aunt Balls, nor will I yet despair to see even you and Mr. Bodham. Present to him my affec- tionate respects, and tell him how much I am obliged to him for his services. Give my love also to all my kindred with you and round about you. Mrs. Unwin joins me in all kind greet- ings, but says that when you see her you will be much disappointed in her. Between friends, she is a little given to Fib on such occasions. — Yours, my dearest Coz —

Wm Cowper.

LADY HESKETH   *pre* Friday, 22 April 1791[1]

Panshanger Collection

My dear Cousin —

Mrs. Harcourt's strange and unaccountable story has now proved to me an occasion of false hope for the last time; hang me if ever I build any thing on it more.[2] When the General sent me news of an unclaim'd Dividend, that story immediately struck into my mind, and I said to myself and to Mrs. Unwin, the lost money is at length come to light. The more we

---

[2] See C to Rose, 29 Apr. 1791.

[1] The references in this letter, which is undated and bears no address, clearly place it in Mar.–Apr. 1791; since John Johnson's visit was to begin on 22 Apr., it would seem that this letter must pre-date that visit by at least a few days.

[2] Perhaps a reference to Sarah Frances Bard Harcourt (d. 1764); see *Ryskamp*, n.5, p. 193. We do not know what the 'strange and unaccountable story' concerns.

thought and the more we reason'd about the matter the more we were convinced it must be so, till at last I gave myself up without reserve to all the agreeable speculations that such a prospect was likely to suggest. This dream was of two days' continuance; then came Sephus's Letter and told me that it *was* a dream. As to Mrs. Unwin, she was sure to behave on the occasion as she behaves on all others, calmly and wisely. She only said — Well — the Lord will provide in his own time — Should it ever be good for you to be rich, he will make you so. But how do you think I behaved myself? Better, I can tell you, than there was any reason to suppose that I should. I folded up the Letter that had just undeceived me, lay'd it on the fire-side shelf with much deliberation, and opening a sheet of Homer that came by the same post, proceeded immediately to the perusal of it. Thus, she behaved like a good Christian as she is, and I like a Philosopher as I am. I had indeed promised my friend Sephus that I would do so, and it was necessary that I should keep my word.

We had a great curiosity to receive from you some account of your Connoscenti, and how your entertainment of that party was conducted.[3] Not that we had or could have any doubt that they would find themselves agreeably situated under your roof, but the manner of managing such an assembly, so unlike all other assemblies, was the circumstance on which I especially wanted to be informed. You have gratified us much by your description of the evening. It is no wonder that it proved a pleasant one, for they must of course be qualified to entertain each other, and you I am sure were equally well qualified to entertain them all. I have much real respect for Mrs. Carter, whom I have always been accustom'd to consider not only as a learned Lady, but as a good one.[4] Blessings on her that she has a friendship for you, which is evident by her giving you counsel.

You have done just the very thing I wish'd you to do in leaving Horace W. without any farther solicitation. Assure yourself, my Dear, that Johnson has been in no fault. Had he been King of these realms he could not have been attended

[3] Lady Hesketh had probably sent C a description of a meeting of some of the 'Blue Stockings' at her house.
[4] See n.5, C to Lady Hesketh, 14–16 Jan. 1787.

and danced after more assiduously, insomuch that I should feel myself hurt should any foot of man, woman or child dance another step in that service; Hurt, not only, nor so much, for my own sake, as for yours. Mind it not my Coz — As you say yourself, we shall do excellently well without him, and when he shall see the List, as some time or other it is probable that he will, he will find that for once in his life at least he has miss'd an opportunity of being in the best company.

Johnny, my dear Johnny, will be here, I expect, on Friday. He has given you I presume an account of his success at Cambridge; success with which he is dissatisfied, but I should be unreasonable indeed were I so. He has sent me a list of as many names as amount to a 100 Guineas, not to mention the honour that I shall receive from most of them. I thank you for subscribing to his country-woman's poems; I knew you would and told him so.[5]

I have drawn on thee for a Cheshire Cheese, value I know not what. Mr. Rose is to send it and thou must make thy payment to Him. You do not mention him, for which reason I presume that he was not at your coterie. I have been close.

I like Barbara's[6] verses well, except that the 4 first are dreadfully ungrammatical. But still I think the manner of these cruel poets, as you justly call them, might be better hit, and were I not a fellow-craft myself, should perhaps attempt it. These are rather too intelligible, and too good, in short there is too much thought in them.

Our alterations proceed with the greatest success, and two beautiful rooms are forming out of desolation and the old store-room. Mr. Frog does his part nobly, gives new deal flooring, new doors, and new and larger windows.

Mrs. U. bids me say, forasmuch as she knows that you interest yourself in her well-being, that she has got rid of the fever that hung on her all the winter, and is better in every respect. With her best affections I remain my Dear, ever yours — W.C.

[5] See n.1, C to John Johnson, 19 Mar. 1791.
[6] Unidentified. C deleted 'Eusebius' and substituted 'Barbara's'.

P.S.

Our Cousin of Totteridge's letter is a most kind one, and I send her a most kind answer.[7] She will perhaps make you acquainted with the contents of it. It accompanies this, to Henry that he may frank it.

Tell the Minister I can't afford to go to war, especially for the sake of an airy nothing call'd the Balance of Europe. God is able to save us, even though the Russian should eat up the Turk to morrow.[8]

JOSEPH HILL   [Wednesday, 27 April 1791][1]

Address: Joseph Hill Esqr. / Wargrove near Twyford / Berkshire
Postmarks: AP/28/91 *and* NEWPORT/PAGNEL
Princeton

My dear friend —

You heap kindness on kindness, and all on the head of a pauper who will never be able to make you any other return than the lean one of acknowledgments. I shall be glad to keep the nest-egg if it can be kept, but I apprehend rather that the approaching summer will go near to addle it. I will not however make free with that precious deposit unless constrained to it by necessity; a supply perhaps may in the mean time arise from some other quarter, and it is even possible that

[7] Unidentified.

[8] 'Catherine's rebuff to the triple alliance raised for Pitt the question whether it was advisable to strengthen his foreign policy yet further. His foreign secretary . . . argued in the cabinet that the triple alliance was England's only refuge from isolation. Therefore Prussia must at all costs be encouraged in activity against Russia . . . an ultimatum [was issued to] Catherine in March 1791; unless she would at once make peace with Turkey, restoring conquered territory, Britain and Prussia would take action against her. Catherine replied that she was not willing to return the city of Oczakov, which she valued as a base on the Black Sea. On 28 March the house of commons was invited to agree that an augmentation of naval forces would be required to enforce their will upon Russia. The address was carried by 93, the opposition resolutions condemning the policy were defeated by 80. Yet on 15 April Pitt drew up new dispatches which conceded to Catherine that Russia might keep Oczakov . . . In August Russia concluded peace on her own terms with Turkey.' J. Steven Watson, *The Reign of George III, 1760–1815* (Oxford, 1960), p. 297.

[1] The address portion of this letter is dated '27 April 1791' in an unknown hand. The top of the first page has been cropped, probably removing a receipt with the date.

Homer himself may yield it, for the negotiation about price can hardly be a long one. You may depend on my doing nothing without first consulting Rose. Apprized as I am of my own insufficiency in the art of bargain-making, I am myself the last man in the world in whom I would place confidence on such an occasion. This, you will acknowledge, implies some prudence, and even some discernment. As to Johnson I am still inclined to think well of him, I mean as to the liberality of his character. He certainly dealt handsomely with me in undertaking to print my Task at his own risque before he had seen a line of it. Then again, he has a good report from all who know him — and thirdly and lastly he gave a handsome price, viz. 800£ to Dr. Darwin for his Loves of the Plants.[2] All these things put together make me hope well of him. A short time however will ascertain the question clearly.

With my best respects to Mrs. Hill I am

most sincerely Yours
Wm Cowper.

SAMUEL ROSE   Friday, 29 April 1791

Address: Samuel Rose Esqr. / Chancery Lane / London.
Postmarks: AP/30/91 *and* NEWPORT/PAGNEL
Princeton

The Lodge
April 29. 1791

My dear Friend —

You have executed your commissions to admiration, and are entitled to all the thanks that can be merited by the purchaser of the best Cheshire cheese I ever tasted. Shoes I have received two pair, but alas they are of the fine weather sort, and the season is so foul that I no sooner set foot in the street than they are wet through. Give yourself however no farther trouble on this article, for before the thicker sort can arrive it is more than probable that the dust may fly.

[2] See n.2, C to Rose, 4 Oct. 1789. For Joseph Johnson's dealings with Darwin concerning payment and copyright, see Gerald P. Tyson, *Joseph Johnson: A Liberal Publisher* (Iowa City, 1979), p. 112.

When you tell me how you have succeeded with Dr. Beattie, tell me at the same time your success with the Mareschal College, and accept, whether you have succeeded or not, my thanks for both applications.[1] I forget if I told you that Mr. Throckmorton had applied through the Medium of the Vice Principal of St. Mary's Hall to the University of Oxford. He did so, but without success. Their answer was that they subscribe to nothing. The Vice Principal however added that when the book should be published, they would all purchase it, and very civilly he subscribed himself. Between the first and second publication of the List 83 names were added, so that with the addition of my Cousin Johnson's acquisitions, together with others made by Henry Cowper, and still others who will probably have enter'd volunteers, we shall, as you say, make a splendid appearance. Pope's subscribers did not amount, I think, to 600, and mine will not fall very short of Five.[2] Noble Doings at a time of day when Homer has no news to tell us, and when all other comforts of life having risen in price, Poetry has of course fallen. I call it a comfort of life to others, because to myself it is become even necessary.

These holiday times are very unfavourable to the Printer's progress. He and all his dæmons are employed in making themselves merry, and me sad, for I mourn at ev'ry hindrance. I lately received from Johnson an offer to purchase the Copy, and graciously consented to sell it to him. It will not be long I presume before he will propose his terms, which, as soon as I shall receive them, I will transmit to You for your consideration.[3] You have been so kind as to say that you will manage the bargain for me, and in truth there is great need that you should, for I am unable to do it myself. He promised me, when I began the work, to deal as liberally

---

[1] James Beattie had been appointed Professor of Moral Philosophy and Logic at Marischal College in 1760. Neither Dr Beattie nor Marischal College subscribed to the Homer.

[2] C ultimately had 498 names. 'The number of [Pope's] subscribers [for the *Iliad*] listed is 575, but one name is repeated . . . The number of copies subscribed for was 654.' 'According to the printed list . . . there were 610 subscribers [for the *Odyssey*] for 1057 sets.' R. H. Griffith, *Alexander Pope, A Bibliography* (2 vols., Austin, 1922-7), I, pt. 1. 41, 121.

[3] C retained copyright and was paid Ł1,000 the following midsummer for an edition of 700 copies.

with me as any man of his trade could possibly do, and I wish for more reasons than one that he may keep his word, but especially for your sake, because in that case he will give you no trouble.

With Johnny of Norfolk's best Compliments and with Mrs. Unwin's, I remain, my dear friend —

Sincerely yours — Wm Cowper.

MRS BALLS   Saturday, 30 April 1791

Address: Mrs. Balls / Swaffham / Norfolk[1]
Postmarks: MA/2/91 *and* NEWPORT/PAGNEL
Princeton

Weston. April 30. 1791.
My dear Cousin,
    I admit all your excuses, and as to my pardons I will keep them for those who need them more. I am not very apt to be angry with my friends, and had no doubt that when your letter should arrive it would give sufficient reasons for its long delay. Yet I say too much when I say that I admit them all, for as to the stupidity that you plead, that is by no means admissible. How could you possibly be stupid so many months together without losing your wits entirely? And that you were in full possession of them when you wrote your last, your Letter itself evinces sufficiently. That apology therefore must be excepted, and the rest are sufficient without it.

    I look forward to the beginning of June with great pleasure, as to a time that will restore to me a near relation with whom I have been merry in the days of my youth, and with whom I shall hope to be cheerful yet again. A relation too, who will be the more welcome, because, till lately, I had no hope that I should see her more. I have great pleasure also in expecting your niece, of whom I conjecture every thing that is amiable and pleasant both in temper and in manners; and thus I think of her, not only because she is of a family every individual of which I have found such, but because she is Johnny's

[1] Mrs Castres Donne had moved to Swaffham, and Mrs Balls was visiting her.

sister, and He cannot be so nearly related to any thing that is not perfectly agreeable. By the way, lest I should forget it I will mention it now. He wishes you by all means to do as you propose, to come together from Swaffham hither, Not only because it will save you so much unnecessary travelling (though that consideration weighs with him as it ought) but also because his sister will in that case have time to rest and refresh herself with you before she proceeds to Cambridge. Whether he means to write to her on this subject or not, is more than I can tell you at present, for he is at this moment in bed and asleep, but I have no doubt that he will because you desire it. I have been myself the subject of all his letters lately, for me he has toiled day and night, and since he began to collect subscriptions to my Homer, seem'd to exist for no other purpose. Neither have [his][2] labours been in vain, for of all my friends and assistants in this cause he has been the most successful.

I would with all my heart, and I wish it on all accounts, that Mrs. Susan Bodham enjoyed better health, for I foresee that as her infirmities deprived me of the sight of my Rose last summer, so they will again in this that is coming. You will think my reason a selfish one, but are we not all selfish in such cases?

Mrs. Unwin bids me present her Love to you, and entreat you to fix no time for your return into Norfolk. You have neither of you a family to call you back, for which reason there can be no need of it. Give my best love to Catharine, and believe me, my dear Coz, most

Affectionately Yours Wm Cowper.

Your nephew is now breakfasting at my elbow, and bids me assure you that he will write this very day to his sister. God give you a good journey to Cambridge, and thence to Weston — Amen![3]

---

[2] The MS is torn at the seal.
[3] Mrs Balls arrived by 15 June, and was still there on 7 July.

CATHARINE JOHNSON — Sunday, 1 May 1791

Postmarks: MA/2/91 *and* NEWPORT/PAGNEL
Formerly Mrs Augusta Donne

May 1st

My dear Cousin —

That you may know somewhat of me at least before you come, I send you my hand-writing, just to tell you that Mrs. Unwin and I expect you here with a pleasure which no pleasure can exceed except what we shall feel on your actual arrival. I learn from your brother that you are in a degree beyond himself apprehensive of strangers; but be not afraid of us, my sweet Catharine, before you come, for we will venture to assure you that you shall have no reason to be so afterward. With Mrs. Unwin's best Love, I am

very affectionately Yours — Wm Cowper.

WALTER BAGOT — Monday, 2 May 1791

Address: The Revd. Walter Bagot / Blithfield near / Litchfield / Staffordshire
Postmark: NEWPORT/PAGNEL
Morgan Library

Weston — May 2. 1791

My dear friend —

Monday being a day in which Homer has now no demands upon me, I shall give part of the present Monday to you. But it this moment occurs to me that the proposition with which I begin will be obscure to you, unless followed by an explanation. You are to understand therefore that Monday being no Post-day, I have consequently no proof-sheets to correct, the correction of which is nearly all that I have to do with Homer at present. I say nearly all, because I am likewise occasionally employed in reading over the whole of what is already printed, that I may make a table of Errata to each of the poems. How much is already printed? say you — I answer — the whole Iliad and almost 17 books of the Odyssey.

Last Thursday I had the pleasure of seeing your Brother Chester once more at Weston. I was carrying a pacquet of Homer to the post and met him soon after I had set forth.

507

He proceeded hither, and in two or three minutes I joined him in my study. After sitting with us about half an hour he insisted on my going forth again in pursuit of my first intention, and walked with me to the bottom of Hoebrook.[1] This I mention as a proof that he has recover'd the use of his leg, which was disabled, as he thinks, neither by rheumatism nor gout, but by the consequence and effect of his fever.

But the pleasure I had in seeing Him, and in seeing him so well, has not been the only one that I have lately received from relations of yours. About a fortnight since, perhaps three weeks, I had a visit from your nephew Mr. Bagot and his Tutour Mr. Hurlock, who came hither under conduct of your niece Miss Barbara.[2] So were the friends of Ulysses conducted to the palace of Antiphates the Læstrygonian by that Monarch's daughter.[3] But mine is no palace, neither am I a giant, neither did I devour any one of the party — On the contrary I gave them Chocolate and permitted them to depart in peace. I was much pleased both with the young man and his Tutour. In the countenance of the former I saw much Bagotism, and not less in his manners. I will leave you to guess what I mean by that expression. — Physiognomy is a study of which I have almost as high an opinion as Lavater himself, the Professor of it, and for this good reason, because it never yet deceived me. But perhaps I shall speak more truly if I say that I am somewhat of an adept in the art, although I have *never studied* it; for, whether I will or not, I judge of every human creature by the countenance, and, as I say, have never yet seen reason to repent of my judgment. Sometimes I feel myself powerfully attracted, as I was by your nephew, and sometimes with equal vehemence repulsed, which attraction and repulsion have always been justified in the sequel.

I have lately read, and with more attention than I ever gave to them before, Milton's Latin poems. But these I must make the subject of some future letter, in which it will be

[1] See n.3, C to Mrs Throckmorton, 2 Feb. 1791.
[2] The visit was actually made on 31 Mar. For Mr Bagot, Mr Hurlock, and Miss Barbara Chester, see notes 4, 5, and 3, respectively, C to Mrs Throckmorton, 1 Apr. 1791.
[3] C's rendition of these events occupies lines 127–62 of his translation of Book X of the *Odyssey*.

ten to one that your friend Samuel Johnson gets another slap or two at the hands of your humble Servant. Pray read them yourself, and with as much attention as I did; then read the Doctor's remarks[4] if you have them, and then tell me what you think of both. It will be pretty sport for you on such a day as this, which is the fourth that we have had of almost incessant rain. The weather, and a Cold the effect of it, have confined me ever since last Thursday. Mrs. Unwin however is well, and joins me in every good wish to yourself and family. — I am, my good friend,

most truly Yours
Wm Cowper.

JOHN BUCHANAN   Wednesday, 11 May 1791

Address: The Revd. Mr. Buchanan
Princeton[1]

Weston — Wed. May 11. 1791

My dear Sir —

You have sent me a beautiful poem, wanting nothing but metre. I would to heaven that you would give it that requisite yourself, for he who could make the sketch cannot but be well qualified to finish. But if you will not, I will; provided always nevertheless that God gives me ability, for it will require no common share to do justice to your conceptions.

I am much Yours   Wm Cowper.

Your little messenger vanished before I could catch him.

---

[4] 'The Latin pieces are lusciously elegant; but the delight which they afford is rather by the exquisite imitation of the ancient writers, by the purity of the diction, and the harmony of the numbers, than by any power of invention, or vigour of sentiment. They are not all of equal value; the elegies excel the odes; and some of the exercises on Gunpowder Treason might have been spared.' *Lives*, ii. 151.

[1] There is a draft of this letter in C's hand in the Panshanger Collection.

[ROBERT SMITH]   Thursday, 12 May 1791

Princeton

Weston-Underwood
May 12. 1791

My dear Sir —

I take the earliest opportunity to acknowledge the receipt of your kind answer to my recommendation, and will take care, with the aid of Mrs. Unwin, that the money shall be given at such times and in such portions as shall make the relief that you have destined to this poor industrious family, most effectual.

I rejoice that a person only of your name, and not yourself, was sinn'd against in the manner that I mention'd and so much resented. Indeed I have had a thousand pangs on the subject of those foolish lines, since I sent them to you; Suspecting, and not without reason, that you might perhaps little thank me for my angry interposition. To say truth, I know not the man in whose cause I should feel myself more fired than in yours, on any such occasion, and because I supposed you unworthily treated, therefore it was that I took the liberty to throw a squib at the offenders without previously consulting you.[1] But I have learn'd by what I have felt, never to be the Author of lines of which you, or any man whom I may respect as much, shall be the subject, without asking his consent for the publication. An injudicious defender is sometimes a man's worst enemy.

With Mrs. Unwin's most respectful Compliments I remain, my Dear Sir,

most truly and affectionately Yours
Wm Cowper

---

[1] Perhaps a reference to *The Task*, iv. 427–8.

MRS THROCKMORTON   Tuesday, 17 May 1791

Address: Mrs. Throckmorton / New Burlington Street / London
Postmarks: MA/18/91 *and* NEWPORT/PAGNEL
Sir Robert Throckmorton

The Lodge
May 17. 1791

My dear Mrs. Frog —

Though you were a whole Letter in my debt I yet had it in continual contemplation to write to you, and should certainly have done so had any thing occurred worthy of communication. But the affairs of our village have proceeded in one even pace ever since your last departure, undisturbed by the least interruption, except that, a night or two since, another drunken party pass'd through it, breaking windows as they went, but not ours. The Doctor also has met with another Lion. Mrs. Unwin and I ent'ring Hill Field on our return from Olney, saw him near the middle of the field and advancing with such heroic strides as he usually makes, toward us. But suddenly a terrible sound was heard from the bottom of Hoebrook. The Doctor stopp'd. In a short time the sound was repeated. The Doctor turn'd short about, and stood with his back toward us. A third time the sound ascended the hill, and the Doctor no longer able to stand his ground set off at his quickest pace and was safe in the house before we could reach it. Presently a horse pass'd us, led by a groom and dress'd in body-cloaths.

I should have answer'd your letter by the Post immediately ensuing the receipt of it, had I not waited for the return of Mr. Palmer from London, who had promised me that he would make enquiry at the General Post Office concerning the probable effect of our Complaint lodged there. I saw him last night and found that he had so done, and the result of his enquiry is that the affair is in the best train possible, that the secretaries are entirely disposed to do us justice, and that the present Occupant at Olney will shortly be superseded. There is accordingly no need that Mr. Frog should trouble himself with any application to Lord Chesterfield[1] on the occasion.

[1] Philip Stanhope, 5th Earl Chesterfield (1755–1815), was joint Postmaster-

Could I spare you without missing you so much as I do, I should be glad that you now and then make a trip to London, were it only that you may fight the battles of Truth and Reason, and correct the erring judgments of the metropolitans. What a Barbarian Lady![2] Her reply to you reminded me of those lines in the Paradise lost.

> So spake the Fiend, and with necessity
> The Tyrant's plea, excused his dev'lish deed.[3]

My bird is washing himself and spurtles my paper, so adieu my Dear Mrs. Frog and believe me with my Love to you and yours — Your affectionate — Wm Cowper.

I grieve that your brother is indisposed. Remember me kindly to him. All will be well I hope both with Him and with me in less than a Century.

Mrs. Unwin sends her best Compliments.

LADY HESKETH   Wednesday, 18 May 1791

Address: Lady Hesketh / New Norfolk Street / Grosvenor Square / London
Postmarks: MA/19/91 *and* NEWPORT/PAGNEL
City Library, Liverpool

The Lodge
May 18. 1971

My dearest Coz —

Has another of thy letters fallen short of its destination, or wherefore is it that thou writest not? One letter in five weeks is a poor allowance for your friends at Weston. One that I received two or three days since from Mrs. Frog has not at all enlighten'd me on this head, for she does not mention thee. Not being able to tell me that she had seen thee, she did not chuse, I presume, to tell me that she had not. But I wander in a wilderness of vain conjecture.

Canst thou tell me to whom I am indebted for a neat Mahogany Pembroke table.[1] I should have concluded that it

---

General from 12. Mar. 1790 to 1798. For some details of the difficulties with the cross-post, see n.6, C to Mrs Throckmorton, 1 Apr. 1791.

  [2] Unidentified.   [3] *Paradise Lost*, iv. 393–4.

    [1] The donor may have been Theadora.

came from thee, from whom all my good things have come, had not the Direction informed me otherwise, by which I learn that it came not primarily from London, but through it from some other Quarter.

Mr. Bean who went to Town on Monday purposes to pay his respects to thee, and to introduce to thee, not me, but my likeness,[2] and if I do not flatter myself, a good one. Perhaps it is a little too young, but not younger than I was once, therefore do not object to it on that account.

I have had a letter lately from New York, from a Dr. Cogswell of that place, to thank me for my fine verses, and to tell me, which pleased me particularly, that after having read the Task, my first volume fell into his hands which he read also and was equally pleased with. This is the only instance I can recollect of a Reader who has done justice to my first effusions, for I am sure that in point of expression they do not fall a jot below my second, and that in point of subject they are for the most part superior. But enough and too much of this. The Task he tells me also has been reprinted in that city.[3]

Mr. Palmer, Drapier of Olney and his Partner Mr. Andrews have both number'd themselves among my subscribers. The former not by his own name, but in the name of his brother, Thomas Palmer Esqr. of Philadelphia.[4] This he has done in order that the more honour may result to thy Cousin, and because unless he had described himself by his trade, which would not have made a handsome figure among Earls, Dukes and Princes, he could not have distinguished himself from John Palmer the Ironmonger over the way, their Christian names being the same.

I know not that I can send thee any more News and breakfast is ready. We have blooming scenes under wintry

[2] 'The earliest known likeness of Cowper, apart from lost portraits of him as a boy, was a profile drawing made by John Higgins in 1791 from a shadow picture. This portrait, which is not a true silhouette but an outline drawing blacked in and touched with white and grey, shows him in a powdered tie-wig and a white cravat which is lying flat, only a small portion being visible over the coat collar.' *Russell*, p. 285.

[3] *The Task* was first printed in New York City in 1787 by Carroll and Paterson; the next New York edition appears to have been in 1796. See *Russell*, pp. 308-9.

[4] 'Thomas Palmer, Esqr.; Philadelphia' and 'Mr. Wm. Andrews, Olney, Bucks.' subscribed for ordinary copies.

skies and with icey blasts to fan them — Adieu, my dearest
Coz — Let me not wait much longer for a line, and believe me
with Mrs. Unwin's affectionate Compliments — ever thine

Wm Cowper.

Johnny has left us a fortnight this day, and is as usual
busied in my cause at Cambridge.

JOHN JOHNSON   Monday, 23 May 1791

Address: John Johnson Esqr. / Caius College / Cambridge
Postmarks: MA/24/91 *and* NEWPORT/PAGNEL
Princeton

Weston-Underwood
May 23. 1791

My dearest Johnny,
Did I not know that you are never more in your element
than when you are exerting yourself in my cause, I should
congratulate you on the hope there seems to be that your
labours will soon have an end. Johnson tells me in the sheet
I received yesterday that the printing of the Odyssey will be
finish'd on Thursday. There remains therefore nothing to
print but the Preface, the Frogs and Mice,[1] the Inscriptions,[2]
and the *List of Subscribers*. The three former I shall send to
London by the Coach on Wednesday, and I write now to
apprize you, lest Johnson should not, that the *latter* can
hardly be got ready and sent too soon. You will remember
that to me you must send it, that I may transmit it free to
Johnson. Let your List be very legible, that I may be able to
correct by it, and let all the names have their proper additions,
that no man who has done honour to me, may lose any of
his honours by me.

[1] C's translation of the mock-heroic poem, *Batrachomyomachia*, at this time
erroneously attributed to Homer, appeared after the *Odyssey* in Volume II of the
translation of Homer. The poem describes in Homeric style the confrontation
between the mice and the frogs. Zeus and Athena debate as to the sides they will
adopt. The frogs are defeated at first but Zeus ultimately intervenes and his
thunderbolts having been of no avail, he sends in crabs to settle the matter.
[2] C is probably referring to the dedications to the Earl Cowper (of the translation of the *Iliad* in Volume I) and the Dowager Countess Spencer (of the translation of the *Odyssey* in Volume II).

514

In a list of 7 or 8 names that I received lately from Lady Hesketh, and which she received from Mrs. Henry Cowper,[3] who received it from Dr. Madan,[4] I find the names of Dr. Jowatt[5] and Dr. Peckard.[6] How this comes to pass I know not, for certainly you cannot have duplicates of those Gentlemen at Cambridge. There is reason enough indeed why Mrs. Alma Mater should account herself happy in having One of each, and I am happy also that the Two she boasts are in the number of my subscribers. The circumstance would not have deserved mention had any thing occurred of more importance.

You will wonder perhaps my Johnny, that Mrs. Unwin by my desire enjoined you secrecy concerning the Translation of the Frogs and Mice. Wonderful it may well seem to you that I should wish to hide for a short time from a few, what I am just going to publish to all. But I had more reasons than one for this mysterious management. That is to say, I had two. In the first place I wish'd to surprize my readers agreeably, and secondly I wish'd to allow none of my friends an opportunity to object to the measure, who might think it perhaps a measure more bountiful than prudent. But I have had my sufficient reward though not a pecuniary one. It is a poem of much humour, and accordingly I found the translation of it very amusing. It struck me too that I must either make it part of the present publication, or never publish it at all. It would have been so terribly out of its place in any other volume.

I long for the time that shall bring you once more to Weston, you and your et cœteras with you. Oh what a month of May has this been! Let never poet, English poet at least, give himself to the praises of May again.

Mrs. Unwin bids me give you her best love. Remember me to Dr. Glynn. Make my best acknowledgments to Dr. Jowatt,

[3] Maria Judith Cowper (1752–1815), daughter of William Cowper of Hertingfordbury (1721 or 1722–69) and Maria Frances Cecilia Madan (1726–97), C's correspondent; she married her first cousin, Henry Cowper, the General's son.

[4] Mrs Henry Cowper's uncle. See n.3, C to Lady Hesketh, 2 May [1790].

[5] The Revd Joseph Jowett (1752–1813), Fellow of Trinity Hall, Cambridge (1773–95), and Regius Professor of Civil Law (1782–1813).

[6] The Revd Peter Peckard (1718–97), Master of Magdalene College, Cambridge (1781–97); he received the degree of DD in 1785. He was an enthusiastic supporter of the abolition of slavery.

and to Mr. Leak[7] for all their kindness to me, and be sure
[to] shut up your subscription directly, take down your
Apollo,[8] and let me have a fair copy of the names as soon
as may be, neither let your seal obliterate a tittle. I am,
dearest Johnny

> most affectionately Yours
> Wm Cowper.

MRS KING   Thursday, 26 May 1791

Address: Mrs. King / Pirten-hall near / Kimbolton / Huntingdonshire
Postmarks: MA/27/91 *and* OULNEY
Princeton

> Weston-Underwood
> May 26. 1791

My dear Madam —

It is high time that I should write, be it only to convince
you that my regard for you will prompt me to it even though
I have not the pleasure of hearing from you. To say truth
we have both been very anxious about you, verily believing
that nothing less than severe indisposition would have kept
you so long silent. If this be the case, I beg that you will
not think of returning me an answer, for though it would give
us the greatest pleasure to hear from you, we should be
sincerely sorry to purchase that pleasure at your expence,
and can only wish for a line on condition that you are able
to write one without encreasing the pain with which I
suppose you afflicted.

With these apprehensions about you I should certainly have
made this enquiry much sooner, would my daily attentions
to what is going forward in the Press have permitted. This
engagement has now been almost of a year's standing, and I
am not even now released from it; but I rejoice to be able to
say that my release is at hand, for the last line of the Odyssey
will be printed this day. There remain the Preface, the List of

---

[7] John Custance Leak (1771–1828), who was admitted to Gonville and Caius
College, Cambridge, in 1788 (LLB, 1794); he was Rector of Little Barningham
from 1802 until his death.

[8] The pasteboards John Johnson had been employing to advertise the Homer.

Subscribers, and 2 or 3 odd matters beside, and then I shall be once more at liberty.

You have not I think forgotten, my dear Madam, that you and Mr. King gave us a hope of seeing you this summer at Weston. In a fortnight we expect some relations of mine from Norfolk; what stay they will make with us is to us unknown at present, but I shall send you the earliest notice of their departure, in the hope that you will supply their place as soon as possible. Years are waning apace, and if we mean to cultivate and improve the intercourse we have begun, there is no time to be lost. Let us not have it to say when we meet in another world, that we might, if we would, have known each other better in this.

It is so long since I wrote my last letter to you, that I cannot at all recollect the date of it, but I seem to remember telling you in it that I had narrowly escaped the greatest of all my terrours, a nervous fever. To say that I escaped it is indeed saying too much, for I question if I am at any time entirely free from it; but I thank God that I escaped the degree of it with which in January I seem'd to be threaten'd. At present I am in pretty good health, yet not quite so well, I think, as in former years at this season. Mrs. Unwin, I believe, is about as well as when she had the pleasure to see you at Weston.

Thus, my dear Madam, I have said all that appears to me, worth saying at present. I have told you how we fare ourselves, and that we are anxious to know how it fares with you. I will add nothing but Mrs. Unwin's best Compliments together with my own, to both our friends at Pirtenhall, and that I am, Dear Madam, affectionately Yours

Wm Cowper.

LADY HESKETH Friday, 27 May 1791

Address: Lady Hesketh / New Norfolk Street / Grosvenor Square / London
Postmarks: MA/28/91 *and* NEWPORT/PAGNEL
Princeton

The Lodge
May 27. 1791

My dearest Coz —

I who am neither dead, nor sick, nor idle, should have no excuse were I as tardy in answering as you in writing. I live, indeed, where leisure abounds, and you, where leisure is not; a difference that accounts sufficiently both for your silence and my loquacity.

When you told Mrs. Howe[1] that my Homer would come forth in May, you told her what you believed, and therefore no falsehood, but you told her at the same time what will not happen, and therefore not a truth. There is a medium between truth and falsehood, and I believe the word, mistake, expresses it exactly. I will therefore say that you were mistaken. If instead of May you had mention'd June, I flatter myself that you would have hit the mark, for in June there is every probability that we shall publish. You will say — Hang the Printer, for it is his fault. But stay, my Dear, hang him not just now, for to execute *Him*, and to find another will cost us time, and so much too, that I question if, in that case, we should publish sooner than in August. To say truth, I am not perfectly sure that there will be any necessity to hang him at all, though that is a matter which I desire to leave entirely at your discretion, alledging only in the mean time that the man does not appear to me, during the last half year, to have been at all in fault. His remittance of sheets in all that time has been punctual, save and except while the Easter holidays lasted, when I suppose he found it impossible to keep his Devils to their business. — I shall however receive the last sheet of the Odyssey to-morrow, and have already sent up the Preface together with all the needful. You see therefore that the publication of this famous work cannot be delay'd much longer.

I thank you for the Eight names, two of which, viz Dr. Peckard, and Dr. Jowatt, how they found their way into Mrs. Henry's list I know not, having received them long since in Johnny's. But it is no matter, we have them, and let that suffice. The former of these good Doctors, as Johnny tells me, has lately published the life of a certain Mr. Nicholas Farrar, and in the margen makes much honourable mention of your Cousin & his doings in verse.[2] Are not you with egg till you see it?

[1] See n.1, C to Lady Hesketh, 26 Feb. 1790.
[2] P. Peckard, *Memoirs of the Life of Mr. Nicholas Ferrar* (Cambridge, 1790), pp. 254–5: 'I shall close this defence of Mr. Ferrar's character with the following

Mrs. U. and I and little Mr. Buchanan were walking together to Ely-ford, while you were entertaining the Frogs. The Evening was the first pleasant one that May had afforded, the Sun set beautifully and the nightingales sang sweetly, and we thought that however happy you might be, you would all have been much happier here.

By the next Hall-cart I shall send you two very neat Land-schapes by our Weston artist, which I will beg you to get framed and glazed for me. We both agree that you can send him nothing better than a waistcoat.

Rose is rather apt to be out of spirits, and I am willing to hope that he was so from constitution when he dined with you, rather than from any clapper-clawing that he had suffer'd at home. I pity him however, for if the temper to which he is yoked, be such, sooner or later he must be clapper-claw'd.

As for Politics I care not a farthing about them. Let who will quarrel, and weep for me, I reck not, having no room in my head for any thing but the slave-bill. That is lost, and all the rest is a trifle.[3] I have not seen Payne's book,[4] but refused to see it when it was offer'd me. No man shall convince me that I am improperly govern'd while I feel the contrary. — Adieu — my dearest Coz — with Mrs. Unwin's affectionate remembrances — I am ever thine —

W Cowper.

A letter the other day from a Mr. Geo. Jermyn of Ipswich,[5] after wand'ring to two or three other persons, found its way to me. He offer'd me his name and two others, but said not a word about first payment or any payment at all, though he desired the books might be sent to him as soon as published.

extract from Mr. Cowper's incomparable, I had almost said divine Poem, entitled, *The Task*, in which he considers the retired, religious man in a very different light from the Author of the Topographia Britannica.' Peckard then goes on to quote lines 906-37 from Book VI of *The Task*.

[3] C is referring to Wilberforce's motion 'to prevent the farther importation of slaves into the British colonies in the West Indies'. The motion was lost on 19 Apr. by a vote of 163 to 88. See John Ehrman, *The Younger Pitt* (1969), pp. 398-9.

[4] Tom Paine's *Rights of Man*. See n. 1, C to Rowley, 1 Feb. 1791.

[5] George Jermyn (*c*.1758-20 Nov. 1799) was a 'bookseller, printer, and stationer, of Ipswich' (*GM* lxix pt. ii (1799), 1088); he subscribed for an ordinary copy of the Homer.

I gave him a civil answer and referred him to my Bookseller. Will you now say that I know nothing of money matters? Who could, could you yourself have acted with more circumspection?

JOHN JOHNSON   Wednesday, 1 June 1791

Address: John Johnson Esqr. / Caius' College / Cambridge
Postmarks: JU/2/91/D *and* NEWPORT/PAGNEL
Barham Johnson

Weston June 1. 1791

My dearest Johnny,

Now you may rest. Now I can give you joy of the period of which I gave you hope in my last, the period of all your labours in my service. But this I can foretell you also. That if you persevere in serving your friends at this rate, your life is likely to be a life of labour. Yet persevere; your rest will be the sweeter hereafter. In the mean time, I wish you, if at any time you should find occasion for him, just such a friend as you have proved to me.

I have sent your List, your numerous and splendid List to Johnson, desiring him to copy it and return it to me, that it may serve me for the correction of the printed copy. I have also given him instructions according to your desire, to send my Homer as a gift to the willing but insufficient men of Sidney, and have given them a place among their brethren.[1] But some precaution in this case will be expedient. It will be necessary that you should intimate to them, or to some of them, by some means or other, that I have actually these gracious intentions toward them, otherwise when they shall receive the volumes there will be danger lest they should think me impertinent and themselves obliged to pay for them.

I have enter'd the name of Dr. James[2] the headmaster of Rugby since I wrote, and have had a letter from a Mr. Jermyn of Ipswich offering me his own and the names of two other

---

[1] 'Sydney College' is listed among the subscriptions from the Cambridge libraries.
[2] The Revd Thomas James (1748–1804) was educated at Eton and King's College, Cambridge (BA, 1771; MA, 1774). In May 1778 he was elected headmaster of Rugby School, where he introduced the Etonian system; he resigned this position in 1794 and in May 1797 was appointed to a prebend in Worcester

persons in his neighbourhood; but he made no mention of either first or last payment though he desired the volumes might be sent immediately on publication. For this reason, and because it was altogether an odd letter, instead of snapping at his proposal I referred him to Johnson. He may take offence perhaps and I may lose him and his friends too; but I saw no remedy; why should not there be Bookswindlers as well as swindlers of every thing else? I have also had a letter from New York, from a certain Dr. Cogswell, unknown to me. He does not write to me on the subject of Homer; I wish he did. But to tell me that my Task has been reprinted in that city and so forth.

And now, my dearest Johnny I have told thee all the news, and have done it with the very pen I used when you were here, unmended and unreleived by any other. Learn œconomy from me.

You promised to be here on the 9th. of June. Keep your promise if possible, but if any thing should happen to alter the day, give us notice, for I cannot bear vain expectation. Give our best love to your Aunt and Sister, whom we are impatient to see, and may God give you all a good journey hither.

> With Mrs. U.'s best love
> Yours ever Wm Cowper.

How must I think & acknowledge the Civilities of Mr. Merrill?[3]

JAMES HURDIS   Monday, 13 June 1791

Hayley, ii. 8–10

> Weston, June 13, 1791.

My dear sir,

I ought to have thanked you for your agreeable and entertaining Letter much sooner: but I have many correspondents who will not be said, nay; and have been obliged of late to give my last attentions to Homer. The very last indeed, for

Cathedral and instituted to the rectory of Harvington. He subscribed for a fine paper copy.

[3] See n.2, C to John Johnson, 26 Nov. 1790.

yesterday I dispatched to Town, after revising them carefully, the proof sheets of subscribers' names; among which I took special notice of yours, and am much obliged to you for it.[1] We have contrived, or rather my Bookseller and Printer[2] have contrived (for they have never waited a moment for me) to publish as critically at the wrong time, as if my whole interest and success had depended on it. March, April, and May, said Johnson to me in a Letter that I received from him in February, are the best months for publication. *Therefore* now it is determined that Homer shall come out on the first of July; that is to say, exactly at the moment when, except a few Lawyers, not a creature will be left in Town who will ever care one farthing about him. To which of these two friends of mine I am indebted for this management, I know not. It does not please, but I would be a Philosopher as well as a Poet, and therefore make no complaint or grumble at all about it. You, I presume, have had dealings with them both — how did they manage for you? And if as they have for me, how did you behave under it? Some who love me, complain that I am too passive; and I should be glad of an opportunity to justify myself by your example. The fact is, should I thunder ever so loud, no efforts of that sort will avail me now; therefore like a good economist of my bolts, I choose to reserve them for more profitable occasions.

I am glad to find that your amusements have been so similar to mine; for in this instance too I seemed to have need of somebody to keep me in countenance, especially in my attention and attachment to animals.[3] All the notice that we

[1] 'The Rev. James Hurdis, M. A. Burwash, Sussex, Fellow of Magdalen College, Oxford.'
[2] Either Deodatus Bye (see *Russell*, p. 163) or John Rivington (see n.4, C to John Johnson, 26 Nov. 1790).
[3] Hurdis's letter of 17 May to C reads in part: 'I was also a great Bird-merchant, & a considerable proficient in the making of Rabbit Hutches and Hen-coops ... The last birds I attempted to rear were a nest of sparrows, which had been by some means dislodged, & left in the open field. They all died save one, & so much gratitude was he possessed of for his board & education, that he felt no inclination to be gone from me. If he escaped from his cage he returned again, and would come when called & perch upon my hand, from the midst of a whole tribe of terrified companions.' This letter is printed in W. F. Tattershall, 'A Literary Discovery, Letters of James Hurdis to Wm. Cowper', *The Sussex County Magazine* (Eastbourne, 1927), pp. 27–8.

lords of the creation vouchsafe to bestow on the creatures, is generally to abuse them; it is well, therefore, that here and there a man should be found a little womanish, or perhaps a little childish in this matter, who will make some amends, by kissing and coaxing, and laying them in one's bosom. You remember the little ewe lamb, mentioned by the Prophet Nathan: the Prophet perhaps invented the tale for the sake of its application to David's conscience;[4] but it is more probable, that God inspired him with it for that purpose. If he did, it amounts to a proof, that he does not over-look, but on the contrary, much notices such little partialities and kindnesses to his *dumb* creatures, as we, because we articulate, are pleased to call them.

Your Sisters[5] are fitter to judge than I, whether assembly-rooms are the places, of all others, in which the ladies may be studied to most advantage. I am an old fellow, but I had once my dancing days, as you have now, yet I could never find that I learned half so much of a woman's real character by dancing with her, as by conversing with her at home, where I could observe her behaviour at the table, at the fire side, and in all the trying circumstances of domestic life. We are all good when we are pleased, but she is the good woman who wants not a fiddle to sweeten her. If I am wrong, the young ladies will set me right; in the mean time I will not teaze you with graver arguments on the subject, especially as I have a hope, that years, and the study of the Scripture, and His Spirit, whose word it is, will, in due time, bring you to my way of thinking. I am not one of those sages who require that young men should be as old as themselves, before they have had time to be so.

With my love to your fair Sisters, I remain, dear Sir,

Yours truly,

W. C.

4 II Samuel, 12: 1–4.
5 See n.1, C to Hurdis, 6 Mar. 1791.

SAMUEL ROSE   Wednesday, 15 June 1791

Hayley, i. 407–8

The Lodge, June 15, 1791.

My dear friend,

If it will afford you any comfort that you have a share in my affections, of that comfort you may avail yourself at all times. You have acquired it by means which, unless I should become worthless myself, to an uncommon degree, will always secure you from the loss of it. You are learning what all learn, though few at so early an age, that man is an ungrateful animal; and that benefits too often, instead of securing a due return, operate rather as provocations to ill treatment. This I take to be the *Summum malum*[1] of the human heart. Towards God we are all guilty of it, more or less; but between man and man, we may thank God for it, there are some exceptions. He leaves this peccant principle to operate, in some degree against himself, in all, for our humiliation, I suppose; and because the pernicious effects of it cannot, in reality, injure him; he cannot suffer by them; but he knows, that unless he should restrain its influence on the dealings of mankind with each other, the bonds of society would be dissolved, and all charitable intercourse at an end amongst us. It was said of Archbishop Cranmer, 'Do him an ill-turn, and you make him your *friend* for ever;'[2] of others it may be said, 'Do them a good one, and they will be for ever your *enemies*.' It is the Grace of God only, that makes the difference.

The absence of Homer, (for we have now shaken hands and parted) is well supplied by three relations of mine from Norfolk. My Cousin Johnson, an Aunt of his, and his Sister. I love them all dearly, and am well contented to resign to them the place in my attentions, so lately occupied by the Chiefs of Greece and Troy. His Aunt and I have spent many a merry day together, when we were some forty years younger; and we make shift to be merry together still. His Sister is a sweet young woman, graceful, good-natured, and gentle, just

[1] 'The highest evil'.

[2] See *Henry VIII*, V. ii. 210–11: 'Do my lord of Canterbury / A shrewd turn, and he's your friend for ever'.

what I had imagined her to be before I had seen her.

Farewell!

W. C.

JAMES COGSWELL   Wednesday, 15 June 1791

Address: Dr. James Cogswell / No. 55 / Queen Street / New York
Historical Society of Pennsylvania (*copy*)

Weston-Underwood
near Olney
Bucks
June 15 1791

Dear Sir —

Your letter and obliging present from so great a distance, deserved a speedier acknowledgment, and should not have wanted one so long, had not circumstances so fallen out since I received them, as to make it impossible for me to write sooner. It is indeed but within this day or two that I have learn'd how by the help of my Bookseller, I may transmit an answer to you. — My Title-page, as it well might, misled you. It speaks me of the Inner Temple, and so I am, but as a member of that society only, not as an inhabitant. I live here almost at the distance of sixty miles from London, which I have not visited these eight and twenty years, and probably never shall again. Thus it fell out that Mr. Morewood[1] had sailed again for America before your parcel reached me, nor should I, it is likely, have received it at all, had not a Cousin of mine who lives in the Temple,[2] by good fortune received it first. He open'd your letter and finding for whom it was intended, transmitted to me both that and the parcel.

Your testimony of approbation of what I have published, coming to me from another quarter of the globe could not but be extremely flattering to me, as was your obliging notice that the Task had been reprinted in your city. Both volumes, I hope have a tendency to discountenance vice, and to promote the best interests of mankind; but how far

[1] *The New York Directory for 1786*, p. 38: 'Morewood & co. merchants, 222 Q[ueen] street'. James Cogswell's surgery was at 219 Queen Street (ibid., p. 24).
[2] Probably Henry Cowper.

they shall be effectual to those invaluable purposes, depends altogether on his blessing whose Truths I have endeavour'd to inculcate. In the mean time I have sufficient proof that Readers may be pleased, may approve, and yet may lay down the book unedified.

During the last five years I have been occupied in a work of a very different nature; a Translation of the Iliad and Odyssey into blank verse, and the work is now ready for publication. I undertook it, partly because Pope's is too lax a version, which has lately occasion'd the learned in this country to call for a new one, and partly because I could fall on no better expedient, to amuse a mind too much addicted to melancholy.

I send you in return for the Volumes with which you have favour'd me, three, on religious subjects, popular productions, that have not been long published, and that may not therefore yet have reached your country. — The Christian Officer's panoply — by a marine officer[3] — The Importance of the Manners of the Great — and — an Estimate of the *Religion* of the Fashionable World.[4] The two last are said to be written by a Lady — Miss Hannah More, and are universally read by people of that rank to which she addresses them. Your manners, I suppose, may be purer than ours, yet it is not unlikely that even among you may be found some to whom her strictures are applicable.

I return you my thanks, Sir, for the volumes you sent, two of which I had read and read with pleasure. Mr. Edward's book,[5] and the Conquest of Canaan.[6] The rest I have not yet had time to read, except Dr. Dwight's Sermon,[7] which

---

[3] *The Christian's Officer's Panoply: Containing Arguments in Favour of a Divine Revelation. By a Marine Officer. With a Recommendation in Favour of the Work, by Sir Richard Hill, Bart.* (1789). A second edition of this work by Andrew Burn (1742–1814) appeared in 1792. The publisher was James Mathews (d. 19 Sept. 1804), A Methodist lay preacher known as 'Bishop Mathews'.

[4] *Thoughts on the Importance of the Manners of the Great to General Society* first appeared in 1788; *An Estimate of the Religion of the Fashionable World* came out in 1791.

[5] Jonathan Edwards's *The Salvation of All Men Strictly Examined* (New Haven, 1790). C's copy is now at the Lilly Library, Indiana University (*Keynes*, 55).

[6] C had reviewed Timothy Dwight's *The Conquest of Canaan, a Poem, In Eleven Books* (Hartford, 1785; reprinted in London by Joseph Johnson in 1788) more than two years before in the Appendix to Volume III (Apr. 1789) of the *Analytical Review* (531–4).   [7] Unidentified.

pleased me almost more than any that I have either seen or heard. I shall always account a correspondence with you an honour, and remain

Dear Sir — your obliged and obedient Servant

Wm Cowper.

JOSEPH JOHNSON [Wednesday, 15 June 1791] [1]

Address: Mr. Johnson Bookseller No. 72 / St. Pauls' Church Yard / London / Post
  paid 8d
Postmarks: PAID/JU/16/91 *and* NEWPORT/PAGNEL
Panshanger Collection

Dear Sir,

You will oblige me if you will be so kind as to put the inclosed into due course of convenyance, and accompany it with the three following books — The Christian Officer's Panoply — which is printed for Matthews No. 18 — the Strand. The Importance of the Manners of the Great — and an Estimate of the Religion of the Fashionable World — These last, I presume, [you] [2] will know where to find without my direction. [I shal]l be your Debtor for them.

It is now high time that I should thank you [for] the endless trouble you have had (and indeed trouble you will still have) in the business of my Homer. I shall be glad for your sake when the Subscription Books are all sent to their proper homes, and hereby promise never to publish more in that way.

Lord Spencer's Books must go, I suppose, to Althorp. Lady Dowager Spencer's to her house near St. Albans which is called I think Hallowell House. And Lord Cowper's to Mr. Henry Cowper's Parliament Office.

I am Dear Sir

Yours Wm Cowper

[1] As the postmark suggests, C must have written this letter requesting books of Johnson for Dr Cogswell on the same day he wrote the letter to Dr Cogswell which was enclosed.
[2] The MS has been cut at the seal.

MRS THROCKMORTON   Saturday, 18 June 1791

Sir Robert Throckmorton

The Lodge
June 18. 1791

My dear Mrs. Frog,

My best information about you is not good enough to ascertain with precision where you are to be found at present; whether you are at Lord Petre's,[1] at Tunbridge, or elsewhere; for various have been the reports concerning your next destination. I have double merit therefore in writing, both because you are a letter in my debt, and because I am not sure that I shall be able to address this to you when I have done. But of this I am, or seem to be tolerably sure, that you will have left London, that scene of constant bustle and engagement, and will consequently, if you seek it in good earnest, be mistress of leisure enough to answer me, should this ever reach you.

I am now, once more, an idle man. This indeed my letter bespeaks, for who that was not idle, would write or think of writing on so forlorn a hope and so absolutely at a venture? But Homer is all printed, the Binders are putting him in boards, and on the first of next month he will make his public entry. Thus are my hands vacant and my head also; vacant indeed to a degree that would be irksome after being so long habituated to employment, had it not fortunately happen'd that just at this moment three Cousins of mine are in the house, who arrived about a week since from Norfolk. Johnny of Norfolk, whom you know; his Sister whom you do not know, but who, I am persuaded, will please you much if you ever should, and an Aunt of theirs in all respects worthy to make the agreeable Duette a Trio. With these my kindred I console myself for the loss of the fine old Greecian, and with these I unbend my mind which may not fare the worse for a little relaxation after such long and constant exercise. They have taken a great liking to Weston, and the world being all before them, where to seek their place of rest,[2] would settle here if it were possible; but after looking to the right and to the left have found nothing that seems

[1] Buckenham, Norfolk.   [2] *Paradise Lost*, xii. 646–7.

very alluring, at least in the shape of a mansion. The empty house in the middle of the village is a dungeon, the house occupied by Mr. Socket[3] is likely to be still so occupied, and the house in which Mr. Morley[4] lived is at present it seems a house that may be said to belong to nobody. On a notion that it was Mr. Frog's property we conducted them to it yesterday, when, after surveying it from top to bottom, they found it such as being put into repair would have suited them, and we well hoped our point accomplished; but in the Evening came the Doctor who dash'd all our hopes by informing us that the house is not Mr. Throckmorton's.

Write to me soon if you love me, and if it be only to tell me that you are well and when we shall see you again. Has your Bill[5] at last succeeded? That it has pass'd I know, but has it pass'd in such a shape as makes it serviceable, or have they dock'd and curtailed it in such a manner as to have made it nothing worth? These are all interesting topics; and now that I have not only written you a letter but furnished you also with materials for an answer, with Mrs. Unwin's best Compliments and Johnny's I shall take my leave, wishing you well at the Hall again and assuring you with great truth that I am affectionately Yours — Wm Cowper.

LADY HESKETH   Thursday, 23 June 1791

Address: Lady Hesketh / New Norfolk Street / Grosvenor Square / London
Postmarks: JU/24/91/D and NEWPORT/PAGNEL
Olney

The Lodge
June. 23. 1791

Send me a draft, my dearest Coz, for as much money as I hope thou hast by this time received on my account, viz from Anonymus, and viz from Wm. Cowper, for we are driven to our last guinea. Let me have it by Sunday's post lest we become absolutely insolvent.

[3] See n.5, C to Newton, 21 Jan. 1788.
[4] Perhaps the man who acted as steward for the Throckmortons and who also had leased from them. See C to Newton, 6 Aug. and 5 Nov. 1785.
[5] The Catholic Relief Act passed on 7 June 1791. See n.2, C to Mrs Throckmorton, 1 Apr. 1791.

23 June 1791

We have received Beef, Tongues and Tea,
And certainly from none but Thee,
Therefore, with all our pow'r of Lungs
Thanks for Beef, and Tea, and Tongues![1]

As I said, so it proves. I told you that I should like our
guests when they had been here a day or two, and accordingly
I like them so well now that it is impossible to like them
better. Mrs. Balls is an unaffected, plain-dressing, good-
temper'd, cheerful, motherly sort of a body, and has the
affection of a parent for her niece and nephew. Her niece is
an amiable young woman in all respects, a handsome likeness
of Johnny and with a smile so like my mother's that in this
Cousin of mine she seems almost restored to me again. I
would that she had better health, but she has suffer'd sadly
in her constitution by diverse causes, and especially by
nursing her father in his last illness, from whose side she
stirr'd not till he expired. Johnny, with whom I have been
always delighted, is also so much in love with me, that no
place in the world will suit him to live in at present, except
Weston. Where he lives, his sister will live likewise, and their
Aunt is under promise to live with them, at least 'till Catharine
shall have attained under her tuition some competent share
of skill in the art of House-keeping. They have look'd at a
house, the next but one to ours, and like it. You may perhaps
remember it. It is an old house with girt[2] casement windows
and has a Fir-tree in the little court in front of it. Here they
purpose to settle if Aunt Bodham, who is most affectionately
attach'd to them all, can be persuaded not to break her heart
about it. Of this there are some hopes, because, did they live
in Norfolk, they would neither live with her, nor even in her
neighborhood, but at 30 miles distance. Johnny is writing
to her now with a view to reconcile her to the measure, and
should he succeed, the house will be hired immediately. It
will please thee, I think, to know that we are likely to have
our solitary situation a little enliven'd, and therefore I have
given thee this detail of the matter.

I told thee, I believe, that my work is to be publish'd on

[1] First published in *Wright*, iv. 81.
[2] To be tied up or secured (*OED* cites this letter in defining 'girt' as an adjective).

530

the first of July. So Johnson purposed when I heard from him last, but whether he will so perform or not must be left to time to discover. I see not what should hinder it. He has not yet made known on what terms he will treat with me for the copy. Perhaps he will stay till he has had opportunity to learn in some measure the world's opinion of it, to which I have no objection. I do not wish more than a just price for it, but should be sorry to take less, and there will be danger either of too much or too little 'till the Public shall have stamp'd its value.

My chief distress at present is that I cannot write, at least can write nothing that will satisfy myself. I have made once or twice a beginning, and disgusted with what I had done, have dropp'd it. I have a subject and a subject for a long work, a subject that I like and that will suggest much poetical matter — Mr. Buchanan gave it me, and it is call'd The Four ages of Man. — But I had need to have many more Ages before me unless I can write on it to better purpose.

With affectionate Compliments from our guests and with Mrs. Unwin's kindest remembrances I remain, Dearest Coz

Ever thine   Wm Cowper.

JOHN NEWTON   Friday, 24 June 1791

Princeton

Weston   June 24. 1791

My dear friend —

Considering the multiplicity of your engagements and the importance, no doubt, of most of them, I am bound to set the higher value on your letters, and instead of grumbling that they come seldom, to be thankful to you that they come at all. You are now going into the country,[1] where I presume you will have less to do, and I am rid of Homer. Let us try therefore if in the interval between the present hour and the next busy season (for I too, if I live, shall probably be occupied

---

[1] Newton and Betsy Catlett travelled more than 750 miles by stage-coach and chaise in the summer of 1791 while St. Mary Woolnoth was undergoing repairs. Bernard Martin, *John Newton* (1950), p. 334.

again) we can contrive to exchange letters more frequently than for some time past.

You do justice to me and Mrs. Unwin when you assure yourself that to hear of your health will give us pleasure. I know not, in truth, whose health and well-being could give us more. The years that we have seen together will never be out of our remembrance, and so long as we remember them we must remember you with affection. In the pulpit and out of the pulpit you have labour'd in every possible way to serve us, and we must have a short memory indeed for the kindness of a friend, could we by any means become forgetful of yours. It would grieve me more than it does to hear you complain of the effects of time, were not I also myself the subject of them. While he is wearing out you and other dear friends of mine, he spares not me, for which I ought to account myself obliged to him, since I should otherwise be in danger of surviving all that I have ever loved, the most melancholy lot that can befall a mortal. God knows what will be my doom hereafter, but precious as life necessarily seems to a mind doubtful of its future happiness, I love not the world, I trust, so much as to wish a place in it when all my Beloveds shall have left it.

You speak of your late loss in a manner that affected me much, and when I read that part of your letter I mourn'd with you and for you; But surely, I said to myself, no man had ever less reason to charge his conduct to a wife with any thing blameworthy. Thoughts of that complexion, however, are no doubt extremely natural on the occasion of such a loss, and a man seems not to have valued sufficiently, when he possesses it no longer, what, while he possess'd it, he valued more than life. I am mistaken too, or you can recollect a time when you had fears, and such as became a Christian, of loving too much, and it is likely that you have even pray'd to be preserved from doing so. I suggest this to you as a plea against those self-accusations which I am satisfied that you do not deserve, and as an effectual answer to them all. You may do well too to consider that had the Deceased been the Survivor, she would have charged herself in the same manner, and I am sure you will acknowledge without any sufficient reason. The truth is that you both loved at least as much as you ought, and, I dare say, had not a friend in the world who did not frequently observe it. To love just enough and not a bit too much, is not for creatures who can do nothing well. If we fail in duties less arduous, how should we succeed in this, the most arduous of all?

As to Jenny Raban[2] we have seen nothing of her. Either she forgot your injunction to call on us, or for some reason or other, did not chuse it. I am glad however to learn from yourself that you are about to quit a scene that probably keeps your tender recollections too much alive. Another place and other company may have their uses, and while your church is undergoing repair, its Minister may be repair'd also.

As to Homer, I am sensible that, except as an amusement, he was never worth my meddling with, but as an amusement he was to be invaluable. As such he served me more than 5 years, and in that respect I know not where I shall find his equal. You oblige me by saying that you will read him for my sake. I verily think that any person of a spiritual turn may read him to some advantage. He may suggest reflections that may not be unserviceable even in a sermon, for I know not where we can find more striking exemplars of the pride, the arrogance, and the insignificance of man, at the same time that by ascribing all events to a divine interposition, he inculcates constantly the belief of a Providence, insists much on the duty of Charity toward the Poor and the Stranger, on the respect that is due to superiors and to our Seniors in particular, and on the expedience and necessity of Prayer and piety toward the Gods. A piety mistaken indeed in its object, but exemplary for the punctuality of its performance. Thousands who will not learn from scripture to ask a blessing either on their actions or on their food, may learn it if they please from Homer.

My Norfolk Cousins are now with us. We are both as well as usual, and with our affectionate remembrances to Miss Catlett I remain Sincerely yours   Wm Cowper.

P.S. On referring to your Letter I perceive that I am too late to catch you in Town. I shall however send mine at a venture.

---

[2] See n.2, C to Newton, 29 Nov. 1788.

LADY HESKETH   Sunday, 26 June 1791

Address: Lady Hesketh / New Norfolk Street / Grosvenor Square / London
Postmarks: JU/27/91/A *and* NEWPORT/PAGNEL
Lehigh University Library

The Lodge
June 26. 1791

Many thanks, my Cousin, for the Bills, which arrived safe with all their accompaniments. Money is never unwelcome here, but at this time is especially welcome, when servants' wages and House-rent call for it. Mrs. Unwin enjoins me particularly to make you her affectionate acknowledgments both for the Bonnet-materials and for directions how to make the Bonnet.

I am glad that Johnson waited on you, and glad that he acquitted himself so well in your presence; glad too that he likes my prose, and fill'd with wonder that he likes my letters, because to Him I have hardly sent any but letters of Jobation.[1] I verily believe that, though a Bookseller, he has in him the soul of a Gentleman. Such strange combinations sometimes happen, and such a one may have happen'd in his instance. We shall see.

Johnny Higgins shall have his waistcoat to-morrow together with a note in which I will tell him all that you say concerning his performances in the Drawing way. Your gift will not be the less acceptable to him because, being in mourning, he cannot wear it at present. It is perfectly elegant and he will always be, and will always have cause to be proud of it. He mourns for his mother[2] who died about 3 weeks since, which when I wrote last I forgot to mention. You knew, I believe, that she had ill health and was subject to violent pains in her stomach. A fit of that sort seized her; she was attended by a nurse in the night, whom she order'd down stairs to get her some broth, and, when the woman return'd, she was dead.

It gives us true pleasure that you interest yourself so much

---

[1] 'A rebuke, reproof, especially one of a lengthy and tedious nature' (*OED*).

[2] On the tablet in Weston Underwood Church Mrs Higgins's epitaph stands beneath this inscription: 'In Memory of Mary Higgins, / The much-loved wife of / Thomas Higgins, who died / On the fourth day of June, / MDCCXCI., aged fifty years.' C wrote an eight-line poem, first published in *Hayley*, commemorating Mrs Higgins.

in the state of our Turnpike. Learn then the present state of it. From Gayhurst to Weston the road is a gravel walk, but Weston itself is at present in a chaotic condition. About three weeks since they dug up the street, and having done so, left it. But it will not continue long in such disorder, and when you see it next you will find the Village wonderfully improved. Already they have fill'd up two abominable ponds more fœtid than any human nostrils could endure; they were to be found, as you must remember, one just under Farmer Archer's window, and the other a little beyond it. Cover'd drains are to be made wherever drains are wanted, and the causey is to be new laid. When all this is done and the road well gravell'd, we will hold our heads as high as any Villagers in the kingdom. — At the present time they are at work on the road from Weston to Olney. Olney is also itself in a state of beautification, and the road between Olney and Bedford is, I believe, nearly finish'd, but that I have never seen. The sooner you come to look at these things with your own eyes the better.

I have hardly left myself room to tell you a story which yet I must tell, but as briefly as possible.

While I reposed myself yesterday evening in the shop of Mr. Palmer, lying at my length on the counter, a labouring man came in. He wanted a hat for his boy, and having bought one at 2 shillings, said he must have a handkerchief for himself, a silk one, to wear about his neck on Sundays. After much bargaining he suited himself with one at last for 4s and 6d. I liked the man's looks, and having just one shilling in my purse I held it to him, saying — Here honest friend, here's something tow'rd paying for your purchase. He took the shilling and look'd at me steadily for a long time saying nothing — At last his surprize burst forth in these words — I never saw such a Gentleman in my life! He then faced about and again was a long time silent; but, at last, turning to me again he said — If I had known you had been so stout I would have had a better. Mr. Andrews told him that the Cutting off would make no difference to him, and he might have a better if he pleased. So he took one at the price of 5s and went away all astonishment at my great bounty. I have learn'd since that he is a very worthy industrious fellow, and has a mother between 70 and 80 who walks every Sunday eight miles to hearing, as they call it, and back again. This is another instance that my skill in physiognomy never deceives me.

Adieu my dearest Coz — with the Love of all here

I remain ever thine   Wm Cowper.

P.S. Since I heard of Mrs. Madan's death, I have thought much of her daughter Sally and rejoice to hear that she is at last provided for.[3]
P.S.

We pack'd the Drawings as well as we could, but the Band-box was old and crazy and was crush'd I suppose in the Hamper. I sent them that you might get them framed at your best leisure, for here we cannot frame them.

JOHN HIGGINS   [Monday, 27 June 1791][1]

Address: Mr. John Higgings Junr
Formerly Hugh Longuet-Higgins

Mr. Cowper presents his Compliments to Mr. Higgins and the following extract from Lady Hesketh's Letter.

'I send a Waistcoat, which I beg you will present in my name to Mr. John Higgins. It is a miserable return for his beautiful Drawings, but he must consider it as the Widow's mite.[2] Did I know any thing that would be useful or acceptable to him either in the Drawing way or in any other, I should be happy to send it him. Pray tell him his performances are approved by every body — People regret that he is born to affluence since it threatens to deprive the world of such a Genius.'

Mr. Cowper will expect the pleasure of Mr. Higgins's company at Tea this afternoon.

Monday

[3] Jane Madan died a year after her husband, Martin, on 15 June 1791 at about the age of 68. Her daughter Sarah married John Thompson on 1 May 1794. A letter of Maria Cowper of 11 Sept. 1792 to her sister, Mrs Maitland, mentions that Sarah had become a Roman Catholic; there is also some evidence that she was of an unruly and extravagant temperament (*The Madan Family*, pp. 120–1).

[1] In his letter to Lady Hesketh of 26 June 1791, C says 'Johnny Higgins shall have his waistcoat to-morrow together with a note'.
[2] See Mark 12: 42.

3 July 1791

JOSEPH JOHNSON   Sunday, 3 July 1791

Panshanger Collection

Weston July 3. 1791

Dear Sir,

This moment return'd from my walk and obliged to prepare for dinner, I have only time to tell you that I have read your letter attentively yet suspect that I do not perfectly understand it.

Do you mean that the whole Subscription money, both first and second payment shall be yours, except the Sums beyond the price of a copy? Out of this money to pay the Printer &c and take the Remainder as your own?[1]

This seems, by the manner in which your proposals are expressed, to be the purport of them, and yet I cannot believe it to be so. Because in that case I should have no other reward of my labours than the Thousand pounds which you propose to give for the copy right. A recompense short of what I have been taught to look for, judging by the sums which have been given not long since for works of much less length and difficulty, and if, I am well inform'd, even by yourself.[2]

I shall wish your speedy answer and
remain in the mean time
Dear Sir — Yours   Wm Cowper.

---

[1] C mentions the terms finally agreed to in his letter to Lady Hesketh of 11 July.

[2] The following outline (Panshanger Collection), in C's hand, is a draft of the missing letter to Joseph Johnson of *pre* 6 July 1791: 'Answer to Johnson's Letter — Wish him still as sincerely as heretofore to consider himself as absolute proprietary by free gift of the Copy-right of my 2 Vols. — Having stood the hazard of gain or loss, he seems to have fairly entitled himself to it, and to have left me without any claim upon him for a remuneration — And with respect to his scheme of sending circular letters to the subscribers, to object to it as having the appearance at least, of begging them to become customers, whatever may be the intention. And would it not answer every purpose to advertize the new edition as printed of a size to match the Homer, without directing that information immediately to them. They can hardly fail to hear of it if the notice be given in all the papers, and if they chuse to add the poems to the Translation will be perhaps more likely to do it thus left to themselves and their own option, than if disgusted, as they are likely to be, by a direct application.'

537

SAMUEL ROSE   Wednesday, 6 July 1791

Address: Samuel Rose Esqr. / Chancery Lane / London / Post pd. / Shilling
Postmarks: PAID/JY/7/91 *and* NEWPORT/PAGNEL
Princeton

Weston July 6. 1791

My dear friend —

Now comes the day of your trouble with which you have long been threaten'd. Mr. Johnson has at length made his offer, with which I seem to have no good reason to be satisfied. I enclose two letters in which it is contained. In explanation of the second letter it is necessary that I should tell you what I wrote in answer to the first.

I ask'd him if he meant to take the whole subscription-money (extra-money excepted) to himself? Adding that if he did, I should account myself but ill recompensed for my labours — or to that effect. In his second letter you will find that his expressions amount to an avowal that he does.

The case therefore stands thus — The whole subscription-money, exclusive of extras, will amount to Ł1144 — The unsubscribed copies being 200 will sell at the advanced price that he proposes for Ł500 more. These sums together make Ł1644.

With this money he means to pay the expences of this first edition — viz — Ł600. And with this money he means to pay me Ł1000 for my copy right. When he has so done Ł44 will remain in his pocket.

This to me has much the appearance of giving me nothing for my copy, or rather it has the appearance of being paid Ł44 for accepting it.

I will not say pardon me for giving you this trouble, because that were to dishonour your friendship and the readiness with which you have undertaken this disagreeable service. On your management for me I shall rely with the most perfect tranquillity, and heartily acquiesce in the result of your negotiation.

I am Dear Sir, most truly and affectionately yours
                                    Wm Cowper
P. S.
I have received yours this moment — nevertheless I send

538

this because it will serve to inform you how I understand, or perhaps misunderstand Johnson's offer. — After all, I can only say as I have already said, that what appears to you to be reasonable will perfectly content me.

I shall be obliged to you if you will desire him to send Mr. Griffiths[1] a copy.

SAMUEL ROSE
Thursday, 7 July 1791

Address: Samuel Rose Esqr. / Chancery Lane / London
Postmarks: JY/8/91 *and* OULNEY
Princeton

Weston Underwood July 7. 1791

My dear friend —

Having given you yesterday only a Postscript in answer to yours, I now sit down less in haste to answer it more at large.

It is very likely that my view of Mr. Johnson's first offer might be both perplex'd and injurious to Him. But such as it was I sent it, and it was the view which not only I, who am a perfect fool in business, but Mrs. Unwin also, and the relations of mine now with me, entertained as well as myself. Aukwardness and extreme incompetence in all business is my misfortune, but avarice I believe is not my fault; and this I say, not to commend myself, but to lighten the labour of your task as much as possible. Troublesome it must be at best, and would be doubly so should I wish for any thing unreasonable. This however is not the case. So far from it that I should be as sorry to receive from Johnson more than he would think himself obliged to give to another, in consideration of any thing past between him and me, as I should be to receive less than on the terms of common market-price I am entitled to.

I am well contented with his second offer, because, considering that the Subscription money will be more than enough to indemnify him, I do not see how he should possibly be a loser by it. Supposing, I mean, the second payments to be made and the remaining copies to find purchasers.

If you see good therefore I am ready to close with him on

[1] Ralph Griffiths of the *Monthly Review*. See n.4, C to Unwin, 12 June 1782.

this second offer, and that done, shall trouble you once more respecting the copy-right. You must advise me what to do with it — whether to keep it 'till the fortune of my work may be more probably conjectured, or whether to sell it now. Whether to dispose of the whole, or to retain a share in it? Direct me in all, for I am in these matters *non compos*.

I wrote to Johnson yesterday after closing my letter to you, and desired him to send a copy to Mr. Griffiths.

You may depend on my taking the first opportunity to select &c, as we agreed should be done when we conversed together on that subject. But the publication of any such remarks on the work as you propose will be a trouble that I presume you will not have to encounter yet. You will know the fittest time.

I write, as it happens, with more interruption, so as hardly to know if I have expressed my own meaning. Give my best love to Mr. Hill if you see him and my thanks, so justly due to him, for the interest he takes in all my matters.

We shall see you I hope in September. — In the mean time I remain with Mrs. Unwin's affectionate remembrances, yours, my dear friend, most truly

Wm Cowper

MRS BODHAM   Thursday, 7 July 1791

Southey, vii. 40–2

Weston Underwood, July 7, 1791.
My dearest Cousin,

Most true it is, however strange, that on the twenty-fifth of last month I wrote you a long letter, and verily thought I had sent it. But opening my desk the day before yesterday, there I found it. Such a memory have I, — a good one never, but at present worse than usual, my head being filled with the cares of publication, and the bargain that I am making with my bookseller.

I am sorry that through this forgetfulness of mine you were disappointed, otherwise should not at all regret that my letter never reached you; for it consisted principally of such reasons as I could muster to induce you to consent to a favourite measure to which you have consented without them. Your kindness, and self-denying disinterestedness on this occasion have endeared you to us all, if possible, still the more, and are truly worthy of the Rose that used to sit smiling on my knee, I will not say how many years ago.

Make no apologies, my dear, that thou dost not write more frequently. Write when thou canst, and I shall be satisfied. I am sensible, as I believe I have already told you, that there is an awkwardness in writing to those with whom we have hardly ever conversed, in consideration of which I feel myself not at all inclined, either to wonder at or to blame your silence. At the same time be it known to you that you must not take encouragement from this my great moderation to write less frequently than you might, lest, disuse increasing the labour, you should at last write not at all.

That I should visit Norfolk at present is not possible: — I have heretofore pleaded my engagement to Homer as the reason, and a reason it was, while it subsisted, that was absolutely insurmountable. But there are still other impediments which it would neither be pleasant to me to relate, nor to you to know, and which could not well be comprised in a letter. Let it suffice for me to say, that could they be imparted, you would admit the force of them. It shall be our mutual consolation that if we cannot meet at Mattishall, at least we may meet at Weston, and that we shall meet here with double satisfaction, being now so numerous.

Your sister is well; Kitty I think better than when she came, and Johnny ails nothing, except that if he eat a little more supper than usual he is apt to be riotous in his sleep. We have an excellent physician at Northampton, whom our dear Catharine wishes to consult, and I have recommended it to Johnny to consult him at the same time. His nocturnal ailment is, I dare say, within the reach of medical advice, and because it may happen sometime or other to be very hurtful to him I heartily wish him cured of it. Light suppers and early rising perhaps might alone be sufficient; — but the latter is a difficulty that threatens not to be easily surmounted.

We are all of one mind respecting you, therefore I send the love of all, though I shall see none of the party till breakfast calls us together. Great preparation is making in the empty house. The spiders have no rest, and hardly a web is to be seen, where lately there were thousands.

I am, my dearest cousin, with best respects to Mr. Bodham, most affectionately yours,

Wm. Cowper.

LADY HESKETH   Monday, 11 July 1791

Address: Lady Hesketh / New Norfolk Street / Grosvenor Square / London
Postmarks: JY/12/91/D *and* NEWPORT/PAGNEL
Princeton

The Lodge
July 11. 1791

My dearest Coz —

Your Draft is safe in our possession and will soon be out of it, that is to say, will soon be negotiated. Many thanks for that, and still more for your kindness in bidding me draw yet again, should I have occasion. None I hope will offer. I have a purse at Johnson's to which, if need should arise, I can recur at pleasure. The present is rather an expensive time with us, and will probably cause the consumption of some part of my loose cash in the hands of my Bookseller.

I am not much better pleased with that Dealer in authors than yourself. His first proposal, which was to pay me with my own money, or in other words, to get my copy for nothing, not only dissatisfied but hurt me, implying, as I thought, the meanest opinion possible of my labours. For that for which an intelligent man will give nothing, can be worth nothing. The consequence was, that my spirits sank considerably below par, and have but just begun to recover themselves. — His second offer, which is to pay all expences and to give me a Ł1000 next Midsummer, leaving the copy-right still in my hands, is more liberal. With this offer I have closed, and Mr. Rose will to-morrow clench the bargain. Josephus understands that Johnson will gain Ł200 by it, but I apprehend that he is mistaken, and that Mr. Rose is right who estimates his gains at One. Mr. Hill's mistake, if he be mistaken, arises from his rating the expences

542

of the Press &c at only £500 — whereas Johnson rates them at Six. Be that as it may, I am contented. If he gains Two, I shall not grudge, and if he gain but One, considering all things, I think he will gain enough.

As to Sephus's scheme of signing the 700 copies in order to prevent a clandestine multiplication of them, at the same time that I fell the wisdom of it, I feel also an insurmountable dislike of it. It would be calling Johnson a Knave, and telling the Public that I think him one. Now, though I do not perhaps think so highly of his liberality as some people do, and I was once, myself, disposed to think, yet I have no reason, at present to charge him with dishonesty. — I must e'en take my chance as other poets do, and if I am wrong'd, must comfort myself with what somebody[1] has said — That Authors are the natural prey of Booksellers.

You judge right in supposing that I pitied the King and Queen of France.[2] I can truly say that, except the late melancholy circumstances of our own (when our Sov'reign had lost his senses, and his wife was almost worried out of hers) no Royal distresses have ever moved me so much. And still I pity them, prisoners as they are now for life, and since their late unsuccessful attempt, likely to be treated more scurvily than ever. Heaven help them, for in their case, all other help seems vain!

· The establishment of our guests at Weston is given up. Not for any impediment thrown in the way by Mrs. Bodham, for she consented with the utmost disinterestedness to the measure, but because on surveying accurately the house in which they must have dwelt, it was found to be so mere a ruin, that it would have cost its value to make it habitable. They could only take it from year to year, for which reason the Landlord would do nothing.

Many thanks for the Mediterranean hint, but unless I were a better Historian than I am, there would be no proportion between the theme and my ability. It seems indeed not to be so properly a subject for one poem, as for a dozen.[3]

[1] Unidentified.
[2] On the evening of 20 June 1791, the royal party escaped from the Tuileries; they were recaptured the next day and sent back to Paris.
[3] C does not seem to have acted on this suggestion.

I was pleased with Bouillie's letter,[4] or to say truth, rather with the principles by which it was dictated. The letter itself seems too much the language of passion, and can only be cleared of the charge of extravagance by the accomplishment of its denunciations. An event, I apprehend, not much to be expected.

We are all well, except poor Catharine, who yesterday consulted Dr. Kerr and to-day is sick of his prescription. Our affectionate hearts all lay themselves at your petitoes, and with Mrs. Unwin's best remembrances I remain for my own peculiar most entirely thine

Wm Cowper.

The Frogs are expected here on Wednesday.

JOSEPH HILL   Tuesday, 12 July 1791

Address: Joseph Hill Esqr. / Great Queen Street / Lincolns Inn Fields / London
Postmarks: JY/13/91/A *and* NEWPORT/PAGNEL
Cowper Johnson

Weston — July 12. 1791

My dear friend —

I learn from a paper of yours enclosed in a letter from Lady Hesketh (and had indeed learn'd it before from Mr. Rose) how much I am obliged to you for your friendly interference in this bargin-making business with Johnson. He stands so fair in the opinion of some who have known him longer than I, not only as an honest book-seller but as a liberal one, that I did well hope for such an offer from him as would save both me and my friends all trouble. But his first offer was such, as considering what he has done in other instances, I hardly know how to account for. At least if it be

---

[4] Probably *Protestation de la noblesse de France, émigrée dans les Pays étrangers, contre la sanction Donnée par le Roi, à la prétendue charte constitutionnelle* (Worms, 1791) by François Claude Amour, Marquis de Bouillé (1739–1800). C is speaking of passages such as (p. 5): 'La liberté est le pouvoir de choisir, sans péril et sans crainte. Cette condition soustraite, la liberté n'existe point. Le premier besoin de l'homme est celui de sa sûreté. Il répugne à la voir menacée. Il n'est pas libre de ne pas fuir les lieux ou les circonstances qui la mettent en danger; dans l'incertitude du choix, sa volonté, entraînée par une force aveugle, embrasse nécessairement le parti le plus sûr, ou du moins rejette celui qu'accompagne un péril évident.'

true, as I have good reason to believe it is, that he gave Dr. Darwin eight hundred pounds for his *Loves of the Plants*,[1] it then seems strange that he should propose to get my Homer for nothing. For to pay me for the copy-right with my own money will certainly bear no other interpretation. His second offer however has made me amends and I am well content with it.

The last was an anxious week with me, not only for the pecuniary interest that I had at stake, but because I was desirous also to obtain such terms as might not disgrace me in the ears of the curious who shall hereafter enquire what I gain'd by my labours. It was irksome to me likewise to feel myself on the edge of a quarrel with a man who has not corresponded with me merely as a Trader in my commodity, but familiarly and almost as a friend. These weighty considerations added to the still more weighty cares that I felt for the success of my work with the Public, were almost too much for me. I have great cause therefore to be thankful both to you and to the Rose who have relieved me from so great a part of my burthen, and have brought this affair to an issue honourable, and therefore perfectly satisfactory to me.

I have nothing to do now but to wait as quiety as I can for the opinion of my readers, and have the better hope of success being conscious of having neglected nothing that might insure it.

> With my best Compliments to Mrs. Hill
> I remain, my Dear friend,
> most sincerely yours
> Wm Cowper

JOHN NEWTON
Friday, 22 July 1791

Address: The Revd. John Newton
Princeton

Weston July 22. 1791

My dear friend —
I did not foresee when I challenged you to a brisker correspondence that a new engagement of all my leisure was

---

[1] See n.2, C to Rose, 4 Oct. 1789 and n.2, C to Hill, [27 Apr. 1791].

at hand. A new, and yet an old one. An interleaved copy of my Homer arrived soon after from Johnson, in which he recommended it to me to make any alterations that might yet be expedient, with a view to another impression. The alterations that I make are indeed but few, and they are also short, not more perhaps than half a line in 2000, but the lines are, I suppose, near 40,000 in all, and to revise them critically must consequently be a work of labour. I suspend it however for your sake till the present sheet be filled, and that I may not seem to shrink from my own offer.

Mr. Bean has told me that he saw you at Bedford, and gave us your reasons for not coming our way. It is well so far as your own comfortable lodging and our gratification were concerned that you did not, for our house is brimfull, as it has been all the summer, with my relations from Norfolk. We should all have been mortified, both you and we, had you been obliged, as you must have been, to seek a residence elsewhere.

I am sorry that Mr. Venn's labours below are so near to a conclusion.[1] I have seen few men whom I could have loved more, had opportunity been given me to know him better. So at least I have thought as often as I have seen him. But when I saw him last, which is some years since, he appeared then so much broken that I could not have imagined he would last so long. Were I capable of Envying, in the strict sense of the word, a good man, I should envy Him, and Mr. Berridge,[2] and yourself, who have spent, and while they last, will continue to spend your lives in the service of the only Master worth serving. Labouring always for the souls of men, and not to tickle their ears as I do. But this I can say — God knows how much rather I would be the obscure tenant of a Lath and plaister cottage with a lively sense of my

---

[1] One of the prominent leaders of the evangelical revival and the author of the enormously popular *The Complete Duty of Man* (first published in 1763), the Revd Henry Venn (see C to Unwin, 11 Sept. 1784) became vicar of Huddersfield in 1759; in 1771, broken down by ill health, he accepted the living of Yelling in Huntingdonshire, which he held until his death.

[2] The Revd John Berridge (1716-93), an evangelical preacher of great power and rigidly held Calvinist views, had been educated at Clare College, Cambridge (BA, 1738; MA, 1742). On 7 July 1755 he was inducted to the college of Everton, Bedfordshire, where he remained until his death.

interest in a Redeemer, than the most admired object of public notice without it. Alas! what is a whole poem, even one of Homer's, compared with a single aspiration that finds its way immediately to God, though clothed in ordinary language or perhaps not articulated at all. These are my sentiments as much as ever they were, though my days are all running to waste among Greeks and Trojans. The night cometh when no man can work,[3] and if I am ordained to work to better purpose, that desireable period cannot be very distant. My day is beginning to shut in, as every man's must who is on the verge of Sixty.

All the leisure that I have had of late for thinking, has been given to the Riots at Birmingham.[4] What a horrid zeal for the church, and what a horrid Loyalty to Government have manifested themselves there! How little do they dream that they could not have dishonour'd their Idol the Establishment more, and that the Great Bishop of Souls himself with abhorrence rejects their service! But I have not time to enlarge — Breakfast calls me — and all my Post-breakfast time must be given to poetry — Adieu — with Mrs. Unwin's best Love to yourself and Miss C, I remain, my dear friend,

most truly yours   Wm Cowper.

WILLIAM BULL   Wednesday, 27 July 1791

Address: The Revd. William Bull / Brighton / Sussex
Postmarks: JY/28/91/D *and* NEWPORT/PAGNEL
Formerly Miss C. M. Bull

Weston July 27. 1791

My dear Mr. Bull —

Mindful of my promise I take the pen, though fearing, and with reason enough, that the performance will hardly be worth the postage. Such as it is however, here it comes, and if you like it not, you must thank yourself for it.

---

[3] John 9: 4.
[4] The riots, of 14–17 July 1791, involved a conflict between sympathizers with the French Revolution celebrating the capture of the Bastille and supporters of the King. C owned a pamphlet entitled *Thoughts on the Late Riot at Birmingham* (1791): *Keynes*, 53.

I have blest myself on your account that you are at Brighton and not at Birmingham, where it seems they are so loyal and so pious that they show no mercy to Dissenters. How can you continue in a persuasion so offensive to the wise and good? Do you not yet perceive that the Bishops themselves hate you not more than the very Blacksmiths of the establishment, and will you not endeavour to get the better of your aversion to red-nosed singing-men and Organs? Come — Be received into the bosom of mother-church, so shall you never want a Jig for your amusement on Sundays, and shall save perhaps your academy from a conflagration.

As for me, I go on at the old rate, giving all my time to Homer, who I suppose was a Presbyterian too, for I understand that the Church of England will by no means acknowledge him for one of hers. He, I say, has all my time, except a little that I give every day to no very cheering prospects of Futurity. I would I were a Hottentot, or even a Dissenter, so that my views of an Hereafter were more comfortable. But such as I am, Hope, if it please God, may visit even me, and should we ever meet again, possibly we may part no more. Then — if Presbyterians ever find the way to heaven, you and I may know each other in that better world, and rejoice in the recital of the terrible things that we endured in this. I will wager sixpence with you now, that when that day comes, you shall acknowledge my story a more wonderful one than yours. Only order your Executors to put sixpence in your mouth when they bury you that you may have wherewithal to pay me.

I have received a long letter from an unknown somebody[1] filled with the highest Eulogiums on my Homer. This has raised my spirits and is the true cause of all the merriment with which I have greeted you this morning. Pardon me, as Vellum says in the Comedy, for being jocular.[2] Mrs. Unwin joins me in love to yourself and your very good son, and we both hope and both sincerely wish to hear of Mrs. Bull's recovery — Yours affectionately — Wm Cowper.

---

[1] Unidentified.
[2] C is referring to Addison's *The Drummer, or The Haunted House* (II. i), a comedy first performed at the Theatre-Royal in Drury Lane in 1716.

WALTER BAGOT   Tuesday, 2 August 1791

Address: The Revd. Walter Bagot
Morgan Library

Weston Augt. 2. 1791

My dear friend —

Although you will not vouchsafe me any other excuse for your silence than that you did not find yourself much in the mood for writing, I have learn'd from your brother Chester that you could have made a better if you would. He told me that you had been very ill, and told me beside that you owed your indisposition to certain liberties that you had taken with yourself in the Quackery-way. Remember, I beseech you, that you are only a spiritual physician by profession, and that to be a good bodily one requires a regular training to the business. Remember also that much as you seem to undervalue the Physiognomical science, it is easier to correct twenty mistaken judgments of men by their faces, than a single physical one. Mrs. Bagot, I hope, will lock up your pill-box. I recommend it to her by all means to do so, for I shall never think you safe or be free from fears about you, so long as you have the management of your own disorders in your own hands. — So now I have treated your physical proficiency as cavalierly as you my phizzical. Iam sumus ergo pares.[1]

I was much obliged, and still feel myself much obliged to Lady Bagot for the visit with which she favour'd me. Had it been possible that I could have seen Lord Bagot too, I should have been completely happy. For, as it happen'd, I was that morning in better spirits than usual, and though I arrived late, and after a long walk, and extremely hot, which is a circumstance very apt to disconcert me, yet I was not disconcerted half so much as I generally am at the sight of a stranger, especially of a stranger Lady, and more especially at the sight of a stranger Lady of quality. When the servant told me that Lady Bagot[2] was in the parlour, I felt my spirits sink ten degrees, but the moment I saw her, at least when I had been a minute in her company, I felt them rise again, and they soon rose even above their former pitch. — I know two Ladies of fashion now whose manners have this effect on me. The

[1] 'Now we are even.'   [2] See n.3, C to Lady Hesketh, 30 Nov. 1785.

Lady in question, and Lady Spencer.[3] — I am a shy animal and want much kindness to make me easy. Such I shall be to my dying day.

Here sit *I*, calling myself *shy*, yet have just publish'd by the *by*, two great volumes of poe*try*.

This reminds me of Ranger's observation in the Suspicious Husband, who says to somebody, I forget to whom — *There is a degree of assurance in you modest men that we Impudent fellows can never arrive at.*[4] Assurance indeed! Have you seen 'em? What do you think they are? Nothing less I can tell you than a Translation of Homer. Of the sublimest poet in the world. That's all. Can I ever have the impudence to call myself shy again?

You live, I think, in the neighborhood of Birmingham. What must you not have felt on the late alarming occasion! You I suppose could see the fires from your windows. We who only heard the news of them, have trembled. Never surely was religious zeal more terribly manifested, or more to the prejudice of its own cause —

Adieu, my dear friend, I am with Mrs. Unwin's best Compliments, ever yours

Wm Cowper.

MRS KING   Thursday, 4 August 1791

Address: Mrs. King / Pertenhall near / Kimbolton / Huntingdonshire.
Postmark: AU/5/91/E
Princeton

Weston-Underwood
Augt. 4. 1791

My dear Madam,

Your last letter, which gave us so unfavorable an account of your health, and which did not speak much more comfortably of Mr. King's, affected us with much concern. Of Dr. Raitt[1] we may say in the words of Milton —

---

[3] See n.5, C to Newton, 31 May 1783. Lady Spencer's visit was made on 22 Nov. 1790 (see C to John Johnson, 26 Nov. 1790).
[4] *The Suspicious Husband*, II. iv. See n.3, C to Chase Price, 21 Feb. 1754. Ranger's remarks are made to Frankly and Bellamy.

---

[1] George Raitt (d. 17 Jan. 1785), who practised at Huntingdon, received the

His long experience did attain
To something like prophetic strain —[2]

For as he foretold to you, so he foretold to Mrs. Unwin, that though her disorders might not much threaten life, they would yet cleave to her to the last, and she and perfect health must ever be strangers to each other. Such was his prediction and it has been hitherto accomplished. Either head-ache or pain in the side has been her constant companion ever since we had the pleasure of seeing you. As for myself, I cannot properly say that I *enjoy* a good state of health, though in general I have it, because I have it accompanied with frequent fits of dejection to which less health and better spirits would perhaps be infinitely preferable. But it pleased God that I should be born in a country where melancholy is the national characteristic, and of a house more than commonly subject to it. To say truth I have often wish'd myself a Frenchman.

N. B. I write this in very good spirits.

You gave us so little hope in your last that we should have your company this summer at Weston, that to repeat our invitation seems almost like teazing you. I will only say therefore that my Norfolk friends having left us, of whose expected arrival here I believe I told you in a former letter, we should be happy could you succeed them. We now indeed expect Lady Hesketh, but not immediately, she seldom sees Weston 'till all its summer beauties are fled, and Red, Brown, and Yellow have supplanted the universal verdure.

My Homer is gone forth, and I can devoutly say — Joy go with it! What place it holds in the estimation of the generality I cannot tell, having heard no more about it since its publication, than if no such work existed. I must except however an Anonymous Eulogium from some man of letters which I received about a week ago. It was kind in a perfect stranger, as he avows himself to be, to relieve me at so early a day from much of the anxiety that I could not but feel on such an occasion. I should be glad to know who he is, only that I might thank him.

degree of Doctor of Medicine at Leyden, and was admitted as Extra-Licentiate of the College of Physicians on 22 Sept. 1749.

  [2] C is paraphrasing *Il Penseroso*, lines 173–4; 'Till old experience do attain / To something like prophetic strain.'

Mrs. Unwin, who is this moment come down to breakfast, joins me in affectionate Compliments to yourself and Mr. King — and I am, my dear Madam,

most sincerely yours
Wm Cowper.

SAMUEL ROSE   Sunday, 7 August 1791

Address: Samuel Rose Esqr.
Princeton

Weston
Augt. 7. 1791.

My dear friend —
   I send you passages for citation, of which you will use just as many as you please and no more.[1] Having occasion to read the whole, in order that I might prepare it for a 2d. edition, I have noted as I went the passage of every book that seem'd to me the fittest of that book for your purpose, designing only that from them all you should make choice of such a number as may be convenient. A glance of your eye will enable you to discriminate which are likely to prove most entertaining to your readers and to strike them most. Thus I have dealt with the Iliad — The citations from the Od— are as you perceive less numerous, and may either be all produced, or only such of them as you shall prefer. I do not send you any of them as better translated than the rest of the work, not being conscious of any difference in this respect, between one part and another, but merely because being distinguishable parts of the Original, if they are well render'd, they will of course do me most honor.
   The references to passages that I call too long for citation may be all strung together in a single paragraph and dispatch'd with one general commendation.
   If you chuse to contrast any of the citations with parallel passages in Pope, I believe it may be very indifferent which. He is every where loose and devious, has seldom much of Homer's spirit, and never any at all of his manner.

---

[1] Such a review was not written. See C to Rose, 20 Aug.

But I would recommend in particular for this purpose the night-scene Simile B. 8.

Perhaps this alone may be sufficient to illustrate the difference between the two versions, and better than more, for comparisons, according to the old adage, are odious, and I would not by invidious ones unnecessarily provoke hostility.

You may perhaps find this business of Reviewing me no disagreeable amusement when the Law will give you leave to attend to it. Wishing that it may prove pleasant, and thanking you heartily for undertaking the service, I

remain my dear friend
most truly yours
Wm Cowper.

Passages for citation from the Odyssey

The Exordium. The departure of Telemachus for Pylus. B. 2. From L. 533 to the end. The story of Proteus. B. 4.
The descent of Mercury to Calypso's isle and the description of it. B. 5. From L. 51 to 87.
The speech of Ulysses to Nausic: B. 6.
Palace and Garden of Alcinous. B. 7. From L. 97 to 162.
The passage of Ulysses between Scylla and Charybdis. B. 12. From L. 237 to 305.
The arrival of Ulysses at his own house. B. 17. From L. 314 to 392.
Penelope's acknowledgment of Ulysses. B. 23. From L. 242 to 284.
Ulysses proving his father and discovering himself to him. B. 24. From L. 203 to 415.

Iliad

Passages for favorable mention tho' too long for citation.

The dispute between Achilles and Agamemnon. Book 1st.
The Catalogue of the ships. B. 2d.
The dialogue between Priam and Helen. B. 3.
Agamemnon's exhortations of the Grecian host. B. 4.

Diomede wounding Venus and the scene that ensues in heaven. B. 5.

The interview between Hector and Andromache. B. 6.

The single combat between Hector and Ajax. B. 7.

The flight of the Greecians with all its circumstances. B. 8.

The conference in the tent of Achilles. B. 9

The whole nocturnal expedition. B. 10.

The speech of Nestor-B. 11

Sarpedon's assault on the barrier and Hector's entrance at the gate. B. 12.

The episodical scene of Idomaneus and Meriones. B. 13

Juno attiring herself — borrowing the Cestus of Venus — engaging the aid of Sleep, and inveigling Jupiter. B. 14.

The whole battle of B. 15

Achilles and Patroclus preparing the Myrmidons for battle. B. 16.

The conflict for the body of Patroclus B. 17

The shield of Achilles. B. 18.

The public reconciliation of Achilles and Agamemnon — B. 19.

The combat of Achilles with Æneas. B. 20.

His conflict with the river Xanthus and the river overcome by Vulcan. B. 21

Hector pursued, slain, and dragg'd by Achilles at his chariot-wheels. B. 22.

The funeral games. B. 23.

Priam conducted by Mercury to the tent of Achilles and the whole ensuing scene. B. 24.

Iliad

Passages for citation.

The descent of Apollo — B. 1. From L. 53 to L. 70.

The assembling of the Greeks — Book 2. Beginning at L. 102 — Ending at L. 116.

The effect of Agamemnon's speech on the multitude. B. 2. Begin at L. 165 — Ending at 180.

The speech of Antenor — B. 3. Begin at L. 239 — Ending at 270.

Pandarus shooting at Menelaus. B. 4. Beginning at L. 121. Ending at 147.

The march of Ajax and his band — B. 4. From 319. to 331

The speeches of Æneas & Pandarus B. 5. From 199 to 254.

Description of the Greeks facing the Trojans. B 5 From 618. to 626.

Paris hasting to overtake Hector B. 6. From 614 to 627.

Hector's challenge: B. 7 From L. 75 to 103.

The night-scene B. 8. From 640 to the end.

The postures of Achilles and Patroclus. B. 9. From 229 to 242.

The apprehension of Dolon by Diomedes and Ulysses. B. 10. From 412 to 445.

The retreat of Ajax. B. 11. From 654 to 688.

The speech of Sarpedeon to Glaucus. B. 12 From 375 to 398.

Neptune's passage from Samothracia to Ægæ and thence to Troy B. 13. From L. 14. to 39.

The Concubitus of Jove and Juno. B. 14. From L. 414 to 425

The speeches of Iris and Neptune B. 15 From 212 to 270.

The pray'r of Achilles — B. 16. From L. 282 to 302.

The rescue of Patroclus' body. B. 17 From 872 to the end.

The appearance of Achilles. B. 18. From L. 248 to 291.

Achilles arming himself — B. 19. From L. 436. to 472.

Description of Achilles slaying the Trojans. B. 20. From 604 to the end.

The exultation of Achilles over Asteropæus. B. 21.

Book 22. The flight of Hector. From L. 152 to 194.

The vision of Patroclus — B. 23. From L. 74 to 132.

Priam chasing the multitude and chiding his sons. B. 24. From L. 302. to 339.

JAMES HURDIS   Tuesday, 9 August 1791

Hayley, ii. 11–13

Weston, August 9, 1791.

My dear sir,

I never make a correspondent wait for an answer through idleness or want of proper respect for him; but if I am silent, it is because I am busy, or not well, or because I stay till something occur that may make my Letter, at least a little better than mere blank paper. I therefore write speedily in reply to yours, being at present, neither much occupied, nor at all indisposed, nor forbidden by a dearth of materials.

I wish always when I have a new piece in hand, to be as secret as you, and there was a time when I could be so. Then I lived the life of a solitary, was not visited by a single neighbour, because I had none with whom I could associate; nor ever had an inmate. This was when I dwelt at Olney; but since I have removed to Weston the case is different. Here I am visited by all around me, and study in a room exposed to all manner of inroads. It is on the ground floor, the room in which we dine, and in which I am sure to be found by all who seek me. They find me generally at my desk, and with my work, whatever it be, before me, unless perhaps I have conjured it into its hiding-place before they have had time to enter. This however is not always the case, and consequently sooner or later, I cannot fail to be detected. Possibly you, who I suppose have a snug study, would find it impracticable to attend to any thing closely in an apartment exposed as mine, but use has made it familiar to me, and so familiar, that neither servants going and coming disconcert me, nor even if a lady, with an oblique glance of her eye, catches two or three lines of my MSS. do I feel myself inclined to blush, though naturally the shyest of mankind.

You did well, I believe, to cashier the subject of which you give me a recital.[1] It certainly wants those *agremens*, which are necessary to the success of any subject in verse. It is a curious story, and so far as the poor young lady was concerned, a very affecting one; but there is a coarseness in the character of the hero that would have spoiled all. In fact, I find it myself a much easier matter to write, than to get a convenient theme to write on.

I am obliged to you for comparing me, as you go, both with Pope and with Homer. It is impossible in any other way of management to know whether the Translation be well executed or not, and if well, in what degree. It was in the course of such a process that I first became dissatisfied with Pope. More than thirty years since, and when I was a

[1] Unidentified further.

young Templar, I accompanied him with his original, line by line, through both poems. A fellow student of mine,[2] a person of fine classic taste, joined himself with me in the labour. We were neither of us, as you may imagine, very diligent in our proper business.

I shall be glad if my Reviewers, whosoever they may be, will be at the pains to read me as you do; I want no praise that I am not entitled to, but of that to which I am entitled I should be loth to lose a little, having worked hard to earn it.

I would heartily second the Bishop of Salisbury[3] in recommending to you a close pursuit of your Hebrew studies, were it not that I wish you to publish what I may understand. Do both, and I shall be satisfied.

Your remarks, if I may but receive them soon enough to serve me in case of a new edition, will be extremely welcome.

W. C.

JOHN JOHNSON

Tuesday, 9 August 1791

Southey, vii. 52

Weston, Aug. 9, 1791.

My dearest Johnny,

The little that I have heard about Homer myself has been equally, or more flattering than Dr. ———'s[1] intelligence, so that I have good reason to hope that I have not studied the old Grecian, and how to dress him, so long and so intensely, to no purpose. At present I am idle, both on account of my eyes, and because I know not to what to attach myself in particular. Many different plans and projects are recommended to me. Some call aloud for original verse, others for more translation, and others for other things. Providence, I hope, will direct me in my choice; for other guide I have none, nor wish for another.

[2] William Alston. See n.5, C to Rowley, Aug. 1758.
[3] John Douglas (1721-1807), Bishop of Salisbury from 1791 to 1807. An eminent divine, he attacked Hume's arguments against miracles in 1752, and he refuted William Lauder's attacks on Milton (see C to Hurdis, 8 Apr. 1792).

[1] Probably Dr Cheatham.

9 August 1791

God bless you, my dearest Johnny.

W. C.

WALTER CHURCHEY   Friday, 12 August 1791

Address: Mr. Walter Churchey Atty. at Law / Hay / Brecon / Post pd. 9d.
Postmark: PAID/AU/13/91
John Rylands Library

Weston-Underwood.
Augt. 12. 1791

Dear Sir —

I am sorry that the names of any friends of yours, names too that you have been at the pains of procuring for me,[1] should have been omitted. I can only assure you that it has not happen'd through any fault of mine, for I immediately transmitted to Johnson all that you transmitted to me. Many omissions and many mistakes have happen'd, and many, I suppose, are always committed on these occasions.

I have this moment received your letter and have this moment written to my Bookseller, telling him all that you have said and giving him all necessary directions. This was my part and I have perform'd it. I am not without hopes of seeing him soon at Weston, in which case I will also endeavour to quicken him vivâ voce; for though by the terms of our contract the concern is now become altogether his own, it is not certain that he will on that account give it the more attention.

I find in my List the name of John Wesley Black Friars road[2] — This, I suppose, can be no other than the name of your late friend the Apostle. I am glad that he approved the specimen, which I am ready to believe he would have approved still more had he seen the amended edition of it.

I am, Dear Sir, with thanks for all past and all intended kindnesses

Much Yours
Wm Cowper

[1] 'Mr. John Powell, Brecon.' is the only name which we can conjecture with some certainty that Churchey supplied.

[2] 'Mr. John Wesley, Blackfriars Road.'; Wesley had died on 2 Mar. 1791.

c.15 August 1791

EDWARD THURLOW   *c.*Monday, 15 August 1791[1]

Fitzwilliam Museum, Cambridge

Answer to Letter 1

My Lord —

A letter reach'd me yesterday from Henry Cowper enclosing another from your Lordship to himself,[2] of which a passage in my work is the subject.[3] It gave me the greatest pleasure. Your strictures are perfectly just, and here follows the speech of Achilles accommodated to them.

Phoenix &c————————————[4]

I have furnish'd myself with an interleaved copy of my Homer which I am preparing for a second edition, should a second ever be wanted, and in this copy I have enter'd the speech as I have here transcribed it.

I did not expect to find your Lordship on the side of rhime, remembering well with how much energy and interest I have heard you repeat passages of the Paradise Lost, which you could not have recited as you did, unless you had been perfectly sensible of their music. It comforts me therefore to know that if you have an ear for rhime, you have an ear for Blank verse also.

It seems to me that I may justly complain of rhime as an

---

[1] On 30 Aug. 1791 C told Lady Hesketh of three letters written by him to Thurlow concerning his translation of Homer. The letter to Lady Hesketh is the first dated reference to the Thurlow letters. C answered the letter he received from Thurlow on the 29th 'immediately'; the other two letters can reasonably be placed about a week apart: *c.*15 Aug. and *c.*22 Aug.

[2] Thurlow's letter to Henry Cowper is also at the Fitzwilliam. It contains no address or postmark, but it is marked in C's hand: 'Lord Chancellor to Hen. C.' In the first paragraph, Thurlow makes his objections to C's translation: 'I have red [*sic*] our Friend's Preface; and believe He is right in many things — but I doubt, whether the melody of a rhimed Line must not be as perfect, as of a blank one. I doubt also, whether the Habit of an English Ear does not require Rhime, at least so far, as sooner to be sensible of measure so marked. and, if He really writes with more ease in Rhime, I doubt whether His objection to the Fetters is true. In revenge I have translated, on the other side, the Speech of Achilles to Pheenix in Rhime, which, I believe, He could burnish in the dull parts, and elevate in the flat, more up to the tone of Homer. But I shall be disappointed, if He does not agree, that It is closer to the Original, than His own; and might be made more so with more skill and care.'

[3] *Iliad*, ix. 758–72 in C's translation.

[4] This is C's copy of his answer to Thurlow's letter, and he has omitted the passage of translation.

inconvenience in translation, even though I assert in the sequel that to me it has been easier to rhime than to write without, because I always suppose a rhiming translator to ramble, and always obliged to do so. Yet I allow your Lordship's version of this speech of Achilles to be very close and closer much than mine. And to say truth, I should like a whole Iliad render'd according to that sample better far than Pope's; because it is Homer and nothing but Homer. But I believe that should either your Lordship or I give them burnish and elevation, your lines would be found, in measure as they acquired stateliness, to have lost the merit of fidelity. In which case nothing more would be done than Pope has done already.

I cannot ask your Lordship to proceed in your strictures though I should be happy to receive more of them. Perhaps it is possible that when you retire into the country, you may now and then amuse yourself with my translation. Should your remarks reach me, I promise faithfully that they shall be all most welcome, not only as yours, but because I am sure that my work will be the better for them.

With sincere and fervent wishes for your Lordship's health and happiness, I remain, my Lord, &c —

SAMUEL ROSE   Saturday, 20 August 1791

Address: Samuel Rose Esqr. / Chancery Lane / London
Postmark: AU/22/91/A
Princeton

Weston. Augt. 20. 1791

My dear friend,

Whatever you do, suffer not this business of Homer to give you a moment's trouble. I cannot endure that you should be in the smallest degree distress'd about it. It is not likely that after an engagement of some years' standing to studies of so very different a nature, you should be able to make a short turn at once to a subject merely classical, without difficulty and inconvenience. I had sagacity enough to foresee that you would find the task a troublesome one, and actually sat down to my desk with a design to relieve you from the burthen of it.

But it is impossible to tell you how much in vain I labour'd. The fear of saying too little, and an equal fear of saying too much, fetter'd my intellects, and made me absolutely unequal to the service.

I am convinced in short, that a Stranger to the author is the only proper person for the purpose, because a stranger alone can feel himself perfectly possessed of the free exercise of his judgment. To a stranger therefore let us leave it. I shall be easy if you will be so. I took my chance on a former occasion, and am as ready to do it now. Be my Reviewer who he may, I am not afraid of him, and if he should even behave himself like an enemy, I had much rather that should be the case, than occasion any anxiety to a friend.

If it be possible that the Repair of your house will afford you and Mrs. Rose an opportunity to breathe a little of our Weston air before Autumn is over, we shall rejoice to receive you, and I am in the mean time affectionately yours

Wm Cowper.

P. S. Mrs. Unwin's best Compliments.
P. S.

I have always intended, and always, while writing, have forgotten to say that on mature consideration I found it expedient to trust Johnson for the well-binding of the Dedication-copies. Had I transferred it to other hands, it seem'd to me that I should unavoidably affront him, and the object was not *tanti*.[1] — In fact, he has acquitted himself in this particular as well as possible. I have, myself, a copy of the best binding which is extremely elegant, and saw yesterday a gentleman who has seen Lord Spencer's copy, which, by his report, is such also.

---

[1] 'Of great importance'.

EDWARD THURLOW   *c.*Monday, 22 August 1791[1]

Charles Ryskamp

My Lord —

We are of one mind as to the agreeable effect of Rhime or Euphony in the lighter kinds of poetry. The pieces which your Lordship mentions would certainly be spoil'd by the loss of it, and so would all such. The Alma would lose all its neatness and smartness, and Hudibras all its Humour.[2] But in grave poems of extreme length, I apprehend that the case is different. Long before I thought of commencing poet myself, I have complain'd and have heard others complain of the wearisomness of such poems. Not that I suppose that tædium the effect of the rhime itself, but rather of the perpetual recurrence of the same pause and cadence, unavoidable in the English couplet.

I hope I may say truly, it was not in a spirit of presumption that I undertook to do what, in your Lordship's opinion, neither Dryden nor Pope would have dared to do. On the contrary, I see not how I could have escaped that imputation had I follow'd Pope in his own way. A closer translation was call'd for. I verily believed that rhime had betrayed Pope into *his* deviations. For me, therefore, to have used his mode of versifying would have been to expose myself to the same miscarriage, at the same time that I had not his talents to atone for it.

I agree with your Lordship that a translation perfectly close is impossible, because time has sunk the original strict import of a thousand phrases, and we have no means of recovering it. But it we cannot be unimpeachably faithful, that is no reason why we should not be as faithful as we can, and if Blank verse afford the fairest chance, then it claims the preference.

Your Lordship I will venture to say can command me nothing in which I will not obey with the greatest alacrity

Eι δυναμαι τελεσαι γε κ, ει τετελεσμενον εστιν[3]

---

[1] For dating, see n.1, C to Thurlow *c.*15 Aug. 1791.
[2] See C to Unwin, 21 Mar. 1784 and n.3.
[3] A variant of this line occurs twice in the *Iliad*. xiv. 196 and xviii. 427: 'My heart bids me fulfil it, if fulfil it I can, and it is a thing that has fulfilment.'

but when, having made as close a translation as even you can invent, you enjoin me to make it still closer, and in rhime too, I can only reply as Horace to Augustus

- - - - - cupidum, pater optime, vires
Deficiunt. - - - - - - - - - - - [4]

I have not treacherously departed from my pattern, that I might seem to give some proof of the justness of my own opinion, but have fairly and honestly adhered as closely to it as I could. Yet your Lordship will not have to compliment me on my success, either in respect of the poetical merit of my lines, or of their fidelity. They have just enough of each to make them deficient in the other.

> Oh Phoenix, father, friend, guest sent from Jove! 〕
> Me no such honours as they yield can move, 〉
> For I expect my honours from above. 〕
> Here Jove has fixt me, and while breath and sense
> Have place within me, I will never hence.
> Hear too, and mark me well — Haunt not my ears
> With sighs, nor seek to melt me with thy tears
> For yonder Chief, lest urging such a plea
> Through love of Him, thou hateful prove to me.
> Thy friendship for thy friend shall brightest shine
> Wounding his spirit who has wounded mine.
> Divide with me the honours of my throne —
> These shall return and make their tidings known,
> But go not thou — thy couch shall here be dress'd
> With softest fleeces for thy easy rest,
> And with the earliest blush of op'ning day
> We will consult to seek our home, or stay.

Since I wrote these I have look'd at Pope's. I am certainly somewhat closer to the Original than he, but farther I say not. — I shall wait with impatience for your Lordship's conclusion from these premisses and remain in the mean time with great truth

My Lord — &c.

Answer 2[5]

---

[4] *Satires*, II. i. 12–13: 'My dear good man, I wish I could but I have not the strength.'

[5] The MS is marked 'Answer 2' in C's hand. It is a copy made by C at the time that he sent the original to Thurlow. There is no signature.

JOHN AND CATHARINE JOHNSON

Saturday, 27 August 1791

Address: John Johnson Esqr. / Swaffham / Norfolk
Postmarks: AU/29/91/D *and* NEWPORT/PAGNEL
Barham Johnson

Weston-Underwood
Augt. 27. 1791

My dearest Johnny —

If my eyes will serve me to write to you I shall be glad, but certain it is that they will not serve me both to do that, and to read your two letters over before I begin. I must answer them therefore as well as I can from memory, and if I forget any thing material, the fault shall be mended hereafter. You will ask what ails my eyes? I answer that they are very weak and somewhat inflamed, and have never indeed been well since that suffusion of bloody memory that happen'd when you were here.[1]

Your first letter I remember gave me some pleasant notices — such as that of your safe arrival in Norfolk, of the improvement of yours and my dear Catharine's health, and of the good tidings you heard at Cambridge concerning the success of my Homerican labours; all these were pleasant intimations and for them all I thank you. The little that I have heard about Homer myself, has been equally or more flattering than even Dr. Cheatham's[2] intelligence, so that I have good reason to hope that I have not grubb'd the pen in vain, nor studied the old Greecian and how to dress him, so long and so intensely, to no purpose. — At present I am idle, both on account of my eyes as aforesaid, and because I know not to what to attach myself in particular. Many different plans and projects are recommended to me. Some call aloud for original verse, others for more translation, and others for other things. Providence, I hope, will direct me in my choice, for other guide I have none, nor wish another.

Elizabeth the poetess is arrived, and shall be distributed to all who have claims upon her.[3] I have not read a line of her

---

[1] We have no further details of the incident.

[2] This is the man mentioned in C's letter to Mrs Balls of 24 Nov. 1790.

[3] Elizabeth Bentley's *Genuine Poetical Compositions* . . . See n.1, C to John Johnson, 19 Mar. 1791.

yet, nor ever shall, unless her type should grow larger, which is not probable, or my eyes stronger.

Mr. Palmer, and Butlin the shoemaker, and Nicols the Taylor shall be paid the first time I go to Olney, which will be either to-day or on Monday. As you went away unpaying, so you went away unpaid. I am in your debt for a hundred Apollos[4] at least, and I know not what beside. I shall have a better memory I hope for these matters when I see you next. — God bless you, my dearest Johnny —

You say well, my dearest Kate, that when you write to me you are afraid of you know not what. I am only a poor author my Dear, not a Critic. You cannot guess what pleasure it gives me that your health is so much improved. God grant the continuance of it, for his gift it is, since means and medicines are chaff, or worse, without his blessing. Give my kindest love to Coz Balls. I am truly sorry that she has been so much indisposed. I thank her for Hayley's poems[5] and will take good care of it as well as of our great Grandsire's poems which I forgot to restore to her.[6] May you soon find yourselves comfortably settled at Dereham, and meet with no more such Landlords as you found in Bucks. Adieu, my dearest Kate, my love to your gold-finch, and tell him I rejoice that Norfolk air agrees with him.

Mrs. Unwin's health is much as usual, and she is always mindful of you all, giving the best proof of it by never ceasing to pray for you. Adieu — I am affectionately and most affectionately with my best remembrances to Mr. and Mrs. Bodham Yours

Wm Cowper.

The Letter to Dr. Kerr goes to-morrow and could not go sooner. No fee will accompany it, because none is wanted.

Johnny seems to forget Kitche's promised coat, but *He* does not forget it. His rags remind him of it continually.
P. S.

My Cousin Balls' note did not come to hand till the day after you were gone, and then I found it at Mr. Palmer's shop when I call'd with a letter for the post.

[4] See n.8, C to John Johnson, 23 May 1791.
[5] Probably the 1785 edition of Hayley's *Poems and Plays*.
[6] The edition of John Donne's poetry which Mrs Balls had sent to C before 9 Sept. 1790. See C's letter to Mrs Bodham of that date.

EDWARD THURLOW   *c.*Monday, 29 August 1791[1]

Huntington Library

My Lord

I haunt you with letters, but will trouble you now with a short line only to tell your Lordship how happy I am that any part of my work has pleased you. — I have a comfortable consciousness that the whole has been executed with equal industry and attention, and am my Lord with many thanks to you for snatching such a hasty moment to write to me, your Lordship's obliged & affectionate

humble Servant
Wm Cowper.[2]

LADY HESKETH   ·   Tuesday, 30 August 1791

Address: Lady Hesketh / Tunbridge / Kent
Postmarks: AU/31/91/C *and* NEWPORT/PAGNEL
Princeton

The Lodge Augt. 30. 1791

My dearest Coz,

The walls of Ogressa's[1] chamber shall be furnish'd as elegantly as they can be, and at little cost, and when you see them you shall cry — Bravo! Bedding we have, but two chairs will be wanting, the servants' hall having engaged all our supernumeraries. These you will either send, or give us commission to buy them. Such as will suit may be found probably at Maurice Smith's of house-furnishing memory,[2] and this latter course I should think the best, because they are of all things most liable to fracture in a waggon.

I know not how it can have happen'd that Homer is such a secret at Tunbridge, for I can tell you his fame is on the wing and flies rapidly. Johnson however seems to be clear from

---

[1] In his letter to Lady Hesketh of 30 Aug., C states: ' . . . yesterday I heard from [Thurlow] again . . . I answer'd this letter immediately . . .'

[2] The MS draft is marked on the verso 'Answer 3' in C's hand and is tipped in before the rear flyleaves of Frederick Locker Lampson-Church's copy of *1785*.

---

[1] A female ogre. *OED* cites the spelling 'ogress'.

[2] See C to Lady Hesketh, 10 Apr. 1786.

blame, and when you recollect that the whole edition is his by purchase, and that he has no possible way to get his money again but by the sale of it, thou thyself wilt think so. A tradesman, an old stager too, may safely be trusted with his own interest.

I have spoken big words about Homer's fame, and bigger than perhaps my intelligence will justify, for I have not heard much, but what I have heard has been pretty much to the purpose. First, little Johnny, going through Cambridge in his way home, learn'd from his tutour there, that it had found many admirers among the best qualified judges of that University, and that they were very liberal of their praises. Secondly — Mr. Rye[3] wrote me word lately that a certain fair (candid) Critic and excellent judge of the county of North-ampton[4] gives it high encomiums. — Thirdly, Mr. Rye came over himself from Gayhurst, yesterday, on purpose to tell me how much he was delighted with it. He had just been reading the Sixth Iliad, and comparing it with Pope and with the Original, and profess'd himself enchanted. Fourthly — Mr. Frog is much pleased with it, and Fifthly — Henry Cowper is bewitch'd with it, and sixthly — so are you and I. Ça suffit —

But now, if thou hast the faculty of erecting thine ears, lift them into the air, first taking off thy cap that they may have their highest possible elevation. — Mrs. Unwin says — No — don't tell her Ladyship all — tell her only enough to raise her curiosity, that she may come the sooner to Weston to have it gratified. But I say, yes — I will tell her all, lest she should be overcharged and burst by the way.

The Chancellor and I, my dear, have had a correspondence on the subject of Homer. He had doubts it seems about the propriety of translating him in Blank Verse, and wrote to Henry to tell him so, adding a translation of his own in rhime of the speech of Achilles to Phoenix in the 9th. book, and referring him to me, who he said could elevate it, and polish it and give it the tone of Homer. Henry sent this Letter to me, and I answer'd it in one to his Lordship, but not meddling with his verses, for I remember'd what happen'd between Gil

---

[3] See n.3, C to Rose, 22 Nov. 1789.
[4] Possibly Rose's uncle, James Clarke, whom Rye knew. See n.2, C to [Rose], [10 Mar. 1788], and C to Rose, 22 Nov. 1789.

Blas and the Archbishop of Toledo.[5] His Lordship sent me two sheets in reply, fill'd with arguments in favour of rhime which I was to answer if I could, and containing another translation of the same passage, only in Blank verse, leaving it to me to give it rhime, to make it close and faithful, and poetical. All this I perform'd as best I could, and yesterday I heard from him again. In this last Letter he says — I am clearly convinced that Homer may be best translated *without* rhime, and that you have *succeeded* in the passages that I have look'd into.

Such is the candour of a wise man and a real scholar. I would to heaven that all prejudiced persons were like him! I answer'd this letter immediately, and here I suppose our correspondence ends. Have I not made a great convert? You shall see the Letters, both his and mine, when you come.

My picture hangs in the study.[6] I will not tell thee what others think of it, but thou shalt judge for thyself.

I altogether approve Mrs. Carter's sentiments on the B——m riots and admire her manner of expressing them.[7] — The Frogs come down to day, bringing Catharina with them. Mrs. Frog has caught cold, as I hear, in her journey, therefore how she may be now I know not, but before she went she was well and in excellent spirits. I rejoice that thy poor lungs can play freely, and shall be happy when they can do the same at Weston. My eyes are weak and somewhat inflamed,

[5] The confrontation was actually between Gil Blas and the Archbishop of Granada and occurs in Book I, Chapter 4. Gil Blas was dismissed by the Archbishop for venturing to criticize rather than praise a speech made by the latter. See C to Unwin, 27 May 1782.

[6] The profile drawing by John Higgins. See n.2, C to Lady Hesketh, 18 May 1791.

[7] Letter CCLXXVIII dated 18 July 1791 in *Letters from Mrs. Elizabeth Carter to Mrs. Montagu, Between the Years 1755 and 1800* (1817) contains the sentiments mentioned by C, and Lady Hesketh probably heard the contents of this letter from her friend, Mrs Montagu: 'I cannot say I was alarmed by any apprehensions of the fourteenth, for I know that as far as human security could prevent mischief, our government had guarded against any tumult. But I felt a very great horror of the general spirit that gave rise to that absurd celebration. Almighty God has so often interposed for the preservation of this kingdom, that on his providence I humbly rely for frustrating the wicked intentions of such as wish to introduce anarchy and rebellion among us, and destroy the happiest establishment that perhaps the world ever saw. It is astonishing that some people, even of sense and virtue, should give any encouragement to the wretches who would contrive our ruin, by praising such execrable performances as Paine's book.' (iii. 327-8).

and have never been well this month past.

Mrs. Unwin is tolerably well, that is, much as usual. She joins me in best love and in every thing that you can wish us both to feel for you. Adieu my dearest Coz —

Ever thine   Wm Cowper

WALTER BAGOT

Tuesday, 6 September 1791

Address: The Revd. Walter Bagot / Blithfield near / Litchfield / Staffordshire
Postmark: NEWPORT/PAGNEL
Morgan Library

Weston-Underwood
Sepr. 6. 1791

My dear friend —

I rejoice that you can so well answer the charge of daring to be your own Physician,[1] and wish you always free from all occasion for a better.

I know not how it happen'd that Johnson disgraced himself by making me a paltry offer in the first instance, for in the second he proposed handsome terms and such as could not be objected to. We are all compounded of Good and Evil, and our behaviour is according to the preponderancy of either at the moment. In him, the Dæmon of avarice prevail'd at first, and, at last, the spirit of Liberality. The terms on which we finally agreed are these. —

He takes the whole subscription, gift-money excepted, together with all the copies unsubscribed for; in consideration of which he pays the expences of the Press &c and me a thousand pounds. The expences amount to about ₤600. — Thus it is that I have disposed of this first edition, and the copy-right remains my own.

I wish you in possession of the volumes because I wait with some impatience for your opinion of them. In the mean time, I will tell you, in order that I may prejudice you as much as possible in their favour, that I have received much encomium from various quarters and those the most respectable, and not from friends only, but from strangers also. In short I am extremely vain, as this paragraph may convince you.

[1] See C to Bagot, 2 Aug. 1791.

Most heartily I give you joy of a little Bagot,[2] spic-and-span new, and of Mrs. Bagot's happy delivery. I do not know what it is to have a son, but suppose it may be matter of great comfort even to Him who had many before. I know however what it is to tremble at the apprehended loss of those who are very dear to us, and therefore so far as Mrs. Bagot is concerned, can sympathize with you most feelingly.

Give my very sincere love to Mr. and Mrs. Chester who I presume are now with you, and to as many of their descendants as are of the party.

I am on the brink of a new literary engagement, and of a kind with which I never meddled before. A magnificent edition of Milton's works (I mean his poetical ones) is about to be published in the Boydel stile, with notes; Fuseli, the Painter, and your humble servant, the Editor.[3] Thus I shall have pass'd through the three gradations of authorship, Poet, Translator, and Critic. Wish me success in this last capacity, and send me what may much contribute to it, any shrewd remarks of your own.

I remain most truly Yours
Wm Cowper

Mrs. Unwin sends her very best respects.

---

[2] Ralph, who would enter holy orders. Walter Bagot already had two sons and three daughters by his first wife, and he was to have five daughters as well as this son by Mary Ward, his second wife.

[3] In Aug. 1790 Joseph Johnson considered embarking on the publication of a Milton Gallery which would rival Boydell's Shakespeare Gallery. Fuseli was to undertake most of the paintings, and a fine edition of Milton was to accompany the illustrations. In addition to a dispute concerning their respective interests in Milton and Shakespeare, Fuseli and Boydell may have been at odds because of Boydell's plans to publish a rival illustrated edition of Milton with illustrations by Romney and a biography of Milton by Hayley. In fact, C and Hayley met and became friends because a newspaper report representing C and Hayley as rivals in writing Milton's life appeared in early 1792, and Hayley wrote about this matter to C on 7 Feb. 1792. Hayley's *Life of Milton*, published by Boydell with only one plate out of ten after Romney and with excerpts from C's translations of Milton, appeared in 1794. Fuseli persevered in his plans, and his Milton Gallery opened in 1799 with 40 paintings (all by Fuseli). See Marcia R. Pointon, *Milton and English Art* (Toronto, 1970), pp. 106-7, 255-60.

JOSEPH JOHNSON   Tuesday, 6 September 1791

Latin and Italian Poems, x

Weston, Sept. 6, 1791.

I have at length brought myself to something like a hope, that I may perhaps prove equal to this business, and in consequence have resolved to attempt it: but must depend on you for my implements. Newton's edition[1] I have, but have nothing more.

JOSEPH JOHNSON   Sunday, 11 September 1791

Southey, xv. 233–4

Weston Underwood, Sept. 11, 1791.

Dear sir,

I have made some alterations in the printed proposals[1] — I should rather say in the wording of them, the reasons of which I need not mention; those for the most material will suggest themselves.

I am very well satisfied with your terms, and shall be glad if the labourer prove worthy of his hire.

I am obliged to you also for liberty given me to draw on you at my pleasure. But my purpose being to leave the bond-money inviolate till time of payment shall arrive, I mean to trouble you at present only with a draft for fifty pounds payable a fortnight after date, which the arrears you mention will make good, whenever paid; that they will be paid is certain, though the time when, is not so. When the whole is received there will be a small surplus in your hands, which I will beg you to remit to me without further demand.

I give you a discharge[2] for Mr. Walter Bagot's twenty pounds' subscription. Lady Walsingham[3] stands in the list as

---

[1] See n.3, C to Henry Cowper, 18 Nov. 1791.

---

[1] See *Russell*, p. 179.

[2] Instead of remitting Bagot's payment to Johnson, C is giving Johnson permission to deduct it from the amount owing to C.

[3] Maria Cowper de Grey (see n.21, *Adelphi*). Her late husband had been created Baron Walsingham on 17 Oct. 1780.

a simple subscriber, which is a mistake: she sent five guineas.

What do you apprehend will be the effect of Boydell's opposition?[4]

> I am, dear Sir, yours,
> Wm. Cowper.

SAMUEL ROSE   Wednesday, 14 September 1791

Hayley, ii. 14–15

> The Lodge, Sept. 14, 1791.

My dear friend,

Whoever reviews me will in fact have a laborious task of it, in the performance of which he ought to move leisurely, and to exercise much critical discernment. In the mean time my courage is kept up by the arrival of such testimonies in my favour, as give me the greatest pleasure; coming from quarters the most respectable. I have reason, therefore, to hope that our periodical judges will not be very adverse to me, and that perhaps they may even favour me. If one man of taste and letters is pleased, another man so qualified can hardly be displeased, and if Critics of a different description grumble, they will not however materially hurt me.

You, who know how necessary it is to me to be employed, will be glad to hear that I have been called to a new literary engagement, and that I have not refused it. A Milton that is to rival, and, if possible, to exceed in splendor, Boydell's Shakespeare, is in contemplation, and I am in the Editor's office. Fuseli is the Painter. My business will be to select notes from others, and to write original notes, to translate the Latin and Italian poems, and to give a correct text. I shall have years allowed me to do it in.

> W. C.

---

[4] See n.3, C to Bagot, 6 Sept. 1791.

WALTER BAGOT   Wednesday, 21 September 1791

Address: The Revd. Walter Bagot / Blithfield near / Litchfield / Staffordshire.
Postmark: NEWPORT/PAGNEL
Morgan Library

Weston-Underwood
Sepr. 21. 1791

My dear friend —

Of all the testimonies in favour of my Homer that I have received, none has given me so sincere a pleasure as that of Lord Bagot. It is an unmixt pleasure and without a draw-back; because I know him to be perfectly and in all respects, whether erudition or a fine taste be in question, so well qualified to judge me, that I can neither expect nor wish a sentence more valuable than his — εἰςο κ αὔτμη

Εν ςτηθεσσι μενει, και μοι φιλα γουνατ᾽ ορωρει.[1]

I hope by this time you have received your volumes and are prepared to second the applauses of your brother, else, woe be to you. I wrote to Johnson immediately on the receipt of your last, giving him a strict injunction to dispatch them to you without delay, but, beast as I was, forgot to order him first to bind them. Pardon me a neglect that I literally blush to think of; I never became sensible of it till this moment, and shall hate myself for the omission whenever I think of it.

My bookseller is no otherwise bound than by promise to print only 700 copies. He assured me that he would play me none of the tricks of his trade, and though my opinion of his religious notions be much like yours, and I hold him to be like most for whom he publishes, extremely heterodox and heretical, yet I found myself obliged to trust him. He had sold some time since a hundred of the unsubscribed-for copies.

I have not a history in the world except Baker's Chronicle,[2] and That I borrow'd 3 years ago from Mr. Throckmorton. Now the case is this. I am translating Milton's third Elegy — his elegy on the death of the Bishop of Winchester. He begins it with saying that while he was sitting alone, dejected, and

---

[1] 'As long as there is breath in my bosom and my [dear] knees can bestow themselves.' C is quoting *Iliad*, ix. 609–10; they are two formulaic lines that occur in various places in Homer.

[2] See n.9, C to Lady Hesketh, 5 Oct. 1787.

musing on many melancholy themes, first, the idea of the plague presented itself to his mind, and of the havoc made by it among the Great — then he proceeds thus —

> Tum memini clarique ducis, fratrisque verendi
> Intempestivis ossa cremata rogis:
> Et memini Heroum quos vidit ad æthera raptos
> Flevit et amissos Belgia tota duces.[3]

I cannot learn from my only oracle Baker who this famous Leader and his reverend brother were, neither does he at all ascertain for me the event alluded to in the second of these couplets. I am not yet possess'd of Wharton who probably explains it,[4] nor can be for a month to come. Consult him for me if you have him, or if you have him not, consult some other, or you may find the intelligence perhaps in your own budget. No matter how you come by it, only send it to me if you can and as soon as you can, for I hate to leave unsolved difficulties behind me.

Mrs. Unwin who is always much obliged to you for your kind mention of her, bids me tell you so and present to you her best respects — I am Ever Yours

Wm Cowper

[3] 'Then I called to mind that famous general and his well-respected brother in arms, whose bones were burned on untimely pyres, and I remembered the heroes that all Belgia had seen snatched up to the skies — Belgia, who wept for her lost leaders.' C is citing lines 9–12 from *Elegia tertia*, which was written for Lancelot Andrewes (1555–1626), Bishop of Winchester (1619–26). The 'famous Leader' was probably 'Ernst von Mansfeld, a mercenary general of a marauding army in the early years of the Thirty Years War, who championed the Protestant cause and was appointed general of Frederick V's army in Bohemia in 1621.' The 'brother in arms' was probably 'Christian of Brunswick, who allied himself to Frederick's cause early in 1622 and, with Mansfeld, defeated the Spaniards at Fleurus, Aug. 1622. He was defeated by Tilly at Stadtlohn in 1623, but came back into the war on the Protestant side in 1625, along with Christian IV of Denmark. He died 16 Jun. 1626.' (Translation of Milton's Latin and information on Mansfeld and Brunswick from *The Poems of John Milton*, ed. John Carey and Alastair Fowler (1968), pp. 49–50, 52.) C's translation, published in *Hayley* (1808), was as follows: 'I, next, deplor'd the fam'd fraternal pair, / Too soon to ashes turn'd, and empty air! / The heroes next, whom snatch'd into the skies, / All Belgia saw, and follow'd with her sighs . . . '

[4] 'I am kindly informed by sir David Dalrymple, "The two Generals here mentioned, who died in 1626, were the two champions of the queen of Bohemia, the Duke of Brunswick, and Count Mansfelt: *Frater* means a Sworn Brother in arms, according to the military cant of those days."' John Milton, *Poems Upon*

In the 1st year of Charles 1st Milton was 17 years of age and then he wrote this elegy.[5] The period therefore to which I would refer you is the 2 or 3 last years of James the 1st.

MR KING   Friday, 23 September 1791

Address: The Revd. Mr. King / Pertenhall near / Kimbolton / Huntingdonshire
Postmarks: SE/24/91/D *and* NEWPORT/PAGNEL
Princeton

Weston-Underwood
Sepr. 23. 1791

Dear Sir —

We are truly concern'd at your account of Mrs. King's severe indisposition, and, though you had no better news to tell us, are much obliged to you for writing to inform us of it and to Mrs. King for desiring you to do it. We take a lively interest in what concerns her. I should never have ascribed her silence to neglect had she neither written to me herself nor commission'd you to write for her. I had indeed for some time expected a letter from her by every post, but accounted for my continual disappointment by supposing her at Edgeware, to which place she intended a visit as she told me long since, and hoped that she would write immediately on her return.

Her sufferings will be felt here 'till we learn that they are removed, for which reason we shall be much obliged by the earliest notice of her recovery, which we most sincerely wish, if it please God, and which will not fail to be a constant subject of prayer at Weston.

I beg you Sir to present Mrs. Unwin's and my affectionate remembrances to Mrs. King in which you are equally a partaker, and to believe me

with true esteem and much Sincerity
Yours Wm Cowper

Several Occasions, ed. Thomas Warton (2nd edn., 1791), p. 434. The first edition appeared in 1785.

[5] Milton was born on 9 Dec. 1608 and composed the poem between Sept. and Dec. 1626 (Charles I's reign commenced on 27 Mar. 1625). The poem is headed 'Anno aetatis 17' in *Poems of Mr. John Milton, Both English and Latin . . . 1645* (1646), its first publication.

SAMUEL ROSE   Tuesday, 4 October 1791

Address: Samuel Rose Esqr. / Chancery Lane / London
Postmarks: OC/5/91/A *and* NEWPORT/PAGNEL
Princeton

The Lodge
Octr. 4th. 1791

My dear friend —
    I am truly sorry for our disappointment (yours I will say as well as ours) and for the cause of it. I had made myself sure of seeing you, and rose this morning full of that pleasant expectation and promising myself an interview with you in few hours. But your excuse is too just for me to be able, however I may regret it, to alledge one word against the reasonableness of it. The next pleasure, I hope, for which I shall be indebted to you now, will be the earliest intelligence you can send us of Mrs. Rose's amended health, and the next to that, the sight of you at Weston once more, which after having miss'd you here so long will be doubly gratifying.[1]

MRS KING   Friday, 21 October 1791

Address: Mrs. King / Pirtenhall / Kimbolton / Huntingdonshire
Postmark: OC/21/91/A
Princeton

Weston Underwood
Octr. 21. 1791

My dear Madam,
    You could not have sent me more agreeable news than that of your better health, and I am greatly obliged to you for making me the first of your correspondents to whom you have given that welcome intelligence. This is a favour which I should have acknowledged much sooner, had not a disorder in my eyes, to which I have always been extremely subject, required that I should make as little use of my pen as possible. I felt much for you, when I read that part of your letter in which you mention your visitors, and the fatigue which, indisposed as you have been, they could not fail to occasion you. Agreeable as you would have found them at another

[1] This note is unsigned.

time, and happy as you would have been in their company, you could not but feel the addition they necessarily made to your domestic attentions as a considerable inconvenience. But I have always said, and shall never say otherwise, that if patience under adversity, and submission to the afflicting hand of God be true fortitude, which no reasonable person can deny, then your sex have ten times more true fortitude to boast than ours, and I have not the last doubt that you carried yourself with infinitely more equanimity on that occasion than I should have done, or any He of my acquaintance. Why is it, since the first offender on earth was a woman, that the women are nevertheless in all the most important points superior to the men? That they are so I will not allow to be disputed, having observed it ever since I was capable of making the observation. I believe on recollection that when I had the happiness to see you here, we agitated this question a little, but I do not remember that we arrived at any decision of it. The Scripture calls you the *weaker vessels*,[1] and perhaps the best solution of the difficulty, therefore, may be found in those other words of scripture. — *My strength is perfected in weakness.*[2] Unless you can furnish me with a better key than this, I shall be much inclined to believe that I have found the true one.

I am deep in a new literary engagement, being retained by my Bookseller as Editor of an intended most magnificent publication of Milton's poetical works. This will ocupy me as much as Homer did, for a year or two to come, and when I have finished it I shall have run through all the degrees of my profession, as Author, Translator and Editor. I know not that a fourth could be found, but if a fourth can be found, I dare say I shall find it.

Mrs. Unwin joins me in best Compliments to yourself and Mr. King, who I hope by this time has entirely recover'd from the cold he had when you wrote, and from all the effects of it. I shall be happy to learn from you that you have had no more attacks of your most painful disorder in the stomach, and remain in the mean time, my Dear Madam,

Your affectionate friend and humble Servant
Wm Cowper

[1] Peter 3:7.   [2] 2 Corinthians 12:9.

CLOTWORTHY ROWLEY   Saturday, 22 October 1791

Address: Clothworthy Rowley Esqr. / Dublin
Postmarks: OC/24/[illegible], OC/27 *and* OULNEY
Princeton

Weston Underwood
Octr. 22. 1791

My dear Rowley —

How often am I to be mortified by hearing that you have been within 60 miles of me, and have taken your flight again to an immeasurable distance? Will you never in one of these excursions to England, (three of which at least you have made since we have had interourse by letter) will you never find your way to Weston? Consider that we are neither of us immortal, and that if we do not contrive to meet before we are 50 years older, our meeting in this world at least will be an affair altogether hopeless. For by that time your travelling days will be over, as mine have been these many years.

I often think of Carr,[1] and shall always think of him with affection. Should I never see him more, I shall never, I trust, be capable of forgetting his indefatigable attention to me during the last year that I spent in London. Two years after, I invited him to Huntingdon where I lived at that time, but he pleaded some engagement, and I have neither seen him nor heard of him, except from yourself, from that hour to the present. I know by experience with what reluctance we move when we have been long fixt, but could he prevail on himself to move hither he would make me very happy, and when you write to him next you may tell him so.

I have to tell you in answer to your question What I am doing, that I am preparing to appear in a new character, not as an Author, but as an Editor. Editor of Milton's poetical works, which are about to be published in a more splendid stile than ever yet. My part of the business is to translate the Latin and Italian pieces, to settle the text, to select notes from others and to [write notes of my own].[2] At present the translation employs me; when that shall be finish'd, I

---

[1] Arthur Carr. See n.4, C to Rowley, 2 Sept. 1762.
[2] These words have been obliterated by a fold in the MS. Words in brackets are supplied from *Southey*, vii. 61.

must begin to read all the books that I can scrape together, of which either Milton or his works are the subject, and that done, shall proceed to my commentary. Few people have studied Milton more, or are more familiar with his poetry than [mys]elf, but I never look'd into him yet [with the e]yes of an Annotator; therefore whether I may expect much or little difficulty I know no more than you do, but I shall be occupied in the business, no doubt, these two years. Fuseli is to be the painter, and will furnish thirty capital pictures to the Engraver.

I have little poems in plenty, but nothing that I can send to Ireland, unless you could put me into a way of conveying them thither at free cost; [for should] you be obliged to pay for them, le jeu ne v[audra pas] les chandelles.[3]

I rejoice that your family are all well[, and in] every thing that conduces to your happin[ess. Adieu,] my good and valued friend, permit me to thank you once more for your kind services in the matter of my subscription, and believe me most truly yours

Wm Cowper.

WALTER BAGOT   Tuesday, 25 October 1791

Address: The Revrd. Walter Bagot / Blithfield near / Litchfield / Staffordshire
Postmark: NEWPORT/PAGNEL
Morgan Library

Weston Underwood
Octr. 25. 1791

My dear friend,

Your unexpected and transient visit, like every thing else that is past, has now the appearance of a dream; but it was a pleasant one, and I heartily wish that such dreams could recur more frequently. Your brother Chester repeated his

---

[3] 'The game would not be worth the candles.' Hugh Percy Jones, *Dictionary of Foreign Phrases and Classical Quotations* (Edinburgh, 1963), p. 278: 'It was an old custom for poor folk to meet in a neighbour's house to play cards. At the end, they each subscribed something towards the expense of the entertainment. If they were stingy, their host found that the gifts were less than the cost of the candle which he had provided.'

visit yesterday, and I never saw him in better spirits. At such times he has, now and then, the very look that he had when he was a boy, and when I see it I seem to be a boy myself, and entirely forget for a short moment the years that have intervened since I was one. The look that I mean is one that you, I dare say, have observed. It is when in a laugh he shuts his eyes quite close and draws his chin into his bosom. Then we are at Westminster again. He left with me that poem[1] of your brother Lord Bagot's which was mentioned when you were here. It was a treat to me, and I read it to my Cousin Lady Hesketh and to Mrs. Unwin, to whom it was a treat also. It has great sweetness of numbers and much elegance of expression, and is just such a poem as I should have been happy to have composed myself about a year ago, when I was loudly call'd upon by a certain nobleman to celebrate the beauties of his villa.[2] But I had two insurmountable difficulties to contend with. One was that I had never seen his villa, and the other, that I had no eyes at that time for any thing but Homer. Should I at any time hereafter undertake the task, I shall now at least know how to go about it, which 'till I had seen Lord Bagot's poem I verily did not. I was particularly charm'd with the parody of those beautiful lines of Milton.

> The song was partial, but the Harmony —
> (What could it less when spirits immortal sing?)
> Suspended Hell, and took with ravishment
> The thronging audience.[3]

There's a Parenthesis for you! The Parenthesis it seems is out of fashion, and perhaps the moderns are in the right to proscribe what they cannot attain to. I will answer for it that had we the art at this day of insinuating a sentiment in this graceful manner, no reader of taste would quarrel with the practise. Lord Bagot show'd his by selecting the passage for his imitation.

I would beat Warton if he were living, for supposing that

---

[1] Unidentified.
[2] Charles Howard, 11th Duke of Norfolk. Probably a reference to 'Audley End'. See C to Lady Hesketh, 23 Jan. 1790 and n.3.
[3] *Paradise Lost*, ii. 552–5.

Milton ever repented of his Compliment to the memory of Bishop Andrews.[4] I neither do, nor can, nor will believe it. Milton's mind could not be narrow'd by any thing, and though he quarrell'd with Episcopacy in the Church of England idea of it, I am persuaded that a good Bishop, as well as any other good man of whatsoever rank or order, had always a share of his veneration.

I learn'd from your brother Chester that you arrived safe at home, and a day sooner than you intended. I rejoice in this, and shall be happy to hear of your health by the first opportunity. Yours my dear friend,

very affectionately — Wm Cowper.

SAMUEL ROSE   Sunday, 30 October 1791

Address: Samuel Rose Esqr. / Chancery Lane / London.
Postmarks: OC/31/91/B *and* OULNEY
British Library

Weston-Underwood
Octr. 30. 1791

My dear friend —

I rejoice that your fears on Mrs. Rose's account are quietted for the present, and sincerely wish that all fears and all occasions of fear that are yet in prospect, may be dispersed in the same manner.

If to have partners of our grief be a source of consolation, as it is generally allow'd to be, then your concern at being witheld from your intended visit to Weston may be alleviated, for I can assure you truly that the disappointment was not all your own.

The Autumn has been a pleasant season at the Hall, and for the pleasures of it we have been much indebted to your

---

[4] See n.3, C to Bagot, 21 Sept. 1791. C is referring to Warton's comment in *Poems Upon Several Occasions*, pp. 439–40: 'Milton, as he grew older in puritanism, must have looked back with disgust and remorse on the panegyric of this performance, as on one of the sins of his youth, inexperience and orthodoxy: for he had here celebrated, not only a bishop, but a bishop who supported the dignity and constitution of the Church of England in their most extensive latitude, the distinguished favourite of Elizabeth and James, and the defender of regal prerogative . . .' C owned a copy of *A Letter to the Rev. Mr. T. Warton on his Late Edition of Milton's Juvenile Poems* (1785): *Keynes*, 61.

profession. The same Triumvirate that enliven'd us last year, have contributed as much to our entertainment this year also. You will guess that I mean Mr. Cruise,[1] Mr. Pitcairne,[2] and Wm. Throckmorton.[3] Could a fourth have been added, you may guess what fourth I mean, I know not that there would have been a wish amongst us for yet another.

You have seen perhaps the beginning of a Review of my Homer in the Gentleman's Magazine for last month.[4] Can you tell me, or can you guess who is the author of it? He says so many handsome things of me, that at times I suspect it to be the work of Nichols himself; but then he seems so much disposed to find fault, that at other times I give it to I know not whom. I ask out of mere curiosity. In the mean time I have received and heard of so many testimonies in my favour given by some of the best judges, that I feel myself arm'd with at least a seven-fold shield[5] against all censure that I can have to expect from others.

I hope, as you hope for me, that I shall find my Miltonic studies agreeable. At present I occupy myself in the translation of his Latin poems, and have just finish'd his 7 elegies.[6] The versification of them is I think equal to the best of Ovid, but the matter of them is almost too puerile for me, who if I wore any beard at all should now wear a grey one. For which reason I am glad that I have done with them.

I thank you for your kind offer of books, but Johnson I imagine will some time or other furnish me with all the needful. I have given him a charge to do so.

Lady Hesketh who is with us joins Mrs. Unwin and myself in best Compliments — You will not I hope let slip the first opportunity you can find to make us amends for your long absence.

I am, my dear friend,

most truly yours　Wm Cowper

---

[1] See n.6, C to Mrs Throckmorton, 19 Feb. 1791.
[2] See n.1, C to Rose, 1 May 1790.
[3] See n.6, C to Lady Hesketh, 3 Nov. 1787.
[4] No. 156, lxi pt. ii (Sept. 1791), 845-6. We do not know the identity of the author.
[5] C's reference is either to the *Iliad*, vii. 222, 245 or to Shakespeare in *Antony and Cleopatra*, IV. xiv. 38.
[6] Published by Hayley in *Latin and Italian Poems*.

When you see Wm. Throck——n next, you will see him in mourning for his mother[7] who died very lately in Wales.

JOSEPH JOHNSON   Sunday, 30 October 1791

Latin and Italian Poems, xxii

Weston, Oct. 30, 1791.

We and the Papists are at present on amicable terms. They have behaved themselves peaceably many years, and have lately received favours from government: I should think therefore, that the dying embers of antient animosity had better not be troubled.[1]

JOHN JOHNSON   Monday, 31 October 1791

Address: [] Johnson Esqr. / East Dereham / []t at the Maid's-head — / []imons[1]
    — Norwich.
Postmark: NO/2/91
Yale (Osborn Collection), Princeton, *and Hayley*, ii.15–16[2]

Weston, Oct. 31, 1791.

My dear Johnny,

Your kind and affectionate Letter well deserves my thanks, and should have had them long ago, had I not been obliged lately to give my attention to a mountain of unanswered Letters, which I have just now reduced to a mole-hill; yours lay at the bottom, and I have at last worked my way down to it.

---

[7] Anna Maria Throckmorton. See n.3, C to Unwin, *c.*20 May 1784.

[1] C is explaining why he is not translating Milton's four Latin poems on the Gunpowder Plot, and 'In Quintum Novembris' ('On the Fifth of November'). He did, however, translate 'In Inventorem Bombardae' ('On the Inventor of Guns') and added the following note: 'The Poems on the subject of the Gunpowder Treason I have not translated, both because they are written with an asperity, which, however it might be warranted in Milton's Day, would be extremely unseasonable now.' *Latin and English Poems,* p. 42.

[1] Mr Simons was the carrier who took the mail from Norwich to Dereham.
[2] Most of this text is taken from *Hayley*. The surviving part of the address; the portion of the sixth paragraph beginning, 'made mention of . . . ' up to and including the seventh paragraph; the portion of the ninth paragraph beginning, 'and playing like an angel . . . ' up to and including the signature are from the Osborn fragment; the postmark and the postscript comprise the Princeton fragment.

It gives me great pleasure that you have found a house to your minds. May you all three be happier in it than the happiest that ever occupied it before you! But my chief delight of all is to learn that you and Kitty are so completely cured of your long and threatening maladies. I always thought highly of Dr. Kerr, but his extraordinary success in your two instances has even inspired me with an affection for him.

My eyes are much better than when I wrote last, though seldom perfectly well many days together. At this season of the year I catch perpetual colds, and shall continue to do so till I have got the better of that tenderness of habit with which the summer never fails to affect me.

I am glad that you have heard well of my Work in your country. Sufficient proofs have reached me from various quarters that I have not ploughed the field of Troy in vain.

Were you here I would gratify you with an enumeration of particulars, but since you are not, it must content you to be told that I have every reason to be satisfied.

Mrs. Unwin, I think, in her Letter to Cousin Balls, made mention of my new engagement. I have but just enter'd on it, and therefore can at present say little about it. It is a very creditable one in itself, and may I but acquit myself of it with sufficiency, will do me honour. The Commentator's part however is a new one to me, and one that I little thought to appear in.

Your Oysters were excellent, as I believe Mrs. Unwin likewise told you, and served us with several suppers. —

Remember your promise that I shall see you in the spring.

The Hall has been full of company ever since you went, and at present my Catharina is there singing and playing like an angel. But you know a Catharina whom, though she neither sings nor plays, I love still better.[3] Tell her so. Remember me with much affection to Cousin Balls, and believe me my dearest Johnny

with all truth and sincerity — Yours
Wm Cowper.

I rejoice that you [   ] poor Kitch who is every day wearing out his workout cloaths in our garden.

[3] C is referring to Catharine Stapleton (see n.1, C to Mrs Throckmorton, 14 May 1789) and Catharine Johnson respectively.

JOSEPH HILL   Monday, 14 November 1791[1]

Address: Joseph Hill Esqr. / Chancery Office / London
Postmarks: NO/15/91/D *and* NEWPORT/PAGNEL
Cowper Johnson

My dear friend —

I thank you for your Harbinger and for all that follow'd. I have waited and wish'd for your opinion with the feelings that belong to the value I have for it, and am very happy to find it so favourable. In my table-drawer I treasure up a bundle of suffrages sent me by those of whose approbation I was most ambitious, and shall presently insert yours among them.

I know not why we should quarrel with compound epithets. It is certain at least that they are as agreeable to the genius of our language as to that of the Greek, which is sufficiently proved by their being admitted even into our common and colloquial dialect. Black-eyed, nut-brown, crook-shank'd, hump-back'd, are all compound epithets, and together with a thousand other such, are used continually even by those who profess a dislike of such combinations in poetry. Why then do they treat with so much friendly familiarity a thing that they say disgusts them? I doubt if they could give this question a reasonable answer, unless they should answer it by confessing themselves unreasonable.

I have made a considerable progress in the translation of Milton's Latin poetry. I give them, as opportunity offers, all the variety of measure that I can. Some I render in heroic rhime, some in stanzas, some in seven, and some in eight syllable measure, and some in blank verse. They will all together I hope make an agreeable miscellany for the English reader. They are certainly good in themselves, and cannot fail to please but by the fault of their translator.

I was sorry to see Lord Craven's[2] death in the papers, knowing him to have been a friend of yours. It seems a plain

---

[1] The top portion of this letter has been removed and the date '14 Novr 91' has been supplied, probably by Hill after he cut off a receipt which also had the date of the letter.

[2] William Craven, Baron of Hampstead Marshall (1737–91), who succeeded to the title in 1769, died at Lausanne on 26 Sept. 1791. His estranged wife, Elizabeth, Baroness Craven (the youngest daughter of Augustus, 4th Earl of Berkeley),

case, according to your account of it, that he died by the accident he met with, and in consequence of that only.

Lady Hesketh and my Fire-side unite with me in wishing for you and yours every thing that you wish for yourselves. Believe me, my dear friend, most truly yours

Wm Cowper

I do not mean to be always in your debt, though in a very emphatical sense I *must* always be so, but next Midsummer will enable me to restore to your purse all that I have taken out of it.

JOHN NEWTON   Wednesday, 16 November 1791

Princeton

Weston Novr. 16. 1791

My dear friend —

I am weary of making you wait for an answer, and therefore resolve to send you one though without the lines you ask'd for. Such as they are, they have been long ready, and could I have found a conveyance for them, should have been with you weeks ago. Mr. Bean's last journey to town might have afforded me an opportunity to send them, but he gave me not sufficient notice. They must therefore be still delay'd till either he shall go to London again, or somebody else shall offer. I thank you for yours which are as much better than mine as gold is better than feathers.

It seem'd necessary that I should account for my apparent tardiness to comply with the obliging request of a Lady, and of a Lady who employed you as her Intermedium. None was

afterwards Margravine of Anspach and Bayreuth and Princess Berkeley of the Holy Roman Empire (1750–1828) provided the following account concerning her husband's demise: 'Upon his Lordship's death . . . a physician, who differed in opinion from the rest concerning the cause of his complaint, requested permission of his son to have the head examined, as he constantly affirmed that the cause existed there. From a blow which he had received on the head in hunting, from a large branch of a tree, eight years before, a deposit of blood was found upon the brain.' *The Beautiful Lady Craven*, ed. A. M. Broadley and Lewis Melville (2 vols., 1913), II. 37.

wanted, as you well assured her, but had there been occasion for one, she could not possibly have found a better.[1]

I was much pleased with your account of your visit to Cowslip Green,[2] both for the sake of what you saw there, and because I am sure you must have been as happy in such company as any situation in this world can make you. Miss More has been always employ'd, since I first heard of her doings, as becomes a Christian. So she was while endeavouring to reform the unreformable Great, and so she is while framing means and opportunities to instruct the more teachable Little.[3] Horace's *virginibus puerisque* may be her Motto, but in a sense much nobler than he has annext to it.[4] I cannot however be entirely reconciled to the though of her being henceforth silent, though even for the sake of her present labours. A pen useful as hers, ought not perhaps to be laid aside. Neither perhaps will she altogether renounce it, but when she has establish'd her schools and habituated them to the discipline she intends, will find it desireable to resume it. — I rejoice that she has a sister like herself, capable of bidding defiance to fatigue and hardship, to dirty roads and wet raiment in so excellent a cause.

I beg that when you write next to either of those ladies, you will present my best Compliments to Miss Martha and tell her that I can never feel myself flatter'd more than I was by her application. God knows how unworthy I judge myself at the same time to be admitted into a collection of which you are a member. Were there not a Crown'd Head or two to keep me in countenance, I should even blush to think of it.

[1] Martha More, familiarly known as Miss Patty (1759?–1819), was the youngest of the five More sisters, and the most constant companion of Hannah, especially in their later years. Patty's request for a poem was passed on to C through Newton, who was well acquainted with her distinguished sister. The poem could not accompany this letter to London because it had to be delivered unfolded, so that Miss Patty could bind it into her book of autographs. When he finally saw C's lines, Newton was not pleased, and C altered the stanza (as his letter to Newton of 20 Jan. 1792, where the revised stanza is quoted, makes clear).

[2] Early in the summer of 1784 Hannah More settled at Wrington Vale in Somerset. 'Here, after submitting plans and drawings to all her friends in turn, she built a cottage which acquired the name of Cowslip Green . . . ': M. G. Jones, *Hannah More* (Cambridge, 1952), p. 125.

[3] In 1791 Hannah More opened schools in Congresbury, Yatton, and Axbridge; she published *Village Politics* in 1792.

[4] *Odes*, III. i. 4. 'To youths and maidens'.

I would that I could see some of the mountains which you have seen, especially because Dr. Johnson has pronounced that no man is qualified to be a poet who has never seen a mountain.[5] But mountains I shall never see, unless perhaps in a dream, or unless there are such in heaven. Nor those, unless I receive twice as much Mercy as ever yet was shown to any man.

I am now deep in Milton, translating his Latin poems for a pompous edition, of which you have undoubtedly heard. This amuses me for the present and will for a year or two. So long I presume I shall be occupied in the several functions that belong to my present engagement.

Mrs. Unwin and I are about as well as usual, always mindful of you, and always affectionately so. Our united love attends yourself and Miss Catlett. Believe me most truly yours

Wm Cowper.

HENRY COWPER   Friday, 18 November 1791

Princeton

Weston-Underwood
Novr. 18. 1791

My dear Henry —

The Mr. Hardy[1] whose letter you sent me, is an unhappy man as the contents of it prove him to be, deranged in his intellects, an enthusiast of the religious kind, and wild with a project of reforming the age, in which he wants me to assist him both with my pen and my purse. His epistle in·short was such as it would have been imprudent in me to answer at any rate, but I am happy that it arrived while Lady Hesketh

---

[5] Probably a reference to this passage: 'Regions mountainous and wild, thinly inhabited, and little cultivated, make a great part of the earth, and he that has never seen them, must live unacquainted with much of the face of nature, and with one of the great scenes of human existence.' *A Journey to the Western Islands of Scotland*, ed. Mary Lascelles (New Haven, 1971), p. 40.

[1] Probably Thomas Hardy (1752–1832), the radical politician, who began about this time to correspond with libertarian societies in England, advocating widespread social and political reform. He founded the London Corresponding Society in 1792. With Horne Tooke and others, he was acquitted of high treason in 1794.

was here, who being acquainted with Captain Hardy his brother,[2] has extricated me from the difficulty by making him acquainted with the affair, and recommending it to him to have recourse to medical assistance as the only means by which the poor man can be benefitted.

You will make us all very happy if you will yourself remove the only objection you have to commenting on my work, which you say is the want of a long conversation with me first. If I am so fast rooted that I cannot be moved, perhaps you are not so, and be you fast rooted as you may, you will not be the first of the kind that has danced after a poet. I will not yield to you in respect of affection and esteem, both which I feel for you most truly, and should be most happy to convince you of it in person.

Perhaps you have Newton's Milton; if so you will oblige me if you will read over a Spectator or two of Addison's which he prefixes to the work.[3] You will there find ennumerated many of those deviations from the common and establish'd rules of Syntax by which in his opinion Milton has ennobled his stile and given it peculiar dignity. Several he mentions, and might have mention'd many more, such as the Infinitive Mood without the Sign of it, the neutral adjective for the adverb &c — Of the latter, the following are instances.[4]

[2] Further unidentified.

[3] In his preface to his 1749 (the 1st) edition of *Paradise Lost* (sig. a2^v–a3), Thomas Newton states: 'It was recommended to me indeed to print entire Mr. Addison's Spectators upon the Paradise Lost, as ingenious essays which had contributed greatly to the reputation of the poem, and having been added to several editions they could not well be omitted in this edition: and accordingly those papers, which treat of the poem in general, are prefixed in the nature of a preliminary discourse; and those, which are written upon each book separately, are inserted under each book, and interwoven in their proper places.' C owned copies of the seventh (1770) and ninth (1790) editions of Newton's volume (*Keynes*, 61); Mr Robert H. Taylor now owns the latter volume. Addison wrote eighteen papers on *Paradise Lost*; they appeared in the Saturday issues of *The Spectator* (Nos. 267, 273, 279, 285, 291, 297, 303, 309, 315, 321, 327, 333, 339, 345, 351, 357, 363, 369) between 5 Jan. and 3 May 1712.

[4] C refers to the fourth *Spectator* paper on *Paradise Lost* (No. 285, 26 Jan. 1712) which reads in part: 'It is not therefore sufficient, that the Language of an Epic Poem be Perspicuous, unless it be also Sublime. To this end it ought to deviate from the common Forms and ordinary Phrases of Speech. The Judgment of a Poet very much discovers it self in shunning the common Roads of Expression, without falling into such ways of Speech as may seem stiff and unnatural; he must not swell into a false Sublime, by endeavouring to avoid the other Extream.' *The Spectator*, ed. Donald F. Bond (5 vols., Oxford, 1965), iii. 11.

——————— and end

Them in his anger, whom his anger saves

To punish *endless*? B.2.L.157.

——————ly

where I shall reign

At thy right hand *voluptuous*. B.2.L.869.

——————ly

But all these points may be better agitated if we can meet, which for every reason would give me the greatest pleasure. But whether we can meet or not, favour me with your remarks and make them freely. I know you will have the candour, if in any case I differ from you, not to place that difference to the account of obstinacy.

Farewell, my dear Henry, Lady H. who seems to look forward to her threaten'd sentence without much trepidation, unites with mine her affectionate and best remembrances to Mrs. Cowper.

Believe me sincerely Yours
Wm Cowper

Your letter being dated from Ham, I supposed you still there, which has occasion'd all these blottings. Lady Hesketh I now understand has learn'd from the General that you have left it.

WALTER CHURCHEY   Wednesday, 23 November 1791

McMaster University

Weston-Underwood
Novr. 23. 1791

Dear Sir —

Your several dispatches have been forwarded to their respective places of destination. I am particularly obliged to you for the last, which I sent off according to your direction on the very day on which I received it. I read it attentively and was much pleased with it; so much, that I made in it only one alteration, and that a very slight one.

If you ever see the Gentleman's Magazine, you will find me reviewed in the two last. The author of the Review treats me with both Compliments and censure. For the former I give him thanks, but do not think him always just in the latter. I abide however by the resolution I told you I had taken, never to set pen to paper in answer to any who may criticize me, say they what they will. In fact, I have no time for controversy even though my own work be in question, being already engaged in a new one which demands, and will for two years to come, my whole attention. The work I mean, is a new Edition of Milton's poetry, on the plan of Boydell's Shakespeare.

I did not add your name to your Critique though you left me at liberty to do so, taking it for granted that had you not rather preferred secrecy, you would have done it yourself.

Perhaps when I confessed myself guilty of here and there an inharmonious line, as I do in my preface, I was more candid than prudent. The number of such is I am persuaded so very small, that had I held my peace, they would never have been objected to me. But I have shot my bolt, and shall be taught by the consequences, on any such future occasion to keep my own counsel. Where I have one line of that sort, Milton has twenty; yet the Iliad and Odyssey are four times as long as the Paradise Lost. I cannot therefore be very culpable in this particular, especially since I have given a reason for the practise which ought either to be answer'd or allowed a good one.

Believe me to be very sensible, as I truly am, of all your friendly attentions to my interest, and assure yourself that I am with great respect and esteem, Dear Sir,

Yours affectionately
Wm Cowper.

I admired your Elegy on the death of Mr. Wesley.[1]

---

[1] 'Lines on the Rev. John Wesley, M.A.' was issued on a small memorial silk card. 'Let others boast of titles, fame, or wealth, / Terrestrial honors, or the age of health — / He, with an uniform consistent Plan, / For seventy years adorned the name of Man: / Toiled in his Masters Vine-yard to the last, / Feared not the future, nor deplored the past; / But like the loved Disciple, worn with years, / He praised his God and died dissolved in tears.'

SAMUEL ROSE   Thursday, 1 December 1791

Address: Samuel Rose Esqr. / Chancery Lane / London
Postmarks: DE/2/91/C *and* OULNEY
Princeton

Decr. 1. 1791

My dear Friend,

On application made this Morning to your last letter but one, with much amazement I perceive that, though you have not reminded me of the omission in your last, it still remains unanswer'd. At least if I have answer'd it, my memory has entirely let slip the matter, which, bad as it is, I think is hardly quite so treacherous. It is a wonder that I should forget so far as to doubt about it, because in that letter you mention your encrease of business, which gave me the sincerest pleasure, and it was my purpose to have told you so immediately, because to express the joy we feel in the success of a friend, is itself a pleasure.

I thank you much for the intelligence sent me by William Throckmorton concerning the sale of my volumes. From Johnson I hear nothing, and should therefore have been left to vain conjectures, and most likely to no very agreeable ones, but for your information. Months ago, I desired him to send me all that either He or Fuseli could collect or think of that might assist me in the Milton way, but he has sent me nothing. I have not indeed as yet perceived the want of such aids, having been hitherto employed merely in translation, but I am now in the middle of the Manso[1] which is the last Latin poem but two, and shall consequently soon see the end of my traductory labours. You will oblige me therefore, if, when you find an opportunity, you will be so good as to remind him that here is an Editor of his at Weston, who has long expected a parcel from him.

Lady Hesketh has been and is still indisposed. Her disorder was at first the rheumatism. She applied a blister, which having only half its effect, has occasion'd her much trouble. She has since applied another, from which we hope better success, but there has not yet been time to ascertain it.

---

[1] 'To Giovanni Battista Manso' appeared in *Latin and Italian Poems*.

If the Christmas Holidays should prove Holidays to you,
we shall hope for the pleasure of seeing you. In the mean
time we often think of you and always with affection. Our
united Compliments attend yourself and Mrs. Rose. Believe
me, my dear Friend

Sincerely yours   Wm Cowper.

I am quite of your mind respecting the propriety of 8vo.[2]

WALTER BAGOT   Monday, 5 December 1791

Address: The Revd. Walter Bagot
Morgan Library

Weston-Underwood
Decr. 5. 1791

My dear friend —
     Your last brought me two cordials; for what can better
deserve that name than the cordial approbation of two
such Readers, as your Brother the Bishop, and your good
friend and neighbour the Clergyman?[1] The former I have
ever esteem'd and honour'd with the justest cause, and am as
ready to honour and esteem the latter as you can wish me
to be, and as his virtues and talents deserve. Do I hate a
Parson? Heaven forbid! I love you all when you are good
for any thing, and as to the rest, I would mend them if I
could, and that is the worst of my intentions toward them.
     I heard above a month since that this first edition of my
work was at that time nearly sold. It will not therefore, I
presume, be long before I must go to Press again. This I
mention merely from an earnest desire to avail myself of all
other strictures that either your good neighbour, Lord Bagot,
the Bishop, or yourself πάντων ἐκπαγλότατ᾽ ἀνδρῶν,[2] may
happen to have made, and will be so good as to favour me
with. Those of the good Evander[3] contained in your last

---

[2] Rose may have suggested that the edition of Milton appear in octavo rather
than quarto, the size employed for the translations of Homer.

---

[1] Unidentified.
[2] This expression occurs three times in the Iliad: i. 146, xviii. 170, and xx.
389. 'The most dreaded of all men.'
[3] Bagot may have cited a passage from the Aeneid, where Evander welcomes

593

have served me well, and I have already in the three different places referr'd to, accommodated the text to them. And this I have done in one instance even a little against the biass of my own opinion.

$$εγω \ δε \ κεν \ αυτος \ ἐλωμαι$$
$$Ελθων \ συν \ πλεονεσσι - \ ^4$$

The sense I had given of these words is the sense in which an old Scholiast has understood them, as appears in Clarke's note in loco. Clarke indeed prefers the other, but it does not appear plain to me that he does it with good reason against the judgment of a very antient commentator and a Greecian. And I am the rather inclined to this persuasion because Achilles himself seems to have apprehended that Agamemnon would not content himself with Briseis only, when he says

But I have *other* precious things on board,
Of *these* take *none* away without my leave. &c[5]

It is certain that the words are ambiguous, and that the sense of them depends altogether on the punctuation. But I am always under the correction of so able a Critic as your neighbour, and have alter'd, as I say, my version accordingly.

As to Milton, the die is cast. I am engaged, have bargain'd with Johnson and cannot recede. I should otherwise have been glad to do as you advise, to make the translation of his Latin and Italian, part of another volume; for, with such an addition, I have nearly as much verse in my budget as would be required for the purpose. This squabble, in the mean time, between Fuseli and Boydell does not interest me at all,[6] let it terminate as it may, I have only to perform my Jobb, and leave the event to be decided by the combatants.

Aeneas to Italy, conducts him to the site of the future Rome, and sends his son back with Aeneas to fight the Latins.

[4] *Iliad*, i. 324–5: 'I will myself go with a larger company and take her . . . ' See Samuel Clarke, *Homeri Ilias Graece et Latine* (2 vols., 1729–32), i. 23, where the scholiastic version is cited as an alternative version.

[5] *Iliad*, i. 300–1; lines 378–9 of C's translation.

[6] See n.3, C to Bagot, 6 Sept. 1791.

Suave mari magno turbantibus æquora ventis
E terrâ ingentem alterius spectare laborem.[7]

> Adieu, my dear friend, I am
> most sincerely Yours
> Wm Cowper

Mrs. Unwin sends her best Compliments.

Why should you suppose that I did not admire the poem you show'd me?[8] I did admire it and told you so, but you carried it off in your pocket, and, so doing, left me to forget it and without the means of enquiry.

I am thus nimble in answering merely with a view to insure to myself the receipt of other remarks in time for a new impression.

MRS BODHAM   Wednesday, 7 December 1791

Address: Mrs. Bodham / South-Green / Mattishall / Norfolk
Postmarks: DE/8/91/E *and* OULNEY
Princeton

> Weston-Underwood
> Decr. 7. 1791

Whether you will be pleased or not, my dearest Rose, that I answer you so speedily, I cannot tell, for my letter will make you my debtor again, and your last will seem to have profited you nothing. But I have a pleasure in scribbling to you, and therefore putting your interest out of the question, shall consider only my own.

It gives me great pleasure that my three wandering Cousins have at last got possession of their new abode, and that they seem to be happy in it. A letter of Johnny's which Lady Hesketh, now with us, received within this day or two, gives us this information. He was well himself at least when he wrote it, if cheerfulness and good spirits are a proof of health, and I conclude that Catharine and her Aunt are well also, since he says nothing to the contrary.

---

[7] *De Rerum Natura*, ii. 1–2: 'Pleasant it is, when over a great sea the winds trouble the waters, to gaze from shore upon another's great tribulation.' Trans. W. H. D. Rouse (1953), p. 85. C has substituted 'ingentem' for 'magnum' found in most editions of Lucretius. [8] See C to Bagot, 25 Oct. 1791.

Though on my own account I could not but regret that these my Cousins found it impossible to settle here, when I consider what an unsuitable mansion they must have had, I am comforted. Weston too, never very Gay, is likely to be a Deserted Village soon. Not deserted indeed by us, but by a family to which it was much more indebted than to ours, for all the appearance of liveliness that it had to boast. I mean the family of the Throckmortons. The Grandfather, old Sir Robert, is dying as we hear, or dead perhaps by this time, Which will occasion the removal of our amiable friends and neighbours to the family seat at Bucklands, in Berkshire. The change will be an unpleasant one to me, for other neighbours we have none, or none with whom we can have much intercourse, and they were the kindest and most agreeable that could be. Let my Cousins therefore rejoice in the sprightlier Dereham, for Weston is likely to be henceforth, at least till the second brother shall marry, almost a solitude.[1]

I beg you to give my best love to Johnny, and to tell him that Kitch's parcel, containing coat, waistcoat &c for him, and a letter for me, arrived safe in the evening of yesterday. Kitch, who will be hereafter, at least on a Sunday, the best dress'd man in Olney and quite a Beau, with features expressive of inexpressible gratitude, entreated me to give his duty and kind love and service in return to Mr. Johnson, and I have hereby acquitted myself of the commission. Tell him too if you please that he shall hear from me soon, and that in the mean time I love him heartily, as I do also his dear Sister and my good Cousin Balls.

Lady Hesketh has been much indisposed for some [   ][2] to all friends in Norfolk.

I have yet another commision for you, my sweet Rose, which is to desire you to express to Mr. Heath[3] when you see him my thanks and obligations for some game which I understand by Johnny's letter is on the wing toward us.

---

[1] Sir Robert died 8 Dec. 1791. George Throckmorton and Catharine Stapleton were married on 29 June 1792.
[2] The bottom portion of this last page of the letter has been cut away, removing three lines of the holograph at this juncture and at the closing part of the letter.
[3] See n.1, C to John Johnson, 26 Nov. 1790.

10 December 1791

JAMES HURDIS   Saturday, 10 December 1791

Hayley, ii. 18–19

Weston, Dec. 10, 1791.

My dear sir,

I am obliged to you for wishing that I were employed in some original work rather than in translation. To tell you the truth, I am of your mind; and unless I could find another Homer, I shall promise (I believe) and vow, when I have done with Milton, never to translate again. But my veneration for our great countryman is equal to what I feel for the Grecian; and consequently I am happy, and feel myself honourably employed whatever I do for Milton. I am now translating his *Epitaphium Damonis*, a Pastoral in my judgment equal to any of Virgil's Bucolics, but of which Dr. Johnson (so it pleased him) speaks, as I remember, contemptuously. But he who never saw any beauty in a rural scene was not likely to have much taste for a Pastoral.[1] *In pace quiescat!*[2]

I was charmed with your friendly offer to be my advocate with the public; should I want one, I know not where I could find a better. The Reviewer in the Gentleman's Magazine grows more and more civil.[3] Should he continue to sweeten at this rate, as he proceeds, I know not what will become of all the little modesty I have left. I have availed myself of some of his strictures, for I wish to learn from every body.

W.C.

---

[1] Johnson devoted a single paragraph in his *Life of Milton* to this poem: 'At his return [from Italy] he heard of the death of his friend Charles Diodati; a man whom it is reasonable to suppose of great merit, since he was thought by Milton worthy of a poem, intituled, *Epitaphium Damonis*, written with the common but childish imitation of pastoral life): *Lives*, ii. 24–5.

[2] 'May he rest in peace.'

[3] See n.4, C to Rose, 30 Oct. 1791. The review reads in part: 'We trust that [Cowper] will not be offended if, in our progress through the works before us, we incidentally point out to animadversion what may appear to us deserving of revision, and capable of improvement . . . Mr. Cowper's work is ushered in by a well-written and very sensible preface, in which he makes the reader acquainted with his design, which is, to exhibit a translation of Homer in blank verse, as most suitable to his purpose . . . The idea is excellent, and calculated to exhibit, what very seldom has appeared, a translation perfect in its kind.' (845)

JOHN BUCHANAN   *c.*Wednesday, 21 December 1791[1]

Princeton

Dear Sir —

I scribble in great haste; am glad you have been heartily
frighten'd by that which so cruelly frighten'd me. Though I
have a house well fill'd with live creatures, I could not go up
stairs after candle light for some nights while we were reading
this Romance,[2] without feeling a cold Rigor in my back and
sinciput.[3] I would not have written it for the world.

We shall be happy to see you whenever it shall suit you to
call — Lady Hesketh has been worse since you were here but
is now better. At present she keeps her chamber.

> All send Compliments I am much
> Yours   Wm Cowper.

Wedy.
Mrs. U. sends many thanks for the sermons.[4]

SAMUEL ROSE   Wednesday, 21 December 1791

Address: Samuel Rose Esqr. / Chancery Lane / London
Postmarks: DE/22/91/[illegible] *and* OULNEY
Princeton

Weston. Decr. 21. 1791

My dear Friend —

It grieves me, after having indulged a little hope that I
might perhaps have the pleasure to see you in the holidays, to
be obliged to disappoint myself. The occasion too is such as
will insure to me your sympathy.

On Saturday last, while I was at my desk near the window,
and Mrs. Unwin at the fire-side opposite to it, I heard her
suddenly exclaim — Oh Mr. Cowper, don't let me fall — I
turn'd and saw her actually falling together with her chair,
and started to her side just in time to prevent her. She was
seized with a violent giddiness which lasted, though with
some abatement, the whole day, and was attended too with

---

[1] The reference to Lady Hesketh in this letter suggests that it was written about
the same time as the letter which follows.
[2] Unidentified.
[3] 'The front part of the head or skull' (*OED*).   [4] Unidentified.

some other most alarming symptoms. At present however she is relieved from the vertigo, and seems in all respects better, except that she is so enfeebled as to be unable to quit her bed for more than an hour in a day.

She has been my faithful and affectionate nurse for many years, and consequently has a claim on all my attentions. She has them, and will have them as long as she wants them, which will probably be, at the best, for a considerable time to come.

I feel the shock as you may suppose in every nerve. God grant that there may be no repetition of it. Another such stroke upon her would, I think, overset me completely. But at present I hold up bravely.

Lady Hesketh is also far from well. She has ventur'd these two last days to dine in the study, else she has kept her chamber above this fortnight. She has suffer'd however by this first sally and has taken cold as I fear'd she would.

Thus are we a house of Invalids, and must wait for the pleasure of receiving you here 'till it shall please God to restore us to health again.

With my best Compliments to Mrs. Rose, and with those of the two Ladies, I remain, my dear friend

most Sincerely yours
Wm Cowper.

SAMUEL TEEDON   Wednesday, 21 December 1791

Address: Mr. Teedon / Olney
Princeton

Dear Sir —

I sent you a verbal message this morning, being at breakfast when the messenger set off. I have now just leisure to say, that except a night almost sleepless, Mrs. Unwin seems considerably amended in her health, but is still very feeble. Her giddiness and sickness seem removed, and her pains, of which she had many, are all much abated.

You will give thanks to God for us, and pray for farther mercies. — I have been much agitated in my spirits, but am as well on the whole as I could expect to be.

I was writing this when yours arrived. Should have written yesterday but had no opportunity.

I thank you, am much obliged to you for all your truly Christian services, and remain

Decr. 21. 1791   Yours   Wm. Cowper.

MISSING LETTERS

Date   *Recipient*

*c.*9 January 1787   General Cowper

In his letter to Lady Hesketh of 8–9 January 1787, C says that he has 'a letter to write to the General . . . '

*c.*12 October 1787   General Cowper

C to Joseph Johnson, 18 October 1787: 'I wrote last week to General Cowper, but have not yet received his answer.'

*c.*6 November 1787   Luke Heslop

C to Hill, 16 November 1787: 'About ten days since I wrote to Archdeacon Heslop, referring him to you.'

*c.*17 November 1787   General Cowper

C to Lady Hesketh, 17 November 1787: 'I write both to the General and to Mr. Hill by this post . . .'

pre 12 March 1788   General Cowper

C to Lady Hesketh, 12 March 1788: 'A few posts since I had a letter from our good friend and Coz the General, in which he kindly offers a recruit my Cellar. An offer accepted joyfully by me . . .'

post 21 March 1788   General Cowper

In his letter to Lady Hesketh of 21 March 1788, C is concerned with his 'poetical effusions' on the 'Slave-trade'. At the beginning of his letter to General Cowper of 27 March 1788, C mentions that a 'Letter is not pleasant which excites curiosity but does not gratify it. Such a letter was my last, the defects of which I therefore take the first opportunity to supply.' C then goes on to transcribe the 'best' of his anti-slavery poems, 'The Morning Dream'. It would seem that C must have written to the General about these poems at about the time he wrote to Lady Hesketh promising to transcribe one of the completed poems and that his 27 March 1788 letter is a fulfilment of a promise made in a missing letter.

*c.*1 May 1788   Mrs Throckmorton

C to Lady Hesketh, 1 May 1788: 'I have had a letter from [Mrs

Date   Recipient

Throckmorton], the brevity of which was the only cause of complaint with which it furnish'd me, though even of That I made no complaint in my answer to it . . . '

c. 15 May 1788   Henry Cowper

C to Lady Hesketh, 19 May 1788: 'I was not aware of my obligations to Henry, neither did at all suspect that He had given his Lordship a Jog on the occasion. Of course when I answer'd his Letter I made him no acknowledgments on that behalf.'

27 May 1788   General Cowper

C to Lady Hesketh, 27 May 1788: ' . . . I write to him [the General] by this Post on purpose to inform him . . . '

10 July 1788   General Cowper

C to Lady Hesketh, 11 July 1788: 'What is become of the General? It is so long since I heard from him that I wonder and am concerned. I wrote to him yesterday.'

c. 26 August 1788   Edward Thurlow

Most of C's letter to Lady Hesketh of this date consists of a transcription of this missing letter.

17 November 1788   John Newton

C. E. Lamb list. This is a list made by C. E. Lamb which was attached to the Ring copies now at Princeton. In his list Lamb enumerated some C to Newton letters whose existence is now known only through his compilation.

30 November 1788   Mrs Hill

C to Samuel Rose, 30 November 1788: 'Having had occasion to write this day to Mrs. Hill I have likewise given myself the pleasure of introducing you to Her.'

pre 25 February 1789 General Cowper

C to Lady Hesketh, 25 February 1789: 'I have written twice to the General and have had no answer.'

c. 21 March 1789   Lady Hesketh

The letter to which C refers at the beginning of his letter to Lady Hesketh of 6 April 1789 is not extant: 'You received I suppose

602

Date	*Recipient*

about a fortnight since, a Letter from me, containing diverse matters of which you have hitherto said nothing. In that Letter I ask'd you what we should do with our verses on the King's recovery . . . '

22 October 1789   John Newton
C. E. Lamb list.

pre 1 February 1790 Clotworthy Rowley
C to Clotworthy Rowley, 1 February 1790: 'I shot a few lines after you to Holyhead according to your desire . . . '

11 April 1790   John Newton
C. E. Lamb list.

7 May 1790   Mr Pearson
C to Mrs Throckmorton, 10 May 1790: 'But I wrote him [Pearson] a letter on Friday . . . informing him that unless he tied up his great mastiff in the day time, I would send him a worse thing, commonly call'd and known by the name of an Attorney.'

c. 1 August 1790   Luke Heslop
C to Joseph Hill, [1 August] 1790: 'I shall at this moment send [Heslop] the joyful news . . . '

c. 14 August 1790   Mrs King
See n.5, C to Mrs King, 14 August 1790.

25 November 1790   John Rivington
C to John Johnson, 26 November 1790: 'Our Press goes on much at the old rate and I wrote yesterday to Rivington the Printer to scold him.'

c. 12 March 1791   Joseph Johnson
C to Lady Hesketh, 12 March 1791: 'Surely we shall get Horace Walpole's name at last, for I wrote, myself, to Johnson about it but a few days ago . . .'

pre 22 April 1791 'Our Cousin of Totteridge'
C to Lady Hesketh, *pre* 22 April 1791: 'Our Cousin of Totteridge's letter is a most kind one, and I send her a most kind answer.'

603

pre 27 May 1791   George Jermyn

C to Lady Hesketh, 27 May 1791: 'A letter the other day from a Mr. Geo. Jermyn of Ipswich . . . found its way to me . . . I gave him a civil answer and referred him to my Bookseller.'

6 July 1791   Joseph Johnson

In his letter to Samuel Rose of 7 July 1791, C refers to a letter to Joseph Johnson written 'yesterday' concerning financial arrangements for the Homer. A summary of this letter is in the Panshanger Collection. See n.2, C to Joseph Johnson, 3 July 1791.

12 August 1791   Joseph Johnson

C to Walter Churchey, 12 August 1791: 'I have this moment received your letter and have this moment written to my Bookseller, telling him all that you have said and giving him all necessary directions.'

1791   John Buchanan

There are probably two missing notes to Buchanan composed between 11 May 1791 and *c.*21 December 1791. Charles Ryskamp owns a list of four notes and one letter which would seem to indicate this. This compilation, in an unknown hand and dated 7 February 1801, includes Note 2 composed on a 'Monday' and Note 3 composed on a 'Tuesd. Mor.'.

LIST OF LETTERS

List of Letters

List of Letters

List of Letters

INDEX

British nobility are listed under titles with cross-references to family names.
Women are listed under their married names with cross-references to maiden names.
Incidental references in the text to important friends and acquaintances are not usually cited.

Index

Barnard, Lewyns Boldero, xxxi
Bastile, 369
Bath, 156, 225, 355, 364, 393, 460
and n.
Battison, Mrs, 220 and n., 236-7
Bean, James, 35n., 59-60, 89, 115-16,
125, 128, 142, 150, 172, 185,
209-10, 232, 267, 293, 309-10
and n., 468, 484, 513, 546, 586
Bean, Mrs James, 142, 172
Beattie, James, 27, 58 and n., 68, 504
Beau, C's dog, 32 and n., 61, 67, 73-4,
77, 119, 160, 189, 192, 198-
202, 211-14, 227, 228n., 244-5,
313, 316, 323, 336-7, 369, 373,
378, 416
Bedford, Francis Russell, 5th Duke of,
194 and n.
Benamor, Dr, 404 and n.
Bentley, Elizabeth, *Genuine Poetical
Compositions* ... 484n., 484-6,
486n., 501, 564-5
Bentley, Richard, *Remarks Upon a Late
Discourse of Free-thinking* ... ,
341 and n.
Berkhamsted, 42-3, 237
Berridge, John, 546 and n.
Bess, C's hare, 221n.
Biddlecombe, Mr, 5
Birch, Selina, 338 and n.
Birmingham, 198; riots there in 1791,
547n., 547-8, 550, 568
Blair, Hugh, 27, 58, 68
Blake, William, xxx
Blithfield, 225, 227
Bodham, Anne (known to C as 'Rose'),
née Donne, biographical sketch,
xix; xxvi-xxvii, 347-8, 352,
359, 368, 378, 386, 393, 395,
398, 401, 433, 445, 505-6, 530,
543
Bodham, Susanna, 395 and n., 498, 506
Bodham, Thomas, xix, 350-1, 393,
395, 398
Bond, John, *Poemata* (edition of
Horace), 345 and n.
books, C's collection of, 126 and n.,
148, 157-8, 317, 483 and n.
Boswell, James, *Journal of a Tour to
the Hebrides,* 289n., 289-90,
298-9
Bouillé, François Claude Amour,
Marquis de, *Protestation de la*

noblesse de France ... , 544
and n.
Bourne, Vincent, 233-4; *Miscellaneous
Poems,* 233-4
Bowyer, William, the younger, xxx
Boydell, John, and his Shakespeare
Gallery, 290 and n., 570 and n.,
572, 591, 594
Brevan, Mary. *See* Mary Churchey
Brighton, 548
Bromley, Sir George, compiler, *A
Collection of Original Royal
Letters* ... , 23-4 and n.
Bromley Chester, Elizabeth Lucy,
née Chester, 96-7 and n., 301
Browne, Isaac Hawkins, *Poems Upon
Various Subjects, Latin and
English,* 284 and n.
Buchanan, John, biographical sketch,
xix-xx; 304, 482, 519, 531
Buckenham, 28 and n., 212, 214, 235,
243, 245, 528
Buckinghamshire, 157, 163, 424, 565
Bucklands, 95, 292, 355, 376, 378,
596
Bull, Francis, xx
Bull, Hannah, *née* Palmer, xx, 548
Bull, John, xx
Bull, Judith, xx
Bull, Thomas, of Weston Underwood,
89 and n., 96, 150
Bull, Thomas Palmer, xxi
Bull, William, biographical sketch, xx;
8, 50, 109, 117, 273, 291, 344
Bull, (at Olney), 465
Bully, a bullfinch, 31 and n., 61, 225
and n., 260
Bunbury, Henry William, 'The Propa-
gation of a Lie', 87n., 87-8
Burke, Edmund, 112n., 112-13, 264;
*Reflections on the Revolution
in France* ... , 458n., 458-9
Burn, Andrew, *The Christian Officer's
Panoply* ... , 526n., 526-7
Burnet, Thomas, *The Theory of the
Earth,* 56 and n.
Burns, Robert, xxviii, 15n., 15-16,
18 and n., 139, 145, 168
Butler, Samuel, *Hudibras,* 562
Butlin, Mr, shoemaker at Olney, 565
Buxton, 228 and n.
Bye, Deodatus, 434n., 439, 442, 471,
497, 504, 518, 522

616

617

Index

Legge, William. *See* Dartmouth, William Legge, 1st Earl of
Legge, William. *See* Dartmouth, William Legge, 2nd Earl of
Leinster, William Robert Fitzgerald, 2nd Duke of, 272 and n.
Le Sage, Alain René, *Gil Blas*, 567-8 and n.
Letts, Jonathan, 131n., 131-2
Leveson-Gower, Granville. *See* Stafford, Granville Leveson-Gower, 1st Marquis of
Livius, George, xxvii
Livius, Maria Dorothy. *See* Maria Dorothy Johnson
Lockhart, John Gibson, xxviii
Lodi, 334 and n.
London, 140, 163, 247, 272, 275-6, 278, 289, 290, 292, 296, 305, 307 and n., 319, 346, 361, 412-13, 496, 513, 525, 528, 578, 586
  I. *Particular buildings, institutions, and places*:
  Amen Corner, 382 and n.
  Bedlam, 164
  Blackfriars' Bridge, 98
  Brooks's Club, 275 and n.
  Coleman's Buildings, 209 and n., 233-4
  Dick's Coffee House, 66 and n.
  Free Masons' Hall, 4 and n.
  Inner Temple, 339, 525
  King's Bench, 191 and n.
  Lock Hospital, xxviii
  Pantheon, 20 and n.
  Pump Court, Middle Temple, 298 and n.
  St. Paul's Cathedral, 272 and n.
  The Temples, Inner and Middle, 121, 305, 385
  Westminster School, 81, 218, 238, 253, 329, 580
  Windmill, in St. John Street, 146, 289, 447
  II. *Particular streets and squares*:
  Edgware, 575
  Great Queen Street, 226, 245, 265
  New Burlington Street, 463
  New Norfolk Street, Grosvenor Square, 364
  Old Palace Yard, 126 and n.

Rathbone Place, 382 and n.
St. Giles, 289
St. James's Place, 278
St. John Street, 30
Longinus, *On the Sublime*, 364 and n.
Louis XVI, King of France, 543 and n.
Lucretius, *De Rerum Natura*, 595n.

Macaulay, Zachary, xxi
Mackenzie, Henry, biographical sketch, xxviii; *The Lounger*, xxviii, 19, 26 and nn., 57, 61, 66 and n., 68; *The Mirror*, xxviii, 26 and nn., 66 and n., 68; 29, 43 and n., 57-8, 71, 73, 456n., 456-7
Mackenzie, Joshua, xxviii
Maclaine, Archibald, 197 and n.
Madan, Jane, *née* Hale, Martin's wife, xxix, 294, 378n., 536 and n.
Madan, Maria Frances Cecilia. *See* Maria Frances Cecilia Cowper
Madan, Martin, biographical sketch, xxviii-xxix; *Thelyphthora*, xxii, xxix, 208, 377-8; *Letters to Joseph Priestley . . .*, 23 and n.; *A New and Literal Translation of Juvenal and Persius . . .*, 293 and n.; xxii, 208, 265, 377-8 and n.
Madan, Penelope. *See* Penelope Maitland
Madan, Sarah (Sally), Martin's daughter, 294, 536 and n.
Madan, Bishop Spencer, Martin's brother, 344n., 370-1, 375 and n., 398, 515
Madan, Spencer, son of above, 375 and n.
Maecenas, 330, 425 and n.
Maitland, Penelope, *née* Madan, 154 and n.
Mann, Theodore Augustus, called the Abbé Mann, 39n., 39-40
Manners, Charles. *See* Rutland, Charles Manners, 4th Duke of
Margate, 292
Marie Antoinette, Queen of France, 543 and n.
Marischal College, 504 and n.
Markham, William, 218 and n., 271, 277n., 277-8
Marquis, C's dog, 31-2
Marriot, Iscah, *née* Haselden, 160, 162, 494, 511

624

Index

Marshall, William, *Planting and Ornamental Gardening*, 419 and n.

Martin, Mr, publican at Woburn, 465-6

Martyn, Thomas, 205 and n., 269-70 and n., 280, 332, 336, 388 and n., 422-3, 435-6, 474

Mathews, James, 526n., 526-7

Mathews, Sarah. *See* Sarah Hill

Mattishall, 445, 464, 541

Menzie, Mr, 272-3

Merrill, John and Joseph, 434 and n., 473, 488

Merry, Robert, 78 and n., 379n., 381

Mesmer, Friedrich Anton, 405n.

Milton, John, 284 and n., 299, 362-3, 575 and n., 581 and n., 589, 591; C's proposed Milton edition, 570 and n., 572-3, 577-9, 582, 584, 588, 591-2, 594, 597; *Paradise Lost*, 71, 78-9 and n., 452, 483, 528n., 559 and n., 580 and n., 590-1; *Lycidas*, 193n., 371n.; *Il Penseroso*, 367n., 551n.; Latin and Italian poems, 508-9, 572, 573-4 and nn., 578, 582, 583 and n., 585, 588, 592 and n., 594, 597 and n.

Minet, Harriet. *See* Harriet Hurdis

Mohammed, 34

Montagu, Elizabeth, *née* Robinson, 159 and n., 161-2, 166-7 and n., 170, 173, 184, 202; *Essay on . . . Shakespeare . . .*, 167 and n.

Montesquieu, 225 and n.; *L'Esprit des lois*, 225 and n.

Montficet, Bernard, *Life and Opinions . . .*, 111 and n.

The Monthly Review, 190 and n., 446 and n.

More, Hannah, 103n., 103-4, 140, 586-7 and n.; *Slavery*, 103n., 103-4, 123; *Thoughts on the Importance of the Manners of the Great . . .*, 103n., 103-4, 123, 129, 153 and n.; 526n., 526-7, 587; *An Estimate of the Religion of the Fashionable World*, 526n., 526-7

More, Martha ('Patty'), 586-7 and n.

Morewood, Mr, 525 and n.

Morgan, Brunton, 3 and n., 225-6

Morgan, Samuel, 3 and n., 225-6

Morley, Mr, 529 and n.

Morley, Mrs or Nanny ('Mrs. Nunnerly'), 427 and n., 467 and n., 494

The Morning Herald, 4, 39 and n., 138, 234 and n., 255, 267, 270n., 274 and n.

Nadir Shah, 40 and n.

Nathan, 523

Newcastle-upon-Tyne, Thomas Pelham-Holles, Duke of, 25 and n.

Newport Pagnel, 46, 48, 69, 117, 124, 170, 229, 292, 295, 445

Newton, Sir Isaac, 353; *Principia*, 71

Newton, John, biographical sketch, xxix-xxx; *Thoughts Upon the African Slave Trade*, 89 and n.; *The Best Wisdom . . .*, 105n., 105-6; Joseph Johnson agrees to publish Newton's previously suppressed Preface to C's *Poems*, 422 and n., 424-5; xviii, 121, 150, 170, 173 and n., 182-3, 184-5, 194, 199, 265, 293, 531 and n., 532

Newton, Mary, *née* Catlett, biographical sketch, xxix-xxx; in bad health, 424, 441; death, 452 and n., 491, 532; 37, 45, 109, 173 and n., 182-3, 194, 199, 210, 234, 240, 310, 320, 344, 404-5

Newton, Thomas, editor of Milton, 571, 589 and n.

New York City, 513 and n.

Nichols, John ('Mr Urban'), biographical sketch, xxx; 8, 161-2, 167, 170, 478 and n., 481, 582

Nicoll, John, 248

Nicols, Mr, the tailor, 565

Norfolk, 235, 352, 367n., 367-8, 392, 398, 412, 433, 455, 477, 492, 517, 524, 530, 541, 545, 551, 564-5

Norfolk, Charles Howard, 11th Duke of, 334-5 and n., 580

Normandy, 225

Northampton, 124, 198, 219 and n., 541

Northumberland, Hugh Percy, 2nd Duke of, 254

Oakes, Dorothy. *See* Dorothy Cowper

625